The Economics of
European Integration

The Economics of European Integration

Fifth edition

Richard Baldwin & Charles Wyplosz

London Boston Burr Ridge, IL Dubuque, IA Madison, WI New York San Francisco
St. Louis Bangkok Bogotá Caracas Kuala Lumpur Lisbon Madrid Mexico City
Milan Montreal New Delhi Santiago Seoul Singapore Sydney Taipei Toronto

The Economics of European Integration, fifth edition
Richard Baldwin & Charles Wyplosz
ISBN-13 9780077169657
ISBN-10 0077169654

Published by McGraw-Hill Education
Shoppenhangers Road
Maidenhead
Berkshire
SL6 2QL
Telephone: 44 (0) 1628 502 500
Fax: 44 (0) 1628 770 224
Website: www.mheducation.co.uk

British Library Cataloguing in Publication Data
A catalogue record for this book is available from the British Library

Library of Congress Cataloging in Publication Data
The Library of Congress data for this book has been applied for from the Library of Congress

Content Acquisitions Manager: Thomas Hill/Emma Nugent
Product Developer: Laura Rountree
Senior Content Product Manager: Jessica Moody
Marketing Manager: Geeta Kumar

Cover design by Adam Renvoize
Printed and bound in the UK by Ashford Colour Press

Dedication

For Sarah, Ted, Julia and Nick - R.B.

In memory of my parents, whose sufferings inspired my yearning for a Europe at peace, and who taught me the pleasure of learning - C.W.

Brief Table of Contents

Detailed Table of Contents

About the Authors

Richard Baldwin is Professor of International Economics at the Graduate Institute, Geneva since 1991, a part-time visiting research professor at the University of Oxford since 2012, Director of CEPR since 2014, and Editor-in-Chief of Vox since he founded it in June 2007. He was Co-managing Editor of the journal *Economic Policy* from 2000 to 2005, Policy Director of CEPR since 2006, and Programme Director of CEPR's International Trade programme from 1991 to 2001. He has previously been a Senior Staff Economist for the President's Council of Economic Advisors in the Bush Administration (1990-1991), on leave from Columbia University Business School where he was Associate Professor. He did his PhD in economics at MIT with Paul Krugman and has collaborated with him on several occasions. He was visiting professor at MIT in 2002/03 and has taught at universities in Australia, Italy, Germany and Norway. He has also worked as consultant for the numerous governments, the Asian Development Bank, the European Commission, OECD, World Bank, EFTA and USAID. The author of numerous books and articles, his research interests include international trade, globalization, regionalism and European integration.

Charles Wyplosz is Professor of International Economics at the Graduate Institute in Geneva where he is also Director of the International Centre for Money and Banking Studies. Previously, he has taught at INSEAD and at the Ecole des Hautes Etudes en Sciences Sociales in Paris. He is a Fellow of CEPR and of the European Economic Association. His main research areas include financial crises, European monetary integration, fiscal policy and regional monetary integration. He is the co-author (with Michael Burda) of the leading textbook *Macroeconomics, A European View* and has published several books and many professional articles. He serves as consultant to many international organizations and governments and is a frequent contributor to public media. He was a Founding Managing Editor of *Economic Policy*. A French national, Charles Wyplosz holds degrees in Engineering and in Statistics from Paris and a PhD in Economics from Harvard University.

Preface

What's up?

Talking about European integration has at times appeared strange during the last few years when disintegration seemed around the corner. As we close this new edition, it seems that the worst is over, but one can never be sure. Over the last three years, between the fourth and fifth editions, the sovereign debt crisis has worsened and then improved. In the first three editions, we noted the many flaws in the integration process, especially those concerning the Eurozone. In the fourth edition, we were lamenting the policy responses to the crisis, pointing out what had to be done. Since then, much has been done, often along the lines that we mentioned. This edition takes stock of these changes, which concern both institutions and policies. The European Union has been transformed, and so has this book.

The most drastic changes concern both the pedagogy and the content. In terms of pedagogy, we have retained the five-part structure but:

- Presentation of the macroeconomic theory has been entirely revised. Chapter 13 now includes a compact presentation of the closed economy centred on the standard *IS–LM* model, except that *LM* is replaced by *MP*, a graphical representation of the Taylor rule, which is arguably what central banks use. It then moves to the open economy version (the Mundell–Fleming model) and introduces the interest arbitrage condition. The remaining chapters make extensive use of this framework, which has become the thread running through Parts IV and V. Chapter 15 also includes an explicit treatment of the theory of central banking.
- Chapter 15, which presents the optimum currency area (OCA), has been entirely redesigned. It presents a more extensive analysis of the benefits accruing from a currency union, including a detailed discussion of central bank independence. The presentation of the OCA criteria is also systematically followed by a critical appraisal.
- A new section has been introduced at the beginning of Chapter 18 to present the characteristics of financial markets and the essential principles needed for the rest of the book.

Concerning content, this edition fully takes on board the many institutional changes that have occurred over the last three years. The book therefore offers an integrated and up-to-date presentation of the European Union. The main changes are:

- The new Stability and Growth Pact, including the Six Pack–Two Pack directives and the Treaty on Stability, Coordination and Governance (TSCG)
- The Banking Union
- The various programmes put in place by the Eurosystem (SMP, LTRO, OMT)
- The enlargement of the Eurozone, which changes the functioning of the Governing Board of the Eurosystem

Obviously, the latest developments are fully covered. The information is included in context within every chapter. Chapter 19, which presents the crisis, has been entirely rewritten, as well as significant portions of Chapters 17 (fiscal policy) and 18 (financial markets). With all relevant data updated, these chapters are effectively new.

What this book is

This is a textbook for courses on European economic integration. Its emphasis is on economics, covering both the microeconomics and macroeconomics of European integration. Understanding European economic integration, however, requires much more than economics, so the book also covers the essential aspects of European history, institutions, laws, politics and policies.

The book is written at a level that should be accessible to second- and third-year undergraduates in economics as well as advanced undergraduates and graduate students in business, international affairs, European studies and political science. Some knowledge of economics is needed to absorb all the material with ease – a first-year course in the principles of economics should suffice – but the book is self-contained in that it reviews most essential economics behind the analysis.

What is in this book

The book is organized into five parts: essential background (Part I), the microeconomics of European integration (Part II), microeconomic policies (Part III), the macroeconomics of monetary integration (Part IV) and macroeconomic policies (Part V).

Part I presents the essential background for studying European integration.

- An overview of the post-Second World War historical development of European integration is presented in Chapter 1. The chapter should be useful to all students, even those who are familiar with the main historical events, as this chapter stresses the economic and political economy logic behind the events.

- A concise presentation of the indispensable background information necessary for the study of European integration is presented in Chapter 2. This includes key facts concerning European economies and a brief review of the EU's legal system and principles (fully updated to reflect the Lisbon Treaty changes). Chapter 2 also presents information on the vital EU institutions and the EU's legislative processes as well as the main features of the EU budget.

- Chapter 3 presents an economic framework for thinking about EU institutions. The first part explains how the 'theory of fiscal federalism' can be used to consider the appropriateness of the allocation of powers between EU institutions and EU Member States. The second part explains how economic reasoning – game theory in particular – can be used to analyse EU decision-making procedures for their efficiency as well as their implications for the distribution of power among EU members. While these are not classic topics in the study of European integration, they are essential to understanding the current challenges facing the EU, such as the 2004 enlargement and the debates around the Lisbon Treaty. This is more relevant than ever as the Eurozone crisis is almost sure to produce a shifting of some competencies from the national level to the supranational level – or, at the very least, a serious debate over such shifts.

Part II presents the microeconomic aspects of European integration.

- An introduction to the fundamental methods of trade policy analysis is presented in Chapter 4. The chapter introduces basic supply and demand analysis in an open economy and the key economic welfare concepts of consumer and producer surplus, and then uses them to study the simple economics of tariff protection.

- An in-depth analysis of European preferential trade liberalization is given in Chapter 5. The focus is on how the formation of a customs union or free trade area affects people, companies and governments inside and outside the integrating nations.

- A thorough study of how the market-expanding aspects of European integration affect the efficiency of European firms is presented in Chapter 6. The main line of reasoning explains how integration in the presence of scale economies and imperfect competition can produce fewer, bigger and more efficient firms facing more effective competition from each other. Again, the ongoing enlargement of the European Union makes this sort of logic more relevant than ever.

- Chapter 7 gives a detailed study of the growth effects of European integration. The emphasis is on the economic logic linking European integration to medium-run and long-run growth effects. Neoclassical and endogenous growth theories are covered to the extent that they help students understand the growth–integration linkages. The basic facts and empirical evidence are also covered.

- Chapter 8 deals with the labour markets. It recalls the basics of labour economics in order to explain unemployment and develop the notion that social requirements may have seriously negative effects in terms of jobs, wages and growth. The chapter uses these insights to study the effects of integration. It deals with many controversial issues such as social dumping and migration, trying hard to stay above the fray by presenting economic analysis as one logic, but not the only one.

Part III presents the main microeconomic policies of the EU.

- Chapter 9 looks at the Common Agricultural Policy (CAP), presenting the economics and facts that are essential for understanding its effects. The chapter takes particular care to examine the economic forces behind recent CAP reform in the light of international trade negotiations (the Doha Round), the eastern enlargement and the reforms that are being discussed for the post-2013 financial period.

- Chapter 10 presents the economics that link European integration to the location of economic activities. This includes a presentation of the main facts on how the location of economic activity has shifted both within and between nations. To organize thinking about these facts – and to understand how EU regional policy might affect it – the chapter presents the location effects of integration in the light of neoclassical theories (Heckscher–Ohlin), as well as the so-called new economic geography. The chapter also presents the main features of the EU's regional policy and considers the implications of the eastern enlargement.

- Chapter 11 covers the basic elements of the EU's competition policy and state aid policy (EU jargon for subsidies). Instead of merely describing the policies, the chapter explains them by introducing the basic economic logic of anti-competitive practices. It has been updated to include several recent cases that illustrate the difficulties of applying simple economics to the complex world of international business.

- Chapter 12 addresses EU trade policy, i.e. its commercial relations with the rest of the world. While trade policy is not as central to the EU as are, say, the CAP and cohesion policies, it is important. The EU is the world's largest trader, and trade policy is probably the only EU 'foreign policy' that is consistently effective. The chapter covers EU trade policy by presenting the basic facts on EU trade, covering the EU's institutional arrangements as concerns trade policy, and finally summarizing the EU's policies towards its various trade partners. It has been fully updated to reflect changes introduced by the Lisbon Treaty.

Part IV continues the approach of Part II by providing the basic principles behind macroeconomic and monetary integration.

- The essential principles needed for the macroeconomic analysis are presented in Chapter 13. This chapter presents the macroeconomic theories and tools needed to analyse monetary integration. It is organized around the Mundell–Fleming model and establishes three principles: interest rate parity, purchasing power parity and the impossible trinity that affects the choice of exchange rate regimes. This chapter can serve either as a refresher for economics students or a (fast) introduction to economics for others.

- The long process of European monetary integration is recounted in Chapter 14. It starts briefly with ancient times when Europe was a de facto monetary union under the gold standard, reviews the Bretton Woods period when Europe's exchange rates were tied together via the US dollar and then moves to the European Monetary System, past and present. The process of euro adoption is briefly reviewed.

- Chapter 15 presents the optimum currency area theory, the framework needed to think about the working of a monetary union. The basis is provided by the principles developed in Chapter 13. Looking at the costs and benefits resulting from sharing a common currency, the theory is essential to understanding what works and does not work in the Eurozone. It is used extensively in further chapters.

Part V is the counterpart to Part III, as it presents the main macroeconomic policies of the EU.

- The main features of the European monetary union are laid out in Chapter 16. This includes a description and analysis of the institutions created by the Maastricht Treaty and how they have evolved since, including during the crisis that started at the end of 2009. It explains the importance attached to price stability and the measures adopted to achieve this objective. The chapter also provides a review of the first decade of the euro up until the crisis.

- Fiscal policy is the last national macroeconomic instrument remaining once national monetary policy has been lost. Chapter 17 looks at the Stability and Growth Pact, designed to deliver just enough budgetary discipline so as not to endanger the overriding price stability objective. Since the first edition of this book, we have underlined the pact's serious shortcomings; the crisis has led to a strengthening of the pact, but fundamental economic and political difficulties remain.

- Chapter 18 deals with the financial markets. It starts with an analysis of financial markets in general. It then explains how and why the financial services industry was transformed by the Single European Act 1986 and by the adoption of a single currency and how it has been fragmented by the crisis. The measures taken to deal with this unexpected development are presented and evaluated, including the creation of the Banking Union. The chapter concludes by questioning whether the euro can challenge the US dollar as a world currency.

- Finally, Chapter 19 offers an overview of the Eurozone crisis. It looks at the global crisis that started in the USA and its transmission to Europe. The next step, the sovereign crisis, is then described and analysed, bringing together much of the material presented in earlier chapters. The policy responses are presented and critically evaluated. The chapter ends with a discussion of the remaining challenges and an analysis of what the break-up of the Eurozone would mean.

How to use this book

The book is suitable for a one-semester course that aims at covering both the microeconomics and macroeconomics of European integration. If the course is long enough, the book can be used sequentially for two courses.

Shorter courses may focus on the trade and competition aspects; they can use only Parts I, II and III. Conversely, a course dealing only with the macroeconomic aspects can use Parts IV and V, and finish with labour market issues as covered in Chapter 8 (which does not really require the previous microeconomic material).

Eclectic courses that focus on theory and cover trade, competition and macroeconomics can use only Chapters 1–8 and 16–19 or just 4–8 and 16–19. Eclectic courses oriented towards policy issues can use, with some additional lecturing if the students are not familiar with basic theory, Chapters 1–2, 9–12 and 16–19. In general, all chapters are self-contained but, inevitably, they often refer to results and facts presented elsewhere.

Each chapter includes self-assessment questions designed to help the students check how well they master the material, and some chapters also provide essay questions which can be given as assignments. We also provide additional readings that are easily accessible to undergraduate students.

The fifth edition continues our tradition of providing many internet links that should allow students and lecturers alike to gain the latest information on the EU's many fast-developing areas. We have observed that the internet is an excellent way to stimulate students' interest by bringing classroom teaching to real issues they see every day in the media. The links we provide go well beyond journalist treatment in a way that allows students to realize the usefulness of the basics they have learned from the text.

Acknowledgements

Our thanks go to the following reviewers for their comments at various stages in the text's development:

Bruno Merlevede, Ghent University
Carsten Hefeker, University of Siegen
Kevin Lawler, University of Durham
Olaf van Vliet, Leiden University
Peter Holmes, University of Sussex
Ralf Fendel, Otto Beisheim School of Management
Shawn Donnelly, University of Twente
Steffen Minter, University of Freiburg

We would also like to thank Ralf Fendel for the material which he provided for the textbook and its accompanying online resources.

Each new edition lengthens our indebtedness to colleagues, former and present students and editors. It also increases our pleasure when the time has finally come to thank them all. In the current and previous editions, a number of colleagues have made useful suggestions and identified mistakes. While we alone are responsible for the remaining old and new mistakes, we thank our reviewers for their no-holds-barred evaluations, which have been both challenging and most useful. We have tried hard to respond to each and every criticism and to follow the many constructive suggestions that we received.

As always, McGraw-Hill has lined up a first-class editing and production team and we would like to thank everyone who was involved. Laura Rountree, the Product Developer, has gently prodded us to deliver and supervised the whole process with firm patience. We also are grateful to Kate O'Leary, the Copy-editor, who helped to improve the quality of the text.

We would also like to thank the students who provided face-to-face feedback while we were teaching the fourth edition material. Richard Baldwin would in particular like to thank the students at the University of Geneva.

Every effort has been made to trace and acknowledge ownership of copyright and to clear permission for material reproduced in this book. The publishers will be pleased to make suitable arrangements to clear permission with any copyright holders whom it has not been possible to contact.

Guided Tour

Introduction

How the European monetary union funct
explained the genesis of this treaty and
difficulties have arisen, which should not
developed countries is a first and it is also
to have got it 100 per cent correct right fr
deal with problems as they arise and one
chapter presents the present situation.

    Section 16.1 lays out the principles t
priority given to price stability and the
to the Eurozone was based on five conve
16.2. The original central banking structu
central banks. Together they make up
governance is presented in Section 16.4,

Chapter introduction

Each chapter opens with an introduction outlining the ideas
and concepts that will be addressed in the following pages.

Maps and diagrams

These are provided throughout the text to show the
geographical impact of changes in EU integration across
the continent.

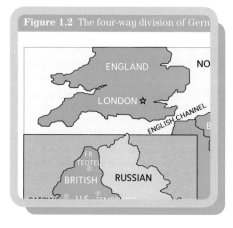

Figure 1.2 The four-way division of Germ

Box 16.5 A challenge from the (

The main risk to central bank independe
creation, a threat to price stability (see B
banks, the Eurosystem has taken bold
of quantities of money and even commit
countries offered combined IMF and Eu
taken the view that these actions bring th
price stability. They have asked the Ger
violate the German constitution (the so-
from financing governments but it is expl
market.[2]

    After more than one year of delibe

Example boxes

Each chapter contains a number of boxes that provide
further examples and explanations of key facts, events or
economic ideas relating to the European Union.

Figures and tables

Figures and tables feature throughout the text to help
illustrate important statistics and data about the European
Union and its Member States.

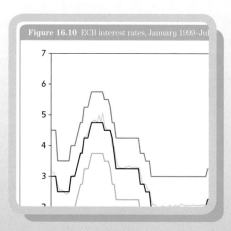

Figure 16.10 ECB interest rates, January 1999–Jul

Chapter summaries

Recaps of the key ideas and discussions are featured at the end of each chapter.

16.8 Summary

The monetary union is an elaborate co
was signed in 1991 and the single cur
currency was not issued until 2002. Th
unique nature of the undertaking.

The main objective assigned to th
an inflation rate close to but below 2 p
pursued only if price stability is not in
granted considerable independence. In
degree of transparency.

Self-assessment questions

1 What shape is the *MP* schedule and how does
  stability and ignores growth? Answer the sam
  growth and disregards price stability.

2 Consider a bank that cares only about price
  flexible exchange rate regime to see what hap

3 A Eurozone member has a fixed exchange
  happens when:
  – when demand for domestic goods declines;
  – when interest rates abroad rise; – when th
  policy.

4 Why are central banks ultimately responsible

Self-assessment questions

Self-assessment questions are included to allow students to test themselves on the economic concepts and facts featured in each chapter.

Essay questions

1 Devise the entry conditions using OCA principl

2 The Eurosystem asserts in its deliberations th
  economic conditions. The reason is that there is
  Discuss this approach and imagine alternative

3 The Maastricht Treaty describes in minute de
  a possible break-up. Imagine that a country is
  Could it leave? How? What could the other cou

4 Why are transparency and accountability so
  difficulties can you envision if the system is
  sufficiently transparent?

Essay questions

Essay questions feature at the end of some chapters and encourage students to write full answers to explore ideas in more detail as practice for exams.

Further reading: the aficionado's

The first decade of the euro as reviewed by the
European Central Bank, www.ecb.int/pub/pc
49ee63d0ce0e8.

And by independent observers:
Aghion, P., A. Ahearne, M. Belka, J. Pisani
on the Eurozone, BRUEGEL, Brussels. Dow
Fatás, A., H. Flam, S. Holden, T. Japelli, I.
Denmark, Sweden and the UK Join?, Stock
www.sns.se.

Further reading, useful websites and references

For students who want to explore key concepts, each chapter contains a list of extra sources to help further research.

Annex: A study

Year	Date	Event	Ex
1948	16 April	OEEC	Or (O
1950	9 May	Schuman Plan	Fro est (E bu Da
1952	1 January	ECSC	Th

Annex

Where appropriate, Annex sections offer further economic explanations, data or background information. The annexes enable further study to complement the chapter, covering more advance concepts and providing greater detail.

Online Learning Centre

Online Learning Centre
www.mheducation.co.uk/textbooks/baldwin

Students – Helping you to connect, learn and succeed

We understand that studying for your module is not just about reading this textbook. It's also about researching online, revising key terms, preparing for assignments and passing exams. The website above provides you with a number of **FREE** resources to help you succeed on your module, including:

- *Self-test questions* to prepare you for mid-term tests and exams
- *Glossary* of key terms to revise core concepts
- *Web links* to online sources of information to help you prepare for class
- **Interactive PowerPoints** to help you understand how to use and interpret diagrams

Lecturer support – Helping you to help your students

The Online Learning Centre also offers lecturers adopting this book a range of resources designed to:

- **Enable faster course preparation** – time-saving support for your module
- **Provide high-calibre content to support your students** – resources written by your academic peers, who understand your need for rigorous and reliable content
- **Allow flexibility** – edit, adapt or repurpose; test in EZ Test or your department's course management system – the choice is yours

The materials created specifically for lecturers adopting this textbook include:

- *Lecturer Outline to support your module preparation, with case notes, guide answers, teaching tips and more*
- *PowerPoint presentations to use in lectures*
- *Image library of artwork from the textbook*

Solutions Manuals providing accuracy-tested answers to the problems in the textbook

To request your password to access these resources, contact your McGraw-Hill Education representative or visit www.mheducation.co.uk/textbooks/baldwin

Test Bank available in McGraw-Hill EZ Test Online

A test bank of hundreds of questions is available to lecturers adopting this book for their module through the EZ Test online website. For each chapter you will find:

- A range of multiple choice, true or false, short answer or essay questions
- Questions identified by type, difficulty and topic to help you select questions that best suit your needs

McGraw-Hill EZ Test Online is:

- **Accessible** anywhere with an internet connection – your unique login gives you access to all of your tests and material in any location
- **Simple** to set up and easy to use
- **Flexible**, offering a choice from question banks associated with your adopted textbook or allowing you to create your own questions
- **Comprehensive**, with access to hundreds of banks and thousands of questions created for other McGraw-Hill titles
- **Compatible** with Blackboard and other course management systems
- **Time-saving** – tests can be marked immediately and results and feedback delivered directly to your students to help them to monitor their own progress

To register for this FREE resource, visit www.eztestonline.com

Let us help make our content your solution

At McGraw-Hill Education our aim is to help lecturers to find the most suitable content for their needs delivered to their students in the most appropriate way. Our **custom publishing solutions** offer the ideal combination of content delivered in the way which best suits lecturer and students.

Our custom publishing programme offers lecturers the opportunity to select just the chapters or sections of material they wish to deliver to their students from a database called CREATE™ at

http://create.mheducation.com/uk/

CREATE™ contains over two million pages of content from:

- textbooks
- professional books
- case books - Harvard Articles, Insead, Ivey, Darden, Thunderbird and BusinessWeek
- Taking Sides - debate materials

Across the following imprints:

- McGraw-Hill Education
- Open University Press
- Harvard Business Publishing
- US and European material

There is also the option to include additional material authored by lecturers in the custom product – this does not necessarily have to be in English.

We will take care of everything from start to finish in the process of developing and delivering a custom product to ensure that lecturers and students receive exactly the material needed in the most suitable way.

With a Custom Publishing Solution, students enjoy the best selection of material deemed to be the most suitable for learning everything they need for their courses – something of real value to support their learning. Teachers are able to use exactly the material they want, in the way they want, to support their teaching on the course.

Please contact **your local McGraw-Hill Education representative** with any questions or alternatively contact Warren Eels **e: warren.eels@mheducation.com**

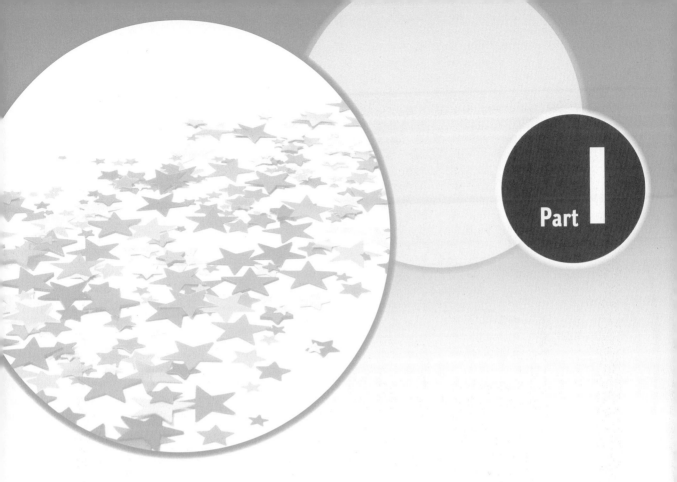

Part **I**

History, Facts and Institutions

Chapter

1

And what is the plight to which Europe has been reduced? . . . over wide areas a vast quivering mass of tormented, hungry, care-worn and bewildered human beings gape at the ruins of their cities and their homes, and scan the dark horizons for the approach of some new peril, tyranny or terror. . . . That is all that Europeans, grouped in so many ancient states and nations . . . have got by tearing each other to pieces and spreading havoc far and wide.

Yet all the while there is a remedy. . . . It is to re-create the European Family, or as much of it as we can, and to provide it with a structure under which it can dwell in peace, in safety and in freedom. We must build a kind of United States of Europe.

Winston Churchill, Zurich, 19 September 1946

History

Chapter Contents

Introduction

The May 2014 European Parliamentary elections saw large gains by anti-EU parties in several nations. These results make it more important than ever to understand how and why Europe arrived at its current state of integration. As Tommaso Padoa-Schioppa – one of the architects of the euro – put it: 'After experiencing political oppression and war in the first half of the twentieth century, Europe undertook to build a new order for peace, freedom, and prosperity. Despite its predominantly economic content, the European Union is an eminently political construct' (2004, 1).

Quite simply, it is impossible to understand today's economic integration without a firm grasp on Europe's post-Second World War history. This chapter presents the main events of European economic integration in chronological order, stressing, wherever possible, the economic and political economy logic behind the events. The Annex provides a chronology 'study guide' to help readers identify the key events and issues.

1.1 Early post-war period

In 1945, a family standing almost anywhere in Europe was in a nation that was recently ruled by a brutal fascist dictator, occupied by a foreign army, or both. As a direct result of these governmental failures, tens of millions of Europeans were dead and Europe's economy lay in ruins. Worse yet, this was not new. If the parents were middle-aged, the Second World War would have been their second experience of colossal European death and destruction. The Second World War was the fourth time in 130 years that France and Germany had been at the core of increasingly horrifying wars. Forgetting about facts like these has allowed politicians such as the UK's Nigel Farage to claim, in 2012, 'When people stand up and talk about the great success that the EU has been, I'm not sure anybody saying it really believes it themselves anymore' (BBC, 2012).

1.1.1 A climate for radical change

As the fog of battle lifted in 1945, it was clear to all that something was desperately wrong with the way Europe governed itself. This opened minds to radical changes – changes that would be absolutely unthinkable in most nations.

It is hard for students born in the 1990s to connect emotionally with the misery and hardship that opened minds to this drastic reconsideration. Yet it is essential to a deep comprehension of the EU in the second decade of the twenty-first century. The web allows students to see photos (see Figure 1.1), watch videos,

---

Figure 1.1 London Hospital in late 1940 and Dresden 1945

© Robert Hunt Library/Mary Evans

© Mary Evans/Epic/Tallandier

read original documents and listen to speeches from the time. The website of the Luxembourg-based Centre Virtuel de la Connaissance sur l'Europe (www.cvce.eu) provides access to a vast range of European documents; go to 'Historical events in the European integration process (1945–2009)'. For powerful photos and videos of Germany's experience, go to http://www.hdg.de/lemo/html/Nachkriegsjahre/ and http://the-world-at-war.npage.de/picture-gallery.html.

Table 1.1 shows some figures on the death and destruction caused by the Second World War. In western Europe, the war killed about 8 million people, with Germans accounting for three-quarters of this total. In central and eastern Europe, over 9 million perished, of whom 6.3 million were Poles. The Soviet Union alone lost over 20 million. The fact that much of the killing was deliberate genocide made it even more horrifying (see www.jewishvirtuallibrary.org for information on the Holocaust).

Table 1.1   Death and destruction in the Second World War

	Death toll	The economic setback: pre-war year when GDP equalled that of 1945
Austria	525,000	1886
Belgium	82,750	1924
Denmark	4,250	1936
Finland	79,000	1938
France	505,750	1891
Germany	6,363,000	1908
Italy	355,500	1909
Netherlands	250,000	1912
Norway	10,250	1937
Sweden	0	(a)
Switzerland	0	(a)
UK	325,000	(a)

(a) GDP grew during the Second World War.

Source: GDP data from Crafts and Toniolo (1996), p. 4; death toll from http://encarta.msn.com

The war also caused enormous economic damage. Figures are difficult to find for central and eastern Europe, but the estimates for western Europe are staggering, as Table 1.1 shows. The war cost Germany and Italy four decades or more of growth and put Austrian and French GDPs back to nineteenth-century levels.

Refugees, hunger and political instability

The economic, political and humanitarian situation in Europe was dire in the years 1945–47, especially in Germany. Food production in 1946 was low and the 1946–47 winter was especially harsh. Hunger was widespread. Food was rationed in most European nations up to the mid-1950s. At times, rations fell to just 900 calories per day in some parts of Germany (2000 calories per day is the standard today). Much of Europe's infrastructure, industry and housing lay in ruins. Many Europeans in these years were dependent on humanitarian aid, in much the same way as people in war-torn African nations are today. The UN Relief and Rehabilitation Administration (UNRRA) spent nearly $4 billion on emergency food and medical aid, helped about 7 million displaced persons return home and provided camps for about a million refugees who did not want to be repatriated.

Politically, western Europe suffered governmental and constitutional crises. The French wartime leader General de Gaulle resigned as president of the provisional government in 1946 over a disagreement on France's new constitution. Italy and Belgium saw bitter internal conflicts over their monarchy. Italy abolished its monarchy in a referendum that involved accusations of communist manipulation. The return of the Belgian king sparked riots. If all this seems like the plot of a B-grade apocalypse movie, you should watch some of the online audiovisual material at www.cvce.eu to see just how real it was. Hunger, riots and refugee camps were commonplace all across western Europe.

1.1.2 The prime question and guiding ideologies

The horror and revulsion arising from this devastation pushed one question to the forefront in the mid-1940s: 'How can Europe avoid another war?' The solutions offered depended on beliefs about the causes of the war; three schools of thought were in evidence:

1 *Germany was to blame.* Guided by this belief, the so-called Morgenthau Plan of 1944 proposed to avoid future European war by turning Germany into 'a country primarily agricultural and pastoral in character' (http://www.worldfuturefund.org). The same thinking guided post-First World War arrangements in Europe. That war was blamed on Germany and the victors were rewarded with territorial gains and financial reparations. The result was a cycle of recovery, resentment and national rivalry that led to the Second World War.

2 *Capitalism was to blame.* Marxism–Leninism blamed capitalism for most of the world's evils, including both world wars. This belief suggested that communism was the solution.

3 *Nationalism was to blame.* The third school blamed the excesses of destructive nationalism for the war. The solution suggested by this belief was tighter integration of all European nations. While calls for a united Europe were heard after the 1914–18 war and during the 1939–45 war, the school's most famous post-war statement was the 1946 'United States of Europe' speech by Winston Churchill (you can listen to it at www.cvce.eu).

School number 3 and the European integration solution ultimately prevailed, but this was far from clear in the late 1940s. Most European nations were either struggling to re-establish their governments and economies or were under direct military occupation. Germany and Austria were divided into US, UK, French and Soviet zones (Figure 1.2). Soviet troops occupied all of central and eastern Europe. In

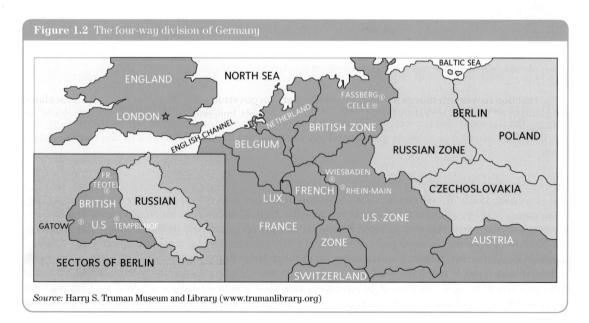

Figure 1.2 The four-way division of Germany

Source: Harry S. Truman Museum and Library (www.trumanlibrary.org)

western Europe, 1945 and 1946 passed with hardly any progress towards the establishment of a post-war architecture. Western European governments' limited governance capacities were overloaded by the dismal humanitarian situation.

Things moved more rapidly in the east. The Soviet Union had already begun to implement its vision of a new Europe during the war. Communism was imposed on the previously independent nations of Estonia, Latvia and Lithuania, and by 1948 communist parties had been pushed to power in every Soviet-occupied country. Communists took power in Albania and Yugoslavia, and were gaining strength in Greece. School number 3 had many adherents in western Europe. In the parliamentary elections of 1946, communists won 19 per cent of the vote in Italy and 29 per cent in France.

1.1.3 Emergence of a divided Europe: the Cold War

America and Britain rejected the Soviet's world vision and the wartime alliance unravelled. The Allies-versus-Axis confrontation was replaced by an East–West confrontation, called the Cold War. By 1947, the USA and Britain had concluded that an economically strong Germany would be essential to the defence of liberal democracy in western Europe. They merged the UK and US zones into 'Bizonia' (September 1947), and France, which had originally favoured the Morgenthau Plan, added its zone in 1948. Germany drew up a constitution in 1948 under the leadership of Konrad Adenauer (see Box 1.1).

Box 1.1   Konrad Adenauer (1876–1967)

Born to a family of modest means, Konrad Adenauer rose to become Mayor of Cologne, a post he was stripped of by the Nazis in 1933. He was President of the 1948 Parliamentary Council that drew up Germany's constitution ('Basic Law') before becoming the first Chancellor (i.e. Prime Minister) of Germany – an office he held from 1949 to 1963. Under his leadership, Germany regained its sovereignty, joined the European Economic Community and NATO, and evolved into a cornerstone of western European democracy and economic strength. Adenauer was a key promoter of close Franco–German cooperation and of Germany's social welfare system.

© Mary Evans/Iberfoto

In reaction to western moves towards creating a German government in their zones, the USSR escalated harassment of western travel to Berlin. Ultimately, the Soviets imposed the famous 'Berlin Blockade' on 24 June 1948. Western powers countered with the equally famous 'Berlin air bridge' (see www.cvce.eu for details and photos). In May 1949, the Federal Republic of Germany was established. The new government agreed to make a military contribution to the western defence effort.

Soviet aggressive promotion of their solution (communism for all) triggered a western reaction that narrowed the three solutions down to two with an 'iron curtain' between them. East of the iron curtain, the post-war architecture was based on communism and one-party politics. To the west, it was built on multi-party democracy, the social market economy and European integration.

The merger of the French, US and UK zones was a defining moment in Europe. Tentative and ideologically-based support for European integration came to be strongly reinforced by western European nations pursuing their own interests. French leaders saw the Franco–German integration as a way of counterbalancing US–UK influence on the Continent while at the same time assuring that a reindustrialized Germany would become an economic partner rather than a military adversary. The UK and the USA supported European integration as the best way to counter the spread of communism in Europe. German leaders embraced European integration as the surest route to re-establishing Germany as a 'normal' nation (Germany was recognized as an independent nation only in 1955). Italian leaders also welcomed European integration, which provided them with an ideological counterbalance to communism and helped shut the door on Italy's fascist past. The Benelux nations (Belgium, the Netherlands and Luxembourg) were happy about anything that reduced the chances of another Franco–German war.

1.1.4 First steps: the OEEC and EPU

From the perspective of European integration, the most important result of the western European effort to resist communism was the so-called Marshall Plan and the Organisation for European Economic Cooperation (OEEC). In reaction to the dire economic conditions in Europe and the attendant threat that communists might come to power in Greece, Italy and France, US Secretary of State (i.e. Foreign Minister) George Marshall announced that the USA would give financial assistance to all European nations 'west of the Urals', if they could agree to a joint programme for economic reconstruction.

Almost immediately, European nations gathered in Paris to study Marshall's proposal (the USSR and the central and eastern European countries eventually withdrew and never received Marshall Plan funds). The conference was intended to determine the amount of aid required and, at US insistence, to create a permanent organization (the OEEC) in which Europeans would cooperate in their mutual economic recovery. A joint programme and organization were duly developed by the Europeans. The US Congress, which was initially reluctant, funded the Marshall Plan in April 1948 after the communist takeover in Czechoslovakia.

The OEEC was established in 1948 with 13 members of the old EU15 (Finland was under Soviet pressure to stay neutral and Spain was under Franco's dictatorship) plus Norway, Iceland, Switzerland, Turkey and the US–UK zone of the Free Territory of Trieste until it was merged with Italy. Germany was still under occupation, but representatives from the western zones participated. From 1948 to 1952, Marshall Plan aid amounted to $12 billion, with half of this going to the UK, France and West Germany. The Soviet bloc's counterpart, the Council of Mutual Economic Assistance (CMEA), was set up in 1949.

The OEEC divided American aid among its members (see Box 1.2), but a far more important role, as far as European history is concerned, was the OEEC's mandate to advance European economic integration. It did this by reducing intra-European trade barriers and improving the intra-European system of payments by establishing the European Payments Union (EPU).

Box 1.2   The European Payments Union (EPU), July 1950 to December 1958

Most European nations were bankrupt after 1945, so trade was generally conducted on the basis of bilateral agreements, often involving barter. The EPU multi-lateralized these bilateral deals. Each month, EPU members added up the deficits and surpluses in their bilateral trade accounts with other EPU members. These were offset against each other so that each nation remained with an overall surplus or deficit with respect to the EPU. The great advantage of this approach was that, since nations no longer owed money to each other directly, the debt-based incentives for importing from or exporting to a particular partner vanished. As a consequence, it was easy to loosen the web of bilateral trade restrictions that had been set up in the early post-war years. In this way, the EPU can be thought of as the real start of post-war European economic integration.

Source: This box is based largely on Eichengreen and de Macedo (2001)

In 1949, the USA demanded that the OEEC make greater efforts to bring about direct European economic integration, especially intra-OEEC trade liberalization. Up to this point, Marshall Plan money was mainly used to finance European countries' dollar deficits in the EPU (see Box 1.2). Responding to this pressure, the OEEC nations removed quantitative restrictions. The OEEC's trade liberalization was important in at least two ways.

First, the liberalization fostered a rapid growth of trade and incomes. The 1950s were marked by a remarkable increase in GDP and the export of manufactured goods, at least on the Continent.

Second, it shifted the mindset of policy makers in a way that eventually opened the door to the European Union. Europe's leaders came to view European integration as an idea that made as much sense economically as it did politically. As Milward (1992) put it: 'The proposals for trade liberalisation and customs unions that were made fell therefore on to a receptive soil.'

In the decades following the First World War, especially during the 1930s, economic growth was viewed as a competition between nations. In this competition, trade barriers played a central role as each nation sought to 'save' its market for its own industrialists. In sharp contrast, the correlation between trade barriers and industrial growth was completely reversed in the 1940s and 1950s. Trade liberalization among western European nations went hand-in-hand with spectacular growth; intra-European imports and exports expanded even more rapidly than output.

1.1.5 The drive for deeper integration

The OEEC was an economic success, but would it prevent another intra-European war? Some OEEC members felt economic integration had to be much deeper to make a future intra-European war unthinkable. The Cold War lent urgency to this drive. With East–West tensions rising steadily, Germany would not only have to be allowed to regain its industrial might, it would have to rearm in order to counter the threat of Soviet territorial aggression. Since many Europeans, including many Germans, were still uncomfortable with the idea of a Germany that was both economically and militarily strong, integrating Germany into a supranational Europe seemed a natural way forward.

1.2 Two strands of European integration: federalism and intergovernmentalism

In 2014, the public debate in many European nations questions whether EU integration has gone too far. This has been an issue for over six decades. While it was clear by the late 1940s that European integration would be the foundation of western Europe's post-war architecture, a serious schism immediately emerged regarding the role of nation-states. Even today, this schism defines the debate over European integration.

1 Some Europeans felt that national sovereignty and the nation-state constituted a fragile system prone to warfare. Since time immemorial, European states had been engaged in intermittent struggles for dominance – struggles that typically involved the invasion of other European nations. As industrialization made killing much more 'efficient', the cost of these struggles rose to the point whereby no one could win. To these thinkers, even democracy was insufficient to prevent horrifying wars. Hitler, after all, gained his first hold on power through democratic means. To prevent another cycle of recovery and national rivalry that might lead to a third world war, nations should be embedded in a *federalist* structure – a supranational organization embodied with some of the powers that had traditionally been exercised exclusively by nations.

2 Other Europeans, led by Britain, continued to view nation-states as the most effective and most stable form of government. To them, European integration should take the form of closer cooperation – especially closer economic cooperation – conducted strictly on an *intergovernmental* basis, i.e. all power would remain in the hands of national officials and any cooperation would have to be agreed unanimously by all participants.

Not surprisingly, the federalist school was most popular in nations that experienced the greatest failures of governance – failures measured in terms of wartime death and destruction (see Table 1.1). This group included Belgium, the Netherlands, Luxembourg, France, Austria, Germany and Italy.

People from nations whose governments avoided foreign occupation and/or catastrophic loss of life tended to maintain their traditional faith in the nation-state. This included the UK, Denmark, Norway and Iceland, as well as the neutrals, Ireland, Sweden and Switzerland. Fascist dictators in Spain and Portugal ruled until the 1970s, so the question was long postponed in the Iberian Peninsula.

1.2.1 Two early extremes: Council of Europe and the ECSC

Intergovernmentalism initially dominated the post-war architecture. In part, this was simply a matter of timing.

The only major European nation with a truly effective, democratic government before 1947 was Britain – a firm believer in intergovernmentalism. The first three organizations – the OEEC, the Council of Europe and the Court of Human Rights – followed the intergovernmental tradition. The OEEC was strictly intergovernmental (i.e. one nation, one vote, with unanimity required to agree anything), and the 1948 'Congress of Europe' established two intergovernmental structures, the Council of Europe (1949) and the Court of Human Rights (1950), both of which continue to function today and are entirely unrelated to the EU.

The first big federalist step came in 1952 with the Schuman Plan inspired by the 'father of European integration', Jean Monnet, but promoted by French Foreign Minister Robert Schuman (see Box 1.3). Schuman proposed that France and Germany should place their coal and steel sectors under the control of a supranational authority.

This was a radical move at the time. Coal and steel were then viewed as the 'commanding heights' of an industrial economy and crucial to a nation's military and industrial strength. Schuman explicitly justified his plan as a means of rendering future Franco–German wars materially impossible.

> ### Box 1.3   Robert Schuman (1886–1963) and Jean Monnet (1888–1979)
>
>
> © European Union, 2014
>
>
> © European Union, 2014
>
> Born in Luxembourg, Schuman studied and worked in Germany until the end of the First World War. He became French when Alsace-Lorraine reverted to France in 1918. He held several positions in the post-war French governments, including Finance Minister, Premier and Foreign Minister. Schuman provided the political push for the European Coal and Steel Community, which most consider to be the wellspring for the European Union. He was also the first President (1958–60) of the European Parliament.
>
> Jean Monnet, born in Cognac in 1888, was a brilliant organizer and as such helped to organize Allied military supply operations in the First and Second World Wars. Near the end of the Second World War he joined Charles de Gaulle's provisional Free French government, and was responsible for the 'Monnet Plan', which is credited with helping France's post-war industrialization. Monnet was a convinced Europeanist and led the European movement in the 1950s and 1960s. Monnet, who is sometimes called the 'father of European integration', was the intellect behind the idea of the ECSC and the first president of its 'High Authority' (precursor of the European Commission) from 1952 to 1955. He continued to push for the European Economic Community and the European Atomic Energy Community (Euratom). He died in 1979.
>
> *Sources:* http://www.hdg.de/lemo/biografie/robert-schuman.html and http://www.hdg.de/lemo/html/biografien/MonnetJean/index.html

Other European nations were invited to join this European Coal and Steel Community (ECSC), and Belgium, Luxembourg, the Netherlands and Italy actually did so. This created a group of nations known simply as 'the Six' – a group that has been the driving force behind European integration ever since. See Box 1.4.

Box 1.4   The European Coal and Steel Community (ECSC)

France and Germany launched the ECSC initiative, inviting other nations to place their coal and steel sectors under its supranational authority. Since coal and steel were critical economic sectors at the time, most nations declined.

The ECSC's structure submerged the role of nation-states to an extent that seems unimaginable from today's perspective. It still represents the 'high-water mark' of European federalism. Crucial decisions concerning such issues as pricing, trade and production in the then-critical coal and steel sectors were placed in the hands of the High Authority. This body, the forerunner of today's European Commission, consisted of officials appointed by the six Member States. The High Authority's decisions, some made by majority voting, were subject to limited control by Member State governments. See Spierenburg and Poidevin (1994) for details on the ECSC.

Times had changed

By the time the ECSC was in operation, Europe was a very different place from what it had been in 1945. The year was 1952 and Cold War tensions were high and rising. Economically, things continued to get better. As Table 1.2 shows, the Six had managed to get their economies back on track, having experienced miraculous growth.

1.2.2 Federalist track: the Treaty of Rome

The ECSC was a success, not so much in that it solved the thorny problems of Europe's coal and steel sectors, but rather as a training scheme for European integration. It showed that the Six could cooperate in a federal structure. The Six as a whole, but especially Germany, continued to grow spectacularly, while East–West tensions continued to mount. The latter made German rearmament an essential component of western Europe's reply to Soviet expansion and ideological commitment to spreading communism.

In 1955, Germany joined western Europe's main defence organization, the North Atlantic Treaty Organization (NATO), and began to rearm in earnest. This triggered a reaction from the Soviet bloc – the USSR and the central and eastern European nations formed the Warsaw Pact to counter NATO. It also brought back the question of deeper European integration.

By 1955, it had become clear that coal and steel were no longer the 'commanding heights' of Europe's economy in economic or military terms. The ECSC might not be enough to ensure that another Franco–German war remained unthinkable. European leaders turned their minds to broader economic integration. Having failed to move directly to political or military integration (see Box 1.5), the natural way forward was broader economic integration.

A key force behind supranationalism was Jean Monnet, who formed a high-powered pressure group – the Action Committee for the United States of Europe – whose membership included leading figures from all the main political parties in each of the Six. The aim was to merge European nation-states into a supranational organization along the lines of the ECSC but much broader in scope.

Table 1.2   Post-Second World War reconstruction

	Back-on-track year (year GDP attained highest pre-Second World War level)	Reconstruction growth (growth rate during reconstruction years, 1945 to back-on-track year) (%)
Austria	1951	15.2
Belgium	1948	6.0
Denmark	1946	13.5
Finland	1945	n.a.
France	1949	19.0
Germany	1951	13.5
Italy	1950	11.2
Netherlands	1947	39.8
Norway	1946	9.7

Source: Nicolas Crafts, Gianni Toniolo, "Postwar growth: an overview", in Nicholas Crafts, Gianni Toniolo (eds), *Economic Growth in Europe since 1945*, (1996) © Centre for Economic Policy Research 1996, published by Cambridge University Press, reproduced with permission

---

Box 1.5   Failed integration, EDC and EPC

Encouraged by the rapid acceptance of the ECSC, federalists pressed ahead with ambitious plans. In the first years of the 1950s, leaders from the Six worked out plans for a supranational organization concerning defence – the European Defence Community (EDC) – as well as for deep political integration – the European Political Community (EPC). This remarkable enthusiasm for supranationality ultimately failed when the French parliament rejected the EDC explicitly, after which EPC plans were dropped.

The ECSC, EDC and EPC proposals were revolutionary by today's standards. When most voters had lived through the traumatic years of the Second World War, radical thinking was mainstream. Today, by contrast, European governments baulk at pooling their sovereignty over comparatively trivial issues such as air traffic control.

Source: Distilled from information on www.cvce.eu

Foreign Ministers of the Six met in Messina in June 1955 to start a process that soon led to the signing, on 25 March 1957, of two treaties in Rome: the first created the European Atomic Energy Community (Euratom); the second created the European Economic Community (EEC). Because the EEC eventually became much more important than Euratom, the term 'Treaty of Rome' is used to refer to the EEC treaty. Britain partook in the preliminary meetings but dropped out in October 1955 as it was not interested in this deep economic integration.

The Treaty of Rome was quickly ratified by the six national parliaments and the EEC came into existence in January 1958. (The institutions of the ECSC, the EEC and Euratom were merged into the 'European Communities', or EC, in 1965.)

The Treaty of Rome committed the Six to extraordinarily deep economic integration (see Chapter 2). In addition to forming a customs union (removing all tariffs and quotas on intra-EEC trade and adopting a common tariff on imports from non-Member nations), it promised free mobility of workers, capital market integration and free trade in services as well as a range of common policies – some of which were to be implemented by a supranational body. The Treaty also set up a series of supranational institutions such as

Figure 1.3 Signing of the Treaty of Rome

© European Union, 2014

the European Parliamentary Assembly (forerunner of the European Parliament), the European Court of Justice and most important of all – the European Commission. See Chapter 2 for details.

1.2.3 Intergovernmental track: from OEEC to EFTA

Formation of the EEC introduced discrimination – preferences is a nice word for the same thing – into European economic integration. Hitherto trade liberalization was extended to all OEEC nations on a non-discriminatory basis. The EEC's customs union meant that tariffs within the EEC would be lower than those charged to third nations. The other 11 OEEC members were side-lined.

Fearing discrimination and marginalization, seven OEEC nations formed their own bloc in 1960, the European Free Trade Association (EFTA). Britain, which was the largest economy in Europe at the time, led this initiative. By the early 1970s, all western European nations had forsaken bilateralism except Ireland, which was in a monetary union with its major trading partner (the UK). Greece and Turkey both applied for associate EEC membership almost as soon as the Treaty of Rome was signed, and Spain signed a preferential trade agreement with the EEC in 1970 (and with EFTA in 1979).

1.2.4 Two non-overlapping circles: Common Market and EFTA

The trade liberalization promised by the Treaty of Rome and the Stockholm Convention (EFTA's founding document) rapidly came into effect in the 1960s. By the late 1960s, trade arrangements in western Europe could be described as two non-overlapping circles (Figure 1.4).

The lowering of intra-EEC trade barriers had an immediate and dramatic impact on trade patterns. During the formation of the customs union (CU), the EEC's share in its own trade rose from about 30 per cent to almost 50 per cent. At the same time, the share of EEC imports coming from six other major European nations remained almost unchanged, falling from 8 to 7 per cent. (More on this in Chapter 5.)

1.3 Evolution to two concentric circles: the domino effect part I

At the beginning of the 1960s, EFTA-based and EEC-based firms had roughly equal access to each other's markets as the preferential tariff cutting had only just begun. As the barriers began to fall within the EEC and within EFTA (but not between the groups), discrimination appeared. This discrimination meant lost

Figure 1.4 A Europe of two non-overlapping circles

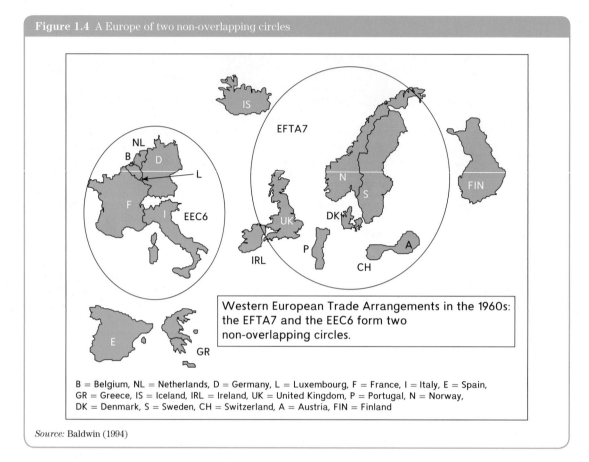

Western European Trade Arrangements in the 1960s: the EFTA7 and the EEC6 form two non-overlapping circles.

B = Belgium, NL = Netherlands, D = Germany, L = Luxembourg, F = France, I = Italy, E = Spain, GR = Greece, IS = Iceland, IRL = Ireland, UK = United Kingdom, P = Portugal, N = Norway, DK = Denmark, S = Sweden, CH = Switzerland, A = Austria, FIN = Finland

Source: Baldwin (1994)

profit opportunities for exporters in both groups. Importantly, the relative economic weight and economic performance of the two circles were far from equal. The GDP – and thus the potential market size – of the six EEC nations was more than twice that of the seven EFTA nations (EFTAns) and the EEC incomes were growing twice as fast. The EEC club was far more attractive to exporters than the EFTA club. Accordingly, the progressive reduction of within-group barriers generated new political economy forces in favour of EEC enlargement, but how did discriminatory liberalization create these forces for inclusion?

Discriminatory liberalization is studied in depth in Chapter 5, but the idea behind these new political economy forces can be illustrated with an anecdote. Two campers in Yellowstone National Park, who have just settled down in their tent, hear the roar of a hungry grizzly bear very close by. One camper sits up and starts putting on his running shoes. The other camper says: 'Are you crazy? You can't outrun a bear!' The first camper, who continues tying his laces, replies: 'Oh, I don't have to outrun the bear. I just have to outrun you.' When it comes to outrunning bears and succeeding in business, relative competitiveness is the key to success. A firm is harmed by anything that helps its rivals.

In the case at hand, closer EEC integration diminished the relative competitiveness of non-EEC firms in EEC markets, thereby harming their sales and profits. Of course, the same happened to EEC firms in EFTA, but given the EEC's much greater economic size, pressures on EFTA members to adjust were much greater than those on EEC nations. This effect helps explain why preferential integration among some nations can change the political economy attitudes of excluded nations. This is what Baldwin (1994, 1995) calls the 'domino theory' of regional integration; the preferential lowering of some trade barriers creates new pressures for outsiders to join the trade bloc and, as the trade bloc gets bigger, the pressure to join grows. As history would have it, the British government was the first to react to the pressure.

1.3.1 First enlargement and EEC–EFTA FTAs

In 1961, the UK applied for EEC membership – just six years after walking away from the Messina talks. There are many reasons for this *volte face*. In the late 1950s, Britain half-expected the EEC to fail just as the EDC and EPC had before it (see Box 1.5). Moreover, British wartime successes hung heavy in the air. Clement Attlee, former UK Prime Minister, dismissed the EEC as 'six nations, four of whom we had to rescue from the other two'. Thinking changed once the EEC was up and working well. UK industries faced the reality of rising discrimination in Europe's largest and fastest-growing markets. The British government had to react; EFTA was not a substitute for free trade access to the EEC6 markets.

Britain's unilateral decision tipped over more dominoes. If the UK was to jump from EFTA to the EEC, the remaining EFTAns would face discrimination in an even larger market (since the EEC is a customs union, the UK would have had to re-impose tariffs on imports from other EFTAns). This possibility led other nations to change their attitude towards membership. In this case, Ireland, Denmark and Norway quickly followed Britain's unilateral move. The other EFTAns did not apply for political reasons, such as neutrality (Austria, Finland, Sweden and Switzerland), lack of democracy (Portugal), or because they were not heavily dependent on the EEC market (Iceland).

While Germany was broadly in favour of UK membership, France was opposed to it. In a renowned January 1963 press conference, French President Charles de Gaulle (see Box 1.6) said 'non' to this first enlargement attempt. The four EFTAns reapplied in 1967 and de Gaulle issued another famous 'non', but, after he retired, the applications were reactivated by invitation of the EEC. After many delays, membership for the four was granted in 1973. At that time, Norway's population refused EEC membership in a referendum.

Box 1.6 Charles de Gaulle (1890–1970)

Charles André Marie Joseph de Gaulle was twice wounded in the First World War and was captured by German forces. A colonel in the French Army when the Second World War broke out, he rose rapidly to brigadier general (the youngest general in the French Army, at age 49). He was strongly opposed to the French surrender in June 1940 (after just two weeks of combat) and broadcast his renowned 'Appeal of June 18' from London. His appeal won over leaders in some of the French Overseas Territories and he created the Free French Movement, which provided an alternative to the collaborationist Vichy Republic led by Marshal Pétain.

After the war, he headed the provisional government, but resigned in 1946, frustrated by the weakness of the president in the new constitution. Like Adenauer, he firmly supported Franco–German cooperation but was a reluctant Europeanist, objecting to supranational organizations such as the ECSC. France, however, had already adopted the Treaty of Rome before his return to power in 1958 under crisis conditions. The general dominated political life and did much to restore French dignity and power. He resigned in 1969 and died the following year.

© Ingram Publishing

The impending departure of four EFTAns to the EEC was anticipated well in advance and triggered a secondary domino effect. The 1973 EEC enlargement meant a swelling of the EEC markets and a shrinking of the EFTA markets. Firms based in the remaining EFTA states would suffer a disadvantage (compared to their EEC-based rivals) in more markets and enjoy an advantage (over their EEC-based rivals) in fewer markets. Accordingly, EFTA industries pushed their governments to redress this situation. The result was a set of bilateral free trade agreements (FTAs) between each remaining EFTAn and the EEC, which took place when the UK and company acceded to the EEC. Notice that this change of heart does need some explaining. The stance of, say, Sweden towards an FTA with the then-EEC was a matter of top-level political calculation.

It may seem strange, therefore, that the calculations of Sweden's political elite led them to sign an FTA in 1972 when they had not found it politically optimal to sign one in the preceding decades. The explanation, of course, is that tighter integration among a nation's trade partners (in this case between the UK, Denmark and Ireland and the EEC) alters the economic landscape facing Swedish exporters. This reshaping of the economic landscape gets translated into a new political landscape. Such forces are in operation today. The 2004 enlargement stimulates demand for free trade with nations on the EU25's new eastern border.

By the mid-1970s, trade arrangements in western Europe had evolved into two concentric circles (Figure 1.5). The outer circle, which encompassed both EFTA and EEC nations, represents a 'virtual' free trade area for industrial products, formed by concatenation of the Treaty of Rome (for intra-EEC trade), EFTA's charter, the Stockholm Convention (for intra-EFTA trade) and individual bilateral FTAs between each EFTA member and the EEC (for EEC–EFTA trade). The inner circle, the EEC, was more deeply integrated.

Figure 1.5 A Europe of two concentric circles

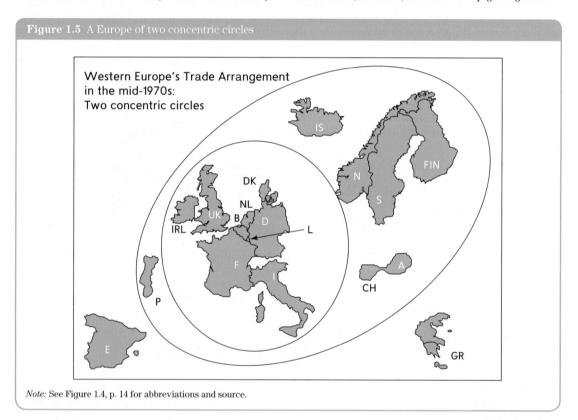

Note: See Figure 1.4, p. 14 for abbreviations and source.

1.4 Euro-pessimism

Although the customs union was implemented smoothly and ahead of schedule, European integration stagnated soon after its completion. The Community was rocked by a series of political crises in the 1960s, soon to be followed by economic shocks in the early 1970s. These created a period known as 'Euro-pessimism' (1973–86).

1.4.1 Political shocks

The spectacularly good economic performance of Europe's economies in the 1950s and 1960s – teamed with the manifest success of European economic integration – went a long way to restoring the confidence of Europeans in their governments' ability to govern (Milward, 1984). So much so that some nations began to regret the promises of deep integration they had made in the Treaty of Rome. Leading this charge for national sovereignty was French President Charles de Gaulle.

The issue came to a head as the final stage in the Treaty of Rome's transition period approached (1 January 1966). At this stage, the voting procedures in the EEC's key decision-making body, the Council of Ministers, were scheduled to switch to majority voting (see Section 3.3.1). For de Gaulle, it was unacceptable that France might have to accept a majority-backed policy even if it had voted against it. In the end, de Gaulle forced the other EEC members to accept his point of view in the so-called Luxembourg Compromise (see Box 1.7). Henceforth, unanimity was the typical rule in EEC decision-making procedures. The insistence

Box 1.7   The 'empty chair' policy and the Luxembourg Compromise

De Gaulle, who had always opposed supranationality, challenged the principle in 1966. The test case came when France opposed a range of Commission proposals including financing of the Common Agricultural Policy. France stopped attending the main Community meetings (the so-called 'empty chair' policy; see Figure 1.6) and threatened to withdraw from the EEC. This marked the end of the post-war climate for radical change, but not the end of the EEC.

Figure 1.6 Crise de la chaise vide, 1965

© European Union, 2014

In exchange for its return to the Council of Ministers, France demanded a political agreement – the Luxembourg Compromise – that de facto overturned the Treaty of Rome's majority voting provisions. Whenever a Member State announced that it felt that 'very important interests' were at stake the voting rule switched to unanimity. In short, this reversed much of the unlimited supranationality that the Six committed themselves to in the Treaty of Rome just ten years before. The Luxembourg Compromise was abolished by the Lisbon Treaty and single-nation moves in the twenty-first century by Britain and others have failed.

Although the Luxembourg Compromise had no legal force, it had an enormous impact. It meant that unanimity was the de facto rule for almost everything. Almost all progress on deeper economic integration was blocked until majority voting was restored in the 1986 Single European Act. The compromise in full reads: 'Where, in the case of decisions which may be taken by a majority vote on a proposal from the Commission, very important interests of one or more partners are at stake, the Members of the Council will endeavour, within a reasonable time, to reach solutions which can be adopted by all the Members of the Council while respecting their mutual interests and those of the Community, in accordance with Article 2 of the Treaty.' For details and background, see http://en.euabc.com/word/640.

on consensus radically reduced the EEC's ability to make decisions (see Chapter 3 on decision-making efficiency) and the problem only got worse as the EEC expanded to nine in 1973.

1.4.2 Failure of monetary integration

The late 1960s saw the USA running an irresponsibly inflationary monetary policy – printing money to pay for the Vietnam War. Since all major currencies were linked to the dollar at the time (via the global fixed exchange rate system called Bretton Woods), US inflation was transmitted into inflation in Europe and elsewhere. This, in turn, led to the gradual breakdown of the global fixed exchange rate system (between 1971 and 1973; see Chapter 14 for details).

Exchange rate stability was widely viewed as a critical factor supporting the rapid post-war growth in trade and international investment and the rising prosperity these brought. It prevented nations from offsetting the market-opening effects of European integration with a competitive devaluation. The EEC searched for ways of restoring intra-European exchange rate stability. It established the Werner Committee, which designed a step-by-step plan for European monetary union by 1980. EU leaders adopted the Werner Plan in 1971.

The economic environment for this new European monetary arrangement could not have been worse. Months after it was launched, the Yom Kippur War in the Middle East triggered an Arab oil boycott of western states. The resulting sharp rise in oil prices had a ruinous economic impact on western Europe. Just as inflationary tendencies were heating up as a result of US actions, the oil shock severely dampened economic activity in Europe and for all of its global trading partners. Most European nations adopted expansionary monetary and fiscal policies to compensate for the economic downturn and these further fuelled inflation. The result was falling incomes and rising inflation known as 'stagflation'. Just as the world was recovering from the 1973 oil shock, the Iranian Revolution produced a second massive oil price hike, in 1979, further aggravating stagflation. A debilitating series of exchange rate crises – caused by these massive external shocks – put the Werner Plan on hold for ever. This monetary integration failure was a key feature of Euro-pessimism.

1.4.3 Failure of deeper trade integration

As tariff barriers fell, Europeans erected new trade barriers. These new barriers consisted of detailed technical regulations and standards, which had the effect of fragmenting the European markets. While these policies, called 'technical barriers to trade' (TBT), undoubtedly inhibited intra-European trade, their announced goal was to protect consumers. EEC leaders had recognized the trade-inhibiting effects of TBTs in the Treaty of Rome (Article 100 requires 'approximation', Euro-speak for harmonization, of national regulations for the 'proper functioning of the common market'). However, as European voters became richer, they demanded tighter regulation of markets and products. The usual machinery of vested-interest politics meant that many of the new standards and regulations tended to protect domestic firms.

The EU first systematically took up the removal of technical barriers in 1969 with its 'General Programme'. This launched what came to be called the 'traditional' or 'old' approach to TBT liberalization. The approach adopted relied on detailed technical regulations for single products or groups of products implemented by unanimously agreed directives. Since unanimity was required, this approach failed. Harmonization proceeded much more slowly than the development of new national barriers. For example, ten years were required to adopt a directive on gas containers made of unalloyed steel and nine and a half years was the average delay for the 15 directives adopted en masse in 1984. In the meantime, Member States were implementing thousands of technical standards and regulations a year.

Stagflation, teamed with the failure of the initiatives to forge deeper monetary and trade integration, created a gloom over the 'European construction'. Many inside and outside Europe suspected that the ideals that had driven European integration since the late 1940s were dying or dead; the stars, so to speak, were falling off the EU flag.

Yet there were some bright spots in European integration during this period.

1.4.4 Bright spots

Spain, Portugal and Greece all adopted democratic governments, thus rendering them eligible for EEC membership. Greece joined in 1981, followed by the Iberians in 1986. The European Monetary System (EMS) started operation in 1978 and was successful in stabilizing intra-EEC exchange rates. EEC financing was put on a firm footing with two budget treaties (1970 and 1975; see Chapter 2 for details). The institutions of the three communities (ESCS, Euratom and EEC) were rationalized by the 1965 Merger Treaty and the EU Parliament was directly elected for the first time in 1979; previously, its members came from the members' national parliaments.

In the USA and Europe, central bankers decided to fight inflation – which had reached double-digit figures in most industrial nations. They did so by inducing a long, hard recession. Between 1981 and 1983 growth was negative or only slightly positive in most of Europe. While inflation rates did decline, this was at the cost of a significant increase in unemployment.

Starting in 1984, economic growth resumed. Political attitudes also changed – in particular, a strenthened belief in market economics began to spread throughout the industrialized world. US President Reagan and British Prime Minister Thatcher are often cited as vanguards, but even the socialist French President Mitterrand adopted a much more favourable attitude towards market-based solutions. While there are many causes for this philosophical shift, the fact that highly interventionist policies had failed to prevent ten years of poor economic performance is surely one of the most important.

1.5 Deeper circles and the domino effect part II: the Single Market Programme and the EEA

This favourable economic climate was matched with the arrival of a talented promoter of European integration, Jacques Delors (see Box 1.8). Delors, President of the European Commission from 1985 to 1994, sought to kick-start European integration by pushing for the 'completion' of the internal market that had been promised in the Treaty of Rome. He dubbed this the 'Single Market Programme'. By July 1987, all Member States had adopted the Single European Act, which is the Community legislation that implemented the Single Market measures (along with many other changes).

Box 1.8   Jacques Delors (1925–)

© European Union, 2014

Jacques Lucien Jean Delors, born in Paris, held a series of posts in banking and the French government. He was heavily engaged in the trade union movement and a devout Catholic. After a stint in the European Parliament, he became Finance Minister under French President Mitterrand. He was President of the European Commission during the most important deepening of European economic integration since the 1950s – an outcome that most observers accredit to his savvy and energy. He was critical to the passing of the 1986 Single European Act, which led to sweeping economic integration.

Delors was also instrumental in the Economic and Monetary Union (EMU), which led to the creation of the euro. Among his many other accomplishments, he pushed through a reform of EU financing and redirected EU spending away from agriculture and towards support for disadvantaged regions.

1.5.1 The Single Market Programme

In 1985, EU firms enjoyed duty-free access to each other's markets; however, they did not enjoy free trade. Intra-EC trade was shackled by a long list of trade-inhibiting barriers such as differing technical standards and industrial regulations, capital controls, preferential public procurement, administrative and frontier formalities, VAT and excise tax rate differences and differing transport regulations, to mention just a few. Although the vast majority of these policies seem negligible individually, the confluence of their effects served to substantially restrict intra-Community trade.

Indeed, many of these barriers were introduced in the 1970s as European nations increasingly adopted standards and regulations that were aimed at protecting consumers, workers and the environment. The free movement of goods was also restricted by national and local government practices such as biased purchasing patterns, exclusive production or service rights, and production subsidies to national champions. Likewise, the free movement of services – which was guaranteed in principle by the Treaty of Rome – was far from being a reality, again largely due to national prudential and safety regulations. Service providers typically were required to possess local certification and the requirements for such certification often varied across nations. Moreover, the certification process was often controlled or influenced by the national service providers, which had an economic interest in excluding foreign competitors via this certification process.

The key changes in the Single Market Programme were designed to reinforce the 'four freedoms' (free movement of goods, services, people and capital) promised by the Treaty of Rome. The concrete steps were:

- Liberalization of trade in goods
- Streamlining or elimination of border formalities
- Harmonization of VAT rates within wide bands
- Liberalization of government procurement
- Harmonization and mutual recognition of technical standards in production, packaging and marketing
- Liberalization of factor trade
- Removal of all capital controls
- Increase in capital market integration
- Liberalization of cross-border market-entry policies, including mutual recognition of approval by national regulatory agencies

The Single European Act also implemented important institutional changes. To clear the decision-making log-jam that had held up similar integration initiatives in the 1970s, the programme included a major change in the EU's decision-making procedures. Decisions concerning Single Market issues would be adopted on the basis of majority voting instead of on a basis of unanimity (see Chapter 3 for a discussion of EU decision-making procedures). This change in voting procedures was part of the so-called new approach to TBT liberalization.

Focus on capital mobility

The most novel aspect of the Single Market Programme was its focus on capital mobility; other features can be viewed as deepening or extending integration initiatives already agreed. Some EU members had unilaterally liberalized capital mobility, but many resisted. The Single Market Programme ruled out all remaining restrictions on capital movements among EU residents by 1988.

It is possible to think of this aspect of the Single Market Programme as unleashing a political economy process that eventually led to the euro. Simple macroeconomic logic (explained in Chapter 13) tells us that, without capital controls, nations must choose between controlling their exchange rate and controlling their monetary policy. Since exchange rate stability was considered paramount, EU members enslaved their monetary policy to achieve exchange rate stabilization in the context of the EMS. But once nations were no longer actively using monetary policy, resistance to centralizing monetary policy decisions in a European central bank was greatly weakened.

1.5.2 The EEA and the fourth enlargement

Since the Single European Act promised much tighter economic integration among EU members, non-EU nations again found themselves threatened by the discriminatory effects of integration in the EU. As in the 1960s and early 1970s, this triggered a domino effect as EFTA firms prompted their governments to offset that discrimination by seeking closer ties to the EU.

In the late 1980s, EFTA governments had decided that they must react to the Single Market. Several considered applying for EU membership (Austria actually did so), while others contemplated bilateral negotiations. Jacques Delors forced the decision in January 1989 by proposing the European Economic Area (EEA) agreement, which essentially extends the Single Market to EFTA economies (apart from agriculture and the Common External Tariff).

Given the political economy forces described above, it is easy to understand why EFTA nations wanted the EEA. Two aspects of the EEA, however, are extraordinary. First, the EEA is unbalanced in terms of the rights and obligations of EFTA nations in relation to future EEC legislation. The EEA commits EFTA nations to accepting future EU legislation concerning the Single Market, without any formal input into the formation of these new laws. Second, the EEA created supranationality among the EFTA nations, a feature that they had resisted since the end of the war.

As it turned out, EFTA nations were not happy with the EEA compromises, especially in the post-Cold War environment, where the East–West political division of Europe appeared to have vanished. By the end of the EEA negotiations, Austria, Finland, Sweden, Norway and Switzerland had applied for EU membership. For them, the EEA was a transitional arrangement. Swiss voters rejected the EEA in December 1992, effectively freezing their EU application. Accession talks with the four EFTAns were successful, however. The EEA thus now consists of the EU27, on one hand, and Norway, Liechtenstein and Iceland, on the other (Norway's voters rejected EU membership by referendum and Switzerland has an EEA-like bilateral deal with the EU).

The Single Market, EEA and plans for monetary union were launched while Cold War politics still mattered. They came to fruition in a very different world.

1.6 Communism's creeping failure and spectacular collapse

The division of Europe into communist and capitalist camps was cemented, quite literally, in 1961 by the construction of the Berlin Wall. While living standards were not too dissimilar to begin with, by the 1980s western European living standards far outstripped those in Eastern Europe and the USSR. Anyone could plainly see that the West's economic system (free markets and an extensive social welfare system) when teamed up with its political system (multi-party democracy and freedom of the press) provided a far better way of life compared to the East's system of planned economies and one-party rule.

While this 'creeping failure' of communism was apparent to the central and eastern European countries (CEECs), Soviet leaders repeatedly thwarted reform efforts via constant economic pressure and occasional military intervention. By the 1980s, the inadequacy of the Soviet system forced changes inside the USSR itself. The USSR adopted a policy of timid pro-market reforms (*perestroika*) and a policy of openness (*glasnost*), which involved a marked reduction in internal repression and diminished intervention in the affairs of the Soviet republics and Soviet-bloc nations.

As far as European integration was concerned, the Soviet foreign policy changes were critical. Pro-democracy forces in the CEECs, which had been repeatedly put down by military force hereto, found little resistance from Moscow in the late 1980s. The first breach came in June 1989 when the Polish labour movement 'Solidarity' forced the communist government to accept free parliamentary elections. The communists lost and the first democratic government in the Soviet bloc took power. Moscow rapidly established ties with the new Polish government.

Moscow's hands-off approach to the Polish election triggered a chain of events over the next 2 years that revolutionized European affairs. Pro-reform elements inside the Hungarian communist party pressed for democratic elections, and, more dramatically, Hungary opened its border with Austria. Thousands of East Germans reacted by moving to West Germany via Hungary and Austria. This set off mass protests against communist repression in East Germany, which culminated in the opening of the border between East and West Germany.

On 9 November 1989, thousands of West and East Berlin citizens converged on the Berlin Wall with pickaxes and sledgehammers to dismantle that symbol of a divided Europe (Figure 1.7). By the end of 1989, democratic forces were in control in Poland, Hungary, Czechoslovakia and East Germany. In 1990, East and West Germany formed a unified Germany and three Soviet republics – Estonia, Latvia and Lithuania – declared their independence from the USSR. By the end of 1991, the Soviet Union itself had broken up, putting a definitive end to its interference in central and eastern Europe. The European Union reacted swiftly to this geopolitical earthquake by providing emergency aid and loans to the fledgling democracies.

Figure 1.7 Solidarity movement and fall of the Berlin Wall

© Mary Evans Picture Library/Interfoto Agentur

1.6.1 Maastricht Treaty, the euro and German unification

The 'political earthquake' caused by the falling of the Berlin Wall also yielded substantial changes within the EU. With the wall gone, unification of the western and eastern parts of Germany was the natural next step, but a unified Germany would be a behemoth. With 80 million citizens and responsible for 30 per cent of Europe's output, Germany would be much larger than France, Britain or Italy. This raised many fears, ranging from a disturbed political balance in the EU to the unlikely, but still scary, spectre of German militarism. Many Europeans, including many Germans, felt that Germany would be best unified in conjunction with a big increase in the forces tying EU members together.

Riding on his success with the Single Market, Jacques Delors seized this historical moment and proposed a radical increase in European economic integration – the formation of a monetary union – a step that he believed would eventually lead to political integration.

The idea was quickly championed by French President François Mitterrand and German Chancellor Helmut Kohl. After extensive negotiations, the EU committed itself to a target of forming a monetary union by 1999 and adopting a single currency by 2002. This commitment was made in the Treaty of Maastricht.

The Maastricht Treaty is covered in depth in Chapter 14, but for the purposes of this chapter it is important to note that the Maastricht Treaty – formally known as the Treaty on European Union – embodied the most profound deepening of European integration since the Treaty of Rome. In addition to committing members to a transfer of national sovereignty over monetary power to a supranational body (the European Central Bank), and abandonment of their national currencies for the euro, the Treaty also:

- created EU citizenship; this included the right to move to and live in any EU state (the Treaty of Rome only guaranteed the right to work in any Member State) and to vote in European and local elections in any Member State;
- locked in the free movement of capital;
- strengthened EU cooperation in non-economic areas, including security and defence policy, law enforcement, criminal justice, civil judicial matters, and asylum and immigration policies;
- enshrined the principle of subsidiarity that was meant to control the transfer of responsibilities from Member States to the European Union;
- strengthened the European Parliament's power over EU legislation;
- introduced the 'Social Chapter' which expanded the EU's social dimension by introducing policies on workers' health and safety, workplace conditions, equal pay and the consultation of employees.

The most historic change was of course the commitment to adopt a single currency. As this subject is covered in great detail in Part V of the book, this chapter deals only with the aspects that are essential to understanding subsequent developments – except those related to the Eurozone crisis, which are dealt with at length in Chapter 19.

Maastricht ratification difficulties

EU treaties such as Maastricht have power because they must be part of each Member State's domestic law, i.e. EU treaties must be ratified by each and every member if they are to come into force. In many EU nations, ratification involves a vote by the national parliament; in others, a referendum. The Maastricht Treaty experienced great difficulties with ratification.

During the negotiations, the British insisted on a formal opt-out from the common currency (the idea was that all other members would have to adopt the euro once they met the criteria) and from the Social Chapter. Even with these provisos, Eurosceptics from his own party nearly brought down British Prime Minister John Major's government during the UK Parliamentary ratification vote. French President François Mitterrand put the Treaty to a referendum expecting a massive 'yes' vote that would bolster the Treaty's prospects (referenda are not mandatory in France), but only 51.4 per cent of the French voted 'yes'. The Treaty was challenged (unsuccessfully) as unconstitutional before Germany's High Court.

More problematic was the fact that Danish voters narrowly rejected the Treaty in a 1992 referendum. After EU leaders agreed to grant Denmark opt-outs on the single currency and defence matters, a second vote on Maastricht was held and the Danes reversed their own veto by voting 'yes'. The Treaty came into force in November 1993.

1.7 Reuniting East and West Europe

Given that almost every other nation in the region had free trade access to the enormous EU market, free trade agreements with the EU were a commercial necessity for the newly free central and eastern European countries (CEECs). Their strategic goal, however, was EU and NATO membership. CEEC leaders felt unsure that the new situation was permanent. If things went wrong in Russia and the iron curtain re-descended, each CEEC wanted to be sure that the curtain would, this time, come down east of its border.

1.7.1 First steps: the Europe Agreements

Each CEEC announced that its goal was to join the EU. The EU, by contrast, was reluctant in the early 1990s. Sidestepping the membership issue, the EU signed Association Agreements (also called Europe Agreements) with Poland, Hungary and Czechoslovakia in 1991. Europe Agreements for other CEECs followed progressively. By 1994, such deals had been signed with Romania, Bulgaria, Albania, Estonia, Latvia and Lithuania.

The Europe Agreements established bilateral free trade between the EU and each individual CEEC. Beyond the removal of tariffs on most industrial goods, a further goal was to make progress towards 'realizing between them the other economic freedoms on which the Community is based'. The adoption of EU laws and practices (competition policy, harmonized standards, etc.) helped the CEECs establish functioning market economies faster than they could have on their own. EFTA negotiated similar bilateral agreements in parallel. Some CEECs also signed trade arrangements among themselves. The goal of EU membership provided an important political anchorage that kept the pro-market reforms on track.

The Europe Agreements stopped short of offering EU membership – reflecting the profound ambivalence that many West Europeans initially felt towards eastern enlargement in the 1980s. For instance, slow action of the parliaments of EU Member States meant that the Europe Agreements signed with Hungary and Poland in December 1991 entered into force only in February 1994. Most of the hesitation was due to the economic nature of the CEEC. The CEECs were poor, populous and agrarian. Since the EU spent 80 per cent of its budget on farms and poor regions, eastern enlargement was viewed as a threat to EU special interest groups.

1.7.2 Copenhagen to Copenhagen: from 1993 accession criteria to EU membership

The EU officially ended its hesitancy in June 1993. In Copenhagen, the EU's key political body – the European Council – decided the associated CEECs could become EU members. The Council laid out the so-called Copenhagen Criteria for membership. These – which are still applied today – are:

- political stability of institutions that guarantee democracy, the rule of law, human rights and respect for and protection of minorities;
- a functioning market economy capable of dealing with the competitive pressure and market forces within the Union;
- acceptance of the Community 'acquis' (EU law in its entirety, including all the treaties and subsequent rules) and the ability to take on the obligations of membership, including adherence to the aims of political, economic and monetary union.

1.8 Preparing for eastern enlargement: a string of new treaties

Once the EU15 leaders confirmed that the CEECs would eventually join, the next order of business was to get EU institutions – which had been designed for 6 members and were straining to work with 15 – ready for a dozen new members. This started a chain of events that eventually ended in adoption of the Lisbon Treaty in December 2009.

The process began formally in December 1993. A treaty-writing exercise (what the EU calls an Intergovernmental Conference, or IGC) had already been scheduled in the 1992 Maastricht Treaty for 1996. The original purpose was something of a 'check-up' halfway into the timetable for monetary union. Building on this, the 1993 Brussels European Council added EU institutional reform to its agenda. The EU was using institutional structures and procedures that had been designed for six members in the late 1950s. By the 1990s, these were proving hard to make work for 15 members; adding another 10 or 12 would require EU institutional reform.

The group set up to propose such changes produced the so-called Westendorp Report. This identified Council of Minister voting and the number of Commission members as areas requiring reform but could not reach agreement on solutions. Agreement on problems and disagreement on solutions marked the four attempts at reform made by the EU over a 16-year period (Amsterdam, Nice, Constitutional and Lisbon Treaties). Moreover, the disagreements it highlights – big member vs. small members, federalists vs. intergovernmentalists, etc. – are exactly those that plagued every step of the decade-long process of reforming EU institutions.

1.8.1 Amsterdam Treaty: cleaning up the Maastricht Treaty

The 1996 IGC produced the Amsterdam Treaty in 1997. Ambitions for the Amsterdam Treaty were high – the mandate was to agree all the necessary enlargement-related reforms highlighted by the Westendorp Report. By this yardstick, it failed.

The Amsterdam Treaty is best thought of as a tidying up of the Maastricht Treaty. The substantive additions included a more substantial role for the EU in social policy formation (UK Prime Minister Tony Blair cancelled the British opt-out). The powers of the European Parliament were modestly boosted, and the notion of flexible integration, so-called closer cooperation, was introduced (see Chapter 2 for details).

The key enlargement-related reforms were not settled but were still pressing, so EU leaders agreed a list called the 'Amsterdam leftovers'. They also agreed to launch a new IGC in 2000.

1.8.2 Nice Treaty: failed attempt to reform EU institutions

After the year-long preparation of the IGC 2000, EU leaders met in Nice in December 2000 to wrap up a new treaty that was supposed to deal with the Amsterdam leftovers. At 4 o'clock in the morning, after the longest EU summit in history, EU leaders announced political agreement on a new treaty.

The result – the Treaty of Nice – was not a success. The critical Amsterdam leftover issues – the size and composition of the Commission, extension of majority voting in the Council of Ministers and reform of Council voting rules – were not fully solved (see Chapter 3 for details). For example, the chairmanship of then-French President Jacques Chirac (France chaired the European Council at the time) was heavily criticized by leaders of the European Parliament and the President of the European Commission, Romano Prodi. Indeed, a few days after the Nice Summit, the European Parliament adopted a resolution that accused the governments of having given 'priority to their short-term national interests rather than to EU interests'. Back then, however, the European Parliament did not have the power to block a new treaty.

Nice Treaty ratification difficulties

The Nice Treaty experienced some trouble with ratification but far less than did the Maastricht Treaty. Only the Irish refused to ratify the Nice Treaty in a referendum. Since a new treaty cannot come into force until all EU members have ratified it, the Irish 'no' had to be addressed. The solution was to make a number of political commitments guaranteeing Irish neutrality and to have all 14 other members ratify the Treaty. Irish voters were then asked to vote again; the second time they said 'yes'.

Note: Sinn Féin opposed the Nice Treaty, but most political parties supported it. Irish voters reversed their decision following EU assurances on military issues.

Incomplete reform

EU leaders at the Nice Summit knew that the Treaty did not fully adjust the EU to the new realities of the coming enlargement. In what had become a familiar pattern, part of the final political deal on the Treaty at Nice was an agreement to hold another IGC to complete the reform process. This 'Declaration on the Future of the Union' highlighted four themes:

1 defining a more precise division of powers between the EU and its members;

2 clarifying the status of the Charter of Fundamental Rights proclaimed in Nice;

3 making the treaties easier to understand without changing their meaning;

4 defining the role of national parliaments in the European institutions.

1.8.3 Eastern enlargement and the Constitutional Treaty

One year after the Nice Summit, the European Council met in the Belgian city of Laeken to adopt the 'Declaration on the Future of the European Union'. This provided an outline for thinking about the new treaty to be written by the IGC in 2004.

In light of the difficult Nice Summit, the Laeken Council also decided on a novel working method. It convened the 'Convention on the Future of Europe', which came to be known as the European Convention, consisting of a large number of men and women representing current and prospective Member States, the national parliaments, the European Parliament and the Commission. The Convention's output was to be the point of departure for the IGC 2004 that would draft the actual treaty (as required by EU law).

As far as its contents are concerned, the 'Laeken Declaration' contains a list of issues that is surprisingly close to that of the 1995 Westendorp Report. The Laeken Declaration, however, included two crucial novelties:

- The Declaration implicitly admits that the Nice reforms were insufficient. In effect, it asks the Convention to reform the Nice Treaty reforms before they have even been implemented (most Nice Treaty changes only took effect after 2004).

- While the Nice Declaration made no mention of a constitution, the word does appear in the Laeken Declaration.[1]

The European Convention, February 2002–July 2003

The European Convention was run by former French President Valéry Giscard d'Estaing with the assistance of two Vice-Chairmen (see Figure 1.8). It started slowly and many early observers expected its large size and ill-defined objectives to result in a muddled outcome.

Figure 1.8 The European Convention was run by its presidium

Presidential podium at the plenary session debate on institutional questions, January 2003. From left to right: Jean-Luc Dehaene (Vice-Chairman, Belgium), Giuliano Amato (Vice-Chairman, Italy) and Valéry Giscard d'Estaing (Chairman, France). © European Union, 2014

However, by mid-2002 President Giscard d'Estaing had redefined the Convention's purpose. The 'Convention on the Future of Europe' was transformed into a constitution-writing convention. The new

---

[1] The Laeken Declaration included the following statement: 'The question ultimately arises as to whether this simplification and reorganization might not lead in the long run to the adoption of a constitutional text in the Union. What might the basic features of such a constitution be? The values which the Union cherishes, the fundamental rights and obligations of its citizens, the relationship between Member States in the Union?'

goal was to present the EU heads of state and government with a fully written constitution. This changed everything. From that point onward, EU members started sending heavyweight politicians in place of low-level representatives. All arguments over the need for a constitution were dropped; discussion turned instead to its content.

Chairman Valéry Giscard d'Estaing was firmly in charge. The Convention's decision-making procedure involved no voting by representatives and indeed no standard democratic procedure of any kind. The Convention adopted its recommendations by 'consensus', with Giscard d'Estaing defining when a consensus existed. The representatives of the candidate countries participated fully in the debate, but their voices were not allowed to prevent a consensus among representatives of the then-15 members of the EU.

These unusual features of the Convention's working method go a long way to explaining the many problems that the Constitutional Treaty was soon to face.

The IGC's failure and the Irish compromise

The process of turning the Convention's draft into an EU treaty (see Figure 1.9) did not start well. Although the draft was presented in July 2003, Italian Prime Minister Silvio Berlusconi (Italy chaired the European Council at the time) convened the IGC only in October 2003. Differences that had been papered over in the Convention emerged immediately – especially the critical Council voting question which had not been openly discussed in the Convention (see Chapter 3 for details). The Italian Presidency failed to bridge the differences – ending hopes that reform would come before enlargement.

Figure 1.9 Toast at the Convention's last Plenary Session, 13 June 2003

Source: © European Union, 2014

All EU members – including the ten members that joined in 2004 – agreed that institutional reform was a must, so the Irish government, which took over the EU Presidency from the Italians, made a new attempt to rewrite the European Convention's rejected draft. Skilful diplomacy by the Irish Presidency and a change of government in Spain permitted a grudging and difficult but ultimately unanimous acceptance of a new draft at the June 2004 summit of EU25 leaders. With this high-level political compromise in hand, the IGC completed its work and the Constitution was signed in Rome in October 2004.

Constitutional Treaty ratification difficulties

For a variety of reasons, five EU nations that would normally have ratified the Constitutional Treaty by parliamentary vote opted for referenda: France, the Netherlands, the UK, Luxembourg and Spain. Two of these – France and the Netherlands – turned in 'no' votes in mid-2005 that derailed the whole process.

The French and Dutch 'nos' were quite a different problem for EU leaders from the Danish and Irish 'nos' on the Maastricht and Nice Treaties. Apart from the fact that the Dutch and French were founding members, the number of no-voters was entirely different. In the first Irish poll on the Nice Treaty, less than a million people voted and only 530,000 said 'no'. In the French referendum, 16 of 29 million French voters said 'no' (see Figure 1.10). Three days later, 4.7 out of 7.6 million Dutch rejected the Treaty. While EU leaders could 'work around' 530,000 Irish no-sayers, it was impossible to ignore over 20 million 'nos'.

Figure 1.10 Posters for the French Constitutional Treaty referendum

© European Union, 2014

In reaction, EU leaders suspended the ratification process and declared a 'period of reflection'.

1.8.4 The Lisbon Treaty

Two inadequate reform attempts (Amsterdam and Nice Treaties), a decade of on-and-off negotiations and four rejections by European voters made it clear that EU institutional reform was not easy and was not popular with EU voters. Why didn't EU leaders just abandon the project? The answer lies in the factors that had been obvious since the 1993 Westendorp Report. An EU of 25 had to reform its institutions if it was to continue functioning effectively and legitimately; the Nice Treaty reforms were not good enough.

Germany re-launches the institutional reform process

The process was re-launched when Germany took on the rotating EU Presidency in 2007. Guided by forceful German leadership, EU leaders declared the Constitutional Treaty to be dead and agreed on the basic outlines of its replacement – the Reform Treaty, which came to be known as the Lisbon Treaty after the city in which it was signed in December 2007.

As EU leaders had been talking about institutional reform since the mid-1990s and the best they could agree on was already in the Constitutional Treaty, EU leaders included all the main Constitutional Treaty reforms in the Lisbon Treaty but packaged them very differently:

- All the grandiloquent language and gestures to supranationalism were dropped.
- All references to symbols of statehood were jettisoned – the flag, the anthem, the Foreign Ministers and the like.
- The word 'constitution' was banished.

The only federalist token was to merge the term 'European Community' with European Union.

Lisbon Treaty ratification difficulties

The idea behind the German repackaging strategy was to avoid referenda in as many nations as possible. By making it more of a technocratic amendment of the existing legal structure, most EU governments felt they would be justified in ratifying the Lisbon Treaty by a vote of the national parliament – the procedure adopted for most treaties by most members since the very beginning. By and large, it worked. The Irish constitution, however, requires a referendum on any law that changes the relationship between Irish law and EU law. Since the Lisbon Treaty certainly meets this criterion, a vote was held in July 2008. The no-voters won by a solid margin.

To justify holding a new vote, the Irish government obtained promises from fellow EU leaders that directly addressed the concerns of certain segments of the Irish electorate. With these promises in hand, the Irish reversed their 'no' in October 2009. The Treaty came into effect in December 2009.

The Lisbon Treaty instituted many important changes. These are addressed at length in Chapters 2 and 3.

1.9 Global and Eurozone crises and institutional responses

European economic integration during the 1990s and much of the 2000s was smooth sailing despite the 'Treaty troubles' discussed above. EU growth was good, unemployment was low and inflation was low and steady. This period has been called the 'Great Moderation'. It seemed that superior monetary policy in all high-income nations was able to avoid important recessions while keeping inflation under control. In Europe, the monetary union was given a good deal of credit for this favourable outcome.

An indicator of these happy economic times was a convergence of Eurozone long-run interest rates with the low levels achieved by Germany (see Figure 1.11). The economic logic is simple. Long-run interest rates reflect the interest rate that investors demand for locking up their money for 10 years or so. Traditionally, nations with unstable monetary and economic policies – Greece, for example – would have to pay higher interest rates to convince investors. During its first decade of existence, the Eurozone erased this difference, as Figure 1.11 shows. By January 2007, for example, there were almost no differences between lending rates to Germany and Greece.

In many nations, the USA included, this situation – and the confidence it inspired – encouraged investors to borrow money to invest. This so-called leverage made the borrowers – be they nations, banks or individuals – susceptible to interest rate rises and/or interruptions in the flow of new borrowing. The USA in particular saw a spectacular rise in lending to home buyers with very poor credit. In autumn 2007, confidence in these so-called subprime loans evaporated, causing huge financial stress for banks and other investors who had made such loans. The US government responded by helping the fragile lenders. However, as we now know, rather than making the problem better, such assistance actually made it worse. The bad debt began to be concentrated in a few banks and other financial institutions.

On 15 September 2008, a major US bank, Lehman Brothers, was caught between a rock and a hard place. It had loans to repay but could not convince enough investors to lend it new money. Instead of bailing out Lehman's, the US authorities decided to allow it to go broke; the idea was to teach other banks that they should be careful. The tactic backfired spectacularly as it set off the largest crisis since the Great Depression – the so-called Global Crisis that is still echoing around the world in 2014. In autumn 2008, all sorts of lenders feared that other banks and financial institutions would go broke and, as a result, almost all lending ceased. Banks, however, have to continually borrow new money to pay off debt previously

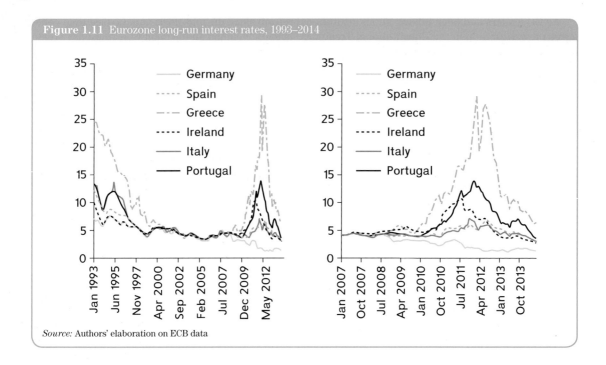

Figure 1.11 Eurozone long-run interest rates, 1993–2014

Source: Authors' elaboration on ECB data

incurred. In other words, the fear of a sudden halt in lending can create a situation whereby the fear of bank insolvency is actually realized. Basically, all large US banks were technically broke. This situation rapidly spread to Europe.

The response of the USA, the UK and other governments could comprise a book of its own, but as far as the Eurozone was concerned, the impact came later. The Lehman wake-up call led investors in Europe to resume their old tactic of charging higher interest rates to weak nations. As the right panel of Figure 1.11 shows, interest rates started to diverge between, for example, Greece and Germany (the right panel is the same as the left panel but shows fewer years for the sake of clarity).

It was into this situation of heightened fragility that the Greek and Irish 'bombs' were thrown. In January 2009, a very large Irish bank (which was heavily over-extended in terms of property loans) essentially went bankrupt. To avoid losses, the Irish government agreed to nationalize the bank. In October 2009, the newly elected socialist premier in Greece announced that his predecessor had 'cooked the books' concerning the size of the Greek national debt and deficit (i.e. the gap between government revenue and spending). These bombs simultaneously made the respective governments much more indebted and raised the interest rate they had to pay on those debts.

As it transpired, these shocks threw Greece and Ireland into what would be considered bankruptcy if they were individuals. The sudden increases in Greek and Irish national debt and the higher interest rates led to questions regarding their solvency as nations. Such doubts led investors to demand higher interest rates, which in turn fuelled fears about their solvency. On top of this, financial markets began to fear that the crisis-struck nations might abandon the euro and allow their currencies to fall in value. This fear simply added to the likelihood of a debt meltdown and thus pushed long-run interest rates even higher.

First Greece and then Ireland asked for emergency loans from other EU nations and the International Monetary Fund (IMF). They did so because they were unable to fund their budget deficits at sustainable interest rates on the financial markets. If they had not received the loans, they would have faced the prospect of defaulting on their debt. As fear spread, so interest on vulnerable governments' debt rose. In other words, the Eurozone crisis spread. The emergency loans to Greece in May 2010 and Ireland in February 2012 were followed by emergency packages for Portugal in May 2011, for Spanish banks in July 2012 and for Cyprus in May 2013.

Parts IV and V cover these events in much greater detail, but for this chapter a key outcome was a massive institutional reform that ended up transferring significant amounts of sovereignty from Eurozone nations to the Eurozone level. The main examples are a sequence of EU laws restricting Eurozone members' ability to run independent tax and spending policies. Eurozone members also agreed to adopt German-style constitutional rules for balanced budgets, going by the evocative names of Six Pack, Two Pack, European Semester and Debt Brake, for example.

On top of these changes affecting national budgetary policies, the Eurozone crisis led to the establishment of a bailout fund called the European Stability Mechanism, common banking oversight for large banks and a procedure for allowing bad banks to go broke without all investors losing all of their money. In short, the seeds of both a banking and a fiscal union were planted by the EU's response to the crisis.

While the Eurozone crisis is far from over, the most intensive and dangerous phase does seem to have passed. The critical moment was when ECB President Mario Draghi announced in a speech that the ECB would do whatever it took to keep the Eurozone from breaking up. From this moment onwards, the very high interest rates started to converge back towards German rates and the immediate fears of a Eurozone break up and national debt defaults faded.

1.10 Summary

It is impossible to summarize 70 years of European integration in a few paragraphs. But it is possible to highlight the main events and lessons as far as the economics of European integration are concerned.

European integration has always been driven by political factors, ranging from a desire to prevent another European war to a desire to share the fruit of integration with the newly democratic nations in central and eastern Europe. Yet while the goals were always political, the means were always economic.

There have been basically three big increases in European economic integration. Formation of the customs union from 1958 to 1968 eliminated tariffs and quotas on intra-EU trade. The Single Market Programme implemented between 1986 and 1992 (although elements are still being implemented today) eliminated many non-tariff barriers and liberalized capital flows within the EU. Finally, the Economic and Monetary Union melded together the currencies of most EU members.

Each of these steps towards deeper integration – but especially the customs union and the Single Market Programme – engendered discriminatory effects that triggered reactions in non-member nations. Just as the knocking down of one domino triggers a chain reaction that leads to the fall of all dominoes, the discriminatory effects of EU integration have created a powerful gravitational force that has progressively drawn all but the most reluctant Europeans into the EU. If there is a lesson to draw from this for the future, it is that the 2004 enlargement is likely to greatly magnify the pro-EU membership forces in the nations further east and south.

In the current decade, the Eurozone crisis has triggered institutional changes that have substantially deepened European integration.

Self-assessment questions

1 Draw a diagram (or diagrams) that graphically shows the major steps in European economic integration, along with dates and the names of the countries involved. Be sure to discuss explicitly the removal of various barriers to the movement of goods, labour and capital.

2 Draw a diagram like Figure 1.4 that shows the current state of trade arrangements in Europe, including all European nations west of the Urals.

3 Make a list of all the EU treaties (with dates) and provide a ten-words-or-less explanation of each treaty's major contribution to European integration.

4 Make a list of the dates of the major stages in the Common Agricultural Policy and its reforms (see europa.eu.int/comm/agriculture/index_en.htm for details).

5 Make a list of the dates of the major stages in the EU structural spending programmes (see http://ec.europa.eu/regional_policy/index_en.cfm for details).

6 What were the main challenges posed by eastern enlargement of the European Union and how was the Treaty of Nice meant to address these challenges?

7 Some European integration experts subscribe to the so-called bicycle theory of integration, which asserts that European integration must continually move forward to prevent it from 'falling over', i.e. breaking down. List a sequence of events from 1958 to 1992 that lends support to this theory.

8 Explain how Cold War politics accelerated European integration in some ways but hindered it in others, such as geographic expansion of the EU.

9 Explain when and by which means the organization that is known as the European Union has changed names since its inception in 1958.

10 Make a table showing the dates of all changes in EU and EFTA membership.

Further reading: the aficionado's corner

For a good, general description of the development of European integration, see:
Urwin, D. (1995) *The Community of Europe*, Longman, London.

Two books that challenge the traditional view that federalist idealism was important in the development of Europe are:
Milward, A. (1992) *The European Rescue of the Nation-state*, Cambridge University Press, Cambridge.
Moravcsik, A. (1998) *The Choice for Europe: Social Purpose and State Power from Messina to Maastricht*, Cornell University Press, Ithaca, NY.

A detailed description of post-war growth can be found in:
Botting, D. (1985) *From the Ruins of the Reich: Germany 1945–1949*, New American Library, New York.
Crafts, N. and G. Toniolo (1996) *Economic Growth in Europe since 1945*, Cambridge University Press, Cambridge.
Jackson, J. (2003) *The Fall of France*, Oxford University Press, Oxford.
Lamfalussy, A. (1963) *The UK and the Six: An Essay on Economic Growth in Western Europe*, Macmillan, London.
Moravcsik, A. (1998) *The Choice for Europe: Social Purpose and State Power from Messina to Maastricht*, Cornell University Press, Ithaca, NY.
Tsebelis, G. (2005) 'Agenda setting in the EU constitution: from the Giscard plan to the pros ratification(?) document', paper presented at the DOSEI conference, Brussels, http://sitemaker.umich.edu/tsebelis/files/giscardagenda.pdf.

Useful websites

The European Parliament's 'factsheets' provide an excellent, authoritative and succinct coverage of many historical institutions, policies and debates. For example, it has pages on the historical development of the Parliament's role, on historical enlargements and on every treaty. See www.europarl.eu.int/factsheets/default_en.htm.

Very detailed information on any topic concerning the EU can be found at http://ec.europa.eu/index_en.htm.

A good glossary can be found at http://europa.eu/legislation_summaries/glossary/.

Details on specific treaties (including handy summaries) can be found at http://europa.eu/about-eu/basic-information/decision-making/treaties/index_en.htm.

For Marxist–Leninist thinking on capitalism, imperialism and war, see this tract by Leon Trotsky at http://www.marxists.org/archive/trotsky/1939/09/ussr-war.htm.

The Truman Library website www.trumanlibrary.org/teacher/berlin.htm is a good source for early post-war background documents online.

The Centre Virtuel de la Connaissance sur l'Europe provides a complete and well-organized website for documents, photos, videos, etc. on virtually every aspect of European integration at www.cvce.eu.

The German Historical Museum (DHM) provides photos and videos of Germany's wartime experience at www.dhm.de/lemo/html/Nachkriegsjahre/DasEndeAlsAnfang/.

References

Baldwin, R. (1994) *Towards an Integrated Europe*, CEPR, London. Freely downloadable from http://heiwww.unige.ch7Baldwin/papers.htm.

Baldwin, R. (1995) 'A domino theory of regionalism', in R. Baldwin, P. Haaparanta and J. Kiander (eds) *Expanding European Regionalism: The EU's New Members*, Cambridge University Press, Cambridge.

BBC (2012) 'Nigel Farage warns of EU "mass unrest" and "revolution", www.bbc.co.uk/news/uk-politics-18014552.

Crafts, N. and G. Toniolo (1996) *Economic Growth in Europe since 1945*, Cambridge University Press, Cambridge.

Eichengreen, B. and J.B. de Macedo (2001) 'The European payments union: history and implications for the evolution of the international financial architecture', in A. Lamfalussy, B. Snoy and J. Wilson (eds) *Fragility of the International Financial System*, P.I.E.-Peter Lang, Brussels.

Milward, A. (1984) *The European Rescue of the Nation-state: 1945–51*, Routledge, London.

Milward, A. (1992) *The European Rescue of the Nation-state*, Cambridge University Press, Cambridge.

Padoa-Schioppa, T. (2004) *The Euro and its Central Bank: Getting United after the Union*, MIT Press, Cambridge, MA.

Spierenburg, D. and R. Poidevin (1994) *The History of the European Coal and Steel Community*, Weidenfeld & Nicolson, London.

Urwin, D. (1995) *The Community of Europe*, Longman, London.

Annex: A study guide to key dates

Year	Date	Event	Explanation
1948	16 April	OEEC	Organisation for European Economic Cooperation (OEEC) established.
1950	9 May	Schuman Plan	French Foreign Minister Robert Schuman proposes the establishment of the European Coal and Steel Community (ECSC). Schuman was inspired by Jean Monnet's vision of building Europe step by step. 9 May is celebrated as the Day of Europe.
1952	1 January	ECSC	The ECSC is established for 50 years; abolished in 2002.
1952	27 May	EDC	'The Six' sign the Treaty establishing the European Defence Community (EDC). The project fails as the French National Assembly rejects the Treaty in 1954.
1953	9 March	EPC	A plan for the European Political Community (EPC) is published.
1957	25 March	EEC	The Six sign treaties in Rome establishing the European Economic Community (EEC) and the European Atomic Energy Community (Euratom). EEC begins 1 January 1958.
1959	21 July	EFTA	European Free Trade Association (EFTA) is established by the Stockholm Convention among Austria, Denmark, Norway, Portugal, Sweden, Switzerland and the UK. EFTA begins 3 May 1960.
1966	1 January	Luxembourg Compromise	De facto voided the Treaty of Rome's majority voting procedures.
1968	1 July	CU completed	Customs union is completed within the EEC and a common external tariff is established.
1969	1–2 December	Failed monetary integration launched	EC leaders agree to establish an Economic and Monetary Union (EMU); to be implemented by 1980.
1972	22 July	EC–EFTA FTAs	Free trade agreements (FTAs) signed with Austria, Iceland, Portugal, Sweden and Switzerland.
1973	1 January	First enlargement	The Six become the Nine as Denmark, Ireland and the UK join the EC. Accession Treaties signed 1 January 1972. EEC signs free trade agreements with Norway (May) and Finland (October).
1978	6–7 July	EMS founded	Bremen European Council establishes the European Monetary System (EMS) and the European currency unit (ECU).
1981	1 January	Second enlargement	Greece joins.

Year	Date	Event	Explanation
1986	1 January	Third enlargement	Spain and Portugal join.
1986	17, 28 February	Single European Act	Single European Act is signed. Treaty enters into force on 1 July 1987.
1990	1 July	EMU stage 1	First stage of Economic and Monetary Union (EMU) begins.
1990	10 October	Germany unites	Germany is united as the former German Democratic Republic länder join the EEC.
1991		First Europe Agreements	EC signs Europe Agreements with Poland, Hungary and Czechoslovakia; Europe Agreements for other CEECs signed by 1995.
1992	7 February	Maastricht Treaty	Treaty on European Union is signed in Maastricht, creating the EU. Treaty enters into force 1 November 1993 after a difficult ratification process in Denmark.
1992	2 May	EEA	Single Market de facto extended to EFTAns via the European Economic Area (EEA).
1993	21–22 June	CEECs can join when ready	EU leaders decide CEECs with Europe Agreements can join when they meet the 'Copenhagen criteria'.
1994	1 January	EMU stage 2	The second stage of EMU begins.
1994	9–10 December	Plan for eastern enlargement	EU agrees strategy on eastern enlargement.
1995	1 January	Fourth enlargement	Austria, Finland and Sweden join the EU.
1997	2 October	Amsterdam Treaty	Treaty signed; comes into force 1 May 1999.
1998	1–2 May	The euro	EU leaders decide 11 to join Eurozone (Austria, Belgium, Finland, France, Germany, Ireland, Italy, Luxembourg, the Netherlands, Portugal and Spain).
1999	1 January	EMU stage 3	Euro becomes a currency in its own right; only electronic currency until January 2002.
2000	7–9 December	Nice Treaty	Treaty is signed; comes into force on 1 February 2003.
2002	1 January	Euro cash	Euro notes and coins circulate.
2002	February	European Convention	Following Laeken Declaration (15 December 2001), the Convention starts; it finishes June 2003.
2003	20 June	Draft Constitution	EU leaders accept the Giscard d'Estaing's draft Constitution as starting point for IGC.
2003	13 December	Draft Treaty rejected	European Council fails to adopt the Italian draft of the Treaty; IGC continues.

Year	Date	Event	Explanation
2004	1 May	Eastern enlargement	Ten new members join (Poland, Hungary, Slovakia, Czech Republic, Slovenia, Estonia, Latvia, Lithuania, Malta and Cyprus).
2004	18 June	Constitutional Treaty signed	Treaty signed. Ratification begins.
2005	30 May	French and Dutch reject Constitution	Constitution rejected; 62% of Dutch voters reject and 55% of French.
2007	1 January	Second eastern enlargement.	Bulgaria and Romania join the EU. Croatia, the Former Yugoslav Republic of Macedonia and Turkey are also candidates for future membership.
2007	13 December	Treaty of Lisbon	Treaty signed; enters into force in 2009.
2008	12 June	Irish reject Treaty of Lisbon	Irish voters reject the Lisbon Treaty in a referendum.
2009	October	Irish accept Lisbon Treaty	Two-thirds of Irish vote 'yes'
2009	January to October	EZ crisis preliminaries	Ireland nationalizes heavily indebted bank and Greece announces its debt and deficit positions are much worse than thought.
2010	May	Greek bailout	Greece is forced to take emergency loans from EU nations and the IMF.
2010	November	Irish bailout	Ireland follows Greece.
2011	May	Portuguese bailout	Portugal requires emergency loans.
2012	July	Spanish bank bailout	Spanish banks require emergency loans.
2012	July	Draghi statement	ECB President Mario Draghi says the ECB will do whatever it takes to resolve the Eurozone crisis and interest rates start to reconverge.
2013	May	Cyprus bailout	Cyprus is forced to default on large depositors in its banks and enter into an IMF programme for restructuring.

Note: Authors' elaboration based on a variety of sources.

In the infancy of societies, the chiefs of the state shape its institutions; later the institutions shape the chiefs of state.

Baron de Montesquieu

Facts, law, institutions and the budget

Chapter Contents

Introduction

The members of the European Union are economically and politically integrated to an extent that is historically unprecedented. In many ways, the EU is already more integrated than loosely federated nations such as Canada and Switzerland. This integration is maintained and advanced by a cocktail of economic, political, historical and legal forces shaped by European institutions, laws and policies. This chapter presents the background information on these institutional features that is essential to the study of European economic integration.

The chapter starts by detailing the extent of European economic integration, before turning to more institutional issues – EU organization, EU law, EU institutions and the legislative process. The chapter then presents basic facts on EU members (population, incomes and economic size), which are essential for understanding the subsequent topic – the EU budget.

2.1 Economic integration in the EU

If markets are so integrated, you can't cook a different soup in one corner of the pot.

Andres Sutt, Deputy Governor of the Bank of Estonia,
on why Estonia wanted to join the Eurozone

The extent and nature of EU economic integration cannot be fully understood without reference to the founders' intentions. The post-war architects of Europe had radical goals in mind when they established the European Economic Community with the 1957 Treaty of Rome (which was re-labelled the 'Treaty on the Functioning of the European Union' by the 2009 Lisbon Treaty).

The Treaty of Rome's main architect, Jean Monnet, headed an influential pan-European group called the Action Committee for the United States of Europe. Having failed with their plans for a European Political Community and a European Defence Community in the early 1950s, they switched to economic integration as the means of achieving their lofty goal (see Chapter 1 for details). This insight is critical to understanding the basic outlines of European economic integration. The various elements were not subjected to individual cost–benefit calculations. The idea was to fuse the six national economies into a unified economic area so as to launch a gradual process that would draw European citizens and their nations into an 'ever-closer union'.[1] In short, economics was to be the road to the 'finalité politique'; namely, politically unified Europe. In the 1940s, when radical thinking was mainstream, this was widely accepted as necessary to prevent another horrific war in Europe.

This section reviews economic integration in today's European Union, organizing the main features according to the logic of a unified economic area.

2.1.1 Treaty of Rome – fountainhead of EU economic integration

The Treaty of Rome was a far-reaching document. It is, in a sense, the bud whose leaves unfolded over 50 years into today's European Union. It laid out virtually every aspect of economic integration that Europe has implemented right up to the 1992 Maastricht Treaty which explicitly added monetary union to EU economic integration. It is also easy to read – unlike today's efforts such as the Lisbon Treaty.

The original Treaty of Rome was written from scratch by highly literate and fairly idealistic politicians and diplomats. Students should at least read the three-page 'PART ONE – Principles' in the original version

---

[1] A clear statement of this can be found in the so-called Spaak Report, 'Rapport des chefs de délégation aux ministres des Affaires étrangères', Bruxelles, 21 April 1956, the outcome of the experts group set up by the Messina Conference. See www.cvce.eu.

Box 2.1   Articles 1, 2 and 3 of the Treaty of Rome

ARTICLE 1. By this Treaty, the High Contracting Parties establish among themselves a EUROPEAN ECONOMIC COMMUNITY.

    ARTICLE 2. The Community shall have as its task, by establishing a common market and progressively approximating the economic policies of Member States, to promote throughout the Community a harmonious development of economic activities, a continuous and balanced expansion, an increase in stability, an accelerated raising of the standard of living and closer relations between the States belonging to it.

    ARTICLE 3. For the purposes set out in Article 2, the activities of the Community shall include, as provided in this Treaty and in accordance with the timetable set out therein:

(a) the elimination, as between Member States, of customs duties and of quantitative restrictions on the import and export of goods, and of all other measures having equivalent effect;

(b) the establishment of a common customs tariff and of a common commercial policy towards third countries;

(c) the abolition, as between Member States, of obstacles to freedom of movement for persons, services and capital;

(d) the adoption of a common policy in the sphere of agriculture;

(e) the adoption of a common policy in the sphere of transport;

(f) the institution of a system ensuring that competition in the common market is not distorted;

(g) the application of procedures by which the economic policies of Member States can be coordinated and disequilibria in their balances of payments remedied;

(h) the approximation of the laws of Member States to the extent required for the proper functioning of the common market;

(i) the creation of a European Social Fund in order to improve employment opportunities for workers and to contribute to the raising of their standard of living;

(j) the establishment of a European Investment Bank to facilitate the economic expansion of the Community by opening up fresh resources;

(k) the association of the overseas countries and territories in order to increase trade and to promote jointly economic and social development.

    Note that the Treaty of Rome has been amended and renamed many times since the 1950s (see Box 2.2); the current name, Treaty on the Functioning of the European Union, is so dull that many writers continue to call it the Treaty of Rome.

(available in many languages on many web pages, such as www.eurotreaties.com). Box 2.1 reproduces verbatim the first three articles.

2.1.2 How to create a unified economic area

The best way to understand European economic integration is not to read the Treaties in detail – they are just too complex. A better way is to think about the founders' goal of an ever-closer union – keeping in mind their 1950s mind-set about the sort of economic integration that would lead to the finalité politique.

    The intention of the Treaty of Rome was to create a unified economic area – an area within which all firms and consumers would have equal opportunities to sell or buy goods and services, and owners of labour and capital would be free to employ their resources in any economic activity anywhere within it.

Box 2.2   Treaty or Treaties of Rome?

Study of European integration is plagued by duplicate names. Many authors use the term the Treaty of Rome, others use Treaties of Rome. In fact two treaties were signed on 25 March 1957 in the Capitol in Rome – The 'Treaty establishing the European Economic Community', which set up the basic economic integration, and another treaty, the 'Treaty establishing the European Atomic Energy Community (Euratom)'.

As the full Treaty names are unwieldy, the abbreviations TEEC (Treaty Establishing the European Community) and Euratom were frequently used. Together they are known as the Treaties of Rome. However, the TEEC turned out to be vastly more important, so 'Treaty of Rome' became the short name for the TEEC.

To complicate things, the 'Treaty establishing the European Economic Community' was renamed the 'Treaty establishing the European Community', or TEC, by the 1992 Maastricht Treaty. The TEC was then re-labelled by the Lisbon Treaty as the 'Treaty on the Functioning of the European Union', or TFEU.

The Maastricht Treaty, which created the European Union (see Section 2.2 for details), is formally called the 'Treaty on European Union', or TEU. This has never been renamed, but the TEU and TEC were often called 'the Treaties'; now 'the Treaties' refers to the TEU and the TFEU.

Creating a unified economic area would, according to the founders' thinking, draw Europeans into ever-closer, ever-deeper economic exchanges (see Box 2.3 for the story of the Treaty's signing). These would, with time, lead Europeans to embrace ever-closer political cooperation and integration. As history shows, the plan worked (see Chapter 1); Europeans in 2014 are integrated on an economic, political, social and cultural level that would have been almost unimaginable in 1957.

The steps necessary to establish this unified economic area are presented below.

Free trade in goods

The most obvious requirement is to remove trade barriers. The Treaty of Rome removed all tariffs and quantitative restrictions among members. Tariffs and quotas, however, are not the only means of discriminating against foreign goods and services. Throughout the ages, governments have proved wonderfully imaginative in developing tariff- and quota-like barriers against foreign goods and services. To remove such 'non-tariff' barriers, and to prevent new non-tariff barriers from offsetting the tariff liberalization, the Treaty included catch-all language that rules out all measures that act like tariffs or quotas.

Common trade policy with the rest of the world

Trade can never be truly free among nations if they do not harmonize their trade policy towards non-members. Understanding this, however, requires a bit of reflection. If members had different tariffs against, say, the USA, there would be an incentive to circumvent them. Dishonest traders could import US goods into the EU nation with the lowest tariff and then re-export duty-free anywhere inside the EU. To prevent this so-called 'trade deflection', the movement of goods within the EU would have to verify that the goods crossing borders actually came from an EU member rather than the USA, or some other third nation. In the real world such controls (called Rules of Origin) act as trade barriers.

The Treaty avoids all this by requiring EU members to adopt a 'common commercial policy'; in other words, identical restrictions on imports from non-members. With these in place, every member can be sure that any product that is physically inside the EU has paid the common tariff and met any common restrictions on, for example, health and safety standards.

Box 2.3   What was really signed in Rome on 25 March 1957?

The Treaty of Rome took 9 months to write, which seems like lightning speed compared to today's treaty-writing negotiations. Writing and ratifying, however, are quite different things. The particular problem in 1957 was the staunch opposition of Charles de Gaulle to supranationality. De Gaulle was not in power when the Treaty was signed but France was in the midst of a political crisis and many believed that de Gaulle would return to power and kill the European project. In the rush to get the ratification process completed under a favourable French government, the signing ceremony in Rome was scheduled even before the agreement was fully fleshed out (e.g. additional Protocols were signed in April 1957).

As Allan Little, the BBC's World Affairs Correspondent, wrote: 'The treaty – still being argued over and translated into four languages until the last minute – was not printed. The six went ahead with the ceremony anyway.' The source for this remarkable piece of historical trivia is Pierre Pescatore, a former EU Court Judge, who was there on 25 March 1957. He told a BBC programme to mark the 50th anniversary of the event: 'They signed a bundle of blank pages. The first title existed in four languages, and also the protocol at the end. Nobody looked at what was in between.' (You can hear Pescatore's remarks, in French, at www.cvce.eu.)

Tariffs are one of the most important restrictions on external trade, so a common commercial policy with respect to tariffs is referred to by the special name 'customs union'.

Ensuring undistorted competition

Even a customs union is not enough to create a unified economic area. Trade liberalization can be offset by public and private measures that operate inside the borders of EU members. For example, French companies might make a deal whereby they buy only from each other. The Treaty therefore calls for a system ensuring that competition in the area is undistorted (more on this in Chapter 11). This includes prohibitions on trade-distorting subsidies to national producers, creation of a common competition policy, harmonization of national laws that affect the operation of the common market and harmonization of some national taxes. Why are all of these necessary to ensure undistorted competition?

- *State aid prohibited.* Production subsidies or other forms of government assistance granted to producers (called 'state aid' in EU jargon) allow firms to sell their goods cheaper and/or allow uncompetitive firms to stay in business. Both effects put unsubsidized firms at a disadvantage. Most forms of 'state aid' are prohibited by the Treaty, although a list of exceptions is specified.
- *Anti-competitive behaviour.* The Treaty prohibits any agreement that prevents, restricts or distorts competition in the area.
- *Approximation of laws* (EU jargon for harmonization). Another source of discrimination stems from product standards and regulations since these can have a dramatic impact on competition and indirectly favour national firms. To reduce this deviation from a unified economic area, the Treaty directs EU members to harmonize such standards and regulations. While this directive was cited in the Treaty of Rome, it did not really start operating until the Single European Act developed a practical way to achieve such harmonization.
- *Taxes.* Taxes applied inside Member States can distort competition directly or indirectly by benefitting national firms. On countering this type of discrimination, the Treaty is weak, requiring only that the Commission consider how taxes can be harmonized in the interest of the common market.

Unrestricted trade in services

Right from the Treaty of Rome, the principle of freedom of movement of services was embraced, although fleshing this into reality has been hard. Services are provided by people and governments have to regulate the qualifications of service providers (e.g. medical doctors). The problem has been to separate prudential regulation of qualifications from protectionist restrictions. This is still a work in progress.

Labour and capital market integration

The Treaty of Rome instituted a common employment and investment area by abolishing barriers to the free movement of workers and capital. This includes a ban on any form of discrimination based on nationality regarding hiring, firing, pay and working conditions. The Treaty also explicitly allows workers to travel freely in search of work. Note that this was not intended to allow free movement of people, only workers. The Single European Act amplified this by requiring the free movement of people, not just workers. For example, it granted British retirees the right to live in Spain even when they were not employed locally.

As for capital mobility, the Treaty focuses on two types of freedom. The first is the right of any Community firm to set up in another Member State. These 'rights of establishment' are essential to integration in sectors with high 'natural' trade barriers, e.g. in sectors such as insurance and banking, where a physical presence in the local market is critical to doing business. The second type concerns financial capital and here the Treaty goes deep. It states that all restrictions on capital flows (e.g. cross-border investments in stocks and bonds, and direct investment in productive assets by multinationals) shall be abolished. It applies the same to current payments related to capital flows (e.g. the payment of interest and repatriation of profits). Very little capital-market liberalization, however, was undertaken until the 1980s since the Treaty provided an important loophole. It allowed capital market restrictions when capital movements create disturbances in the functioning of a Member State's capital market. Moreover, it did not set a timetable for this liberalization. Capital market liberalization only became a reality 30 years later with the Single European Act and the Maastricht Treaty.

Exchange rate and macroeconomic coordination

Fixed exchange rates were the norm when the Treaty of Rome was written, and throughout the late 1940s and 1950s nations occasionally found that their fixed exchange rate level induced their citizens to purchase a value of foreign products and assets that exceeded foreigners' purchases of domestic goods and assets. Such situations, known as balance-of-payments crises, historically led to many policies – such as tariffs, quotas and competitive devaluations – that would be disruptive in a unified economic area. To avoid such disruptions, the Treaty of Rome called for mechanisms for coordinating members' macroeconomic policies and for fixing balance-of-payments crises. This seed in the Treaty of Rome eventually sprouted into the euro, the Stability and Growth Pact and the European Central Bank. See Chapters 17 and 18 for details.

Common policy in agriculture

From a logical point of view, it might seem that a unified economic area could treat trade in agricultural goods the same way as it treats trade in services and manufactured goods. From a political point of view, however, agriculture is very different and the EU has explicitly recognized this right from the beginning.

In the 1950s, Europe's farm sector was far more important economically than it is today. In many European nations, a fifth or more of all workers were employed in the sector. Moreover, national policies in the sector were very important and very different across nations. In reaction to the great economic and social turmoil of the 1920s and 1930s, most European nations had adopted highly interventionist policies in agriculture. These typically involved price controls teamed with trade barriers (Milward, 1992). Moreover, in the 1950s, the competitiveness of the Six's farm sectors differed massively. French and Dutch farmers were far more competitive than German farmers. If the Six were to form a truly integrated economic area, trade in farm goods would have to be included. However, given sharp differences in farm competitiveness among the Six, free trade would have had massively negative effects on many farmers, although, as usual with free trade, the winners would have won more than the losers would have lost.

These simple facts prevented the writers of the Treaty of Rome from including more than the barest sketch of a common farm policy. They did, however, manage to agree on the goals, general principles and a two-year deadline for establishing the common policy. The Common Agricultural Policy came into effect in 1962 (see Chapter 9).

2.1.3 Omitted integration: social policy and taxes

The Treaty of Rome was enormously ambitious with respect to economic integration, but it was noticeably silent on two politically sensitive areas that might naturally be part of creating a unified economic area:

- Harmonization of social policies (the set of rules that directly affects labour costs such as wage policies, working hours and conditions, and social benefits).
- Harmonization of taxes.

Subsequent treaties have pushed social integration further but not anywhere near as deep as economic integration. Harmonization of taxes has advanced only slightly since the 1950s. This section considers the economic and political logic behind these omissions.

Social policy

Social harmonization is very difficult politically since even the original six members of the EEC held very different opinions on what types of social policy should be dictated by the government. France, for example, was much keener on the equal treatment of woman than was Italy. Since social policies very directly and very continuously touch citizens' lives, opinions are strongly held. In addition to social harmonization being significantly more difficult politically, there are economic arguments suggesting that it is not necessary.

Does European economic integration demand harmonization of social policies?

This question has been the subject of an intense debate for decades. From the very beginning there were two schools of thought:

- *The harmonize-before-liberalizing school.* This school holds that international differences in wages and social conditions provide an 'unfair' advantage to countries with more laissez-faire social policies. The thinking here is easy to explain. If nations initially have very different social policies, then lowering trade barriers will give nations with low social standards an unbalanced advantage, assuming that exchange rates and wages do not adjust.
- *The no-need-to-harmonize school.* This school argues that wages and social policies are reflections of productivity differences and social preferences – differences that wage adjustments will counter. This school rejects calls for harmonization and notes that, in any case, social policies tend to converge as all nations get richer. The thinking here is that wages adjust to offset any systematic differences. For instance, if one nation requires that firms provide their workers with longer holidays than another, workers in the former will produce less in a year and will thus earn less. The competitiveness effect of the costly social regulation is offset by lower wages.

Tax policy

Like social policies, tax policy directly touches the lives of most citizens. This means that a nation's tax policy is the outcome of a hard-fought political compromise between broad groups of citizens, firms and labour unions, all of whom are well-informed and fully engaged. Given this, EU leaders have

always found it difficult politically to harmonize taxes, and this situation started with the Treaty of Rome which made taxation a matter of national concern except for taxes that acted like subsidies or trade barriers.

2.2 EU structure pre- and post-Lisbon

The 2009 Lisbon Treaty simplified the structure of the EU. However, a great deal of writing on the EU refers to the old structure – or explains the new structure with reference to the old structure. Thus students have to learn both the old and new systems if they want to be able to follow today's discussion on European integration. Fortunately, they are not too different and understanding the motives behind the old structure makes it easier to understand the motives behind the new structure.

2.2.1 The EU's pre-Lisbon structure

Up to the 1992 Maastricht Treaty (formally its title was the Treaty on European Union, or TEU), things were simple. There was the European Economic Community (EEC) that mattered a lot and a couple of other Communities (Coal and Steel, and Euratom) that did not. The Maastricht Treaty took a big leap forward in economic integration with the monetary union, but it also pushed forward a broadening of European integration ambition. The members, however, were somewhat suspicious that this new broadening might get out of hand if the European Commission and European Court continued to push for an 'ever closer Europe'. To counter this, EU members insisted that the Maastricht Treaty put in place some 'fire breaks'.

More specifically, up to the 1992 Maastricht Treaty, most integration initiatives were subject to the Treaty of Rome's supranational decision-making procedures; for example, majority voting on EU laws which implied that any law passed had to be implemented by all members, even members who voted against it. Moreover, the European Court was the ultimate authority over disputes involving all such laws and the Court's rulings occasionally had the effect of boosting integration (see the Cassis de Dijon case in Chapter 4 for a famous example).

This supranationality created two related problems – an understanding of which provides a logical framework that makes sense of the unusual structure of the EU pre-Lisbon and helps build an understanding of why the Lisbon changes are important.

The first problem concerned the old schism between federalists and intergovernmentalists (see Chapter 1). On the one hand, some EU members – the 'vanguard' – wished to spread European integration to areas that were not covered in the original Treaties, such as harmonization of social policies and taxation. On the other hand, another group of members – call them the 'doubters' – worried that supranational decision-making procedures were producing an irresistible increase in the depth and breadth of European integration that forced their citizens to accept more integration than they wanted. Germany is an example of the vanguard and Britain an example of the doubters.

The vanguard called this irresistible increase the 'Community method' while the doubters called it 'creeping competences' ('competence' is the EU jargon for policy areas where EU-level policy takes the lead over Member States' national policies).

To the doubters, a particularly worrisome feature was the EU Court's ability to interpret the Treaty of Rome and subsequent amendments. The Treaty of Rome says that the EU can make laws in areas not mentioned in the Treaty, if the Court rules that doing so is necessary to attain Treaty objectives. The Treaty objectives, however, are extremely far-reaching; the first line of the Treaty of Rome's Preamble says that the members are 'determined to lay the foundations of an ever closer union among the peoples of Europe'. Doubters worried that the Treaty's ambitious objectives combined with the Court's ability to sanction law-making in areas not explicitly mentioned in the Treaties opened the door to essentially unlimited transfers of national sovereignty to the EU level.

The second problem concerned integration that was taking place outside of the EU's structure due to differences between the vanguard and the doubters. The Schengen Accord is the classic example. While the free movement of people is an EU goal dating back to 1958, some members (e.g. Britain) held up progress towards passport-free travel. In 1985, five EU members signed an agreement ending controls on their internal frontiers. This was completely outside of the EU's structure and many observers feared that such ad hoc arrangements could undermine the unity of the Single Market and possibly foster tensions among EU members. A more recent example is the 2005 Prüm Treaty on police cooperation, which was signed outside the EU umbrella by seven EU members.

Both problems were addressed by the rather complex structure EU members set up with the Maastricht Treaty.

2.2.2 Maastricht and the three pillars as fire breaks

The Maastricht Treaty drew a clear line between supranational and intergovernmental policy areas by creating a 'three-pillar' organizational structure. The deep economic integration – basically the integration in the Treaty of Rome, Single European Act and the monetary union part of the Maastricht Treaty – were placed in the supranational 'first pillar'. The intergovernmental policies – foreign and

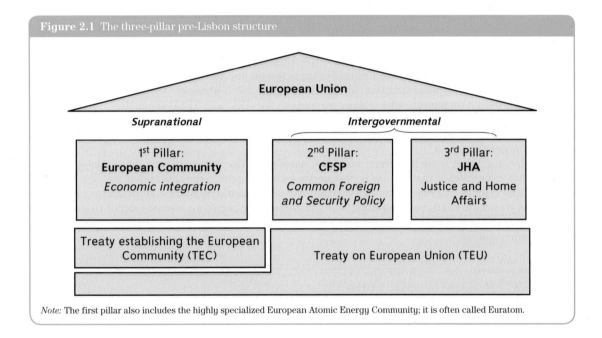

Figure 2.1 The three-pillar pre-Lisbon structure

Note: The first pillar also includes the highly specialized European Atomic Energy Community; it is often called Euratom.

defence matters (second pillar) and police, justice and other 'home affairs' (third pillar) – are under the European Union 'roof' but were not subject to supranationality in terms of decision making and EU Court rulings (see Figure 2.1).

The three-pillar structure solved the two problems mentioned above. The clear distinction between supranational and intergovernmental cooperation allowed initiatives like Schengen to be brought under the EU's wing without forcing every member to join. This greatly reduced the resistance of Britain and other doubters to further discussion of closer integration in areas like police cooperation and foreign policy cooperation.

The key, as far as the doubters were concerned, is that Maastricht put Member States clearly in control in second- and third-pillar areas. There was no possibility of the Court or Commission using their authority to force deeper integration on reluctant members in pursuit of the duties assigned to them by the Treaty of Rome.

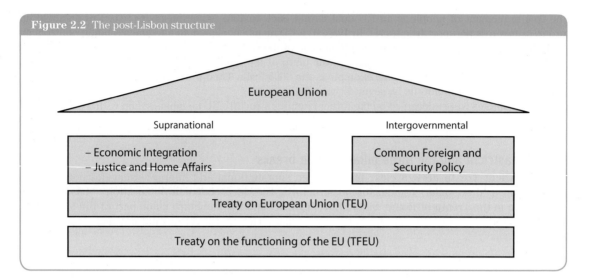

Figure 2.2 The post-Lisbon structure

2.2.3 Post-Lisbon organization: two pillars in a single organization

One of the most radical things in the Lisbon Treaty is the de jure removal of the three-pillar structure. It was replaced by a two-pillar structure, as shown in Figure 2.2. It abolishes the European Community, replacing the term 'Community' with 'Union' throughout the TEU and TFEU (henceforth 'the amended Treaties' for short). Some writers refer to this as the removal of the pillar structure because there is now just one organization and it has what lawyers call 'legal personality' (it can sign agreements with nations and organizations).

However, the basic need that some members have for a fire break against deeper integration in second-pillar issues meant that Lisbon is best understood as merging the third pillar into the first. The new structure (Figure 2.2) essentially has two pillars – a supranational pillar and an intergovernmental pillar. It is therefore worth learning about the old three-pillar structure in some detail to understand which of today's EU policies are governed by supranationality (see Box 2.4) and which are governed by intergovernmentalism.

Box 2.4   Supranationality in the EU

Supranationality arises in the EU in three main ways:

1 The Commission can propose new laws that are then voted on by the Member States (in the Council of Ministers) and the European Parliament. If passed, these new laws bind every Member State, even those that disagree with them.

2 The Commission has direct executive authority in a limited number of areas – the most prominent being competition policy. For instance, the Commission can block a merger between two EU companies even if their governments support the merger (see Chapter 11 for details).

3 The rulings of the European Court of Justice can alter laws, rules and practices in Member States, at least in limited areas (see the Factortame case discussed in Section 2.3.2 for an example).

The Lisbon Treaty basically merged the third-pillar issues into the first pillar with all its supranationality, although exceptions are included article by article so it is more difficult to draw the broad picture.

2.3 EU law

One of the most unusual and important things about the EU is its supranational legal system. This is a direct implication of the EU's unusual degree of economic integration. Implementing and maintaining a unified economic area requires a legal system of some kind since disputes over interpretation and conflicts among various laws are inevitable.

By the standards of every other international organization in the world, the European legal system is extremely supranational. For example, even the highest courts in EU Member States must defer to decisions by the EU's Court of Justice on matters concerning the interpretation of EU law. The EU is very much like a federal state in this respect. Just as the decisions of lower courts in France, Germany and Italy can be overturned by those nations' supreme courts, the EU's Court of Justice has the ultimate say on questions concerning European law.

Before the Lisbon Treaty, the deep, supranational aspects of EU law only applied to first-pillar issues, i.e. where supranationality was the agreed principle. While the Lisbon Treaty removed the pillars, it did not remove the distinction between areas where the EU law's deep supranationality applies and areas where it does not. Now, however, the default option is that it applies to all areas except those areas explicitly excluded.

The topic of EU law is as intricate as it is fascinating. This section presents the barest outlines of the subject, focusing on the elements that are essential for understanding the decision-making process in particular and the economics of European integration more generally. Note that this section is largely based on *The ABC of European Union Law* by Claus-Dieter Borchandt, which is free to download. It has been fully updated to reflect Lisbon Treaty changes. This book is the best online introduction to the subject.

2.3.1 'Sources' of EU law

The legal systems of most democratic nations are based on a constitution. The EU does not have a constitution, so where did these principles come from? As is true of so many things in the EU, a complete answer to this question would fill a book or two, but the short answer is easy: the Treaty of Rome created the Court and the Court created the legal system and its principles.

The Treaty of Rome commits Member States to a series of general economic and political goals, and it transfers important elements of national sovereignty to the European level in perpetuity. For example, after 1958 Member States no longer had the right to control their external trade policy and there was no legal way for them to quit so this loss of sovereignty was permanent.

The Treaty was not very specific when it came to setting up the legal system. The Treaty establishes the Court of Justice and states that its general task is to 'ensure observance of law and justice in the interpretation and application of this Treaty' (Article 164 in the original Treaty). It then goes on to define the Court's composition and to assign the Court a few specific tasks.

The Treaty of Rome was also not specific enough to deal with the many issues that came before the Court. The Court reacted to the lack of specificity in the Treaty by creating the Community's legal system via case law. That is to say, it used decisions relating to particular cases to establish general principles of the EC legal system.

EC law is now an enormous mass of laws, rules and practices that has been established by Treaties (primary law), EU laws (secondary law) and decisions of the Court (case law).

2.3.2 EU legal system: main principles

Since the EC legal system was not created by any single document, its principles were never officially proclaimed before the Lisbon Treaty. The 'principles' of EC law were thus general patterns that various jurists have discerned from the thousands of pages of primary, secondary and case law, and different jurists list different principles.

Three principles that are always mentioned are 'direct effect', 'primacy of EC law' and 'autonomy' of the EC legal system. These were first established in two landmark cases in 1963 and 1964 (see Box 2.5). These three have been explicitly confirmed in the Lisbon Treaty (see below for details).

Box 2.5   Two cases that established the EC legal system

The EC legal system was not explicitly established in any Treaty, so the Court used some early cases to establish three key principles. Since these principles arose in the course of real-world cases, it can be difficult to precisely distinguish among the three principles in the two cases.

***Van Gend & Loos v Netherlands*, 1963.** In this case, the Dutch company Van Gend & Loos brought an action against its own government for imposing an import duty on a chemical product from Germany which was higher than duties on an earlier shipment; the company claimed that this violated the Treaty of Rome's prohibition on tariff hikes on intra-EC trade. The Dutch court suspended the case and asked the EC Court to clarify. The EC Court ruled that the company could rely on provisions in the Treaties when arguing against the Dutch government before a Dutch court.

Plainly, this case has an element of direct effect and primacy. The Dutch government had one rule – the higher tariff rate – while the Treaty had another (no increase allowed). The EC Court said the Treaty provision trumped the national provision. Moreover, the EC Court said that the Dutch court should consider the Treaty directly rather than, for example, the Dutch Parliament's transposition of the Treaty's principles into Dutch law. In effect, the Court said that the Treaty was Dutch law as far as the Dutch court was to be concerned. This was new, since normally a national court can consider only national law when judging a case.

The European Court also took the opportunity to write down its thoughts on the fundamental nature of the EC legal system. In the *Van Gend & Loos v Netherlands* decision, it wrote: 'The Community constitutes a new legal order of international law for the benefit of which the States have limited their sovereign rights, albeit within limited fields, and the subjects of which comprise not only Member States but also their nationals.'

***Costa v ENEL*, 1964 decision by the Court of Justice.** The next year, the Court expanded its view of the EC legal system in a case involving a dispute over 1925 lire – about one euro! In 1962, Italy nationalized its electricity grid and grouped it under the National Electricity Board (ENEL in Italian). Mr Flaminio Costa, a shareholder of one nationalized company, felt he had been unjustly deprived of his dividend and so refused to pay his electricity bill for 1925 lira. The non-payment matter came before an arbitration court in Milan but since Mr Costa argued that the nationalization violated EC law, the Milan court asked the European Court to interpret various aspects of the Treaty of Rome.

The Court took the opportunity to go way beyond the question at hand. In its judgement, the Court stated the principle of autonomy and direct effect:

- 'By contrast with ordinary international treaties, the EEC Treaty has created its own legal system which . . . became an integral part of the legal systems of the Member States and which their courts are bound to apply.'
- 'Member States have limited their sovereign rights, albeit within limited fields, and have thus created a body of law which binds both their nationals and themselves.'

Relying on the logic of what the Treaty of Rome implied – at least implicitly – the Court established the principle of primacy.

- '[T]he law stemming from the Treaty, an independent source of law, could not, because of its special and original nature, be overridden by domestic legal provisions, however framed, without being deprived of its character as Community law and without the legal basis of the Community itself being called into question. The transfer by the States from their domestic legal system to the Community legal system of the rights and obligations arising under the Treaty carries with it a permanent limitation of their sovereign rights, against which a subsequent unilateral act incompatible with the concept of the Community cannot prevail.'

The Court's justification was that if EC law were not supreme, the objectives of the Treaty could not be met: 'The executive force of Community law cannot vary from one State to another in deference to subsequent domestic laws, without jeopardising the attainment of the objectives of the Treaty.'

'Direct effect'

'Direct effect' is simple to define – it means that Treaty provisions or other forms of EU law such as directives can create rights which EU citizens can rely upon when they go before their domestic courts. This is radical. It means that EC laws must be enforced by Member States' courts, just as if the law had been passed by the national parliament. A good example is the case of a Sabena air stewardess (as they called female flight attendants in the 1970s) who claimed that she was paid less and had to retire earlier than male flight attendants. Although this was not a violation of Belgian law at the time, the EC Court ruled in 1976 that the Treaty of Rome (which provides for equality of pay between the sexes) had the force of law in Belgium, or in legal terms, it had direct effect. The stewardess won the case.

The principle of direct effect is quite unique. For example, when New Zealand ratifies the Kyoto Protocol, it is agreeing to certain obligations, but New Zealand courts ignore these obligations unless they are implemented by a law passed by the New Zealand parliament. Even more unusual is that this 'direct effect' notion applies to EU laws passed by majority voting, e.g. directives. This means that, even if a Member State government votes against a particular law, that law automatically has the force of law, so its national courts must treat the EU law as if it were a national law. Importantly, there are complex conditions for a Treaty provision to have direct effect, so not everything in every Treaty is automatically enforceable in Member States.

The logical necessity of this principle is straightforward. If laws agreed in Brussels could be ignored in any Member State, the EU would fall into a shambles. Each member would be tempted to implement only the EU laws it liked. This would, for example, make it impossible to create a single market or ensure the free movement of workers.

Primacy of EC law

This principle, which means that Community law has the final say, is not in the Treaty of Rome and indeed appears explicitly for the first time only in the rejected Constitutional Treaty (it is included in the Lisbon Treaty). It was, nonetheless, a principle that had been generally accepted by all EU members even before the Lisbon Treaty. It was repeatedly used to overturn Member State laws.

One classic example of this principle is the 1991 Factortame case, which confirmed the supremacy of EC law over UK law. The UK's Merchant Shipping Act of 1988 had the effect of forbidding a Spanish fishing company called Factortame from fishing in UK waters. Factortame asserted in UK courts that this violated EC law, and asked the UK court to suspend the Merchant Shipping Act until the EC Court could rule on the matter (this often takes a couple of years). Under UK law, no British court can suspend an Act of Parliament. The EC Court ruled that under EC law, which was supreme to UK law, a national court could suspend laws which contravened EC law. Subsequently, the highest UK court did strike down the Merchant Fishing Act.

The logical necessity of this principle is just as clear as that of direct effect. Simplifying for clarity's sake, 'direct effect' says that EC laws are automatically laws in every Member State. Primacy says that when EC law and national, regional or local laws conflict, the EC law is what must be enforced.

Autonomy

Most European nations have several layers of courts – local, regional and national. The lower courts, however, do not exist independently of the higher courts, and often the higher courts depend upon the lower courts (e.g. in some nations, the high court can rule only after the case has been tried at a lower level). The EC legal system, however, is entirely independent of the Member States' legal systems according to the principle of autonomy.

2.4 The 'Big-5' institutions

There are many EU agencies, bodies and committees, but one can achieve a very good understanding of how the EU works by knowing about the 'Big-5'. Somewhat confusingly, their names tend to be changed in each new treaty. Using the current names as defined in the Lisbon Treaty, these are:

- the European Council (heads of state and governments);
- the Council of the European Union (member nations' ministers), often called by its old name, the Council of Ministers;
- the European Commission (appointed eurocrats);
- the European Parliament (directly elected);
- the EU Court (appointed judges).

On the other institutions, see Borchandt (2010). The European Central Bank and related institutions are now equally important, but they are intentionally separate from the Big-5. They are dealt with in Parts IV and V.

The relations between and basic roles of the Big-5 are summarized schematically in Figure 2.3.

2.4.1 The European Council

The European Council is comprised of the EU's national leaders and as such is the highest political-level body in the EU. It provides political guidance to the EU as a whole, but especially to the European Commission. All EU major strategic choices are made by the European Council, sometimes in cooperation with the European Parliament. To facilitate cooperation with other EU bodies, the President of the European Commission, and the High Representative of the Union for Foreign Affairs and Security Policy attend the meetings but don't vote.

The European Council meets at least twice a year – and in recent years at least four times (see Box 2.6). The most important meetings come in June and December at the end of each 6-month term of the Presidency of the EU. These June and December meetings are important, high-profile media events – the one aspect of the EU that almost every European citizen has seen on television.

Most important EU initiatives and policies are instigated by the European Council. For example, it provides broad guidelines for EU policy and thrashes out the final compromises necessary to conclude the most sensitive aspects of EU business, including reforms of the major EU policies, the EU's multi-year budget plan, treaty changes and the final terms of enlargements. This body is by far the most influential institution because its members are the leaders of their respective nations. Moreover, it usually takes decisions by consensus, so its decisions have the implicit backing of every EU national leader.

Following the Lisbon Treaty, the European Council is now chaired by a president selected by the Council itself, who serves a 2.5 year term.[2] The first President, Herman van Rompuy, served until November 2014

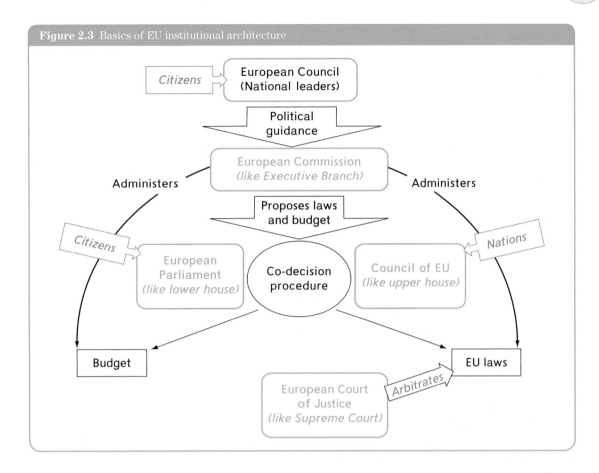

Figure 2.3 Basics of EU institutional architecture

(see Box 2.7). The President leads preparations for European Council meetings and ensures follow-through on its decisions. The President represents the EU at international summits in the area of foreign and security policy.

The 'Conclusions' and lack of legislative power

The most important decisions of each Presidency are contained in a document known as the 'Conclusions of the Presidency', which is published at the end of each European Council meeting. Students who want to track the EU's position on a particular topic – be it the need for a constitution or its position on Zimbabwe – will do well to start with the Conclusions (go to www.european-council.europa.eu).

One peculiarity of the EU is that the most powerful body by far – the European Council – has no formal role in EU law-making. The political decisions made by the European Council are translated into law following the standard legislative procedures (more on this below).

Confusingly, the European Council and the Council of the EU (what was called the Council of Ministers before Lisbon) are often both called 'the Council'. Moreover, neither of these Councils should be confused with the Council of Europe, which is an international organization set up in the 1940s and entirely unrelated to the EU.

---

[2] The President is selected on the basis of so-called qualified-majority voting (a system of weighted votes with large nations getting more weight). Chapter 3 describes this voting system in full. Before the Lisbon Treaty, the European Council was chaired by the head of the nation holding the Presidency of the EU. As the Presidency of the EU rotated every 6 months, and different members had different priorities, the European Council's effectiveness tended to be undermined. Specifically, this rotation made long-term planning and multi-year efforts difficult to organize and carry through.

Box 2.6 A typical European Council meeting, 27 June 2014

European Council meetings are often followed closely by the media. The 27 June 2014 meeting was especially well covered since it saw a conflict between UK Prime Minister David Cameron and most other EU leaders over the nomination of Jean-Claude Juncker as the next President of the European Commission. The photo shows (left to right) an angry-looking David Cameron, Danish Prime Minister Helle Thorning-Schmidt and Commission President José Manuel Barroso.

© European Union, 2014

But that headline event was not the only thing addressed at the meeting. The leaders started by considering Eurozone governance issues, and issues related to justice and home affairs, energy security and climate change. They also met with Ukrainian President Petro Poroshenko and adopted the strategic priorities for the EU in the following years. As if that was not enough, on the same day agreements were signed with Georgia and Moldova, and the signature process for Ukraine's Deep and Comprehensive Free Trade Area agreement completed.

Box 2.7 Herman van Rompuy, first President of the European Council (2009–14)

Once the Lisbon Treaty came into effect in December 2009, EU leaders asked one of their own to become the first long-term President of the European Council – then-Belgian Prime Minister Herman van Rompuy. A life-long politician with a degree in economics (and a penchant for haiku poetry), he espouses modesty and 'quiet determination'.

Van Rompuy has worked largely behind the scenes to make the European Council's reactions to various events – especially the Eurozone crisis – more effective and expedient. His first appointment and then reappointment for a second term (until 30 November 2014) were unanimously agreed upon by EU leaders.

© European Union, 2014

2.4.2 The Council of the EU

The Council is the EU's main decision-making body. Its official name is the Council of the European Union (since the Lisbon Treaty) but it was called the Council of Ministers for most of the EU's history (and many people still use that name). Almost every piece of legislation is subject to its approval. The Council consists of one representative from each EU member. The national representatives must be authorized to commit their governments to Council decisions, so Council members are the government ministers responsible for the relevant area – the finance ministers on budget issues, agriculture ministers on farm issues and so on.

The Council is where the Member States' governments assert their influence directly. Since all EU governments are elected (democracy is a must for membership) and the Council members represent their governments, the Council is the ultimate point of democratic control over the EU actions and law-making. Although the European Parliament is elected directly, very few Europeans know the name of their Member of the European Parliament (MEP). European voters do, however, know the name of their Prime Minister – and will hold him or her accountable if something goes seriously wrong in the EU.

The Council is responsible for certain supranational areas (see Figure 2.2). To meet these responsibilities, it has the power to:

- Pass European laws (jointly with the European Parliament; see Section 2.5). Most of the laws passed concern measures necessary to implement the Treaties or simply to keep the vital parts of the EU running smoothly (the internal market, the Common Agricultural Policy, etc.).

- Coordinate the general economic policies of the Member States in the context of the Economic and Monetary Union (EMU; see Chapter 16 for details).

- Pass final judgement on international agreements between the EU and other countries or international organizations (a power it shares with the European Parliament).

- Approve the EU's budget, jointly with the European Parliament.

In addition to these tasks linked to economic integration, the Council takes the decisions pertaining to Common Foreign and Security Policies (CFSPs). To the average European, these are some of the most visible actions of the Council.

Although the Council is a single institution, it follows the somewhat confusing practice of using different names to describe itself according to the matters being discussed. For example, when the Council addresses European and Monetary Union (EMU) matters it is called the Economic and Financial Affairs Council, or Ecofin to insiders. One particularly important group is the Eurogroup comprising the finance ministers of the Eurozone nations. It meets the day before the Ecofin meeting to discuss matters because only Eurozone nations vote on issues relating to the euro in Ecofin.

Decision-making rules

The Council has two main decision-making rules. On the most important issues – such as Treaty changes, the accession of new members and setting the multi-year budget plan – the Council must decide unanimously. However, on most issues, the Council decides on the basis of a form of majority voting called 'qualified majority voting' (QMV). These rules are extremely important for understanding how Europe works, so they are the subject of extensive analysis in Chapter 3.

Presidency of the EU

One EU Member State at a time holds the Presidency, with this office rotating every 6 months. The Presidency nation sets the EU basic agenda and chairs all the Council of Ministers meetings except those dealing with foreign affairs and security policy, which are chaired by the High Representative of the Union for Foreign Affairs and Security Policy (more on this position below).

The High Representative of the Union for Foreign Affairs and Security Policy

This is a new post created by the Lisbon Treaty. The High Representative of the Union for Foreign Affairs and Security Policy (High Representative for short) attends Council of EU meetings, European Council meetings and Commission meetings. The Lisbon Treaty also created the European External

Action Service to assist the High Representative. This is a new organization; its roles and form are still evolving. Its most obvious manifestation is the EU Delegations (something like an embassy) in about 150 non-EU nations.

The first High Representative, Catherine Ashton, was appointed in 2009 for a 5-year term (see Box 2.8).

Box 2.8   Catherine Ashton, first High Representative (2009–14)

Cathy Ashton was serving as the EU Trade Commissioner when she was elevated to the new post in 2009. Apart from her time as Trade Commissioner, she had no foreign affairs experience and had held the Trade Commissioner slot only since 2008. Previously, she worked in the Labour government of Tony Blair before being appointed as Leader of the House of Lords. She was made a life peer with the title of baroness in 1999. She was born to a working-class family with roots in Lancashire coal mining; she was the first person in her family to attend a university.

Her term ended in November 2014.

© European Union, 2014

2.4.3 The Commission

The European Commission is best thought of as the executive branch of the EU, but with a twist. It is also charged with 'safeguarding' the Treaties. Indeed, since the EU's foundation, it has been a key driving force behind deeper and wider European integration – often pushing, pulling and prodding EU Member States towards the goal of an ever-closer union. The body, based in Brussels, has three main roles:

1 to propose legislation to the Council and Parliament;
2 to administer and implement EU policies;
3 to provide surveillance and enforcement of EU law in coordination with the EU Court.

As part of its third role, it is responsible for ensuring that the Treaties are implemented and enforced.

The Commission also represents the EU at some international negotiations, such as those relating to World Trade Organization (WTO) trade talks. The Commission's negotiating stances at such meetings are closely monitored by EU members.

Commissioners and the Commission's composition

The European Commission is made up of one Commissioner from each EU member.[3] This includes the President and two Vice-Presidents. The current Commission President, Jean-Claude Juncker (a former Prime Minister of Luxembourg), was selected in 2014 to replace the outgoing President, José Manuel Barroso (a former Prime Minister of Portugal). Commissioners, including the President of the Commission, are appointed all together and serve for 5 years (see Box 2.9).

The appointments are made just after European Parliamentary elections and take effect in the January of the following year. The current Commission's term ends in 2014. The new commissioners had not been appointed at the time this edition went to press.

---

[3] The original intention of the Lisbon Treaty was to reduce the number of Commissioners to less than the number of Member States, but a political promise made by EU leaders to Ireland annuls that goal, so there will be one Commissioner per member for the foreseeable future.

The President of the European Commission from 2014 to 2019 will be Jean-Claude Juncker. A former Prime Minister of Luxembourg from 1995 to 2013, he was previously the first permanent President of the Eurogroup from 2005 to 2013 – a span which included the outbreak and policy responses to the Eurozone crisis. Juncker studied law but never practised as a lawyer because he entered politics straight out of university.

© European Union, 2014

Commissioners are effectively chosen by their own national governments, but the choices are subject to political agreement by other members and the President of the Commission. The Commission as a whole and the Commission President individually must also be approved by the European Parliament.

Each politically appointed Commissioner is in charge of a specific area of EU policy. In particular, each runs what can be thought of as the EU equivalent of a national ministry. These 'ministries', called Directorates-General, or DGs in EU jargon, employ a relatively modest number of international civil servants.

The Commission as a whole employs about 24,000 people, which is fewer than those who work for the city of Vienna. Just as in national ministries, Commission officials tend to provide most of the expertise necessary to administer and analyse the EU's vastly complex network of policies since the Commissioners themselves are typically generalists.

Commissioners are not supposed to act as national representatives. They are forbidden from accepting or seeking instruction from their country's government. In practice, Commissioners are generally quite independent of their home governments, but since they have typically held high political office in their home nations, they are naturally sensitive to issues that are of particular concern back home. This ensures that all decisive national sensitivities are heard in Commission deliberations. You can find the Commissioner from your own nation at ec.europa.eu/index_en.htm – along with all the others and their respective areas of responsibility.

The Commission has a great deal of independence in practice and often takes views that differ substantially from the Member States, the Council and the Parliament. However, it is ultimately answerable to the European Parliament since the Parliament can dismiss the Commission as a whole by adopting a motion of censure. Although this has never happened, a censure motion was almost passed in 2005. In 1999 a similar near-censure triggered a sequence of events that ended in mass resignation of the Commission led by President Jacques Santer.

Legislative powers

The Commission's main law-making duty is to prepare proposals for new EU legislation. These range from a new directive on minimum elevator safety standards to the reform of the Common Agricultural Policy (CAP). Neither the Council nor the Parliament can adopt legislation until the Commission presents its proposals, except under extraordinary procedures. This monopoly on the 'right to initiate' makes the Commission the gatekeeper of EU integration. It also allows the Commission occasionally to become the driving force behind deeper or broader integration. This was especially true under the two Delors Commissions that served from 1985 to 1994 and pushed forward the Single European Act and the Maastricht Treaty.

Commission proposals are usually based on general guidelines established by the Council of Ministers, the European Council, the Parliament or the Treaties. A proposal is prepared by the relevant

Directorate-General in collaboration with other DGs concerned. In exercising this power of initiative, the Commission consults a very broad range of EU actors, including national governments, the European Parliament, national administrations, professional groups and trade union organizations. This complex consultation process is known in EU jargon as 'comitology'.

Executive powers

The Commission is the executive in all of the EU's endeavours, but its power is most obvious in competition policy. Chapter 11 explains in more detail how the Commission has the power to block mergers, to fine corporations for unfair practices and to insist that EU members remove or modify subsidies to their firms. The Commission also has substantial latitude in administering the Common Agricultural Policy, including the right to impose fines on members that violate CAP rules.

One of the key responsibilities of the Commission is to manage the EU budget, subject to supervision by a specialized institution called the EU Court of Auditors. For example, while the Council and Parliament decided the programme-by-programme allocation of funds in the EU's current multi-year budget (Financial Perspective in EU jargon), the Commission basically decides the year-by-year indicative allocation of Structural Funds across members.

Decision making

The Commission decides, in principle, on the basis of a simple majority. The 'in principle' proviso is necessary because the Commission makes almost all of its decision on the basis of consensus. The reason is that the Commission usually has to get its actions approved by the Council and the Parliament. A Commission decision that fails to attract the support of a very substantial majority of the Commissioners will almost surely fail in the Council and/or Parliament.

2.4.4 The European Parliament

The Parliament has two main tasks: sharing legislative powers with the Council of Ministers and the Commission; and overseeing all EU institutions, but especially the Commission. The Parliament, on its own initiative, has also begun to act as the 'conscience' of the EU, for example condemning various nations for human rights violations via non-binding resolutions.

The Lisbon Treaty boosted the power of the Parliament substantially, making it equal to the Council on most types of EU legislation. Especially noteworthy are the Parliament's new powers over the budget (in particular, agricultural spending where previously the Parliament had little say, and some Justice and Home Affairs issues). The European Parliament also gets an increased role in Treaty revision, an increased role in the selection of senior EU leaders and a right of refusal for most international agreements, including trade agreements.

In 2014, the European Parliament significantly stretched its power by effectively usurping the European Council's right to nominate the next President of the European Commission. Under the Lisbon Treaty, the European Council nominates the Commission President and the Parliament accepts or rejects this nomination. The Lisbon Treaty, however, included some vague language about the European Council taking account of the outcome of the European Parliamentary elections. Parliament proceeded to announce 'lead candidates' at the head of each major party and indicated that the Council should appoint the lead candidate from the party that won the most votes. In the 2014 elections, the centre-right party won about 29 per cent of the vote. However, as the voter turnout was just 43 per cent, the centre-right received votes from something like 12 per cent of the eligible EU voters (29 per cent of 43 per cent). Despite this meagre showing, the centre-right group claimed that their victory meant that the European Council should nominate their lead candidate, Jean-Claude Junckers. Britain strongly opposed both the procedure in general and the candidate in particular (see Box 2.9), but Junckers was appointed and will replace José Barroso as the next Commission President.

Organization

The European Parliament (EP) has about 750 members who are directly elected by EU citizens in special elections organized in each Member State every 5 years (most recently in May 2014). The number of

Members of European Parliament (MEPs) per nation varies with population, but the number of MEPs per million EU citizens is much higher for small nations than for large. For example, in the 2014–19 Parliament, Luxembourg has 6 MEPs and Germany has 96, despite the fact that Germany's population is about 160 times that of Luxembourg.

The latest elections saw continued dominance of the centre-right and centre-left parties, the EPP and S&D, respectively (see Table 2.1). There was, however, a significant increase in the explicitly anti-European integration candidates elected. The number of anti-EU MEPs rose in 16 of the 28 EU Member States, with the number doubling in Greece, Poland, Austria, Finland and Denmark. Even Germany elected seven anti-EU MEPs. In all, the strongly Eurosceptic parties won about 15 per cent of seats. It is a very diverse group and was unable to form an effective bloc. A number of these parties banded together in the 'Europe of Freedom and Direct Democracy' grouping.

Table 2.1   Results of the 2014 Parliamentary election by party groups

Party group name	Result (%)
Group of the European People's Party (EPP)	221 MEPs, 29
Group of the Progressive Alliance of Socialists and Democrats (S&D)	191 MEPs, 25
European Conservatives and Reformists (ECR)	70 MEPs, 9
Alliance of Liberals and Democrats for Europe (ALDE)	67 MEPs, 9
European United Left/Nordic Green Left (GUE/NGL)	52 MEPs, 7
The Greens/European Free Alliance (Greens/EFA)	50 MEPs, 7
Europe of Freedom and Direct Democracy (EFDD)	48 MEPs, 6
Non-attached Members (NI) – Members unattached to a political group	52 MEPs, 7

Turnout in European Parliamentary elections has fallen steadily, from 62 per cent since the first election in 1979 to 43 per cent in 2014. This is quite low compared to the turnout for national government elections.

MEPs are supposed to represent their local constituencies, but the Parliament's organization has evolved along classic European political lines rather than along national lines (for details, see Noury and Roland, 2002). The European Parliament election campaigns are generally run by each nation's main political parties and MEPs are generally associated with a particular national political party. Although this means that over a hundred parties are represented in the Parliament, fragmentation is avoided because many of these parties have formed political groups. As in most EU Member States, two main political groups – the centre-left and the centre-right – account for two-thirds of the seats and tend to dominate the Parliament's activity. The centre-left grouping in the European Parliament is called the Party of European Socialists, the centre-right group is called the European People's Party.

National delegations of MEPs do not sit together. As in most parliaments, the European Parliament's physical, left-to-right seating arrangement reflects the left-to-right ideology of the MEPs. These party groups have their own internal structure, including chairs, secretariats, staffs, and 'whips' who keep track of attendance and voting behaviour. The political groups receive budgets from the Parliament. Details on the size and national composition of the European Parliament can be found on http://www.elections2014.eu/en.

Location

The Parliament is not located in Brussels, the centre of EU decision making, but in Strasbourg (Figure 2.4) owing to France's dogged insistence (the Parliament's predecessor in the European Coal and Steel

Figure 2.4 The European Parliament's building in Strasbourg (it also has buildings in Brussels and Luxembourg)

© iStock.com/ LUke1138

Community, the Common Assembly, was located in Strasbourg since it was near to the heart of the coal and steel sectors). Equally determined insistence by Luxembourg has kept the Parliament's secretariat in Luxembourg. Since Brussels is where most of the political action occurs, and is also the location of most of the institutions that the Parliament is supposed to supervise, the Parliament also has offices in Brussels (this is where the various Parliamentary committees meet).

The staffs of the Parliament's political groups work in Brussels. It is not clear how much this geographic dispersion hinders the Parliament's effectiveness, but the time and money wasted on shipping documents and people among three locations occasionally produces negative media attention.

2.4.5 Court of Justice

In the EU, as in every other organization in the world, laws and decisions are open to interpretation and this frequently leads to disputes that cannot be settled by negotiation. The role of the Court of Justice (often known by its pre-Lisbon Treaty name, the European Court of Justice, or the 'EU Court') is to settle these disputes, especially disputes between Member States, between the EU and Member States, between EU institutions, and between individuals and the EU. As discussed above, the EU Court is the highest authority on the application of EU law.[4]

As a result of this power, the Court has had a major impact on European integration. For example, its ruling in the 1970s on non-tariff barriers triggered a sequence of events that eventually led to the Single European Act (see Chapter 4 for details). The Court has also been important in defining the relations between the Member States and the EU, and in the legal protection of individuals (EU citizens can take cases directly to the EU Court without going through their governments).

The Court, which is located in Luxembourg (Figure 2.5), consists of one judge from each Member State. Judges are appointed by common accord of the Member States' governments and serve for 6 years. The Court also has eight 'advocates-general' whose job is to help the judges by constructing 'reasoned submissions' that suggest what conclusions the judges might make. The Court reaches its decisions by majority voting. The Court of First Instance was set up in the late 1980s to help the EU Court with its ever-growing workload.

---

[4] The Lisbon Treaty lumps three EU courts (the Court of Justice, the General Court and the Civil Service Tribunal) under the label Court of Justice of the European Union; the first one is by far the most important.

Figure 2.5 Headquarters of the European Court of Justice in Luxembourg

© iStock.com/fuchs-photography

2.5 Legislative processes

The European Commission has a near-monopoly on initiating the EU decision-making process. That is to say, it is in charge of writing proposed legislation, although it naturally consults widely when doing so. More importantly, this right of initiative affords the Commission a good deal of power over which new legislation is considered. For example, if France and Germany want a particular EU law to be passed, they have to first convince the Commission that it would be a good idea.

Once developed, the Commission's proposal is sent to the Council for approval. Most EU legislation also requires the European Parliament's approval, although the exact procedure depends upon the issue concerned. (The Treaties specify which procedure must be used in which areas.)

The main procedure is called the 'ordinary legislative procedure'. The Parliament and the Council have equal power in terms of approval/rejection and amendment.[5] The details of the ordinary legislative procedure are highly complex (see Box 2.10) but simple in concept. The Commission writes a proposed law and before it can be enacted (i.e. become law) both the Parliament and the Council have to approve it. But the Parliament and the Council can amend the proposed law, so the process works in sequence (so there is only one version of the proposal at any one time). This can lead to a couple of rounds of revisions. In any case, both bodies have to agree the same version if the proposal is to be enacted. The Council acts on the basis of a weight-majority system and the Parliament on the basis of a simple majority of MEPs voting.

An excellent online video that readers may find useful can be found at: http://www.iiea.com/blogosphere/making-eu-law--a-video-infograph. The Parliament also has a pretty good infographic at http://www.europarl.europa.eu/aboutparliament/en/0081f4b3c7/Law-making-procedures-in-detail.html.

2.5.1 National parliaments

Member States' parliaments are not part of the EU institutional superstructure, but the Lisbon Treaty gives them a heightened role in guarding against competence creep, i.e. the EU overstepping its authority and legislating in areas where it should not. For example, if a sufficient number of national parliaments

---

[5] Before Lisbon, the Council had more power as there were several important areas in which Parliament was only 'consulted' or was ignored altogether. The areas over which Parliament gained power include immigration, criminal judicial cooperation, police cooperation, and trade and agricultural policy.

Box 2.10 The ordinary legislative procedure in detail

An elaborate consultation process between the Commission and other relevant EU bodies, business groups, labour unions, other civil society groups and in some cases foreign governments and international organizations is the first step. The Commission then drafts a proposed law and sends it to the European Parliament. The Parliament get to act first; it either accepts the proposal or amends it. The proposal is updated to include any parliamentary amendment and sent to the Council. The Council approves the Parliament's position or suggests amendments. If the Council approves, the law (as amended by the Parliament) is adopted. If the Council amends it, the law is sent back to the Commission, which then approves or disapproves of the amendments.

The European Parliament then has 3 months to react (this is called the Second Reading). It can either accept the Council's amendments, provide further amendments of its own or reject the Council's amendments. In the first case, the law with the Council amendments becomes law (this also happens if the Parliament fails to act within 3 months). In the last case, the law is rejected and the process is stopped. In the middle case, another round is needed.

The amended law again goes to Commission (to get its opinions of the amended proposal) and then on to the Council. The Council has three options: accept, reject or amend. The outcome in the 'accept' or 'reject' cases are, as would be expected, either enactment (since both bodies approved the same proposal) or rejection of the proposal (see Figure 2.6). To avoid indefinite back-and-forth amendments, if the Council amends the proposal at this stage, the whole thing goes to a Conciliation Committee, which tries to hash out a compromise that both sides can agree to. If it manages such a compromise, it goes back to both the Parliament and the Council for a final yes-or-no vote; no further amendments are possible. The Conciliation Committee has 6 weeks to reach agreement; beyond that time period, the law is rejected and the process stopped.

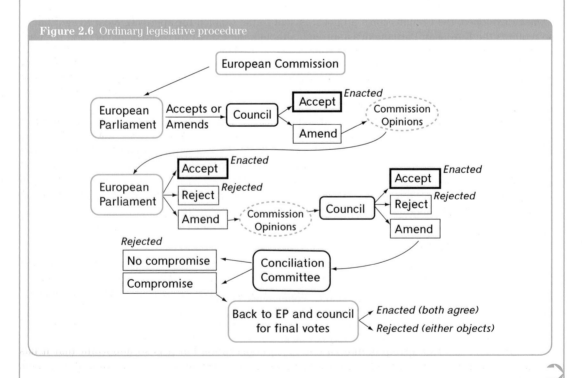

Figure 2.6 Ordinary legislative procedure

The exact voting rules are complex but basically the Parliament acts on the basis of a simple majority (50 per cent of the MEPs voting) and the Council acts on the basis of a weighted voting scheme called 'qualified majority' (see Chapter 3 for details). The Commission's voice is also influential since the Council must act unanimously to accept an amendment that the Commission disapproves.

There are also a couple of legislative procedures that rarely arise (see Box 2.10).

The other 'special legislative procedures' foreseen in the Lisbon Treaty are re-labellings of existing procedures that were created to reduce the power of the Parliament on matters that are especially sensitive (mostly on grounds of national sovereignty). These are:

- *Consultation procedure.* Here, the Council can adopt legislation based on a proposal by the European Commission after merely consulting the European Parliament. Consultation is still used for legislation concerning internal market exemptions and competition law.
- *Consent procedure.* This procedure (which used to be called the assent procedure) allows the Council to adopt legislation (proposed by the Commission) after obtaining the consent of Parliament. In this way, Parliament can reject the law but it cannot formally propose amendments. The procedure applies to things like the admission or withdrawal of members.

is convinced that a legislative initiative would better be taken at a local, regional or national level, the Commission either has to withdraw it or clearly justify why it does not believe that the initiative is in breach of the principle of subsidiarity.

While national parliaments are mentioned in several places, the clearest examples are in the creation of what are known as 'yellow and orange cards'. These give national parliaments the right to express concerns on subsidiarity directly to the institution that initiated the proposed legislation. Under the 'yellow card' procedure, any parliament can, within 2 months of the release of a draft law, submit an opinion that the law violates the principle of subsidiarity. This triggers a voting system among national parliaments. If at least one-third of national parliaments approve the opinion, the Commission has to reconsider the law. The Commission can persevere but it must justify its actions.

The 'orange card', which applies to the ordinary legislative procedure, is tougher. If a majority of available parliaments votes against a proposed law, the Commission must review the law as before but, in addition to the Commission providing justification, the European Parliament and Council must also consider the national parliaments' objections. Plainly these measures give no direct power to the national parliaments, but any law that attracted a yellow or orange card would surely be subjected to brutal media scrutiny. The idea is that possible media scrutiny would deter the Commission from proposing such laws in the first place or encourage it to modify them to meet the concerns.

2.5.2 Enhanced cooperation

The tension between the 'vanguard' members, who wish to broaden the scope of EU activities, and the 'doubters', who do not, led to the introduction of a new type of integration process called 'enhanced cooperation'. This allows subgroups of EU members to cooperate on specific areas while still keeping the cooperation under the general framework of the EU.

However, the conditions for starting new enhanced cooperations are so strict that few such initiatives have come into force. One involves divorce law and the other patent law (see Box 2.11).

In some ways, the Eurogroup is like an enhanced cooperation but it is so important that it has its own set of rules – and these rules are evolving as the EU responds to the global and Eurozone financial crises.

Box 2.11   Divorce and the first enhanced cooperation

Divorce is never an easy thing, but it can get nightmarishly complicated with a mixed nationality couple with children. Even within the EU, divorce laws vary widely – from the no-fault, automatic policy of secular Sweden to devotedly Catholic Malta's lack of recognition of divorce – and it is not always clear which laws should apply.

The EU tried to simplify things and avoid spouses engaging in a trying and costly search for the 'best' set of divorce laws by agreeing a regulation (known as Rome III) that would specify which laws apply. The absolute refusal of Sweden and Malta to agree to the regulation (which must be agreed unanimously since such legal cooperation is a third-pillar issue) induced a subset of nations to proceed by requesting an enhanced cooperation on the matter. The group included Austria, France, Greece, Hungary, Italy, Luxembourg, Romania, Slovenia and Spain from the beginning; Germany, Belgium, Portugal and Lithuania are considering joining the initiative.

2.6 Some important facts

EU nations are very different, one from another. This simple fact is the source of a large share of the EU's problems, so it is important to understand it in detail. This section covers the facts on population, income and economic size. Students can easily find the most up-to-date figures for this section in the freely downloadable data from the Eurostat website, epp.eurostat.ec.europa.eu.

2.6.1 Population and income

There are about 500 million EU citizens, a figure that is substantially larger than the corresponding US and Japanese figures, but substantially smaller than those of China and India. The EU28 nations vary enormously in terms of population, as the upper panel of Figure 2.7 shows. The differences are easier to remember when the nations are grouped into big, medium, small and tiny – where these categories are established by comparison with the population of well-known cities:

- The 'big' nations are defined here as having 35 million people or more – clearly more people than even the largest city in the world (Jakarta's population is about 26 million while the Greater Tokyo area has over 30 million). In the EU there are six big nations: Germany, the UK, France, Italy, Spain and Poland. Germany is substantially larger than the others, more than twice the size of the smallest in the group. The total population of the 'Big-6' accounts for about 70 per cent of the 505 million people in the EU28 nations. Turkey, with whom the EU started membership negotiations in October 2005, has over 75 million inhabitants. This exceeds the population of all EU nations except Germany and, given the projected decline in the German population and rapid population growth in Turkey, the ordering is likely to be reversed within a few years.

- The 'medium' nations are defined as having populations of between 7 and 12 million, something like that of a really big city, say, Paris with its surroundings. There are eight medium members (Greece, Portugal, Belgium, the Czech Republic, Hungary, Sweden, Austria and Bulgaria).

- The 'small' nations have populations along the lines of a big city, ranging from Madrid (5.4 million) to Lyons (1.6 million). The nine Member States in this range are Denmark, Finland, Slovakia, Ireland, Croatia, Lithuania, Slovenia, Latvia and Estonia.

- The 'tiny' nations have populations that are smaller than those of a small city like Genoa. The list comprises Cyprus, Luxembourg and Malta.

- The only nations that fall between these categories are the Netherlands (with 17 million) and Romania (with 20 million).

Figure 2.7 Population and income per capita (PPS), 2013

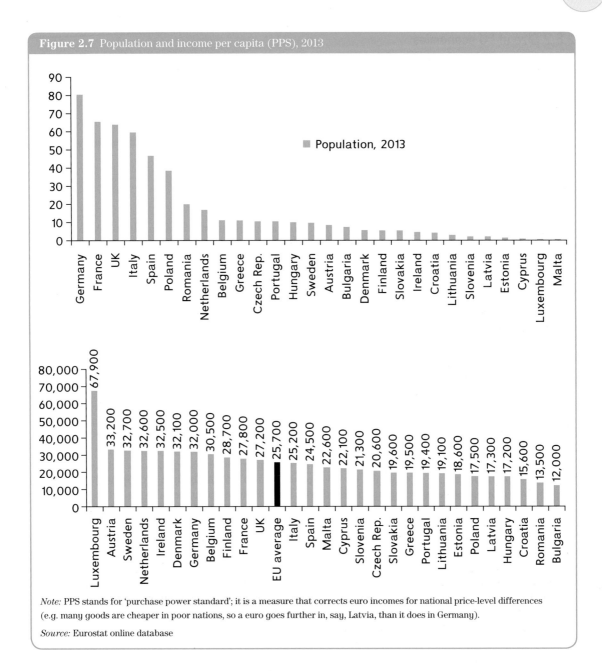

Note: PPS stands for 'purchase power standard'; it is a measure that corrects euro incomes for national price-level differences (e.g. many goods are cheaper in poor nations, so a euro goes further in, say, Latvia than it does in Germany).

Source: Eurostat online database

The average income level of the people in these nations also varies enormously. Again, it is useful to classify the nations into three categories – high, medium and low. Luxembourg is in a super-rich class by itself; Luxembourgers are more than twice as rich as the French and Swedes. One explanation for this is that Luxembourg is, economically speaking, a medium-sized city and incomes in cities tend to be quite high. The high-income category – defined as incomes above the EU27 average (about €26,000 in 2013) – includes ten of the EU28 nations. In the medium-income category there are four relatively poor 'old' members (Italy, Spain, Greece and Portugal), ten new members (Malta, Cyprus, Slovenia, the Czech Republic, Slovakia, Lithuania, Estonia, Poland, Latvia, Hungary and Croatia). Low-income nations, defined as those with per-capita incomes of less than 60 per cent of the EU average, are Romania and Bulgaria.

2.6.2 Size of EU economies

The size distribution of European economies is also very uneven, measuring economic size with total GDP. Just six nations, the 'Big-5' (Germany, the UK, France, Italy and Spain) and the Netherlands, account for more than 80 per cent of the GDP of the whole EU. The other nations are small, tiny or minuscule, using the following definitions:

- 'Small' is an economy that accounts for between 1 and 3 per cent of the EU27's output.
- 'Tiny' is one that accounts for less than 1 per cent of the total.
- Minuscule is one that accounts for less than one-tenth of 1 per cent.

2.7 The budget

The EU budget is the source of a great deal of both solidarity and tension among EU members, so a full understanding of the EU requires some knowledge of this area. This section looks at the following questions in order. What is the money spent on? Where does it come from? Who gets the most on net? How does the budget process work?

2.7.1 Expenditure

Total EU spending is now over €130 billion. While this sounds like a lot to most people, it is really fairly small – only about 1 per cent of total EU27 GDP – just €270 per EU citizen. The first priority here is to study how this money is spent. We look first at spending by area and then spending by EU member.

Expenditure by area

As with so many things in Europe, understanding EU spending in all its detail would take a lifetime, but understanding the basics takes just a few minutes. Starting at the broadest level, the EU spends its money on farming, poor regions and other things. These categories, however, attract a great deal of criticism, especially – as we shall see in Chapter 9 – that much of the agriculture money is given to large landowners.

Under Commission President Barroso the names of all main spending categories were changed to make them sound more positive. For example, the EU spends almost half its budget on payments to farmers despite the sector's meagre contribution to EU growth, income and employment. To make this sound more in line with a forward-looking, dynamic EU, these expenditures were labelled 'Sustainable Growth: Natural Resources'.

The easiest way to remember the facts is to turn to plain English and focus only on the biggest areas (see Figure 2.8), which are farming (42 per cent) and poor regions (33 per cent). The rest is split among many different uses – the biggest being R&D and Training (12 per cent) and Administration (6 per cent). Spending on agriculture and poor regions is so important that we have written separate chapters dealing with each, so we do not go into further detail here (see Chapter 9 on agriculture and Chapter 10 on poor regions).

Historical development of EU spending by area

The EU's spending priorities and level of spending have changed dramatically since its inception in 1958. The EU budget grew rapidly, but started at a very low level (just 8/100ths of 1 per cent of the EEC6's GDP). EU spending was negligible until the late 1960s, amounting to less than €10 per EU citizen. This changed as the cost of the Common Agricultural Policy (CAP) started to rise rapidly in the 1960s and Cohesion spending started to rise in the 1980s. From the early 1970s to the early 1990s, the budget grew steadily as a fraction of EU GDP, starting from about 0.8 per cent and rising to 1.2 per cent in 1993. Since the 1994 enlargement, the budget as a share of GDP has remained quite stable at about 1 per cent.

CAP spending began in 1965 and soon dominated the budget. For almost a decade, farm spending regularly took 80 per cent or more of total expenditures; at its peak in 1970, it made up 92 per cent of the budget! From the date of the first enlargement, 1973, Cohesion spending began to grow in importance, pushing down Agriculture's share in the process. Indeed, the sum of the shares of these two big-ticket items

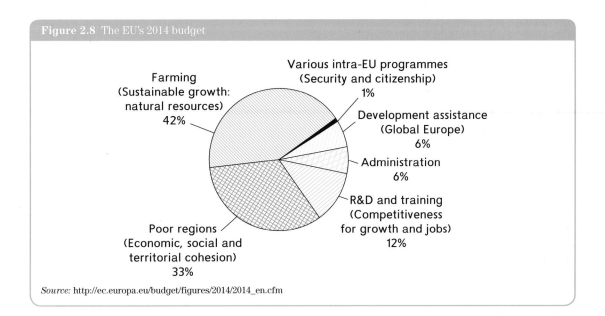

Figure 2.8 The EU's 2014 budget

Source: http://ec.europa.eu/budget/figures/2014/2014_en.cfm

has remained remarkably steady, ranging between 80 and 85 per cent of the budget. In a very real sense, we can think of Cohesion spending as steadily crowding out CAP spending over the past three decades.

2.7.2 Expenditure by type by member

By far the most important benefit gained from EU membership is economic integration. By comparison, the financial transfers involved in EU spending are minor. Remember that the whole budget is only about 1 per cent of EU GDP and the net contributions (payments to the EU minus payments from the EU) are never greater than one-tenth of 1 per cent. Be this as it may, many people are interested to see which members receive the largest shares of EU spending. Many EU disputes, after all, are over budget matters.

The amount and type of EU spending varies quite a lot across members (see Figure 2.9). Poland and Spain are the top recipients, with most of their money coming from EU payments to farmers and poor regions. There are a few other noteworthy patterns too, however:

- Farming receipts are important for members with relatively large farm sectors like Denmark and Ireland.
- Spending on poor regions is more important for the poorer Member States such as the central and eastern European members).
- Almost all of Luxembourg's and Belgium's receipts come from administrative spending.
- The UK has remarkably low receipts for its size; Belgium, with a sixth of Britain's population, gets the same total.

Readers may find it instructive to download the data themselves and search for abnormalities in their own nation's receipts.

2.7.3 Revenue

The EU's budget must, by law, be balanced every year. All of the spending discussed above must be financed each year by revenues collected from EU members or carried over from previous years. The system is designed so that each EU member pays a bit less than 1 per cent of their GDP (see Figure 2.10). Some observers find this anomalous since taxation in most nations, especially in Europe, is progressive, i.e. the tax rate that an individual pays rises with his or her income level.

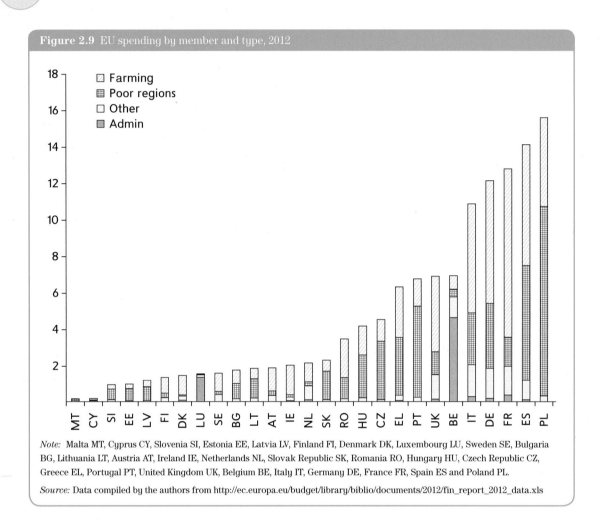

Figure 2.9 EU spending by member and type, 2012

Note: Malta MT, Cyprus CY, Slovenia SI, Estonia EE, Latvia LV, Finland FI, Denmark DK, Luxembourg LU, Sweden SE, Bulgaria BG, Lithuania LT, Austria AT, Ireland IE, Netherlands NL, Slovak Republic SK, Romania RO, Hungary HU, Czech Republic CZ, Greece EL, Portugal PT, United Kingdom UK, Belgium BE, Italy IT, Germany DE, France FR, Spain ES and Poland PL.

Source: Data compiled by the authors from http://ec.europa.eu/budget/library/biblio/documents/2012/fin_report_2012_data.xls

Up to 1970, the EU's budget was financed by annual contributions from the members. A pair of treaties in the 1970s and a handful of landmark decisions by the European Council established the system we have today in which there are four main sources of revenue. (See Box 2.12 for further details.) This revenue is known as 'own resources' in EU jargon.

There are four main types of revenue. Two of the four have long been used, and indeed in the early days of the Union they were sufficient to finance all payments. These so-called traditional own resources are:

- Tariff revenue stemming from the Common External Tariff (CET). Although trade within the EU is tariff-free, tariffs are imposed on imports from non-member nations. This money accrues to the EU rather than to any particular member.

- 'Agricultural levies' are tariffs on agricultural goods that are imported from non-members. Conceptually, these are the same as the previous category (they are both taxes on imports from third nations) but are viewed as distinct since the levies are not formally part of the CET. Historically, the level of these tariffs has fluctuated widely according to market conditions (they were part of the CAP's price support mechanism; see Chapter 9).

The importance of these two revenue items has fallen over the years to the point where they are no longer major items (together, they make up only one-seventh of the revenue needs). This reduced importance

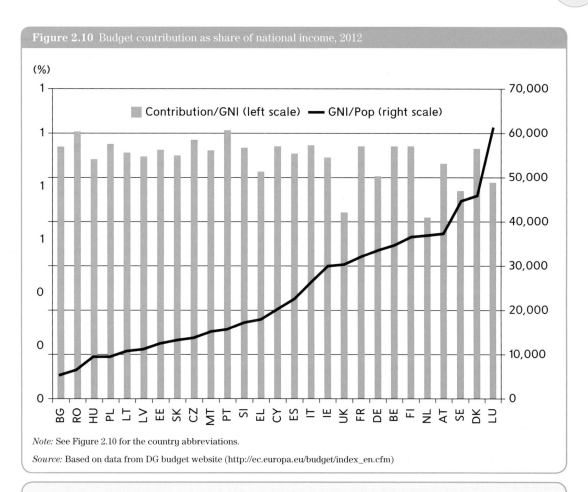

Figure 2.10 Budget contribution as share of national income, 2012

Note: See Figure 2.10 for the country abbreviations.

Source: Based on data from DG budget website (http://ec.europa.eu/budget/index_en.cfm)

Box 2.12   Milestones in the EU budget procedure

1958–70. The EU's budget was financed by contributions from its members.

April 1970. The Luxembourg European Council. The 'own resources' system is introduced. These included customs duties, agricultural levies (i.e. variable tariffs) and a share of VAT revenue collected by EU members. The Treaty of July 1975 refined and reinforced the system, establishing the European Court of Auditors to oversee the budget and giving the European Parliament the formal right of rejection over annual budgets.

1975–87. This period was marked by sharp disputes over the budget contributions and ever-expanding CAP spending. The UK's Margaret Thatcher in particular complained repeatedly about the UK's position as the largest net contributor.

1984. The Fontainebleau European Council. The VAT-based revenue source was increased and the UK was awarded its famous 'rebate'.

1988. Delors I package. This reform established the basis of the current revenue and spending system. It introduced a fourth 'own resource' based on members' GNPs, established an overall ceiling on EU revenue as a percentage of the EU's GNP and started reducing the role of VAT-based revenue. The package, decided at the Brussels European Council in June, also established the EU's multi-year budgeting process whereby a Financial Perspective sets out the evolution of EU spending by broad categories. Substantively, the Financial Perspective adopted provided for a major reorientation of

EU spending from the CAP to Cohesion spending; Cohesion spending was doubled and CAP spending growth was capped.

1992. Delors II package. The Edinburgh agreement of December 1992 increased the revenue ceiling slightly, to 1.27 per cent, and further reduced the role of VAT-based revenue. It also adopted a new Financial Perspective for 1993–99, which amplified the shift of EU spending priorities away from the CAP and towards Cohesion.

1999. Agenda 2000 package. The Berlin European Council adopted the 2000–06 Financial Perspective. There were no major changes on the revenue side and the only major change on the spending side was the creation of a new broad category, 'Pre-accession' expenditures, meant to finance programmes in central and eastern European nations and provide a reserve to cover the cost of any enlargements in this period.

2005. After a failure to reach agreement at their June 2005 Summit, the issue of setting the seven-year Financial Perspective for the 2007–13 period fell to the UK Presidency. The basic idea was to move spending slowly away from agriculture, to make the spending on poor regions more coherent and concentrated, and increase spending on competitiveness measures such as R&D. The 2004 and 2007 enlargements, however, added 12 new members with below-average incomes and many farmers, so large changes in budget priorities proved politically impossible.

stems from the way that the level of the CET has been steadily lowered in the course of WTO rounds (e.g. the 1986–94 Uruguay Round). Moreover, EU enlargement and the signing of free trade agreements with non-members means that a very large fraction of EU imports from non-members is duty free. The level of the agricultural levies has also been reduced in the context of CAP reform. The third and fourth types of own resources provide most of the money. They are:

- 'VAT resource'. As is often the case when it comes to tax matters, the reality is quite complex, but it is best thought of as a 1 per cent value added tax. The importance of this resource has declined and is set to decline further.

- GNP-based. This revenue is a tax based on the GNP of EU members. It is used to top up any revenue shortfall and thus ensures that the EU never runs a deficit.

The other revenue sources have been relatively unimportant since 1977. Now, they include items such as taxes paid by employees of European institutions (they do not pay national taxes), fines, and surpluses carried over from previous years. Until the 1970s budget treaties came fully into effect, 'miscellaneous' revenue included direct member contributions, which were a crucial source of funding in the early years.

2.7.4 Budget process

The budget is decided and controlled jointly by the European Parliament, the Council and the Commission. To avoid delays and problems, the EU's annual budget is guided by a medium-term agreement on spending priorities called the 'Multiannual Financial Framework'. The current framework sets out broad spending guidelines for the annual budgets from 2014 to 2020 (you can download it from http://ec.europa.eu/budget/mff/lib/data/MFF2014-2020.xls).

The procedure for drawing up the annual budget (as laid down in the Treaties) calls for the Commission to prepare a preliminary draft budget. The Commission's draft is presented to the Council for amendments and adoption. Once it has passed the Council, the budget goes to the European Parliament, which has some power to amend it. After two readings in the Council and the Parliament, it is the European Parliament that adopts the final budget, and its President who signs it. For more information, see http://ec.europa.eu/budget/mff/introduction/index_en.cfm.

2.8 Summary

This chapter covered seven very different topics.

Economic integration

The economic integration in the EU was designed to create a unified economic area in which firms and consumers located anywhere within it would have equal opportunities to sell or buy goods throughout the area, and where owners of labour and capital would be free to employ their resources in any economic activity anywhere in the area. Such integration is implemented via the 'four freedoms' – the free movements of goods, services, people and capital.

EU organization

The organization of the EU changed after the 2009 Lisbon Treaty from a three-pillar to a two-pillar system. The first pillar (supranational decision making and the authority of supranational institutions such as the Commission and European Court) encompasses economic integration and some areas of Home and Justice Affairs. The other pillar includes areas in which EU integration proceeds on an intergovernmental basis, such as the Common Foreign and Security Policy. The treaties governing these areas are the Treaty on European Union (TEU) and the Treaty on the Functioning of the EU (TFEU).

Law

The EU is unique in that it has a supranational system of law. That is, on matters pertaining to the European Community, EU law and the European Court take precedence over Member States' laws and courts. The key principles covered were 'direct effect', 'primacy' and 'autonomy'.

Institutions and legislative procedures

While there are many EU institutions, only five really matter for most things. These are the European Council, the Council of Ministers, the Commission, the Parliament and the Court.

These five institutions work in concert to govern the EU and to pursue deeper and wider European economic integration. Under the main legislative procedure, now called the 'ordinary legislative procedure', the Commission proposes draft laws which have to be approved by the Council of Ministers and the European Parliament before taking effect. The three bodies work in sequence to ensure there is only one version of a proposed law at any one time. Most EU legislation has to be turned into national law by each Member State's parliament.

Facts

A dominant feature of the EU members is their diversity in size and income levels.

Budget

The EU budget is rather small, representing only 1 per cent of the EU's GDP. It is spent mainly on a set of agricultural programmes known as the Common Agricultural Policy (roughly 40 per cent of the budget) and on poor regions in the EU (roughly a third of the budget). The budget is funded through four complicated mechanisms but the result is that each EU member pays roughly 1 per cent of its GDP to the Commission, regardless of its income level.

Self-assessment questions

1 Draw a diagram like Figure 2.7 which includes the role of the national Parliaments.
2 Draw a schematic representation of the steady deepening of EU economic integration.
3 Draw a diagram that shows the main steps (and dates) in the development of the Big-5 EU institutions. (Hint: You may have to turn to the websites referred to in the text to find the dates.)

4 Develop an easy way of remembering the names of all EU15 members (e.g. there are four big ones, four small ones, four poor ones and three new ones). Do the same for the 12 newcomers that joined between 2004 and 2007.

5 Explain in 25 words or fewer the difference between EC law and EU law.

6 List the main sources of EU revenue and the main spending priorities. Explain how each of these has developed over time.

7 Explain why it is important that the European Court's rulings cannot be appealed in Member States' courts.

8 Make a table recording the major changes to each of the Big-5 institutions implied by the Lisbon Treaty.

Further reading: the aficionado's corner

For more economic statistics on Europe, see the most recent issue of the *Eurostat Yearbook*. This is well-organized and provides directly comparable figures for all EU members. Eurostat, which used to charge for data, now allows free downloads of most data series. Much of the same information can be found in the Statistical Appendix to the Commission publication, *European Economy*. The OECD also provides an excellent statistical overview in its 'OECD in figures'. You can download the latest issue for free from www.oecd.org.

On EU law, an excellent source is *The ABC of Community Law* by **Borchandt** (2010); this eBook can be freely downloaded. It is still the best freely downloadable text and has been fully updated to reflect changes instituted by the 2009 Lisbon Treaty.

Another well-written and succinct source is 'The European Union Today', published by the UK's House of Lords and written by **Maxine Hill and Matthew Purvis** (11 June 2010). Go to http://www.parliament.uk/business/publications/research/briefing-papers/LLN-2012-003/the-european-union-today.

Two other good sources of further information on the budget and a discussion of the many options and conflicts are:

Notre Europe (a think tank established by Jacques Delors): http://www.eng.notre-europe.eu/011015-97-European-Budget.html.

Bruegel (a Brussels-based think tank on European economic issues):

http://www.bruegel.org/publications/publication-detail/publication/760-the-long-term-eu-budget-size-or-flexibility/.

Useful websites

The European Parliament's factsheets provide excellent, up-to-date, authoritative and succinct coverage of EU law, institutions, decision-making procedures and the budget process. It is a really great place to start when you are trying to figure out how or why or what the EU does in any area ranging from marine conservation to banking union: http://www.europarl.europa.eu/aboutparliament/en/displayFtu.html.

The most exhaustive (but also exhausting) source for information on EU law is the Commission's excellent website: http://europa.eu/legislation_summaries/.

References

Baldwin, R. et al. (2001) *Nice Try: Should the Treaty of Nice be Ratified?*, CEPR, London.

Borchandt, K.-D. (2010) *The ABC of European Union Law*. Download from http://europa.eu/documentation/legislation/pdf/oa8107147_en.pdf.

House of Lords (2008) 'European Union Committee: 10th Report of Session 2007–08, The Treaty of Lisbon: an impact assessment'. Download from www.publications.parliament.uk/pa/ld200708/ldselect/ldeucom/62/62.pdf.

Milward, A. (1992) *The European Rescue of the Nation-state*, Cambridge University Press, Cambridge.

Mongelli, F.P., E. Dorrucci and I. Agur (2007) 'What does European institutional integration tell us about trade integration?', *Integration and Trade (IADB)*, 11(26).

Noury, A. and G. Roland (2002) *European Parliament: Should It Have More Power?*, *Economic Policy*, 17(53): 279–319.

Open Europe (2008) 'Open Europe parliamentary briefing #5: Foreign policy and defence'. Download from www. openeurope.org.uk/research/cfspbriefing.pdf.

Nothing is more difficult, and therefore more precious, than to be able to decide.

Napoleon Bonaparte

Decision making

Chapter Contents

Introduction

A great debate is raging in Europe: What is the appropriate division of powers between the EU and its member nations? It was fuelled and focused by British Premier David Cameron's pledge to repatriate some decision-making powers that were previously shifted to EU institutions. The debate takes on an historic importance since he linked the outcome to an in-or-out referendum on EU membership for Britain.

> *There is a growing frustration that the EU is seen as something that is done to people rather than acting on their behalf. . . . People are increasingly frustrated that decisions are taken further and further away from them. . . . We are starting to see this in the demonstrations on the streets of Athens, Madrid and Rome. We are seeing it in the parliaments of Berlin, Helsinki and the Hague.*

David Cameron, UK Prime Minister, 23 January 2013

In responding to the speech, Guido Westerwelle, German Foreign Minister, said: 'Germany wants an ambitious reform of the economic and monetary union. In such decisive issues as the future of the common currency, we do not need less, but more integration.' But he quickly added that there were limits: 'Not all and everything must be decided in Brussels and by Brussels.' And the core practical issue was signalled by Swedish Foreign Minister, Carl Bildt: 'Flexibility sounds fine, but if you open up to a 28-speed Europe, at the end of the day there is no Europe at all. Just a mess.'

While David Cameron has revived the debate, he did not invent it. His concern that the EU has too much power find many historical echoes. In the 1960s, French President Charles de Gaulle boycotted EU meetings and threatened to take France out of the EU over similar issues. In the 1990s, the notion of 'subsidiarity' arose to address German Länder concerns that their powers – granted to them by the German constitution – were being usurped by EU treaties. Indeed, there has been a massive shift in the consensus on the need to centralize more powers.

The tension arises since centralization started life as a key goal – perhaps the primary goal – of the nascent EU. The opening sentence of its founding document – the 1958 Treaty of Rome – declares that the European Union is 'Determined to lay the foundations of an ever-closer union among the peoples of Europe.' But after five decades and a massive pooling of sovereignty, the appetite for more centralization is greatly diminished.

Enthusiasm for deeper integration has notably cooled. When EU law was massively revised by the 2009 Lisbon Treaty, the famous phrase 'ever closer union' was demoted to the thirteenth paragraph. Moreover it was diluted and qualified with a caution on centralization. The phrase is now completed with 'in which decisions are taken as closely as possible to the citizen in accordance with the principle of subsidiarity'.[1] Reflecting such concerns, Lisbon created a formal role for Member State Parliaments in policing subsidiarity. This takes the form of an 'early warning mechanism' whereby a third of national parliaments can issue a 'yellow card' against a proposed EU law on the grounds that it violates the principle of subsidiarity.

This chapter presents frameworks that should help the reader think at a more abstract and analytical level about this great debate. The chapter is organized around two major questions:

1 Who should be in charge of what? That is, which decisions should be taken at the EU level and which should be taken at the national or sub-national levels?

2 Is the EU-level decision-making procedure efficient and legitimate?

In answering these questions we shall examine the EU's actual practice and develop a number of specific analytical tools. Moreover, we shall look at proposed reforms of the system in response to recent and future enlargements that challenge the EU's decision-making structure.

---

[1] Readers can find the Treaties conveniently collected at http://europa.eu/about-eu/basic-information/decision-making/treaties/index_en.htm.

3.1 Task allocation and subsidiarity: EU practice and principles

Governments set policies in many areas – speed limits on roads, school curriculums, monetary policy, taxation, import taxes on Chinese T-shirts, development of nuclear weapons, deployment of troops abroad, etc. Plainly, not all of these policies are made by the same level of government. Most European nations have at least three levels of government (local, provincial and national) and EU members have a fourth level of government, the EU.

Although European nations differ in their attitude towards internal centralization (e.g. France tends to centralize many more issues than does Belgium), there is usually a fairly clear allocation of tasks to the four levels of government in each nation. Typically, local speed limits are set by the local government, but motorway speed limits are determined at the national level. Anything to do with military matters is dealt with at the national level, but local nature reserves are likely to be addressed at the provincial level.

In short, there seems to be a 'method to the madness' – some systematic thinking. But what is the logic behind this allocation of tasks? This is the main question we turn to now. We begin by covering the existing EU principles that guide the allocation of policies between the EU and Member States and briefly cover their practice. The next section presents an analytic framework for organizing thinking about the appropriate allocation of tasks among the various levels of government.

3.1.1 Introduction to 'competences'

In EU jargon, this task allocation is called the question of 'competences'. Areas in which the EU alone decides are known as 'exclusive competences' or 'Union competences'. Those areas in which responsibility is shared between the EU and Member States are called 'shared competences'. There are two types of shared competence: those whereby members cannot pass legislation in areas where the EU has already done so and those whereby the existence of EU legislation does not hinder members' rights to make policy in the same area (see Table 3.1, for examples). The third type is a 'supporting, coordinating or complementary competence' (EU Constitution, Article 1-17) whereby the EU can pass laws that support action by members. The most common names are 'supporting competence' and 'supporting action'. Finally, tasks whereby national or sub-national governments alone decide are called 'national competences'.

Some tasks and decisions are clearly assigned to the EU, such as competition policy whereby the EU has the final say on, for example, mergers that affect the European market. Others are clearly assigned to Member States, such as the secondary school curriculum. A great number, however, are shared between the EU and Member States. As is true of so many things in the EU, the exact dividing lines are unclear. The Lisbon Treaty substantially improved clarity on this point, but much is still open to interpretation.

The basic source of ambiguity is that areas of exclusive Union competence are defined partly by reference to functional descriptions. For example, the Union has exclusive competence when it comes to international agreements when it is 'necessary to enable the Union to exercise its internal competence, or insofar as its conclusion may affect common rules or alter their scope'. Plainly, the meaning of 'necessary' would be open to interpretation in many cases. The Treaties' objectives are ambitious, so this proviso puts a great many tasks in the grey area between Community competence and national competence. Often, the dividing line has been established by the European Court.

Task allocation is further blurred by the so-called flexibility clause, which allows the EU to obtain additional competences when necessary; however, this requires an elaborate procedure (see the 'Flexibility clause' section below).

3.1.2 Principle governing the allocation of competences

The touchstone principle is that the EU has no powers intrinsically. Article 1 of the Treaty on European Union says that it is the members that confer competences on the EU in order to attain objectives they have in common. This is the 'principle of conferral', i.e. the default option is that competences remain with the members.

While the limits of EU competences are governed by the principle of conferral, the use of these is governed by the principles of 'subsidiarity' and 'proportionality'. Both words have distinct meanings in the EU.

Table 3.1   Allocation of competences to the EU

Exclusive	Shared		Support, coordinate or supplement
Customs union	Exclusive if EU has policy	Non-exclusive	Certain human health policies
Competition policy	Internal market	R&D policies	Industry
Eurozone monetary policy	Certain social policy	Outer space policies	Culture
Conservation of marine resources	Cohesion policy	Development cooperation	Tourism
Common commercial policy	Agriculture and fisheries	Humanitarian aid	Education and training
	Environment		Civil protection and disaster prevention
	Consumer protection		Administrative cooperation
	Transport		Coordination of economic, employment and social policies
	Energy		Common foreign, security and defence policies
	Old third pillar 'Area of freedom, security and justice'		
	Certain public health polices		

Source: The main provisions are in TEU Articles 1, 4, 5, 6, Protocol No. 2

Subsidiarity and proportionality

The principle of subsidiarity pursues two contrasting goals: (1) to allow the EU to act if a problem cannot be adequately addressed by national policies alone, and (2) to guard national sovereignty in those areas that cannot be dealt with more effectively at the EU level. The overarching goal is thus to keep decisions as close to the citizen as possible without jeopardizing win–win cooperation at the EU level. As Borchardt (2010) puts it, 'when it is not necessary for the EU to take action, it is necessary that it should take none'.

The principle of proportionality comes into play when EU action is necessary, i.e. when the objectives of the Treaties can be better achieved at the EU level or in an area in which the EU has exclusive competence. In such situations, the proportionality principle says that the EU should undertake only the minimum necessary actions.

Here is an example of how the subsidiarity and proportionality principles work. The uncoordinated setting of VAT rates would hinder the smooth functioning of the internal market by, for example, leading to massive cross-border shopping driven by VAT differences. The principle of subsidiarity thus suggests that coordinating action at the EU level would be better than uncoordinated action at the national level. In short, the EU should do something to harmonize VAT rates. The principle of proportionality, however, suggests that all that is needed is *some* harmonization, *not complete* harmonization. In keeping with the principle of proportionality, the EU agreed to minimum and maximum VAT rates but let members decide their own rates within the band.

Practically, these principles mean that the 'burden of proof' lies on the instigators of EU legislation. They must make the case that there is a real need for common rules and common action in the area and that the proposed rules or actions restrict national sovereignty as little as possible.

Flexibility clause

The conferral principle says that the EU can act only in areas in which Member States have conferred power to it in the Treaties; however, there are situations when a new challenge – one not foreseen in the Treaties – arises that requires action at the EU level. One way to deal with this would be to require a Treaty modification each time such things arose. As Chapter 1 showed plainly, changing treaties can be a long and tricky process.

3.1.3 Competences in practice

The Treaties as amended by the Lisbon Treaty spell out the EU's competences more clearly and more explicitly than was the case before. Indeed, this is one of its major accomplishments. Table 3.1 lists the areas in which the EU has competences. All other areas are exclusive competences of the members since any power not explicitly conferred upon the EU remains with the members. Importantly, TEU Article 6 explicitly states that inclusion of the Charter of Fundamental Rights does not extend the EU's competences in any way.

The biggest switch, as noted in Chapter 2, is that of Home and Justice Affairs from intergovernmental treatment (i.e. whereby the EU had no competences at all) to shared competence. This is a natural follow-on from decades of tight economic integration. Europeans are just more tied up with each other, and so many face cross-border legal issues that rarely arose in the last century – things like marriage contracts, retirement plans and house buying.

The third category – support, coordinate or supplement – is new and very useful as the Commission has increasingly turned to this sort of 'soft law' approach in the face of resistance to more direct policies. For example, when it comes to competitiveness, it provides frameworks and benchmarking structures that help members coordinate without actually requiring them to do anything specifically. By putting this category of action into the Treaties, the legal status of such actions was clarified.

3.2 Understanding the task allocation theory of fiscal federalism

The last section considered EU principles and practices, but it did not explain the logic underpinning them. This section uses economic reasoning to help readers understand the allocation of tasks in a systematic way. Of course, practice and theory differ – as Albert Einstein is alleged to have said, 'The difference between theory and practice is greater in practice than it is in theory' – but most readers will find it easier to remember the practice if they understand the underpinning logic.

This section presents a framework for thinking about the most appropriate level of government for each type of task. A complete consideration of this question, however, would take us into subjects (political science, sociology, national identity, etc.) that are too far afield for this book. The main line of thinking presented here is called the theory of 'fiscal federalism'. Even though this provides only an incomplete approach to the question, it proves to be a very useful framework for organizing one's thinking about the basic trade-offs.

3.2.1 The basic trade-offs

We focus on five important considerations when thinking about the appropriate allocation of policy-making tasks to the various levels of government. In the real world, the five blend together in complex ways. To clarify our thinking, however, we consider each in isolation. The first concerns local diversity.

Diversity and local informational advantages

When people have very different preferences, centralized decision making creates inefficiencies. There are both obvious and subtle aspects to this point.

The obvious aspect is that a single, centrally chosen policy will typically be a compromise. By definition, a compromise will not be the right policy for everybody. Take the example of road speed limits. Suppose the German federal government could choose only one speed limit for the whole country. The result would be a limit that was too slow for the autobahn but too fast for residential neighbourhoods. (Of course, for some policies, choosing one policy for the whole nation might reduce costs but we put that aside for clarity's sake and deal with it below under 'Scale economies'.)

The subtle aspect concerns local information about diverse situations and preferences. The speed limit example seemed strained since the federal government could set different speed limits for different roads. The subtle point is that, if many different limits are to be set, local governments are probably better at determining which limit to apply to which roads in their localities. This is basically an issue of the cost of acquiring the information necessary to adapt policies to local conditions and preferences. As a general principle (to which there are many exceptions), local governments can acquire such information more cheaply and so the decision-making task should be allocated to the local level.

The general idea is more concretely illustrated in Box 3.1.

Box 3.1   Economic inefficiency of a one-size-fits-all policy

To illustrate this general idea more concretely, we turn to Figure 3.1. (The figure employs supply and demand analysis and the notion of consumer surplus; see Chapter 4 if you are unfamiliar with this type of reasoning.)

Figure 3.1 Diversity of preferences and decentralization

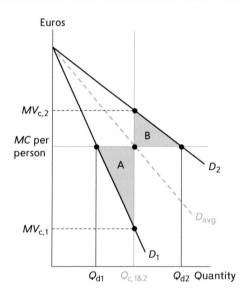

Note: The diagram assumes that individuals in each region are identical and the governments are 'benevolent'.

Technical note: The MC per person = MV criterion is identical to Samuelson's famous sum of MV condition since $MC/N = MV$ implies $MC = N * MV$, where N is the number of people in the region.

The figure shows demand curves for a particular public service. One is for an individual located in region 1 (marked as D_1) and the other for a person in region 2 (marked as D_2). We assume that, for some reason, people in the two regions have different preferences for public services. For example, if we are talking about the density of public bus services, people in region 2 might live in a city where commuting by car is difficult, so they prize bus services more highly than the people in region 1. These relative preferences can be seen from the fact that D_1 is below D_2; from the consumer surplus analysis in Chapter 4, this means that the marginal value of a slight increase in the density of bus services is lower for individuals in region 1 than it is in region 2.

To start the analysis, we work out the level of bus services that would be provided if the levels were chosen separately by the region 1 and region 2 governments. The region 1 government would best serve its citizens by choosing the level whereby a typical region 1 person's marginal value of a denser bus service (i.e. more buses per day and/or more routes) was just equal to the per-person cost of providing the extra service. In the panel, this optimal level is Q_{d1} for region 1 (the $_d$ stands for decentralized and the $_1$ for region 1). Region 2's government would choose a higher level, namely, Q_{d2}. (This assumes, for simplicity, that the marginal cost is constant at all levels of service and identical across regions.)

Contrast this with the situation whereby the policy decision is centralized so that the same level is chosen for both regions. In this case, the central government would look at the average preference for bus services as reflected by the average demand curve marked as D_{avg}. Using the same reasoning as with local governments, the optimal average provision is shown by $Q_{c,\,1\&2}$.

How do these two situations compare in terms of people's welfare? Taking the decentralized choice as the initial situation, the figure shows that people in both regions are made worse off by centralizing the decision. The people in region 1 are forced to pay (via their taxes) for a level of bus service that is too high for their preferences. The loss to a typical region 1 person is given by the triangle 'A' since this measures – for each extra increase in Q – the gap between the marginal value of the denser service and the marginal cost. The marginal value is given by the demand curve D_1 and the marginal cost is given by the *MC per person* line. Region 2 residents also lose, but for them the loss stems from the fact that they would like a denser service than is provided when decision making is centralized. In particular, area B shows their losses since it measures, for each unit reduction of Q, the gap between their marginal value (given by D_2) and the marginal cost (given by *MC per person*).

In summary, the diagram shows the rather straightforward point that choosing a one-size-fits-all policy leads to an inferior outcome when people have diverse preferences. If the Q_s are chosen separately for the two regions, there is no reason to centralize the decision. It will typically be cheaper for local authorities to determine what is optimal for their region. More specifically, suppose it costs X euros more for the central authorities to get the information than it would cost local authorities. Since the decision would be the same in both cases (Q_{d1} and Q_{d2} are chosen), the centralized decision making is worse since taxpayers will have to pay the extra information-gathering cost, X.

Scale economies

The advantage of localized decision making in terms of information efficiency is really quite a robust result. Yet in many situations there are offsetting cost savings from a one-size-fits-all policy that arise from scale economies, i.e. the notion that the per-person cost of a service falls as more people use the service.

For example, in the case of bus services, it seems reasonable to believe that the cost per kilometre of bus service tends to fall as the number of buses gets larger. A large bus company can more easily ensure that the right number of drivers is available, the fixed cost of a maintenance centre can be spread over more buses, and the per-bus cost of administration may fall – at least up to a point – when the bus company is larger. Imagine an extreme situation where every bus in, say, Paris was owned and operated by separate companies versus the situation where all the buses were owned by a single company. Surely the latter would be more efficient in terms of costs.

To sum up, economies arising from joint decision making tend to favour centralization, while diversity of preferences and local information advantages favour decentralization. We turn next to another key issue that arises when the decisions made in one region affect people in other regions. In economics jargon, these are called 'spillovers'.

To understand the economics of the scale versus diversity trade-off, see Box 3.2.

Box 3.2   Economic gains from scale versus losses from one-size-fits-all

The widespread presence of scale economies in the provision of public services – transport services, medical services, etc. – tends to favour centralization. To see this point, we refer to Figure 3.2. The diagram focuses only on the impact of centralization on the typical region 1 individual. In the decentralized situation the marginal cost per person of a denser bus service is shown by the line marked *MC p.p. (decentralized)*. In the case of centralized services, the marginal cost is lower, namely, *MC p.p. (centralized)* due to scale economies.

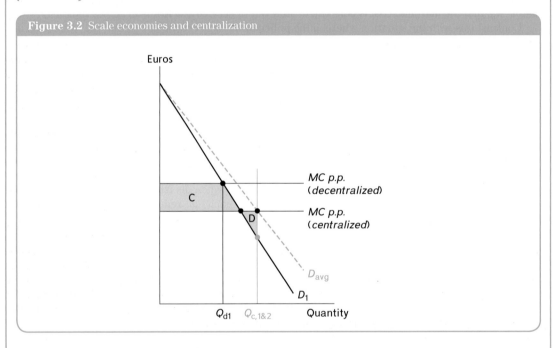

Figure 3.2 Scale economies and centralization

The figure shows that there is a trade-off between having the level of service precisely adjusted to local preferences and having a lower service cost due to scale economies. When the decision is local, the optimal provision is – as in Figure 3.1 – Q_{d1}. When it is centralized, the marginal cost is lower so the intersection of marginal value of the average citizen (D_{avg}) and marginal cost is at $Q_{c,1\&2}$. As before, the level that is optimal for the average citizen is not right for region 1 people, so there is inefficiency; again, this is measured by a triangle, marked D in Figure 3.2. This inefficiency, however, is offset by the gain from scale economies. That is, the region 1 person faces a lower marginal cost; the benefit of this is shown by the four-sided area, C. (The gain is just like a price reduction in standard consumer surplus analysis; see Chapter 4 for details.)

It appears, from the figure, that the gain from scale economies outweighs the loss from one-size-fits-all decision making. But, of course, if the scale economies were less important (i.e. the *MC* fell by less) or preferences were more diverse (i.e. the D_{avg} curve was further from the D_1 curve), then decentralization would be the superior outcome. The analysis for region 2 is quite similar and so it is omitted for the sake of brevity.

Spillovers

The next major consideration guiding task allocation is 'spillovers', i.e. an economic side-effect, known in economics jargon as an 'externality'.

Many public policy choices involve multi-region effects. National defence is one extreme. The presence of an army almost anywhere in the country deters foreign invasion for the country as a whole, so all the nation's citizens benefit from the army. It would be silly in this case to have taxpayers in each city decide separately on the army's size since, in making their decision, each set of taxpayers is likely to undervalue the nationwide benefit of a slightly bigger army. This is why the size of the army is a decision that is made at the national level in almost every nation. This is an example of what are called 'positive spillovers', i.e. where a slightly higher level of a particular policy or public service in one region benefits citizens in other regions.

A similar line of reasoning works when there are negative spillovers, i.e. when one region's policy has a negative effect on other regions. A good example of this is found in taxation. The value added tax (VAT) rate is set at the national level in all EU nations, so consider why this is so. If the VAT were chosen by each region, regions might be tempted to lower their VAT rate in an attempt to lure shoppers. For example, if the VAT in the centre of Frankfurt were 25 per cent, one of its suburbs might set its VAT at, say, 15 per cent in order to draw shoppers to its shops. In fact, if this tax undercutting were effective enough, the suburb would actually see its tax collection rise. (If the rate reduction was more than matched by an increase in local sales, the total VAT collected by the suburb would increase.) Of course, if the suburb's tax-cutting worked, Frankfurt would probably have to respond by lowering its rate to 15 per cent. In the end, both Frankfurt and the suburb would charge VAT rates below what they would like, but neither would gain shoppers by doing so. This negative spillover is so famous that it has a name: 'race to the bottom'. Again, the solution that is adopted by most nations is to set the VAT rate at the national level, but this time it is done to avoid negative spillovers.

As it turns out, cross-border shopping is not much of a problem in most parts of the EU, so there is little incentive to completely harmonize VAT rates at the EU level. The EU does, however, require VAT rates to fall within a wide band so that the maximum difference between VAT rates cannot be massive.

In summary, the existence of important negative or positive spillovers suggests that decisions made locally may be suboptimal for the nation (or EU) as a whole. The very existence of spillovers, however, does not force centralization. First, it may be possible to take account of the spillovers via cooperation among lower-level governments. This does not work for all policies, however, since cooperation is very difficult to sustain when the policies are difficult to observe directly and the spillovers are difficult to quantify. Moreover, even if decentralized cooperation does not work well, one may still resist centralization when there are big differences in preferences. A very interesting case study in this sort of fiscal federalism trade-off concerns the EU's different treatment of general VAT and extra sales taxes, or excise taxes on alcohol and tobacco. National preferences within the EU vary enormously when it comes to alcohol and tobacco, so although there is at least as much an argument for partly harmonizing these taxes as there is for harmonizing general VAT rates, the EU has never been able to do so. See Box 3.3 for details.

Box 3.3 Beer, cigarettes and VAT harmonization

Since 1 January 1993, EU travellers have been allowed to buy unlimited quantities of alcohol and tobacco (for their own use) in any Member State, and, as long as they pay taxes due in the Member State where they bought the goods, no additional taxes are due when they return home. This has posed some problems for British fiscal authorities since Britain has some of the highest 'sin' taxes in Europe.

While there has been some progress towards the harmonization of excise duties across the EU (incorporated into EC directives adopted on 19 October 1992), this effort consists of establishing specific minimum rates that are quite low. As House of Commons (2002) notes: 'The sheer variation in duty rates between countries made any closer form of harmonisation politically infeasible.' For example, in the

such policies are very diverse. In Spain, for example, the primary form of labour market protection for workers is employment protection legislation, i.e. laws that make it difficult to fire workers. Germany relies much more on unemployment benefits. Given this divergence of national preferences, the losses from a one-size-fits-all policy would be likely to outweigh any gains in efficiency or avoidance of negative spillovers. Of course, one can argue with this and it is impossible to settle the argument scientifically. For example, German labour unions insisted that nationalized, one-size-fits-all wage bargaining should also apply to the eastern Länder despite the great diversity of economic conditions, and they insisted on the same homogeneity of labour market laws.

Most non-economic policies are decided at the national level. For example, most foreign policy, defence policy, internal security and social policies are made at the national level. Of course, various nations cooperate on some of these policies – a good example is the agreement between France, Germany, Spain and the UK to produce a common military transport plane – but the decision making is allocated to the national level and cooperation is voluntary.

Roughly speaking, the old first-pillar policies (i.e. economic integration; see Section 2.2.3 in Chapter 2 on the old pillar structure) are where there are important spillovers; where national preferences are not too great and common policies tend to benefit from scale economies. The theory of fiscal federalism thus helps us to organize our thinking about why such policies are centralized.

The old second-pillar policies – common foreign and security policies – are marked by enormous scale economies. For example, unifying all of Europe's armies would result in a truly impressive force and allow Europe to develop world-class weapon systems. However, second-pillar policies are also marked by vast differences in national preferences. Some EU members – France and the UK, for example – have a long history of sending their young men to die in foreign lands for various causes. Other EU members – such as Sweden and Ireland – shun almost any sort of armed conflict outside their own borders. Given this diversity of preferences, the gains from scale economies would be more than offset by adopting a one-size-fits-all policy. Because of this, the only common EU policies in these areas are those arrived at by common consent, i.e. by cooperation rather than centralization.

The old third-pillar policies lie somewhere between first- and second-pillar policies, both in terms of the gains from scale economies and in terms of the diversity of preferences. As discussed above, many Europeans find themselves, or their pensions, or their marriages, or their land purchases subject to multiple legal jurisdictions. Thus the uncoordinated nature of such national laws is increasingly creating negative spillovers. Moreover, as Europeans' incomes converge upwards, there is a strong tendency for the differences in their legal preferences to converge. Both reasons – narrower preference differences and more people affected by negative spillovers – can be taken as the underlying reason why the Lisbon Treaty essentially merged the old first and third pillars. As explained in Chapter 2 in detail, it did so by formally removing the pillars, but it maintained a sharp distinction between supranational and intergovernmental areas of cooperation by specifying the nature of the cooperation that applies article-by-article in the Treaties.

3.3 Economic view of decision making

The previous sections looked at factors affecting the allocation of tasks between the EU and its Member States. This abstracted from the actual process by which EU-level decisions are made. In other words, we simplified away the question of how decisions were made at the EU level in order to study the issue of which decisions should be made at the EU level.

In this and subsequent sections we reverse this simplification, focusing on the question of how the EU makes decisions. In particular, we shall concentrate on how the decision-making mechanisms affect the EU's ability to act, the distribution of power among EU nations and democratic 'legitimacy'.

Efficiency, power and legitimacy are inherently vague concepts. To make progress, we adopt the tactic of progressive complexity. That is, we start by taking what may seem to be a very shallow view of political actors and their motives. These simplifying assumptions allow us to develop some very precise measures of efficiency, legitimacy and national power in EU decision making. The benefit is that these precise measures permit us to comment on how efficiency and legitimacy have evolved in the EU and how they evolved with the 2004 and 2007 enlargements and how they will evolve when the Lisbon Treaty rules come into effect.

Before turning to the measures, however, we consider the decision-making rules in detail.

3.3.1 Qualified majority voting

The EU has several different decision-making procedures but the main one is the 'ordinary legislative procedure' discussed in Chapter 2. This requires the Council to adopt the legislation by 'qualified majority voting' (which is universally known as QMV). The European Parliament, by contrast, adopts laws by a simple majority. As the Parliament's voting is straightforward – the usual 50 per cent majority threshold with one vote per Member of Parliament – we focus on the Council's voting rules.

The rules from 2004 to 2014: Nice Treaty QMV

The rules governing Council voting from 2004 to 2014 were set out in the Nice Treaty. While these are in theory no longer relevant, a last-minute political compromise means that an EU member can invoke the Nice Treaty rules up to 2017.[2]

The Nice Treaty QMV rules mean that each Member State's minister casts a certain number of votes in the Council. More populous members have more votes, but less than population proportionality would suggest. For example, Sweden has 10 votes and 9 million citizens while France has 6 times more citizens but only 29 votes; Cyprus has about 10 per cent of the Swedish population but 40 per cent as many votes (four versus ten). See Figure 3.3. If a proposal is to pass the Council, it must receive 'yes' votes for members that have at least 255 of the 345 total votes, i.e. about 74 per cent. But that is not all. There are two additional thresholds – one concerning the number of yes-voters and the other concerning the share of EU population that they represent. The number-of-members threshold is 50 per cent and the population threshold is 62 per cent.

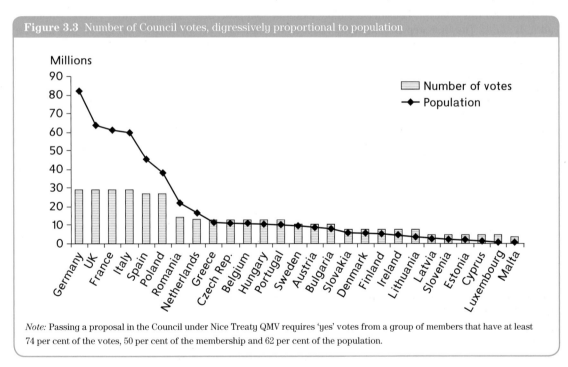

Figure 3.3 Number of Council votes, digressively proportional to population

Note: Passing a proposal in the Council under Nice Treaty QMV requires 'yes' votes from a group of members that have at least 74 per cent of the votes, 50 per cent of the membership and 62 per cent of the population.

3.3.2 EU ability to act: decision-making efficiency

From the mid-1990s right up until the Lisbon Treaty, EU leaders struggled to reform EU institutions in preparation for eastern enlargement – specifically the addition of 12 new members to an existing club of 15. The process is now complete and the Lisbon Treaty has created a new QMV procedure that takes effect in 2014. The goal of this long series of reform attempts was to keep the EU's decision-making procedures 'efficient' and democratically legitimate. We deal first with decision-making efficiency.

---

[2] See Baldwin (2007) for a discussion of this compromise.

In economics, 'efficiency' usually means an absence of waste. In the EU decision-making context, the word has come to mean 'ability to act'. While 'ability to act' is more specific than efficiency, it is still a long way from operational. For instance, on some issues the EU finds it very easy to make decisions, yet on others it finds it impossible to find a coalition of countries that would support a particular law. The perfect measure of efficiency would somehow predict all possible issues, decide how the members would line up into 'yes' and 'no' coalitions, and use this to develop an average measure of how easy it is to get things done in the EU. Such predictions, of course, are impossible given the uncertain and ever-changing nature of the challenges facing the EU.

An alternative approach, which we shall study here, sounds strange at first, but is really the best way of thinking systematically about the issue. Rather than trying to predict details of decision making on particular topics, we adopt a 'veil of ignorance'. That is, we focus on a randomly selected issue – random in the sense that no EU member would know whether it would be for or against the proposition.

A quantitative measure of efficiency: passage probability

The specific measure we focus on is called the 'passage probability'. The passage probability measures how easy it is to find a majority under a given voting scheme. Specifically, it is the number of all possible winning coalitions divided by the number of all possible coalitions. The idea is that, if each conceivable coalition of voters is equally likely, then the measure tells us the likelihood of approving a randomly selected issue; that is why it is called the passage probability. The idea behind assuming all coalitions are equally likely is that, on a randomly selected issue, each voter is as likely to say 'yes' as he or she is to say 'no'.

To explain this concept, consider a simple example. Suppose there are only three voters, whom we call A, B and C. The first step is to identify all possible coalitions, i.e. all possible arrays of 'yes' and 'no' votes. With three voters, there are eight possible coalitions. All eight are listed in the first three columns of Table 3.2. To keep things really simple, suppose that the three nations all have ten votes. The fourth column shows the number of 'yes' votes for each of the eight coalitions. The fifth column checks whether each coalition would win, assuming it takes 50 per cent (i.e. at least 15 votes) to pass the proposal.

Table 3.2   Passage probability in a simple example

A	B	C	Vote allocation #1		Vote allocation #2	
			10 votes each	Qualified majority (50%)?	20 votes to A, 5 to B and 5 to C	Qualified majority (50%)?
Yes	Yes	Yes	30	Yes	30	Yes
No	Yes	Yes	20	Yes	10	No
Yes	No	Yes	20	Yes	25	Yes
Yes	Yes	No	20	Yes	25	Yes
No	No	Yes	10	No	5	No
Yes	No	No	10	No	20	No
No	Yes	No	10	No	5	No
No	No	No	0	No	0	No
Passage probability (50% majority threshold) (%)				50.0		37.5
Passage probability (70% majority threshold) (%)				12.5		37.5

The passage probability is calculated in the second to last row. With the simple equal vote allocation #1, half of all possible coalitions pass the proposal, so the passage probability is 50 per cent.

To illustrate the usefulness of the passage probability concept, consider what would happen to this organization's ability to act if the allocation of votes became more concentrated, but there was no change in the majority threshold. For example, say that nation A now has 20 votes and nations B and C only 5 each. Just thinking intuitively, one would be hard put to form a judgement on whether the shift from 10 votes each to the 20, 5, 5 allocation would make it harder or easier to pass a random proposal. With the passage probability, however, we see that the second allocation of votes leads to fewer ways of forming a winning coalition and so the change in vote allocation reduces decision-making efficiency.

The second thing that affects the passage probability is the majority threshold. It is intuitively obvious that raising the threshold makes it harder to find a coalition. Comparing the last two rows confirms this intuition. For vote allocation #1, raising the threshold from 50 per cent (i.e. 15 votes) to 70 per cent (21 votes) lowers the passage probability from 50 to 12.5 per cent. However, the details matter. Note that under allocation #2, the higher threshold does not make it any harder to find winning coalitions. The point is that there are no coalitions with a number of votes that lies between the old threshold (15 votes) and the new higher threshold (21 votes).

When looking at the real EU Council, the principle is the same, but the calculations are much, much more tedious. The main point is that the number of possible yes/no coalitions among 27 votes is 2 raised to the power of 27, which is a very big number – over 134 million. To find the passage probability, one needs a computer and the right software.

The level of the passage probability is affected by the number of members, the distribution of votes and, above all, the majority threshold. It is important to note, however, that the exact level of the passage probability is not very important. As Chapter 2 explained, most EU legislation is proposed by the European Commission, and the Commission often refrains from introducing legislation that is unlikely to pass.

Historical efficiency and Treaty of Nice reforms

It is interesting to see how the EU's efficiency has changed over time. Above all, it is interesting to see how enlargement affects the EU's decision-making efficiency.

The five left-most bars in Figure 3.4 show the passage probability for qualified majority voting (QMV) in the historical EUs with 6, 9, 10, 12 and 15 members. These indicate that, although efficiency has been

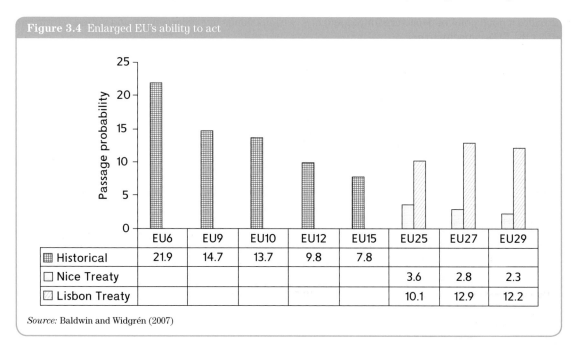

Figure 3.4 Enlarged EU's ability to act

	EU6	EU9	EU10	EU12	EU15	EU25	EU27	EU29
Historical	21.9	14.7	13.7	9.8	7.8			
Nice Treaty						3.6	2.8	2.3
Lisbon Treaty						10.1	12.9	12.2

Source: Baldwin and Widgrén (2007)

declining, past enlargements have only moderately hindered decision-making efficiency. The 1994 enlargement lowered the probability only slightly, from 10 to 8 per cent, and the Iberian expansion lowered it from 14 to 10 per cent. The figures also hide the fact that the Single European Act, which took effect in 1987, greatly boosted efficiency by shifting many more decisions from unanimity to qualified majority voting.

Notice that the 2004 enlargement greatly reduces the passage probability. This is true even with the Nice Treaty voting reforms (which were supposed to maintain the enlarged EU's ability to act). In fact, the Nice Treaty's complex rules made matters slightly worse than they would have been with no reform at all. The results show that accepting 12 newcomers without reform would dramatically reduce efficiency, cutting the current passage probability by something like a third, from 7.8 to 3.6 per cent.

This point, which became widely accepted after 2001, was why EU leaders asked the European Convention to reconsider the EU's decision-making rules – the request that eventually led to the Lisbon Treaty's new double-majority rule for the Council. Note that the decision-making rules in the Parliament and Commission were not viewed as problematic and thus were not reformed in the Constitution or the Lisbon Treaty.

The role of the Commission and Parliament

In the mainstay legislative process, the ordinary legislative procedure (i.e. the old codecision procedure), both the Commission and the Parliament play critical roles. But they do not really affect decision-making efficiency.

The Commission proposes legislation and drafts the first version. This gives it a good deal of power, as will be discussed in more depth below. But it has always had this power, so the increasing difficulty of passing EU legislation is not related to the Commission's role. A more plausible link would be with the enlargement of the European Parliament. After all, if enlarging the Council makes it harder to pass laws, doesn't enlarging the Parliament do the same thing?

To address this, it is necessary to realize a special feature of the 50 per cent majority rule that the Parliament uses. When the winning coalition needs only half the votes, the passage probability is unrelated to the number of voters. Upon reflection, this is obvious. There is an almost unfathomable number of possible yes/no coalitions in the 785-member Parliament (2 raised to the power of 785 is something like 2 with 236 zeroes after it), but when you only need half to win, it is clear that half of all coalitions will be winners. Thus the passage probability is always 50 per cent regardless of the number of voters.[3] This is why we can ignore the Parliament when considering the passage probability.

Of course, in the real world things are much more complex than the passage probability, but this concept provides a good point of departure for judging how various things like enlargement and voting reform can affect the EU's capacity to act.

3.4 The distribution of power among EU members

The next aspect of EU decision making that we address is the distribution of power among EU members. As with efficiency, there is no perfect measure of power. The tactic we adopt relies on the law of large numbers. That is, we look to see how likely it is that each member's vote is crucial on a randomly drawn issue. Before turning to the calculations, however, we lay out our specific definition of power.

For our purposes, power means influence, or, more precisely, the ability to influence EU decisions by being in a position to make or break a winning coalition in the Council. Of course, no one has absolute power in the EU, so we focus on the likelihood that a Member State will be influential. On some things Germany's vote will be crucial, on others it will be irrelevant, and the same goes for all other members. What determines how likely it is that a particular nation will be influential?

The most direct and intuitive measure of political power is national voting shares in the Council. Under current EU rules, each Member State has a fixed number of votes in the Council. Up to the 2004 enlargement, 87 Council-of-Minister votes were divided among the 15 EU nations, with large nations receiving more votes than small ones (see Chapter 2 for details). It seems intuitively plausible that nations with more votes are more likely to be influential on average, so the first power measure to try is a nation's share of Council votes. But how can we tell if this power measure captures anything real? See Box 3.4.

---

[3] This is not exactly true with an odd number of voters but the difference is negligible.

Box 3.4　Why Parliament reform does not affect national power distributions

Most EU legislation must be approved by both the Council and the Parliament. As it turns out, the allocation of seats in the European Parliament does not affect national power, per se. The reason rests on three facts: (1) the national distribution of Council votes and MEP seats is quite similar, as Figure 3.5 shows; (2) to pass the Council, a proposal must garner at least 71 per cent of votes; and (3) to pass the Parliament, a proposal needs to win only half of the MEP votes.

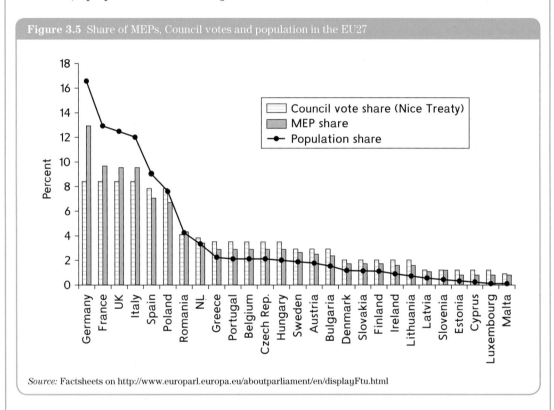

Figure 3.5 Share of MEPs, Council votes and population in the EU27

Source: Factsheets on http://www.europarl.europa.eu/aboutparliament/en/displayFtu.html

　　To illustrate how these three facts affect the Parliament's power from a purely national perspective, we must cover a few preliminaries. First, we start with a simple assumption – that MEPs act as national representatives and indeed that their votes are controlled directly by national governments (obviously this is false, but going to this extreme helps to build intuition for more realistic cases). Second, recall that we define power as the ability to break a winning coalition, so the question is: 'Can a nation use the votes of its MEPs to block a coalition that it cannot otherwise block?' If the answer is 'no', then the votes of MEPs do not affect a nation's power, even under the extreme assumption that MEP votes are controlled by governments. And, of course, if national power is not affected by MEP votes when they are directly controlled, national power is certainly not affected when the MEPs vote according to their own conscience. Finally, we assume that each nation's share of Council votes is identical to its share of MEP votes (rather than just similar). Under these assumptions, we can think of the actual procedure as a double-majority system. To pass, a proposal needs to attract the votes of Member States that have at least 50 per cent of MEP votes and 71 per cent of Council votes.

　　Now here is the main point. The first criterion is redundant since the Council vote threshold is higher than the MEP threshold. That is, since the distributions of Council and MEP votes are assumed to be identical, any coalition that has 71 per cent of Council votes will automatically have 71 per cent of MEP votes, which is plainly more than the 50 per cent necessary. Some careful thought and a little mental gymnastics reveal the implications of this for national power; there are no instances when a nation's MEP votes increase its power to block. In every instance where it can block on the basis of MEP votes, it can also block on the basis of Council votes.

Even under a more realistic view of the process, the same conclusion holds. The fact that the distribution of MEP votes is similar to the distribution of Council votes, teamed with the fact that the Council threshold is much higher than the Parliament's threshold, means that MEPs' votes could never increase a nation's ability to block, even if the MEPs voted on strictly national lines.

Interestingly, this suggests one indirect reason why the Parliament has tended to form cross-national coalitions. If they acted on purely national lines, MEPs would, on typical issues (i.e. where the national government accurately represents the national view), act as rubber-stampers. If they form cross-national coalitions, they may bring something new to the process.

An important caveat to all this is the fact that EU nations are made up of diverse groups. Since some groups are less well-represented in their nation's government than they are in the European Parliament (e.g. labour unions when a right-wing government is in power), having more seats means that these special-interest groups will have a larger say in EU decision making.

For a more detailed analysis, see Bindseil and Hantke (1997).

3.4.1 Empirical evidence on the relevance of power measures

One cannot measure a nation's power in EU decision making directly, but the exercise of power does leave some 'footprints' in the data. Budget allocations are one manifestation of power that is both observable and quantifiable. To check whether our power measure is useful, we see if it can help to explain the budget allocation puzzles we discussed in Chapter 2.

To understand why our power measure should be related to outward signs of power such as the budgetary spending allocation, we need to briefly review the budget process that was explained in detail in Chapter 2. We then discuss 'back scratching' and 'horse trading'.

The annual budget must be passed by both the Council and the European Parliament. These annual budgets, however, are constrained by medium-term budget plans called Multiannual Financial Frameworks (the current one covers 2014–20). Adopting a Framework requires unanimity in the Council, but the annual budgets are passed on the basis of a qualified majority. For both the Multiannual Financial Framework and the annual budgets, the Parliament's voting is on the basis of a simple majority (i.e. 50 per cent). As it turns out, the European Parliament does not matter from a national power perspective. This notion is explained in detail in Box 3.4. For this reason, we focus solely on voting shares in the Council.

As already pointed out, most Council decisions are made on the basis of qualified majority voting. Since the Council decides many issues each year, and members do not care dearly about all of them, countries tend to trade their votes on issues that they view as minor in exchange for support on an issue that they view as major, even if the two issues are totally unrelated. This sort of natural activity is referred to by the colourful names of 'back scratching' and 'horse trading'.

Now that we have discussed the background, we can turn to the main reasoning. Citizens in EU nations, or at least some citizens, benefit when EU money is spent in their district. Successful politicians, responding to the desires of their citizens, use their political clout to direct money homewards. For example, suppose that countries ask for a little 'gift' each time they find themselves in a position that is critical to a winning coalition. In the data, the 'gift' ends up as EU spending, but the actual mechanism could be subtle, say a more favourable treatment in the allocation of EU subsidies to hillside farmers, a more generous allocation of milk quotas or inclusion of reindeer meat in the CAP's price support mechanism. In this light, it seems natural that a country's power measure would equal its expected fraction of all special gifts handed out.

If one goes to the cynical extreme and views the whole EU budget as nothing more than a pile of 'gifts', then our power measures should meet the EU's budget allocation perfectly. If high-minded principles such as helping out disadvantaged regions also matter, then the power measure should only partially explain the spending pattern.

As it turns out, voting power goes a long way towards solving the 'puzzle' of EU budget allocation discussed in Chapter 2. Statistical evidence by Kauppi and Widgrén (2004) shows that, although standard elements do matter – such as a member's dependency on farming and its relative poverty – voting power always turns out to be an influential determinant of budget allocations.

3.4.2 Voting shares as a power measure: the shortcomings

While voting shares are a natural measure of power, they have problems. To illustrate the potential pitfalls of voting weights as a power measure, consider a 'toy model' of the Council. Suppose there are only three countries in this toy model – imaginatively called A, B and C – and they have 40, 40 and 20 votes, respectively. Decisions are based on a simple majority rule (+50 per cent to win). If we used voting weights as a measure of power, we would say that countries A and B, each with their 40 votes, were twice as powerful as C with its 20 votes. This is wrong.

With a bit of reflection you can convince yourself that all three nations are equally powerful in this toy Council. The point is that any winning coalition requires two nations, but any two nations will do. Likewise, any pair of nations can block anything. As a consequence, all three nations are equally powerful in the sense that they are equally likely to make or break a winning coalition.

The level of the majority threshold can also be important in terms of power. For example, continuing with our toy model, raising the majority rule from 50 to 75 per cent would strip nation C of all power. The only winning coalition that C would belong to is the grand coalition A&B&C, but here C would not be able to turn it into a losing one by leaving the coalition. Therefore C's vote can have no influence on the outcome. Again, voting shares in this example would give a very incorrect view of power.

More generally, power – i.e. the ability to make or break a winning coalition – depends upon a complex interaction of the majority threshold and exact distribution of votes. Indeed, the useless-vote situation in which nation C found itself in our second example actually occurred in the early days of the EU. See Box 3.5 for details.

Box 3.5   Luxembourg's useless vote, 1958–73

The 1957 Treaty of Rome laid down the rules for qualified majority voting in the EEC6. The big three – Germany, France and Italy – got four votes each, Belgium and the Netherlands got two each, and Luxembourg got one. The minimum threshold for a qualified majority was set at 12 of the 17 total votes.

A little bit of thought shows that the Treaty writers did not think hard enough about this. As you can easily confirm, Luxembourg's one vote never matters. Any coalition (group of 'yes' voters) that has enough votes to win can always win with or without Luxembourg. According to formal power measures, this means that Luxembourg had little power over issues decided on a QMV basis. As Felsenthal and Machover (2001) write: 'This didn't matter all that much, because the Treaty of Rome stipulated that QMV would not be used until 1966; and even in 1966–72 it was only used on rare occasions. Still, it seems a bit of a blunder.' It all changed post-1973, when the weights were altered to allow for the accession of Britain, Denmark and Ireland. Indeed, since then Luxembourg's votes have turned out to be crucial in a surprisingly large number of coalitions. Maybe that is why Luxembourg has the highest receipt per capita in the EU despite being the richest nation by far.

Source: This box is based on Felsenthal and Machover's excellent eBook (2001), which provides a much more in-depth look at voting theory.

Simple counterexamples such as these led to the development of several more sophisticated power indices. We shall focus on the 'Normalized Banzhaf Index'.

3.4.3 Power to break a winning coalition: the Normalized Banzhaf Index

In plain English, the Normalized Banzhaf Index (NBI) gauges how likely it is that a nation finds itself in a position to 'break' a winning coalition on a randomly selected issue. By way of criticism, note that the set-up behind the NBI provides only a shallow depiction of a real-world voting process. For instance, the questions of who sets the voting agenda, how coalitions are formed and how intensively each country holds its various positions are not considered. In a sense, the equal probability of each coalition occurring and each country switching its vote is meant to deal with this shallowness. The idea is that all of these things would average out over a large number of votes on a broad range of issues. Thus, this measure of power is really a very long-term concept. Another way of looking at it is as a measure of power in the abstract. It tells us how powerful a country is likely to be on a randomly chosen issue. Of course, on particular issues, various countries may be much more or much less powerful.

The easiest way to understand this concept more deeply is to calculate it for our simple example in Table 3.2. To make it interesting, we take the uneven vote allocation case (#2) and assume a 70 per cent majority threshold, so winning takes 21 votes. As before, we line up all eight possible coalitions and decide which are the winning ones (Table 3.3). These are the first three. Then we ask who the critical players are in these winning coalitions – critical in the sense that they would turn the winning coalition into a losing coalition if they changed their vote. In the first coalition, only A is critical since the defection of either B or C would not change the outcome; nation A and the remaining other nation would have enough votes to win. In the second and third coalitions, where the majority is narrower, both nations are critical, namely, A and C in the second and A and B in the third.

Table 3.3 Critical players with a 70 per cent majority threshold

A	B	C	Yes votes	70% majority?	Critical player(s)
Yes	Yes	Yes	30	Yes	A
Yes	No	Yes	25	Yes	A, C
Yes	Yes	No	25	Yes	A, B
Yes	No	No	20	No	
No	Yes	Yes	10	No	
No	No	Yes	5	No	
No	Yes	No	5	No	
No	No	No	0	No	

Thus there are five situations in which a nation would find itself critical. Nation A finds itself in this situation three of the five times, while B and C are critical in only one of the five times. Thus, in this sense, A is more powerful than B and C. The NBI for A is three-fifths, while it is one-fifth for B and C.

The calculation of NBI for all EU members is a topic that may fascinate some readers, but it is not essential to our study of EU decision making, so we relegate its discussion to Box 3.6.

Box 3.6   Calculating the Normalized Banzhaf Index (NBI)

The mechanical calculation of the NBI is easy to describe and requires nothing more than some patience and a PC with lots of horsepower. To work it out, one asks a computer to look at all possible coalitions (i.e. all conceivable line-ups of 'yes' and 'no' votes) and identify the winning coalitions. Note that listing all possible coalitions is easy to do by hand for low numbers of voters; in a group of 2 voters there are only 4, in a group of 3 there are 8. However, the general formula for the number of all possible coalitions for a group of n voters is 2^n, so determining which coalitions are winners by hand quickly becomes impractical; in the EU15, 32,768 coalitions have to be checked. In the EU27, the number is over 134 million. The computer's next task is to work out all the ways that each winning coalition could be turned into a loser by the defection of a single nation. Finally, the computer calculates the number of times each nation could be a 'deal breaker' as a fraction of the number of times that any country could be a deal breaker. The theory behind this is that the Council decides on a vast array of issues, so the NBI tells us how likely it is that a particular nation will be critical on a randomly selected issue.

For the EU15, it turns out that the theoretically superior power measure (NBI) is not very different from the rough-and-ready national vote-share measure. The measures are also quite similar for EU27. Readers who distrust sophisticated concepts should find their confidence in the Banzhaf measure bolstered by this similarity – and the same applies to readers who distrust rough-and-ready measures.

3.4.4 Power shifts in 2014 (or 2017)

The fate of the Lisbon Treaty was ultimately settled in 2009 and the new voting rules are finally about to come into effect. At the insistence of Poland, however, the new voting rules can be suspended at the wish of a single member up to 2017 (TFEU Protocol No. 35); if this suspension is requested, the old Nice rules apply.

The NBI is a useful tool for understanding both Poland's problems with the Lisbon rules and many of the struggles among Member States over EU institutional reforms – past, present and future. A good example can be found in the switch between the Nice Treaty voting rules (which are in effect today) and those of the Lisbon Treaty.

As pointed out in Chapter 1, the Nice, Constitutional and Lisbon Treaties all had a very hard time getting accepted by EU leaders. Much of the difficulty turned on the voting rules in the Council. Specifically, the voting rule proposed by Giscard d'Estaing was included in the Italian President's draft presented to the European Council in December 2003. This was rejected for many reasons, but the main sticking point was the power changes implied, especially for Spain and Poland. Council voting rules were also one of the hardest issues in the 2004 discussions that finalized the Constitutional Treaty. Finally, after the Constitution had been abandoned, the deal on its replacement (Lisbon Treaty) was hung up on the Council voting issue right until the end.

Switching from the current rules in place (those in the Nice Treaty) to the Lisbon Treaty rules changes the power distribution between large and small nations. The Lisbon Treaty would grant some additional power to the smallest states, but it would provide a huge boost to Germany's power. Since power is measured by shares and shares must add to 100 per cent, the German and tiny-nation power gains must be paid for by the other members. As Figure 3.6 shows, Spain and Poland will be the big losers, but the middle-sized EU Member States will also suffer as a result of the Lisbon rules.

Figure 3.6 Winners and losers under the Nice and Lisbon voting rules

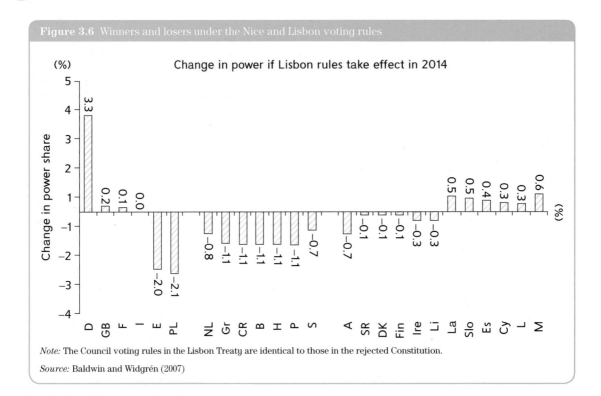

Note: The Council voting rules in the Lisbon Treaty are identical to those in the rejected Constitution.

Source: Baldwin and Widgrén (2007)

3.5 Legitimacy in EU decision making

The EU is a truly unique organization. Nowhere else in the world has so much national sovereignty been transferred to a supranational body. As Chapter 1 pointed out, the massive death and destruction of two world wars is what led the EU's founders to contemplate this transfer, but the continual willingness of the current generation of Europeans to accept it depends upon much more practical considerations. One consideration is the EU's ability to deliver results, but another important consideration is the democratic legitimacy of the EU's decision-making process.

3.5.1 Thinking about democratic legitimacy

What makes a decision-making system legitimate? This is a difficult question so it helps to start with an extreme and obviously illegitimate voting scheme and to think about why it seems illegitimate. Almost every European would view as illegitimate a system that allowed only landowning males the right to vote. Why? Because those without votes would find it unjust. And if the landowning men were forward looking, they would also find it illegitimate since they or their male offspring might one day lose their land. In short, a good way to think about legitimacy is to apply the 'in the other person's shoes' rule. A system is legitimate if all individuals would be happy with any other individual's allocation of voting power, which, if you think about it, requires equality. Equal power per citizen is thus a very natural legitimacy principle.

But what constitutes a citizen? In the EU there are two answers: nations and people. The EU is a union of states, so each state is a citizen and should thus have equal voting power. The EU is also a union of people, so people are citizens and so each person should have equal voting power. This makes it impossible to apply the equality principle in a simple manner. Note that there is a more classical way to phrase this same point. Democracy, it has been said, is the tyranny of the majority. To avoid this tyrannical aspect, democracies must have mechanisms that protect the rights and wishes of minorities. Indeed, many nations provide mechanisms for giving disadvantaged groups larger than proportional shares of power, but the starting point for such departures is one vote per person. In the EU, the over-weighting of small nations' votes was one such mechanism. For example, equality of power per person would grant Germany 2000 per cent more power than Ireland; equality per member would grant Luxembourgers 160 times more power per person than Germans. Given the dual-union nature of the EU, neither extreme is legitimate.

Using the NBI described above, we have a very precise (albeit crude) measure of 'power per person' and 'power per nation'. The 'fair' power distribution for the union-of-states view is trivial; in the EU27, each member should get 1/27th of the power. For the union-of-people view, power should be distributed such that each EU citizen has equal power regardless of nationality. As it turns out, the Nice Treaty voting rules favoured the equal-power-per-person view (since it shifted power to big nations). The Constitutional Treaty rules had a less clear-cut impact because they greatly boosted Germany's power but also boosted the power of EU members with populations below that of a medium-large city.

3.6 Summary

Just to continue to operate, the EU must make a steady stream of decisions to adjust to the ever-changing economic and political landscape. This chapter looked at the EU decision-making process from two perspectives. First, it considered the EU's current allotment of 'competences' between the EU and national government levels. In terms of actual practices and principles, the key points were:

- Policy making is categorized into areas in which the EU has 'exclusive competence', i.e. where the decision is made only at the EU level; areas in which competence is shared; areas in which the EU can undertake supporting, coordinating or complementary actions; and areas in which the EU has no competence, i.e. where decisions are made only at the national or sub-national level.

- The allocation of policy areas to these categories is determined by the Treaties and, when necessary, by decision of the European Court. This allocation, however, is blurred since the Treaties do not always refer to specific fields. Sometimes they refer only to areas by functional description, e.g. the internal market, which themselves are only vaguely defined (or at least vague from a legalistic perspective). To clarify the allocation, the EU operates on the principle of subsidiarity and proportionality, which says that unless there is a good reason for allocating a task to the EU level, all tasks should be allocated to national or sub-national governments, and even then the EU should take only the minimum necessary action. The old three-pillar structure of the EU helped to clarify the allocation; namely, first-pillar (Community pillar) issues were under EU competences while second- and third-pillar issues were not. The Lisbon Treaty removed the pillars, but essentially merged the old first and third pillar into one supranational area while keeping the old second pillar (foreign and defence policy) as intergovernmental.

The chapter also presented a framework for thinking about how tasks should be allocated between various levels of government (theory of fiscal federalism). This framework stresses four trade-offs that suggest whether or not a particular decision should be centralized:

- Diversity and information costs favour decentralized decision making
- Scale economies favour centralization
- Democracy-as-a-control-device favours decentralization
- Jurisdictional competition favours decentralization

The second part of the chapter considered the EU decision-making process in more detail, focusing on efficiency (i.e. the EU's ability to act), national power shares and democratic legitimacy. These three concepts are inherently vague, but the chapter assumes a series of simplifications that enable us to present precise measures of all three. Of course, the necessary simplifications mean that the resulting measures provide only shallow indications of efficiency, power and legitimacy; however, they do at least provide a concrete departure point for further discussion. These measures were:

- *Efficiency.* We measured efficiency using 'passage probability', i.e. the likelihood that a randomly selected issue would win a 'yes' vote in the Council. We showed that enlargement has continually lowered the EU's passage probability, but that the 2004 enlargement lowered it by a large and unprecedented amount. We also saw that the voting reforms established in the Treaty of Nice will make matters worse, even though they were intended to maintain decision-making efficiency.

- *National power distributions.*   We showed that the voting shares of small nations far exceed their population shares. Interpreting voting shares as a measure of power, this says that power in the EU is biased towards small nations. We also showed that this allocation of power goes a long way to explaining why actual EU spending patterns seem strange, i.e. that several rich nations receive above-average receipts per capita. This section also presents a more sophisticated measure of power called the Normalized Banzhaf Index, which measures the probability that a given nation will find itself in a position whereby it can break a winning coalition.

- *Legitimacy.*   This is by far the vaguest of the three concepts. The approach we adopt is to check whether the allocation of votes in the EU's Council lines up against two notions of legitimacy. If the EU is viewed as a union-of-people, a natural yardstick is equal power per citizen. If the EU is viewed as a union-of-states, the natural metric is equal power per Member State. Under the principle of equal power per EU citizen, the mathematics of voting tells us that this requires that the Council's votes per country rise with the square root of the country's population. The benchmark of equal power per EU Member State requires an equal number of votes per nation.

Self-assessment questions

1 List the main trade-offs stressed by the theory of fiscal federalism. Discuss how the tension between negative spillovers and diversity can explain the fact that the EU has adopted only very limited harmonization of social policies. (Hint: See the Annex in Chapter 1.)

2 In many European nations, the trend for the past couple of decades has been to decentralize decision making from the national level to the provincial or regional level. How could you explain this trend in terms of the theory of fiscal federalism?

3 Using the actual Council votes that came into force after the 2004 enlargement, list five blocking coalitions that you might think of as 'likely'. Do this using the Nice Treaty definition of a qualified majority. Do the same using the qualified majority definition proposed in the draft Constitutional Treaty.

4 The formal power measure discussed in the chapter assumes that each voter has an equal probability of saying 'yes' or 'no' on a random issue, and that the votes of the various voters are uncorrelated. That is, the likelihood that voter A says 'yes' on a particular issue is unrelated to whether voter B says 'yes'. However, in many situations, the votes of a group of voters will be correlated. For example, poor EU members are all likely to have similar views on issues concerning spending in poor regions. Work out how this correlation changes the distribution of power (defined as likelihood that a particular voter can break a winning coalition). To be concrete, assume that there are 5 voters (A, B, C, D and E), each has 20 votes, the majority rule is 51 per cent and A and B always vote the same way.

5 Using the definition of legitimacy proposed in the text (equal power per person), try to determine whether the US Congress is 'legitimate'. Note that the US Congress has two houses: the Senate and the House of Representatives. In the Senate, each of the 50 states has 2 Senators, while the number of Representatives per state is proportional to the state's population.

Further reading: the aficionado's corner

More wide-ranging introductions to fiscal federalism applied to the European Union can be found in:

Dewatripont, M. et al. (1995) *Flexible Integration: Towards a More Effective and Democratic Europe*, CEPR Monitoring European Integration 6, CEPR, London.

Berglof, E. et al. (2003) *Built to Last: A Political Architecture for Europe*, CEPR Monitoring European Integration 12, CEPR, London.

The latter includes a general discussion that applies the theory to the Constitutional Treaty.

For an opinionated view on what decisions should be allocated to the EU, see:

Alesina, A. and Wacziarg, R. (1999) *Is Europe Going too Far?*, Carnegie-Rochester Conference on Public Policy. Although this contains several factual errors concerning EU law and policies, it provides a highly cogent application of the theory of fiscal federalism to decision making in the EU.

To learn more about formal measures of power and legitimacy, see:

Felsenthal, D. and M. Machover (2001) *Enlargement of the EU and Weighted Voting in the Council*, www.lse.ac.uk.

For historical power distributions, see:

Laruelle, A. and M. Widgrén (1998) 'Is the allocation of voting power among EU Member States fair?', *Public Choice*, 94: 317–39.

See also:

Baldwin, R. (1994) *Towards an Integrated Europe*, CEPR, London.

Baldwin, R., E. Berglof, F. Giavazzi and M. Widgrén (2001) *Nice Try: Should the Treaty of Nice be Ratified?*, CEPR Monitoring European Integration 11, CEPR, London.

Begg, D. et al. (1993) *Making Sense of Subsidiarity: How Much Centralization for Europe?* CEPR Monitoring European Integration 4, CEPR, London.

Peet, J. and K. Ussher (1999) *The EU Budget: An Agenda for Reform?* CER Working Paper, February.

Useful websites

Extensive explanation and use of formal voting measures can be found on the 'European Voting Games' website: http://www.esi2.us.es/~mbilbao/eugames.htm.

You can find software for calculating voting power indices at: http://homepages.warwick.ac.uk/~ecaae/index.html.

References

Baldwin, R. (2007) 'Stranger than fiction: The voting rules in the Reform Treaty are a victory for Poland', VoxEU.org, 24 June 2007.

Baldwin, R. and M. Widgrén (2007) 'Pandora's (ballot) box', CEPR Policy Insight No.4, www.cepr.org/pubs/policyinsights.

Bindseil, U. and C. Hantke (1997) 'The power distribution in decision making among EU Member States', *European Journal of Political Economy*, 13: 171–85.

Bolkestein, F. (2004) 'UK in dock after booze-cruise blitz', http://www.thefreelibrary.com/UK+in+dock+over+booze-cruise+blitz.-a0123434735.

Borchardt, K.-D. (2010) *The ABC of European Union Law*. Download from http://europa.eu/documentation/legislation/pdf/oa8107147_en.pdf.

Felsenthal, D. and M. Machover (2001) *Enlargement of the EU and Weighted Voting in the Council*. LSE eBook on www.lse.ac.uk.

House of Commons (2002) 'Crossborder shopping and smuggling'. House of Commons Library, Research Paper 02/40, London.

Kauppi, H. and M. Widgrén (2004) 'What determines EU decision making? Needs, power or both?', *Economic Policy*, 19(39): 221–26.

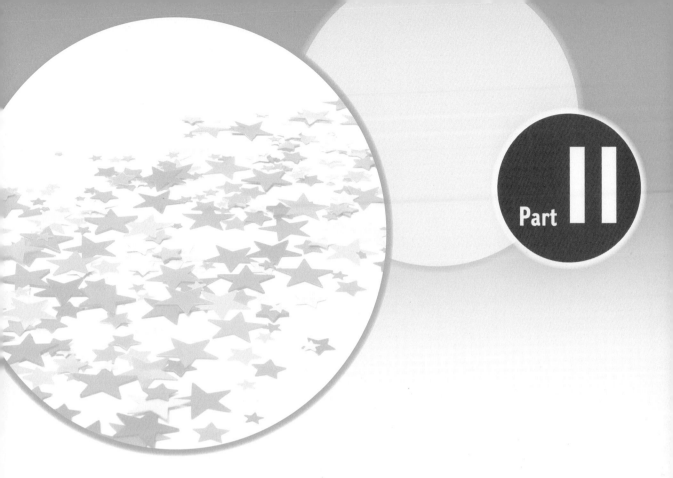

The Microeconomics of
European Integration

Everything should be made as simple as possible, but not simpler.

Albert Einstein

Essential microeconomic tools

Chapter Contents

Introduction

This chapter presents the tools that we shall need when we begin our study of European economic integration in the next chapter. The tools are simple because we make a series of assumptions that greatly reduce the complexity of economic interactions.

The primary simplification in this chapter concerns the behaviour of firms. In particular, all firms are assumed to be 'perfectly competitive', i.e. we assume that firms take as given the prices they observe in the market. Firms, in other words, believe that they have no impact on prices and that they could sell as much as they want at the market price. A good way of thinking about this assumption is to view each firm as so small that it believes that its choice of output has no impact on market prices. This is obviously a very rough approximation since even medium-sized firms – the Danish producer of Lego toys or the Dutch brewer of Heineken, for example – realize that the amount they can sell is related to the price they charge.

The second key simplification concerns technology, in particular scale economies. Scale economies refer to the way that per unit cost (average cost) falls as a firm produces more units. Almost every industry is subject to some sort of falling average cost, so considering them (in Chapter 6) will be important, but a great deal of simplification can be gained by ignoring them. This simplification, in turn, allows us to master the essentials before adding in more complexity in subsequent chapters.

4.1 Preliminaries I: supply and demand diagrams

Assessing many economic aspects of European integration is made clearer with the help of a simple yet flexible diagram with which to determine the price and volume of imports, as well as the level of domestic consumption and production. The diagram we use – the 'import supply and import demand diagram' – is based on straightforward supply and demand analysis. But to begin from the beginning, we quickly review where demand and supply curves come from. Note that this section assumes that readers have had some exposure to supply and demand analysis; our treatment is intended as a review rather than an introduction. Readers who find it too brief should consult an introductory economics textbook such as Mankiw (2011).

Well-prepared readers may want to skip this section, moving straight on to Section 4.2.

4.1.1 Demand curves and marginal utility

A demand curve shows how much consumers would buy of a particular good at any particular price. Generally speaking, consumers strive to spend their money in a way that maximizes their material well-being. Their demand curve is thus based on some sort of optimization exercise. To see this, the left-hand panel of Figure 4.1 plots the 'marginal utility' curve for a typical consumer, i.e. the 'happiness' (measured in euros) that consumers would get from consuming an extra unit of the good given that they are already consuming a certain number of units. For example, if we are considering the demand for cups of coffee, the marginal utility curve shows how much extra joy a consumer gets from having one more cup starting from any given number of cups already consumed. Typically the extra joy from an extra cup falls with the number of cups bought per day. For example, if the consumer buys very few cups of coffee per day, say c' in the diagram, the gain from buying an extra one is likely to be pretty high, for example mu' in the diagram. If, however, the consumer buys lots of cups already, then the gain from one more is likely to be much lower. This is shown by the pair, c'' and mu''.

This marginal utility curve allows us to work out how much the consumer would buy at any given price. Suppose the consumer could buy as many cups as she likes at the price p^*. How many would she buy? If the consumer is wise, and we assume she is, she will buy cups of coffee up to the point where the last one bought is just barely worth the price. In the diagram, this level of purchase is given by c^* since the marginal benefit (utility) from buying an extra cup exceeds the cost of doing so (the price) for all levels of purchase up to c^*. At this point, the consumer finds that additional cups would not be worth the price. For example, the marginal utility from buying c^* plus one cups of coffee would be below p^*. As usual, one gets the market demand for cups of coffee by adding all consumers' individual marginal utility curves horizontally (e.g. if the price is p^* and there are 100 identical consumers, market demand will be 100 times c^*).

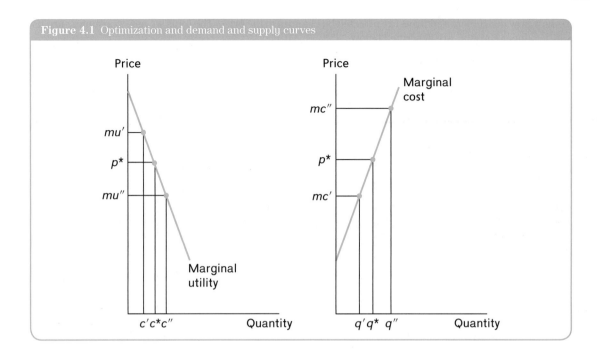

Figure 4.1 Optimization and demand and supply curves

A key point to retain from this is that the price that consumers face reflects the marginal utility of consuming a little more.

4.1.2 Supply curves and marginal costs

Derivation of the supply curve follows a similar logic, but here the optimization is done by firms. The right-hand panel of Figure 4.1 shows the 'marginal cost' curve facing a typical firm (assume they are all identical for the sake of simplicity), i.e. the extra cost involved in making one more unit of the good. While the marginal cost of production in the real world often declines with the scale of production, allowing for this involves consideration of scale economies and these, in turn, introduce a whole range of complicating factors that would merely clutter the analysis at this stage. To keep it simple, we assume that firms are operating at a point where the marginal cost is upward sloping, i.e. that the cost of producing an extra unit rises as the total number of units produced rises. The curve in the diagram shows, for example, that it costs mc' to produce one more unit when the production level (e.g. the number of cups of coffee per day) is q'. This is less than the cost, mc'', of producing an extra unit when the firm is producing q'' units per year.

Using this curve we can determine the firm's supply behaviour. Presuming that the firm wants to maximize profit, the firm will supply goods up to the point where the marginal cost just equals the price. For example, if the price is p^*, the firm will want to supply q^* units. Why? If the firm offered one less than q^* units, it would be missing out on some profit. After all, at that level of output, the price the firm would receive for the good, p^*, exceeds the marginal cost of producing it. Likewise, the firm would not want to supply any more than q^* since, for such a level of output, the marginal cost of producing an extra unit is more than the price. Again, we get the aggregate supply curve by adding all the firms' individual marginal cost curves horizontally.

A key point here is that, under perfect competition, the price facing producers reflects the marginal production cost, i.e. the cost of producing one more unit than the firm produces in equilibrium.

4.1.3 Welfare analysis: consumer and producer surplus

Since the demand curve is based on consumers' evaluation of the happiness they get from consuming a good and the supply curve is based on firms' evaluation of the cost of producing it, the curves can be used

to show how consumers and firms are affected by changes in the price. The tools we use, 'consumer surplus' and 'producer surplus', are described below.

Consumers buy up to the point where their marginal utility just equals the price. For all other units bought, the marginal utility exceeds the price. This means that the consumer gets what is known as 'consumer surplus' from buying c^* units at price p^* (see Figure 4.2). In words, this says that consumers get more (in terms of utility) than they pay for. How much? For the first unit bought, the marginal unit was mu' but the price paid was only p^*, so the surplus is the area shown by the rectangle 'a'. For the second unit, the marginal utility was somewhat lower (not shown in the diagram), so the surplus is lower; specifically, it is given by the area 'b'. Doing the same for all units shows that buying c^* units at p^* yields a total consumer surplus equal to the sum of all the resulting rectangles. If we take the units to be very finely defined, the triangle defined by the points 1, 2 and 3 gives us the total consumer surplus. Box 4.1 discusses a real-world illustration of consumer surplus.

Figure 4.2 Deriving consumer and producer surplus

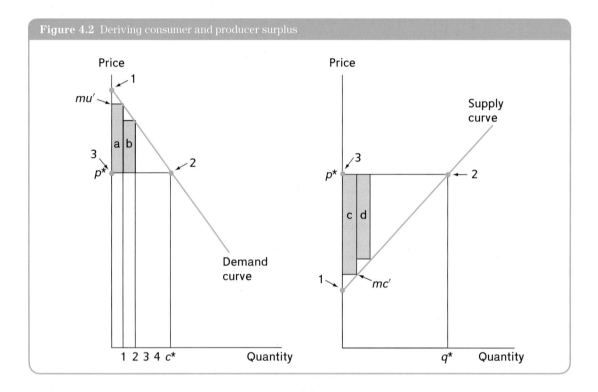

Box 4.1   Consumer surplus and Swiss Rail's Half Fare Card

Switzerland's wonderful rail system can be expensive, so many tourists buy the Half Fare Card; in 2011, it cost 85 GBP for a one-month pass. The fact that people pay to get unlimited access to a lower price is an example of consumer surplus in action. To see this, ask yourself what would be the maximum you would pay for being able to buy half-price tickets. For example, suppose you were planning a two-week trip that involved 20 individual train trips. Suppose the average price was 10 GBP, so you would spend 200 GBP without the card. With the card you spend only 100 GBP, so you would be willing to pay up to 100 pounds for a Half Fare card. In fact, you would probably be willing to pay a bit more than 100 GBP since at the lower per-trip price (i.e. 5 GBP versus 10), you would probably take a few trips more than you found optimal at the full price.

An analogous line of reasoning shows us that the triangle formed by points 1, 2 and 3 in the right-hand panel gives us a measure of the gain firms get from being able to sell q^* units at a price of p^*. Consider the first unit sold. The marginal cost of producing this unit was mc' but this was sold for p^* so the firm earns a surplus, what we call the 'producer surplus', equal to the rectangle 'c' in the right-hand panel. Doing the same exercise for each unit sold shows that the total producer surplus is equal to the triangle defined by points 1, 2 and 3.

By drawing similar diagrams on your own, you should be able to convince yourself that a price rise increases producer surplus and decreases consumer surplus. A price drop does the opposite.

4.2 Preliminaries II: introduction to open-economy supply and demand analysis

This section introduces the 'workhorse' diagram – the open-economy supply and demand diagram – that is essential to our study of European economic integration. Well-prepared readers may consider skipping, moving straight on to the tariff analysis in Section 4.3. The diagram, however, is used throughout this chapter and the next, so even advanced students may wish to briefly review the diagram's foundations; if nothing else, such a review will help with the terminology.

4.2.1 The import demand curve

We first look at where the import demand curve comes from; Figure 4.3 facilitates the analysis.

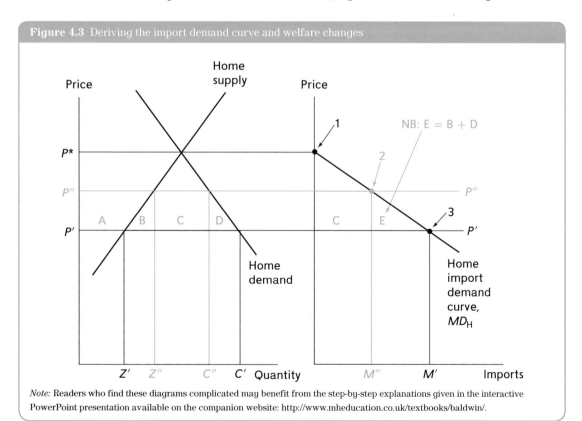

Figure 4.3 Deriving the import demand curve and welfare changes

Note: Readers who find these diagrams complicated may benefit from the step-by-step explanations given in the interactive PowerPoint presentation available on the companion website: http://www.mheducation.co.uk/textbooks/baldwin/.

The left-hand panel of the diagram depicts a nation's supply and demand curves for a particular good. As usual, the domestic price is on the vertical axis; quantity is on the horizontal axis. If imports of the good were banned for some reason, the nation would only be able to consume as much as it produced. The result

would be a market price of P^* since this is the price where the amount that consumers want to buy just matches the amount that firms want to produce. Plainly, import demand is zero at P^* (for simplicity, we assume that imported and domestic goods are perfect substitutes). This zero-import point is marked in the right-hand panel as point 1; this diagram has the same price on the vertical axis, but plots imports on the horizontal axis.

How much would the nation import if the price were lower, say, P'? The first thing to note is that the import price will fix the domestic price. Imports are always available at P', so no consumer would pay more than P'. Of course, domestic producers must match the import competition, so P' becomes the domestic price.

The second thing to note is the impact of P' on consumption, production and imports. Consumption demand would be C' and domestic production would be Z'. As C' exceeds Z', consumers buy more than domestic firms are willing to produce at P'. The 'excess' demand is met by imports. That is to say, imports are the difference between C' and Z' (in symbols, $M' = C' - Z'$).

What this tells us is that import demand at P' is M'. This point is marked in the right-hand panel of the diagram as point 3. Performing the same exercise for P'' yields point 2, and doing the same for every possible import price yields the import demand curve, i.e. the amount of imports that the nation wants at any given domestic price. The resulting curve is shown as MD_H in the right-hand panel. (For convenience, we often call the nation under study 'Home' to distinguish it from its trade partner which we call 'Foreign'.)

Welfare analysis: MD curves as the marginal benefit of imports

When studying European economic integration, a critical question that arises time and again is the extent to which a policy raises or lowers nations' welfare. In answering such questions, it is useful to know how to carry out welfare analysis with the import demand curve.

Consider a rise in the import price from P' to P''. As argued above, the higher import price means the domestic price rises by the same amount. The corresponding equilibrium level of imports drops to M'', since consumption drops to C'' and production rises to Z''. We can see the welfare analysis in the left-hand panel using the standard notions of consumer and producer surpluses (see Section 4.1). Specifically, the price rise lowers consumer surplus by $A + B + C + D$. The same price rise increases producer surplus by A. The right-hand panel shows how this appears in the import demand diagram. From the left-hand panel, the import price rise means a net loss to the country of $B + C + D$, since the area A cancels out (area A is a gain to Home producers and a loss to Home consumers). In the right-hand panel, these changes are shown as areas C and E; as it turns out, area E equals area $B + D$.

A powerful perspective: trade volume effects and border price effects

It proves insightful to realize that the MD_H curve shows the marginal benefit of imports to Home. Before explaining why this is true, we show that it is a useful insight. As we saw above, Home loses areas C and E when the price of imports rises from P' to P''. Area C is easy to understand. After the price rise, Home pays more for the units it imported at the old price. Area C is the size of this loss. (Say the price rise was €1.2 per unit and M'' was 100; the loss would be €1.2 times 100; geometrically, this is the area C since a rectangle's area is its height times its base.) Understanding area E is where the insight comes in handy. Home reduces its imports at the new price and area E measures how much it loses from the drop in imports. The marginal value of the first lost unit is the height of the MD_H curve at M''. But since Home had to pay P' for this unit, the net loss is the gap between P' and the MD_H curve. If we add up the gaps for all the extra units imported, we get the area E. The jargon terms for these areas are the 'border price effect' (area C) and the 'import volume effect' (area E).

To understand why MD_H is the marginal benefit of imports, we use three facts and one bit of logic: (1) the MD_H curve is the difference between the domestic demand curve and the domestic supply curve; (2) the domestic supply curve is the domestic marginal cost curve, and the domestic demand curve is the domestic marginal utility curve (see Section 4.1 if these points are unfamiliar); and (3) the difference between domestic marginal utility of consumption and domestic marginal cost of production is the net gain to the nation of producing and consuming one more unit. The logical point is that an extra unit of imports leads to some combination of higher consumption and lower domestic production, and this leads to some combination of higher utility and lower costs; the height of the MD_H curve tells us what that combination is.

Or, to put it differently, the nation imports up to the point where the marginal gain from doing so equals the marginal cost. Since the border price is the marginal cost, the border price is also an indication of the marginal benefit of imports.

To see these points in more detail, see the interactive PowerPoint presentations available on this book's Online Learning Centre, http://www.mheducation.co.uk/textbooks/baldwin/.

4.2.2 The export supply curve

Figure 4.4 uses an analogous line of reasoning to derive the import supply schedule. The first thing to keep in mind is that the supply of imports to Home is the supply of exports from foreigners. For simplicity's sake, suppose that there is only one foreign country (simply called 'Foreign' hereafter) and its supply and demand curves look like the left-hand panel of the figure. (Note that the areas in Figure 4.4 are unrelated to the areas in Figure 4.3.)

As with the import demand curve, we start by asking how much Foreign would export for a particular price. For example, how much would it export if the price of its exports was P'? At price P', Foreign firms would produce Z' and Foreign consumers would buy C'. The excess production (equal to $X' = Z' - C'$) would be exported. (Note that, as in the case of import demand, the export price sets the price in Foreign; Foreign firms have no reason to sell for less since they can always export, and competition among Foreign suppliers would prevent any of them from charging Foreign consumers a higher price.) The fact that Foreign would like to export X' when the export price is P' is shown in the right-hand panel at point 2.

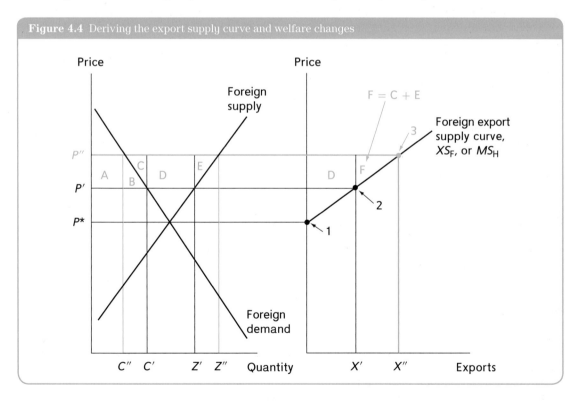

Figure 4.4 Deriving the export supply curve and welfare changes

As the price for Foreign exports (i.e. Home's import price) rose, Foreign would be willing to supply a higher level of exports for two reasons. The higher price would induce Foreign firms to produce more and Foreign consumers to buy less. For example, the price P'' would bring forth an import supply equal to X'' (this equals $Z'' - C''$); this is shown as point 3 in the right-hand panel. At price P^*, exports are zero. Plotting all such combinations in the right-hand panel produces the export supply curve XS_F. We stress again the simple but critical point that the Foreign export supply is the Home import supply, thus we also label XS_F as MS_H.

Welfare

The left-hand panel also shows how price changes translate into Foreign welfare changes. If the export price rises from P' to P'', consumers in Foreign lose by A + B (these letters are not related to those in the previous figure), but the Foreign firms gain producer surplus equal to A + B + C + D + E. The net gain is therefore C + D + E. Using the export supply curve XS_F, we can show the same net welfare change in the right-hand panel as the area D + F. Note that the insight from the MD_H curve extends to the XS_F curve, i.e. the XS_F curve gives the marginal benefit to Foreign of exporting.

This review of import supply and demand was very rapid – probably too rapid for students who have never used such diagrams and probably too slow for students who have. For those who find themselves in the first category, interactive PowerPoint presentations that go over the diagram in greater detail are available at www.mheducation.co.uk/textbooks/baldwin.

4.2.3 The workhorse diagram: *MD–MS*

The big payoff from having an import supply curve and an import demand curve is that it permits us to find the equilibrium price and quantity of imports. The equilibrium price is found by putting together import demand and supply as shown in the left-hand panel of Figure 4.5; we drop the 'H' and 'F' subscripts for convenience.

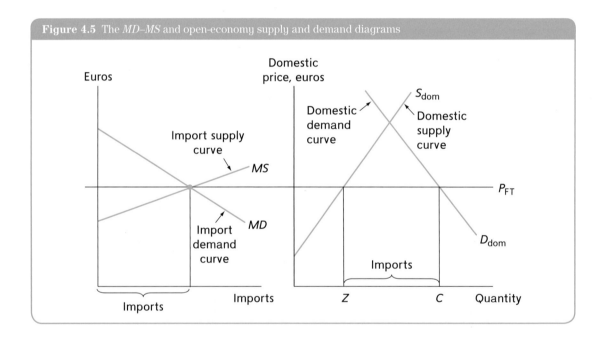

Figure 4.5 The *MD–MS* and open-economy supply and demand diagrams

Assuming imports and domestic production are perfect substitutes, the domestic price is set at the point where the demand and supply of imports meet, namely, P_{FT} (FT stands for free trade). While the import supply and demand diagram, or *MD–MS* diagram for short, is handy for determining the price and volume of imports, it does not permit us to see the impact of price changes on domestic consumers and firms separately. This is where the right-hand panel becomes useful. In particular, we know that the market clears only when the price is P_{FT}, so we know that Home production equals Z and Home consumption equals C. The equilibrium level of imports may be read off either panel. In the left-hand panel, it is shown directly; in the right-hand one, it is the difference between domestic consumption and production.

Having explained these basic microeconomic tools, we turn now to using them to study a simple but common real-world problem – the effects of a tax on imports from all nations. Such taxes are called tariffs.

4.3 MFN tariff analysis

To build from simple to complex, we preface the analysis of preferential trade liberalization in Europe with a simpler example, but one that nevertheless is useful for understanding the world. That is, we introduce the basic method of analysis and gain experience in using the diagrams by first studying the impact of removing the simplest type of trade barrier – a tariff that is applied to imports from all trade partners. We call this a non-discriminatory liberalization.

Although this is not what happened when Europe integrated economically, we first look at the non-discriminatory case since it is less complex. An extra benefit of taking this detour is that it helps us understand the effects of the EU lowering its common external tariff – as it does in the context of world trade talks (see Chapter 12). For historical reasons, a non-discriminatory tariff is called a 'most favoured nation' tariff, which provides the handy abbreviation, MFN.

4.3.1 Price and quantity effects of a tariff

The first step is to determine how a tariff changes prices and quantities. To be concrete, suppose that the tariff imposed equals T euros per unit.

The first step in finding the post-tariff price is to work out how the tariff changes the MD–MS diagram; here, Figure 4.6 facilitates the analysis. (See Section 4.2 if you are unfamiliar with the MD–MS diagram.)

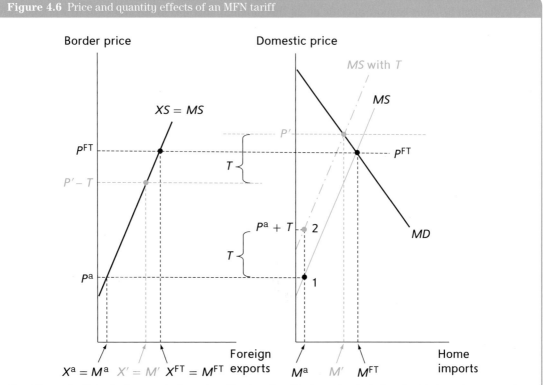

Figure 4.6 Price and quantity effects of an MFN tariff

Note: Observe the distinction between the domestic and border prices. The domestic price is the price that domestic consumers pay for the good. The border price is the price foreign producers receive when they sell the good to Home. They can differ because of the tariff (a tariff is nothing more than a tax on imports). When you buy a coffee at a café for, say, 1 euro, the café owner does not get the full euro because the owner has to pay a tax, called the VAT, on your purchase. As a result, the price that the café owner receives is only 80 cents (the VAT is 20 per cent in this example) even though you pay 100 cents. In exactly the same way, foreigners receive a price (the border price) that equals the domestic price minus the tariff.

The right-hand panel of Figure 4.6 shows the pre-tariff import demand and import supply curves as *MD* and *MS*, respectively. The left-hand panel shows the foreign export supply curve as *XS*. Note that the vertical axis in this right-hand panel shows the domestic price, while the vertical axis in the left-hand panel shows the border price – the difference between the two is simple, but critical (see the note to Figure 4.6).

A tariff shifts up the MS curve

Imposition of a tariff has no effect on the *MD* curve in the right-hand panel since the *MD* curve tells us how much Home would like to import at any given *domestic* price. By contrast, imposing a tariff on imports shifts up the *MS* curve by *T*. The reason is simple. After the tariff is imposed, the domestic price must be higher by *T* to get Foreign to offer the same quantity as it offered before the tariff. Consider an example. How much would Foreign supply before the tariff if the Home domestic price before the tariff were P^a? The answer, which is given by point 1 on the *MS* curve, is M^a. After the tariff, we get a different answer. To get Foreign to offer M^a after the tariff, the domestic price must be $P^a + T$ so that Foreign sees a border price of P^a.

Having shown that the tariff shifts up the *MS* curve, consider next the tariff's impact on equilibrium prices and quantities.

The new equilibrium prices and quantities

Even without a diagram, readers will surely realize that a tariff raises the domestic price and lowers imports. After all, a tariff is a tax on imports and it is intuitively obvious that putting a tax on imports will raise prices somewhat and lower imports somewhat. Why do we need a diagram?

The diagram helps us be more specific about this intuition; this specificity allows us to work out how much the nations gain or lose from the tariff. Returning to our analysis, note that, after the tariff, the old import supply curve is no longer valid. The new import supply curve, labelled *MS with T*, is what matters and the equilibrium price is set at the point where the new import supply curve and the import demand curve cross. As intuition would have it, the new price – marked P' in the diagram – is higher than the pre-tariff price P^{FT} (as already noted, FT stands for free trade). Because of the higher domestic price, Home imports are reduced to M' from M^{FT}. To summarize, there are five price and quantity effects of the tariff:

1 The price facing Home firms and consumers (domestic price) rises to P'.
2 The border price (i.e. the price Home pays for imports) falls to $P' - T$; this also means that the price received by Foreigners falls to $P' - T$.
3 The Home import volume falls to M'.

The other two effects cannot be seen in Figure 4.6, but are obvious to readers who worked through Figure 4.3. The higher domestic price stimulates production and discourages consumption. Specifically:

4 Home production rises.
5 Home consumption falls.

There are also production and consumption effects of the tariff inside the exporting nation. Since the border price falls, Foreign production drops and Foreign consumption rises. We could see this explicitly if we put a diagram like the left-hand panel of Figure 4.4 to the left of the diagram in Figure 4.6. You may want to do this as an exercise to test your familiarity with the diagrams.

4.3.2 Welfare effects of a tariff

Having worked out the price and quantity effects, it is simple to calculate the welfare effects of the tariffs; that is to say, who wins, who loses and by how much. The analysis is really just a combination of what we did in Figures 4.3 and 4.4; this is done in Figure 4.7. The left-hand panel shows Home's supply and demand, the middle panel shows the world market for imports and the right-hand panel shows the Foreign supply and demand. We start with Home.

As shown in Figure 4.7, the MFN tariff raises the Home price of the good (to P') while lowering the border price (to $P' - T$). Home consumers lose A + B + C + D, Home producers gain A and Home government

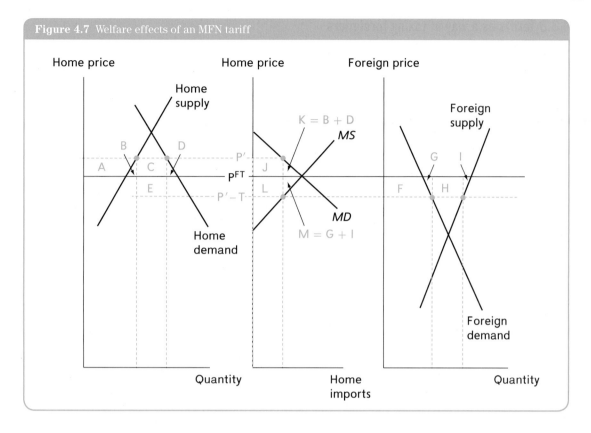

Figure 4.7 Welfare effects of an MFN tariff

gains tariff revenue C + E. The net Home welfare effect is +E − B − D. This can be positive or negative depending upon the size of the tariff (you can show that it will be negative for very large tariffs, but positive for sufficiently small tariffs).

Turning to Foreign, we see that Home's tariff has lowered the border price facing Foreign exporters and this in turn brings down the price faced by Foreign producers and consumers. Foreign consumers gain F while Foreign firms lose F + G + H + I. There is no change in tariff revenue (the tariff is paid to the Home government), so the net impact on Foreign is –G − H − I. This is plainly negative regardless of the tariff's size.

A useful condensation

The first time one works through these welfare calculations, it is useful to consider the full distributional effects as we did in Figure 4.7. (i.e. the impact on consumers, producers and government revenue). Yet, once one is familiar with the diagrams, it is convenient to condense the analysis into a single diagram, like the centre panel in Figure 4.7. This lets us show the overall welfare effects of a Home tariff on both nations. Using the area labels in the centre panel, Home's welfare changes by +L − K, Foreign's welfare changes by −L − M, so world welfare falls by −K − M.

To summarize, we find:

- The tariff reduces Foreign welfare since it means it sells less and receives a lower price.
- The tariff creates private-sector winners and losers (Home firms gain, Home consumers lose), but the losers (consumers) lose more than the gainers (firms) gain.
- Home collects tariff revenue equal to J + L.
- The overall Home welfare change is +L − K; this net effect may be positive or negative; the relative sizes of L and K depend upon the slopes of the *MD* and *MS* curves and on the size of *T*.
- The global impact of the tariff, adding Home and Foreign welfare changes together, is definitely negative.

4.3.3 Tariffs as a way of taxing foreigners

The result that a tariff might make the Home country better or worse off is worth looking at from a different angle. The two parts of Home's net welfare impact, namely, $+L - K$, represent very different kinds of changes.

- The area L is the 'border price effect', i.e. the gain from paying less for imports

We can also think of it as the amount of the new tariff revenue that is borne by foreigners. This statement requires some explaining. In the real world, the importing firm pays the whole tariff, so one might think that the importing firm bears the full burden of the import tax. This would be wrong. Part of the burden is passed on to Home residents via higher prices. How much? Well, pre-tariff, the domestic price was P^{FT} and post-tariff it is P', so the difference shows how much of the tariff is passed on to Home residents. Since this price hike applies to a level of imports equal to M', we can say that the share of the tariff revenue borne by Home residents is area J. Using the same logic, we see that some of the tariff burden is also passed back to Foreign suppliers. The before-versus-after border price gap is P^{FT} minus $(P' - T)$ and this applies to M' units of imports. So area L is a measure of how much of the tariff revenue is borne by foreigners.

- Area K is the 'trade volume effect', i.e. the impact of lowering imports

Here is the argument. The *MD* curve shows the marginal benefit to Home of importing each unit (see Section 4.2 if this reasoning is unfamiliar to you). Given this, the gap between the *MD* curve and P^{FT} gives us a measure of how much Home loses for each unit it ceases to import. The area of the triangle C is just all the gaps summed giving the change in imports.

- To put it differently, area L represents Home's gain from taxing foreigners while area K represents an efficiency loss from the tariff

Given all this, we can say that if T raises Home welfare, then it does so only because the tariff allows the Home government to indirectly tax foreigners enough to offset the tariff's inefficiency effects on the Home economy. That is, T causes economic inefficiency at Home but T is also a way of exploiting foreigners. Since the exploitation gains may outweigh the inefficiency effects, Home may gain from imposing a tariff.

4.3.4 Global welfare effects and retaliation

The global welfare impact is simply a matter of summing up effects; as we saw, it is negative and equal to $-K - M$.

Put in this way, the possibility that Home might gain from a tariff is clearly suspect. For example, if Home and Foreign were symmetric and both imposed tariffs, both would lose the efficiency triangle K and the gain to Home of L on imports would be lost to Home on its exports to Foreign. Home would also lose the deadweight triangle M on exports, so the net loss to each of the symmetric nations would be $-K - M$.

In short, protection by all nations is worse than a zero-sum game. It is exactly this point that underpins the economics of WTO tariff-cutting negotiations. If only one nation liberalizes, it might lose. If, however, the nation's liberalization is coordinated with its trading partners' liberalization, the zero-sum aspect tends to disappear.

4.4 Types of protection: an economic classification

Tariffs are only one of many types of import barrier that European integration has removed. The first phase of EU integration, 1958–68, focused on tariff removal, but the Single Market Programme that was started in 1986 focused on a much wider range of non-tariff barriers.

While there are several methods of categorizing such barriers, it proves useful to focus on how the barriers affect so-called trade rents. A tariff, for instance, drives a wedge between the Home price and the border price (i.e. the price paid to foreigners). This allows someone (in the tariff case it will be the Home government) to indirectly collect the 'profit' from selling at the high domestic price while buying at the low border price. For historical reasons, economists refer to such profits (area A + B in Figure 4.8)

Figure 4.8 Home welfare effects of import protection

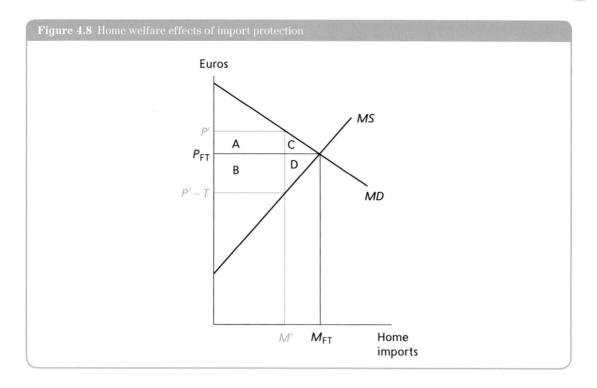

as 'rents'. When it comes to welfare analysis, we must watch the trade rents closely. For some import barriers, Home residents get the rents, but for others no rents are created, or foreigners get them. This distinction is highlighted by distinguishing three categories of trade barrier: domestically captured rent (DCR) barriers; foreign captured rent (FCR) barriers; and 'frictional' barriers. We consider them in turn.

4.4.1 DCR barriers

Tariffs are the classic DCR barrier. Here, the Home government gets the trade rents. From a Home nationwide welfare perspective, however, it does not really matter whether the government, Home firms or Home consumers earn these rents, as long as the rents are captured domestically. What sorts of barrier other than tariffs would lead to domestically captured rents? Some forms of quotas are DCR barriers. A quota is a quantitative limit on the number of goods that can be imported per year. To control the number of foreign goods entering the country, the government hands out a fixed number of import licences and 'collects' one licence per unit imported. The price and quantity effects of a quota that restricts imports to M' in Figure 4.8 are identical to the effects of a tariff equal to T. The point is that, if imports are limited to M', then the gap between domestic consumption and production can be no more than M', implying that the domestic price must be driven up to P'. Another way to say this is that T is the 'tariff equivalent' of the quota. Now consider the trade rents. With a quota, whoever has the licence can buy the goods at the border price $P' - T$ and resell them in the Home market for P'. This earns the licence holders A + B. If the government gives the licences to Home residents, then the quota is a DCR barrier. If it gives them to foreigners, the quota is an FCR barrier.

4.4.2 FCR barriers

A prime example of an FCR barrier is a 'price undertaking' in the context of an anti-dumping tariff. Under EU law, the Commission can impose a tariff on a non-member nation if that nation's firms are selling goods below cost in the EU market (so-called dumping). In some cases, an anti-dumping tariff is imposed but in other cases no tariff is imposed and the exporting firm promises to raise its price instead. These promises are called 'price undertakings'.

For example, if the agreed level were P' from Figure 4.8, the price undertaking would have the same price and quantity effects as a tariff, T. Importantly, however, the undertaking allows foreign producers, rather than the Home government, to garner the rents A + B. Throughout the industrialized world, and in the EU in particular, it is very common for trade barriers to be arranged so that foreigners earn the rents. One reason is that trade rents are used as a kind of gift to soothe foreign companies and governments that are likely to be angered by the imposition of a trade barrier.

Finally, note that an FCR barrier harms EU welfare more than a DCR barrier. Specifically, the welfare cost of an FCR is always negative, i.e. –A – C, instead of being ambiguous, i.e. B – C. Moreover, the foreign welfare impact is now A – D, so an FCR may end up helping foreigners!

4.4.3 Frictional barriers

An important type of trade barrier that still remains inside the EU consists of what are sometimes called 'technical barriers to trade' (TBTs). Western European countries often restrict imports by subjecting them to a whole range of policies that increase the real cost of buying foreign goods. Some examples are excessive bureaucratic 'red-tape' restrictions and industrial standards that discriminate against foreign goods. One of the most famous examples is discussed in Box 4.2.

Box 4.2   *Cassis de Dijon*: a history-making technical barrier to trade

One very common type of frictional barrier concerns health and safety regulations that have the side effect of hindering trade. Perhaps the most famous of these was a German regulation that forbade the importation of certain low-alcohol spirits, including the sweet French liqueur, Cassis – used in the famous white wine cocktail, Kir. This regulation was challenged before the EU's Court of Justice as a barrier to trade. When challenged on this regulation, the German government argued that the prohibition was necessary to protect public health (since weak spirits more easily promote alcohol tolerance) and to protect consumers (since consumers might buy weak spirits, thinking they were strong). In 1979, the Court ruled that the measure was not necessary since widespread availability of low-alcohol drinks (e.g. beer) in Germany made the prohibition ineffective in furthering public health. It also found that putting the alcohol content on the label was sufficient to protect consumers, so the import ban was not necessary for their protection. This Court ruling resulted in the frictional barrier being removed. More importantly, it established the basic principle known as 'mutual recognition' whereby goods that are lawfully sold in one EU nation shall be presumed to be safe for sale in all EU nations. Exceptions to this principle require explicit motivation. By the way, the formal name for this Court case is *Rewe-Zentral AG v Bundesmonopolverwaltung für Branntwein*; no wonder it's called *Cassis de Dijon*.

Since frictional barriers are bad for a nation, one may ask why they are so prevalent. Box 4.3 provides one explanation.

Box 4.3   Why do frictional barriers arise so often?

Government agencies charged with formulating and enforcing standards are often 'captured' by special-interest groups from the regulated industries. Moreover, the Home firms that are to be subjected to the standards often play an important role in setting the standards. For example, when regulating a highly technical field such as elevators, the government (which probably does not employ many full-time elevator experts) naturally asks the opinions of domestic firms that produce elevators. With an eye to their foreign competitors, they quite naturally push for standards that raise the cost of imported goods more than the cost of locally produced goods.

An example can be found in the paper industry. Sweden and Finland produce paper mainly from new trees, while French and German paper producers use a lot of recycled paper and rags. In the early 1990s, the EU was considering a regulation that would require all paper sold in the EU to contain a certain fraction of recycled paper. This sounds like a 'public interest' regulation. However, it also would have had the effect of eliminating the resource-based advantage of Swedish and Finnish firms, much to the joy of French and German firms. In other words, it would have raised the real cost of imports (since the Nordic producers would have had to switch to less efficient techniques). As it turns out, it is not clear which production method is 'greener'. Recycling paper requires lots of chemicals that may be released into the environment, while establishing more tree farms is, well, green – a point that was not raised by French and German paper producers.

As a result of Finland and Sweden joining the EU, the regulation was not adopted, but this shows the subtle mixing of public interest and protectionism that inevitably arises when nations adopt regulations and standards. Of course, nations do need health, safety, environmental and industrial standards, so we cannot eliminate frictional barriers by simply abolishing all regulation. This is one of the issues tackled by the EU's 1992 programme.

One important class of frictional – i.e. cost-creating – barriers involves industrial and health standards that are chosen at least in part to restrict imports. For example, some countries refuse to accept safety tests that are performed in foreign countries, even in highly industrialized nations. This forces importers to retest their products in the local country. Beyond raising the real cost of imported goods, this sort of barrier delays the introduction of new products. While this clearly harms consumers, Home producers may benefit since it may give them time to introduce competing varieties. Another example involves imposing industrial, health, safety or environmental standards that differ from internationally recognized norms. It is often difficult to know objectively whether an unusual regulation or standard represents a valid 'public interest' concern or whether it is just a protectionist device. In fact, both motives are usually behind the adoption of such measures.

Regardless of why such policies are adopted, they have the effect of protecting Home producers or service providers. Home firms design their products with these standards in mind, while foreign firms, for whom the Home market may be relatively unimportant, are unlikely to do so. Bringing imported products into conformity raises the real cost of imports.

For example, all cars sold in Sweden must have wipers for the headlights. While this policy may have some merit as a safety regulation (in the old days Sweden had lots of dusty rural roads), it also has the effect of raising the price of imported cars more than it raises the price of Swedish cars. From the drawing board onwards, all Volvo and Saab models – and their production facilities – are designed with these headlight wipers in mind. For other car makers, take Renault as an example, the Swedish market is far too small to really matter. The design of Renaults and Renault's mass production facilities are not optimized for the installation of headlight wipers. Consequently, while it is expensive to put headlight wipers on both Swedish and French cars, it is much more so for French cars. This gives the Swedish car makers an edge in Sweden. Similar sorts of barrier give the French an edge in their domestic market.

4.5 Sources of competitiveness differences

The diagrams in Section 4.3 assumed that the two nations incurred different costs when producing the good whose quantity appears on the horizontal axis (see Figure 2.7, for example). But where do such cost and price differences come from?

A major part of international trade theory is concerned with exactly this question. In that literature it is called the question of 'sources of comparative advantage'. This section introduces some basic notions of comparative advantage theory to help readers understand the real-world sources of these price differences.

4.5.1 Traditional comparative advantage made simple

Comparative advantage analysis starts with a sector-by-sector comparison of the competitiveness of individual nations. To structure our thinking about sectoral competitiveness, it is useful to focus on a simplistic notion of competitiveness – one where cheaper means more competitive. To keep things simple, we brush aside all cost considerations apart from labour productivity and wages. The Home nation's cost of producing a particular good is the number of hours required to produce and sell one unit of the good and Home's wage.

For example, if it takes workers in a UK factory a total of 7 hours to produce an electric fan, and the UK wage is, say, 5 GBP per hour, then the fan costs 35 GBP. Under the assumption of perfect competition, the price on the market would be 35 GBP. Suppose the same electric fan takes 20 hours to make in an Italian factory (since Italian factories are less productive in this example), and the Italian wage is 12 euros an hour, the Italian-made fan would cost 140 euros.

Which fan is cheaper? The answer depends upon the exchange rate, i.e. the number of euros per pound. If the exchange rate (EUR/GBP) is 2.00 euros per pound, then converting the GBP price to euros implies that the British-made fan would cost 70 euro – cheaper than the 140 euro price of the Italian-made fan. This is what we mean when we say Britain is more competitive than Italy in terms of fans.

The same sector-by-sector comparison is made for four goods in Table 4.1, namely, electric fans, espresso machines, jet engines, and designer silverware. In each case, illustrative hours-per-unit are listed for the two nations. To calculate prices, the table also includes the two nations' wages, and an illustrative exchange rate. The British wages are converted from pounds to euros for the calculation. The second- and third-to-last columns show the calculated prices. The final column shows the ratio of the Italian price to the UK price (both in euros).

Table 4.1   Example of sector-by-sector competitiveness

	Hours needed in:		Wages (local currency)		Exchange rate	Wages in euros		Prices in euros		Price ratio
	UK	Italy	UK (GBP)	Italy (EUR)	EUR per GBP	UK	Italy	UK	Italy	Italy/ UK
Electric fan	7	20	5	12	2	10	7	70	140	2.000
Espresso machine	10	13	5	12	2	10	7	100	91	0.910
Jet engine	1300	3000	5	12	2	10	7	13,000	21,000	1.615
Designer silverware	23	15	5	12	2	10	7	230	105	0.457

Sources of sector-by-sector competitiveness

The relative price is a measure of the UK's competitiveness sector by sector because, when the Italian price is high compared to the British price, it is the UK good that is more competitive. It is instructive to think about the relative price (e.g. 140/70) in a slightly different way. To start with, observe that the relative price depends upon two things:

- relative labour productivity (i.e. hours needed in Italy over hours needed in the UK);
- relative wages measured in a common currency.

Relative productivity is something that changes quite slowly as it depends upon the nations' industrial histories, general level of scientific and technological know-how, management efficiency and experience in making the goods concerned – to mention just a few factors.

Figure 4.9 shows some actual numbers for the UK and Italy, and Germany and Poland for comparison. Specifically, labour productivity is here measured as total GDP divided by total hours worked. Since 2000, all of these have risen in national currency terms (the left-hand panel of Figure 4.9). The German and Italian numbers show GDP measured in euros. Plainly, workers in German factories are more productive and this is the main reason wages are higher in Germany than Italy. Both sets of workers have seen increasing productivity and this underpins the ability of industry to raise wages every year without losing competitiveness. The UK numbers show GDP per hour worked in pounds and the Polish in zlotys, so they cannot actually be compared directly to the euro-based numbers.

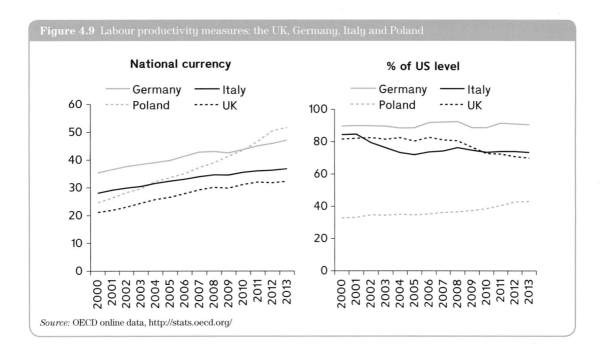

Figure 4.9 Labour productivity measures: the UK, Germany, Italy and Poland

Source: OECD online data, http://stats.oecd.org/

The right-hand panel of Figure 4.9 shows the labour productivities (i.e. GDP per hour worked) converted to a common basis (US dollars) and then compared to US productivity. What it shows is that Germany has maintained its labour productivity at about 90 per cent of the US level since 2000. The UK and Italy, by contrast, have seen a significant decline. Poland, while starting at a much lower level than the other three, is clearly catching up. Again, this is the main reason Polish wages and incomes are rising much faster than those in western Europe.

The relative wage also moves. But what is the 'right' relative wage? The answer is that the relative wages adjust to ensure that Italy and the UK, or both, are competitive in some sectors but not all. Returning to the illustrative example, Figure 4.10 facilitates the discussion. The dark bars in the chart plot the relative price numbers for the four goods listed in the last column of Table 4.1, when we took the relative Italian-to-UK wage (measured in euros) to be 7/10. The line at 1.0 is relevant since if the bar is above this, the UK is the lower-cost producer (i.e. competitive in the sector). If the bar is below 1.0, Italy is the one that is competitive in the sector (i.e. the low-cost producer). When the relative wage is 7/10 as assumed in Table 4.1, each nation is competitive in two sectors.

Now consider what the situation would look like if the exchange rate were 1.0 euros per GBP. Before turning to calculations, think about what this would do to the relative competitiveness of Italy and the UK. If wages remained constant in local terms (euros and pounds), then the exchange rate change (from 2 euros to 1 euro per point) would raise the relative price of Italian labour. Or looking at it from the British perspective, it would make UK wages appear to fall – relative to Italian wages – by 50 per cent, namely, from 10 to 5 euros. Plainly, this will tend to improve UK competitiveness in all sectors.

To identify the degree of change, we can re-do the price calculations using this simple formula:

$$\frac{\text{Italian price}}{\text{UK price}} = \frac{\text{Italian hours needed}}{\text{UK hours needed}} \times \frac{\text{Italian wage (€)}}{\text{UK wage (£)}} \times \frac{1}{\text{€'s per £}}$$

The answers are listed above the light bars in Figure 4.10 (diligent readers should work this out for themselves). The results show that Italy would be uncompetitive in all sectors at this 1.0 exchange rate. Surely this is not an equilibrium because it would mean that Italy imports everything and exports nothing.

Figure 4.10 Illustration of the relative wage that balances competitiveness

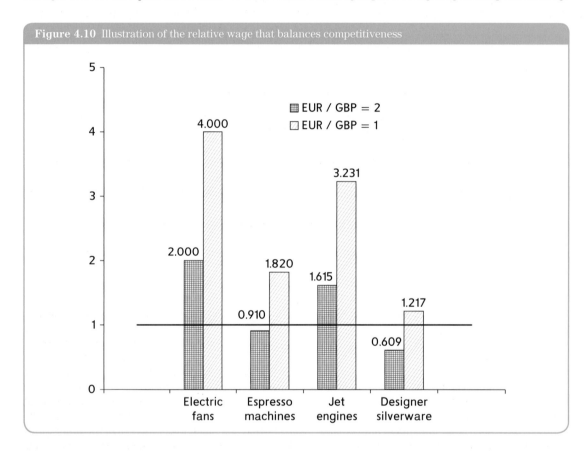

The real-world mechanisms for arriving at the equilibrium relative wage are complex. Explaining them would fill a few more chapters. But even without a full understanding, our simple 'thought experiment' serves to elucidate the basic considerations. If Italian workers are too expensive relative to UK workers – taking into account their relative productivity – then Italy would have no exports to pay for its imports. In equilibrium, the relative wage will adjust so that each nation is competitive in some sectors. When exchanges rates can move – as is the case for the EUR/GBP rate – then some of the adjustment can come from changes in the number of euros to the pound. When exchange rates are locked-in – as they are among the Eurozone nations – the only way to adjust national competitiveness is to change wages directly. Doing so can be painful, as the recent Eurozone crisis has shown.

4.5.2 Other sources of competitiveness

The simple illustration above looks only at labour productivity and the price of labour (i.e. the wage). In reality, many other things affect the competitiveness of goods – product quality and reliability, for example. These help explain why most Europeans will pay more for a Volkswagen than they will for a similar car made by Renault. Quality and reliability themselves are the outcome of complex factors and interactions among these factors. Since quality is hard to measure and hard to change, simple microeconomics typically ignores it by assuming that only prices matter.

Another example is the cost of other inputs such as energy. This competitiveness factor has been in the news recently due to big changes in the US shale gas and oil industry. The rapid growth in shale gas output has pushed down natural gas prices in the USA. This has helped the competitiveness of sectors that use a lot of these inputs. A 2014 VoxEU.org column (Mathieu et al., 2014) discusses how this development has shifted US sector-by-sector competitiveness. In sectors like plastics and nitrogen fertilizers – for which oil and gas represent 25 to 40 per cent of total costs – the lower price of this input has massively boosted US sectoral competitiveness. Other inputs such as managers, skilled technicians, engineers and software programmers can also vary in price across nations and vary in importance by sector and so these too are considered important sources of comparative advantage.

4.5.3 Summary

The partial equilibrium diagrams in the rest of the chapter take the competitiveness of Home and Foreign as given. Specifically, national competitiveness is reflected in the relative heights of the domestic supply curves (recall that these are really the marginal cost curves so a higher supply curve means higher costs). This section provides a rationale for why some nations will be more competitive in some sectors while other nations will be competitive in others.

The bottom-line insight is simple. For many reasons, the sectoral profiles of national costs differ across nations. Some nations are really good at engineering goods, others in design-intensive goods, and yet others in labour-intensive goods. Given these different cross-sector, national profiles, relative wages adjust so that each nation is cost-competitive in some sectors but not all.

4.6 Summary

This chapter presented the essential microeconomic tools for trade policy analysis in the simplified world in which we assume there is no imperfect competition and no scale economies. The two most important diagrams are the open-economy supply and demand diagram (right-hand panel of Figure 4.5) and the *MD–MS* diagram (left-hand panel of Figure 4.5). The *MD–MS* diagram provides a compact way of working out the impact of import protection on prices, quantities and overall Home and Foreign welfare. The open-economy supply and demand diagram allowed us to consider the distributional impact of import protection, i.e. to separate the overall effect into its component effects on Home consumers, Home producers and Home revenue.

The chapter also discussed types of trade barrier in Europe and classified them according to what happens to the trade 'rents'. Under the first type, DCR barriers, the rents go to domestic residents; with FCR barriers, the rents go to foreigners; and with frictional barriers, the rents disappear. European integration consisted primarily of removing DCR barriers up until the mid-1970s. Subsequent goods-market liberalization has focused on frictional barriers.

The final topic was a quick introduction to the intuition behind the sources of comparative advantage, i.e. the reasons why nations are competitive in some but not all sectors.

Self-assessment questions

1 Using a diagram like Figure 4.8, show the full Foreign welfare effects of imposing a Home tariff equal to *T*, i.e. show the impact on Foreign producers and Foreign consumers separately.
2 In August 2005, EU clothing retailers such as Sweden's H&M complained about the new EU restrictions on imports from China that were imposed after complaints from clothing producers based in Italy, France, Spain, Portugal and Greece. Use a diagram like Figure 4.8 to explain the positions of the various EU interest groups.

3 One way to think about the slope of the *MS* curve is in terms of the 'size' of the home nation. The idea is that the demand from a very small nation has a very small impact on the world price. For example, Switzerland could probably increase its oil imports by 10 per cent without having any impact on the world oil price. Using a diagram like Figure 4.7, show that the welfare costs of imposing an MFN tariff are larger for smaller nations, interpreting this in terms of the *MS* curve's slope. Show that when the *MS* curve is perfectly flat, the welfare effects are unambiguously negative.

4 Using a diagram like Figure 4.8, show that a country facing an upward-sloping *MS* curve can gain – starting from free trade – from imposing a sufficiently small tariff. (Hint: Starting from a small tariff, the rectangle gains and triangle losses both increase in size as the tariff gets bigger, but the rectangle gets bigger faster.) Show that any level of a frictional or FCR barrier lowers Home welfare.

5 Using the results from the previous exercise, consider the impact of Home imposing a tariff on Foreign exports and Foreign retaliating with a tariff on Home's exports. Assume that the *MS* and *MD* curves for both goods (Home exports to Foreign and Foreign exports to Home) are identical. Starting from a situation in which Home and Foreign both impose a tariff of *T*, show that both unambiguously gain if both remove their tariffs, but one nation might lose if it removed its tariff unilaterally. By the way, this exercise illustrates why nations that are willing to lower their tariffs in the context of a WTO multilateral trade negotiation are often not willing to remove their tariffs unilaterally.

6 Using a diagram like Figure 4.5, show that an import tariff equal to *T* has exactly the same impact on prices, quantities and welfare as a domestic consumption tax equal to *T* and a domestic production subsidy equal to *T*. (Hint: A production subsidy lowers the effective marginal cost of domestic firms and so lowers the domestic supply curve by *T*.)

7 Using a diagram like Figure 4.7, show the impact on quantities, prices and welfare when Home has no tariff but Foreign charges an export tax equal to *T*.

8 Using a diagram like Figure 4.5, show the impact on quantities, prices and welfare when Home has no tariff but Foreign imposes an export quota with a tariff-equivalent of *T*.

9 Using a diagram like Figure 4.7, show that the welfare effects of a quota that restricts imports to *M'* are exactly the same as a tariff equal to *T*; assume that each quota licence (i.e. the right to import one unit) is sold by the government to the highest bidder.

Further reading: the aficionado's corner

Every undergraduate textbook on international economics has a chapter on tariff analysis that covers the same material as this chapter. One particularly accessible treatment can be found in:

Krugman, P. and M. Obstfeld (2005) *International Economics*, 7th edition (or earlier), HarperCollins, New York.

For much more on the economics of trade protection, see:

Vousden, N. (1990) *The Economics of Trade Protection*, Cambridge University Press, Cambridge.

Useful websites

The World Bank's website provides extensive research on trade policy analysis. This includes many papers on non-discriminatory trade policy but also a very large section on preferential trade arrangements under the heading of 'regionalism'. See www.worldbank.org.

The Commission's website on trade issues can be found at http://ec.europa.eu/trade/. It has lots of information on the latest changes to EU trade policy.

References

Mankiw, G. (2011) *Principles of Economics*, 6th edition (or earlier), South Western Publishing, New York.

Mathieu, M., T. Spencer and O. Sartor (2014) 'Economic analysis of the US unconventional oil and gas revolution', http://www.voxeu.org/article/limited-economic-impact-us-shale-gas-boom.

[T]he ideas of economists and political philosophers, both when they are right and when they are wrong, are more powerful than is commonly understood. Indeed the world is ruled by little else. Practical men, who believe themselves to be exempt from any intellectual influences, are usually the slaves of some defunct economist.

John Maynard Keynes, 1935

The essential economics of preferential liberalization

Chapter Contents

Introduction

This chapter begins our study of the microeconomics of European integration, focusing on the preferential (i.e. discriminatory) aspects. This is critical since discrimination (the nicer word is preferential) is the heart and soul of European economic integration. Over the past six decades, Europe has liberalized trade and factor markets – but not with everyone. By 1968, EU members charged zero tariffs on all imports from each other, while imposing significant tariffs on imports from the USA, Canada and Japan. Likewise, the Single Market Programme instituted the principle of mutual recognition of product standards on a discriminatory basis. In principle, goods made and sold in one EU nation could be sold in all EU nations, but this privilege did not extend to goods made in third nations. Discriminatory effects also played a central role in the political economy of European integration – especially the domino effects discussed in Chapter 1.

The main goal of this chapter is to provide a framework for analysing the essential economics of preferential liberalization. As usual, we start simple and add complexity as we go. For simplicity's sake, we continue with the last chapter's simplifying assumptions of no imperfect competition and no increasing returns (NICNIR). While these assumptions are both monumentally unrealistic, they are pedagogically convenient. They allow us to study the main economic logic of discriminatory liberalization without having to invest a lot of time in learning new tools (that is postponed until the next chapter).

5.1 Analysis of unilateral discriminatory liberalization

The simplest form of preferential liberalization is a unilateral preferential liberalization, so we turn to this first. Specifically, this section looks at what happens when a nation removes its tariff on imports from only one of its trading partners. We postpone consideration of changes in partner tariffs until the next section. This two-step approach is useful for two distinct reasons:

- While European economic integration almost always involves two-way integration (e.g. France and Germany lowered their tariffs against each other's exports at the same time during the 1960s), the analysis of a two-way (i.e. reciprocal) liberalization is basically an easy extension of the analysis of a one-way (i.e. unilateral) liberalization.

- The EU extends unilateral preferences to almost every developing nation in the world; the analysis in this section is directly applicable to EU programmes such as 'Everything but Arms' (which removes tariffs and quotas on imports from the world's poorest nations) and the Generalized System of Preferences. (More on these in Chapter 12.)

5.1.1 The basic logic in words: Vinerian insights

Before turning to diagrams – which may strike some readers as complex – it is worth presenting the basic economic logic in words. This helps boost intuition for the diagrams. It may also be sufficient for readers in a hurry.

There are only three elemental effects we really need to understand in relation to preferential liberalization:

- The first general point, namely, 'Smith's certitude', was made by Adam Smith.

When a nation 'exempt[s] the good of one country from duties to which it subjects those of all other . . . the merchants and manufacturers of the country whose commerce is so favoured must necessarily derive great advantage' (as quoted in Pomfret, 1997).

The economic logic behind Smith's certitude is straightforward and easily illustrated with an example of a world where firms from two nations – call them Partner and Rest-of-World (RoW) – are competing in a third nation – call it Home. Without preferences, Home charges the same tariff on imports from Partner and RoW. Now suppose Home unilaterally removes tariffs on imports from Partner but not from RoW. The fruits of this reduced import tax will – as usual with tax removals – be shared between consumers and producers. Home consumers will see lower prices and Partner exporters will see higher prices. The higher border price for Partner firms induces them to sell more to Home. Plainly, this is good for Partner – its firms sell more and obtain a higher price. In short, Smith's certitude stems from the fact that Partner firms enjoy a rise in both prices and sales to Home.

- The second elemental effect was identified when Gottfried Haberler (1937) asserted that third nations – those excluded from the preferences – must lose; this is 'Haberler's spillover'.

Haberler's spillover can be illustrated with the same simple case. To remain competitive in the Home market while still paying the tariff, RoW firms must accept a lower pre-tariff price for their exports since their post-tariff price must match the competition's price. This pushes them down their export supply curve so RoW exports fall. Thus Haberler's spillover shows up as RoW exports suffer a drop in both prices and sales to Home. Or to put it differently, what is preference to Partner (Smith's certitude) is discrimination to RoW (Haberler's spillover).

As we shall see in the next sections, Smith's certitude and Haberler's spillover are the linchpins of the political economy of the traditional view of regionalism.

- The third elemental effect is called Viner's ambiguity.

Jacob Viner (1950) demonstrated that preferential liberalization might harm the preference-giving nation; this is 'Viner's ambiguity'. Viner, who was blissfully ignorant of post-war mathematical economics, couched his argument in the enduring but imprecise concepts of 'trade diversion' and 'trade creation' (see Box 5.1). The basic economics nevertheless is clear from his terms. Discriminatory liberalization is both 'liberalization' – which removes some price wedges and thus tends to improve economic efficiency and Home welfare – and 'discrimination' – which introduces new price wedges and thus tends to harm efficiency and welfare. Viner associated the liberalization part with 'trade creation' and the discriminatory part with 'trade diversion'. It is not possible to say a priori whether the sum of these effects is positive or negative, i.e. its sign is ambiguous.

Box 5.1   Terminology in detail: trade creation, trade diversion

If one were to sneak into the bedroom of almost any famous international economist, shake them awake and shout loudly, 'Free trade area – good or bad?', the first words out of their mouth would surely include 'trade creation and trade diversion'. Indeed, these terms are so influential that, despite their shortcomings, one really must know them.

It should be clear to readers who have worked through the RTA diagram that this terminology fails to capture all welfare effects of discriminatory tariff liberalization, and, as we shall see in Section 5.2.3, it is completely useless when it comes to the type of barriers European integration has addressed since the mid-1970s, i.e. non-tariff barriers. One economist who has studied the history of 'customs union theory' suggests that the terms persist because they are 'highly effective tools of focusing policy makers' attention on the ambiguous welfare effects of RTAs' (Panagariya, 1999).

Economists have dealt with the incompleteness of Viner's terms in two ways. Some stretch the original meaning of his terms to cover the full effects in the simplest case where the *MS* curves are flat (see the Annex at the end of this chapter). Others have introduced new jargon – adding terms like 'internal versus external trade creation' and 'trade expansion'. All this variance in literary interpretation is possible because Viner did not use diagrams in his book and certainly no maths, so there is some debate over exactly what he meant. The most convincing translation of Viner's words into modern economics was undertaken by Nobel Laureate James Meade in his famous 1955 book, *The Theory of Customs Unions*. That book employed a general approach based on the powerful toolkit developed by, among others, Paul Samuelson, Kenneth Arrow, James Mirrlees, and Meade himself. Namely, he breaks down net welfare effects into what we have called trade volume effects and border price effects.

See Box 5.2 for further details on the thinkers behind these three elementary effects.

5.1.2 The RTA (regional trade arrangement) diagram

To get a deeper and clearer understanding of the economics of preferential liberalization, it is necessary to turn to diagrams. The diagrams, unfortunately, are more complex than those in the previous chapter for

---

Box 5.2 Smith, Haberler and Viner

The three men responsible for the elemental effects were all interesting characters. Adam Smith, who died in 1790, is seen as the father of economics because his 1776 book, *The Wealth of Nations*, defined the basic approach to markets that is at the heart of modern economic thinking. Not content with launching economics, he was also a social philosopher and a leading figure in the Scottish Enlightenment – a collaborator of David Hume.

Gottfried Haberler was born in 1900 in Austria where he earned degrees in political science and law before moving to Harvard University in the 1930s. His most famous work reformulated the case for free trade based on the concept of opportunity cost. As part of this, he invented the production possibility frontier. He was the thesis adviser of the father of one of this textbook's authors (Richard Baldwin).

Smith	**Haberler**	**Viner**

© Library of Congress Prints and Photographs Division [LC-US Z62.17407]	© Archive of the University of Vienna	© Princeton University Library

Jacob Viner, born in 1892, grew up in Montreal, earning his first degree at McGill and then a PhD at Harvard. He taught at the Universities of Chicago, Stanford, Yale and Princeton, and twice at the Graduate Institute of International and Development Studies in Geneva (where both the authors of this textbook teach today). Apart from his elemental contribution to the analysis of preferential trade liberalization, he introduced the long-run and short-run cost curves used in every economics textbook today. At Chicago and Princeton, many students were frightened by the thought of studying under him. His most famous student was Milton Friedman.

---

one simple reason – we need a minimum of three nations in the analysis (Home, Partner and RoW). Our first task is to extend the workhorse *MD–MS* diagram from Chapter 4 to allow for two sources of imports. Figure 5.1 shows how.

Before starting, we note that the theory of preferential liberalization is often taught using an additional simplifying factor called the 'small economy' assumption. While this simplifies the analysis of Viner's ambiguity from the perspective of the Home country, it also assumes away the critical impact that preferential liberalization has on other nations (Smith's certitude and Haberler's spillover). Interested readers can find this case in the Annex at the end of the chapter.

Free trade equilibrium

We open our study of the RTA diagram by working out the free trade equilibrium. That is to say, we want to identify the equilibrium price and quantities when no tariff is imposed by Home. To find the free trade price, we need to find the intersection between the *MD* curve and the *MS* curve, as in Chapter 4. But what is the *MS* curve with two trade partners?

The two leftmost panels of Figure 5.1 show the export supply curves for two individual countries, which we call Partner and RoW. (To minimize complications, we assume that Partner and RoW are identical, so

Figure 5.1 The RTA diagram

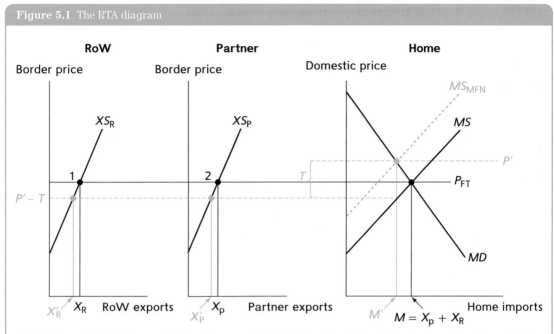

Note: Readers who find the diagrams in this section somewhat involved may benefit from the step-by-step explanations available in the interactive PowerPoint presentation on the Online Learning Centre.

their XS curves are identical.) Because there are two suppliers of imports, we must aggregate them in the standard microeconomics way, namely, by forming the horizontal sum of the two export supply curves. This summed curve is shown as MS in the right-hand panel. Note that the MS curve is flatter than XS_P or XS_R since a given price increase will raise supply from both Partner and RoW.

With the MS curve in hand, we see that the free trade equilibrium price is P_{FT} (as before, FT stands for 'free trade'), i.e. the point at which MS and MD intersect. The corresponding level of imports is M, as shown. As we shall be interested in changes to the imports coming from Partner and RoW, we identify the initial free imports. We do this by using each supplier's XS curve to see how much would be offered at the price P_{FT}. The answers are given by points 1 and 2 in the diagram, namely, X_R and X_P (the subscripts R and P stand for RoW and Partner, respectively).

MFN tariff with two import suppliers

Working out the free trade equilibrium was just the first step. Next we have to see what would happen to prices and quantities if Home applied a non-discriminatory tariff (i.e. an MFN tariff as described in Chapter 4). The reason we do this is to be able to have a baseline for comparison when we study – in the third step – what happens when Home removes the tariff but only on imports coming from Partner.

What happens when Home imposes a tariff equal to T on imports coming from both nations? As always, the first task is to find how the tariff affects the MS curve. As we saw in Chapter 4, an MFN tariff shifts the MS curve up by T since the domestic price would have to be T higher to elicit the same quantity of imports after the tariff is imposed. The new MS curve is shown in the diagram as the curve marked MS_{MFN}. As usual, imposing a tariff does nothing to the MD curve (see Chapter 4 if this point is not obvious).

The intersection of MS_{MFN} and MD tells us that the post-tariff equilibrium domestic price for imports is P' and the new import level is M'; with P' as the new domestic price, the new border price is $P' - T$. At this border price, both import suppliers are willing to supply less, namely, $X_{R'}$ and X_P, as shown in the diagram. See Chapter 4 if the concept of 'border price' is not familiar to you.

Finally, we are ready for the third step – an analysis of a discriminatory unilateral liberalization by Home.

5.1.3 Price and quantity effects of discriminatory liberalization

What happens when Home removes T but only for imports from Partner, i.e. when Home unilaterally liberalizes on a preferential basis?

To answer this, we start, as always, by working out the impact of the preferential liberalization on the MS curve. The new MS curve, which we will call MS_{RTA}, is shown in Figure 5.2 (here RTA stands for 'preferential trade arrangement').

Figure 5.2 Price and quantity effects of unilateral, discriminatory tariff liberalization

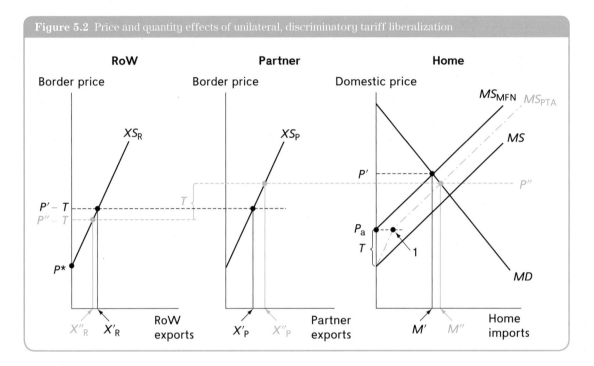

The position of the MS_{RTA} is quite intuitive. After the preferential tariff liberalization, half of Home's import suppliers get duty-free access; the other half pays T. It seems natural, therefore, that MS_{RTA} lies halfway between the free trade MS_{FT} and the MFN tariff MS_{MFN}. One small qualification is necessary, however; considering this helps us see how MS_{RTA} is constructed.

The tariff prevents RoW firms from exporting until the domestic price in Home rises above the price marked P_a in Figure 5.2. When Home's domestic price is below P_a, the border price faced by RoW exports is below their zero-supply price (marked as P^* in the diagram). Partner-based firms, by contrast, would export when Home's domestic price is slightly below P_a since they face Home's domestic price (not the Home price minus the tariff). As a consequence, Partner firms – but only Partner firms – will supply imports at the domestic price P_a and this corresponds to the point marked 1 in the diagram. Thus the MS_{RTA} curve is Partner's XS curve up to point 1. After that, both foreigners supply imports, so the MS_{RTA} resumes its normal slope.

The domestic price change and conflicting border price changes

Having worked out the new MS curve, namely, MS_{RTA}, we are ready to find the new equilibrium price. This is, as always, given by the intersection of the MD and MS_{RTA} curves, namely, P''. This is the new, post-RTA domestic price. As you might have expected even without going through the analysis, the new domestic price is lower than the old MFN tariff price. After all, imports from Partner can now enter duty free.

The impact on the border price is twofold because only RoW continues to pay the tariff. For Partner-based firms, the liberalization means that they now face Home's domestic price, P'', so for them the border price is P''. For RoW-based firms, which still have to pay T, the border price is $P'' - T$. This means that RoW sees its border price fall (this is the price-part of Haberler's spillover). Partner firms see the border rise (this is the price-part of Smith's certitude). The source of this conflicting border price change is the fact that RoW must cut its border price to remain competitive in relation to Partner firms' exports, which benefitted from T's removal.

Next we consider the quantity effects.

Supply switching

Given that Partner firms see a price rise, they increase exports from $X_p' X_p''$ (this is the quantity-part of Smith's certitude). RoW exports fall from $X_R' X_R''$ because their border price has fallen (this is the quantity-part of Haberler's spillover). This combination of higher Partner sales and lower RoW sales is known as 'supply switching' or 'trade diversion'. Defining it directly, supply switching occurs when a discriminatory liberalization induces the Home nation to switch some of its purchases to import suppliers who benefit from the RTA and away from suppliers based in nations that did not benefit from the RTA.

Did this sort of supply switching actually occur in Europe? When the EEC eliminated tariffs on a discriminatory basis during the formation of its customs union between 1958 and 1968, supply switching did indeed occur – as described in Box 5.3. We discuss more recent econometric evidence for other regional trade agreements (RTAs) in Section 5.5.

Box 5.3 The supply-switching effects of the formation of the EEC customs union

Figure 5.3 shows the trade volume effects that occurred when the EEC6 removed their internal tariffs between 1958 and 1968. In the left-hand panel, the columns show the import shares broken down into intra-EEC6 imports, imports from six other European nations (the ones who joined in the EU's first three enlargements) and the rest of the world.

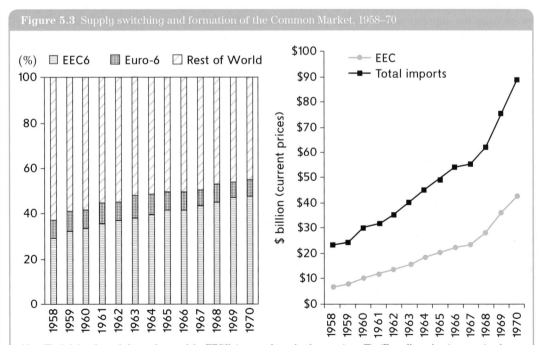

Figure 5.3 Supply switching and formation of the Common Market, 1958–70

Note: The left-hand panel shows shares of the EEC6's imports from the three regions. The 'Euro-6' are the six countries that had joined the EU by the mid-1980s: the UK, Ireland, Denmark, Spain, Portugal and Greece.

Source: http://epp.eurostat.ec.europa.eu/portal/page/portal/international_trade/introduction © European Union, 1995–2014

Note that, as the EEC6 share of exports to itself rose from about 30 per cent in 1958 to about 45 per cent in 1968, the share of EEC imports from other nations had to fall. Part of the displacement occurred with respect to imports from other non-EEC European nations. As the dark bars show, the import share from six other western European nations (the UK, Ireland, Portugal, Spain, Denmark and Greece) fell during this period by a small amount, from 8–9 per cent to 7 per cent. The main displacement came from the rest of the world, mainly imports from the USA. The right-hand panel, however, shows that imports from all sources were in fact growing rapidly. Thus we have to interpret the 'supply switching' as a relative thing. That is, if the customs union had not been formed, imports from non-EEC6 members would have risen even faster.

Summary: price and quantity effects

To summarize, the price and quantity effects are:

- Home's domestic price falls from P' to P''.
- The border price falls from $P' - T$ to $P'' - T$ for RoW imports.
- The border price rises from $P' - T$ to P'' for Partner imports.
- RoW exports fall.
- Partner exports rise.
- Total Home imports rise from M' to M''.

These price and quantity effects may seem strange at first – especially the fact that Home buys more imports from the supplier whose border price has risen. This strangeness is simple to understand. The discriminatory liberalization distorts price signals so that Home consumers are not aware of the fact that Partner goods cost the nation more than RoW goods. To the Home consumer, imports from the two sources cost the same, namely, P'. Supply switching is created by the behaviour of firms: partner firms see a higher border price and thus sell more; RoW firms see a lower border price and thus sell less.

Interested readers may want to add a fourth panel to the diagram by drawing a standard open-economy supply and demand figure for Home to the right of the *MD–MS* panel. Doing so allows you to see that Home production falls and Home consumption rises as a result of the domestic price drop.

5.1.4 Welfare effects

Having worked out the price and quantity effects, we are ready to study the welfare consequences for Home, Partner and RoW. As it turns out, showing the welfare implications in the same figure as the price and quantity effects would complicate the diagram too much. Thus Figure 5.4 reproduces the previous figure but omits unnecessary lines to reduce the 'clutter factor'. As we saw in Chapter 4, all welfare effects stem from price and quantity changes, so these are all that we really need to keep track of.

The welfare effects on foreigners are straightforward. Partner gains D since it gets a higher price and sells more. In other words, Partner experiences a positive border price effect and a positive trade volume effect (see Chapter 4 if you are not familiar with these terms). RoW's losses are E for the reverse reasons; it gets a lower price and sells less (a negative border price effect and a negative trade volume effect).

Home's welfare effects are slightly more complex due to the conflicting border price changes. The direct way of gauging Home's net welfare effect is to use the concepts of 'trade volume effects' and 'border price effects' that were introduced in Chapter 4. This direct approach is also the easiest way to remember the Home welfare effects and it is the easiest way to understand them, so this is what we do in Figure 5.4. Some readers, however, may benefit from working through the welfare impact using the indirect method of adding up the separate impacts on consumer surplus, producer surplus and tariff revenue (see Box 5.4). The two methods lead to the same answer.

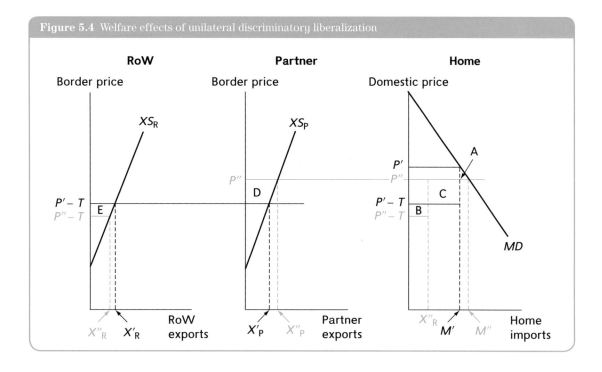

Figure 5.4 Welfare effects of unilateral discriminatory liberalization

---

Box 5.4   Home welfare effects of discriminatory tariff cutting in detail

Here, we consider the 'gross' welfare implications of the price and quantity changes derived in Figure 5.4. To see consumer and producer surplus separately, we put the rightmost panel from Figure 5.4 in the left-hand panel of Figure 5.5 and add to it a right-hand panel consisting of a standard open-economy supply and demand diagram. (As we are focusing on Home welfare, we shall drop the two Foreign panels.) Turn first to the right panel. The drop in the domestic price from P' to P'' raises consumer surplus by $D + A_2 + A_1 + A_3$, but lowers producer surplus by D (see Chapter 4 if this reasoning is unfamiliar). The net change in the private surplus (i.e. producer and consumer surplus combined) is $A_2 + A_1 + A_3$. The change in tariff revenue is slightly more involved than usual. Originally, the tariff revenue was $A_1 + B_1 + C$ (i.e. T times M'). After the RTA, the tariff revenue is $B_1 + B$ since T is charged only on X_R''. Thus, the change in tariff-revenue is $B - A_1 - C$. Adding the private surplus change and the net revenue change, we find that the net impact on Home is: $A_2 + A_1 + A_3 + B - A_1 - C$. Cancelling, this becomes $A_2 + A_3 + B - C$. In Chapter 4 we showed that $A_2 + A_3$ equals A in the left-hand panel, so the net effect is just $A + B - C$, as in Figure 5.4.

Following the direct analysis, we note that the preferential tariff liberalization has increased imports. By the usual reasoning (see Chapter 4), the increase in imports raises Home welfare, with the exact measure being the gap between the MD curve and P'' summed over all the extra units imported. This equals the area marked A in Figure 5.4.

Consider next the conflicting border price effects using these key facts: (1) Home imports amounted to M' before the RTA; (2) after the RTA, an amount equal to X_R'' comes from RoW; and

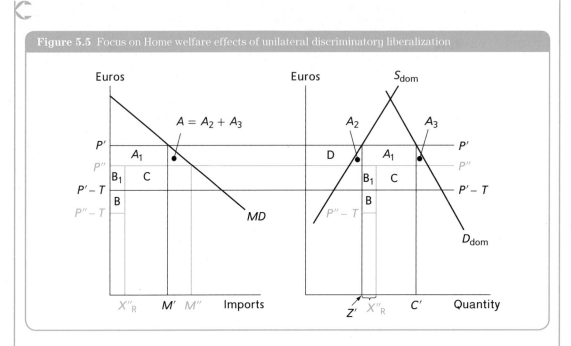

Figure 5.5 Focus on Home welfare effects of unilateral discriminatory liberalization

(3) the rest of M', namely, $M' - X''_R$ comes from Partner. Next we line up these quantities with the relevant price changes:

- The goods coming from RoW have fallen in price, so Home gains on these. The exact size of the gain is just the amount of imports affected times the price drop; in the figure, this gain equals area B.
- The goods coming from Partner have risen in price, so Home experiences a loss. The size of the loss is again the amount of imports affected (namely, $M' - X''_R$) times the price rise, namely, the difference between $P' - T$ and P''. Graphically, this is area C.

What about the border price effect on the extra imports, $M'' - M'$? The border price effect does not apply to these units; since Home did not import them to begin with, it does not make sense to talk about how much more or less they cost post-liberalization. The welfare impact of the extra imports shows up in the trade volume effect, i.e. area A.

Putting together the trade volume effect and the border price effects, Home's overall welfare change is equal to the areas A plus B minus area C. A key point to remember is that this welfare effect may be positive or negative (this is Viner's ambiguity).

Summary: welfare effects

To sum up:

- Partner gains area D (Smith's certitude).
- RoW loses area E (Haberler's spillover)
- Home's welfare changes by $A + B - C$, which may be positive or negative (Viner's ambiguity).

As Figure 5.4 is drawn, the net welfare impact looks negative. Interested readers should be able to show that discriminatory liberalization will lead to a welfare gain if T is large enough. Moreover, as usual with tax analysis, the slopes of the supply and demand curves also affect the size of the welfare effects.

5.2 Analysis of a customs union

Until now we have considered only unilateral tariff cuts. European integration, however, involves reciprocal, i.e. two-way, preferential liberalizations, so it is important to think through the case of two-way preferential liberalization. In our simple model, that means Home and Partner both set their tariffs to zero on each other's exports.

As it turns out, the study of a customs union is an easy stretch of the unilateral RTA analysis. The main extra insight we gain from studying a customs union (a free-trade agreement with a common external tariff) arises from the fact that a customs union (CU) is systematically more favourable for participating countries than unilateral liberalization schemes since Home exporters gain from Partner tariff cuts.

To keep things simple, we shall look at the formation of a CU between Home and Partner, assuming that all three countries (Home, Partner and RoW) are symmetric initially in all aspects, including the MFN tariff they initially impose on all imports. To do this carefully, we must address the question of the three-nation trade pattern. Again to streamline the analysis, we adopt the simplest combination that permits us to study the issues. This leads us to assume that three goods are traded (goods 1, 2 and 3). Each country produces all three goods, but cost structures are such that each nation exports two of the three goods while importing the remaining one. The trade pattern, shown schematically in Figure 5.6, entails Home importing good 1 from Partner and RoW, and Partner importing good 2 from Home and RoW.

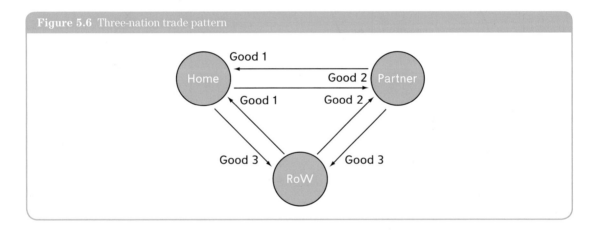

Figure 5.6 Three-nation trade pattern

5.2.1 Price and quantity effects

A customs union is formed between Home and Partner when Home eliminates T on imports of good 1 from Partner, and Partner eliminates T on imports of good 2 from Home. The tariffs facing RoW exports are not changed, and since Home's and Partner's MFN tariffs were identical to start with, there is no need to harmonize their tariffs applied to RoW; T becomes the common external tariff.

We first address the price and quantity effects. Plainly, the impact of Home's discriminatory liberalization is exactly the same as the impact shown in Figure 5.2, so there is no need to repeat it here. The impact of Partner's discriminatory liberalization of imports of good 2 from Home can also be seen using the same diagram. Here is the key point.

A moment's reflection reveals that, given the assumed symmetry of nations, what happens to Home's exports when Partner lowers its barriers is exactly what happened to Partner's exports when Home lowered its barriers. We can, therefore, rely on analysis with which we are already familiar. More specifically, the price of good 2 in Partner falls from P' to P'' (see Figure 5.2) but the border price facing Home exporters when they sell good 2 to Partner rises – from $P' - T$ to P''. Nothing happens to domestic prices in RoW (since they did not liberalize), but RoW exporters face a lower border price for their exports to Partner. The trade volume effects are similarly simple. Partner imports rise from M' to M'' and Home exports to Partner rise; using the terminology from Figure 5.2, Home exports to Partner rise from X_F' to X_F'' RoW's exports to Partner fall, as in Figure 5.2.

5.2.2 Welfare effects

The welfare effects are also just a matter of adding up the effects illustrated above. On Home's import side (i.e. in the market for good 1), Home gains the usual $A + B - C$ in the right-hand panel of Figure 5.7. On Home's export market (good 2), Home's situation is shown in the left-hand panel, so it gains area D. The welfare effects on Partner are identical to this, as a result of the assumed symmetry of goods and nations.

It is useful to study the welfare effects a bit more closely, using Figure 5.8. This diagram shows only the two liberalizing nations, Home and Partner. To be concrete, suppose this is the market for good 1, which

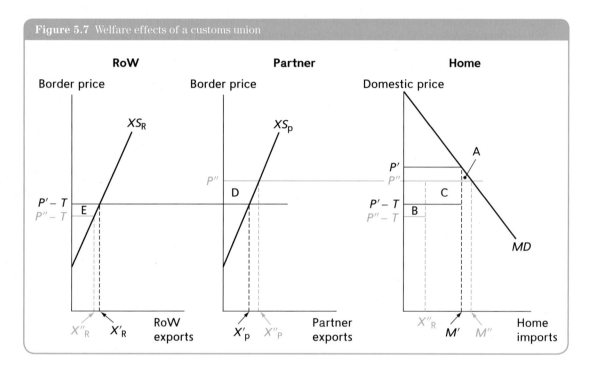

Figure 5.7 Welfare effects of a customs union

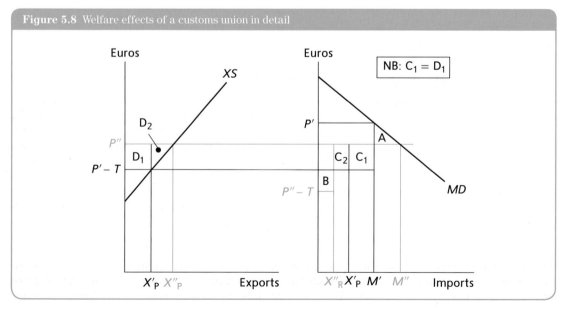

Figure 5.8 Welfare effects of a customs union in detail

Home imports and Partner exports. The diagram is based on the two right-most panels of Figure 5.7 but we have added further detail to the areas. In particular, the trade price loss associated with area C is here split into two parts, C_1 and C_2, for a good reason.

Recall that Home loses $C_1 + C_2$ because the tariff cut raised the price it paid for imports from Partner (from $P' - T$ to P''). The first area, C_1, identifies how much it pays for the units it continues to import from Partner ($M' - X'_P$). Home's loss of C_1, however, is exactly matched by a gain to Partner of the same size; the higher price for the X'_P units transfers C_1 from Home to Partner. The key point is that, because C_1 is just a transfer between CU members, Home's loss of C_1 on its imports of good 1 will be offset by a gain of $D_1 = C_1$ on its exports of good 2 to Partner. After all, Partner also lowers its tariff against Home exports, so we know that Home will gain an area exactly equal to C_1 in its exports of good 2. In addition, Home will gain D_2 in its export market.

Area C_2 is quite different. It identifies the direct cost of the supply switching (trade diversion), so there is no offset gain on the export side. More specifically, recall that, from pre-CU symmetry, we know that RoW exports to Home pre-CU were equal to X'_{P*} After the CU, RoW exports are X''_R so the difference, X'_P, X''_R, measures the amount of supply switching. This quantity is multiplied by the price change ($P' - T$ to P'') to get the welfare cost of the supply switching.

In summary, using the fact that $D_1 = C_1$, the net gain to Home is $+A + B + D_2 - C_2$. This net welfare effect may still be negative, but it is clear that the welfare change from a CU is more positive (or less negative) than the welfare change from a unilateral discriminatory liberalization with Partner.

The losses to RoW from the CU are twice the size of their losses shown in Figure 5.7, since they lose E both on the exports of good 1 to Home and on the exports of good 2 to Partner. Readers who find this reasoning a bit complex may benefit from the step-by-step explanations in the interactive PowerPoint presentations that can be freely downloaded from http://graduateinstitute.ch/home/research/centresandprogrammes/ctei/ctei_people/baldwin_home/economics-of-european-integratio.html.

General equilibrium effects: second-order terms of trade changes

Lastly, we must consider the indirect or second-round implications of the CU.

RoW experiences a reduction in the value of its exports, yet has not reduced the value of its imports from Home and Partner. While this sort of trade deficit may be sustainable in the short run, eventually RoW must turn the situation around. In the real world, this is usually accomplished by a real depreciation of its currency (or a terms of trade worsening if it is in a monetary union). This makes all RoW exports to Home and Partner cheaper and simultaneously makes imports from those two countries more expensive. Both changes have positive welfare implications for the Home and Partner countries; they earn more on their exports to RoW and pay less for their imports from RoW. This is a further negative trade price effect for RoW stemming from the general equilibrium effects of the CU between its trading partners. Such effects, however, are likely to be small.

5.2.3 Customs unions versus free trade agreements

The 1957 Treaty of Rome committed the six original EU members to eliminating all tariffs and quotas on trade among themselves but it also committed them to completely harmonizing their tariffs on imports from non-member nations. In reaction to this customs union, other western European nations formed another trade bloc – known as the European Free Trade Association (EFTA) – in 1960. This was not a customs union, only a free trade area since EFTA members did not adopt a common external tariff. (See Chapter 1 for details.)

What are the key differences between a customs union and a free trade area? Why did the EEC go for a customs union while EFTA went for an FTA? We address these questions in order, starting with the main economic differences.

Stopping tariff cheats: 'trade deflection' and 'rules of origin'

When tariffs between two nations are zero, yet they charge two different tariffs on imports from third nations, firms have an incentive to cheat on tariffs. Take our three-nation example. If all Home–Partner trade is duty free, yet Home charges a 10 per cent tariff on imports from RoW while Partner charges only a 5 per cent tariff on goods coming from RoW, Home-based buyers of RoW goods would be tempted to import the goods first into Partner (thus paying only a 5 per cent tariff) and then to import them duty free from Partner to Home. To thwart this practice – known as trade deflection – Home and Partner have two choices. They can eliminate the temptation by harmonizing their external tariffs (thus turning their FTA into a customs union), or they can stay with the FTA but restrict duty-free treatment to goods that are actually *made* in Home or Foreign. The set of rules that enforce the latter option are called 'rules of origin'.

One problem with rules of origin, and thus with FTAs, is that it can be difficult to know where a product is made in today's highly globalized markets. Personal computers made in, say, Switzerland will contain components from all over the world. The Swiss company may be doing little more than customized assembly of parts from the USA and Asia. In the extreme, it may be doing nothing more than opening the box of a US-made computer and putting in an instruction manual translated into, say, Norwegian. Should the full value of this computer be given duty-free treatment when it is exported to Norway? (Switzerland and Norway are both EFTA members.)

The costs of rules of origin

For manufactured goods, the EU's basic rule of origin is that some fixed percentage of the product's value-added – say 50 per cent – must be done in the exporting nation. For example, if Switzerland exports a specialized type of computer set-up to Germany but imports the monitors and computers from Asia, then the Swiss export will only qualify for zero-tariff treatment if the final price of the good is more than 50 per cent higher than the value of the imported components. For many products, the rules can be much more complex.

Because they can be very expensive to comply with, rules of origin can act as trade barriers, or as barriers that de facto nullify the benefits of a de jure trade agreement. A good example of this can be seen in the EU's unilateral preference schemes for developing nations. Brenton and Manchin (2003) show that only one-third of EU imports from developing countries that were – in principle – eligible for preferences actually entered the EU market with reduced duties. The reason is that the EU's rules of origin in developing nations' exports (e.g. textiles and clothing) are very difficult and expensive to comply with, so the developing nation exporters prefer to pay the EU's high common external tariff rather than comply with the rules of origin and pay zero tariff.

An additional problem with rules of origin is that they can end up as hidden protection. Since rules of origin are specified at the product level, they can be difficult for non-experts to evaluate – just as is the case with technical barriers to trade. As a consequence, rules of origin are usually written in consultation with domestic firms that have an incentive to shape the rules into protectionist devices.

One great advantage of a customs union like the EU is that firms do not have to demonstrate the origin of a product before it is allowed to cross an intra-EU border duty free. Any good that is physically in Germany was either made in Germany or paid the CET when it entered. In either case, the good deserves duty-free passage into France, or any other EU member, without any documentation at all.

5.2.4 Political integration and customs unions

Most preferential trade arrangements in the world are free trade agreements rather than customs unions, like the EU. The reason is simple – political integration. Getting a group of nations to agree on a common external tariff at the launch of a customs union is difficult, but the real problems begin as time passes. For instance, if one member nation believes its industry is being undercut by some non-member nation which is exporting its goods at a price that is below cost (so-called dumping), it may want to impose tariffs to offset the dumping. In a customs union, all nations must agree on every dumping duty since external tariffs must always remain constant. Likewise, nations typically reduce their tariffs in the context of GATT/WTO negotiations. For a customs union, this requires all members to agree on a common negotiating position on every single product.

In practice, keeping the Common External Tariff (CET) common requires some integration of decision making. In the EU, the Commission formally has the power to set tariffs on third-nation goods (even though it naturally consults with Member States before doing so), but very few groups of countries are willing to transfer that amount of national sovereignty. As a result, most trade blocs, including EFTA and the North American Free Trade Agreement, are free trade areas rather than customs unions.

Another way to 'solve' the decision-making problem is for the members to let one nation decide everything. This is the case in all the successful customs unions in the world apart from the EU. For example, South Africa is the dominant nation in the Southern African Customs Union and Switzerland is the dominant nation in the Swiss–Liechtenstein customs union.

5.3 How large are EU tariff preferences

The reasoning heretofore has given the impression that tariff preferences really matter. But how big are tariff preferences inside the EU? A background paper prepared for the World Trade Organization's flagship report in 2011 (Carpenter and Lendle, 2010) gives the exact numbers.

The figures in Table 5.1 show the shares of intra-EU trade that take place under various ranges of tariff preferences. Note that the tariff preference is just the tariff charged to non-members since the tariff inside the EU is always zero. For example, if the non-member tariff (i.e. the MFN tariff) is 10 per cent on a particular type of good, then the preference margin inside the EU is 10 per cent (the external tariff minus the internal tariff). The table identifies five classes of these preferences: high (above 20 per cent), medium (10–20 per cent), low (5–10 per cent), very low (positive but below 5 per cent), and no preference at all since the MFN tariff is zero.

As we can see, the preferences vary a good deal across products but are not very high on average. The top row shows the number of preferences for all intra-EU trade taken together. Only 10 per cent of all intra-EU trade has preferences over 10 per cent and about a third (34 per cent) has no preference at all. About half has a preference of 10 per cent or less (17 per cent plus 38 per cent).

The lack of high preference is even more marked for the high trade volume products such as transportation equipment, machinery, chemical products, and base metals. Together these account for about 60 per cent of all intra-EU trade. None of these have more than 5 per cent of the trade subject to preferences over 10 per cent.

The situation is quite different, however, when it comes to agricultural goods. Two-thirds of all intra-EU trade in animal products have preferences over 20 per cent and the figures are similarly high (although not as extreme) for vegetable products and prepared food, beverages and tobacco.

Table 5.1   Tariff preferences on intra-EU trade

	Above 20%	10–20%	5–10%	0.1–5%	0% (zero MFN)
Total intra-EU	4	6	17	38	34
Machinery	0	4	2	59	35
Transport equipment	4	4	52	38	3
Chemical products	0	0	17	29	53
Base metals	0	0	11	34	54
Prepared food, beverages and tobacco	22	20	12	7	13
Animal products	67	15	5	3	5
Vegetable products	19	19	23	8	18

Source: Carpenter and Lendle (2010)

5.4 Frictional barriers: the 1992 Programme

Heretofore we have dealt with tariff liberalization. This was an important part of early European economic integration, but after the free trade agreements between the EU and EFTA nations were signed in 1973, tariff liberalization was a minor part of intra-European economic integration (see Chapter 1 for details).

Since the mid-1970s – and especially since the 1986 Single European Act – most of the economic integration in Europe has involved the removal of 'frictional' barriers to trade. As Chapter 4 explained, this type of barrier hinders trade without raising revenue. Frictional barriers often involve intricate differences between national regulations, so a critical frictional-barrier-liberalizing element of the 1986–92 Single Market Programme was the mutual recognition principle that made it difficult for EU members to use health, safety and environmental regulations as subtle forms of trade barrier.

This section extends the basic Figure 5.4 reasoning in a way that allows us to study the impact of preferential frictional barriers liberalization. At a basic level, this is easy to do since frictional barriers can be conceptualized as tariffs where the tariff revenue is thrown away. As we shall see, for such barriers Smith's certitude and Haberler's spillover still hold, but Viner's ambiguity disappears.

5.4.1 Price and quantity effects

To keep things simple, we continue to work with the simplified reality of three nations, and we assume that they all initially impose a frictional barrier whose tariff equivalent is T. Note that the 'tariff equivalent' is a useful way of measuring the importance of a frictional barrier since it identifies the size of the tariff, T, that would drive an equivalent wedge between the border price and the Home price.

To be specific, we assume that Home and Partner fully remove the frictional barrier on each other with no change in the frictional barrier applied to RoW–Home or Partner–RoW trade. In this sense it is a preferential frictional barrier liberalization.

Not surprisingly, the price and quantity effects of the preferential liberalization are very similar to those discussed in Figure 5.2. After all, a frictional barrier can be thought of as a tariff where the tariff revenue is thrown away. The only change concerns the border price.

As discussed in Chapter 4, the importer's and exporter's border prices differ with a frictional barrier. In particular, the importer's border price (i.e. what the importing nation actually pays for the imports) is higher than that of the exporter's border price (i.e. what the exporter actually gets paid for the export). In particular, the difference is T and it reflects the real costs involved in overcoming the frictional barrier. Given this, frictional barrier liberalization lowers Home's border price while at the same time raising the border price faced by Partner's exporters.

Using the Figure 5.7 terms, the reciprocal, preferential frictional barrier liberalization:

- lowers Home's domestic price from P' to P'';
- lowers Home's border price from P' to P'';
- raises the price received by Partner exporters from $P'' - T$ to P'';
- lowers the price received by RoW exporters from $P' - T$ to $P'' - T$.

The quantity effects follow from the price changes. Namely:

- Home imports rise from M' to M''.
- Partner exports rise from X'_P to X''_P.
- RoW exports fall from X'_R to X''_R.

Combining the last two, we see that supply switching still occurs.

5.4.2 Welfare effects

The welfare effects on Home are simple. As with tariffs, the change in Home private surplus equals areas $F + A$ in Figure 5.9. This is not offset by a loss in tariff revenues, as was the case in Figure 5.4; this is why Viner's ambiguity fails in the frictional barrier case. Removing frictional barriers – even on a preferential

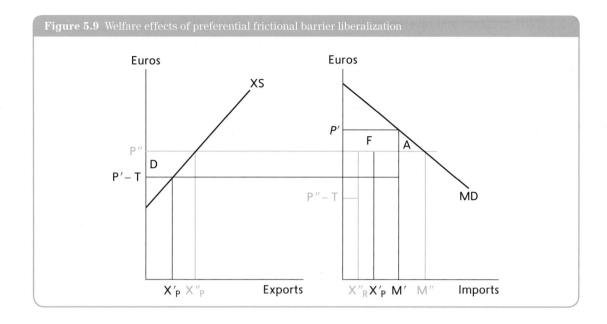

Figure 5.9 Welfare effects of preferential frictional barrier liberalization

basis – always lowers the price that the nation pays for its imports. Although both Partner and RoW exporters see changes in the prices they receive for exports to Home, and this leads to supply switching, this 'trade diversion' has no welfare consequences for Home.

Since we are looking at a reciprocal liberalization like the Single European Act, we have to also consider the changes that affect Home's and RoW's exporters to Partner (i.e. in the good-2 market using the Figure 5.6 labels). In this market, Home is an exporter to Partner, and the welfare effect is also positive. Home exporters get a higher price and sell more, so they gain the area D.

Thus the overall welfare effect of the reciprocal, preferential frictional barrier liberalization FTA is +D + F + A for Home, and the same for Foreign by symmetry. RoW loses the equivalent of area E from Figure 5.4 twice (once on its exports to Home and once on its exports to Partner). A key point is that Viner's ambiguity has disappeared. With frictional barriers, any kind of liberalization will lead to positive border price effects and positive trade volume effects since the border price equals the domestic price with frictional barriers.

5.5 Deep regionalism, the Eurozone and 'soft preferences'

Apart from those on agricultural products, EU tariffs are very low, and indeed nations around the world have lowered tariffs substantially. Nevertheless, EU external trade liberalization is proceeding by focusing on 'beyond-tariff' issues – things that are very much related to the Single Market reforms discussed in Chapters 1 and 2.

Regional integration initiatives that go beyond mere tariff cutting are called 'deep' trade agreements. With so many non-EU nations signing deep agreements, new thinking has developed about the impact of these nominally 'preferential' trade agreements. One very recent example is the Trans-Atlantic Trade and Investment Partnership (TTIP) between the EU and the USA (see Box 5.5, later in this chapter). The logic presented in the preceding chapters can be used to analyse the likely effects.

If the TTIP is signed and implemented, its effect on trade is projected to differ substantially from the traditional three effects: Smith's certitude, Haberler's spillover, and Viner's ambiguity (see Egger et al. (2014) for a detailed analysis). The key is to view the beyond-tariff liberalizations as if they were frictional barrier changes of the type studied in Figure 5.9, but with some new elements. As it turns out, intuition is best developed by considering a very different change – the introduction of the euro.

5.5.1 Trade creation and reverse trade diversions: trade effects of the euro

The common currency lowered the cost of, say, French firms doing business in Germany. For one thing, they no longer had to hold two bank accounts (one for French francs and one for deutschemarks). For another, the firms didn't have to worry about exchange rate changes, or changing money. Plainly, we can think of this as a reduction of a frictional barrier, as studied in Figure 5.9. But this is not the end of the story.

The euro also made it easier for third-nation firms – say, Japanese or British firms – to do business with Eurozone members. Before the euro, a Japanese firm that wanted to sell specialized GPS sports watches in Germany would have had to establish a bank account in Germany and set up internal arrangements to deal with the deutschmarks it received. For a market the size of Germany this might be worthwhile, but for one the size of Austria, the Japanese firm might not find all this effort worthwhile. The euro's introduction, however, removed the extra cost. The monetary union makes it possible to sell in euros to all Eurozone markets at no extra cost. In this way, we can think of the euro – which otherwise might be thought of as a preferential economic integration – as a non-discriminatory removal of frictional barriers.

This is 'reverse trade diversion'. That is to say, the euro's introduction boosted French–German trade by lowering costs, but it did not do so at the expense of third-nation firms. The seemingly preferential change actually boosted EU imports from third nations rather than decreasing them, as the supply-switching logic would have led us to believe. Another interesting outcome is that, by getting third-nation firms – like the Japanese GPS manufacturer – used to using euros, it actually became easier for EU firms to export to Japan. Empirical estimates of the trade effects of the euro confirm that these trade creation and reverse trade creation effects actually occurred. See the VoxEU column by Frankel (2008) for details.

5.5.2 Trade effects of TTIP

Policy changes that lead to such effects have been called 'soft preferences' to distinguish them from the hard preference we saw when tariffs were removed preferentially (e.g. the analysis in Figure 5.1).[1] Consider what soft preferences might look like under the sort of regulatory convergence that is an important part of the TTIP negotiating agenda (see Box 5.5).

Box 5.5   The Trans-Atlantic Trade and Investment Partnership

The EU and the USA account for nearly half the world's income and output. Bilateral trade in goods and services is worth 2 billion euros a day. They have fairly similar economic and political structures and values but both worry about their competitive positions in a world of emerging economies, most notably China, India, Russia and Brazil. In this light, a trans-Atlantic trade deal seems quite natural and indeed it attracted head-of-state level interest on both sides of the ocean.

The Transatlantic Trade and Investment Partnership (TTIP) was launched in June 2013 with a view to concluding a deal that addresses a broad range of bilateral trade and investment issues. Originally the agreement was to be struck within two years – but the deadline keeps moving. In 2014 no end was in sight and the deal was struggling with political opposition in both Europe and the USA – especially as expressed by the US Congress. It remains to be seen whether the TTIP will get a new lease of life or be shelved by the new European Commission and the USA after its midterm elections.

But what is there to liberalize? The EU and the USA lowered most tariffs during the 60 years of GATT talks (GATT, General Agreement on Tariffs and Trade, is what the WTO used to be called) and may lower them further if the current WTO talks ever conclude (WTO talks that were supposed to finish within a three-year period are now into their thirteenth year). Three-quarters of EU imports from the USA pay tariffs of under 2.5 per cent and 40 pay no tariff at all. In the other direction, the numbers are 77 per cent (US tariffs under 2.5 per cent on EU goods) and 50 per cent (already duty free).

---

[1]   See Baldwin (2014) for details and more examples.

The answer is found in European history. As so often happens in global trade matters, the TTIP negotiators are broaching issues that were tackled inside the EU almost three decades ago. The EU discovered that its 1968 customs union was not enough to ensure free trade since tariffs are often not the biggest trade barriers. The whole Single European Act was premised on the idea that freeing commerce within Europe required tackling many 'behind the border barriers' (BBBs). Likewise, the main obstacles to greater trans-Atlantic commerce (trade, services, investment, etc.) are regulatory. Recent estimates suggest that these obstacles act like 20–30 per cent tariffs – in other words, tariff-free does not mean free trade.

With this precedent in mind, the TTIP is trying to tackle barriers by: substantively reducing duties and tariffs on agricultural and industrial goods; opening service markets so that EU and US firms can compete on equal terms; allowing firms to bid for public contracts; improving access and transparency on government purchases; enabling EU firms to import energy and other raw materials from the USA; and ensuring that specialized food and drink products from regions in the EU can be marketed as such in the USA.

Source: Based on Wilton Park (2014)

If the EU and USA adopt one standard on, for example, automotive air-conditioners, EU and US air-conditioner firms will get lower-cost access to each other's markets since they only have to produce to one standard instead of two. Apart from eliminating extra paperwork, testing and certification, the longer production runs should reduce average costs too due to greater scale economies (Chapter 6 covers these in detail). In Figure 5.10 this is shown by the dark arrows indicating a reduction in regulatory-linked trade costs among TTIP members (the USA and EU).

Importantly, the regulations for things like air-conditioners are not nation-specific. That is, the test is whether an air-conditioner meets the standard – regardless of where it is made. Thus, firms in other nations also gain lower-cost access since now they too only have to produce to one standard for both the EU and US markets. This means that non-TTIP firms also benefit from accessing TTIP markets – even though the policy change was wrought in a bilateral agreement. This is shown in Figure 5.10 by the light blue

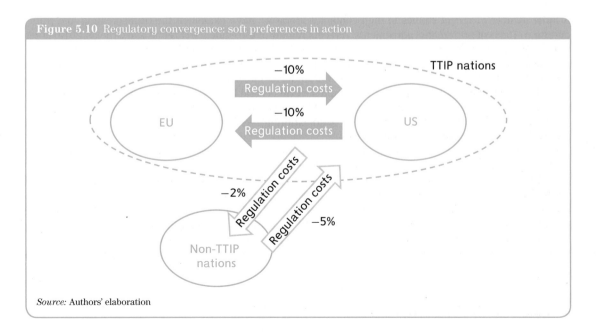

Figure 5.10 Regulatory convergence: soft preferences in action

Source: Authors' elaboration

arrow from a non-TTIP nation to TTIP nations. Finally, as the non-TTIP firms adapt to the new harmonized standard it is very likely that TTIP firms will have an easier time than before in selling to non-TTIP nations.

The numbers in the diagram are illustrative, but they are not too far off the numbers being used to simulate the impact of the TTIP (see Egger et al., 2014).

5.6 WTO rules

The world trading system is governed by a set of rules overseen by the World Trade Organization (WTO). The most important guiding principle of the GATT/WTO is non-discrimination in trade policy, i.e. the so-called most favoured nation principle, or MFN for short. This says that nations should, in principle, impose tariffs on a non-discriminatory basis. Of course, all of the preferential liberalization discussed above contradicts this principle – so why is it allowed? As it turns out, the GATT created an explicit loophole for FTAs and customs unions. Allowing this loophole was important for some of the early GATT members since they wished to maintain existing preferential arrangements (especially Britain's Commonwealth Preferences).

The loophole, formally known as Article 24, specifically allows preferential liberalization, subject to a few restrictions, the most important of which are:

- Free trade agreements and customs unions must completely eliminate tariffs on 'substantially all trade' among members.
- The phase-out of tariffs must take place within a reasonable period.

Although there are no hard definitions, 'substantially all trade' is usually taken to mean at least 80 per cent of all goods and a 'reasonable period' is taken to be ten years or less.

For a customs union, there is the additional requirement that the common external tariff (CET) 'shall not on the whole be higher or more restrictive' than before the customs union. That is, when forming the customs union, the members cannot harmonize the CET to the highest level of any member. In the case of the EEC's customs union formation, external tariff harmonization generally involved a reduction in French and Italian tariffs, a rise in Benelux tariffs and little change in German tariffs.

5.7 Empirical studies of supply switching

A large number of recent studies in the economics literature have examined the trade-creating and trade-diverting effects of preferential agreements. A recent review of the evidence (Freund and Ornelas, 2010) notes that most studies find evidence of trade creation and little or no evidence of trade diversion for most RTAs.

However, the EU may be an exception. Magee (2008) uses data from the late twentieth century to estimate the creation/diversion effects of 15 separate RTAs including NAFTA, the 1986 enlargement of the EU, and 1992 bilateral RTAs between the EU and several central European nations. Of the eight RTAs that were found to have positive trade creation effects, only two were found to be trade-diverting. Those two were the 1986 EU enlargement, and the EU Association agreements with central and eastern European countries in the early 1990s.

A more recent study using twenty-first century data measures trade creation and diversion for many RTAs around the world (Acharya et al., 2011). Their estimates show that most RTAs – including the EU and EFTA – had positive trade-creation effects and reverse trade-diversion effects, i.e. the RTAs raised the partners' imports from each other and from nations outside the agreement. This is not consistent with our study of the economic effects of a preferential tariff liberalization; however, it is consistent with the idea that many of today's RTAs – especially the EU and EFTA – are really pursuing frictional barrier liberalization that tends not to be discriminatory for the reasons discussed in Section 5.5.

For a recent discussion of the evidence, see the VoxEU.org column by Jeffery Bergstrand (2008), which explains some of the technical difficulties involved in estimating the impact of trade agreements.

The impact of deep RTAs on trade is more recently examined in empirical work. The seminal paper here is that of Orefice and Rocha (2014), who show that deep RTAs tend to foster trade in production networks among their members, with the average effect being 12 percentage points. They also note that their findings (linking production sharing and deep RTAs) help to explain the seemingly paradoxical rise of deep integration while preference margins are shrinking. The idea is that partners are not primarily exchanging market access, they are eliminating beyond-tariff barriers to trade and investment.

Complementary findings are presented by Acharya et al. (2011) – see Figure 5.11. Their estimates, which are based on the period after the massive unilateral tariff liberalization that was largely completed, show a curious pattern of trade creation and diversion. The estimated trade creation and diversion are plotted in Figure 5.11.

Figure 5.11 Recent estimates of trade creation and trade diversion

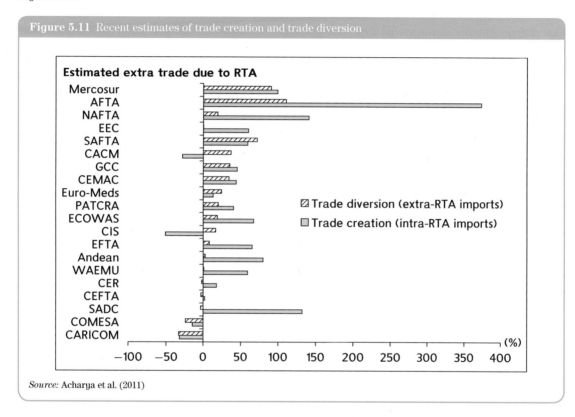

Source: Acharya et al. (2011)

The most striking finding is that almost all the RTAs have led to reverse trade diversion, i.e. external trade creation. This makes no sense in the old Vinerian analytic framework since the tariff preference for partners is tariff discrimination for third nations. Rather, we see that the RTAs are creating trade for members and non-members alike.

The most likely explanation is that the RTAs are liberalizing frictional barriers in a way that lowers them for all, but more for members than non-members. Taken together, this suggests that RTAs are acting more like general trade liberalization schemes – but schemes that are slanted toward members. In the case of COMESA and CARICOM, the RTAs seem to be acting as general trade restriction schemes.

A different tack is taken by Antràs and Foley (2011). They analyse the impact of the ASEAN FTA (AFTA) on the level and nature of US multinational firms' activity. They find that the FTA boosted the number of US firms investing in AFTA, boosted the size of the affiliates and increased the sales of these affiliates within ASEAN markets. While this is not a direct connection between twenty-first century RTAs and supply-chain trade, it illustrates how RTAs can have effects via very non-Vinerian channels, in this case investment.

Summary

The empirical evidence suggests that tariff preferences are no longer the dominant aspect of regionalism in the twenty-first century. Studies carried out with recent data find that RTAs are associated with modest trade-creation and reverse trade-diversion. This suggests that standard Viner analysis is incorrect or incomplete.

The most likely explanation is that the combination of GATT negotiations and unilateral liberalization by developing nations has greatly reduced the importance of tariff preferences. Thus we should think of RTAs less in terms of tariff preferences and more in terms of their impact on frictional barriers and twenty-first century trade disciplines. The few papers that directly test the impact of twenty-first century trade agreements concur on the fact that deep RTAs tend to foster and be fostered by twenty-first century trade.

5.8 Summary

This chapter introduced the verbal logic and graphical methods necessary to study preferential trade liberalization in an NICNIR setting. After going over the preliminaries, we studied the price and quantity and welfare effects of the formation of a customs union. The main technical points are:

- Formation of a preferential trade arrangement, such as the EEC's customs union or EFTA's free trade area, tends to lower domestic prices and raise imports overall, but the discriminatory aspects of these liberalizations also produce supply switching, that is to say, a switch from non-member suppliers to member-based suppliers.

- The welfare effects of any trade liberalization, including RTA liberalization, can be captured by standard public-finance concepts, which we here call trade volume effects and border price (or trade price) effects.

- The welfare impact of preferential tariff liberalization is ambiguous for the liberalizing nations; this is called Viner's ambiguity. The deep fundamental reason is that RTAs are discriminatory liberalizations; the liberalization part – what Viner called trade creation – tends to boost economic efficiency, while the discrimination part – what Viner called trade diversion – tends to lower it. The impact on excluded nations is always negative.

- Estimates of the welfare impact of trade liberalization in the NICNIR setting are inevitably very small. This suggests to most observers that one has to look to more complicated frameworks if one is to understand why trade liberalization in general, and European integration in particular, matter.

The bigger lessons from the chapter concern the way in which the economic analysis helps us to understand the big-think trends in European integration. The NICNIR framework helped us to study the impact of discriminatory liberalization on outsiders in an intellectually uncluttered setting. This helps us to understand why outsiders always reacted to the deepening and widening of EU integration. As we showed, preferential liberalization definitely harms excluded nations since it leads them to face lower prices for their exports to the customs union and lower export sales. It seems natural, therefore, that the outsiders would react either by forming their own preferential arrangements (as happened in the 1960s with EFTA), or by deepening the integration between outsiders and the EU (as outsiders did in the 1970s and again in the 1990s), or by joining the EU (as nine formerly outsider western European nations had done by 1994).

Self-assessment questions

The NICNIR was the backbone of 'customs union theory' for years, so quite a number of extensions and provisos were put forth in the NICNIR setting. Some of them are still insightful and the following exercises illustrate the basic points.

1 (Kemp–Wan theorem) Starting from a situation like that shown in Figure 5.1, where the three nations are symmetric in everything, including the initial MFN tariff T, suppose that Home and Partner form a customs union *and* lower their common tariff against RoW to the point where the new, post-liberalization border price facing RoW exporters is the same as it was before the liberalization, i.e. $P' - T$. Show that this 'Kemp–Wan' adjustment ensures that Home and Partner gain while RoW does not lose from this CU-with-CET-reduction scheme.

2 (Cooper–Massell extended) We can think of a preferential unilateral liberalization in the following roundabout manner. Home lowers its tariffs to zero on an MFN basis, but then raises it back to T on imports only from RoW. Now suppose that Home faces a flat MS curve for imports from both Partner and RoW (this is the 'small country' case). Moreover, suppose that Partner's MS is somewhat above that of RoW's.

   First work out the welfare effects on Home. (Hint: This is covered in the Annex.)

   Second, show that Home would gain more from a unilateral MFN liberalization than it would from a unilateral preferential liberalization. (Historical note: Taking their NICNIR analysis as definitive, this result led Cooper and Massell to suggest that small countries must join customs unions for political reasons only. You can see that this is only a partial analysis by realizing that a customs union also lowers tariffs facing Home-based exporters.) Try to figure out how Home gains from Partner's tariff removal on Home-to-Partner exports. After doing this, see if you can say definitely whether Home gains more from unilateral free trade or from joining the customs union. You should also be able to show that the optimal policy for a small nation is to have unilateral free trade *and* join every FTA that it can.

3 (Large partner rule of thumb) Redo the FTA formation exercise from the text, assuming that RoW is initially a much smaller trading partner of Home and Partner in the sense that most of Home's imports are from Partner and most of Partner's imports are from Home when all three nations impose the initial MFN tariff, T. Show that the 'net border price effect' (area $B - C_1 - C_2$ in Figure 5.8) is smaller when RoW is initially a less important trade partner of Home and Partner nations. (Hint: Focus on the Home country and start with a diagram like Figure 5.1. Keep the vertical intersections of XS_P and XS_R at the same height, but make the XS_R steeper and the XS_P flatter in a way that does not change P''; our thanks to Jonathan Gage for help with this problem.)

4 (Growth effects and RoW impact) Suppose that signing an FTA between Home and Partner produces a growth effect that raises their income level and thus shifts their MD curves upwards. Use a diagram like Figure 5.4 to show how big the upward shift would have to be to ensure that RoW did not lose from the Home–Partner FTA. (In the 1970s, this was the informal explanation for why the EEC6 formation did not lead to trade diversion.) Can you show the welfare impact of this growth on Home?

5 (Hub-and-spoke bilateralism) Using RTA diagrams, show what the price, quantity and welfare effects would be of a hub-and-spoke arrangement among three nations. (Hub-and-spoke means that country 1 signs FTAs with countries 2 and 3, but 2 and 3 do not liberalize trade between them.) Assume that there are *only* frictional barriers in this world, that initially all import barriers have a tariff equivalent of T, and that the FTAs concern only frictional barrier liberalization. Be sure to look at the price, quantity and welfare impact on (i) a typical spoke economy (2 or 3) and (ii) the hub economy.

6 (Sapir, 1992) Consider a situation in which Home and Partner have formed a customs union but have not eliminated frictional barriers between them. Specifically, assume that all trade flows among Home, Partner and RoW are subject to frictional trade barriers equal to T' and additionally the tariff on trade between the CU and RoW is equal to T''. Show that eliminating frictional barriers inside the CU might harm welfare since it leads to a reduction in the amount of tariff revenue collected on imports from RoW.

7 Suppose Home has no trade barriers, except anti-dumping measures. These antidumping measures take the form of price undertakings, i.e. instead of Home imposing a tariff on RoW and Partner imports, Home requires Partner and RoW firms to charge a high price for their sales to Home. Show the price, quantity and welfare effects of imposing this import price floor (look at all three nations). Next, show the price, quantity and welfare effects of removing the price undertaking (i.e. allowing free trade) only for imports from Partner. Be sure to illustrate the impact on all three nations. (Hint: The price undertaking is a price floor, so it does not act just like a tariff; be very careful in constructing the MS_{RTA} for this situation.)

Further reading: the aficionado's corner

The modern study of European economic integration began life under the name of 'customs union theory' with **Viner** (1950). Viner's seminal text triggered a flood of work. At the time, tariffs were the key trade barriers and theorists had few tools for dealing with imperfect competition, so the early literature focused on tariff removals in the NICNIR setting. For a highly readable survey of this literature, see:

Pomfret, R. (1986) 'The theory of preferential trading arrangements', *Weltwirtschaftliches Archiv*, 122: 439–64.

A review of pre-Vinerian literature is provided by:

O'Brien, D.P. (1975) 'Classical monetary theory', in *The Classical Economists*, Clarendon Press, Oxford, pp. 140–69.

Following Viner's theory, which associated welfare effects with changes in trade flows, early empirical studies focused on trade creation and diversion. Surveys of this literature include:

Mayes, D. (1978) 'The effects of economic integration on trade', *Journal of Common Market Studies*, XVII: 1–25.

Srinivasan, T.N., J. Whalley and I. Wooton (1993) 'Measuring the effects of regionalism on trade and welfare', in K. Anderson and R. Blackhurst (eds) *Regional Integration and the Global Trading System*, Harvester Wheatsheaf for the GATT Secretariat, London, pp. 52–79.

Winters, L.A. (1987) 'Britain in Europe: a survey of quantitative trade studies', *Journal of Common Market Studies*, 25: 315–35.

A more extensively graphic presentation of pre- and post-1958 trade flows in Europe can be found in:

Neal, L. and D. Berbezat (1998) *The Economics of the European Union and the Economics of Europe*, Oxford University Press, London.

See also:

Baldwin, R.E. and A. Venables (1995) 'Regional economic integration', in G. Grossman and K. Rogoff (eds) *Handbook of International Economics*, Volume III, North-Holland, Amsterdam.

Mankiw, G. (2000) *Principles of Economics*, Thomson Learning, New York.

Useful websites

While the EU's customs union has been completed for over three decades, some policy issues occasionally arise. See the Commission's website for details: http://europa.eu.int/comm/taxationcustoms/.

The history of EFTA's free trade area can be found at www.efta.int/.

Further information on WTO rules concerning preferential trade arrangements can be found at www.wto.org.

References

Acharya, R., J.-C. Crawford, M. Maliszewski and C. Renard (2011) 'Landscape', in J.-P. Chauffour and J.-C. Maur (eds) *Preferential Trade Agreement Policies for Development: A Handbook*, World Bank Publications, Washington, DC, Chapter 2.

Antràs and C.F. Foley (2011) 'Poultry in motion: a study of international trade finances practices', NBER Working Papers 17091, National Bureau of Economic Research, In.

Baldwin, R. (2006) *In or Out: Does it Matter? An Evidence-based Analysis of the Trade Effects of the Euro*, Centre for Economic Policy Research, London.

Baldwin, R. (2014) 'The impact of mega-regionals: the economic impact', in *Mega-regional Trade Agreements: Game-changers or Costly Distractions for the World Trading System?*, World Economic Forum, July.

Bergstrand, J. (2008) 'How much has European economic integration actually increased members' trade?', VoxEU.org, 6 September, http://www.voxeu.org/article/european-economic-integration-and-trade-how-big-was-boost.

Brenton, P. and M. Manchin (2003) 'Making EU trade agreements work: the role of rules of origin', *The World Economy*, 26(5): 755–69.

Carpenter, T. and A. Lendle (2010) 'How preferential is world trade?', CTEI Papers, No. 2010-32, http://graduateinstitute.ch/files/live/sites/iheid/files/sites/ctei/shared/CTEI/working_papers/CTEI-2010-32.pdf.

Cooper, C. and D. Massell (1965) 'Towards a general theory of customs unions in developing countries', *Journal of Political Economy*, 73: 256–83.

Frankel, J. (2008) 'The euro at ten: why do effects on trade between members appear smaller than historical estimates among smaller countries?', VoxEU.org, 24 December.

Freund, C. and E. Ornelas (2010) *Regional Trade Agreements*, Policy Research Working Paper Series 5314, World Bank.

Haberler, G. (1937) *The Theory of International Trade with its Applications to Commercial Policy*, Macmillan, New York.

Kemp, M. and H. Wan (1976) 'An elementary proposition concerning the formation of customs unions', *Economic Journal*, 6: 95–97.

Magee, C.S.P. (2008) 'New measures of trade creation and trade diversion', *Journal of International Economics*, 75(2): 340–62.

Meade, J. (1955) *The Theory of Customs Unions*, Oxford University Press, London.

Orefice, G. and N. Rocha (2014) 'Deep integration and production networks: an empirical analysis', *World Economy*, 37(1): 106–36.

Panagariya, A. (1999) 'Preferential trade liberalization: the traditional theory and new developments', *Journal of Economic Literature*, 37: 287–331.

Pomfret, R. (1997) *The Economics of Regional Trading Arrangements*, Clarendon Press, London.

Sapir, A. (1992) 'Regional integration in Europe', *Economic Journal*, 102(415): 1491–506.

Viner, J. (1950) *The Customs Union Issue*, Carnegie Endowment for International Peace, New York.

Wilton Park (2014) 'Transatlantic Trade and Investment Partnership (TTIP)', Wilton Park Conference report, 17–18 February, WP No. 1307, https://www.wiltonpark.org.uk/conference/wp1307/.

Annex: Discriminatory liberalization: small country case

This Annex presents the classic analysis of unilateral preferential tariff liberalization for the so-called 'small country' case. Here 'small country' means nothing more than ignoring the price effects on all foreign nations – Partner and RoW alike. In particular, simplifying means that the import supply curve (MS) in Figure A5.1 is flat so the world price never changes. In this case, we do not need the MS–MD diagram discussed above.

Figure A5.1, which allows for two potential sources of imports (countries A and B), helps to organize the reasoning. To set the stage, suppose that Home initially imposes a tariff of T on imports from A and B. (Goods produced in the countries A, B and Home are perfect substitutes.) The Home nation is assumed to face a flat import supply curve from both countries. The idea behind this simplification is that Home is so small that it can buy as much or as little as it wants without affecting the price. Specifically, the import supply curves from A and B are the flat curves at the levels P_A and P_B. We can see that country A producers are more efficient since they can offer the goods at a lower price. That is, importing from A costs Home consumers $P_A + T$, while importing from B costs $P_B + T$. Plainly, all imports initially come from the cheaper supplier, namely, A.

Adding together the three sources of supply (Home, A and B), we find the pre-liberalization total supply curve to be TS_1. Because it is the horizontal sum of the Home supply curve and the two import supply curves, it follows the Home supply curve up to $P_A + T$ and, beyond that, it follows A's import supply curve. The equilibrium Home price (i.e. the price facing Home consumers and producers) is $P_A + T$, since this is where total supply meets demand. The border price, namely, the price that Home as a country pays for imports, is P_A.

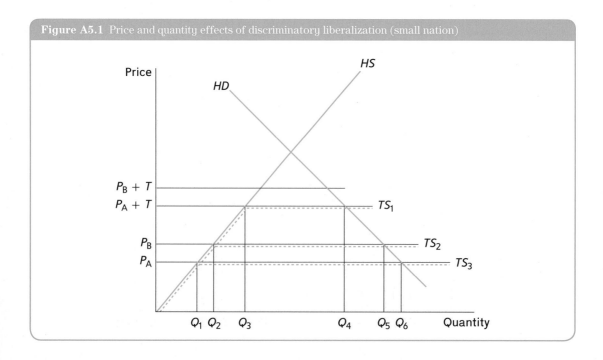

Figure A5.1 Price and quantity effects of discriminatory liberalization (small nation)

Next, we ask what would happen if the tariff were removed on a discriminatory basis; that is to say, if it were removed on imports from only A or only B. Both cases must be considered. We turn now to the price, quantity and welfare effects of the two cases.

A5.1 Price and quantity analysis, liberalization with low-cost country

In the first case, the liberalization is applied to Home's current trading partner, namely, A. The total supply curve becomes TS_3, so the Home price falls to P_A. Home consumption rises, Home production falls, imports rise and nothing happens to the border price of imports. To summarize:

- The price in the Home market of both imports and Home import-competing goods falls to P_A.
- Home production falls from Q_3 to Q_1.

  Home consumption rises from Q_4 to Q_6.

- The import volume rises from the difference between Q_3 and Q_4 to the difference between Q_1 and Q_6.
- The border price (i.e. the price of imported goods before the imposition of the tax) remains unchanged at P_A.

With some thought, it is clear that discriminatory liberalization with the low-cost country has the same impact as an MFN liberalization. After all, both types of liberalization remove the tariff on all imports (the preferential tariff cut leaves the tariff on goods from B, but no imports come from B before or after the liberalization).

A5.2 Welfare analysis: liberalization with low-cost country

As with the price and quantity analysis, in this case the welfare analysis is identical to that of non-discriminatory liberalization. Home consumer surplus rises and Home producer surplus falls because of the liberalization. Since more units are consumed than produced domestically, the sum of consumer and producer surpluses rises. Part of this gain is offset by a loss in tariff revenue. Using Figure A5.2 to be more precise:

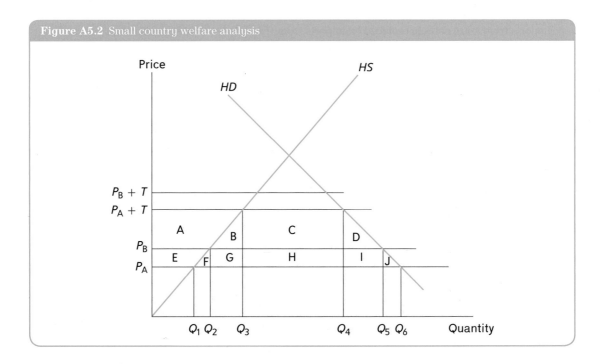

Figure A5.2 Small country welfare analysis

- Consumer surplus rises by the sum of all areas, A through J.
- Producer surplus falls by the area A + E.
- Government revenue falls by C + H.
- The net effect is unambiguously positive and equal to (B + F + G) and (D + I + J).

A5.3 Liberalization with high-cost country: supply switching

The analysis is only slightly trickier when the preferential trade arrangement is signed with the high-cost country.

Graphically, as shown in Figure A5.1, this results in a total supply curve of TS_2 and a Home price of P_B. Recall that since country B is the high-cost supplier (i.e. P_B is above P_A) nothing was imported from B initially. Granting duty-free access to goods from B artificially changes the relative competitiveness of goods from A and B – at least in the eyes of Home consumers. Goods from B cost P_B while goods from A cost $P_A + T$. Quite naturally, Home importers of goods will divert all their import demand from A towards B. We call this the 'supply-switching' effect of discriminatory liberalization; it is the first of two elements that arise with discriminatory liberalization but do not arise with non-discriminatory liberalization. Note, however, that discriminatory liberalization does not always lead to supply switching. It can only do so when it is done with the high-cost country.

The second novel aspect of discriminatory liberalization is the border price impact. That is, as consumers switch from the low-cost source to the high-cost source (country B), the Home border price rises. We call this the 'border price' effect, or the import-price-rising effect. The importance of this price change should be clear – such liberalization will raise the cost of imports to the country as a whole.

To summarize, there are six price and quantity effects:

1 The preferential liberalization increases competition from imports and thereby forces down the Home price of locally made and imported goods to P_B.
2 Consumption rises to Q_5.
3 Some high-cost Home production is replaced by lower-cost imports. This amount is equal to $Q_3 - Q_2$.
4 The new Home production level is Q_2.
5 Imports from A are entirely replaced by imports from B and the level of imports rises.
6 The border price rises. That is to say, Home now pays more for its imports (namely, P_B) than it did before (namely, P_A).

A5.4 Welfare analysis: liberalization with high-cost country

When the tariffs come down only on imports from the country that initially sells nothing to Home, the welfare effects turn out to be ambiguous. To summarize using Figure A5.2, there are three welfare effects of a discriminatory liberalization of a tariff (or any DCR barrier):

1 Home consumers gain the area A + B + C + D.
2 Home producers lose area A.
3 All tariff revenue is lost. This lowers Home welfare; the change being $-C - H$.

The net effect is B + D − H. This may be positive or negative; discriminatory tariff liberalization therefore has ambiguous welfare effects. This is the so-called Viner ambiguity. Notice that the net welfare impact depends only on the change in the quantity of imports (which rises in this case) and the change in the price of imports (which also rises in this case).

The countries of Europe are too small to give their peoples the prosperity that is now attainable and therefore necessary. They need wider markets.

Jean Monnet, 1943

By its size – the biggest in the world – the single market without frontiers is an invaluable asset to revitalize our businesses and make them more competitive. It is one of the main engines of the European Union.

Jacques Delors, July 1987

Market size and scale effects

Chapter Contents

Introduction

Market size matters. From its very inception in the 1950s, an important premise behind European economic integration was the belief that unification of European economies would – by allowing European firms access to a bigger market – make European firms more efficient and this, in turn, would allow them to lower prices, raise quality and gain competitiveness in external markets.

This chapter explores the economic logic of how European integration can lead to fewer, larger firms operating at a more efficient scale and facing more effective competition. The EU policy responses to these changes – notably the enforcement of rules that prohibit unfair subsidization of firms and rules restricting anti-competitive behaviour – are studied in Chapter 11. In the EU, such policies are called, respectively, 'state aids' policy and 'competition policy'.

6.1 Liberalization, defragmentation and industrial restructuring: logic and facts

We start the chapter by verbally explaining the logic that links European integration to industrial restructuring before presenting some facts on mergers and acquisitions (M&As) and the effects on competition.

Europe's national markets are separated by a whole host of barriers. These included tariffs and quotas until the Common Market was completed in 1968 and tariffs between the EEC and EFTA until the EEC–EFTA free trade agreements were signed in 1974. Yet, even though intra-EU trade has been duty free for over three decades, trade among European nations is not as free as it is within any given nation. Many technical, physical and fiscal barriers still make it easier for companies to sell in their local market than in other EU markets. While most of these barriers seem trivial or even silly when considered in isolation, the confluence of thousands of seemingly small barriers serves to substantially restrict intra-EU trade. As a result, EU firms can often be dominant in their home market while being marginal players in other EU markets (think of the European car market). This situation, known as market fragmentation, reduces competition, which, in turn, raises prices and keeps too many firms in business. Keeping firms in business is not, of course, a bad thing in itself. The problem is that it results in an industrial structure marked by too many inefficient small firms that can get away with charging high prices to cover the cost of their inefficiency. Owing to the absence of competition, poor and/or low-quality services and goods may also accompany the high prices (think of the European telephone service before liberalization).

Tearing down these intra-EU barriers defragments the markets and produces extra competition. This 'pro-competitive effect', in turn, puts pressure on profits and the market's response is 'merger mania'. That is, the pro-competitive effect squeezes the least efficient firms, prompting an industrial restructuring whereby Europe's weaker firms merge or are bought out. Ultimately, Europe is left with a more efficient industrial structure, with fewer, bigger, more efficient firms competing more effectively with each other. All this means improved material well-being for Europeans as prices fall and output rises. In some industries, restructuring may be accompanied by a sizeable reallocation of employment, as firms cut back on redundant workers and close inefficient plants and offices (a painful process for workers who have to change jobs). In other industries, however, liberalization can unleash a virtuous circle of more competition, lower prices, higher sales and higher employment.

In the remainder of this chapter we work through the logic of what was just presented informally. Schematically, the steps can be summarized as: liberalization $\rightarrow$ defragmentation $\rightarrow$ pro-competitive effect $\rightarrow$ industrial restructuring. The result is fewer, bigger, more efficient firms facing more effective competition from each other.

6.1.1 Some evidence

As the verbal explanation made clear, the cutting edge of the scale effects turns on the pro-competitive effect and this can be measured by the price–cost ratio. A study of French manufacturing data calculated the price–cost ratio shown in Figure 6.1 (Bellone et al., 2008). The authors calculate that implementation of the Single Market Programme and its follow-up in the Economic and Monetary Union treaty (Maastricht Treaty) lowered the margin by 4 to 5 percentage points.

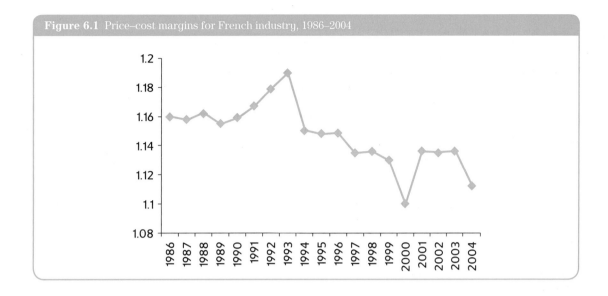

Figure 6.1 Price–cost margins for French industry, 1986–2004

Econometric evidence from Allen et al. (1998a, 1999b) suggests that the Single Market Programme reduced price–cost margins by 4 per cent on average, in line with the estimate for France. This impact varied from quite high, e.g. −15 per cent in the office machinery sector, to quite small, e.g. −0.1 per cent in brewing. It is noteworthy that in the auto sector – a sector that was granted a bloc exemption from the Single Market Programme – the price–cost margin actually rose.

Another study, Badinger (2007), used data on 10 EU Member States over the period 1981–99 for each of 3 major industry groups (manufacturing, construction and services) and 18 more detailed industries to test whether the EU's Single Market Programme reduced firms' price–cost mark-ups, i.e. had a pro-competitive effect. He found mark-up reductions for aggregate manufacturing and construction. In contrast, mark-ups have risen in most service industries since the early 1990s. He suggests that this latter finding confirms the weak state of the Single Market for services and suggests that anti-competitive defence strategies have emerged in EU service industries.

More recently, Chen et al. (2009) found evidence of a pro-competitive effect from economic integration using disaggregated data for EU manufacturing over the period 1989–99. They found that foreign import penetration has a strong competitive effect, with prices and mark-ups falling and productivity rising.

6.2 Theoretical preliminaries: monopoly, duopoly and oligopoly

To study the logic of European integration's impact on scale and competition we need a simple yet flexible framework that allows for imperfect competition. The framework we employ below – the *BE–COMP* diagram – assumes a knowledge of simple imperfect competition models, so by way of preliminaries, we briefly review the simplest forms of imperfect competition – monopoly, duopoly and oligopoly (see Box 6.1 for background on Joan Robinson who pioneered this thinking). Advanced readers may want to skip this section and move directly to the *BE–COMP* diagram in Section 6.3, but since it introduces notation and basic concepts, even advanced readers may find it useful.

As usual, we start with the simplest problem – namely, the decision faced by a firm that has a monopoly. The monopoly case is easy because it avoids strategic interactions. When a firm is the only seller of a product, it can choose how much to sell and what price to charge without considering the reaction of other suppliers. The only restraint a monopolist faces is the demand curve. A downward-sloping demand curve is a constraint because it forces the monopolist to confront a trade-off between price and sales; higher prices mean lower sales. When considering the impact of European integration on imperfectly competitive firms, we need to determine how various policy changes will alter prices and sales. The first step in this direction is to see what determines a monopolist's prices and sales in a closed economy. The natural question then is: 'What is the profit-maximizing level of sales for the monopolist?'

An excellent way to proceed is to make a guess at the optimal level, say, Q' in the left-hand panel of Figure 6.2. Almost surely this initial guess will be wrong, but what we want to know is whether Q' is too low or too high. To this end, we calculate the profit earned when Q' units are sold at the highest obtainable price, namely, P'. The answer is A + B, since the total value of sales is price times quantity (area A + B + C) minus cost (area C).

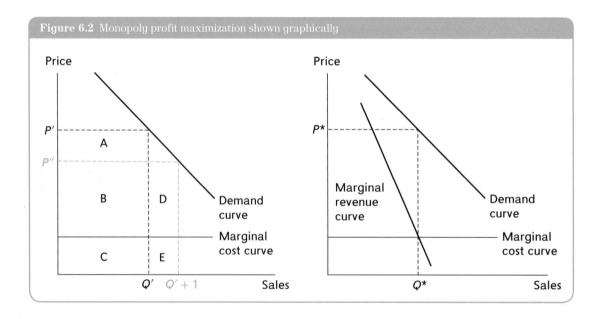

Figure 6.2 Monopoly profit maximization shown graphically

Would profits rise or fall if the firm sold an extra unit? Of course, to sell the extra unit, the firm will have to let its price fall a bit to P''. The change in profit equals the change in revenue minus the change in cost. Consider first the change in revenue. This has two parts. Selling the extra unit brings in extra revenue (represented by areas D + E), but it also depresses the price received for all units sold initially (lowering revenue by an amount equal to area A). The net change in revenue – called 'marginal revenue' for short – is given by the areas D + E minus area A. The change in cost – called marginal cost for short – is area E. Plainly, profit only increases if the extra revenue (D + E – A) exceeds the extra cost E, i.e. if D – A is positive. As it is drawn, D – A appears to be negative, so marginal revenue is less than marginal cost at $Q' + 1$. This means that raising output from Q' would lower profits, so the initial guess of Q' turned out to be too high.

To find the profit-maximizing level using this trial-and-error method, we would consider a lower guess, say, Q' minus 4 units, and repeat the procedure applied above. At the profit-maximizing level, marginal revenue just equals marginal cost. This level must be optimal since any increase or decrease in sales will lower profit. Increasing sales beyond this point will increase cost more than revenue, while decreasing sales would lower revenue more than cost. Both would reduce profit.

The right-hand panel of Figure 6.2 shows an easier way to find the point at which marginal revenue equals marginal cost. The diagram includes a new curve, called the marginal revenue curve. This shows how the marginal revenue (measured in euros) declines as the level of sales rises. (It declines since area A from the left-hand panel gets very small for low levels of sales.) At the sales level marked Q^*, marginal revenue just equals marginal cost. The firm charges the most it can at this level of sales, and this is P^*. These are the profit-maximizing levels of sales and price.

6.2.1 Lessons

Several deep aspects of imperfect competition come through even in the monopoly case. First, in setting up the problem, we had to assume things about the firm's beliefs concerning the behaviour of other economic agents. In this case, the monopolist is assumed to believe that consumers are price-takers and that the trade-off between prices and sales depends only on the demand curve (rather than, for example, on the reaction of firms in other markets). Second, the critical difference between perfect and imperfect competition comes out clearly. As part of the definition, perfectly competitive firms are assumed to take the price of their output as given (a classic example is a wheat farmer who cannot set his own price; he just sells at the current market price). This means that such firms are assumed to be ignorant of the fact that selling more will depress the market price. In terms of the diagram, perfectly competitive firms ignore area A, so they maximize profits by selling an amount where price equals marginal cost. Of course, any increase in sales would have some negative impact on price, so it is best to think of perfect competition as a simplifying assumption that is close to true when all firms have market shares that are close to zero. By stepping away from this simplification, imperfect competition allows firms to explicitly consider the price-depressing effect – area A – when deciding how much to sell.

6.2.2 Duopolist as monopolist on residual demand curve

The monopoly case is instructive, but not very realistic – most European firms face some competition. Taking account of this, however, brings us up against the strategic considerations discussed above. The convention we adopt to sort out this interaction is the so-called Cournot–Nash equilibrium that won John Nash a Nobel prize (see Box 6.2). That is, we assume that each firm acts as if the other firms' outputs are fixed. The equilibrium we are interested in is where each firm's expectations of the other firms' outputs turn out to be correct, i.e. no one is fooled. This no-one-fooled notion proves to be somewhat difficult to comprehend in the abstract but, as we shall see below, it is easy in specific applications.

The residual demand curve shortcut

Since firms take as given the sales of other firms, the only constraint facing a typical firm is the demand curve shifted to the left by the amount of sales of all other firms. In other words, each firm believes it is a monopolist on the shifted demand curve (we called the shifted demand curve the 'residual demand curve'). This realization is handy since it means that we can directly apply the solution technique from the monopolist's problem; the only change is that we calculate the marginal revenue curve based on the residual demand curve instead of the demand curve.

This trick is shown in Figure 6.3 for a competition between two firms producing the same good – a situation that economists call 'duopoly'. For simplicity, we assume that the firms have the same marginal

---

Box 6.2   John Nash (1928–)

© Office of Communications, Princeton University

Early work on imperfect competition (see Box 6.1) was hampered by the problem of strategic interactions among firms. The 'Nash equilibrium' was the concept that cleared away confusions and opened the door to thousands of books and articles on imperfect competition.

The brilliant but troubled creator of the Nash equilibrium concept is a mathematician whose career has attracted an unusual amount of public attention. Since Nash's path-breaking publications have been interspersed with periods of paranoid schizophrenia, Hollywood found it easy to cast him in the cherished stereotype of a mad genius, making his life the subject of a big-budget film entitled *A Beautiful Mind* in 2001. The basis of the Nash equilibrium concept was his 1950 article entitled 'Non-cooperative games'. Just 27 pages long, it earned him the Nobel Prize in economics in 1994. An autobiographical account of his life is available on www.nobel.se/economics/laureates/1994/index.html.

---

cost curves. Taking firm 2's sales as given at Q_2, firm 1 has a monopoly on the residual demand curve labelled RD_1. Firm 1's optimal output in this case is X'_1 (since at point A_1, the residual marginal revenue curve, RMR_1, crosses the marginal cost curve, MC). The right-hand panel shows the same sort of analysis for firm 2. Taking firm 1's output as fixed at Q_1, firm 2's optimal output is X'_2.

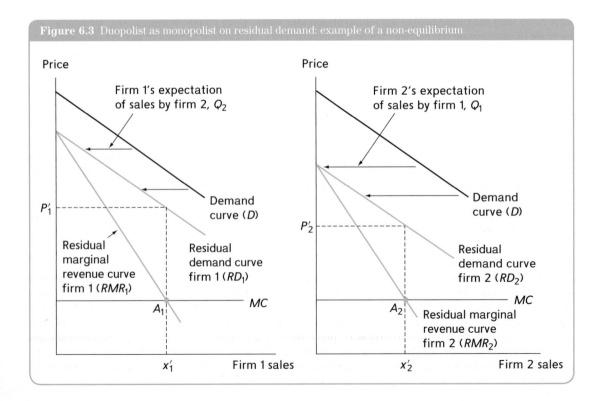

Figure 6.3 Duopolist as monopolist on residual demand: example of a non-equilibrium

Note that the situation in Figure 6.3 is not an equilibrium. To highlight the importance of the difference between expected and actual outcomes, the diagram shows the solutions of the two firms when their expectations about the other firm's output do not match the reality. The consistent-expectations outcome, i.e. the Nash equilibrium, is shown in Figure 6.4, but we first consider why Figure 6.3 is not an equilibrium.

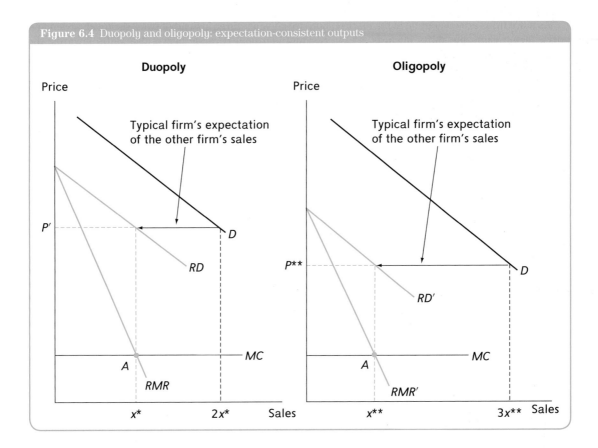

Figure 6.4 Duopoly and oligopoly: expectation-consistent outputs

As drawn, X_1' and X_2' are not a Cournot–Nash equilibrium since the firms' actual output levels do not match expectations; firm 1 produces X_1', which is greater than what firm 2 expected (namely, Q_1), and likewise, firm 2 produces X_2', which is greater than what firm 1 expected (namely, Q_2).

We can also see the problem by observing that the implied prices are not equal. If X_1' and X_2' were actually produced by the firms, then firms would not be able to charge the prices they expected to charge. In other words, this is not an equilibrium because the outcome is not consistent with expectations.

Finding the expectation-consistent equilibrium

How do we find the expectation-consistent set of outputs? The easiest way is to use the assumed symmetry of firms. In the symmetric equilibrium, each firm will sell the same amount. With this fact in mind, a bit of thought reveals that the residual demand curve facing each firm must be half of the overall demand curve. This situation is shown in the left-hand panel of Figure 6.4 for a duopoly. Some facts to note are that: (1) the optimal output for a typical firm is x^*, given by the intersection of RMR and MC; (2) the total sales to the market are $2x^*$ and at this level of sales the overall market price (given by the demand curve, D) is consistent with the price each firm expects to receive given the residual demand curve, RD; and (3) the outputs of the identical firms are equal in equilibrium.

6.2.3 Oligopoly: Cournot–Nash for an arbitrary number of firms

While allowing for two firms was more realistic than allowing for one firm only, studying the impact of European integration on mergers and acquisitions requires us to allow for an arbitrary number of firms. In economists' jargon, this situation is called an oligopoly. As it turns out, this situation is straightforward to deal with when firms are symmetric. The right-hand panel of Figure 6.4 shows the argument for the case of three firms.

As more firms are competing in the market (here we consider three instead of two), the residual demand curve facing each one shifts inwards, so the residual marginal revenue curve also shifts inwards; the new curves are shown in the right-hand panel as RD' and RMR'. The implication of this shift for prices is clear. The new $RMR = MC$ point occurs at a lower level of per-firm output and this implies a lower price. In equilibrium (i.e. where outcomes match expectations), each of the three firms produces an identical amount, identified as x^{**} in the diagram, and charges an identical price, p^{**}.

Given that we have worked through the 1, 2 and 3 firm cases, readers should be able to see what would happen as the number of firms continues to rise. Each increase in the number of competitors will shift inwards the RD facing each one of them. This will inevitably lead to lower prices and lower output per firm.

Of course, this analysis is just formalizing what most readers would expect. If one adds more competitors to a market, prices will fall along with the market share of each firm. As is so often the case, the brilliant concepts are simple.

6.3 The *BE–COMP* diagram in a closed economy

To study the impact of European integration on firm size and efficiency, the number of firms, prices, output and the like, it is useful to have a diagram in which all of these things are determined. The presentation of this diagram, which actually consists of three sub-diagrams, is the first order of business. To keep things simple, we begin with the case of a closed economy. The diagram is an extensive elaboration of one originally used by Nobel Laureate Paul Krugman (see Box 6.3).

Box 6.3   Paul Krugman (1953–)

Photo: M.Olsson, Copyright
© Nobel Media AB (2008)
Nobelprize.org

Building on the work of John Nash (see Box 6.2), Paul Krugman introduced imperfect competition and increasing returns to international trade theory. This introduction profoundly changed the way we think of international trade, so much so that the literature he started is now called the 'new trade theory' (even though Krugman did his early work on this in 1979!).

The *BE–COMP* diagram, which is inspired by a diagram that Krugman called the *PP–CC* diagram, is most closely related to his work with James Brander, a professor at the University of British Columbia (Brander and Krugman, 1983), which focuses on imperfect competition as a cause of trade.

In recent years, Krugman has been widely known for his opinion pieces published in the *New York Times* and his blog at http://krugman.blogs.nytimes.com/.

You can read more about why he got the Nobel Prize at www.voxeu.org/index. php?q=node/2463 or on the Nobel site at http://nobelprize.org/nobel_prizes/economics/laureates/2008/press.html.

Source: www.princeton.edu/~paw/web_exclusives/more/more_06.html

---

The heart of the *BE–COMP* diagram is the sub-diagram in which the number of firms and the profit-maximizing price–cost margin are determined. As usual, the equilibrium will be the intersection of two curves, the *BE* curve and the *COMP* curve. We start by presenting the *COMP* curve.

6.3.1 The *COMP* curve

It is easy to understand that imperfectly competitive firms charge a price that exceeds their marginal cost; they do so in order to maximize profit. But how wide is the gap between price and marginal cost, and how does it vary with the number of competitors? These questions are answered by the *COMP* curve.

If there is only one firm, the price–cost gap – what we call the 'mark-up' of price over marginal cost – will equal the mark-up that a monopolist would charge. If there are more firms competing in the market, competition will force each firm to charge a lower mark-up. We summarize this 'competition-side' relationship between the mark-up and the number of firms as the '*COMP* curve' shown in Figure 6.5. It is downward-sloping since competition drives the mark-up down as the number of competitors rises, as explained above. We denote the mark-up with the Greek letter μ, pronounced mu, since 'mu' is an abbreviation for mark-up. We call it the *COMP* curve since the size of the mark-up is an indicator of how competitive the market is.

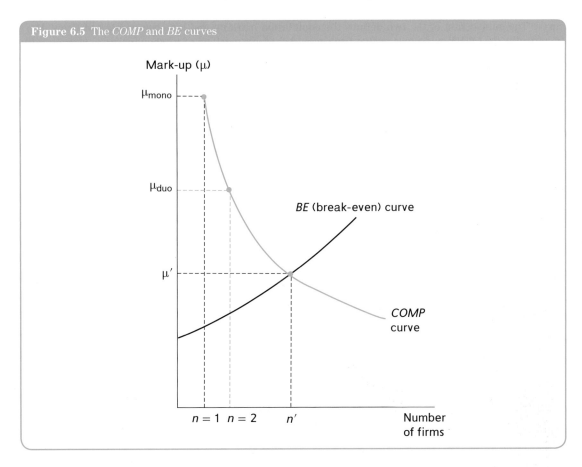

Figure 6.5 The *COMP* and *BE* curves

While this intuitive connection between price and marginal cost may suffice for some readers, extra insight is gained by considering the derivation of the *COMP* curve in more detail. This is done in the Annex.

6.3.2 The break-even (*BE*) curve

The mark-up and number of firms are related in another way, summarized by the *BE* curve.

When a sector is marked by increasing returns to scale, there is only room for a certain number of firms in a market of a given size. Intuitively, more firms will be able to survive if the price is far above marginal cost, i.e. if the mark-up is high. The curve that captures this relationship is called the 'break-even curve', or zero-profit curve (*BE* curve, for short) in Figure 6.5. It has a positive slope since more firms can break even when the mark-up is high. That is to say, taking the mark-up as given, the *BE* curve shows the number of firms that can earn enough to cover their fixed cost, say, the cost of setting up a factory.

Again, this intuitive presentation of the *BE* curve will suffice for many readers, but might well raise questions in the minds of more advanced readers. These questions are addressed in the Annex.

6.3.3 Equilibrium prices, output and firm size

It is important to note that firms are not always on the *BE* curve since they can earn above-normal or below-normal profits for a while. In the long run, however, firms can enter or exit the market, so the number of firms rises or falls until the typical firm earns just enough to cover its fixed cost. By contrast, firms are always on the *COMP* curve since firms can change prices quickly in response to any change in the number of firms.

With this in mind, we are ready to work out the equilibrium mark-up, number of firms, price and firm-size in a closed economy using Figure 6.6. The right-hand panel combines the *BE* curve with the *COMP* curve. The intersection of the two defines the equilibrium mark-up and long-run number of firms. More specifically, the *COMP* curve tells us that firms would charge a mark-up of μ' when there are n' firms in the market, and the *BE* curve tells us that n' firms could break even when the mark-up is μ'. The equilibrium price is – by definition of the mark-up – just the equilibrium mark-up plus the marginal cost, *MC*. Using the *MC* curve from the left-hand panel, we see that the equilibrium price is p' (this equals μ' plus *MC*). The middle panel shows the demand curve and this allows us to see that the total level of consumption implied by the equilibrium price is C'.

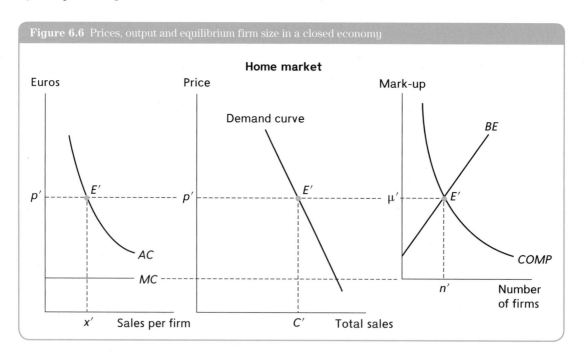

Figure 6.6 Prices, output and equilibrium firm size in a closed economy

The left-hand panel helps us to find the equilibrium firm size, i.e. sales per firm, which we denote as x'. This sub-diagram shows the average and marginal cost curves of a typical firm. As a little bit of reflection reveals, a typical firm's total profit is zero when price equals average cost (when price equals average cost, total revenue equals total cost). Since we know that total profits are zero at the equilibrium and we know the price is p', it must be that the equilibrium firm size is x' since this is where the firm's size implies an average cost equal to p'.

In summary, Figure 6.6 lets us determine the equilibrium number of firms, mark-up, price, total consumption and firm size all in one diagram. With this in hand, we are now ready to study how European integration has sparked a wave of industrial restructuring.

6.4 The impact of European liberalization

European integration has involved a gradual reduction of trade barriers. The basic economic effects of this gradual reduction can, however, be illustrated more simply by considering a much more drastic liberalization – taking a completely closed economy and making it a completely open economy. To keep things simple, we suppose that there are only two nations, Home and Foreign, and that these nations are identical. Since they are identical, we could trace through the effects looking at either market, but we focus on Home's market for convenience.

6.4.1 No-trade-to-free-trade liberalization

The immediate impact of the no-trade-to-free-trade liberalization is to provide each firm with a second market of the same size and to double the number of competitors in each market. How does this change the outcome?

The competition aspect of the liberalization is simple to trace out. The increased number of competitors in each market makes competition tougher. In reaction, the typical firm will lower its mark-up in each market to point A in Figure 6.7.

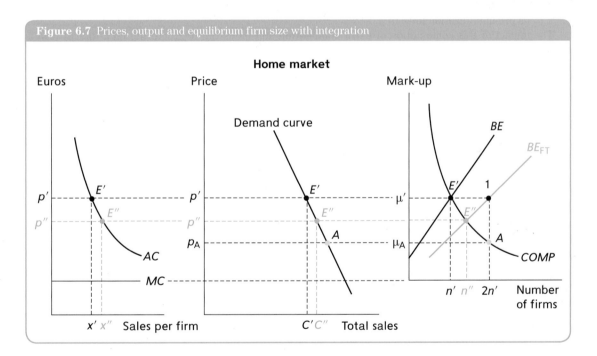

Figure 6.7 Prices, output and equilibrium firm size with integration

The doubling of the market size facing each firm also has an important effect. The liberalization adds a new market for each firm, so it makes sense that more firms will be able to survive. To see how many more firms can survive, we work out the impact of the liberalization on the BE curve. As it turns out, the liberalization shifts the BE curve to the right, specifically to BE_{FT}, as shown in the diagram. Why? Shifting BE to the right means that at any given mark-up more firms can break even. This is true since as the market size increases the sales per firm increase, thus providing a higher operating profit per firm at any given level of mark-up.

The size of the rightward shift is determined without difficulty. If there were no changes in the mark-up (there will be in the new equilibrium, but ignore this for the moment), then double the number of firms could break even since each firm would be selling the same number of units. In other words, the new BE curve must pass through the point marked '1' in the diagram; at point 1, the mark-up is μ', the number of firms

is $2n'$, and logic tells us that this combination of μ and n would result in all firms breaking even. Point 1, however, is merely an intellectual landmark used to determine how far out the *BE* curve shifts. It is not where the economy would be right after liberalization since the mark-up would immediately be pushed down to μ_A.

Because the increase in competition would immediately push down the mark-up to μ_A, the two newly integrated markets will initially be at a point that is below the *BE* curve. We know that all firms will be losing money at point A since the actual mark-up (μ_A) is less than what would be needed to have all $2n'$ firms break even. Now, this loss of profit is not a problem in the short run since firms only need to break even in the long run. Indeed, the profit losses are what would trigger the process of industrial restructuring that will eventually reduce the number of firms.

The corresponding effect on prices is shown in the middle diagram as the move from E' to A and then to E''. Before explaining this, observe that the middle panel shows the demand curve for Home only, so the no-trade-to-free-trade liberalization does not shift the demand curve. The Foreign market has an identical demand, but since exactly the same thing goes on in Foreign, we omit the Foreign demand curve to reduce the diagram's complexity.

As mentioned above, the initial impact of the extra competition ($2n'$ firms selling to the Home market instead of n') pushes the equilibrium mark-up down to μ_A, so the price falls to p_A. Thus during this industrial restructuring phase, the price would rise to p'' (from p_A), but this rise does not take the price all the way back to its pre-liberalization level of p'.

The impact of this combination of extra competition and industrial restructuring on a typical firm is shown in the left-hand panel. As prices are falling, firms that remain in the market increase their efficiency – i.e. lower their average costs – by spreading their fixed cost over a larger number of sales. Indeed, since price equalled average cost before the liberalization and in the long run after liberalization, we know that the price drop is exactly equal to the efficiency gain. In the left-hand panel, this is shown as a move from E' to E''. Increasing returns to scale are the root of this efficiency gain. As the equilibrium scale of a typical firm rises from x' to x'', average costs fall.

To summarize, the no-trade-to-free-trade liberalization results in fewer, larger firms. The resulting scale economies lower average cost and thus make these firms more efficient. The extra competition ensures that these savings are passed on to lower prices. It is useful to think of the integration as leading to two steps.

Step 1. Short term: defragmentation and the pro-competitive effect (from E' to A)

We start with the short-term impact, that is to say, the impact before the number of firms can adjust. Before the liberalization, each market was extremely fragmented in the sense that firms in each nation had a local market share of $1/n'$ and a zero share in the other market. After the liberalization, the market share of each firm is the same in each market, namely, $n'/2$. This elimination of market fragmentation has a pro-competitive effect, which is defined as a decrease in the price–cost mark-up. This is shown in the right-hand panel of Figure 6.7 as a move from E' to A. The short-term impact on prices and sales can be seen in the middle panel as a drop from p' to p_A.

Step 2. Long term: industrial restructuring and scale effects (from A to E'')

Point A is not a long-term equilibrium since the operating profit earned by a typical firm is insufficient to cover the fixed cost. We see this by noting that point A is below the *BE* curve and this tells us that the mark-up is too low to allow $2n'$ firms to break even. To restore a normal level of profitability, the overall number of firms has to fall from $2n'$ to n''. In Europe, this process typically occurs via mergers and buy-outs, but in some cases the number of firms is reduced by bankruptcies. As this industrial consolidation occurs, the economy moves from point A to point E''. During this process, firms enlarge their market shares, the mark-up rises somewhat and profitability is restored.

Welfare effects

The welfare effects of this liberalization are quite straightforward. The four-sided area marked by p', p'', E' and E'' in the middle panel of Figure 6.8 corresponds to the gain in Home consumer surplus. As usual, this

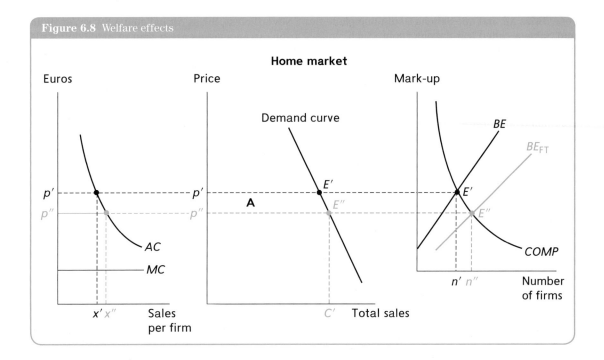

Figure 6.8 Welfare effects

gain can be broken down into the gain to consumers of paying a lower price for the units they bought prior to the liberalization, and the gains from buying more (C'' versus C''). Note that the exact same gain occurs in the Foreign market (not shown in the diagram).

As it turns out, this four-sided region labelled A in Figure 6.8 is Home's long-term welfare gain because there is no offsetting loss to producers and there was no tariff revenue to begin with. Firms made zero profits before liberalization and they earn zero profits after liberalization. Note, however, that this long-term calculation ignores the medium-term adjustment costs. These costs, which stem from the industrial restructuring, can be politically very important. Indeed, many governments attempt to thwart the restructuring by adopting a variety of policies such as industrial subsidies and various anti-merger and anti-acquisition policies (discussed further in Chapter 11). We should also note that the welfare gains shown can be rather substantial. Roughly speaking, the percentage gain in real GDP equals the share of the economy affected (industry in the EU, for instance, accounts for about 30 per cent of output) times the percentage drop in price.

6.4.2 Slow and fast adjustments

The discussion above has shown that the integration initially leads to big price reductions and large profit losses. These profit losses are eliminated as the number of firms fall and profits are restored to normal levels. During this industrial restructuring process, prices rise slightly. This sequence of steps – sometimes called industry 'consolidation' or an industry 'shake-out' – is relevant to some industries, for example air travel. Here, Europe's liberalization has resulted in large profit losses for many European airlines and big price reductions for consumers. At first, airlines were reluctant to merge – largely because most airlines were government-owned and their governments were willing to use taxpayer euros to cover the losses. More recently, however, European airlines are rationalizing their costs by forming cooperative alliances. While the actual number of firms has not yet fallen, the number of planes flying a particular route is reduced. For example, before the two firms went bankrupt, cooperation between Swiss Air and Sabena meant that, instead of having two planes flying the Geneva–Brussels route (one Swiss Air and one Sabena), only one plane flew. Nevertheless, Swiss Air called it a Swiss Air flight and Sabena called it a Sabena flight. Such 'code-sharing' arrangements are a way of achieving scale economies without actually eliminating a national carrier. Interestingly, both airlines eventually went bankrupt but the Swiss and Belgian governments stepped in to create replacement airlines, Swiss and SN Brussels Airlines.

In other industries, firms anticipate the increased competition and undertake the mergers and acquisitions quickly enough to avoid big losses. European banking is an example. The introduction of the euro and continuing liberalization of the banking sector mean that European banks will have to become fewer and bigger in order to break even. However, instead of waiting for profit losses to become intolerable, banks have launched a record-breaking series of mergers and acquisitions. In terms of Figure 6.8, this would look like a move from E' directly to E'''.

6.4.3 Empirical evidence

There is ample empirical evidence that European industry is marked by fewer, bigger, more efficient firms since the Single Market Programme. Unfortunately, there is little direct evidence in Europe that industry consolidation was caused by market integration, although this is what most economists believe is the obvious explanation. More direct evidence linking market size with efficiency and competition can be found in Campbell and Hopenhayn (2002). The authors study the impact of market size on the size distribution of firms in retail-trade industries across 225 US cities. In every industry examined, establishments were larger in larger cities. The authors conclude that their results support the notion that competition is tougher in larger markets and this accounts for the link between firm size and market size.

6.5 Summary

Three main points have been made in this chapter:

- One very obvious impact of European integration has been to face individual European firms with a bigger 'home' market. This produces a chain reaction that leads to fewer, bigger, more efficient firms that face more effective competition from each other. Understanding the economic logic driving this chain reaction is the main goal of this chapter. This logic can be summarized as follows. Integration defragments Europe's markets in the sense that it removes the privileged position of national firms in their national markets. As a result, all firms face more competition from other firms in their national market, but at the same time they have better access to the other EU markets. This general increase in competition puts downward pressure on price–cost mark-ups, prices and profits. The profit-squeeze results in industrial restructuring, a process by which the total number of firms in Europe falls. The lower prices and lower number of firms mean that the average firm gets larger and this, in turn, allows firms to better exploit economies of scale. This efficiency increase, in turn, permits the firms to break even despite the lower prices.

- The industrial restructuring is often politically painful since it frequently results in layoffs and the closure of inefficient plants. Governments very often attempt to offset this political pain by providing 'state aid' to their national firms. Such state aid can be viewed as unfair and the perception of unfairness threatens to undermine EU members' interest in integration. To avoid these problems, the founders of the EU established rules that prohibited state aid that distorts competition. The Commission is charged with enforcing these rules. These rules are covered in Chapter 11.

- Industrial restructuring raises another problem that led the EU's founders to set out another set of rules. As integration proceeds and the number of firms fall, the temptation for firms to collude may increase. To avoid this, the EU has strict rules on anti-competitive practices. It also screens mergers to ensure that mergers will enhance efficiency. Again, the Commission is charged with enforcing these rules. These rules are also covered in Chapter 11.

Self-assessment questions

1 Suppose that liberalization occurs as in Section 6.4 and the result is a pro-competitive effect, but instead of merging or restructuring, all firms are bought by their national governments to allow the firms to continue operating. What will be the impact of this on prices and government revenues? Now that the governments are the owners, will they have an incentive to continue with liberalization? Can you imagine why this might favour firms located in nations with big, rich governments?

2 Use a three-panel diagram, like Figure 6.6, to show how the number of firms, mark-up and firm size would change in a closed economy if the demand for the particular good rose, i.e. the demand curve shifted out.

3 Using your findings from Question 2, you should be able to consider the impact of a no-trade-to-free-trade integration between a large and a small nation, where size is defined by the position of the demand curve (the demand curve in the large nation will be further out than the demand curve for the small nation). To do this, you will need two of the three-panel diagrams of the Figure 6.6 type to show the pre-integration situation. Then use a three-panel diagram of the Figure 6.7 type to show what happens to prices, firm size and the number of firms in the integrated economy. Note that you will want to show both demand curves in the middle panel. As usual, assume that all firms have the same marginal cost. What does this analysis tell you about how integration affects firms in small nations versus large nations?

4 Consider a sequence of EU 'enlargements' where each enlargement involves a no-trade-to-free-trade addition of one more member. Specifically, suppose there are three initially identical economies, each of which looks like the one described in Section 6.3. Initially, all nations are closed to trade. Now consider a no-trade-to-free-trade integration between two of the nations (just as in Section 6.4.1). Then consider a no-trade-to-free-trade integration of a third nation. (Hint: The second step will be very much like the integration between unequal-sized economies explored in Question 3.) Calculate how much the third nation gains from joining and compare it to how much the existing two-nation bloc gains from the third nation's membership. Who gains more in proportion to size: the 'incumbents' or the 'entrants'?

Essay questions

1 When the Single Market Programme was launched in the mid-1980s, European leaders asserted that it would improve the competitiveness of European firms vis-à-vis US firms. Explain how one can make sense of this assertion by extending the reasoning in this chapter.

2 Has the strategy of defragmenting Europe's markets worked in the sense of promoting bigger, more efficient firms facing more effective competition? Choose an industry, for example telecoms, chemicals, pharmaceuticals or autos, and compare the evolution of the EU industry with that of the USA or Japan. You can find information on these and many more industries on the Commission website: http://ec.europa.eu/enterprise/policies/industrial-competitiveness/index_en.htm

3 Some EU members allow their companies to engage in 'anti-takeover' practices. Discuss how differences in EU members' laws concerning these practices might be viewed as unfair when EU industry is being transformed by a wave of mergers and acquisitions.

4 Describe the historical role that the scale economies argument played in the economic case for deeper European integration. Start with the Spaak Report (see www.ena.lu) and the Cockfield Report, Completing the Internal Market, White Paper, COM(85) 310 final (you can find it in French, 'Livre blanc sur l'achèvement du marché intérieur', on http://www.cvce.eu/ under the subject 'The Delors White Paper').

Further reading: the aficionado's corner

Consideration of imperfect competition and scale effects was made possible in the 1980s with development of the so-called new trade theory:

Helpman, E. and P. Krugman (1985) *Market Structure and Foreign Trade: Increasing Returns, Imperfect Competition and the International Economy*, MIT Press, Cambridge, MA.

Helpman, E. and P. Krugman (1989) *Trade Policy and Market Structure*, MIT Press, Cambridge, MA.

The new theory was naturally applied to the analysis of the Single Market Programme when it was first discussed in the mid-1980s. Many of the classic studies are contained in:

Winters, L.A. (1992) *Trade Flows and Trade Policies after '1992'*, Cambridge University Press, Cambridge.

A synthetic, graduate-level survey of this literature is provided by:

Baldwin, R. and A. Venables (1995) 'Regional economic integration', in G. Grossman and K. Rogoff (eds) *Handbook of International Economics*, North-Holland, New York.

An alternative presentation of the theory and a thorough empirical evaluation are provided by:

Allen, C., M. Gasiorek and A. Smith (1998a) 'European Single Market: how the programme has fostered competition', *Economic Policy*, 13(24): 441–86.

Other useful works are:

Brander, J. and P. Krugman (1983) 'A "reciprocal dumping" model of international trade', *Journal of International Economics*, 15 (November): 313–21.

Mas-Colell, A., M. Whinston and J.R. Green (1995) *Microeconomic Theory*, Oxford University Press, New York.

Useful websites

A large number of evaluations of the Single Market, most of which employ ICIR frameworks, can be found on http://ec.europa.eu/economy_finance/publications/. The document *The Internal Market: 10 Years without Frontiers* is especially useful. This site also posts the annual *State Aids Report*, which provides the latest data on subsidies.

References

Allen, C., M. Gasiorek and A. Smith (1998a) 'European Single Market: How the programme has fostered competition', *Economic Policy*, 13(24): 441–86.

Allen, C., M. Gasiorek and A. Smith (1998b) 'The competition effects of the Single Market in Europe', *Economic Policy*, 13(27): 439–86.

Badinger, H. (2007) 'Has the EU's Single Market programme fostered competition? Testing for a decrease in markup ratios in EU industries', *Oxford Bulletin of Economics and Statistics*, 69(4): 497–519.

Bellone, F., P. Musso, S. Antipolis, L. Nesta and F. Warzynski (2008) 'L'effet pro-concurrentiel de l'intégration européenne: une analyse de l'évolution des taux de marge dans les industries manufacturières françaises', OFCE, N° 2008–09, Paris.

Brander, J. and P. Krugman (1983) 'A "reciprocal dumping" model of international trade', *Journal of International Economics*, 15 (November): 313–21.

Campbell, J. and H. Hopenhayn (2002) *Market Size Matters*, NBER Working Paper 9113, Cambridge, MA.

Chen, N., J. Imbs and A. Scott (2009) 'The dynamics of trade and competition', *Journal of International Economics*, 77(1): 50–62.

Helpman, E. and P. Krugman (1985) *Market Structure and Foreign Trade: Increasing Returns, Imperfect Competition and the International Economy*, MIT Press, Cambridge, MA.

Annex: Details on the *COMP* and *BE* curves

A6.1 *COMP* curve in detail

Consider how the profit-maximizing mark-up changes when the number of firms increases. To keep the reasoning concrete, consider an increase from 1 firm (the monopoly case) to 2 firms (the duopoly case).

The solid lines in the left-hand panel of Figure A6.1 show the usual problem for a monopolist, with the demand curve marked as *D* and the marginal revenue curve marked as *MR*. (See Section 6.2 if you are not familiar with the monopolist case.) The profit-maximizing output, x_{mono}, is indicated by the point *A*, i.e. the intersection of marginal cost (marked as *MC* in the diagram) and marginal revenue (marked as *MR* in the diagram). The firm charges the most it can for the level of sales $x$mono, i.e. p'. The price–marginal cost mark-up (called the mark-up for short) equals $p' - MC$, as shown. We can also see the size of operating profit (i.e. profit without considering fixed cost) in the diagram since it is, by definition, just the monopolist mark-up times the monopoly level of sales x_{mono}. In the diagram, this is shown by the area of the box marked by the points p', A', A and *MC*.

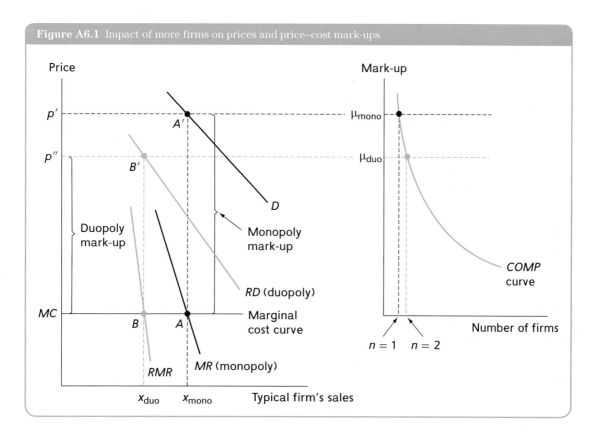

Figure A6.1 Impact of more firms on prices and price–cost mark-ups

When a second firm competes in this market, we have a duopoly rather than a monopoly. To solve this, we adopt the standard 'Cournot–Nash' approach of assuming that each firm takes as given the output of the other firm(s). Practically speaking, this means that each firm acts as if it were a monopolist on the 'residual demand curve', i.e. the demand curve shifted to the left by the amount of other firms' sales (marked as *RD* in the diagram). The exact equilibrium price and output are found by identifying the intersection of

the residual marginal revenue curve (*RMR*) and the marginal cost curve; again, firms charge the highest possible price for this level of sales, namely, p''. In drawing the diagram, we have supposed that the two firms have identical marginal cost curves (for simplicity), so the outcome of the competition will be that each firm sells an equal amount. You can verify that p'' is the price that the full demand curve, D, says would result if two times x_{duo} were sold.

The net result of adding an additional firm is that the price drops from p' to p'' and thus lowers the equilibrium mark-up. We also note that more competition lowers the level of sales per firm, although the sum of sales of the two competing firms exceeds the sales of a monopolist. Finally, note that adding in more firms lowers each firm's operating profit since it reduces the mark-up and sales per firm. The duopoly operating profit is the duopoly mark-up times x_{duo}; this is shown by the area p'', B', B, MC in the diagram.

Here we have looked only at the switch from one to two firms, but it should be clear that continuing to add in more firms would produce a similar result. As the number of firms rose, the residual demand curve facing each firm would shift inwards, resulting in a lower price, lower level of output per firm and, most importantly, a lower price–cost margin, i.e. a lower mark-up. In the extreme, an infinite number of firms would push the price down to marginal cost, eliminating the price–cost margin and all operating profits; each firm would be infinitely small (this is why perfectly competitive firms are sometimes called atomistic).

A6.2 *BE* curve in detail

While the positive link between mark-up and the break-even number of firms is quite intuitive, it is useful to study the relationship more closely. To keep the reasoning as easy as possible, we consider the simplest form of increasing returns to scale, namely, a situation in which the typical firm faces a flat marginal cost curve and a fixed cost of operating. The fixed cost could represent, for example, the cost of building a factory, establishing a brand name, training workers, etc.

This combination of fixed cost and flat marginal cost implies increasing returns since the typical firm's average cost falls as its scale of production rises, as shown in the left-hand panel of Figure A6.2.

Figure A6.2 The *BE* curve in detail

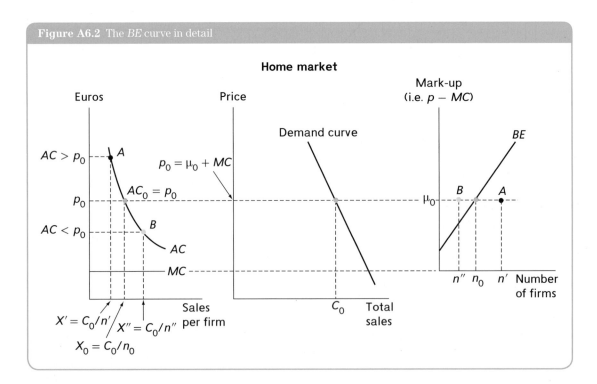

If a firm is to survive in this situation, it must earn enough on its sales to cover its fixed cost. The amount it earns on sales is called its 'operating profit', and this is simply the mark-up times the level of sales. For example, if the mark-up (i.e. price minus marginal cost) is €200 and each firm sells 20,000 units, the operating profit per firm will be €4 million. As we shall see, this simple connection between the mark-up, sales and operating profit makes it quite easy to figure out the number of firms that can break even at any given mark-up.

Since all firms are identical in this example, a given mark-up implies that the price will also be given; specifically, it will equal the mark-up plus marginal cost. For example, if the mark-up is μ_0 as in Figure A6.2, then the price will be $p_0 = \mu_0 + MC$. At this price, the demand curve tells us that the level of total sales will be C_0. Finally, we again use the symmetry of firms to work out the level of sales per firm; this will be total sales divided by the number of firms, which, in symbols, is C_0/n. To see how many firms can break even when the mark-up is μ_0, we turn to the left-hand panel in the diagram. With a little thought, you should be able to see that a firm will make zero total profit (i.e. operating profit plus the fixed cost) when its average cost exactly equals the price. Using the average cost curve, marked as *AC* in the left-hand panel, we see that the typical firm's average cost equals price when the sales of the typical firm equal x_0. Because we know that sales per firm will be C_0/n, we can work out the number of firms where the sales per firm just equal x_0. In symbols, the break-even number of firms, call this n_0, is where C_0/n_0 equals x_0.

It is instructive to consider what would happen if the mark-up were μ_0, but there were more than n_0 firms, say, n' firms, in the market. In this case, the sales per firm would be lower than x_0, namely, $x' = C_0/n'$, so the typical firm's average cost would be higher and this means that the average cost of a typical firm would exceed the price. Plainly, such a situation is not sustainable since all the firms would be losing money (earning operating profits that were too low to allow them to cover their fixed cost). This case is shown by point *A* in the left-hand panel of the diagram. The same point *A* can be shown in the right-hand panel as the combination of the mark-up μ_0 and n'; we know that at this point firms are not covering their fixed cost, so there would be a tendency for some firms to exit the industry. In the real world this sort of 'exit' takes the form of mergers or bankruptcies. The opposite case of too few firms is shown in the right- and left-hand panels as point *B*; here, firms' average cost is below the price and so all are making pure profits (i.e. their operating profit exceeds the fixed cost). Such a situation would encourage more firms to enter the market.

To work out all the points on the *BE* curve, we would go through a similar analysis for every given level of mark-up. The logic presented above, however, makes it clear that the result would be an upward-sloping *BE* curve.

*. . . Europe faces a moment of truth.
Either we recognise that 'business as
usual' will consign us to a gradual
decline or we take the bold and
ambitious course of sustainable growth.
. . . Measures to promote growth and get
the most out of our Single Market have
been given priority. European spending
has been re-oriented towards growth-
releasing investment.*

**José Manuel Barroso, Outgoing President
of the European Commission in 2014**

Growth effects and factor market integration

Chapter Contents

Introduction

EU growth has been abysmal since the Global Crisis exploded in 2008 and the Eurozone Crisis started in 2010. But this is not the sort of growth dealt with in this chapter. The crisis-linked slowdowns are mostly likely to be transitory – although 'transitory' in this case may end up being a decade. What we are talking about here is long-run growth in normal, non-crisis times. This involves an analytic 'change of gears'.

The two previous chapters looked at 'allocation effects' of European integration, i.e. the impact on the efficiency with which economic resources within nations are allocated across economic activities. Allocation effects are 'one-off' in the sense that a single policy change leads to a single reallocation of resources. European leaders, however, have long emphasized a different type of economic effect – the growth effect. Growth effects operate in a way that is fundamentally different from allocation effects; they operate by changing the rate at which new factors of production – mainly capital – are accumulated, hence the name 'accumulation effects'.

Factor market integration is another channel by which European integration can change the supply of productive factors within EU members. Under EU rules, citizens of any EU nation may work in any other EU nation. Similar rules guarantee the free movement of capital, so this aspect of European integration can – in principle – alter the amount of productive factors employed in any given EU member. Or, to put it differently, capital and labour movements can look like an allocation-of-resources effect from the EU perspective, but like an accumulation effect from the national perspective. This chapter therefore also studies the economics of factor market integration.

7.1 The logic of growth and the facts

The link between European integration and growth rests on the logic of growth. The logic of growth is simple, but widely misunderstood, so before looking at the facts, we briefly present the logic of growth in words.

7.1.1 The logic of growth: medium-run and long-run effects

Economic growth means producing more and more every year. Per-capita growth means an annual rise in the output per person. In most western European nations, output per capita rises at between 1 and 3 per cent per year in normal times. How does this happen?

If a nation's workers are to produce more goods and services year after year, the economy must provide workers with more 'tools' year after year. Here 'tools' is meant in the broadest possible sense – what economists call capital – and three categories of capital must be distinguished: physical capital (machines, etc.), human capital (skills, training, experience, etc.) and knowledge capital (technology).

Given this necessity, the rate of output growth is hitched straight to the rate of physical, human and knowledge capital accumulation. Most capital accumulation is intentional and is called investment. Accordingly, we can say that European integration affects growth mainly via its effect on investment in human capital, physical capital and knowledge capital. The qualification 'mainly' is necessary since integration may unintentionally affect accumulation, for instance by speeding the international dissemination of technological progress (this is especially important in central European nations).

Growth effects fall naturally into two categories: medium term and long term. An instance of medium-term effects is 'induced physical capital formation'. For all the reasons documented in the previous chapters, European integration improves the efficiency with which productive factors are combined to produce output. As a side effect, this heightened efficiency typically makes Europe a better place to invest, so more investment occurs. The result is that the initial efficiency gains from integration are boosted by induced capital formation. While the above-normal capital formation is occurring, the economies experience a medium-term growth effect. This growth effect is only medium term, since it will eventually peter out; as the amount of capital per worker rises, the gain from investing in each further unit of capital diminishes.

Eventually the gain from investing in an extra unit reaches the cost of doing so and the above-normal capital formation stops. A good example of this is the investment boom that Spain experienced around the time of its accession to the EU.

Long-term growth effects involve a permanent change in the rate of accumulation, and thereby a permanent change in the rate of growth. Since the accumulation of physical capital faces diminishing returns, long-run growth effects typically refer to the rate of accumulation of knowledge capital, i.e. technological progress.

To summarize the logic of growth effects schematically: European integration (or any other policy) → allocation effect → improved efficiency → better investment climate → more investment in machines, skills and/or technology → higher output per person. Under medium-run growth effects, the rise in output per person eventually stops at a new, higher level. Under long-run growth effects, the rate of growth is forever higher.

7.1.2 Post-war European growth: the evidence

Any informed discussion of European integration and economic growth must begin with a fistful of overarching facts. We first cover these facts before setting out a prima facie case that European integration has, broadly speaking, been favourable to growth in the post-war period.

Phases of European growth

By historical standards, continuous economic growth is a relatively recent phenomenon. Before the Industrial Revolution, which started in Great Britain in the late 1700s, European incomes had stagnated for a millennium and a half. As Figure 7.1 shows, at the beginning of the first millennium, per capita incomes hardly above the bear minimum for survival – guesstimated by the great growth scholar Angus Maddison to be $400 per year in 1990 dollars. By the end year 1000, European incomes had fallen back to the survival minimum. From 1500, Western European incomes climbed extremely slowly. The rising European incomes reflected massive economic and political transformations as feudalism's rural/agrarian focus evolved toward a more urban and market based-economy – a change known as the Commercial Revolution. The industrial revolution brought modern growth and incomes skyrocketed. The chart shows that the cumulative income growth between 1900 and 1913 was as large as that won in the five centuries after the turn of the first millennium.

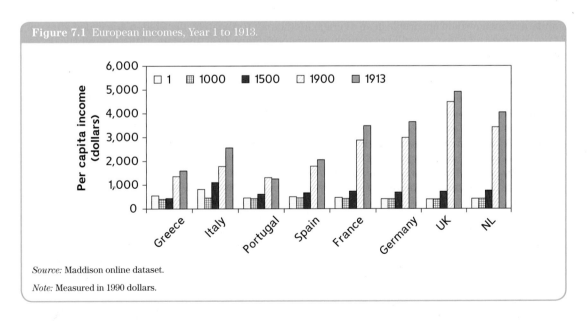

Figure 7.1 European incomes, Year 1 to 1913.

Source: Maddison online dataset.

Note: Measured in 1990 dollars.

With industrialization, which had spread to most of continental Europe by 1870, incomes began to rise at a respectable rate of something like 2 per cent per year. Growth rates, however, were hardly constant from this date – four growth phases are traditionally defined, as Table 7.1 shows. During the 1890–1913 period (often called the *Belle Époque*) real GDP grew at 2.6 per cent. This is considered to be a very good

Table 7.1   European growth phases, 1890–1992

Period	Real GDP	Real GDP per capita	Real GDP per hour
1890–1913	2.6	1.7	1.6
1913–1950	1.4	1.0	1.9
1950–1973	4.6	3.8	4.7
1973–1992	2.0	1.7	2.7
Whole period 1890–1992	2.5	1.9	2.6

Notes: Figures are annual average percentages for 12 nations (Austria, Belgium, Denmark, Finland, France, Germany, Italy, Netherlands, Norway, Sweden, Switzerland and the UK, all adjusted for boundary changes).

Note that the 1950–73 period is the aberration. Both before and after this period, growth rates were just under 2 per cent per annum (excluding the unusual 1913–50 period). The Golden Age was also the most intensive period of European integration and it was this correlation that first started economists thinking about the growth effects of European integration.

Source: Nicolas Crafts, Gianni Toniolo, "Postwar growth: an overview", in Nicholas Crafts, Gianni Toniolo (eds), *Economic Growth in Europe since 1945*, (1996) © Centre for Economic Policy Research 1996, published by Cambridge University Press, reproduced with permission

growth rate, and is enough to double GDP every 27 years. Since population was also growing rapidly in this period, real GDP per person rose at only 1.7 per cent per annum. These rates were approximately halved during the 1913–50 period (i.e. from the First World War until the end of the post-Second World War reconstruction period). Despite this, the GDP per hour worked accelerated slightly to 1.9 per cent since the average hours worked per year fell with the introduction and spread of labour unions and social legislation.

The period from 1950 to 1973 is called the Golden Age of growth; throughout the world, but especially in Europe, growth rates jumped. Real GDP growth rates more than tripled and per-capita GDP growth almost quadrupled. At this pace, per-capita incomes would double every 18.6 years, implying that the material standard of living would quadruple in an average lifetime. Unfortunately, the Golden Age ended after only 23 years for reasons that are still not entirely understood. Since 1973, the date of the first oil shock, per-capita incomes have progressed at only 1.9 per cent per year. However, as the working week has been further shortened during this period, GDP-per-hour-worked continued to progress at a respectable 2.7 per cent per annum.

Growth performance during the 1913–50 period was far from homogeneous. This phase, which Crafts and Toniolo (1996) aptly call the 'second Thirty Years War', contains the two world wars and the Great Depression, each of which was responsible for massive income drops. It also, however, contains the most spectacular growth phase that Europe has ever seen, namely, the years of reconstruction, 1945–50. Table 7.1 shows various aspects of this 'reconstruction period' for 12 European nations. The first point (a point we also made in Chapter 1) is that the Second World War caused enormous economic damage. It cost Germany and Italy four decades or more of growth and put Austrian and French GDPs back to nineteenth-century levels. Despite this, recovery was remarkably rapid. By 1951, every European nation was back on the pre-war growth path. This resurgence was due to a short period of truly astonishing growth. All the growth rates were double digit (except Belgium's); France, for instance, grew at almost 20 per cent a year for four consecutive years and the Netherlands grew at almost twice that pace for two years. To a large extent, however, this rapid growth is a bit of an illusion. It consisted of merely setting back up, or repairing, production facilities created in earlier years. This also indicates that much of the Second World War drop in GDP was due to the temporary disorganization of Europe's economy rather than permanent destruction.

7.1.3 Are growth and European integration related?

As the verbal logic of growth presented above suggests, growth is affected by a myriad of factors. To isolate the impact of integration on growth requires statistical methods – regression analysis – that are standard in the scientific literature on trade and growth. The consensus in this literature is that economic integration is good for income growth, although the exact relationship is not fully understood. The literature on European integration per se is much less developed. A recent pair of papers by Harald Badinger (2005, 2008)[1] suggest that, although there is no long-run (i.e. permanent) boost to growth, tighter European integration does produce a sizeable medium-run growth effect.

The point is illustrated in Figure 7.2. In reality, European integration did occur and this produced the income growth we can observe in the data. To work out the fraction of this income that was due to an integration-induced growth effect, one needs to simulate what income would have been *without* European integration. The difference is the medium-run growth effect.

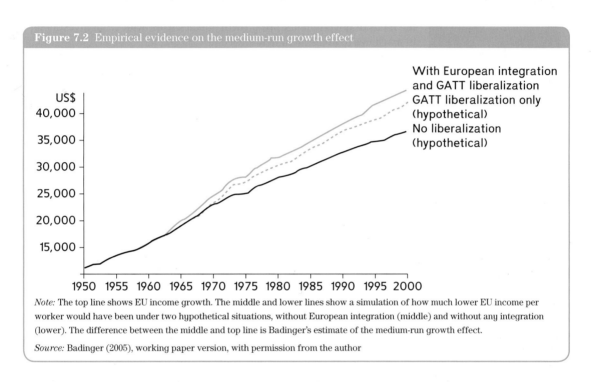

Figure 7.2 Empirical evidence on the medium-run growth effect

Note: The top line shows EU income growth. The middle and lower lines show a simulation of how much lower EU income per worker would have been under two hypothetical situations, without European integration (middle) and without any integration (lower). The difference between the middle and top line is Badinger's estimate of the medium-run growth effect.

Source: Badinger (2005), working paper version, with permission from the author

We turn now to a more careful consideration of *how* integration might affect growth. Establishing such an analytical framework is useful to understanding the growth–integration link, but more importantly, it allows us to make more pointed predictions that can be confronted with the data.

7.2 Medium-term growth effects: induced capital formation with Solow's analysis

Spain's accession to the EU in the mid-1980s and Estonia's accession in 2004 were accompanied by an investment boom that raised their GDP growth by several percentage points for a few years. In this section, we consider ways of understanding how EU membership could yield such a medium-term growth bonus.

The key to the medium-term growth bonus is 'induced capital formation'. That is to say, integration induces firms to raise the level of capital per worker employed. For the moment, we focus exclusively on the machine per worker (i.e. physical-capital to labour) ratio, so the first step is to identify a means of determining the equilibrium capital/labour ratio. The approach we adopt was discovered by Nobel Laureate Robert Solow in the 1950s (see Box 7.1). It assumes that people save and then invest a fixed share of their income.

---

[1] Also see Henrekson et al. (1997), Coe and Moghadam (1993) and Italianer (1994).

Box 7.1 Robert Solow (1924–)

© Donna Coveney/MIT

Robert Solow's most famous contributions to economics, published in the late 1950s, revolutionized thinking about the causes of growth. Before Solow, the dominant thinking was that capital accumulation by itself was the driving force of growth. What Solow showed was that capital accumulation was induced by technological progress, so the ultimate growth driver was technological progress. This simple realization shifted the focus of governments' pro-growth policies worldwide from investment in machines to investment in knowledge.

A brilliant and precocious student (he enrolled at Harvard at 16 years old and started teaching at MIT two years before finishing his PhD), Solow as a professor turned out to be an excellent teacher who devoted an inordinate amount of time to students. He is also famous for being one of the wittiest living economists. Writing about Milton Friedman's hardline views on the importance of money, Solow wrote, 'Everything reminds Milton of the money supply. Well, everything reminds me of sex, but I keep it out of the paper' (see www.minneapolisfed.org for further pithy examples in a 2002 interview). In 1987, Solow won the Nobel Prize.

7.2.1 Solow diagram

To keep things easy, we start by viewing the whole EU as a single, closed economy with fully integrated capital and labour markets and the same technology everywhere.

We begin our study of the logic linking growth and integration by focusing on the connection between GDP-per-worker and capital-per-worker. When a firm provides its workers with more and better equipment, output per worker rises. However, output per worker does not increase in proportion with equipment per worker. To see this, consider the example of the efficiency of your studying and your personal capital/labour ratio. The most primitive method of studying would be just to go to lectures and listen. Buying some paper and pencils would allow you to take notes and this would enormously boost your productivity in terms of both time and quality. Going further, you could buy the book and again this would boost your productivity (i.e. the effectiveness per hour of studying) but not as much as the pencils and paper. It would also be nice to have a calculator, a laptop, high-speed connection to the internet at home and a laser printer of your own.

Each subsequent increase in your 'capital' would boost your effectiveness, but each euro of capital investment would provide progressively lower increases in productivity. As it turns out, this sort of 'diminishing returns' to investment also marks the economy as a whole. Raising the capital/labour ratio in the economy increases output per hour worked, but the rate of increase diminishes as the level of the capital/labour ratio rises.

This sort of less-than-proportional increase in efficiency is portrayed by the GDP/L curve. This shows that raising the capital/labour ratio (K/L, which is plotted on the horizontal axis) increases output per worker, but a 10 per cent hike in K/L raises GDP/L by less than 10 per cent. This is why the curve is bowed downwards in Figure 7.3. (Alternatively, think of the curve as rising less rapidly than a straight line.)

The GDP/L curve shows us what output per worker would be for any given K/L; but what will the K/L be? The equilibrium K/L ratio depends upon the inflow and outflow of new capital per worker. The inflow is investment – firms building new factories, buying new trucks, installing new machines, etc. The outflow is depreciation – factories, trucks and machinery break down with use and must be repaired or replaced. The equilibrium K/L is where the inflow of new investment just balances depreciation of capital. The reason is simple. If the flow of savings exceeds the depreciation of capital, then K/L rises. If depreciation outstrips investment, K/L falls. The next step is to find the inflow and outflow of capital.

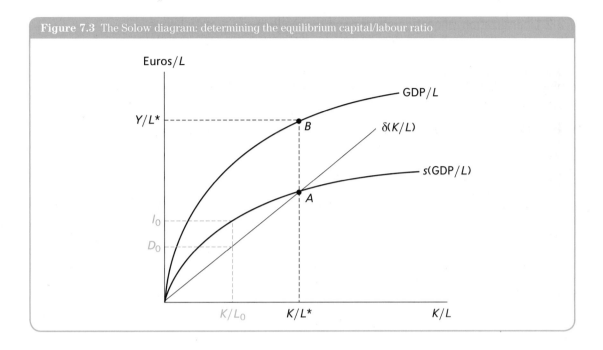

Figure 7.3 The Solow diagram: determining the equilibrium capital/labour ratio

Solow simply assumed that people save and invest a constant fraction of their income each year, so the inflow of capital is just a fraction of GDP/L; in the diagram, this constant savings and investment fraction is denoted as s, so the inflow-of-capital curve is marked as $s(GDP/L)$. (In European nations, s is somewhere between 20 and 35 per cent.) The investment-per-worker curve has a shape that is similar to that of the GDP/L curve but it is rotated clockwise since the savings are a fraction of GDP/L. As for depreciation, Solow made an equally simple assumption. He assumed that a constant fraction of capital stock depreciates each year. In the figure, the constant fraction of the capital stock that depreciates each year is denoted with the Greek letter 'delta', δ. (In Europe, something like 12 per cent of the capital stock depreciates each year.) The depreciation per worker line is shown as $\delta(K/L)$. It is a straight line since the amount of depreciation per worker increases in proportion to the amount of capital per worker.

The important point in the figure is A, the crossing of the $s(GDP/L)$ curve and the $\delta(K/L)$ line. This occurs at K/L^*. At this capital/labour ratio, the inflow of new investment just balances the outflow. For a ratio below K/L^*, the capital/labour ratio would rise since investment outstrips depreciation. For example, if K/L were K/L_0, then the inflow would be I_0 and the outflow would be D_0. Since I_0 is higher than D_0, the amount of new capital per worker installed would be greater than the amount of capital per worker lost to depreciation. Naturally, the capital/labour ratio would rise. With more capital being installed for a ratio higher than this, depreciation surpasses investment, so K/L would fall. The last thing to work out is the output per worker implied by the equilibrium K/L. The answer, which is given by the GDP/L curve at point B, tells us that output per worker in this equilibrium will be Y/L^*.

Although it is not essential to our main line of analysis, we finish our discussion of the Solow diagram with a consideration of long-run growth. The main point that Solow made with his diagram was that the accumulation of capital is not a source of long-run growth. Capital rises up to the point where the K/L ratio reaches its equilibrium value and then stops, unless something changes. To explain the year-after-year growth we see in the modern world – about 2 per cent per year on average – Solow relied on technological progress. He assumed that technological advances would rotate the GDP/L curve upwards year after year, pulling the $s(GDP/L)$ curve up with it. As can be easily verified in the Solow diagram, such progress will lead to an ever-rising output per worker and an ever-rising capital/labour ratio. When we look at the growth effects of European integration, we shall be referring to growth that is higher than the growth that would have otherwise occurred due to technological progress.

We next use the Solow diagram to study how European integration might boost growth.

7.2.2 Liberalization, allocation effects and the medium-run growth bonus

The verbal logic of growth effects is straightforward. Integration improves the efficiency of the European economy by encouraging a more efficient allocation of European resources. Not surprisingly, this improved efficiency also makes Europe a better place to invest and thus boosts investment beyond what it otherwise would have been. The extra investment means more tools per worker, and this raises the output per worker. As workers get more tools than they would have without integration, output per worker rises faster than it would have done otherwise. To put this differently, integration produces extra growth as the capital/labour ratio approaches its new equilibrium output. This is the medium-run growth bonus introduced by Baldwin (1989). It is medium term since the higher growth disappears once the new equilibrium capital/labour ratio is reached.

Medium-run growth bonus in detail

Figure 7.4 allows us to portray the logic in more detail. The first step is to realize how 'allocation effects' of European integration alter the diagram. For all the reasons presented in Chapters 4 to 6, European integration has improved the effectiveness with which capital, labour and technology are combined to produce output. To take one concrete example, we saw that integration can lead to fewer, more efficient firms. From the firm-level perspective, this improved efficiency means lower average cost. From the economy-wide perspective, the improved efficiency means that the same amount of capital and labour can produce more output. How can we show this in the Solow diagram?

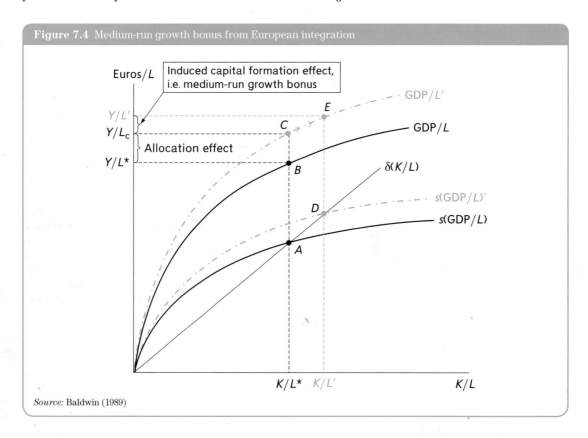

Figure 7.4 Medium-run growth bonus from European integration

Source: Baldwin (1989)

The positive allocation effect shifts the GDP/*L* curve to the dashed line marked GDP/*L*′. The new GDP/*L* curve is the old one rotated up counter-clockwise since the improved efficiency means that the economy is able to produce more output, say, 2 per cent more, for any given capital/labour ratio. This is the first step. The impact of the higher efficiency on output is shown by point *C*. That is, holding the capital/labour ratio constant at K/L^*, output would rise from Y/L^* to Y/Lc. This is not the end of the story, however, since K/L^* is no longer the equilibrium capital/labour ratio. This brings us to the second step.

The shift in the GDP/L curve up to GDP/L' also shifts up the investment curve to s(GDP/L)'. After all, the fixed investment rate now applies to higher output and so generates a higher inflow of investment for any given capital/labour ratio. This is shown in the diagram by the dashed curve s(GDP/L)'. Since the inflow has risen, K/L^* is no longer the equilibrium. At K/L^*, the inflow exceeds the outflow, so the economy's capital/labour ratio begins to rise. The new equilibrium is at the new intersection of the inflow and outflow curves, namely, point D, so the new equilibrium capital/labour ratio is K/L'. The rise from K/L^* to K/L' is called 'induced capital formation' and reflects the fact that improved efficiency will tend to stimulate investment.

What are the growth implications? As the capital/labour ratio rises from K/L^* to K/L', output per worker rises from Y/Lc to Y/L'. This is shown in the diagram as the movement from point C to point E. Since the capital stock builds up only slowly, the movement between C and E can take years. The key to the second step is to realize that the rise in output per worker between C and E would show up as faster than normal growth until the economy reaches point E. At that time, the growth rate would return to normal.

Summary in words

In words, the integration-causes-growth mechanism is: integration → improved efficiency → higher GDP/L → higher investment-per-worker → economy's capital/labour ratio starts to rise towards new, higher equilibrium value → faster growth of output per worker during the transition from the old to the new capital/labour ratio. This is the so-called medium-term growth bonus from European integration.

When it comes to welfare, however, it is important to note that higher output is not a pure welfare gain. In order to invest more, citizens must save more and this means forgoing consumption today. Consequently, the higher levels of consumption made possible tomorrow by the higher K/L ratio are partly offset by the forgone consumption of today.

7.2.3 Other medium-run growth effects: changes in the investment rate

The Solow diagram relied on an extremely convenient simplifying assumption – a constant investment rate. Unfortunately, taking the investment rate as given severely limits the range of growth effects that we can study. As the introduction pointed out, the basic logic of growth rests on the decision to invest in new physical capital (machines), new human capital (skills) and/or new knowledge capital (innovations). Many growth effects operate by altering the costs and/or benefits of investing and thus by altering the investment *rate*, what we called s in the diagram. For instance, many people claim that the euro makes it easier, cheaper and safer to invest in Europe. If this turns out to be true, the extra investment would boost growth at least in the medium term, but how would we get this into the Solow framework?

If European integration raises the investment rate from, say, s to s', the inflow of capital curve, namely, s(GDP/L), will rotate upwards, as shown in Figure 7.5. This change would in turn alter the equilibrium capital/labour ratio. Following the logic we considered above, the inflow of capital at the old capital/labour ratio K/L^* would exceed the outflow, so the capital stock per worker would rise to the new equilibrium shown by point C in the diagram. As before, the rising K/L would raise output per worker from Y/L^* to Y/L' (these Y/L^* and Y/L' are unrelated to those in previous figures). During this process, growth would be somewhat higher than it would have otherwise been.

This shows that it is straightforward to illustrate this second type of growth effect in the Solow diagram. We postpone our discussion of how various aspects of European integration might raise the investment rate to Section 7.3, where we consider EU capital market integration.

7.2.4 Evidence from EU accessions

Western Europe grew rapidly in the post-war period and experienced rapid integration. The problem, however, is that it is very difficult to separate the effects of European integration from the many other factors affecting growth. One natural experiment is to look at what happened to nations that joined the EU. These nations experienced a rather sudden and well-defined increase in economic integration when they

Figure 7.5 European integration and the investment rate

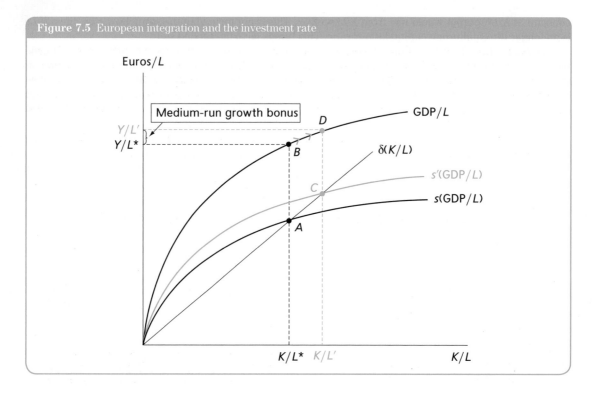

joined. In particular, we shall look at the impact of EU membership on Portugal and Spain (which joined in 1986), Latvia, Lithuania and Estonia (which joined in 2004), and Greece (which joined in 1981).

The logic sketched out above explains how integration may raise a nation's steady-state capital stock. What sort of 'footprints' would this leave in the data? First, heightened efficiency makes investment more worthwhile, i.e. it tends to raise the real return to capital. Moreover, this will normally be associated with an increase in the profitability of existing capital and this, in turn, should show up in the average behaviour of the stock market (as long as the stock market reflects a broad sample of firms). An important caveat comes from the fact that liberalization usually harms some firms and sectors even when it is beneficial for the nation as a whole. If the stock market is dominated by, say, state-controlled 'white elephants' that will face increased pressure in a more liberal economy, a drop in the stock market index may accompany the enlargement. Second, the Solow diagram is too simple to distinguish between domestic and foreign investors, but we presume that an improvement in the national investment climate should attract more investment from both sources. These two effects are likely to leave three kinds of 'footprint' in the data:

1 Stock market prices should increase.
2 The aggregate investment to GDP ratio should rise.
3 The net direct investment figures should improve.

Portugal and Spain

The case that EU membership induced investment-led growth is the strongest for the Iberians. Following restoration of democracy in the mid-1970s, Portugal and Spain applied to the EU in 1977, with membership talks beginning in 1978. The talks proved difficult, so accession occurred only in 1986. Growth in Portugal picked up rapidly and stayed high both during the negotiations and after accession; and between 1977 and 1992, Portugal expanded 13 per cent more than France (the country we have chosen as a 'control'). In Spain, however, growth was worse than that of France until accession. From 1986, it picked up significantly and between 1986 and 1992 Spain's cumulative growth edge over France amounted to 7.5 per cent, about the same as Portugal's.

As the lower panel of Figure 7.6 shows, much of this rapid growth was due to a higher rate of physical capital formation. Portugal's investment rate responded strongly and quickly to the combination of democracy and the prospect of EU membership. The importance of membership probably stems from some mixture of reduced uncertainty concerning the nation's stability and the prospect of improved market access. Note, however, that as a member of EFTA, Portugal already had duty-free access to the EU market for industrial goods. The pattern of the Spanish investment rate, in contrast, did not differ significantly from that of our 'control' country until accession actually occurred. At that point, however, the Spanish investment-rate pattern does follow the predictions of integration-induced investment-led growth.

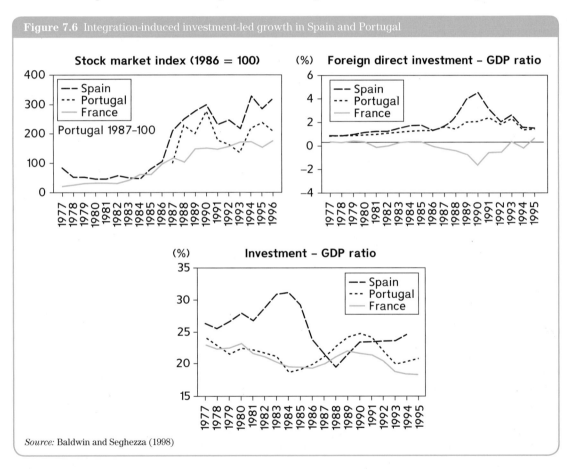

Figure 7.6 Integration-induced investment-led growth in Spain and Portugal

Source: Baldwin and Seghezza (1998)

The top-left panel of the figure shows the same pattern for the stock market price indices. Spain's index tracked that of France until accession but thereafter showed signs of a significant improvement in the investment climate. Portuguese data are available only from 1987, but clearly show a better-than-average performance in subsequent years. The top-right panel displays the evidence for net foreign direct investment. Here the prospect of membership and domestic market-oriented reforms boosted the attractiveness of Spain and Portugal as industrial locations. Note that the boom in Portuguese foreign direct investment came only after accession.

The Baltic States

Latvia, Lithuania and Estonia were republics of the USSR until 1991. Upon independence they approached the EU to establish closer ties. From the mid-1990s it was clear that they would eventually become EU members and would certainly be part of the first enlargement wave. As history would have it, that wave came in 2004.

Since these nations were under strict communist rule until 1991 – and thus their economies were subject to central planning – data for the 1990s is a confusion of factors. These nations were making the difficult transition from a planned socialist economy to European-style social market economies. At the same time, they were preparing for EU membership and signing a series of trade agreements with the EU, EFTA, each other, Finland, Sweden, etc. From 2000, however, we see the clear signs of investment-led growth, as shown in Figure 7.7. The investment to GDP ratio was far above that of France (again included as a control) and rising. There is no jump when enlargement came since the 2004 enlargement was widely anticipated more than a year in advance. The drop in investment from 2007 is a consequence of the global economic crisis that started with the subprime mortgage crisis in the USA.

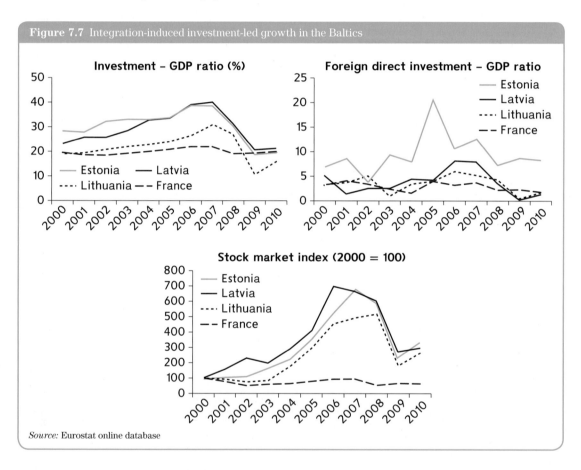

Figure 7.7 Integration-induced investment-led growth in the Baltics

Source: Eurostat online database

The facts supporting FDI are not as convincing as they were for Spain when it comes to Latvia and Lithuania. The case of Estonia – which shares close lingual, historical and geographic ties with high-tech and high-wage Finland – is quite clear. Once it was apparent that property rights in Estonia would be forced to meet EU standards, Estonia experienced a big inward surge of FDI, especially from Finland and Sweden. The evidence from stock markets is quite clear. As EU membership approached, investors bid up the price of Baltic companies – a sign that EU accession was improving the investment climate in the Baltics.

Greece

As in the case of Portugal and Spain, the Greek accession (1981) came just after a period of undemocratic governments. However, unlike the Iberians, Greece continued its pervasive state controls of the economy.

These controls prevented the Greek economy from reacting flexibly to any shock, and EU membership turned out to be one such example. Moreover, the poor macroeconomic management of the Greek economy further harmed the investment climate. The high and unstable inflation rate provides an example. While most European nations brought inflation down during the 1981–91 period, the Greek inflation rate hardly moved (from 25 per cent in 1981 to 20 per cent in 1991). Moreover, during this period inflation fluctuated greatly, jumping up or down by more than 3 percentage points in a single year in five out of the ten years.

Given this background, it is not surprising that we find no evidence of investment-led growth in Greece. Figure 7.8 shows the Greek numbers for the 5 years prior to, and 10 years subsequent to, accession. None of the figures suggest that EU membership had any impact on our three indicators.

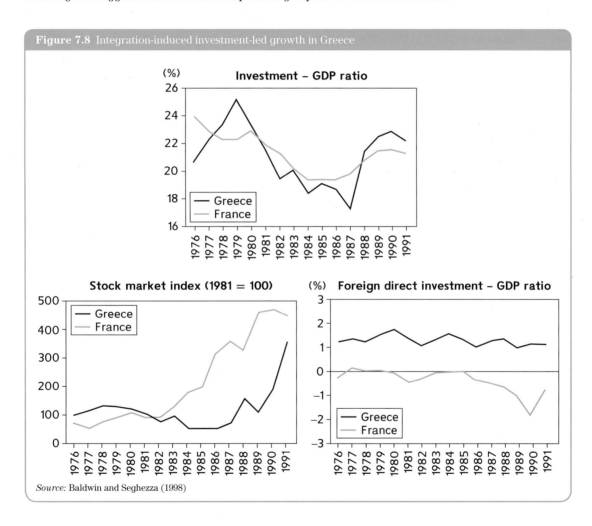

Figure 7.8 Integration-induced investment-led growth in Greece

Source: Baldwin and Seghezza (1998)

The sharp contrast between the Greek case and the others provides an important lesson. While integration may improve the investment climate in a nation, this can certainly be offset by other factors.

7.3 Long-term growth effects: faster knowledge creation and absorption

Up to this point we have focused on physical capital. Here, we focus on knowledge capital, i.e. technology. Although both technology and machines are capital in the sense that they provide a flow of productive services over time, there is an enormous difference between the two. The most important, for our purposes,

concerns diminishing returns. It is easy to see that raising the physical capital is subject to diminishing returns. Is knowledge capital subject to the same effects? The answer is clearly no.

The stock of knowledge per worker has risen steadily at least since the Enlightenment in the seventeenth century. Moreover, even as the knowledge stock rises, there seems to be no tendency for the usefulness of more knowledge to diminish. In the late nineteenth century, at the end of a particularly impressive burst of innovation called, by some, the second industrial revolution, the chief of the US Patent Office made the famously incorrect statement that Congress should close the Patent Office since everything had already been invented.

This myopic viewpoint seems humorous exactly because knowledge, by its very nature, does not seem to be subject to the same sort of limits as physical capital. As we shall see, when we focus on knowledge capital instead of physical capital, diminishing returns can disappear and accumulation can continue forever. This realization led in the 1990s to what is called 'endogenous growth theory'. See Box 7.2 for information on the intellectual pioneers in open-economy endogenous growth.

Box 7.2   Two endogenous growth pioneers: Gene Grossman and Elhanan Helpman.

Some of the early endogenous growth work was done by Paul Romer, now a professor at Stanford University, but the international aspects that are relevant to European integration were worked out by Gene Grossman and Elhanan Helpman in 1990.

A graduate of the Bronx High School of Science (which lists eight Nobel Prize winners among its alumni), Gene Grossman was one of many MIT PhD students who studied growth under Bob Solow. Elhanan Helpman is an Israeli economist who did his PhD at Harvard and teaches there after spending many years at the University of Tel Aviv. The Grossman-Helpman collaboration was born out of their mutual interest in trade theory.

They focused on the innovation sector as the producer of ever accumulating knowledge stock. While the basic mechanism had long been understood information, their key breakthrough was to mathematically model the process in an open economy. To make one-time investments in knowledge pay off, knowledge owners had to be able to price output above marginal cost. As pointed out in Chapter 6, this in turn required an amenable, general equilibrium framework that allowed for increasing returns and imperfect competition. The so-called new trade theory – of which both Grossman and Helpman were pioneers – provided exactly the tools necessary. The marriage of these tools with the conceptual realization that growth is driven by endogenous innovation led to a wealth of insights and empirical methods that transformed economists' understanding of the growth process.

As we pointed out in Section 7.2.1, technological progress shifts the GDP/L curve up in the Solow diagram and this raises output per worker in exactly the same way as we saw in the Figure 7.4 analysis. In short, we can think of technological progress as an allocative efficiency gain that comes every year, but instead of the gain being driven by European integration, it is driven by technology.

From this perspective, it is clear that the rate of technological progress is the key to understanding the long-term growth rate. The key point from our perspective is that, in principle, European integration can alter the rate of technological progress.

7.3.1 Solow-like diagram with long-term growth

To study this possibility in closer detail, we draw a Solow-like diagram where we focus on knowledge capital accumulation, rather than physical capital accumulation. The key difference is that knowledge capital does not face diminishing returns, so the GDP/*L* curve rises in a straightline fashion with respect to the knowledge-per-worker ratio, referred to as *K/L* in Figure 7.9 (note that the *K/L* here is not the same as *K/L* in the previous figures; it is knowledge capital per worker instead of physical capital per worker).

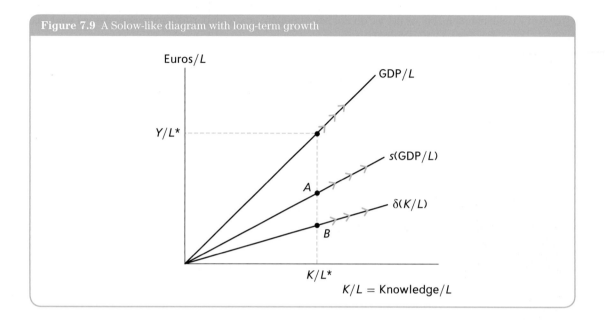

Figure 7.9 A Solow-like diagram with long-term growth

To keep things simple, we continue to assume that each nation invests a constant fraction of its national income in the accumulation of knowledge capital – this rate (referred to as *s* in the diagram) could be measured by the fraction of a nation's income invested in R&D, i.e. typically something like 3 to 5 per cent in European nations. To see how the total investment in new knowledge changes with the knowledge/labour ratio (*K/L*), we plot *s*(GDP/*L*) as before. However, now it is a straight line since the GDP/*L* curve is a straight line.

We also continue to assume that depreciation is constant in the sense that a given fraction of the national knowledge capital stock 'depreciates' each year. When it comes to knowledge, we usually say the knowledge capital has become obsolete rather than saying it has depreciated, but the wording does not change the logic. In both cases, a certain fraction of the capital becomes worthless every year.

As drawn in Figure 7.9, the investment rate exceeds the depreciation rate at all levels of *K/L*. For example, at a moment in time when the *K/L* ratio equals *K/L**, the amount of new knowledge capital per worker that is created is given by point *A*, while the amount of knowledge per worker that becomes obsolete is *B*. Since the inflow of new knowledge exceeds the outflow, the knowledge capital stock rises. This is shown by the arrow on the horizontal axis that suggests that *K/L* will continually rise.

As *K/L* rises for ever, the output per worker will rise for ever, along with the amount of new knowledge created and the amount of new knowledge that depreciates. These points are shown by the arrows on the GDP/*L* line, the *s*(GDP/*L*) line and the δ(*K/L*) line.

The diagram does not let us directly see how fast output per worker is rising, but it is easy to work this out. The further *s*(GDP/*L*) is above δ(*K/L*), the larger is the annual net addition to *K/L*. Thus as *s* rises, the nation will accumulate knowledge capital faster, and thus its income will rise faster.

Does European integration affect the long-term growth rate?

The evidence on long-term growth effects of European integration is much harder to find. The overarching fact is that long-term growth rates around the world, including those in Europe, returned to their pre-Golden Age levels. Since the level of European integration was rising more or less steadily during the whole post-war

period, one would have to tell a complicated story to explain how the long-run growth rate returned to its pre-integration average, if integration strongly boosted long-run growth. Badinger (2005) confirms this with statistical evidence (also see Deardorff and Stern, 2002). For this reason, it is probably best to focus on medium-term growth effects, i.e. investment booms that are associated with European integration.

The experience of the new Member States will provide an important opportunity for testing the growth effects of EU membership, but as yet we do not have enough data to undertake serious statistical analysis.

7.4 Summary

The logic of accumulation effects of European integration is based on the fundamental logic of economic growth. A nation's per-capita income can rise on a sustained basis only if its workers are provided with a steadily rising stock of physical, human and/or knowledge capital. Consequently, European integration will affect the growth rate only to the extent that it affects the rate of accumulation of physical, human and knowledge capital.

The chapter focused on two basic mechanisms through which European integration affects capital accumulation:

- In so far as European integration makes the European economy more efficient, i.e. leads to a positive allocation effect, it raises output and this – assuming a constant investment rate – leads to more investment. The end result of this higher level of investment is a higher long-term equilibrium capital stock and thus a higher equilibrium income per person.

- European integration may also raise the investment rate by making investment less risky. As with the previous effect, the end result is a higher capital stock and a higher output per worker.

Examples of this integration-induced investment-led growth are fairly common.

Long-term growth effects were also studied. The underlying mechanism is the same as for medium-term growth effects, but because knowledge capital does not face diminishing returns, an increase in investment in knowledge (R&D) can lead to a permanent increase in the growth rate. There is little empirical evidence that European integration has had a major impact on long-term growth rates in Europe.

Self-assessment questions

1 When the German reunification took place, Germany's labour force rose much more than its capital stock (since much of East Germany's capital stock was useless in the market economy). Use a diagram to analyse what the medium-term growth effects should have been. Go on the internet to find out what actually happened to German growth after reunification.

2 It is often said that the prospect of EU membership made central European nations a better, safer place to invest. Using the Solow diagram, show how this would affect medium-term growth in these nations. What sort of 'footprints' would this leave in the data?

3 Use a diagram to analyse the medium-term growth effects of the following situation. Assume: (1) Serbia's K/L was pushed below its long-term equilibrium by war damage to its capital stock, and (2) the EU signs a free trade agreement with Serbia that has two effects: (2a) it increases the efficiency of the Serbian economy (allocation effect), and (2b) it raises the Serbian investment rate (s) but only temporarily, for, say, 10 years. (i) Show what (1), (2a) and (2b) would look like; (ii) show where the Serbian economy would end up in the long run (i.e. after s returned to its normal rate); and (iii) show how the integration would affect Serbia's growth path.

4 Just after the Second World War, the economies of the Six experienced massive destruction of physical capital. Although many workers also died, the war tended to do more damage to the capital stocks than it did to the labour force. Use a diagram to illustrate how this may help explain the 'miraculous growth' in the late 1940s and 1950s.

Further reading: the aficionado's corner

An extensive description and analysis of growth in Europe can be found in:

Crafts, N. and G. Toniolo (1996) *Economic Growth in Europe since 1945*, Cambridge University Press, Cambridge.

An alternative presentation of the Solow model, one that allows for several extensions such as population growth and continuous technological progress, can be found in:

Mankiw, G. (2000) *Principles of Economics*, Thomson Learning, New York.

An advanced treatment of neoclassical and endogenous growth can be found in:

Barro, R. and X. Sala-i-Martin (1995) *Economic Growth*, McGraw-Hill, New York.

Other useful works are:

Baldwin, R. and R. Forslid (2001) 'Trade liberalization and endogenous growth: a q-theory approach', *Journal of International Economics*, 50: 497–517.

References

Badinger, H. (2005) 'Growth effects of economic integration: evidence from the EU member states', *Weltwirtschaftliches Archiv*, 141(1): 50–78.

Badinger, H. (2008) 'Technology- and investment-led growth effects of economic integration: a panel cointegration analysis for the EU-15 (1960–2000)', *Applied Economics Letters*, 15(7): 557–61.

Baldwin, R. (1989) 'The growth effects of 1992', *Economic Policy*, 9: 247–82.

Baldwin, R. and E. Seghezza (1998) 'Regional integration and growth in developing nations', *Journal of Economic Integration*, 13(3): 367–99.

Cameron, R. and L. Neal (2003) *A Concise Economic History of the World*, Oxford University Press, Oxford.

Coe, D. and R. Moghadam (1993) 'Capital and trade as engines of growth in France', *IMF Staff Papers*, 40: 542–66.

Deardorff, A. and R. Stern (2002) *EU Expansion and EU Growth*, Ford School of Public Policy, Working Paper 487.

Henrekson, M., J. Torstensson and R. Torstensson (1997) 'Growth effects of European integration', *European Economic Review*, 41(8): 1537–57.

Italianer, A. (1994) 'Whither the gains from European economic integration?', *Revue Economique*, 3: 689–702.

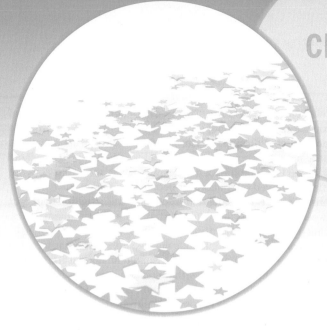

Chapter

8

As the extent of economic integration approaches that of the United States, labour market institutions and labour market outcomes may also begin to resemble their American counterparts. . . . Full and irreversible economic integration may call for harmonization of social and labour-market institutions within the European Union.

Giuseppe Bertola, 2000

Economic integration, labour markets and migration

Chapter Contents

Introduction

For most people, a good job is an essential element of a good life. This is why employment is a critical political and economic issue throughout Europe. Rightly or wrongly, European citizens expect Europe to improve their lot. The failure to deliver full employment throughout Europe, therefore, is a major failure. Even though labour market policies remain a national prerogative, this failure challenges the whole integration process. The rejection of the Constitution is a symptom of a widespread discontent that does not spare Europe and its institutions. The job difficulties faced by millions of people throughout the continent are due to poor national policies and institutions, but can European integration make the situation better, or worse? This chapter explores the linkages between jobs and European integration. It covers two main topics: unemployment, and how it is related to trade integration, and migration, one of Europe's four freedoms.

The chapter starts by describing the situation of the European labour markets. It shows that in many countries unemployment is high and employment is low. We next present a simple analytical framework that explains the unemployment phenomenon. This framework shows that socially desirable features of the labour market have serious economic costs. Put differently, social protection results in labour market rigidities. With these basics in place, we next examine the impact of European integration on Europe's labour markets. We show that economic and labour market integration encourages labour market flexibility. The last section looks at migration. Migration is another form of integration. From an economic point of view, it allows for a more efficient allocation of resources. But it also helps build up a better understanding of people. In contrast to widespread fears of huge migratory movements, the evidence is that Europeans move little.

8.1 European labour markets: a brief characterization

In contrast to goods markets, which are deeply integrated, the labour markets of the Eurozone remain distinct. There are two main reasons for that. First, there is not much 'trade' in labour, because migration within the EU is very limited. Second, each country has its own social customs, a historical heritage that leads to very different legislations and practices. As a result, we cannot talk of a 'European labour market'; there are as many markets as there are countries. Still, on average, the EU is generally not doing well. Figure 8.1 shows

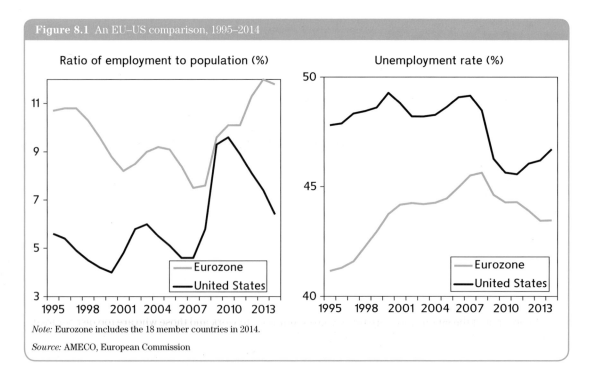

Figure 8.1 An EU–US comparison, 1995–2014

Note: Eurozone includes the 18 member countries in 2014.

Source: AMECO, European Commission

two measures of labour market performance (see Box 8.1 for an explanation of these and other definitions). The employment-to-population ratio is the percentage of the working-age population (conventionally set at 15 to 64 years) that has a job. The average employment-to-population ratio in the EU27 countries is growing, but remains significantly below the US rate. In 2008, the EU27 employment-to-population ratio stood at 69 per cent. This means that 31 per cent of the working-age population does not have a proper job. Some of these people may be disabled. The others are not working for two main reasons: some cannot find a job; others are not interested in looking for work, in some cases because they are taking care of the household. The right-hand chart shows the unemployment rate, the percentage of people who want to work but do not find a job. It is higher in Europe than in the USA. It is also the case that more Europeans are apparently not keen to work. Labour is a country's most precious input, because it is its people and their talents and because each country spends considerable resources to educate its population. A non-employment rate of 31 per cent thus represents a massive waste of talent and a huge loss in income. Just as bad is that those who do not have a job feel estranged from society.

Box 8.1   Labour market concepts

Categories

A country's total population can be broken down into several categories (Table 8.1). The first distinction is between the total population and the working-age population, conventionally defined as all valid people from 15 to 64 years old. Thus the working-age population excludes the young, the retired and the invalid.

Table 8.1   Decomposition of the population of the EU28 countries (millions), 2014

Employed (1)	Unemployed (2)	Labour force (3)=(1)+(2)	Out of the labour force (4)	Employment-age population (5)=(3)+(4)	Population (6)
225	35	259	76	336	510

Source: AMECO, European Commission

The working-age population (N) can be decomposed into three groups: (1) those who are employed (E); (2) those who are unemployed (U); and (3) those who are out of the labour force (O):

$$N = E + U + O$$

The labour force includes the employed and the unemployed:

$$L = E + U$$

and the working-age population is the sum of the labour force and the others:

$$N = L + O$$

People out of the labour force are those who do not want to work and those who are too discouraged even to seek a job and thus qualify as unemployed.

Ratios

The unemployment rate (u) is the ratio of the number (U) of people who declare themselves unemployed (they have no job and are actively looking for one) to the labour force (L):

$$u = \frac{U}{L}$$

The employment rate (e) is the remaining proportion of the labour force, composed of those who hold jobs:

$$e = \frac{E}{L} = 1 - u$$

The participation rate (p) is the ratio of the labour force to the working-age population:

$$p = \frac{L}{N} = 1 - \frac{O}{N}$$

The employment-to-population ratio, which is shown in Figures 8.1 and 8.2, is the proportion of people of working age who hold a job:

$$eR = \frac{E}{N} = \frac{E}{L}\frac{L}{N} = ep$$

How are people counted?

This is not an innocuous question. Each country carries out census polls and other formal population-counting procedures. The employed, E, are identified from firms reporting taxes and various welfare contributions, and from surveys. The unemployed, U, are identified either through polls or because they are officially registered as such (the difference matters as each country has its own procedure; the International Labour Office produces harmonized data based on surveys). This leaves those out of the labour force, O, as a residual ($O = N - E - U$). Precision is not the name of the game as the black market can include 10 or 20 per cent of the working-age population.

An important distinction is between voluntary and involuntary unemployment. In principle, people who do not want to work are classified as out of the labour force (O). In practice, however, things are less clear cut: some people counted in U are really voluntarily unemployed or actually employed, whereas others counted in O are involuntarily unemployed. Three main reasons explain this discrepancy. First, some unemployed people are really working in the black market (they are counted in U whereas they should be in E). Second, being unemployed opens the door to a range of welfare payments, mainly unemployment insurance benefits. It is believed that these benefits enable workers to be choosier and to reject some job offers or to search less than would otherwise be the case; yet, they must identify themselves as involuntarily unemployed either by registering or when polled. Finally, some people who have searched for a job for a long time become discouraged and simply drop out of the labour force (i.e. they are counted in O whereas they really are in U).

Note: These concepts are further defined and explained in International Labour Organization (ILO) publications. See www.ilo.org.

While, on average, European labour markets underperform, the situation varies considerably from one country to another. This is illustrated in Figure 8.2, which displays the average employment-to-population ratios and the unemployment rates during 2010–14 for each EU country as well as for similar non-EU countries. The countries with the best-performing labour markets are closer to the top-left corner,

Figure 8.2 Employment-to-population ratios and unemployment rates in 2010–14: EU28 and comparable non-EU countries

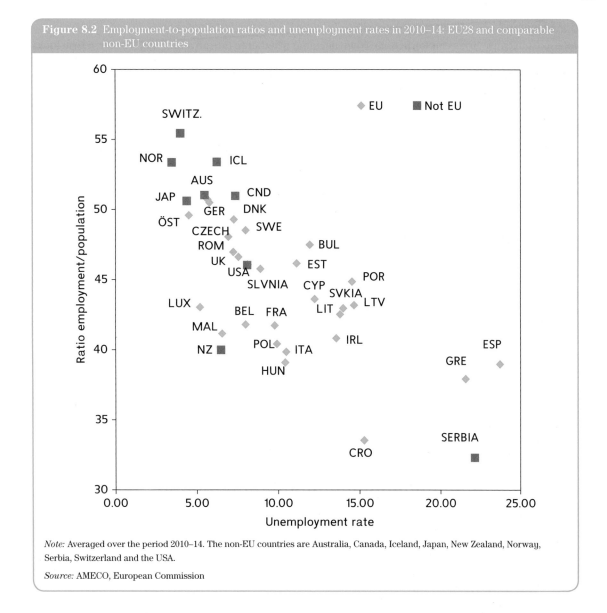

Note: Averaged over the period 2010–14. The non-EU countries are Australia, Canada, Iceland, Japan, New Zealand, Norway, Serbia, Switzerland and the USA.

Source: AMECO, European Commission

while poorly performing countries appear in the bottom-right corner. Most of the countries with the best performing labour markets are non-EU members. With the exception of Serbia, the poorly performing countries are all EU members.

8.2 Labour markets: the principles

We start with the essential tools that will guide us throughout this chapter. We look at the demand for labour by firms, at the supply of hours of work by individuals, and ask why unemployment is a general feature. This question leads us to realize that the labour market is a very special market, similar to none other.

8.2.1 Demand

Jobs exist because firms employ people. When deciding whether to hire an additional worker, a firm looks at the cost and the benefit. The cost is the wage, to which must be added the various contributions that most governments impose (contributions to health, unemployment and retirement programmes). As we will think in terms of hours of work, let us call this total the hourly wage cost. The benefit is the additional output that the worker will deliver, which is called the marginal productivity of labour – because we look at the margin, the output from one more hour of work. A key feature of labour productivity is that it declines as more hours are being performed. One reason is that, at any point of time, the equipment available in the firm is given, so that more workers will have to share it. Another reason is that longer hours mean that workers get tired and equipment is used up faster and breaks down more often. The principle of declining labour marginal productivity is captured in Figure 8.3 by the downward-sloping curve labelled *MPL*.

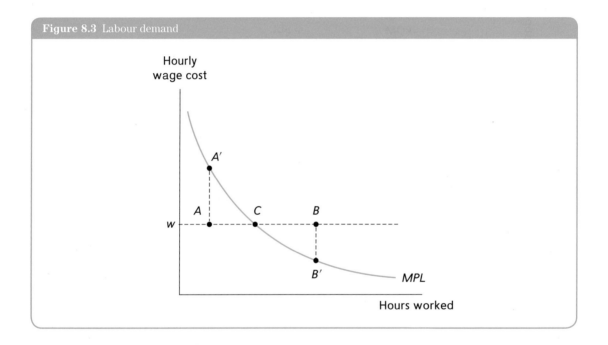

Figure 8.3 Labour demand

Now imagine a firm facing an hourly labour cost w. If it chooses to buy the number of hours corresponding to point A in Figure 8.3, its cost is lower than its benefit, which corresponds to point A'. Hiring one more hour is therefore highly profitable, and there is no reason for the firm not to do so and move rightward from point A. How far? Imagine that the firm goes all the way to point B, where the hourly labour cost is now higher than the marginal productivity of labour, as point B' indicates. Hiring more hours would entail losses. Reducing one hour would mean saving on the wage bill by w and giving up output by MPL, hence a saving for the firm. This means that the firm does well by moving leftward from point B. Clearly, the best position is at point C, on the MPL curve. If w rises, the point corresponding to point C will move up the MPL curve. This shows that the firm will always hire the number of hours that corresponds to the marginal productivity of labour. Put differently, the MPL curve represents the firm's demand for labour.[1]

---

[1] Note that the marginal productivity is measured in units of output. To be comparable, we also need to measure wage costs in the same units, e.g. one hour of work gets you three beers or one-thousandth of a car, more generally a portion of GDP. We consider here the real wage, which is represented as the ratio of the nominal wage W to the price level P, $w = W/P$.

8.2.2 Supply

Labour is supplied by people. As we all know too well, work is tiring and less pleasurable than leisure. This is why we ask for remuneration. How much we ask will depend on our skills and personal characteristics, including our inclination to stay at home. We consider the 'average' worker, so we ignore these personal characteristics. Instead, we ask what has to happen to the wage to convince the average worker to work one more hour. If the worker is unemployed, ignoring for the time being any welfare income such as unemployment benefits, almost any salary is better than nothing. If the worker already works quite a lot, one more hour is not that attractive and it will take a fairly good salary to convince her to stay longer on the job. This reasoning suggests that the supply of labour can be represented by an upward-sloping curve, as shown in Figure 8.4. The curve is steeper, the choosier the worker is.

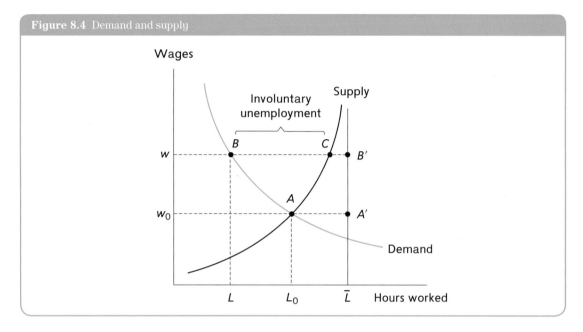

Figure 8.4 Demand and supply

8.2.3 Equilibrium and more realism

Equipped with the demand and supply apparatus, we are tempted to conclude that the outcome occurs at point A in Figure 8.4 where demand and supply meet.[2] Note that, in this situation, both firms and workers are perfectly satisfied with the situation. In particular, the total amount of work L_0 corresponds precisely to what workers are willing to supply at the going wage w_0. That does not mean that every worker has a job or that every employed person works full time. Such a case of full employment corresponds to $\bar{L}$. The distance AA' represents unused labour or unemployment. This is a special form of unemployment, however, for these hours are voluntarily not worked. Given the wage rate, some people do not wish to work at all or to work long hours – this is the meaning of the supply curve.

If, as Figure 8.4 presumes, the labour markets operated like other markets, there would be no involuntary unemployment. This is why equilibrium at point A is unrealistic. Since in every country a number of people are involuntarily unemployed, we have to admit that this is not a good description of real-life labour markets. Indeed, labour markets are very special, and for a good reason. The goods that are bought and sold on this market are people's time, talent and effort. Quite obviously, these are not standard goods.

Looking at Figure 8.4, we see that involuntary unemployment can only occur if workers are not on their supply curve. More precisely, they must be kept involuntarily somewhere to the left of the supply

---

[2] Here, we ignore the various charges that make wage costs different from what workers take home. Section 8.3.3 shows how to deal with this issue.

curve. On the other hand, firms are usually on, or close to, their demand curve. True, firms can have more workers than they want because they are forbidden to dismiss workers or, on the contrary, they may be unable to find all the workers that they need. But these are transient and limited departures, and we can safely ignore them. This all means that, in order to explain involuntary unemployment, we have to imagine that the economy lies on the labour demand curve somewhere up above point A, for example at point B. In this case, employment is L, and the distance BC measures involuntary unemployment while CB' captures voluntary unemployment.

How can point B be a lasting equilibrium? The salient feature of point B is that the wage w is above its no-involuntary-unemployment level w_0. The challenge, therefore, is to understand why such an outcome is possible. If the labour market were a market like all others, the wage rate would decline until it reached $w0$. This is not what happens. Somehow, wages do not move up and down, and they very rarely move down. A number of characteristics explain this feature:

- Salaries, the price of labour, are not set like the price of oil or corn, through bidding. They are collectively negotiated by representatives of employers and employees.

- Negotiations take place at more or less regular intervals and agreements hold for periods that usually extend to one year or more. Thus labour markets react slowly to changing conditions.

- Wage contracts are often regulated. For example, in many countries minimum wage legislation hampers downward adjustments.

- Conditions under which workers are hired and dismissed are also the object of specific legislation and customs.

- Unemployment benefits, designed to limit the hardship of becoming unemployed, can backfire, as explained below.

8.2.4 The economics of collective negotiations

The most crucial feature, perhaps, is the collective nature of labour negotiations. We now amend the demand–supply diagram to illustrate their economic effects. Workers resort to a collective representation – let's call it a trade union for the sake of simplicity – because it allows them to achieve better wages. If the arrangement works – if it did not, it would not have survived – the trade union's action delivers a higher wage than individual workers would achieve on their own. In Figure 8.5 we distinguish between the

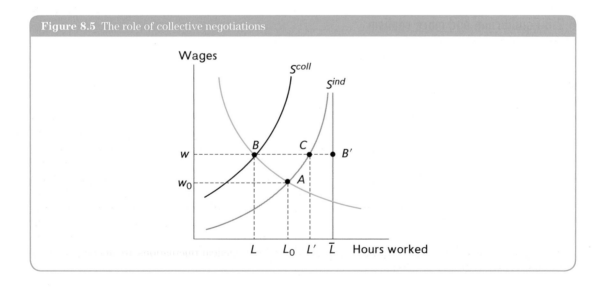

Figure 8.5 The role of collective negotiations

individual supply curve S^{ind}, which describes how individuals trade off income from work against leisure time, and a collective supply curve S^{coll}, which lies above the previous one.

Point A shows the outcome of the free interplay of individual demand and supply in the labour market in the absence of any rigidity: employment is L_0, the real wage is w_0 and there is no involuntary unemployment. With collective negotiations, the outcome of the negotiation is now represented by point B. As collective negotiations raise the real wage to w, firms respond by aiming at production processes that are less labour intensive and employment declines to L. Note that, at the new, higher wage level w, the amount of labour that workers wish to supply increases to L', corresponding to point C. The result is involuntary unemployment represented by the distance BC. This unemployment is collectively voluntary, however.

Why is this feature of labour markets so widespread? The workers who negotiate wages are, by definition, those who hold a job. They are the insiders. Reducing their own wages would allow some of those currently unemployed, the outsiders, to find jobs. But outsiders have no voice in the negotiations and the insiders have no interest in accepting wage cuts. This is why point B is stable in the sense that there is no mechanism that would change the situation. From a social and political viewpoint, this is understandable. The overwhelming majority of workers are employed since the highest unemployment rates rarely exceed 10–15 per cent, at least in the developed countries. Democratically, therefore, they support an institution that delivers higher wages, even at the cost of unemployment. In return, the insiders ask for assistance for the unemployed. Unemployment benefits are usually financed, partly at least, through taxes paid by the employed, who then feel that the outcome is beneficial to them and fair to the unemployed. Yet, from a strict economic point of view, these arrangements can be analysed as rigidities that prevent the labour markets from being flexible enough to avoid involuntary employment, sometimes on a very large scale, as Table 8.1 shows.

Collective negotiations provide a first explanation of the involuntary unemployment phenomenon, but many other common features conspire to make things worse. This is the case of high and, especially, long-lasting, unemployment benefits. These benefits have an obvious justification. Losing a job is already a traumatic experience; at least those who face this hardship, and their families, should live decently until they find a new job. But experience shows that a by-product of these benefits is that unemployed people feel less pressure to take up new jobs, and therefore remain unemployed for longer periods of time, which further lessens the pressure on insiders to allow for more wage flexibility. Figure 8.6 shows that, in many EU countries, a large number of people remain unemployed for more than one year. This is an important example of the fact that many European countries have long attached more weight to social protection than to economic efficiency. They tend to run socially generous but economically inefficient unemployment programmes. Some countries have found a way of combining both concerns. This is the case in the Scandinavian countries, which provide generous unemployment benefits coupled with the obligation to take up job offers.

8.2.5 The cyclical impact of wage rigidity

An important implication of wage rigidity can be seen by considering the case of a cyclical downturn when the wage is fixed at w. We start in Figure 8.7 from a situation where employment takes place at point B, with involuntary unemployment measured by BC. Now imagine that the economy slows down, for reasons explained in Chapter 17. Firms cannot sell all their products. Given that their equipment is in place anyway – their stock of capital cannot be reduced – the marginal product of labour declines and the demand for labour shifts down from D to D'. If the wages were perfectly flexible, we would have started at point A and moved to point A'. Employment and wages would have declined, voluntary unemployment would have risen but there would still be no involuntary unemployment. With wages rigidly maintained at w, we move to B', employment declines from L to L' and involuntary unemployment rises to $B'C$. It is easy to imagine the opposite case of an economic expansion, which would result in higher employment and lower involuntary unemployment. We see that wage rigidity explains the fact that cyclical fluctuations are accompanied by variations in involuntary unemployment.

Figure 8.6 Long-term unemployment, 2014

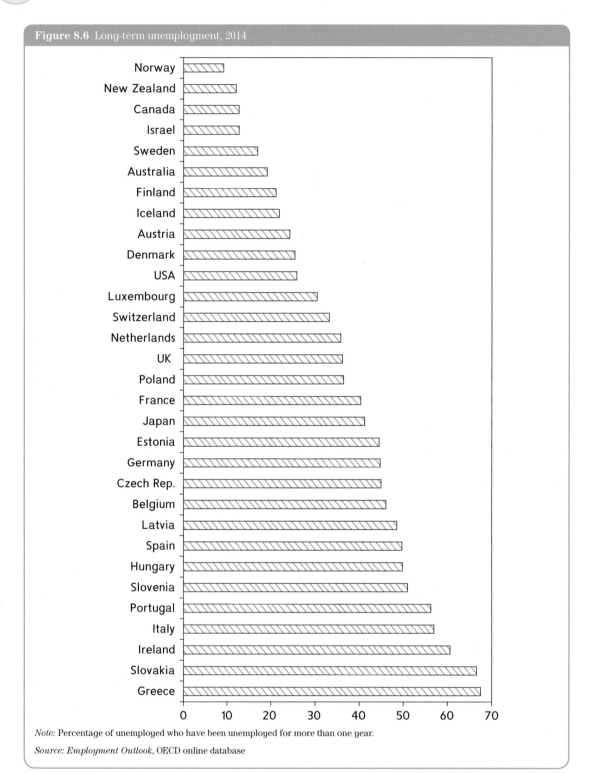

Note: Percentage of unemployed who have been unemployed for more than one year.

Source: Employment Outlook, OECD online database

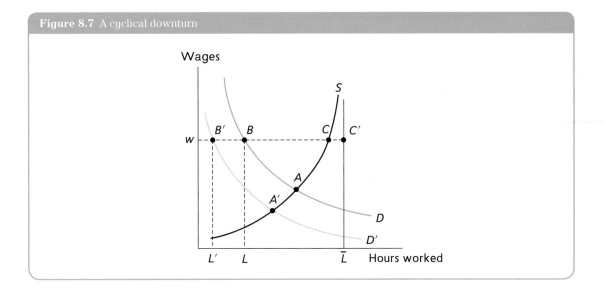

Figure 8.7 A cyclical downturn

8.3 Effects of trade integration

The previous chapters have focused on the effects of the Single Market on the goods and services markets and on overall economic growth. This section looks at the effects on the labour markets. In order to compete in the goods and services markets, producers must fight on all fronts; first and foremost, their production costs. Production costs include three main components: labour costs, the price of equipment and the price of materials.

Both equipment and material costs are largely determined internationally (since domestically produced goods must compete with imports) and therefore are not a source of comparative advantage. Labour costs, which typically amount to over 50 per cent of total production costs, on the other hand, are a key source of competitiveness. Competition in the goods market, in turn, has deep implications for the labour markets. Through goods markets, national labour markets indirectly compete against each other. This section examines some implications of this observation.

8.3.1 Economic effects of trade integration

Chapter 4 shows the distortionary effects of barriers to trade. When these barriers are eliminated, Chapter 5 shows that protected import-competing industries shrink while export industries expand. In terms of the analysis above, this can be seen as shifts in the labour demand curve that take place at the sectoral level.

If the labour markets are fully flexible, wages should rise in the industries that expand and they should decline in the industries that shrink. This, in turn, should trigger workers to move from the shrinking to the expanding industries, until wages are the same in both sectors. Wages could rise or decline, depending on the relative importance of the various adjustments, but there would still be no involuntary unemployment.[3]

A more realistic description must recognize the labour market rigidities presented in Section 8.2. As an illustration, we can either assume that wages are downward-rigid, as in Section 8.2.3, or think of the distinction between individual and collective labour supply, as in Section 8.2.4. We do both in Figure 8.8, where we imagine that trade opening separates out the economy into two broad sectors, an expanding one and a contracting one. Additionally, we take the extreme case where workers are specialized and cannot move from one sector to the other, at least not until they have undergone retraining.

---

[3] The Heckscher–Ohlin theory predicts that wages will increase if the country is capital-intensive relative to its trading partners and that wages will decrease if labour is relatively more abundant. This reasoning ignores the subsequent impact on capital accumulation.

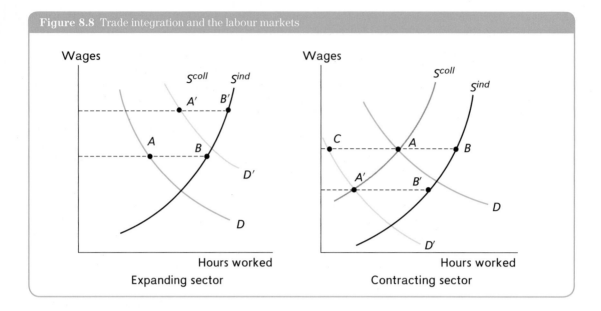

Figure 8.8 Trade integration and the labour markets

The initial situation is represented by point *A* in both charts. With collective labour bargaining, involuntary unemployment is measured by *AB* in each sector. The left-hand chart describes the expanding industry, where the demand for labour increases and the curve shifts from *D* to *D'*. The opposite happens in the contracting sector, shown in the right-hand chart. The new situation is represented by points *A'* in both charts and involuntary unemployment is measured by *A'B'*. It is not clear whether involuntary unemployment increases or decreases, both in each sector and in total. If the S^{coll} and the individual labour supply S^{ind} curves are parallel, there is no unemployment effect. There is a priori no reason to expect trade integration to raise or lower unemployment. This lines up with the facts. As previously noted, the tighter integration of European markets has been accompanied by steady or rising unemployment rates in some EU members such as France and Germany, but falling unemployment rates in members such as the UK, Sweden and Spain.

The only clear effect is that wages rise in the first sector and they decline in the second one. This may be seen as a source of growing inequality if wages were previously higher in the now-expanding sector, but inequality could be declining in the opposite case. At the very least, workers in the contracting sector may see the impact of trade integration as unfair.

We can briefly also consider what happens if, in addition, wages are downward-rigid, meaning that they can rise but not decline, because of legislative arrangements, social customs or the prevalence of minimum wage legislation. This does not matter for the expanding sector, since wages there increase. In the contracting sector, however, downward wage rigidity implies that the outcome is found at point *C* and involuntary unemployment, measured by *CB*, unambiguously increases.

In the end, trade integration does affect unemployment, unless the rigidities are severe. In that case, unemployment and inequalities are likely to rise. Yet trade is being blamed for creating unemployment. In fact, trade is only the messenger, which reveals the adverse effects of underlying distortions. This message, however, is very difficult to convey – the analysis presented here is far from trivial – and protectionism is never far below the surface. This is one reason why Europe's ability to dismantle *all* trade barriers is rather exceptional.

8.3.2 Institutional effects of trade integration

Labour market distortions are almost always related to institutional arrangements that reflect a country's political and social history. These institutions imply various degrees and forms of rigidity, with various effects on productive efficiency and unemployment. Such a deep change as European integration is unlikely to leave the institutions untouched. This section shows that labour market institutions and economic integration interact, with influences running in both directions:

- Economic integration affects the nature of labour market institutions. These institutions arise from a compromise between economic and social imperatives, reached under conditions that prevail at some point in time. When faced with deep economic integration, labour market institutions become a strategic characteristic in the quest for competitiveness, i.e. economic effectiveness. The ability of firms to compete across borders on the Single Market depends on the ability of employers and employees to react adequately to adverse shocks. In addition, if the labour markets are too inflexible, integration may result in job losses with no job gains and possibly even no general economic gain either. This changes the incentives that justified the initial institutional arrangements and, quite likely, opens the way to labour market reforms that raise the effectiveness of labour markets. Figure 8.1 shows that, indeed, some progress has been achieved in the EU.

- Labour market institutions affect integration. Economic integration almost always creates winners and losers, but typically the winners win more than the losers lose. Europeans' willingness to elect leaders who push ever-deeper integration hinges critically on their belief that labour market institutions along with social safety nets will spread the net benefits of integration and dampen the pain felt by the losers. In the absence of some degree of fairness, broad political support for ever-closer economic integration is unlikely to be maintained in EU nations.

One important question is how national labour market institutions stand to be affected by the process of EU integration. In principle, since trade competition becomes competition among national social arrangements, survival of the fittest should guarantee that, eventually, all European states will gravitate towards the most efficient arrangements. This principle, however, must face the fact that European integration can be challenged, and even possibly reversed, if it is perceived as unfair.

8.3.3 Economics of 'social dumping'

A good example of this situation is the widely held view that European integration undermines valuable social protection, a view summarized as 'social dumping'. Indeed, workers in many of the older Member States (EU15) are convinced that competition from the 12 new Member States (EU12) will force a reduction in the level of social protection that they enjoy today. At the time they joined, wages were much lower in the EU12 countries (see Table 8.2) and in some of them the level of social protection was also considerably lower than in the EU15.

There is nothing new here; it is an old, old concern. It was, for example, the crux of a major debate over the shape of the Treaty of Rome in the 1950s. In the early 1950s, French workers worried that lax social policy in Italy and Germany would undermine French social policy. Half a century later, in 2005, French workers voted against the European Constitution, partly because they feared competition from the famed 'Polish plumber'. As history would have it, since the 1950s social protection of workers rose spectacularly throughout western Europe despite (or maybe because of) the deep integration between nations that initially had very different wage and social protection levels. Much the same is happening now in the EU12 countries. Table 8.2 shows that the wage gap is often narrowing.

Such fears lead to calls for social harmonization. The leaders of the six founding nations of the European Union already worried about 'social dumping'. Yet, they decided that harmonization of most social policies was not a necessary component of European integration. The economic logic behind this judgement continues to affect EU policy, so it is worth considering in some detail.

To get a handle on the basic issues, we start by making strong assumptions to radically simplify the range of issues at hand. We will add back in some important aspects of reality after having established the basic points. Taking the example of France, we start by supposing that, as in Section 8.2.3, labour markets operate like other markets, so the wage adjusts to make sure that there is no involuntary unemployment. Moreover, to keep things simple, suppose France starts without any social policies and initially is closed to trade. The equilibrium, shown in the left-hand panel of Figure 8.9, is where the real wage is w and the employment level is L.

Table 8.2   Median net earnings (annual), 2004–13

	2004	2006	2008	2010	2012
Bulgaria	729	961	1,308	1,536	1,799
Czech Republic	2,617	3,427	4,671	4,897	5,103
Estonia	–	–	4,046	4,041	4,588
Latvia	1,393	1,916	3,109	2,919	3,219
Lithuania	1,602	2,074	2,967	2,798	2,982
Hungary	2,724	3,061	3,560	3,457	3,113
Poland	2,229	2,776	3,717	3,515	3,599
Romania	944	1,431	2,066	2,068	2,084
Slovenia	–	–	5,953	6,513	6,758
Slovakia	–	–	3,715	4,035	4,133
Germany	13,129	13,267	14,098	14,706	15,254
France	11,968	12,745	13,672	14,050	14,443
UK	17,133	18,256	16,733	16,036	18,170
EU27	10,729	11,300	11,662	11,986	12,697

Source: http://epp.eurostat.ec.europa.eu/statistics_explained/index.php/Wages_and_labour_costs

Figure 8.9 Social policy and distortions

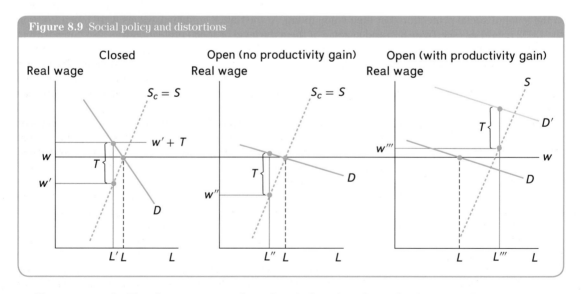

Now suppose the French government adopted a whole series of social policies, e.g. limits on working hours, obligatory retirement benefits, maternity leave, sick leave, 6 weeks of annual holiday, etc. These policies would undoubtedly be good for most workers. Indeed, most Europeans view these as necessities, not luxuries. Yet, however good these policies are for workers and society at large, they are expensive for firms. To be specific, suppose that they raise the cost of employing workers by T euros per hour. What happens to wages and employment? The demand schedule shifts vertically down by T, since labour cost has increased by that amount. The new equilibrium wage paid to workers – this is called the 'take-home' pay – with the general policy will be w'.[4] It is useful to think of the social policy 'tax' being paid partly by consumers (in the form of higher prices) and partly by workers (in the form of lower take-home wages). The firms we consider here are competitive and so cannot bear any part of T (they earn zero profits both before and after T is imposed).

Why does the take-home wage fall when social policies are imposed? Firms hire workers up to the point where marginal labour productivity is equal to the wage cost, as explained in Section 8.2.1. This cost includes wage and non-wage costs, such as the cost of social policies. Firms cannot pay higher labour costs if they want to avoid losing money. Given this iron law of the labour market – firms hire workers up to the point where all included employment costs equal the workers' value to the firm – everything that raises non-wage labour costs must force down the take-home pay of workers. In essence, the social policies are a way of 'forcing' workers to take part of their remuneration in the form of non-wage 'payment', e.g. 4 weeks of paid holiday or generous sick leave, instead of in the direct form of take-home pay.

Next, consider the impact of freeing trade in goods between France and other nations. As far as the labour market is concerned, freer trade has two main impacts:

1 As discussed at length in Chapters 4, 5, 6 and 7, trade tends to boost the productivity of an economy. It does so by allowing a nation's capital and labour to be allocated more efficiently. For example, Chapter 6 showed how freer trade produced fewer, larger, more efficient firms that faced more effective competition from each other.

2 Trade also tends to flatten the demand curve since it heightens the competition between national firms and foreign firms. For example, if real wage costs rise by €100 per week, firms will have to raise prices. The negative impact of higher prices on output, and therefore employment, is greater in the presence of foreign competition. Or, to put it more directly, greater integration of goods markets means that workers in different nations compete more directly with each other.

We begin with the second concern since this is closest to the everyday concerns of many workers in Europe. The middle panel in Figure 8.9 shows the impact of the flatter demand curve on French labour. The way the diagram is drawn, openness per se would have no impact if there were no social policy. Without the tax T, wage and employment levels would be as in the closed economy case (i.e. w and L). The non-wage costs, i.e. T, however, change things. Since labour demand is now more responsive to total labour costs, the take-home wage of French workers will fall more, to w'' rather than w', when T is imposed. The reason is simple. Greater openness gives consumers a wider range of options. When T is imposed, more of it gets paid by workers than by consumers. In other words, the greater price sensitivity forces workers to bear more of the burden of the social-policy 'tax'.

The result that greater openness reduces wages flies in the face of Europe's experience. The incomes of European workers have been growing steadily as European markets have become more tightly integrated. Moreover, as discussed in Chapter 7, some of the fastest income growth occurred in the 1960s when European trade integration was proceeding at its fastest pace. How can we explain this? The efficiency-enhancing effects of trade integration are the answer.

The third panel in Figure 8.9 shows the labour market implications of trade-induced efficiency gains. As productivity rises, the value of workers to firms rises and this is demonstrated as a shift up the demand curve to D'. Now we see that, even if trade integration makes the demand curve flatter, the shift up in the labour demand curve more than offsets flattening. In the figure, the take-home wage has risen to w'' and employment has increased to L''.

So far we have put the issue of unemployment to the side by assuming that the labour market clears. To consider unemployment, we allow the 'collective' labour supply curve (S^{coll}) and the individual labour supply curve (S^{ind}) to differ, as in Section 8.2.4. This is done in Figure 8.10, which corresponds to the second panel of Figure 8.9. The initial position is characterized by unemployment U, with employment L and supply

---

[4] Readers who have taken a good course in microeconomics will recognize this as the analysis of the 'incidence' of the 'tax' T.

L_s. The social policy distortion reduces employment to L' and supply to L'_s. The effect on unemployment is not clear, however, and this is also the case of the trade-opening effect, as we have already seen in Section 8.3.1. Here again, trade integration has no direct impact on unemployment, only on employment.

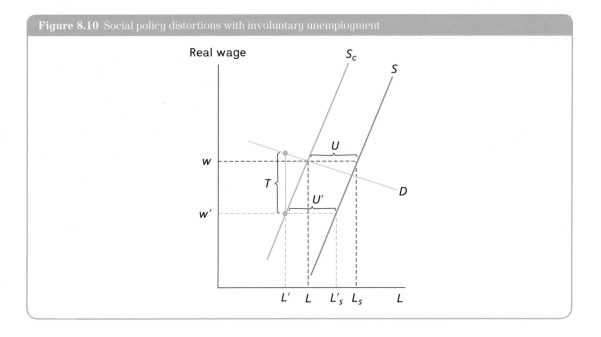

Figure 8.10 Social policy distortions with involuntary unemployment

What has all this got to do with social dumping? What we have shown is that the total cost of employing workers – wage and non-wage costs – is tied to the productivity of workers. If governments raise social policy standards, the economy will adjust by lowering employment and reducing the wages (of course, wages rarely fall; what would happen is that wages would rise more slowly than productivity for a number of years, as happened in France when the 35-hour week was introduced). When an economy is more open, the wage and employment adjustments tend to be greater, other things equal. Or, to put it more colloquially, the anti-employment effects of social policies are magnified by greater openness.

This does not necessarily put pressure on social policies. The key point is that the same mechanism is at work in France's trade partners. If the other nations have lower social policy standards, their workers will have higher take-home pay than otherwise, since the foreign firms hire workers up to the point where their total labour cost matches their workers' productivity. Social harmonization would result in lower wages in these countries but would have little impact on the competitive pressures facing French employers. Turning this around, the same logic tells us that lowering French social policy standards would not boost French competitiveness in anything but the short run.

The upshot of all this should be clear. The logic of competition ties the sum of wage and non-wage costs to workers' productivity. The founders of the EU therefore believed that the division between wage and non-wage costs could be left to the choice of each Member State exactly because this division has only a moderate impact on external competitiveness.

8.4 Migration

Along with the other freedoms of movement (goods, services, capital), the free movement of workers is the cornerstone of EU integration and has been so since its inception in the 1950s. The goal is both economic and political. Allowing workers to move freely within the Union should enhance economic efficiency by allowing workers to find the jobs that best suit their skills and experience, while simultaneously allowing firms to hire the most appropriate workers. On a political level, the architects of the EU hoped that mobility would foster mutual understanding among the peoples of Europe. As many readers will know from first-hand experience, the fact that many young Europeans spend some time living, studying or working in other EU nations has had a big impact on the way Europeans view each other. This section considers European migration. We start with some facts.

8.4.1 Some facts

We start with global migration patterns. Figure 8.11 presents the net migration record – the excess of immigrants over emigrants, so that negative numbers indicate an outflow of workers while positive numbers mean an inflow – of continents since the 1950s, with forecasts for the period 2005–10. The figure confirms that people move from 'the South' to 'the North' and increasingly so. It also shows that Europe has switched from net emigration to net immigration. This is explained by Europe's spectacular growth during the late 1950s and the 1960s, which brought about conditions of full employment and led governments and firms to seek out foreign labour. The turnaround of Europe's economic fortunes, starting with the 1973 recession, temporarily stopped the evolution, but the trend has been resumed. This pattern reflects the two basic reasons why people leave their countries: (1) they flee poverty and (2) they flee political instability and related violence. In general, political instability breeds poverty.

Figure 8.11 Net migration rates, 1950–2010

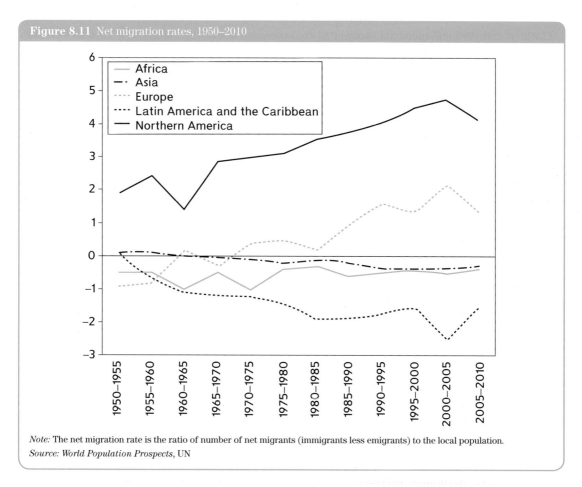

Note: The net migration rate is the ratio of number of net migrants (immigrants less emigrants) to the local population.
Source: World Population Prospects, UN

Global numbers should not conceal important differences within Europe. For decades, southern Europe (Italy, Spain, Portugal and Greece) and south-eastern Europe (mainly Turkey) were prime sending nations, while the northern European nations (the EEC6 less Italy plus the Nordic and Alpine countries) were big

receiving nations. Since the early 1980s, with growth picking up, the southern European nations have become net importers as well. Some of this migration involves the return of Spanish, Italian and Portuguese workers who had previously emigrated, but it also reflects an increasing inflow of non-European workers from places such as Africa or Latin America. Within Europe, Turkey has been joined in its role as a provider of migrants by central and eastern European nations that dropped, by the end of the 1980s, general restrictions on emigration imposed by their previous regimes.

Migration within the EU is, in principle, free. Yet, when the EU was expanded in 2004, special provisions were temporarily imposed on the 10 new members to limit migration from these countries to the incumbent 15 members. Similar restrictions were imposed on Bulgaria and Romania upon accession in 2007. We return to this issue in Section 8.4.4. Box 8.2 explains why fears of massive immigration from central and eastern Europe have been unjustified. In fact, seven out of ten foreign workers in EU Member States are from non-EU countries. The policies that govern labour flows from non-member nations are entirely national – the EU does not try to impose what might be called a common external migration policy. To put it differently, being part of the EU's common labour market does not seem to matter very much for migration.

Box 8.2   The flood that was not to be

The 2004 and 2007 enlargements brought 12 countries and about 100 million new citizens into the European Union. Table 8.2 shows that most workers in the EU12 countries are paid substantially less in their home nations than they would get if they held similar jobs in the EU15. According to the principles laid out in Section 8.2.1, this difference is primarily due to higher labour productivity in the EU15. The income gap between the east and the west in Europe is approximately 50 per cent when adjusted for higher prices in the west; at current exchange rates, the income gap is even larger. This raised the prospect of massive east–west migration, but this possibility has not become reality.

Direct bilateral flow numbers are not available (and data on migration are notoriously unreliable), so we proceed in an indirect way. Table 8.3 reports net migration flows. It is likely that gross outflows from the EU12 to the EU15 countries were significantly larger, since most EU12 countries have also witnessed immigration from the rest of the world, including from the CIS (Commonwealth of Independent States) countries of the former Soviet Union, as well as from some southern European countries. Net outflows have declined in all EU12 countries, several of which have actually become net immigration countries. Looking at the EU15 countries, net inflows mostly declined between 1997–2003 and 2004–07, in spite of sustained flows from the rest of the world. A good example is Spain, which has seen rising immigration from Latin America. The main exceptions are Austria, Finland and Ireland, each one being a special case of its own.

Why didn't the flood happen? One possible reason is that most EU15 nations negotiated long transition periods during which EU12 citizens cannot move freely into their labour markets. But countries that opened their borders, such as Ireland, Sweden and the UK, report no or little increase in net inflows. Most likely, the low migration numbers reflect the fact that the 'New Europeans' share much of the 'Old Europeans'' resistance to moving (see Chapter 11). With the prospect that the EU12 countries are likely to catch up with the EU15 countries, the incentives to leave home, family and friends, to wade into a new culture with another language, have been too limited to trigger large-scale migration.

Being part of a common labour market does not seem to be the key to determining the origin of migrants. Migrants from EU nations make up a much higher percentage of foreign workers in Norway and Switzerland than they do in France and Germany. This shows that the discriminatory liberalization implied by the free mobility of workers within the EU (i.e. workers from one EU nation are free to work in any other EU nation, but they need special permission to work in non-EU nations such as Norway) is not a dominant factor in determining migration patterns. This contrasts sharply with discriminatory liberalization of goods. As Chapter 5 shows, the composition of imports is strongly influenced by implementation of the customs union.

Table 8.3 Net immigration before and after enlargements (1000s of people)

	Belgium	Denmark	Germany	Ireland	Greece	Spain	France	Italy
1997–2003	164	71	1146	193	302	2596	853	1197
2004–2007	202	42	237	245	162	2558	358	1753
	Luxembourg	Netherlands	Austria	Portugal	Finland	Sweden	UK	Total EU15
1997–2003	27	266	164	344	32	143	924	6522
2004–2007	12	−60	179	131	40	157	842	5557
	Bulgaria	Czech Rep.	Estonia	Cyprus	Latvia	Lithuania	Hungary	
1997–2003	−213	32	−14	41	−33	−96	97	
2004–2007	−1	174	1	52	−5	−28	71	
	Malta	Poland	Romania	Slovenia	Slovakia			
1997–2003	17	−497	−592	18	−14			−186
2004–2007	7	−79	−23	29	17			262

Note: A positive number indicates net immigration; a negative number signals net emigration.

Source: Eurostat online database

There is nothing really new here. We already mentioned that, in the 1950s and 1960s, nations across north-western Europe were experiencing such rapid growth that industry found itself short of workers. Individual nations responded by facilitating inward migration from many different nations. Not surprisingly, nations that wanted to 'import' workers found it easiest to induce migration from nations with low wages and relatively high unemployment. The fact that Spain, Portugal and Greece were not at the time members of the EU did little to hinder the flow of their workers into EU members such as Germany. Indeed, German immigration policy in the 1960s was at least as welcoming to Turks and Spaniards as it was to southern Italians. Moreover, nations such as Sweden and the UK, whose industries also experienced labour shortages, managed to attract migrants – including some migrants from EU nations such as Italy – even without being part of the Common Market. In short, the western European policies that fostered the big migration flows in the 1960s were basically unrelated to the policies of the Common Market.

8.4.2 Economics of labour market integration

Labour migration is probably the most contentious aspect of economic integration in Europe. In most western European nations, popular opinion holds immigrants responsible for high unemployment, abuse of social welfare programmes, street crime and deterioration of neighbourhoods. As a result, a number of explicitly anti-immigration political parties have fared well in elections. How does immigration affect the sending and receiving nations, and who gains and who loses from it?

Simplest framework

We start with the simplest analytical framework that allows us to organize our thinking about the economic consequences of labour migration. We start with the case where migration is not allowed between two nations (Home and Foreign) that initially have different wages. Figure 8.12 shows a situation in which workers initially earn better wages in Home than in Foreign. The length of the horizontal schedule represents total labour available in both countries, L in Home and L^* in Foreign. For the time being, we will assume full employment, $L + L^*$ in total, for both countries. The marginal productivity of labour in Home is measured on the left vertical axis. The corresponding MPL curve is downward sloping as employment in Home is measured along the horizontal axis from left to right. The foreign marginal productivity of labour is measured on the right vertical axis. The corresponding MPL^* curve seems upward sloping, but it is not, since employment in Foreign is measured in the opposite of the usual direction, from right to left. Initially, the situation in Home is represented by point Q, with wage w and employment L. Point Q^* describes the initial situation in Foreign, with wage w^* and employment L^*.

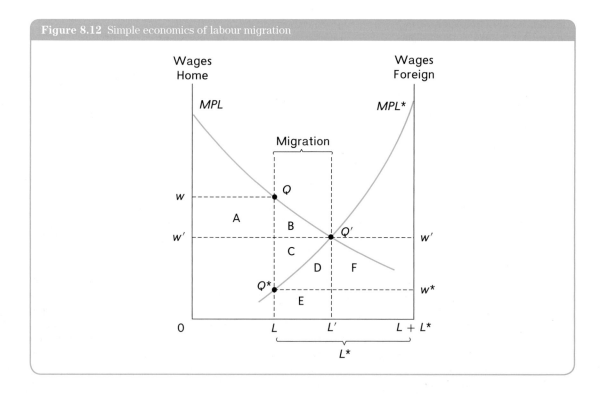

Figure 8.12 Simple economics of labour migration

Now allow migration. Given the wage difference, labour will flow from Foreign to Home. This will push down wages in Home and thus harm the Home workers – while benefiting Home capital owners. The opposite happens in Foreign. As some Foreign labour moves to Home, Foreign wages tend to rise, making the remaining Foreign workers better off – and Foreign capital owners worse off. If there is no impediment – legal, personal reticence or other – migration will go on until wages are equalized. This is represented by point Q', with wages w' in both countries.

We find that, in each country, some lose and some gain from migration, but what about each country? Start with Home country. We need to understand the impact of migration on the earnings of workers and capital-owners. To that effect we look at Figure 8.13, which enlarges the Home country situation around point Q. The area under the *MPL* curve represents total Home output. The reason follows directly from the definition of the marginal product of capital. The first unit of labour employed produces output equal to the height of the *MPL* curve at the point where $L = 1$. The amount produced by the second unit of capital is given by the level of *MPL* at the point where $L = 2$, and so on. Adding up all the heights of the *MPL* curve at each point yields the area under the curve.

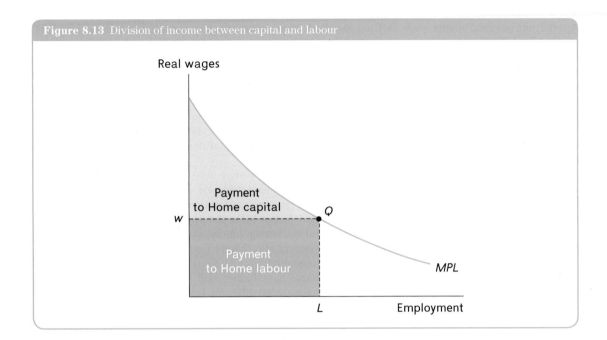

Figure 8.13 Division of income between capital and labour

The total earnings of Home labour is just the wage rate w times the amount of labour L, which is measured in Figure 8.13 by the rectangle below and to the left of point Q. Since we are assuming that capital and labour are the only two factors of production in this simple world, capital receives all the output that is not paid to labour. Graphically this means that capital's income corresponds to the triangle between the *MPL* curve and the w line.

With this in hand, we turn now to the welfare effects of capital flows. We saw that the 'native' Home workers lose. As they move from Q to Q′, their wages decline by $w - w'$. Their loss is represented by the rectangle marked A in Figure 8.12. Home capital-owners increase their earnings by area A plus the triangle B. Thus the total economic impact on Home citizens is positive and equal to the triangle B. Another way of seeing that Home gains from migration is to note that the immigrant workers raise total output in Home by the areas B + C + D + E, but some of it, equal to areas C + D + E (i.e. w' times the labour flow $L^* - L'$), does not benefit 'native' workers since it is paid out to the immigrants.

The Foreign workers who remain in their country see their wages rise from w^* to w'. The size of this gain is shown by rectangle F. With production falling, Foreign capital-owners lose by D + F. Combining all these losses and gains, the factors of production that remain in Foreign lose overall by an amount measured by triangle D. However, if we count the welfare of the emigrant workers as part of Foreign's welfare, the conclusion is reversed. Foreign workers abroad used to earn E, now they receive C + D + E, so they gain C + D. Altogether, Foreign gains by an amount equal to the triangle C.

In short, while migration creates winners and losers in both nations, collectively both nations gain. The deep reason for this has to do with efficiency. Without labour mobility, the allocation of productive factors was inefficient. For example, on the margin, Foreign workers were less productive. Migration improves the overall efficiency of the EU economy and the gains from this are split between Home and Foreign. Foreign gets area C; Home gets area B. This all assumes that there is no unemployment to start with and therefore seems unrealistic; we return to this issue in Section 8.4.3 below.

Broader interpretation: complementarity vs. substitutability

The analysis above classifies all productive factors into two categories: capital and labour. It is important to note, however, that for most EU nations we should interpret 'capital' as including 'human capital', i.e. highly educated workers. The reason has to do with the economic notion of 'complementarity' versus 'substitutability'. Consider the example of how productive factors combine to produce hotel services. Apart from material inputs such as food and bed linen, hotels require unskilled workers (cleaners, etc.), skilled workers (managers, marketing people, etc.) and capital (the building, furniture, etc.). In a country such as Norway, unskilled labour is very costly so hotels are very expensive; consequently there are relatively few hotels. If Norway allowed hotels to hire foreign workers at lower wages, some factors would be hurt – the unskilled workers who earned high wages before the immigration – but other factors would be helped. Skilled workers and capital would find that their rewards rise. As the price of hotel rooms fell, the hotel industry would expand, raising the demand for highly skilled workers and capital. In this situation, we say that unskilled workers are complements to skilled workers and capital: demand for skilled workers and capital rises as the supply of unskilled workers increases and their price falls.

The point of this is to put the losses to domestic labour in perspective. Immigrants often have a skill mix that is very different from that of domestic workers. Skilled domestic workers can thus be thought of as belonging to 'capital' in Figure 8.12 and thus winning from immigration. In France and Germany, for example, immigrants often work at jobs, e.g. in factories, that boost the productivity of native workers in related fields such as management, finance, sales and marketing. Indeed, immigrants often fill jobs that no native would take, such as kitchen workers, street sweepers, etc.; this is an extreme form of complementarity in which there are no economic losers in the receiving nation.

We can look at the opposite case, when immigrants have higher skill levels than the average native worker. In these cases, the analysis of immigration is somewhat different. Instead of shifting L from Foreign to Home, migration shifts 'capital'. Graphically this raises the *MPL* curve in Figure 8.12 for Home and lowers it for Foreign. The reason is that the presence of more skilled workers tends to raise the productivity of unskilled workers. If you want a mental picture of this process, think of American entrepreneurs coming into Ireland and starting businesses that hire Irish workers away from the farm sector. Again, we see that immigration can be a win–win situation for the receiving nation.

Another insight from the notion of complementarity is that of micro-level matching. Some immigrants may have very specific skills that are lacking in the receiving nation. Since these workers do not compete with native workers, or compete with very few native workers, such immigration is usually less contentious since it creates few losers. This level of matching among countries can proceed to an even lower level. For example, even within a single company, the experiences of workers vary, and free mobility of labour may make it easier to move workers into jobs that best fit their experience. Again, it is entirely possible that everyone gains from such matching. More generally, immigrants who have skills that are complementary to the skill mix in the receiving nation are typically less likely to create losers in the receiving nation.

Empirical evidence

So much for the theory. What does the evidence tell us? Given the importance of immigration in the various national debates in Europe, economists have done a great deal of work estimating the impact of migration on the wages of domestic workers. Generally, these studies find that a 1 per cent rise in the supply of workers via migration changes the wages of native workers by between 1 and –1 per cent, with most studies putting the figure in the even narrower range of ±0.3 per cent. There are two key points to take away from these findings. First, it is not obvious that immigration always lowers wages. Since nations tend to let in workers who have skills that are complementary to those of domestic workers, the impact is often positive. Second, whether it is slightly positive or slightly negative, the impact is quite small. Again, this outcome is due in part to the fact that countries tend to restrict the types of labour inflow that would have large negative effects on wages.

Table 8.4 provides some information regarding the complementarity/substitutability issue. It shows the education levels of workers employed in the EU15 countries, according to where they come from, in percentages of all employed workers. Immigrants from the other EU15 countries are generally better educated and occupy higher-skill jobs than the natives. This suggests micro-level matching and explains why this type of immigration is not controversial. Immigrants from outside the EU are complementary in the opposite direction: they are often less educated and fill in elementary tasks/jobs. Immigrants from the EU10 – the 10 countries that acceded in 2004 – are in-between as far as education is concerned and they tend to accept less-skilled jobs.

Table 8.4   Education level and skills of immigrant workers in the EU15 countries in 2005 (% of total)

	Overall EU employed	Immigrant workers from:		
		EU15	EU10	Outside EU
Education				
Low	27	15	15	36
Medium	47	41	63	40
High	26	44	22	23
Occupation				
High-skilled white collar	40	55	16	20
Low-skilled white collar	26	24	28	25
Skilled manuals	25	12	27	21
Elementary tasks	10	9	30	35

Source: Survey of the European Union, OECD, September 2007

8.4.3 Unemployment
Framework

One common belief is that immigrants cause unemployment. The framework presented in the previous section cannot help us assess this view since it explicitly assumes that all workers get jobs. Instead, we use the framework presented in Section 8.2.4 and apply it to the employment of native workers. In Figure 8.14, in the absence of immigration, the labour market is at point A and involuntary unemployment is AB.

Now suppose that some immigrants enter the country. We have to imagine how the immigrants will operate in the labour market. One extreme assumption is that the immigrants are willing and able to perform the same jobs as natives but at a wage that is below the union-set wage w. Being cheaper, they displace the native workers. The demand curve for native workers shifts to the left from D to D'. The idea here is that firms first hire cheap immigrants and then turn to the native market to fulfil any remaining demands. The distance AC measures the share of employment taken over by immigrant workers. The result is that the market moves to point A'. The union-set wage and native employment fall to w' and L', respectively. Two points are worth stressing. First, even in this extreme case – where firms are able to hire immigrants at below market wages – the drop in native employment $(L - L')$ is less than the number of immigrants (AC). As a consequence, total employment, counting both natives and immigrants, rises. This dampening is due to the drop in native wages, which allows firms to produce more output and therefore expand jobs.

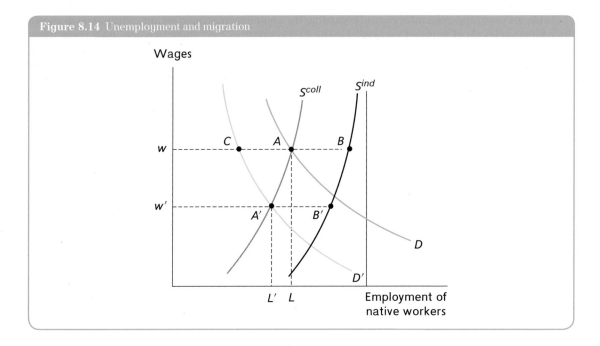

Figure 8.14 Unemployment and migration

Second, there may be no change in unemployment. Because unemployment is a result of the labour market's structure, immigration will affect unemployment only to the extent that it affects the structure of the labour market. In the particular example shown in the diagram, where the two labour supply curves S^{ind} and S^{coll} are drawn as parallel, there is no change in the number of unemployed natives. In that case, the drop in wages from w to w' decreases the number of native workers who want to work at the going wage by as much as the drop in native employment. If we had not drawn the two supply curves as parallel, we would have got a different answer.[5] The main point, however, is that if immigration is to affect unemployment, it must do so by altering labour market structure.

Another possible assumption is the opposite one: that immigrants participate in the labour market in exactly the same way as do native workers. In this case (not shown in the diagram), both curves S^{ind} and S^{coll} shift to the right. The results would be qualitatively identical to those shown in Figure 8.14. There would be some drop in the wage and some increase in employment. Since the true impact of immigrants on national labour markets is probably somewhere between these two extremes, it seems reasonable to believe that the standard impact of immigration will be some increase in employment, some decrease in wages and an ambiguous effect on unemployment.

Empirical evidence

The empirical evidence on the effect of immigration on unemployment is mixed. A visual inspection of Figure 8.15 does not suggest any link. Some studies have found that immigrants increase the chance of unemployment for some groups of workers, but have the opposite effect on other groups of workers. This is clearly linked to the complements and substitutes analysis. Other authors find little or no effect of immigration on the risk of being unemployed. In summary, the empirical evidence we have to date does not support the notion that immigration has large, negative effects on European labour markets. As usual, this lack of convincing evidence is due in part to the fact that countries tend to pick and choose their immigrants, presumably with a view to avoiding large negative effects on employment and/or unemployment.

---

[5] How are the curves in reality? Truth is, we don't know. The proof of the pudding is in the eating, namely, in the empirical evidence discussed below.

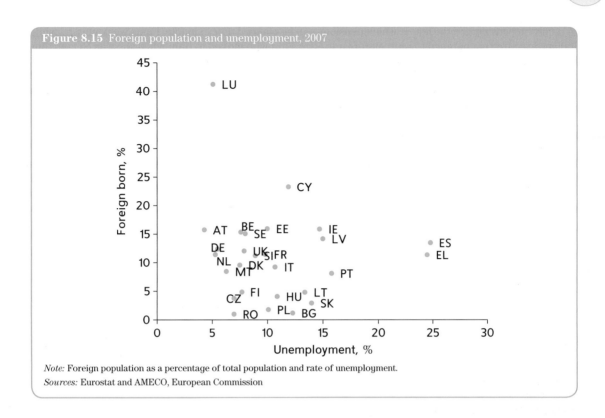

Figure 8.15 Foreign population and unemployment, 2007

Note: Foreign population as a percentage of total population and rate of unemployment.

Sources: Eurostat and AMECO, European Commission

8.4.4 Barriers to mobility

Two key results emerge: (1) immigration is likely to raise employment and national income; and (2) immigration is unlikely to affect unemployment in either direction. These results provide a strong endorsement for the fundamental principle of freedom of movement of workers within the EU. Few people take advantage of this opportunity as can be seen from the low share of the foreign-born population in most EU nations (Figure 8.15, vertical axis). One reason is that EU citizens do not regard freedom of establishment as an attractive option. Another is that, in spite of the stated policy, there remain a large number of barriers, some explicit, most implicit.

The first barrier is the explicit temporary arrangement concerning the new EU members, except Cyprus and Malta. Starting in 2004, all countries may apply restrictive measures for up to seven years following accession. Except Ireland, the UK and Sweden, all EU15 countries and Hungary chose to implement this clause. In 2006, obviously reassured that migration was moderate, a number of countries allowed unrestricted entry from the 2004 acceding countries.

Other implicit barriers concern social protection. Health insurance does not raise serious difficulties since any EU worker is allowed to enter the local system upon settlement, paying local dues and receiving equal treatment. In order to simplify the transition process, a European Health Card was introduced in 2004.

The situation is more complicated as far as pension rights are concerned. The principle is simple: workers collect pension rights wherever they go; upon retirement, they apply to their country of residence to establish their pension rights on the basis of work performed anywhere in the EU. However, the rights acquired in each country of previous residence are assessed on the basis of that country's system. This 'detail' means that pension rights act as a strong barrier to mobility. The reason is that rules to accumulate rights differ widely from one country to the next. This concerns, in particular, the length of time required to receive a pension and the age at which pensions can be claimed. For example, Finns work until 67 while Italians are often encouraged to retire before age 60. A Finn who moved to Italy when she was 50 may thus be pushed into retirement at age 57, with a minimal Italian pension, and she will not receive the complement from Finland until ten years later. The situation is even worse than that. The agreement concerns general pensions, not those tied to a company or a profession. In several countries, such occupational pensions represent the larger share of retirement income.

Similarly, unemployment benefits discourage mobility. Existing agreements allow an unemployed worker who moves elsewhere within the EU to keep receiving the benefits for up to three months. Imagine the case of a worker who moves from a high to a low unemployment country after having lost his job. If he does not find a job within three months of arrival, he loses his unemployment benefit and is without income. This is a powerful deterrent to migration. The rule might seem strange, but it is designed to discourage 'welfare tourism' – the possibility that people move not to seek jobs but to gain access to generous welfare payments.

A last barrier worth mentioning concerns the regulated professions. Obviously, not everyone can set himself up as a medical doctor. In principle, the EU countries recognize each other's qualifications, so doctors, architects, nurses or lawyers can practise anywhere they wish. But the rule does not apply to all regulated professions. For instance, in order to open a hairdressing salon in France, one has to satisfy surprisingly exacting conditions, which rule out all other European hairdressers.

These are examples of the many barriers that limit labour mobility within Europe. Add languages and customs, distance from home, frequent housing shortages, and you start understanding why the freedom of establishment is not delivering. The European Commission is regularly advancing proposals to beat back all regulatory barriers, but many initiatives fail because myriads of local private interests – such as French hairdressers – are opposed to the free entry of competitors.

8.5 Summary

This chapter has dealt with two related topics: the link between trade integration and labour markets and migration, and the view that the EU may be moving to a single integrated labour market. Both issues are politically sensitive but there is surprisingly little substance behind widely held fears that workers systematically get the wrong end of the stick.

Relative to comparable advanced economies, many European countries exhibit low rates of employment and high rates of unemployment. This represents a waste of our most precious resources and a source of anxiety. The situation, though, is very uneven, reflecting the diversity of labour market arrangements inherited from each country's history. Labour market regulations are needed to protect workers but many of them introduce rigidities that prevent the achievement of full employment.

European integration affects the labour markets in two main ways:

- Trade integration indirectly leads to competition between labour markets. It affects the labour markets in two ways. It creates winners and losers and it shifts production patterns, which require labour market flexibility to avoid job losses. In general, countries with more flexible labour markets have a comparative advantage in goods markets. This has led countries with more rigid markets to complain about social dumping, as they resist economic pressure to reform their labour markets. The principle remains that labour markets and social policies are a national prerogative. Theory and evidence support this principle.

- The EU treaty guarantees the freedom of movement of workers. Here again, many citizens fear that competition from foreign workers will lower wages and create more unemployment. The fear is commonplace in the EU15 countries where wages are much higher than in the EU12 countries. Theory and evidence suggest that these fears are largely misplaced. In fact, for a number of cultural and institutional reasons, there is too little mobility of workers in Europe, in spite of the general principle of freedom of movement.

Self-assessment questions

1 Explain what happens to a firm's profits as it moves in Figure 8.3 from point A to point B.

2 Using Figure 8.4, explain what happens to voluntary and involuntary unemployment as workers individually ask for higher wages for the same amount of work. Answer the same question using Figure 8.5, assuming that there is no change in the collective supply of labour.

3 The following figure depicts the evolution of the unemployment rate in France and in the UK, distinguishing between a trend and deviations from the trend. In the UK, the rate tends to deviate more from its trend than in France. Can you explain this pattern?

Unemployment rates in France and the UK (% of labour force)

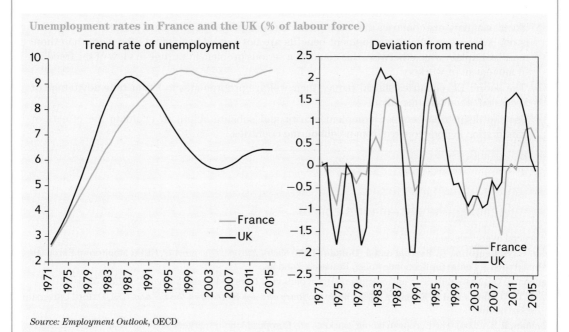

Source: *Employment Outlook*, OECD

4 Figure 8.8 shows the effect of trade integration in the presence of collective bargaining. What would things look like in the absence of collective bargaining but when wages are downward-rigid?

5 Same question as (4) but looking at the effects of migration in Figure 8.14.

6 Explain why the immigration of low-skilled workers can hurt native low-skilled workers and benefit high-skilled workers.

7 Capital accumulation and technological innovations raise the marginal productivity of capital. Graphically, in Figure 8.13 the *MPL* curve shifts up. Starting from point Q, consider two cases: (a) wages rise but employment remains unchanged at L; (b) employment increases but wages rise. Compare the changes to the income shares of capital and labour and interpret your results.

8 Looking at Figure 8.2, there seems to be a weak inverse relationship between the unemployment rate and the employment-to-population ratio. Why? And why is this relationship not tighter?

Essay questions

1 'Compared to Americans, Europeans care more about equity than efficiency.' Comment.

2 It is argued – and it is the case in some countries – that the minimum wage should be set at different levels for the young, for the older, for the unskilled or for particular industries. Evaluate this argument.

3 The distinction between voluntary and involuntary unemployment is not as clear-cut as presented in this chapter. Explain why, providing examples.

4 'Hard line' trade unions push for higher wages while 'cooperating' trade unions push for more jobs. What do these differences imply for the working of the labour market and for output? (Hint: Capture the distinction in terms of the shape of the S^{coll} curve.)

5 'Social magnets' are countries that offer generous unemployment and other welfare benefits. This is one key reason why unemployment benefits are not served to migrants for more than three months. Explain why, otherwise, this could be a serious problem in Europe in view of the freedom of movement of workers.

6 'The poorer EU countries should reduce their welfare programmes to better take advantage of accession.' Evaluate this advice.

7 Use the distinction between complementarity and substitutability to evaluate the effects of immigration in your country from neighbouring countries.

Further reading: the aficionado's corner

For general overviews, see:

Bean, C., S. Bentolila, G. Bertola and J. Dolado (1998) *Social Europe: One for All?*, CEPR Monitoring European Integration 8, Centre for Economic Policy Research, London.

Blanchard, O. (2006) 'European unemployment: the evolution of facts and ideas', *Economic Policy*, 45: 5–60.

Boeri, T., M. Burda and F. Kramarz (2008) *Working Hours and Job Sharing in the EU and USA*, Oxford University Press, Oxford.

Freeman, R.B. (2004) 'The European labour markets: are European labour markets as awful as all that?', *CESifo Forum*, 5(1): 34–39.

Nickell, Stephen (2006) "A Picture of European Unemployment: Success and Failure" in: Martin Werding (ed.) *Structural Unemployment in Western Europe: Reasons and Remedies*, MIT Press: 9-52.

Portugal, P. and J.T. Addison (2004) 'The European labour markets: disincentive effects of unemployment benefits on the paths out of unemployment', *CESifo Forum*, 5(1): 24–30.

The articles collected in: **Bertola, G., T. Boeri and G. Nicoletti (eds)** (2001) *Welfare and Employment in a United Europe*, MIT Press, Cambridge, MA.

On the trade-off between economic efficiency and social concerns, see:

Atkinson, A. (1999) *The Economic Consequences on Rolling Back the Welfare State*, MIT Press, Cambridge, MA.

On trade unions, see:

Calmfors, L., A. Booth, M. Burda, D. Checchi, R. Naylor and J. Visser (2001) 'What do unions do in Europe? Prospects and challenges for union presence and union influence', in T. Boeri, A. Brugiavini and L. Calmfors (eds) *The Role of Unions in the Twenty-first Century*, Oxford University Press, Oxford.

Checci, D. and C. Lucifora (2002) 'Unions and labour market institutions in Europe', *Economic Policy*, 35: 361–408.

On migration, see:

Boeri, T. and H. Brücker (2005) 'Why are Europeans so tough on migrants?', *Economic Policy*, 44: 629–704.

Diez Guardia, N. and K. Pichelmann (2006) *Labour Migration Patterns in Europe: Recent Trends, Future Challenges*, Economic Papers No. 256, European Commission. Download from http://ec.europa.eu/economy_finance/publications/publication644_en.pdf.

European Commission, *Job Mobility Action Plan*. Download from http://europa.eu/rapid/press-release_IP-07-1879_en.pdf

Hatton, T. (2007) 'Should we have a WTO for international migration?', *Economic Policy*, 50: 339–84.

Nickell, S. (2007) *Immigration: Trends and Macroeconomic Implications*, Nuffield College, Oxford. Download from www.bis.org/publ/bppdf/bispap50f.pdf

OECD (2007) *Survey of Europe*, September.

To find a job in the EU, got to the European Commission's job mobility portal EURES: https://ec.europa.eu/eures/page/homepage.

Useful website

The website of the Rodolfo de Benedetti Foundation, dedicated to European labour market issues: www.frdb.org.

Reference

Bertola, G. (2000) 'Labour markets in the European Union', *Ifo-Studies*, 46(1): 99–122.

Table 9.1   Importance of agriculture, 1955 vs. 2009

	Agriculture's share of GDP (%)		Agriculture's share of employment (%)	
	1955	**2009**	**1955**	**2009**
Belgium	7.9	0.6	9.3	1.5
Luxembourg	9.3	0.2	19.4	1.4
Netherlands	11.4	1.3	13.2	2.8
Germany	8.0	0.5	18.5	1.7
France	11.4	1.2	26.9	2.9
Italy	20.7	1.5	40.0	3.7
EEC6	11.5		21.2	
UK	4.8	0.5	4.6	1.1
Denmark	18.4	0.7	24.9	2.5

Sources: European Commission (2011) and Zobbe (2001)

by the 1950s. Comparing the numbers for 1955 and 2009 for Britain versus the other nations, it is clear that the downsizing of farming has been a much bigger headache on the Continent. This goes a long way to explaining why Britain has always had a problem with the EU's agricultural policy, which was basically designed for nations in very different situations.

To a large extent, the CAP has been a programme aimed at buffering the worst pain of this inevitable downsizing. As the agricultural sector changes, so too must the CAP.

The CAP is a policy that is in the politically painful process of moving from one simple economic logic to another simple economic logic. This suggests that the best way to understand the CAP is to study the CAP's original simple economic logic before discussing the unintended problems that are driving EU leaders to reform the CAP towards its new simple economic logic.

Once we have these analytic organizing frameworks in place, we consider the details of the CAP's policy instruments and commodity regimes.

9.1 The old simple logic: price supports

The early CAP was designed to ensure that farmers would get at least a minimum price for their output. In economics jargon, it established a price 'floor'. Such prices were set for many farm products, including grains, dairy products, beef, veal and sugar. For most of the CAP's existence, these prices were between 50 and 100 per cent higher than world prices; dairy and sugar prices were even higher.

How does a government enforce a price floor?

- One way is to impose an administrative price and make it a crime to sell for less.

This rarely works when there are millions of sellers and buyers as black markets and corruption tend to undermine the official price.

- The CAP, instead, chose a market-based system called 'market intervention'.

The CAP promised to buy unlimited amounts of food at the price floor, so the market price could never be lower. Such purchases, however, were only the last resort. Up until the 1970s, the EU imported most farm products, so it could raise their domestic price with tariffs – as we saw in Chapter 4. Given this, the best way

to understand the simple logic of the early CAP is to use the standard open-economy supply and demand diagram introduced in Chapter 4.

9.1.1 Basic price-floor diagram for a net importer

The economics of the tariffs used to raise EU food prices above the price floor are quite similar to the standard tariff analysis presented in Chapter 4. The CAP tariffs were called 'variable levies' since they changed daily with the world price, which itself fluctuated due to shifts in world supply and demand. The tariff was adjusted to ensure that imports never pushed EU prices below the price floor; for example, when the world price is P^w (see Figure 9.2), the tariff necessary to achieve the price floor is T. When the world is higher, say, $P^{w\prime}$, as shown in the diagram, the tariff only need to be $T\prime$.

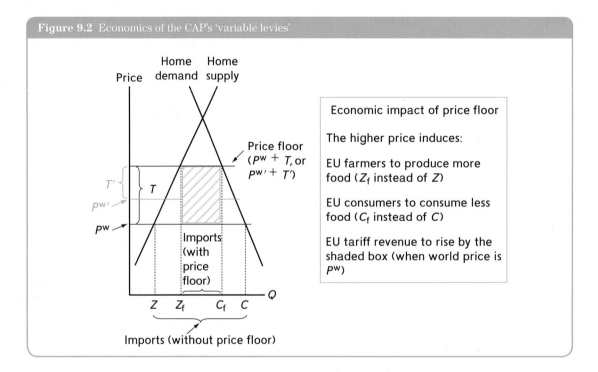

Figure 9.2 Economics of the CAP's 'variable levies'

As we saw in Chapter 4, the domestic price ends up as the world price plus the tariff, for example, $P_w + T$. At this price, all domestic production (equal to Z_f) is sold at the price floor, where the subscript 'f' indicates 'floor'. Domestic consumption is C_f and the difference between consumption and production equals the level of imports. In words, the variable levy raises the EU price by taxing imports.

The food tax and subsidy interpretation

Readers will gain great insight into all the complicated politics of the CAP and the problems that arise from different thinking on tariffs. As it turns out, any tariff can be thought of as an all-in-one package consisting of (1) free trade in the presence of (2) a consumption tax equal to T and (3) a production subsidy equal to T. Figure 9.3 facilitates the analysis.

With free trade (i.e. no tariff), the domestic price would be P^w but consumers would see this price plus the tax T (so they'd actually pay $P^w + T$). A production subsidy means that the government pays farmers T euros per kilo of food they sell at the market price P^w, so farmers would produce as they would when the price was $P^w + T$. Since consumers and producers see the same price as with the tariff, they consume and produce exactly the same amounts (C_f and Z_f). This implies that imports are also the same, namely, C_f minus Z_f.

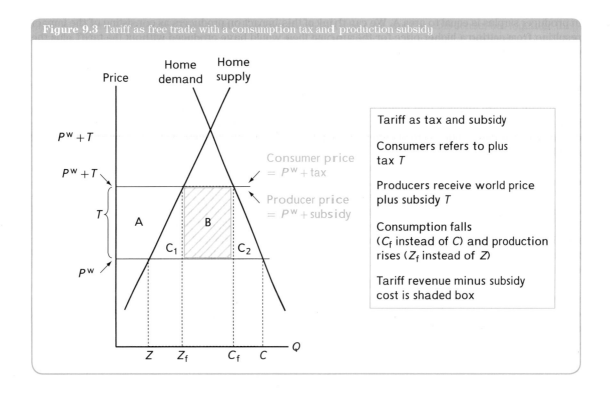

Figure 9.3 Tariff as free trade with a consumption tax and production subsidy

Tariff as tax and subsidy

Consumers refers to plus tax T

Producers receive world price plus subsidy T

Consumption falls (C_f instead of C) and production rises (Z_f instead of Z)

Tariff revenue minus subsidy cost is shaded box

What about the tariff revenue? There is no tariff and thus no tariff revenue, but there is revenue from the consumption tax. The revenue from the consumption tax is the level of consumption C_f times the tax T (equal to areas $A + C_1 + B$ in the diagram). The consumption tax revenue, however, is offset by subsidy expenditure. The cost of the production subsidy payment to farmers is production Z_f times T (equal to areas $A + C_1$ in the diagram). The difference between the new revenue and the new expenditure is exactly B – the amount of the tariff revenue. Or to put it differently, the government's receipt net of its payments for its tax-and-subsidy policy equals $(C_f - Z_f) \times T$, just as with the tariff.

The insight payoff

This way of looking at the price floor is insightful since it makes quite plain that EU consumers were the ones paying the CAP's price floor. Part of what they pay goes to domestic farmers (area A) and part to the EU budget (areas B and C_1). It also helps us understand the political difficulties encountered as the EU tried to reform the system.

As we shall see, most of the reform involved lowering the price floor – which is equivalent to lowering the subsidy to farmers. Plainly, they would resist such a cut unless it was compensated somehow. Providing such compensation is the source of many sticky issues in CAP reform. Moreover, it is clear that such reforms are not going to save much money. In 2014, farmers were paid directly by the EU with something called 'direct payments' instead of being paid indirectly via artificially high prices. Despite this, the shift from price supports to direct payments can still be win–win. EU consumer surplus rises by $A + C_1 + B + C_2$ while the direct payments necessary to fully compensate the farmers is just $A + C_1 + B$.

Aggregate welfare effects

The overall welfare effects of the tariff are familiar from Chapter 4. Figure 9.2 provides a recap of the analysis. The higher price ($P_w + T$ instead of P_w) means that consumer surplus falls by $A + C_1 + B + C_2$. The first part, $A + C_1 + B$, reflects the higher cost that consumers pay for the food they continue to consume. The second part, C_2, is what they lose from the tariff-induced drop in consumption. For producers, the gain

This uneven-distribution point is critical – the key to many of the CAP's paradoxes – so it is worth presenting it from another angle. Few readers will be familiar with modern farming, but everyone has been to a food store. Box 9.1 presents an analogy by considering what would happen if CAP-like policies were used to support the owners of European food stores.

Box 9.1   An analogy with hypothetical support for food stores

In most European nations, there are many, many food stores, but food sales are dominated by huge supermarket chains. Simplifying to make the point, we can think of there being two types of store: small, family-run stores and hypermarkets. The small stores are much more numerous, but since many people do their main food shopping at hypermarkets, the total sales of the many small stores is only a fraction of the hypermarkets' sales. To be concrete, suppose that the hypermarkets account for only 20 per cent of the total number of stores, but account for 80 per cent of sales. Now suppose that small, family-owned stores experienced severe problems and the EU decided to support them. However, instead of subsidizing only the small stores, the EU decides to subsidize the sales of *all* food stores. Plainly, 80 per cent of the subsidies would go to the hypermarkets that did not need them. Once the hypermarkets got used to the billions, you can bet that they would engage in some pretty fierce politicking to hold on to the money. Moreover, the public might support the policy in the belief that the funds are helping the millions of small, family-owned stores.

In summary, the distributional consequences of using price floors to support the EU farm sector are quite regressive:

- The benefits of price supports go mainly to the largest EU farms because large farms produce a lot (and the support is tied to level of production) and because large farms tend to be more efficient (so their costs are lower). Since the owners of large farms tend to be rich, the benefits of a price floor are systematically biased in favour of large, rich farmers.

- Since price floors are paid for by consumers (they are the ones that have to pay the higher price), and food tends to be more important in the budget of poor families than it is in the budget of rich families, price floors are in essence paid for by a regressive consumption tax.

9.2 Changed circumstances and CAP problems

When the CAP was first implemented in 1962, its price-support based design was a politician's dream. Producers were happy, consumers were happy, and the programme paid for itself (indeed, it produced a profit). Specifically:

- The price floors provided higher and more stable prices to farmers, so they were happy.

- The booming growth of the 1960s (see Chapter 7) was biased towards industry and cities, so raising farm incomes fostered 'social cohesion'.

- Food production rose and stabilized, which was viewed as an important achievement at the time because many remembered food shortages and hunger.

- The variable tariffs even generated revenue for the EU budget.

Because average incomes were rising so rapidly – much faster than food prices – the share of people's income spent on food actually fell. Readers should also note that many Europeans felt and still feel a great deal of empathy with farmers. They view agriculture as a form of economic activity unlike others.

The CAP's 'honeymoon', however, was soon to end.

9.2.1 The 'green' revolution

The post-war period saw revolutionary advances in the application of science to agriculture. Crops and farm animals were selectively bred to boost yields. A whole agrochemical industry sprang up, producing pesticides to control insects, herbicides to control weeds and chemical fertilizers to boost soil fertility. Huge planting and harvesting machines were developed to save labour. Strange as it may seem today, this chemical-, energy- and machine-intensive technology was known as the 'green revolution'.

Since the CAP rewarded output, EU farmers – especially those with large farms – switched to these new, more intensive farming methods. The result was impressive. EU farm production rose rapidly – so much so that the EU switched from being a net importer to a net exporter in most farm products.

In most sectors, this sort of rapid productivity growth would be a cause for celebration. In European agriculture, it was called the 'supply problem'. Other European sectors that have experienced rapid technological progress – e.g. telecoms – saw rapid price falls as the efficiency gains were passed on to consumers. The political power of the EU farm lobby, however, was strong enough to prevent this. EU food prices continued to be fixed far above the world price.

9.2.2 Negative consequences of the 'supply problem'

This combination of high, fixed prices and rapid technological progress created a whole cascade of problems that triggered a series of CAP reforms – the latest of which was implemented in 2014. To understand these, we study the impact of a price floor in the presence of a positive supply shock. Figure 9.6 shows the situation. Technological improvements shifted the supply curve down (recall that the supply curve is marginal cost, so cost-lowering technology shifts the whole curve downwards; see Chapter 4).

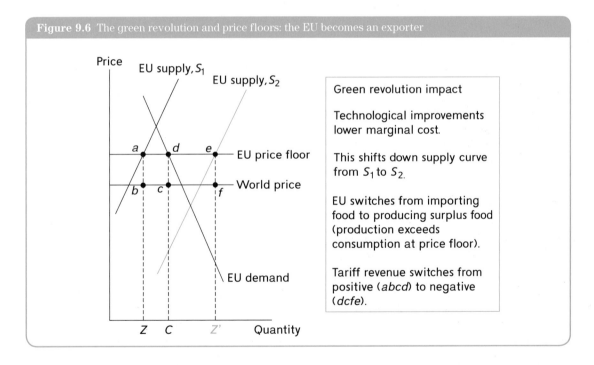

Figure 9.6 The green revolution and price floors: the EU becomes an exporter

Before the supply shift, the EU was a food importer and the price floor worked as in Figure 9.2. After the shift, the EU supply curve is S_2 with the price floor in place, so the EU has surplus food production; production level Z' exceeds the consumption level, C.

Some facts showing the impact on the EU food trade balance are shown in Figure 9.7, using wheat to illustrate the points. The rapidly rising line shows how the green revolution boosted yields (i.e. output per hectare) on a sustained basis. As area harvested changed little, output rose along with the rising yields. As consumption rose more slowly than production, the EU switched from importing wheat to exporting it around the late 1970s.

This simple switch trigger a cascade of problems.

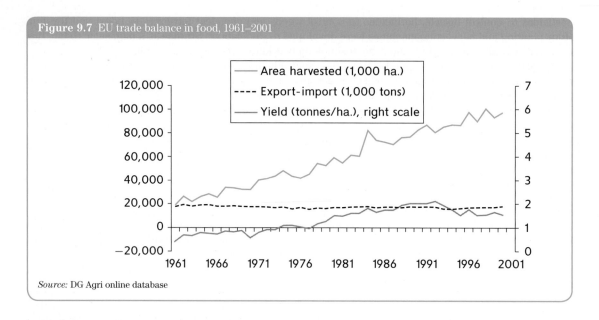

Figure 9.7 EU trade balance in food, 1961–2001

Source: DG Agri online database

The budget problem

The immediate difficulty was budgetary. Since the EU was no longer a food importer, the price floor could not be maintained with a variable tariff. The CAP had to directly buy food at the price floor; specifically it had to purchase at the price floor (i.e. Z' minus C in Figure 9.6) all the food that EU consumers didn't want. In short, the CAP rapidly turned from a money-maker to a money drain as the EU had to dole out large sums to buy the 'excess' food.

Although the CAP came into operation in 1962, it did not incur a positive expenditure until 1965. After this, however, its cost and share of the budget started to grow exponentially, rising from 8 per cent in 1965 to 80 per cent in 1969 (Figure 9.8). Fights over how to pay for these hindered EU cooperation throughout the 1970s and early 1980s.

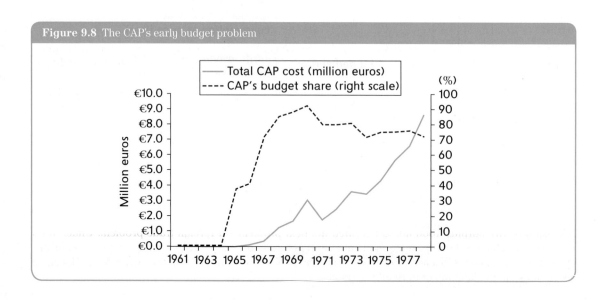

Figure 9.8 The CAP's early budget problem

The disposal problem: wheat, beef and butter mountains

Initially, the surplus production was viewed as a temporary problem. The food was stored in the hope that next season the consumption would exceed production. The stored food was viewed as a buffer stock. This was not to be.

High and stable prices teamed with steady technological progress made investment in agriculture very attractive. The supply curve continued to shift outwards, so the EU were forced to continue buying food. The EU found itself the owner of what the media called 'wheat, beef and butter mountains'. In 1985, the EU had 18.5 million tonnes of cereals stored, about 70 kilos for each of its citizens. Much of this food rotted, causing a major public relations problem (paying high prices for food and then allowing it to rot certainly looks bad).

Apart from the cost of buying all this food, the EU also faced the problem of what to do with it. When the food 'surpluses' first appeared, the EU viewed them as temporary. To reduce the budget and disposal problems, the EU sold the food at subsidized prices. Some was sold to non-standard consumers within the EU. For example, a sixth of the wheat crop in 1969 was rendered unfit for human consumption and sold as animal feed at a subsidized price. The major destinations for the subsidized sales were foreign markets. This practice of buying high domestically and selling cheap abroad is called 'dumping', although the EU jargon for it is 'export restitution' or 'export subsidies'.

The cost of such export subsidies can be thought of as 'negative tariffs'. That is, instead of buying at the low world price and selling at the high support price, the EU was buying high at the support price and selling low at the world price. The cost is shown in Figure 9.6 as area $dcfe$. Technically, this was done by paying large corporations to undertake the buy-high-sell-low business. This is why companies like Tate & Lyle routinely received billions of euros from the CAP. The payments are called export subsidies.

Readers will realize that the EU needed high tariffs and border controls to make the price floor work even when it was exporting. Although no imports come into the EU with the tariff set such that the support price equals the world price plus the tariff, they would if the tariff were removed. Every farmer in the world would like to sell at the EU's price floor instead of the world price; thus to reserve the higher price only for EU producers, the world price plus the EU tariff must exceed the price floor. For an example of the sort of smuggling that can result, see Box 9.2.

Box 9.2   Swiss border guards catch meat smugglers

'Buy low and sell high' is a sure way to make money. Unfortunately, two men were arrested in December 2012 as they sought to put this theory into practice. Under pressure from Switzerland's powerful 'cow lobby', the nation keeps beef prices very high – even higher than those in the EU. The men were caught smuggling 151 kilos of sausages, 110 kilos of chicken, 57 kilos of lamb and large quantities of poultry-burgers from Germany.

The plan was to deliver the meat to a family farm, which would then resell it in the Swiss market. This is hardly a unique occurrence. In the same year, Swiss customs guards caught a man smuggling in vans 1.4 tonnes of Dutch beef and 1.5 tonnes of ham and cheese.

Source: Based on an online news story by Malcolm Curtis, 18 December 2012. http://www.thelocal.ch/20121218/basel-border-guards-nab-meat-smugglers

---

Dumping and international objections

Disposing of EU 'surplus' food abroad created the next problem – a foreign trade problem. Under WTO rules for manufactured goods, dumping is normally not permitted, especially when the practice is driven by government export subsidies. However, before the 1994 Uruguay Round agreement, the WTO placed no restrictions on the dumping of agricultural goods.

The EU's food dumping drove down world food prices. As we saw in Chapters 4 and 5, a drop in the world price is a gain for net importers but a loss for net exporters. While the world's net food importers did not complain, EU dumping infuriated the world's large food exporters: Argentina, Australia, Bolivia, Brazil, Chile, Colombia, Costa Rica, Guatemala, New Zealand, Paraguay, the Philippines, South Africa, Thailand, Uruguay, Canada and – most importantly – the USA.

By shutting off EU markets to the exports of non-members, the CAP reduced the world price of food as well as reduced the volume of non-members' exports. As the EU's food surplus grew, and the EU started to subsidize its exports, non-members were further harmed.

Many countries impose some form of import protection on food, so while the CAP's tariffs were harmful to the world market, they were not viewed as particularly out of line with the rest of the world's practice. The subsidized export of food, however, was more unusual. Additionally, the USA and the EU were, at the time, the only major subsidizers and often engaged in subsidy wars. We shall return to the international impact of the CAP several times in the rest of this chapter.

The farm income problem

A somewhat paradoxical effect of this rapid technological progress was a shrinking of employment in the farm sector – the 'farm income problem'. Despite its massive budgetary cost and high implicit tax on European food consumers, the CAP failed to bring the reward to farming in line with the incomes of average EU citizens. In 1990, the income from farming per agricultural worker averaged less than 40 per cent of the income per worker in the EU12 economy as a whole (European Commission, 1994). While most farm family income was augmented by some non-farm earnings, farming was not a very attractive activity.

Farmers showed their discontent with the CAP by 'voting with their feet', i.e. quitting the sector. The number of farms and farmers has declined steadily since the CAP's inception (Figure 9.9). This is the truest indication that the average EU farmer found that, even with CAP support, farm incomes were not keeping up with those in the rest of the economy.

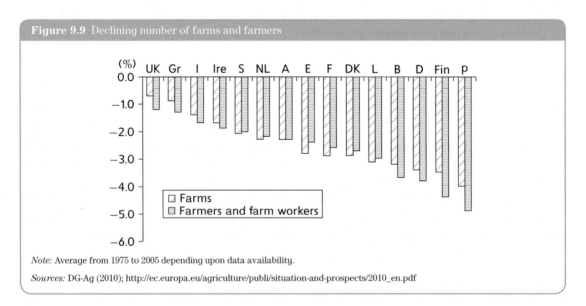

Figure 9.9 Declining number of farms and farmers

Note: Average from 1975 to 2005 depending upon data availability.

Sources: DG-Ag (2010); http://ec.europa.eu/agriculture/publi/situation-and-prospects/2010_en.pdf

Inequality across farm size

The big-versus-small logic illustrated in Figure 9.5 was magnified by green revolution technology. Much of the new innovations worked best for large-scale farms, so the output of large farms increased more than that of small farms. This exacerbated the unequal distribution of CAP support.

Table 9.2 shows just how uneven the payments were in 2011. The payment size categories are on the left; they range from less than 0 euros (i.e. these farmers actually owed the CAP money!) to over half

Table 9.2   Extremely uneven distribution of CAP payments, EU27, 2011

Size of payment (euros)	1000 recipients	Average payment (euros)	Cumulative share of recipients (%)	Cumulative share of payments (%)
< 0	13.7	824	0.2	0.0
> 0 and < 500	2,847.7	250	37.6	1.7
> 500 and < 1,250	1,582.3	807	58.4	4.9
> 1,250 and < 2,000	671.7	1,585	67.2	7.6
> 2,000 and < 5,000	996.5	3,187	80.3	15.5
> 5,000 and < 10,000	577.9	7,082	87.9	25.7
> 10,000 and < 20,000	433.2	14,212	93.6	41.0
> 20,000 and < 50,000	364.6	30,736	98.4	68.9
> 50,000 and < 100,000	93.0	66,954	99.6	84.4
> 100,000 and < 200,000	16.7	119,528	99.8	89.3
> 200,000 and < 300,000	5.7	171,469	99.9	91.8
> 100,000 and < 200,000	2.9	221,665	99.9	93.4
> 200,000 and < 300,000	1.7	276,555	99.9	94.5
> 300,000 and < 500,000	2.6	380,738	100.0	97.0
> 500,000	1.5	806,719	100.0	100.0

Source: http://ec.europa.eu/agriculture/statistics/agricultural/2013/index_en.htm, Table 3.6.1.14

a million euros. What the figures show is that 58 per cent of farmers got less than 1250 euros. While that will sound like a nice amount of money to most readers, it is peanuts when it comes to running a business, or farm. For these farms, the CAP is not really helping. At the other extreme, 1500 recipients got, on average, 806,719 euros. As these are large farms, these are almost sure to be run as modern industrial agricultural corporations. For them, the CAP is probably not really necessary – although, as the old saying goes, 'rich or poor, it's always nice to have money'.

Table 9.2 also shows the share of CAP that goes to big and small recipients. Notice that 80 per cent of the farms get only 15 per cent of the money. That means that the 85 per cent of the money remaining goes to just 20 per cent of the farms. To put it starkly, big farms find the CAP hugely profitable, but for the vast majority of farmers the CAP payments are just enough to keep them on the edge of bankruptcy.

Industrialization of farming: pollution and animal welfare

The 'industrialization of farming' that came with green-revolution technology had a negative impact on the environment and animal welfare. As the public's concerns over both reawakened in the 1980s and 1990s, these harmful effects of the CAP eroded public support for it.

The CAP harmed the environment in many ways. It induced farmers to apply more fertilizers and pesticides, and put more cows to graze on each hectare of land. The resulting decline in semi-natural habitats harmed wildlife numbers and diversity. Land under cultivation expanded in ways that had damaging effects on soil structure. The CAP's subsidization of particular crops (e.g. cereals, oilseeds, peas and beans) and livestock enterprises (e.g. dairy) encouraged 'monocultures', which further reduced biodiversity. Water quality suffered from the nitrates and phosphates in chemical fertilizers, which over-stimulated water

plants and led to the clogging up of lakes and so on. Where pork and beef production are particularly intensive, such as in the Netherlands, animal manure is the problem.

Animal welfare and 'factory farming'

Just as science improved crop yields, science has also been applied to boost the efficiency of animal products – meat, eggs, milk, etc. Efficiency in this sense typically means producing the most meat at the least cost. Doing so has involved studying the most efficient density of animals, the use of antibiotics to control disease and promote growth, the scientific design of animal feed and the breeding of higher-yielding, disease-resistant animals. While raising farm productivity, these practices have moved modern farming a very long way from the pastoral scenes still in the minds of many Europeans.

Some aspects of industrial farming became known to the wider public as the result of two animal diseases. BSE, known as 'mad cow' disease, was spread by the practice of processing the carcasses of dead cows (some of which had the disease) into feed that was then given to healthy cows. Outbreaks of 'foot and mouth' disease also occasionally occur and, to contain them, large numbers of animals are destroyed to mitigate the economic consequences. The disease does not kill the animals but renders them uneconomical.

Some Europeans reacted strongly against this 'factory farming' as inhumane treatment of animals. While there are some extremists, the concern has become quite mainstream. For instance, a million EU citizens signed a 1991 petition to the European Parliament calling for animals to be given a new status in the Treaty of Rome as sentient beings. The petition worked. The Lisbon Treaty includes animal protections: 'Member States shall, since animals are sentient beings, pay full regard to the welfare requirements of animals' (Article 13 of EFEU).

Concern for developing nations

The last problem facing the CAP was the growing realization that the dumping of food on the world market was harming the prospects of developing nations. The dumping of sugar and protection of cotton were particularly harmful to some of the world's poorest nations. As EU citizens started to realize this, attitudes began to change.

See Box 9.3 for a discussion of the impact of the EU sugar policy on Mozambique.

Box 9.3 EU sugar policy and Mozambique

The CAP's sugar policy is one of the oldest and most complex EU policies. EU sugar prices are maintained at about three times the world price, but not for all production. At the high price, many EU farmers would find it profitable to switch to growing sugar beet. EU leaders recognized this impending 'supply problem' from the beginning, so the amount of sugar for which farmers receive the high price is capped. Since the EU produces more sugar than it consumes at the high prices, the EU has to subsidize the export of the excess, but again, not for all production. The EU sets a quota for the maximum amount of exports it will subsidize; anything beyond this must be sold at world prices. One strange thing about EU sugar policy is that it actually taxes EU farmers in order to raise the money for the export subsidies. High EU tariffs shut off almost all imports, but again with an exception. The EU allows entry for some imported sugar from its former colonies, the so-called ACP (African, Caribbean and Pacific) nations, but the EU must re-export it, with subsidies, since it already produces more sugar than it consumes. Note that more than half of the EU's sugar is grown in Germany and France.

All this manipulation has made the EU the world's largest exporter (accounting for approximately two-fifths) of white sugar. EU subsidies depress the world price and its tariffs deny other nations the opportunity to sell in the EU market. Taken together, the CAP's sugar policy has a powerfully negative impact on poor countries, especially on poor nation farmers – a group that tends to be the poorest people in poor countries.

By way of illustration, the non-governmental organization Oxfam has highlighted the impact of EU sugar policies on Mozambique (2002, www.oxfam.org.uk). It points out that per-capita income in Mozambique is under 250 euros per year and two-thirds of the population live below the poverty line. The 80 per cent of the population that lives in rural areas relies mainly on agriculture for their living, with sugar production being the single largest source of jobs in the country. Oxfam estimates that Mozambique is one of the lowest-cost producers of sugar in the world, with a production cost under 300 euros per tonne. Removal of EU sugar tariffs would help Mozambique directly, but even a cessation of export subsidies would be welcome. For example, the EU exports almost a million tonnes of sugar to Algeria and Nigeria, nations that would otherwise be natural markets for Mozambique's sugar.

Since 2006, the system has been becoming less distortionary, with support prices falling by about 40 per cent. The reform increased EU imports to the benefit of developing country sugar exporters. However, the developing nation exporters that get limited preferential access to the EU market are harmed by it (the ACP nations; see Chapter 12 for details). These exporters face the same price reduction.

9.3 The simple economic logic of the new CAP

The EU is moving to a new simple CAP logic. Below we discuss some of the milestones in the transition between the old and new simple logic, but first we explain the economics and politics of the new logic. This involves three steps, each corresponding to one of the three elements of the new system: (1) support prices lowered to the world price level, (2) farmers compensated for the lower prices with 'decoupled direct payments', and (3) a new linking of the payments to social concerns, particularly the environment, animal welfare and rural development.

9.3.1 The logic of price cuts

Adam Smith's book *The Wealth of Nations*, published in 1776, contains a simple solution to all the CAP's problems, which all stem from the fact that the EU was producing too much food given world market conditions. Overproduction, in turn, was due to the fact that EU prices were above the world price. The obvious solution was to let Smith's 'invisible hand' guide production and consumption instead of politically-set support prices. This simple solution – lowering the support price to the world price, or eliminating the price floor all together and allowing the free-market price in food – is the first part of the new CAP logic.

The welfare gain from this cut-the-price reform is positive, as can be seen in Figure 9.10. The lower price would raise consumer surplus by the area $a + b$, while lowering producer surplus by $a + b + c$. Additionally, the cost of the 'negative tariff' (i.e. export subsidy) would be eliminated, adding an area of gain equal to $b + c + d$. In total, EU welfare would rise by $(a + b) - (a + b + c) + (b + d + d)$, which equals area $b + d$.

While eliminating or lowering the price floor would have solved the problem and raised EU welfare on aggregate, this 'Adam Smith reform' was not politically feasible. The EU farm lobby was, and is, just too powerful.[1] Although there are few EU farmers – less than 5 per cent of the population even back in the 1970s – their political power was, and still is, enormous. To EU farmers who have earned millions from the EU since the 1960s, the CAP resembled a personal gold mine. Just as real gold-mine owners hire armed guards to protect their investment, EU farmers were willing to spend millions on the politicking necessary to guard their 'gold mine', i.e. prevent prices from being lowered without compensation.[2]

---

[1] It is important to note that the EU's special treatment of farmers was not unusual. In the early 1990s, the EU's generosity was only in the middle of the OECD pack. OECD (2004) reports that the subsidy equivalent per EU farmer was $13,000, less than half the amount for EFTA members (Sweden, Switzerland, Norway, Finland and Austria) and about equal that of the USA and Japan.

[2] See http://ec.europa.eu/agriculture/fin/directaid/2006/annex1_en.pdf for details.

9.3.2 Price cuts compensated by 'decoupled direct payments'

The political solution was to provide compensation that would, in essence, 'bribe' farmers into allowing CAP reform to proceed. This added the second element to the new CAP logic. In EU jargon, this compensation is termed 'decoupled direct payments'. The 'direct payment' part is self-explanatory; the 'decoupled' part indicates that payment of the money is not linked to food production levels.

As it turns out, such price-cuts-with-compensation are win–win. To see this, recall how the price support was like a combination of a consumption tax and a production subsidy. In this light, the simple cut-the-price reform would have removed both the tax and the subsidy. The cut-prices-and-compensate reform removes the consumption tax and replaces the production-linked subsidy with a decoupled subsidy.

In terms of Figure 9.10, the cut-prices-and-compensate reform lowers the price that both consumers and producers see in terms of the old price floor and the world price. This reduces EU output to Z', raises EU consumption to C', thus eliminating the need for the EU to buy unwanted food and dump it on the world market. Full compensation of farmers would cost $a + b + c$ (equal to their loss in producer surplus), but this would still make the whole reform a net winner for EU consumers and the EU as a whole. Consumer surplus would rise by $a + b$ and the producer surplus reduction would be exactly offset by the compensation, leaving tax revenue implications. EU taxpayers would save $(b + c + d)$ from eliminating the export subsidy, but have to pay $(a + b + c)$ in compensation. EU welfare would thus rise by $(a + b) + (0) - (a + b + c) + (b + d + d)$, where the (0) shows the impact on EU producers. The sum of this is the same as the cut-the-price reform, namely, a gain equal to the area $b + d$.

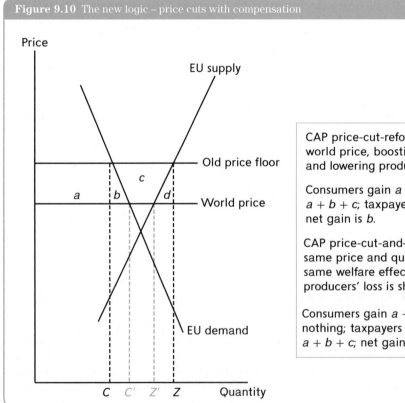

Figure 9.10 The new logic – price cuts with compensation

Price

EU supply

Old price floor

c

a | b | d

World price

EU demand

C C' Z' Z Quantity

CAP price-cut-reform: price falls to world price, boosting consumption to C' and lowering production to Z'.

Consumers gain $a + b$; producers lose $a + b + c$; taxpayers gain $b + c + d$; net gain is b.

CAP price-cut-and-compensate reform: same price and quantity effects, and same welfare effects except the producers' loss is shifted to taxpayers.

Consumers gain $a + b$; producers lose nothing; taxpayers gain $b + c + d$ but lose $a + b + c$; net gain is $b + d$.

This result should not surprise readers who fully understand the logic in Chapter 4. Since the compensation is – from the EU-wide perspective – just one group of EU citizens transferring money to another set of EU citizens, it has no impact on EU-level welfare. From an aggregate welfare point of view, cut-the-price and cut-the-price reform-with-compensation are identical.

9.3.3 Linking direct payments to environmental and animal welfare goals

This cut-and-compensate reform made sense in the short run. Most Europeans would agree that some sort of transitional compensation was owed to farmers. After many years, however, the moral case for compensation began to fade. The first steps towards the new logic happened in 1992 – before most readers of this book were born. By the 2000s, the payments started to look more like unjustified transfers. Two developments extenuated this impression. First, since the direct payments were made to named farms and farmers, the inequality documented in Table 9.2 became very transparent. One could even see how much the Queen of England received in CAP payments (see Box 9.5). Second, the money started going to millions of farmers in central and eastern Europe, who had never experienced the price cuts in the first place. They were being compensated for losses they had never incurred.

One reaction would have been to shift EU spending from farms to other areas, say, R&D schemes to deal with youth unemployment, or development aid to Africa. The political power of the farmers, however, prevented this. The political solution was to justify the payments on social grounds, such as protecting the environment, promoting animal welfare, encouraging rural development, etc. In essence, the 'decoupled' direct payments were recoupled to something other than farm output.

Box 9.4 Money and the extraordinary political power of EU farmers

To understand how much big EU farmers would spend to resist simple price cuts, consider the numbers involved, taking the EU 2007–13 budget package as an example. This package allocated 330 billion euros to payments to farmers and the cost of keeping farm prices high. There are only 12.6 million people working in the farm sector. If the money were divided evenly, that would be about 26,000 euros per person – certainly something worth fighting for.

The money, however, is not distributed evenly, as Table 9.2 showed. Most of the money goes to the largest farm owners. For example, in 2006, the EU25 paid 33.1 billion euros to 7.3 million farmland owners, with about 70 per cent of the money going to just 10 per cent of these (the ones with the largest landholdings). Small farmers earned much less from the CAP but, without the higher prices, many would be driven out of farming altogether.

In a nutshell, the CAP meant loads of cash for the happy few (large farms) but it was a matter of survival for the 80 per cent of EU farmers with small operations. In addition to the cold-hearted political logic of cash, part of the farmers' disproportionate power stems from the warm-hearted feeling that the average European has towards the sector; opinion polls show that most EU citizens approve of CAP spending in general.

Box 9.5 Queen Elizabeth's CAP receipts

The list of English CAP recipients (the Scottish and Welsh governments refuse to release the information) includes some of the richest people in the realm. The Duke of Westminster, whose net worth is about €7 billion, received about €1 million over two years, the Duke of Marlborough got €1.5 million over the same period, and the Queen and Prince Charles received more than €1.5 million each, according to the data. The royal family is also a major landowner in Scotland (for which the data is still secret), so this is probably a serious underestimate. Multinational corporations, however, received even more. At the head of the subsidy list is the multinational corporation Tate & Lyle. It received more than 10 times the payments received by Queen and Prince Charles, some €180 million (most of this was spent on dumping sugar on the world market). Nestlé got €30 million. Overall, there were 24,525 names on the list, but half of the money went to the top 2000 recipients. Or, to put it differently, half the money was divided among the 22,500 smallest farms. See *The Guardian* newspaper's website (http://image.guardian.co.uk/sys-files/Guardian/documents/2005/03/23/CAP.pdf) for a full list. A similar list can be downloaded for Denmark from www.dicar.dk.

9.4 CAP reform

Up to the mid-1980s, the primary way of dealing with higher CAP costs was to increase contributions from Member States. This was understandable. The CAP was not very expensive from the aggregate viewpoint (less than half a per cent of EU GDP) and it was essentially European governments paying each other's farmers. The Germans paid more than they received while the reverse was true for the French and Italians. The British negotiated a 'rebate' in 1984 to reduce their net payment.

This political balance changed when Spain and Portugal joined in 1986. As discussed in Chapter 3, this altered the politics in the Council in critical ways. The CAP did little to help Spanish and Portuguese farmers since their climates prevented them from producing the goods that the CAP supported most, i.e. dairy, sugar, wheat, rice and beef. The newcomers, who were reluctant to see their national contributions to the budget rise year after year in order to subsidize the production of rich northern European farmers, teamed up with the two incumbent poor nations (Ireland and Greece) to shift EU spending priorities towards 'structural spending' in poor nations (see Chapter 3 for further details). One option would have been to expand the EU budget to pay for the extra structural spending, but the EU net contributors (especially Germany, Denmark and the UK) opposed this. EU leaders decided instead to find ways of capping CAP costs, so to speak.

From 1986 to the present, the CAP has been repeatedly reformed. Although the details are complex, the basic trend is simple. EU leaders were gradually guiding the CAP from the old simple logic of prices explained in Section 9.1 to the new simple logic explained in Section 9.3.

For most of this period, the overall level of support to farm incomes did not fall, as Figure 9.11 shows. The producer subsidy equivalent (PSE), which is calculated by the OECD, shows the sum of all supports to EU farmers from the CAP and national sources. The chart shows both the level (billions of euros) and the PSE as a share of total farm output. Up until the mid-2000s, the total cost of the CAP was steady and it has fallen only moderately since. The PSE percentage, by contrast, has been on a clear downward trajectory since 1998. The difference indicates that EU agricultural output is falling more slowly than total PSE payments.

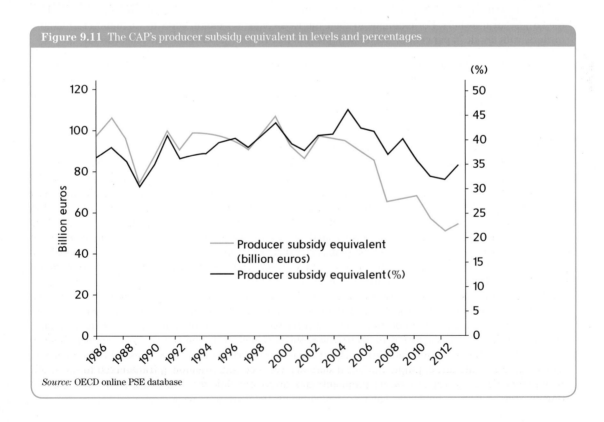

Figure 9.11 The CAP's producer subsidy equivalent in levels and percentages

Source: OECD online PSE database

9.4.1 Ad hoc supply control attempts

This situation posed a reform dilemma. Lowering farm prices dealt with the political roadblock discussed in the previous section, but buying all the excess food was too expensive. The EU's first reaction was to try to work around the problem, dealing with the surplus situation without fundamentally changing the price-floor system. As the European Commission (1994) puts it, the 1983 to 1991 period involved 'years of experimentation' with supply controls.

The CAP during this period became fantastically complex. Fortunately, most of these experiments have been dropped, so most students of European integration have no need to study their details. What is important is the outcome of these new policies. The CAP's share of the budget began to fall to meet the new political imperative of spending more of the EU budget on poor members and regions.

These ad hoc supply control policies, however, failed to address the supply problem. The wheat and butter mountains continued to grow along with subsidized exports, and, despite this, average farm incomes continued to fall relative to the EU-wide average.

9.4.2 The MacSharry reforms

The first really big reform was driven by pressure from the EU's trade partners who were fed up with seeing the market for their exports ruined by export subsidies (the USA also subsidized its exports). The issue came into sharp relief when the global trade talks, known as the Uruguay Round, failed in December 1991 when the EU refused to commit to phasing out its export subsidies and open its agriculture markets. Since these global trade talks were viewed as vital to European exporters of goods, services and intellectual property, Europe's highest-powered exporters started to push for CAP reform. The political power of poor regions who wanted to use the money and European exporters who wanted the Uruguay Round to succeed were sufficient to get a major reform accepted by the Council of Ministers. The resulting reform package (the MacSharry reforms) put the CAP on the road to the economic logic of Figure 9.9. All subsequent reforms to date have followed its main outlines.

There have been three major CAP reforms since the MacSharry package, which pushed the basic MacSharry logic even further. All involved further price cuts that were compensated by direct payments to landowners. The first resulted from the March 1999 meeting of the European Council in Berlin. The prime driver of this reform was the need to get the CAP ready for eastern enlargement and to prepare it for a falling budget share in the 2000–06 Financial Perspective. The second came in 2003. The third was embodied in the new 2014–20 Multiannual Financial Framework.

9.4.3 The 2003 CAP reform and 2008 Health Check

The driving force was the current WTO trade talks (the so-called Doha Development Agenda). Developing countries were reluctant to start new WTO talks and were only convinced when the EU members and other rich nations promised in November 2001 to liberalize agricultural markets as part of the Doha Round. With the crucial mid-term meeting of ministers scheduled for September 2003 in Cancun, Mexico, the EU had to come up with a reform of the CAP that would allow it to fulfil its liberalization pledge. The Cancun meeting ended in failure. Although there is plenty of blame to go round, many observers believe that the meagre liberalization contained in the CAP reform was at least one major reason for the failure. The 2003 reform has been followed up by a series of sector-specific reforms in recent years.

In 2008, the EU undertook a reform with a peculiar name, the 'Health Check'. This agreement pushed the market orientation of the CAP even further and took a big step towards liberalizing one of the most resistant sectors – dairy. The reform abolished arable set-aside (i.e. paying farmers to not grow food). It is also relaxing the restrictiveness of milk quotas gradually, with the goal of eliminating them in 2015. Moreover, the unfairness of the direct payments was mitigated under the name of 'modulation'. This means that some direct payments to farmers are reduced and the money transferred to the Rural Development Fund. Lastly, the direct payments are no longer linked to the production of a specific product.

9.5 Today's CAP

Today's CAP has two pillars. The first concerns direct payments and the cost of the remaining price supports. The second is called 'Rural Development'. The precise implementation of both pillars is delegated to Member States' Ministries of Agriculture – the idea being that the national ministries would have better knowledge of local conditions and constraints. Substantial reforms to this basic system are being phased in between 2014 and 2020.

We address the first pillar first.

9.5.1 CAP's first pillar: direct payments and market intervention

A key goal of the 2014–20 reforms is to achieve 'convergence', i.e. a more equal distribution of support. Previous CAP reforms had adjusted the level of direct payments according to a farm's historical production as a means of calibrating the amount of 'compensation' paid to each farmer for the price cut. The new system aims to achieve a more equal allocation across Member States and across farmers within each Member State. This will mean a clear and genuine convergence of payments not only between Member States, but also within Member States. As part of this, Member States will use a uniform payment per hectare by the start of 2019.

Another innovation is to tie the direct payments more clearly to environmental goals by insisting that 30 per cent of each member's budget allocation ('national envelope' in CAP jargon) be conditional on the adoption of sustainable farming practices. This is a step beyond the existing milder requirement that all recipients respect minimum environmental and animal welfare standards. These requirements are known as 'cross-compliance' rules. These are complex and vary somewhat from nation to nation. There are two basic categories: 'Good agricultural and environmental conditions' (soil protection, avoidance of overgrazing, etc.), and 'Statutory management requirements' (wildlife protection, avoidance of ground water pollution, etc.).

Basic Payment Scheme

The main vehicle for giving money directly to EU farms is called the 'Basic Payment Scheme' and it accounts for 70 per cent of each member's direct payments. Within this, there is flexibility for Member States to grant certain famers more money according to a series of criteria such as young farmers, small farmers, and farmers who have land with natural constraints.

The new CAP takes one step back towards the old pre-reform system by allowing members to tie a limited amount of aid to the production of a specific product. The total amount, however, should be less than about one-tenth of the national envelope. It takes a step forward, in contrast, in that it seeks to prevent abuses of the system that occurred in the past, such as golf courses claiming CAP subsidies. While this was a positive move, the Commission had proposed a much stronger 'active farmer' condition to prevent payments to 'sofa farmers' and absentee landlords and the like. The farm lobby overruled them, however, arguing that it would be too burdensome administratively to prove eligibility if the criteria included things like being actively engaged in farming activities or farming forming a significant share of the farmer's income.

Market interventions: eliminating left over price support and supply control measures

While most CAP expenditures had long ago moved away from manipulating market outcomes via price floors and production quotas, two of the most politically powerful lobbies – dairy farmers and sugar beet growers – had managed to hold on to production quotas and high prices. The new CAP eliminates the quotas for milk in 2015 and for sugar in 2017.

The CAP's protection scheme for EU sugar producers has long been derided as one of the most obvious cases of the CAP harming the interests of some of the world's poorest people (see Box 9.3), so this is a welcome step.

9.5.2 CAP's second pillar: rural development

For many years, successive CAP reforms have moved money away from directly paying farmers and towards paying for rural development schemes. Member States design their own multi-year programmes but these must be drawn from a menu of measures specified at EU level. The CAP 2014–20 requires Member States to spend about a third of this money on land management projects and schemes linked to climate change.

The multi-year programmes are to target six priorities areas: (1) improving innovation and knowledge transfer, (2) boosting agricultural competitiveness, (3) promoting food-chain integration, including processing and marketing, (4) helping ecosystems, (5) encouraging the transition to a low-carbon economy, and (6) promoting social inclusion, poverty reduction and economic development in rural areas.

9.6 Remaining problems

Today's CAP shares some of the problems discussed above. For example, not all of the payments are fully decoupled, so production distortions persist in some sectors. Moreover, with or without the CAP, the most productive farming is industrial farming and this almost inevitably involves chemical and energy usage that harms the environment.

9.6.1 Social inequality and CAP payments

The complete decoupling of the single payments is good economics, as we saw in Figure 9.10, but it poses what might be called a public relations problem for the CAP as a whole. Full decoupling turns the single payment into a subsidy to farmland ownership. Since many of the EU's landowners are not those who actually farm it, the CAP is increasingly looking like an excuse for paying very large sums of money to rich landowners. Paying millions of euros to wealthy landowners is not what most Europeans view as a good idea. For a long time the allocation of the payments remained a secret; however, using new 'freedom of information' laws, journalists forced some governments to reveal who was getting the cash. Such recipients included Queen Elizabeth II and other royalty (Box 9.5).

The Commission is set against this iniquitous allocation of CAP money and has tried many times to trim payments to the largest landowners. As part of its campaign, it has begun to publish annual data on the size distribution of payments in each Member State. Moreover, as part of the EU's new transparency goals, the Commission adopted a rule in March 2008 that requires the full name, municipality and postal code of every recipient. The first full list came out in April 2009. A good deal of information is already available on the Commission's web page on the CAP (ec.europa.eu/agriculture/funding/index_en.htm).

This sort of transparency puts a political bomb under the massive payments to rich landowners. Local media is likely to highlight the anomalies. For example, we have already seen that some of the ministers in charge of reforming the CAP are in fact receiving CAP payments (Box 9.6). Increasingly, CAP spending will be seen as welfare for the rich and support for first-pillar payments is likely to erode.

Box 9.6   Government ministers receiving CAP payments

In the Dutch and Danish cases, a scandal has emerged involving politicians charged with overseeing the CAP actually receiving some of the money personally. For example, 4 of the 18 Danish ministers or their spouses, including the Farm Minister, received CAP money. The biggest scandal to date, however, involved the Dutch Farm Minister Cees Veerman. He receives about €190,000 annually in CAP subsidies for the farms he owns.

The scandal was revealed when British Premier Tony Blair suggested a reform of the CAP in the summer of 2005. The Dutch Prime Minister Jan Peter Balkenende at first supported Blair, but Veerman threatened to resign in protest if Balkenende backed Blair. According to an *International Herald Tribune* article (19 August 2005), a spokesman for the Dutch Ministry of Agriculture claimed that there was no connection between Veerman's cash receipts and his opposition to CAP reform. One can question this assertion, since Veerman referred to his farms as 'my pension', according to a report in *The Guardian* newspaper.

This makes it easier to understand why governments have opposed the release of detailed information on who is getting the taxpayers' money. As more EU nations reveal the names of CAP recipients, the pressure to reform the welfare-for-rich-landowners aspect of the CAP is likely to grow. One proposal put forth several times by the European Commission (and rejected by the Council) would put an upper limit on the payment per farm.

The linking of these payments to environmental and animal welfare concerns is a popular conception, but the details matter and these will eventually be more widely publicized. The key point is that the payments are not linked to *new* environmental and animal welfare regulations; rather, they are linked to regulations that the farmers should already have been following. This is not done in other industries. For instance, the EU does not provide millions to the auto industry and threaten to take them away if they don't comply with environmental regulations.

9.6.2 Farmers only get about half of the CAP's support

Another problem with the CAP is that a great deal of the money ends up in the hands of people other than farmers. An OECD study in 2003 examining the actual beneficiaries of the reformed CAP found that much of the support actually ends up in the pockets of input suppliers such as non-farming landowners and agrochemical firms.

When it comes to direct payments based on hectares, one euro of payment ends up having a minimal impact on the earning of farm household labour. Since the payments are tied to the land, it is the land price that soaks up most of the subsidy. This is not a problem for farmers who owned their land before the area payments were instituted, but about 40 per cent of EU farmland is not owned by the people who farm it.

The OECD calculates that about 45 cents of every euro of direct payment benefits non-farming landowners instead of farmers. The other major CAP policy – market price support – does even worse. Farmers get only 48 cents in the euro, with 38 cents going to real resource costs and input supplies.

9.7 Summary

The CAP started in the 1960s as a way of guaranteeing EU farmers high and stable prices. Because agricultural technology advanced rapidly, and because the high prices encouraged farm investment, EU food production rose rapidly, much faster than EU food demand. As a consequence, the EU switched from being an importer of food to being an exporter of food. This change meant that supporting prices required much more than keeping cheaper foreign food out with high tariffs. The EU began to purchase massive amounts of food – an operation that became very expensive, consuming over 80 per cent of the EU's budget in the 1970s. Since the EU had no use for the food it bought, it disposed of the surplus by storing it or dumping it on the world market. The former was expensive and wasteful; the latter had serious international repercussions since it tended to ruin world markets for farmers outside the EU.

A combination of budget constraints and pressure from EU trade partners forced a major reform of the CAP in the 1990s, the so-called MacSharry reform. This reform lowered guaranteed prices, and thus reduced the amount of food the EU had to buy, but it compensated farmers for the price-cut by providing them with direct payments. This type of price-cut-and-compensate reform was developed further by the so-called Agenda 2000 reforms and the June 2003 reforms.

The economic impact of the CAP is quite unusual at first glance. Despite high prices and massive subsidies, the EU farming population continues to decline because CAP support is distributed in an extraordinarily unequal way. The largest farms, which are typically owned by rich citizens or corporations, receive most of the money, while the small farms get very little. In short, CAP payments to most EU farms are too small to prevent many farmers from quitting. Yet, despite the small size of most payments, the total cost of the CAP is huge because payments to big farms are big. The MacSharry and Agenda 2000 reforms did little to change this because the direct payments are related to farm size.

The CAP was seriously reformed in 2003, followed by a plethora of related reforms in 2005 and 2008. These moved the CAP a long way from a price-support system towards an income-support system with market-determined prices. This has solved many of the trade conflicts that arose from the EU's dumping and it has eliminated the food mountains.

The CAP reforms for 2014–20 complete most of the transition from the old simple system of price supports to the new simple system of direct payments that are decoupled from food production but linked to socially useful goals such as respect for the environment and animal welfare. Nevertheless, a very large share of the money is just given to people who own rural land. Since land ownership is quite concentrated, this ends up as a transfer from the average EU taxpayer to large landowners – even if the most recent reform made some modest progress on limiting large payments to large farms. This policy is increasingly difficult to justify when conditions of austerity are forcing governments to cut back spending on schools, innovation policies, pensions, etc.

The basic problem, to be tackled in future reforms, is the dilemma created by decoupling payments that were created to subsidize the production of food. Without the link to farm output, the CAP struggles to ensure that payments go only to 'farmers', as conventionally understood. This in itself raises the question of whether support for rural Europe should not be encompassed within more general social cohesion and development schemes, such as those discussed in Chapter 10.

Self-assessment questions

1 In 2003, the world wheat price is above the CAP's target price so the price floor has become a price ceiling. (i) Using a diagram like Figure 9.2, show how the EU could implement the price ceiling with an export tax. (ii) What are the effects of this in the EU and in the rest of the world (prices, quantities and welfare)?

2 Some developing nations accuse the EU of using technical standards for food (pesticide content, etc.) as a barrier to trade. Suppose they are correct. Use diagrams to show how you would analyse the impact of such protection on EU and RoW welfare. (Hint: See Chapter 4's analysis of 'frictional' barriers.)

3 Before the UK adopted the CAP, it supported its farmers with a system of 'deficiency payments', which is the agro-jargon for production subsidies. Using a diagram like Figure 9.2, analyse this policy assuming that the import of food was duty free, but the government directly paid farmers the difference between the market price and a target price for each unit of food they produced. Be sure to consider the implications for world prices, UK production and UK imports, as well as the welfare implications for UK farmers, consumers and taxpayers.

4 Suppose that the EU allowed free trade in food and subsidized production on small farms only. Analyse the price, quantity and welfare implications of this policy using a diagram.

5 The text mentions that since direct payments are tied to the land, it is the land price that soaks up most of the subsidy. Use a classic supply and demand diagram to demonstrate this result. (Hint: This is a standard exercise in what is known as the 'incidence of a tax' since a subsidy is just a negative tax.)

6 The European Commission has proposed putting an upper limit on the total direct payment per farm of approximately €300,000. What would be the impact of this on prices, output and the distribution of farm incomes?

Further reading: the aficionado's corner

A wide-ranging and accessible consideration of the CAP can be found in:

Hathaway, K. and D. Hathaway (eds) (1997) *Searching for Common Ground. European Union Enlargement and Agricultural Policy*, FAO, Rome.

An excellent account of why so few Europeans manage to capture such a large share of the budget is provided in:

Anderson, K. (2010) *The Political Economy of Agricultural Price Distortions*, Cambridge University Press, Cambridge.

Other useful works are:

ERS (1999) *The EU's CAP: Pressures for Change*, US Department of Agriculture Economic Research Service, International Agriculture and Trade Reports, WRS-99 – 2. Download from http://www.ers.usda.gov/publications/wrs-international-agriculture-and-trade-outlook/wrs992.aspx

EU Court of Auditors (2000) *Greening the CAP*, Special Report No. 14/2000.

European Commission (1994) *EC Agricultural Policy for the 21st Century*, European Economy, Reports and Studies, No. 4.

European Commission (1999) *Agriculture, Environment, Rural Development: Facts and Figures – A Challenge for Agriculture*, DG Agriculture. Download from http://ec.europa.eu/agriculture/envir/report/en/.

Farmer, M. (2007) *The Possible Impacts of Cross Compliance on Farm Costs and Competitiveness*, Institute for European Environmental Policy, 21, January.

Halverson, D. (1987) *Factory Farming: The Experiment That Failed*, Animal Welfare Institute, London.

Milward, A. (1992) *The European Rescue of the Nation-state*, University of California Press, Berkeley, CA.

Moehler, R. (1997) 'The role of agriculture in the economy and society', in K. Hathaway and D. Hathaway (eds) *Searching for Common Ground: European Union Enlargement and Agricultural Policy*, FAO, Rome, www.fao.org/docrep/W7440E/w7440e00.htm.

Molle, W. (1997) *The Economics of European Integration*, Ashgate, London.

Nevin, E. (1990) *The Economics of Europe*, Macmillan, London.

Swinnen, J. (2002) *Towards a Sustainable European Agricultural Policy for the 21st Century*, CEPS Task Force Report No. 42, Brussels.

Useful websites

For a non-institutional view of the CAP, and a series of readable and informative essays, see http://members.tripod.com/~WynGrant/WynGrantCAPpage.html.

The Commission's website http://europa.eu.int/comm/agriculture/ provides a wealth of data and analysis, although much of it is politically constrained to be fairly pro-CAP. The US government's Agricultural Department provides even more analysis and tends to be more openly critical of the CAP; the pages of the Economic Research Service are especially informative. See http://www.ers.usda.gov/publications/wrs-international-agriculture-and-trade-outlook/wrs992.aspx#.VDvgvPmSy40.

Every year, the OECD publishes an excellent report on the agricultural policy of all OECD members (this includes the CAP). For the latest figures and exhaustive analysis, see www.oecd.org.

References

DG-Ag (2010) 'Situation and prospects for EU agriculture and rural areas', Note to file. Download from http://ec.europa.eu/agriculture/publi/situation-and-prospects/2010_en.pdf.

European Commission (1994) *EC Agricultural Policy for the 21st Century*, European Economy, Reports and Studies, No. 4.

European Commission (2013) *Rural Development in the EU Statistical and Economic Information, Report 2013*, DG Agriculture, http://ec.europa.eu/agriculture/statistics/rural-development/2013/index_en.htm.

IMF (2002) *World Economic Outlook*, September. Download from www.imf.org.

International Herald Tribune (2005) 'Dutch minister got farm subsidy', 19 August.

OECD (2003) *Farm Household Income: Issues and Policy Responses*, OECD, Paris.

OECD (2004) *Analysis of the 2003 CAP Reform*, OECD, Paris.

Oxfam (2002) 'Stop the dumping', Oxfam Briefing Paper 31. Download from www.oxfam.org.uk/resources/policy/trade/downloads/bp31_dumping.pdf.

Zobbe, H. (2001) *The Economic and Historical Foundation of the Common Agricultural Policy in Europe*, Working paper, Royal Veterinary and Agricultural University, Copenhagen. Download from www.flec.kvl.dk/kok/ore-seminar/zobbe.pdf.

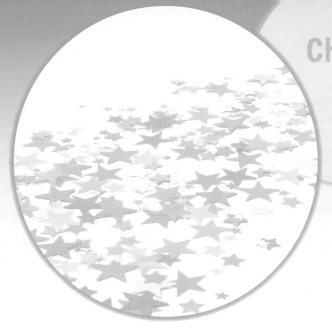
[T]he Community shall aim at reducing disparities between the levels of development of the various regions and the backwardness of the least favoured regions or islands, including rural areas.

Treaty on the European Union, Maastricht, 1992

Location effects, economic geography and regional policy

Chapter Contents

Introduction

When deeper European economic integration took off in the 1950s, rural Europe was really poor. Electricity and telephones were far from standard in rural households and many were without indoor plumbing. Europe as a whole was booming, but cities and a few industrial regions were leaving rural Europe behind. The EU's founders made a concern for rural Europe one of the key goals of European integration. As the 2004 and 2007 enlargements added large swathes of poor rural areas to the EU, helping Europe's rural communities remains a touchstone of today's EU.

This chapter looks at the facts, theory and policy connecting European integration to the location of economic activity in Europe.

10.1 Europe's economic geography: the facts

Regional incomes in the EU follow a clear pattern. Rich regions are located close to one another and form the 'core' of the EU economy. Poor regions tend to be geographically peripheral (see Combes and Overman, 2004, for more details). These points are made clear in Figure 10.1, which shows a map of Europe's night-time light pollution. Since light pollution lines up very closely with economic activity at this scale, we can think of such pollution as revealing the spatial distribution of economic activity. The 'heart of Europe' is clearly made up of western Germany, the Benelux nations, north-eastern France and south-eastern England. This region contains only one-seventh of the EU's land but a third of its population and half of its economic activity. It is the economic centre of Europe. Roughly speaking, the concentration of economic activity drops as one moves away from the core, although the map shows that there is also a massive concentration of economic activity in northern Italy and various hot spots in Iberian and Nordic regions.

Figure 10.1 Europe at night – light 'pollution'

© National Oceanic and Atmospheric Administration (NOAA)

The map also serves to make an important point about nations and regions. The focus of our analysis in the earlier chapters has been on nations' economies and the integration of nations. Looking at Figure 10.1, it is not hard to see that national borders are not really the best way to think about economic activity in Europe. In short, regions matter.

Although distance is continuous, when we discuss the economics below we frequently refer to the 'core' and the 'periphery'. The core is the regions with the brightest lights in Figure 10.1, the rest is the periphery. Plainly, it is very blunt to put regions into just two categories, but it proves analytically convenient.

10.1.1 Why does peripherality matter?

Why should anyone care about the location of economic activity? There are, after all, very few people in northern Finland. Why is it a problem that there is also very little economic activity there? For reasons we discuss below, incomes tend to be lower for people living in the periphery regions – although, as always, there are exceptions, especially around key but remote cities such as Rome, Madrid, Dublin, Edinburgh, Stockholm and Helsinki (see Figure 10.2). Note that:

- Most regions in the 12 new members have incomes that are below those of the EU15 nations. The differences are stark. The poorest region in the EU27 is Severozapaden in Romania, which has a per-capita income that is 28 per cent of the EU27 average. The richest region, Inner London, had an average income that is 343 per cent higher than the EU27 average.

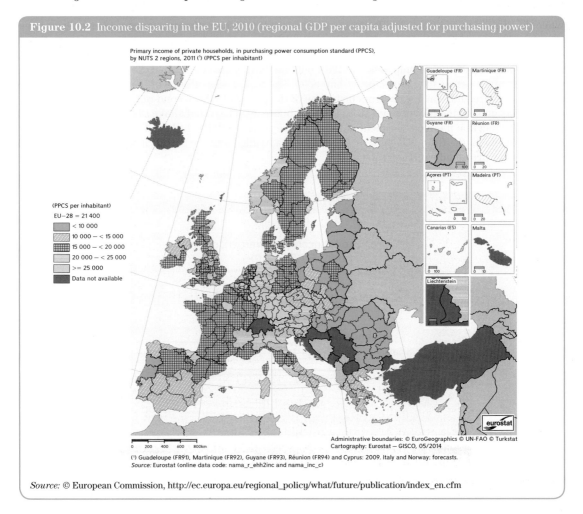

Figure 10.2 Income disparity in the EU, 2010 (regional GDP per capita adjusted for purchasing power)

Primary income of private households, in purchasing power consumption standard (PPCS), by NUTS 2 regions, 2011 (¹) (PPCS per inhabitant)

(PPCS per inhabitant)
EU−28 = 21 400

< 10 000
10 000 − < 15 000
15 000 − < 20 000
20 000 − < 25 000
>= 25 000
Data not available

Administrative boundaries: © EuroGeographics © UN-FAO © Turkstat
Cartography: Eurostat – GISCO, 05/2014

(¹) Guadeloupe (FR91), Martinique (FR92), Guyane (FR93), Réunion (FR94) and Cyprus: 2009. Italy and Norway: forecasts.
Source: Eurostat (online data code: nama_r_ehh2inc and nama_inc_c).

Source: © European Commission, http://ec.europa.eu/regional_policy/what/future/publication/index_en.cfm

● Apart from the western-most and southern-most parts of the Continent, none of the EU15 regions have incomes below 75 per cent of the EU27 average. Although it is not shown on the map, the northern extremes of the Continent would also have very low incomes if it were not for the colossal income transfers and special programmes undertaken by Sweden and Finland. One of the most striking things about the map is how regional incomes seem to fall in relation to the region's distance from the 'heart of Europe' (again apart from the Nordic cases).

The wide disparity in income levels is a problem from a social point of view, but it is also a problem from the political perspective. Large income gaps between regions foster bitter political disputes that can hinder cooperation on things such as European integration. Giving the poorer regions hope that they will catch up is an important role for the EU's regional policies.

The disadvantages of the poor regions range much further than low incomes. A range of standard indicators of social misfortune suggest that many of Europe's poor regions have a variety of problems. For instance, the poor regions also often have higher levels of youth unemployment and long-term unemployment and lower levels of investment and education.

Much more detail on the state of the regions is available in the 'Eurostat regional yearbook', for example Eurostat (2013). Eurostat's online database also allows you to generate your own custom-made maps based on unemployment, income, tertiary education and so on.

10.1.2 Evolution over time: narrower national differences, wider regional differences

While the dispersion of income levels across nations is still very high, the gaps among EU members have been steadily narrowing, as Figure 10.3 shows. The EU15 members have on average seen a significant convergence of their incomes with the EU15 average (shown in each year as EU15 = 100). Note that Sweden, Finland and Austria only joined in 1995, but had participated in much of the economic integration with the EU even before they joined (see Chapter 1). The real success stories are Spain, Portugal, Greece and, above all, Ireland, which went from being one of the poorest to the second-richest Member State. The obvious exception to the convergence story is Luxembourg, which started above average and continued to diverge. The fact that it is a net recipient of EU funds (see Chapter 3) has little to do with this performance; most of it is due to the Grand Duchy's development of a highly lucrative financial service sector based in part on its low taxes and banking secrecy.

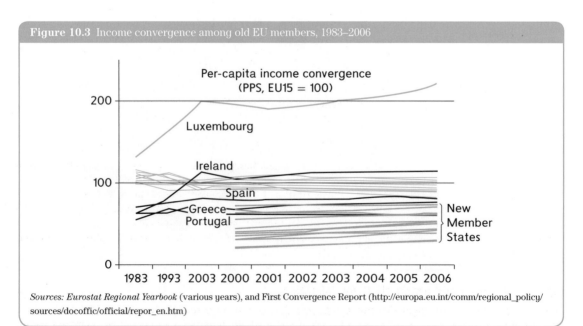

Figure 10.3 Income convergence among old EU members, 1983–2006

Sources: Eurostat Regional Yearbook (various years), and First Convergence Report (http://europa.eu.int/comm/regional_policy/sources/docoffic/official/repor_en.htm)

The convergence of the new Member States is also clear in the chart, although the process has been gradual and their membership in 2004 did not lead to any visible jump.

Divergence within nations

The convergence across nations, however, hides an important trend. Income inequality across regions within each EU nation has been rising steadily. We can see this clearly by taking the example of the UK. The left-hand map in Figure 10.4 shows the distribution of per-capita income in 1995, region by region. The right-hand map shows the same for 2005. To ease comparison between 1995 and 2005, we look at each region's per-capita income compared to the UK average. Thus a region with a per-capita income equal to 100 is just at the UK average, while those with figures below 100 have below-average incomes. In 1995, Greater London was the only region with more than 140 (i.e. more than 40 per cent above the UK average). Two other regions – Scotland and the region below London – had above-average incomes. All the rest had below-average incomes. In 2005, London retained its first place but Scotland was no longer above average. Additionally, two of the regions in the west saw their incomes drop below 90 per cent of the average. Overall, there is a clear increase in regional inequality between 1995 and 2005.

Figure 10.4 GDP per capita in British regions, 1995 vs. 2005

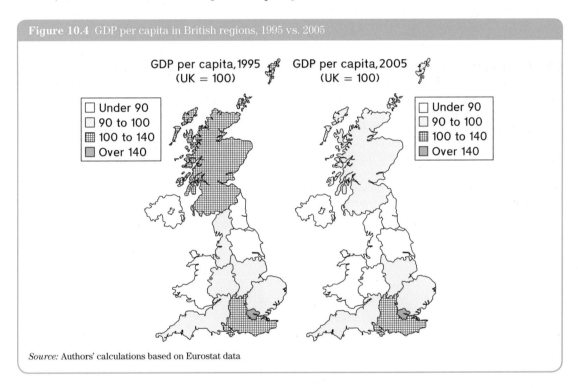

Source: Authors' calculations based on Eurostat data

A similar pattern holds generally across the EU. For example, Poland has been growing rapidly during this time and in fact all regions saw their incomes rise. However, some regions – such as Warsaw – grew much faster than others, so their share of Polish GDP rose. Roughly speaking, regions with low per-capita incomes have lost out in the race for national GDP shares. In short, inequality among regions within EU nations has risen. There are many exceptions, as always. For instance, western French regions have seen their GDP shares rise, as have some of the poorer parts of southern Italy, but even in equalitarian Sweden, the northern regions have shrunk relative to the rest of the nation.

10.1.3 Integration and production specialization

The evidence presented up to this point suggests that European economic integration has had only a modest impact on the location of economic activity as a whole, with the many changes occurring within

nations rather than across nations. Lumping together all economic activity (i.e. measuring activity by total GDP), however, may hide changes in the composition of economic activity within each nation or region. European integration may have encouraged a clustering of manufacturing by sector rather than by region. To explore this possibility, we look at regions' and nations' industrial structures and their evolution. We focus on industry since it is difficult to get comparable data on services.

Figures for European nations

Using a particular measure of specialization – called the Krugman specialization index – we look at how different the industrial structures are in various European nations and how they have evolved. The Krugman index tells us what fraction of manufacturing activity would have to change sector in order to make the particular nation's sector-shares line up with the sector-shares of the average of all other EU15 nations.

The indices for the EU27 are shown in Table 10.1. Since almost all the changes are positive, we conclude that the industrial structures of most nations are diverging from the average EU industrial structure. In other words, taking the EU average as our standard, most European nations experienced an increase in the extent to which they specialized in the various manufacturing sectors. The only major exception is that of Spain, whose industrial structure became substantially more similar to the EU average over this period.

Table 10.1   Specialization by nations, 1980–1997

	1980–83 (%)	1988–91 (%)	1994–97 (%)
Ireland	62	66	78
Greece	58	66	70
Finland	51	53	59
Denmark	55	59	59
Portugal	48	59	57
Netherlands	57	55	52
Sweden	39	40	50
Belgium	35	38	45
Italy	35	36	44
Germany	31	35	37
Austria	28	28	35
Spain	29	33	34
UK	19	22	21
France	19	21	20
EU15 average (weighted)	30	33	35

Source: Midelfart-Knarvik et al. (2002)

How important is this increase in specialization? To take one example, Ireland's index in 1970–73 was 70 per cent, which means that 35 per cent of total production would have to change sector to bring it into line with the rest of the EU. Ireland's index had increased by 8 per cent by 1997, so by that year 38 per cent of Ireland's manufacturing would have to change sector to get in line with the EU average. For most EU nations, the change has been fairly mild, to the order of 5 or 10 per cent.

10.1.4 Summary of facts

To summarize, the facts are:

- Europe's economic activity is highly concentrated geographically at the national level as well as within nations.
- People located in the core enjoy higher incomes and lower unemployment rates.
- While the income equality across nations has narrowed steadily with European integration, the geographical distribution of economic activity within Member States has become more concentrated (taking income per capita as a measure of economic activity per capita).
- As far as specialization is concerned, European integration has been accompanied by only modest relocation of industry among nations, at least when one lumps all forms of manufacturing together.
- The little movement that there has been tends to lean in the direction of manufacturing activities having become more geographically dispersed across nations, not less.
- Most European nations have become more specialized on a sector-by-sector basis.
- At the sub-national level, we see that industry has become more concentrated spatially.

10.2 Theory part I: comparative advantage

We now turn to the economic logic that connects European integration and the location of economic activity, focusing on two aspects in particular: specialization at the international level and agglomeration at the international level.

To keep things simple, we consider each effect in isolation, using a separate framework for each. The first framework focuses on natural differences among European nations – what economists call comparative advantage. The second framework – which is presented in the following section – focuses on the tendency of closer integration to encourage the geographic clustering of economic activity.

10.2.1 Comparative advantage and specialization

Opening up trade between nations raises economic efficiency. This is just the 'magic of the market'. When trade is very difficult, each nation has to make the most of what it consumes. Trade allows nations to 'do what they do best and import the rest'. Trade allows a nation to concentrate its productive resources in sectors where it has an edge over other nations. The jargon word for the edge is 'comparative advantage'. This consequence of liberalization can have important effects on the location of industry because it encourages a nation-by-nation specialization. The main purpose of this section is to explain how comparative advantage and European economic integration help explain the type of industrial specialization that happened in Europe in the 1980–97 period and is likely to continue into the future.

An example

To see the basic idea more clearly, think about what Europe would look like without any trade. European nations have different supplies of productive factors – and different types of goods use factors in different proportions – so without trade the output of a nation would be largely determined by its supplies of factors. Focusing on labour supplies, consider the current distribution of labour among EU members, dividing labour into three types: those with little education (less than secondary), those with at least secondary education, and highly educated workers (researchers). To make the numbers comparable, we compute each nation's supply of low-education workers relative to its total supply of workers and compare this to the same ratio calculated for the EU as a whole (EU's supply of low-educated labour to overall labour) – and we do the same for the other two labour types.

The numbers are shown in Figure 10.5. For example, we see that Portugal's supply of low-education workers (divided by Portugal's total supply of workers) is 83 per cent above the EU average. Germany's is 52 per cent below the EU average. Now consider what this means for the price of a good that uses low-education labour intensively, such as clothing. Without any trade, Germany and Portugal would have to

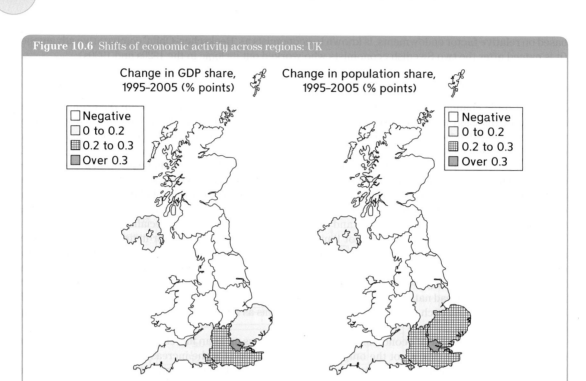

Figure 10.6 Shifts of economic activity across regions: UK

Note: All UK NUTS1 regions grew in nominal terms in this period, but since some grew faster than others the share of total UK GDP rose in the fastest-growing regions and fell in others.

Source: Authors' calculations on Eurostat data downloaded September 2008

10.3.1 Agglomeration and dispersion forces in general

The logic of economic geography rests on two pillars – dispersion forces and agglomeration forces. Agglomeration forces promote the spatial concentration of economic activity while dispersion forces discourage such concentration. The spatial distribution of economic activity at a moment in time depends upon the balance of the pro-concentration (agglomeration) forces and anti-concentration (dispersion) forces. The main question we want to answer is: 'How does European integration affect the equilibrium location of an industry?' To set the stage for the equilibrium analysis, we first consider dispersion and agglomeration forces in isolation.

Dispersion forces

Dispersion forces favour the geographic dispersion of economic activity. Land prices are the classic example. The price of land – and therefore the price of housing, office space, etc. – is usually higher in built-up areas, such as Central London, than it is in rural areas, such as North Wales. What this means is that if everything else were equal, firms and workers would prefer to locate in less built-up areas. Of course, we know other things are not equal, but the forces that make built-up areas more attractive are called agglomeration forces and we put them aside for the moment to focus on dispersion forces. Dispersion forces counteract agglomeration forces by increasing the attractiveness of less-developed regions. In addition to land prices, there are several other forms of congestion-based dispersion forces; these get their name from the fact that living in a congested area has many downsides (light, noise and air pollution, etc.).

While congestion-based dispersion forces are important in the real world, we shall ignore them in our theory. There are two very good reasons for this. First, such dispersion forces are not changed by European economic integration. Thus, when we go to see how European integration affects the geographic dispersion of economic activity, consideration of such forces will not add anything important. Second, including such forces in our theory complicates matters, so for simplicity's sake we put them aside. (See Box 10.2 for what happens when they are put back into the framework.)

The only dispersion force we consider is the so-called local competition force. That is, given trade costs and imperfect competition, firms are naturally attracted to markets where they would face few locally based competitors. For example, an entrepreneur thinking about setting up a new convenience store is likely to choose a location that is far from other competitors. In seeking to avoid local competition, firms spread themselves evenly across markets. In this way, local competition tends to disperse economic activity.

Agglomeration forces

An agglomeration force exists when the spatial concentration of economic activity creates forces that encourage further spatial concentration. This definition is more circular than the straight-line chain of causes and effects usually presented in economics. This circularity, however, is the heart of the subject. To return to the question of causality raised by the comparison of maps in Figure 10.6, the answer is that workers move because the jobs concentrate *and*, at the same time, the jobs concentrate since workers concentrate.

There are many agglomeration forces, but some of them operate only on a very local scale. These explain, for instance, why banks tend to group together in one part of London while dance clubs cluster in another part of the city. The study of agglomerations at this level – it is called urban economics – is fascinating, but it is not the level of agglomeration that interests us. European policy is concerned with the impact of European integration on agglomeration at the level of regions and nations. At this geographic level, many of the city-level agglomeration forces are unimportant. The two most important agglomeration forces that operate across great geographical spaces are called demand linkages and cost linkages (also known as backward and forward linkages, respectively).

Demand-linked and cost-linked agglomeration forces

To illustrate the circular-causality logic of demand-linked and cost-linked agglomeration forces as simply as possible, we make a couple of bold assumptions. First, we assume that firms will choose one location (see Box 10.1 for the economics behind this assumption). Second, we assume that there are only two possible locations, a region called 'north' and a region called 'south'. The demand-linked circular causality rests on market-size issues (hence its name). Firms want to locate where they have good access to a large market. Consider the UK example again. In 2005, much but not all UK demand was in southern England. If a firm locates in the north, it incurs high shipping costs when selling to southern customers, although it has low costs when selling to customers in the north. (It is cheaper to sell to nearby customers.) Since there are more customers in the south, northern firms can reduce their shipping by moving to the south. This is where the circular causality of demand linkages starts. Other things equal, firms want to be in the big market.

Box 10.1 How scale economies force manufacturing firms to choose a location

By definition, a firm that is subject to scale economies is one whose average cost – i.e. the per-unit cost – of producing a good falls as the scale of production rises. This means that firms whose production is subject to scale economies will benefit from concentrating production in a single location – think of it as a single factory, rather than setting up a factory near every market. For example, contrast the production of car engines, which is marked by huge scale economies, with the production of cheese, which is economical even at fairly low levels of output (there are thousands of these around Europe). Owing to scale economies, most European car companies make all engines of a particular type in a single factory located somewhere in Europe. The reason is that the per-engine cost of production is much lower in big factories. When it comes to cheese, however, the cost reduction from having a single massive cheese factory would not lower per-kilo production costs by much. For this reason, companies tend to put cheese factories near the milk production rather than ship massive quantities of milk to a massive cheese factory.

The causality becomes circular because the movement of firms from the small market in the north to the big market in the south makes the big market bigger and the small market smaller. The reason is that, by moving to the south, the firms create jobs in the south and this induces workers to move to the south. This affects market size since workers tend to spend their incomes locally. For example, when a firm leaves Dijon to set up in Paris, it moves jobs to Paris. This makes it somewhat harder to get a job in Dijon and somewhat easier to get a job in Paris, so this move encourages workers to move to Paris. We call this an 'agglomeration force' since spatial concentration (the Dijon-to-Paris move) of economic activity creates forces (the change in market sizes) that encourage further spatial concentration.

The basic idea is illustrated in Figure 10.7. It is useful to separate two things that are closely related: market size (i.e. 'south market as a share of total market', or the spatial distribution of firms), and firm location (i.e. 'share of firms in the south', or the spatial distribution of firms).

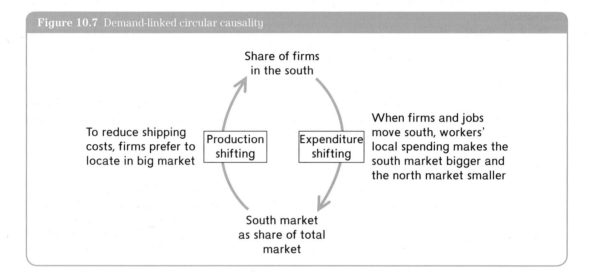

Figure 10.7 Demand-linked circular causality

Starting from the left arrow, we see that the market size affects the location of firms. The logic rests on firms' desire to minimize shipping costs. The right arrow shows that the location of firms affects relative market size. The logic is simply that firms employ workers and workers tend to spend their incomes locally. If no dispersion forces were in operation, this circular causality would continue until the north was entirely empty of jobs and firms.

This brings us to the second major type of agglomeration force: cost-linked circular causality. This agglomeration force works in a fashion that is similar to demand-linked circular causality, but it involves production costs rather than market size.

It is a fact that, in the modern economy, firms buy plenty of things from other firms. These range from raw materials and machinery to specialized services such as marketing, accounting and IT services. Since it is cheaper to find and buy such input from firms that are nearby, the presence of many firms in a location tends to reduce the cost of doing business in that location. Thinking this through, we can see that a similar circular causality will encourage agglomeration. Figure 10.8 helps explain this.

The figure separates two things that are closely related but worth keeping distinct: firm location (i.e. 'share of firms in the south', or the spatial distribution of firms), and the cost-advantage of producing in the big market (i.e. 'cost of producing in the south', or the spatial distribution of production costs).

Starting from the left arrow, we note that, if many firms are already in the south, then doing business in the south will – all else equal – be cheaper than doing business in the north. This production-cost differential influences the location of firms. The right arrow shows how the relocation of firms from the north to the south tends to improve the business climate in the south and worsen it in the north, at least in terms of the range of available inputs. Again, if there were no dispersion forces (e.g. wages in the north being lower than those in the south), this circular causality would empty out the north entirely.

Figure 10.8 Cost-linked circular causality

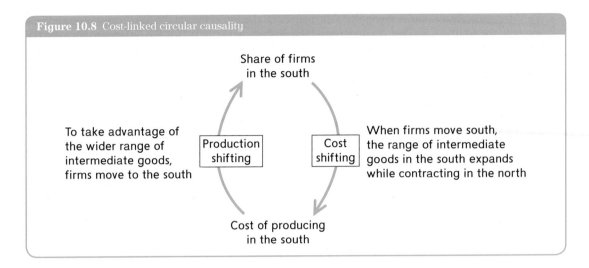

In other words, cost-linked circular causality describes the way in which firms are attracted by the presence of many suppliers in the big market and how firms moving to the big market widens the range of suppliers and thus makes the big market even more attractive from a cost-of-production point of view.

10.3.2 The locational effects of European integration

European integration affects the balance of agglomeration and dispersion forces in complex ways. Such complexity is important for understanding the real world since – as the facts presented above show – the locational effects of European integration are far from simple. The best way to understand this complex logic, however, is to follow the principle of progressive complexity. We start with a set of simplifying assumptions that allow us to focus on the critical logical relationships. Once we have understood this logic in a simplified setting, we add back in complicating factors.

A very simple analytic framework

To simplify, we start by assuming away all dispersion forces except 'local competition'. We also assume away cost-linked circular causality (by assuming firms buy no intermediate inputs). This leaves us with only one pro-agglomeration consideration and one pro-dispersion consideration:

- The pro-agglomeration force is that firms would, all else equal, prefer to locate in the big market in order to save on trade costs, i.e. to be close to more of their customers than they would be if they were located in the small market.
- The pro-dispersion force is that firms would, all else equal, prefer to be in the market where there are few local competitors and that means locating in the small market.

The final simplifying assumption is that we ignore the circular causality in the demand-linked agglomeration force. One way to think of this is by supposing that workers spend all their income in their native region regardless of where they work. Thus the south market starts out bigger, but firms moving to the south does not make the market bigger.

To study the balance of the agglomeration and dispersion forces, it helps to have a simple diagram. Figure 10.9 serves this purpose. The diagram plots the strength of agglomeration and dispersion forces on the vertical axis. The horizontal axis plots the share of all firms that are located in the big region, i.e. the south. Thus:

- The 'agglomeration force' line is flat since we assume away circular causality for simplicity's sake. The market-size difference does not vary with the share of firms in the south, so the strength of the agglomeration force as we move out along the agglomeration force line does not change.

- The 'dispersion force' line is rising since the benefit of staying in the small region rises as more firms move to the southern market. To understand the positive slope, note that the difference between the degree of local competition in the north and in the south increases as a higher share of firms move to the south. For example, suppose there were only four firms. When they are split 2–2 between the regions, the local competition is even. When they are split 3–1, the local competition is more intense in the region with three firms (the south). Finally, if the split is 4–0, then the difference in local competition is even greater. Connecting these observations, we see that the dispersion force (i.e. the attractiveness of the small market) rises as the share of firms in the south rises. Graphically, this means that the 'dispersion force' curve is upward-sloping.

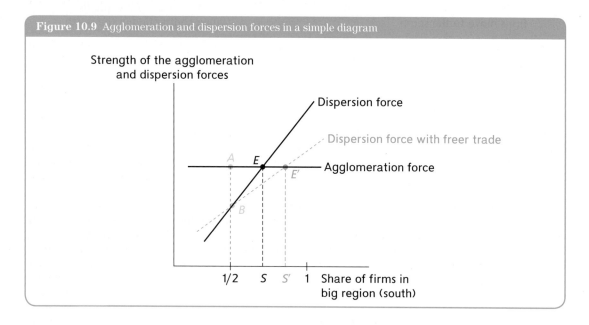

Figure 10.9 Agglomeration and dispersion forces in a simple diagram

The locational equilibrium is shown by point E; this is where the share of firms in the south rises to the point where incentives to agglomerate are just balanced by incentives to disperse. It is instructive to consider why other points are not the equilibrium. For example, consider the point where half the firms are in the north. For this equal distribution of firms, the strength of the agglomeration force is shown by point A; the strength of the dispersion force is shown by point B. Because A is greater than B, we know that the agglomeration force – i.e. the force leading more firms to move to the south – is stronger than the dispersion force – i.e. the force leading firms to move to the north. As a consequence, having only half the firms in the south cannot be an equilibrium. Moreover, since the agglomeration force is stronger than the dispersion force, some firms will move from the small north to the big south.

As firms move southward, the gap between the agglomeration force and the dispersion force narrows. The location equilibrium is where the two forces just offset each other, namely, point E, where the share of firms in the south is S. Although it is not shown in the diagram, readers can easily convince themselves that points to the right of point E involve a situation where the dispersion forces are larger than the agglomeration forces so the share of firms in the big region would tend to fall back to point E.

The location effects of tighter European integration

Finally, we come to the main subject of this section: How does tighter economic integration affect the location of industry inside a nation? We think of greater economic integration as lowering shipping costs. Note that here we are speaking of the trade costs among regions within a nation. Such cost reductions come with improvements in technology and improvements in transportation infrastructure and competition. All of these are fostered directly and indirectly by various elements of European integration. This is especially true for EU regional spending on roads, airports, seaports – the sort of thing we discuss below. It is worth noting, however, that such within-nation integration would proceed even without European integration. For the purposes of the diagram, we do not care about the exact reason trade costs are falling; we simply assume they do fall and trace out the impact on the spatial dispersion of firms.

How do we show the trade cost reduction in the diagram? The first point is that the agglomeration force line does not move. The agglomeration force is based on the fact that the northern market is bigger and this fact does not change when trade becomes freer. Nothing happens to the 'agglomeration force' line.

Freer trade, however, has a very direct effect on the 'dispersion force' curve. The source of the dispersion force is that trade costs protect firms located in the small market from competition from firms located in the big market. It is clear, then, that something will happen to the dispersion force line. To get a handle on this, consider a very particular point on the line, the point where the share of firms in the big region is ½. At this point, the level of trade costs has no influence on the relative attractiveness of the two regions. Whether trade costs are high or low, the degree of local competition in the two markets will be identical. The thrust of this is that the dispersion force line must always pass through point B in the diagram. Any change will be a rotation of the line around point B.

For points to the right, the dispersion force line must come down. The reason is that, with more firms in the south than the north, the advantage of being in the low-competition north (low competition since there are fewer firms there) is reduced by lower trade costs. In other words, the lower trade costs provide less protection against competition from south-based firms. For this reason, the local competition advantages of being in the north are reduced. Since this is true for all points to the right of ½, this shows up graphically as a clockwise rotation of the 'dispersion force' line around the ½ point.

Given that the dispersion-force curve rotates clockwise and the agglomeration-force curve stays put, the new locational equilibrium is at point E'. Note that this involves a higher share of firms in the big region. In other words, free trade promotes the agglomeration of economic activity in the initially big region. As we saw in Figure 10.2, this within-nation concentration of economic activity is a widespread phenomenon in Europe.

The simplifying assumptions above made it very easy to study integration's impact on the location of economic activity in Figure 10.9. While it assumed away many important factors affecting the location of economic activity, it is sufficient for understanding the basic economic logic of how tighter European integration can be expected to favour the location of industry in Europe's core regions. Some readers, however, will want to explore the economics of this in greater depth. Box 10.2 shows how some factors can be included in a modified version of Figure 10.9.

Box 10.2 Considering additional complicating factors

As it turns out, it is not very difficult to add back in a number of complicating factors that we assumed away to start with.

For example, we can easily allow for circular causality in the agglomeration force. We do this by drawing the agglomeration-force line as upward-sloping (Figure 10.10). If the line slopes upward, it says that the strength of the agglomeration force rises as a larger share of firms move to the big southern region. This addition raises an extra complication concerning the impact of freer trade. Freer trade rotates the dispersion-force line as in the text; however, now it also reduces the agglomeration force for any level of firms in the north. The reason is clear; the agglomeration force stemmed from the fact that locating in the big market helps a firm reduce its shipping costs. Since lower overall shipping costs narrow this difference between the markets, the agglomeration-force line shifts down. The complication is that there is now a graphical possibility that the new E' will be to the left of the old E. A careful study of the logic shows that this cannot occur. Roughly speaking, the free trade reduces the agglomeration forces by less than the dispersion forces so the new location equilibrium involves more spatial concentration.

Figure 10.10 Allowing for circular causality

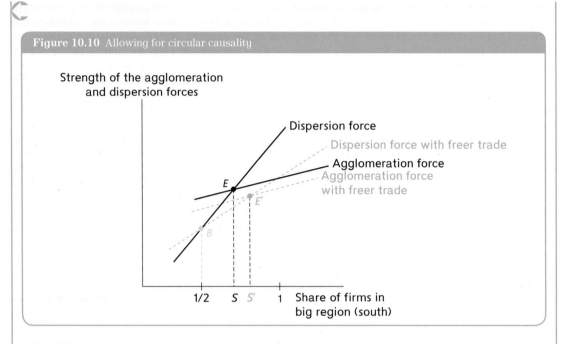

We can consider other dispersion forces by shifting the dispersion-force curve up or twisting it at the ends. For dispersion forces that are not related to the share of firms in the north, the dispersion-force curve is shifted up vertically. For example, it could be that one region is intrinsically more pleasant to live in. Since the impact of this on location does not depend upon the share of firms in the south, we allow for such forces by shifting the curve either up or down. Interested readers can easily check that a downward shift will increase the equilibrium share of firms in the south. Other dispersion forces, however, are related to the share of firms. For example, the concentration of firms in southern England drives up the wages of workers in this region. Other things equal, this acts as a dispersion force in that it discourages some firms from moving to the south. We can reflect this in the diagram by rotating the dispersion-force line counter-clockwise around the ½ point.

10.4 Theory part III: putting it all together

The facts presented above showed that European integration was accompanied by location effects within nations that are quite different from those between nations. European integration seems to be associated with a more even dispersion of economic activity in the sense that per-capita GDP figures tended to converge nation by nation. Within nations, however, the opposite has happened. In most Member States, regional disparities have grown as European integration has deepened. The theory presented above helps us to understand the difference. The key factor is the mobility of capital and labour.

While there are few remaining restrictions on intra-EU labour flows, workers seldom move across national borders in the EU. Labour mobility between regions within a nation is higher, but still not enormous – as we can see with the huge variation in regional unemployment rates. However, labour mobility has not always been low within nations. The post-war period, for example, saw a massive shift of the population from rural to urban regions and this often involved a move across regional boundaries. Moreover, other productive factors are more mobile; for example, capital and skilled workers are quite mobile between regions within the same nation.

Oversimplifying to make the point, think of all factors as perfectly mobile within nations, but perfectly immobile across nations. In this case, removing barriers to trade allows nations to specialize in the sectors in which they have a comparative advantage. The resulting efficiency gain allows all nations to increase their output. Moreover, deeper aspects of integration, such as foreign direct investment and mobility of students, suggest that European integration would also be accompanied by a convergence of national technology frontiers to the best practice in Europe, with the technological laggards catching up with the technological leaders. Both of these factors would promote a convergence of per-capita incomes across European nations. Importantly, the lack of factor mobility across nations means that agglomeration forces are not dominant at the national level. That is to say, the cycles of circular causality that might lead all economic activity to leave a region have no chance of starting. This conclusion must be modified to allow for sector-specific clusters. Even if productive factors do not move across national boundaries, agglomeration forces operating at the sectoral level could result in nations specializing in particular industries. For example, deeper integration could foster greater geographic clustering of, say, the chemicals industry and the car industry, but in the end each nation ends up with some industry.

By contrast, the much greater mobility of factors within nations permits backward and forward linkages to operate. As one region grows, it becomes attractive to firms for both demand and cost reasons, so more firms and more factors move to the region, thereby fuelling further growth.

10.4.1 Regional unemployment

The analysis so far has assumed that wages are flexible enough to ensure full employment of all labour. Since regional unemployment is a serious problem in Europe, we turn to the economic logic connecting delocation and unemployment. As usual, we follow the principle of progressive complexity by starting simple.

If wages were adjusted instantaneously across time and space, we would have no unemployment. The wage rate paid for each hour of work would adjust so that the amount of labour that workers would like to supply at that price just matched the amount that firms would like to 'buy' (hire). In this hypothetical world, the wages would instantaneously jump to the market-clearing level, i.e. the level where labour supply matches labour demand. Things are not that simple, however.

For many reasons, most European nations have decided to prevent the wage – the 'price' of labour – from jumping around like the price of crude oil or government bonds. (See Chapter 8 for a more formal treatment of unemployment.) All sorts of labour market institutions, ranging from trade unions and unemployment benefits to minimum wages and employment protection legislation, mean that the price of labour is systematically stabilized at a level that exceeds the market-clearing wage level. The direct logical consequence is that workers systematically want to offer more labour at the going wage than firms are willing to hire; this is the definition of unemployment. As in any market, if the price is fixed too high, the amount offered for sale will exceed the amount that is bought.

In most European nations, there is a strong spatial element to this price-fixing of labour. Take Germany, for example. For many reasons, labour productivity in the eastern Länder is lower than it is in the western Länder. Thus, firms would only be willing to employ all the eastern labour offered if wages were lower in the east. However, German labour unions have methodically prevented eastern wages from falling to their market-clearing level, either in an attempt to avoid downward pressure on their own wages or, more charitably, in the spirit of solidarity with the eastern workers who actually do get employed. Whatever the source of regional wage inflexibility, its logical consequence is regional unemployment. Moreover, since firms can leave a region much more easily than workers, a continual within-nation clustering of economic activity will tend to be associated with high levels of unemployment in the contracting regions and low levels in the expanding regions.

Finally, it should be clear that this sort of mismatch of migration speeds (firms move faster than workers) – teamed with a lack of regional wage flexibility – has the effect of creating an agglomeration force. A little shift of industry raises unemployment in the contracting region and lowers it in the expanding region. Since unemployment is an important factor in workers' migration decisions, the initial shift makes workers more likely to migrate to the expanding region. Such migration, however, changes the relative market sizes in a way that tends to encourage more firms to leave the contracting region. (For a detailed account of geographical clustering of unemployment in Europe, see Overman and Puga, 2001).

10.4.2 Peripherality and real geography

Our theoretical discussion has intentionally simplified physical geography considerations by working with only two nations, both of which are thought of as points in space. Real-world geography, of course, is

much more interesting and this matters for the location of economic activity. We can use the basic logic of demand-linked agglomeration forces to consider how one can put real geography back into the picture.

As discussed above, firms that want to concentrate production in a single location tend, other things being equal, to locate in a place that minimizes transportation costs. With only two markets, this means locating in the bigger market, but when the economic activity is spread out over real geography, the answer can be less obvious. However, the fact that economic activity is highly concentrated in Europe makes the problem easier. As the map in Figure 10.2 showed, the core of Europe is fairly compact from a geographical point of view, i.e. it is concentrated in the northeast corner of the continent. This is why it is useful to abstract Europe's geography as consisting of two regions, the core and the periphery, what we called the north and the south in the previous section.

There are many complicating factors, however. For example, despite the Alps forming a wall between northern Italy and the big French, German and UK markets, northern Italy has quite good road access thanks to several tunnels and passes through the mountains.

Economists have a way of taking account of the various real-geography features, known as the accessibility index (also called the market potential index); see Figure 10.11 for a recent example. The

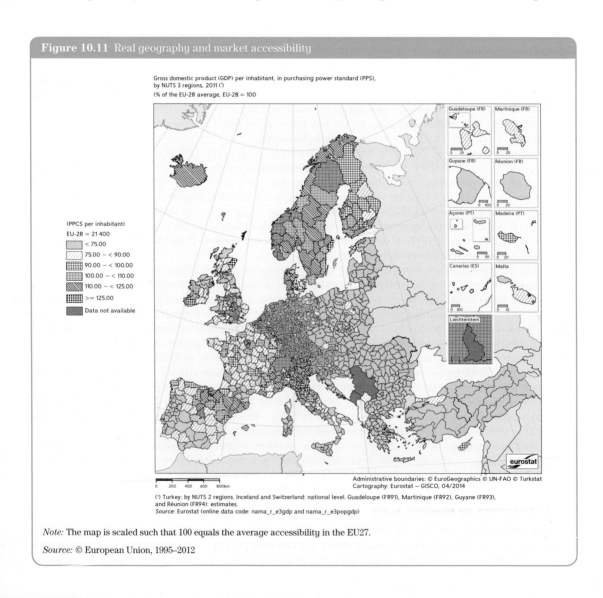

Figure 10.11 Real geography and market accessibility

Gross domestic product (GDP) per inhabitant, in purchasing power standard (PPS), by NUTS 3 regions, 2011 (¹)
(% of the EU-28 average, EU-28 = 100

(PPCS per inhabitant)
EU-28 = 21 400
< 75.00
75.00 − < 90.00
90.00 − < 100.00
100.00 − < 110.00
110.00 − < 125.00
>= 125.00
Data not available

0   200   400   600   800km

Administrative boundaries: © EuroGeographics © UN-FAO © Turkstat
Cartography: Eurostat – GISCO, 04/2014

(¹) Turkey: by NUTS 2 regions. Inceland and Switzerland: national level. Guadeloupe (FR91), Martinique (FR92), Guyane (FR93), and Réunion (FR94): estimates.
Source: Eurostat (online data code: nama_r_e3gdp and nama_r_e3popgdp)

Note: The map is scaled such that 100 equals the average accessibility in the EU27.

Source: © European Union, 1995–2012

accessibility index for each region measures the region's closeness to other regions that have a lot of economic activity. For example, to calculate the accessibility of the region that contains Paris, the Ile de France, one calculates how long it would take to get from the centre of Paris to the main urban centre of every other region in the EU (the calculation varies somewhat according to the form of transport used; the map here works with road transportation). Finally, one weights each of these transport times by the destination region's share of the EU's total economic activity. Adding up these weighted times gives us an idea of how close Paris is to the bulk of EU economic activity. Doing the same for every other region gives us an index of accessibility by region.

10.5 EU regional policy

Most Europeans care about disadvantaged regions as part of their general preference for social cohesion. Indeed, reducing regional inequality has been a headline goal of the European Union since its inception in the later 1950s and this was reaffirmed in the Lisbon Treaty. Article 174 of the Treaty of Lisbon states:

> *In order to promote its overall harmonious development, the Union shall develop and pursue its actions leading to the strengthening of its economic, social and territorial cohesion. In particular, the Union shall aim at reducing disparities between the levels of development of the various regions and the backwardness of the least favoured regions.*

This section reviews the main aspects of EU regional policy, which has developed gradually over the last six decades. See Her Majesty's Government (2014) for a succinct history of EU cohesion policy, which is here taken as a synonym for regional policy.

10.5.1 Instruments, objectives and guiding principles

In its latest long-term budget plan, the so-called Multiannual Financial Framework for 2014–2020, the EU is committed to spending a third of its budget on cohesion policy. How is this money allocated? Here, we just touch upon the main points. Interested readers can find well-written documentation of the full details at http://ec.europa.eu/regional_policy/index_en.htm.

The guiding light for cohesion spending in the period 2014–20 will be the 'Europe 2020 Strategy' for 'smart, sustainable and inclusive growth'. This 10-year strategy was introduced by the European Commission in 2010 with the explicit goal of overcoming the global and Eurozone crises. It has 11 thematic objectives – 3 under smart growth, 4 under sustainable growth and 4 under inclusive growth (see Table 10.2). EU nations negotiate partnership agreements ('Operational Programmes') with the European Commission on how they will use EU funds to help deliver the Europe 2020 strategy.

The new cohesion policy for 2014–20 will involve thousands of projects. These will range from improving transport and telecommunication links with remote regions, helping small and medium-sized enterprises in disadvantaged regions, cleaning up the environment, and improving education attainment and skill levels.

Every region in the EU is eligible for cohesion spending of one type or another, but the bulk of the money, about 80 per cent, goes to poor regions. Specifically, about two-thirds goes to regions whose incomes are less than 75 per cent of the EU27 average – the so-called less developed regions. Another 13 per cent goes to 'transition' regions whose incomes are between 75 and 90 per cent of the EU27 average. The remaining 20 per cent can be spent in all other regions, i.e. those with incomes above 90 per cent. Something like 3 per cent of the money is earmarked for cross-region projects that reduce the negative effects of borders. This 'European Territorial Cooperation' helps regions work together to address common problems such as pollution in the Baltic Sea and cross-border use of hospitals.

10.5.2 Allocation by Member State

Spending per nation is set down in the Multiannual Financial Framework for 2014–2020. As Figure 10.12 shows, a rough negative correlation exists between high receipts per capita and high incomes. Estonians get the highest receipts, at €2,700, while the Dutch get the least, at just €84 per capita spread over the seven years.

Introduction

Competition among firms is the heart and soul of the social market economy. It is what turns the profit motive into a socially beneficial urge. Competition, however, has and always has had a tendency to break down. In his 1776 masterpiece on market economics, *The Wealth of Nations*, Adam Smith wrote: 'People of the same trade seldom meet together, even for merriment and diversion, but the conversation ends in a conspiracy against the public, or in some contrivance to raise prices.' A strong competition policy encourages the process of rivalry among firms, which in turn boosts more choice for consumers, lower prices and higher quality. Competition also fosters an efficient allocation of resources and incentivizes innovation.

Deeper European economic integration – together with more general trends such as WTO trade liberalization and globalization – has put European manufacturing and service sector firms under a great deal of pressure. As discussed in Chapter 6, the long-run outcome of this heightened competitive pressure is typically a reshaped industry marked by fewer, bigger, more efficient firms engaged in more effective competition among themselves. However, in the short and medium run firms may be tempted to collude in order to avoid or postpone industrial restructuring, and Member State governments may be tempted to provide subsidies that delay the necessary but painful restructuring.

The founders of the European Union understood that pressures to collude and subsidize would arise in the course of economic integration. They also understood that anticipation of such unfair practices could reduce political support for economic integration in all nations; an 'I will not liberalize since the others are not playing fair' feeling could halt all deeper integration, especially in the sectors where it is most critical, i.e. those marked by important scale economies and imperfect competition.

To guard against these pressures, broad prohibitions were written into the Treaty of Rome on private and public policies that distort competition. Such strictures have been at the core of EU policy ever since. Of course, the Treaty of Rome has several provisions that have not been followed seriously, and the founders understood that this is frequently the fate of many provisions in many treaties. Yet, the Treaty writers felt that enforcing fair play in the internal market was so important that EU competition policy required special institutional arrangements – arrangements that would ensure that political expediency would not hinder the maintenance of a level playing field. Again, this practice continues even today.

To this end, the Treaty grants the European Commission the sole power (exclusive competence in EU jargon; see Chapter 2) to regulate the EU's competition policy. The Commission's decisions can be overturned by the EU Court but they are not subject to approval by the Council (i.e. what was called the Council of Ministers before the Lisbon Treaty) or the European Parliament. Of course, the Commission is not a 'Lone Ranger' in such matters. It continuously consults with Member States, especially via their respective competition authorities, but the Commission has the final word on whether mergers are allowed, whether particular business practices are allowed, and whether aid provided by Member States to firms is allowed. We can say that competition policy is one area where the Member States have truly transferred substantial sovereignty to a supranational level. The Lisbon Treaty confirmed the special position of competition policy and the control of state aid.

This chapter opens by providing an introduction to the economics of anti-competitive practices by private firms and subsidies by governments. It then proceeds to discuss the EU's actual policies.

11.1 The economics of anti-competitive behaviour and state aid

Before turning to how the European Commission regulates competition and state aid, it is important to understand the economics that lead private firms to engage in anti-competitive behaviour and what the effects of this are on the broader economy. This is the task we turn to first. Here, we study basic issues using the framework introduced in Chapter 6. The discussion here assumes readers have mastered the *BE–COMP* diagram, which is explained at length in Chapter 6.

11.1.1 Allowing collusion in the *BE–COMP* framework

As the EU's Single Market becomes less fragmented, firms experience greater competition, which forces them to restructure in a way that lowers their costs. Frequently, such adjustments involve waves of mergers and acquisitions. An alternative, however, is for the firms to collude in order to avoid or postpone industrial restructuring. Or, to put it more directly, in many sectors firms face the choice between perishing or engaging in anti-competitive behaviour; some firms choose the latter. See Box 11.1 for some examples.

Box 11.1 Examples of cartels

In July 2014, the German antitrust authority, BKA, fined 21 sausage producers over 300 million euros for fixing the prices of sausages. Thirty-three individuals were also penalized. The BKA determined that the collusion had occurred for a decade, with price-fixing deals struck on the telephone or in the Hotel Atlantic Kempinski – a five-star hotel in Hamburg. While exact prices were not agreed, the conspirators set price ranges. The cartel was uncovered with the help of an anonymous tip. Eleven of the companies involved admitted wrongdoing and cooperated with the authorities.

Other German food producers have also been caught colluding. In February 2014, BKA fined three German sugar producers 280 million euros for market manipulation and April saw 11 breweries fined 340 million euros for price fixing. The fined breweries accounted for half of German beer sales.

Interested readers can find details of the latest convictions on http://ec.europa.eu/competition/cartels/cases/cases.html.

Theory

While firms reacting to competitive pressure by price-fixing may be understandable, doing so is illegal under EU law and economically harmful for Europe as a whole. In a nutshell, allowing collusion among firms can result in too many, too small firms that must charge high prices to compensate for their lack of efficiency. The high prices result in lower demand and production. Thus protecting existing firms can end up reducing the overall level of industrial production.

One very clear real-world example was seen in telecoms services. Before liberalization, each European nation had its own monopoly provider; services were expensive since firms were small and as a result consumers did not spend much on telecoms. Since liberalization, competition has forced a massive industrial restructuring, a massive increase in the size of firms and a massive reduction in the price of services. The result has been a boom in the amount of telecoms services produced and consumed in Europe.

We illustrate this general point with an extended version of the *BE–COMP* framework from Chapter 6.

The BE–COMP diagram

Reviewing it briefly, the *BE–COMP* diagram, shown in Figure 11.1, has three panels:

1 The middle panel shows the demand curve facing the sector in a typical nation (the diagram assumes that there are two identical nations; the middle panel shows the demand curve for one of them – the Home market). This panel is used for keeping track of consumer surplus and the connection between price and industry-wide production (which must equal consumption). For example, in the closed-economy case, the long-run price is P'. This means that total consumption must equal C'. This in turn means that total production must be C'.

2 The left-hand panel shows the average and marginal cost curves for a typical firm (all firms are identical). The diagram assumes that firms enter or exit until all pure profit is eliminated, i.e. until price equals average cost. This panel is used to keep track of the typical firm's size, x, and its efficiency, as measured by its average cost (lower average cost means higher efficiency). The long-run equilibrium firm size is deduced from the long-run equilibrium price since we know that pure profits are zero in the long run, so the long-run price must equal the average cost of the typical firm. The average cost curve, AC, thus tells us how large the typical firm must be to have an average cost equal to the long-run equilibrium price. For example, if the long-run price is P', the typical firm size must be x' to ensure that price equals average cost.

3 The right-hand panel shows two equilibrium relationships between the mark-up and the number of firms. Recall that the mark-up is price minus marginal cost and that we denote it with the Greek letter μ,

pronounced 'mu'. The number of firms is denoted n. The $COMP$ curve shows the equilibrium combinations of μ and n assuming normal competition; as expected, more firms corresponds to more competition and thus a lower mark-up. The BE (break-even) curve is upward sloping since, as the number of firms rises, the sales per firm fall and so firms would need a higher mark-up in order to cover their fixed costs.

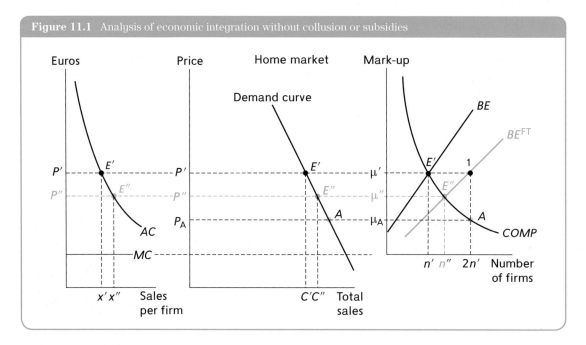

Figure 11.1 Analysis of economic integration without collusion or subsidies

The equilibrium in the three panels identifies the equilibrium number of firms, n, mark-up, μ, price, P, firm size, x, and total output/consumption, C.

As in Chapter 6, we model European integration as a no-trade-to-free-trade liberalization between two identical nations. The equilibrium with no trade is marked by E'; the one with free trade between the two identical nations is marked E'. There are two immediate and very obvious effects from the no-trade-to-free-trade liberalization:

1 *Market size*: post-integration, each firm has access to a second market of the same size.

2 *Degree of competition*: post-integration, each firm faces twice the number of competitors.

The market-size effect shifts the BE curve to the right, specifically out to the point marked '1' (see Chapter 6 for a detailed explanation). The competition aspect is the simplest to illustrate in the diagram, Figure 11.1. Immediately upon opening the markets, i.e. before the industry has had time to adjust, the number of firms is $2n'$. Thus the typical firm will lower its mark-up in each market to point A – assuming, of course, that firms do not collude (recall that the $COMP$ curve shows the mark-up under normal competition).

The extra competition forces mark-ups down to point A, and this pushes prices down to P_A. At this combination of sales per firm and mark-up, all firms begin to lose money (i.e. A is below the relevant break-even line, BE^{FT}). This 'profit pressure' forces industrial reorganization (mergers, acquisitions and bankruptcies) that gradually reduces the number of firms to the new long-run equilibrium number, n''. Note that after this long-run 'industry shake-out', firms are bigger and more efficient (the left-hand panel shows that x has increased to x'' and average cost has decreased to P''); they are also facing more effective competition than before the liberalization (the right-hand panel shows that the price–cost margins drop to μ'').

To summarize in words, deeper European integration boosts the degree of competition and this in turn requires the industry to consolidate so as to better exploit scale economies. Naturally, this consolidation involves the exit of some firms. The classic examples are telecoms, airlines, banking and autos, where market integration has resulted in a wave of mergers.

The key point as far as competition policy is concerned is that deeper European integration will generally be accompanied by a long-run reduction in the number of firms. This is important for two reasons:

- First, it means that Europe must be even more vigilant to ensure that the fewer bigger firms do not collude.
- Second, it means that firms may be tempted to engage in anti-competitive practices in order to avoid or delay the industrial restructuring.

We turn now to showing what anti-competitive practices look like in the *BE–COMP* diagram. Box 11.2 provides a real example of how four firms conspired to raise the price of beer in the Netherlands.

Box 11.2   Collusion in the Dutch beer market

The Commission convicted four brewers of running a cartel in the Netherlands (the Heineken group, Grolsch, Bavaria and the InBev group). Beer is big business for the Dutch; yearly consumption is something like 80 litres per inhabitant! The four brewers involved sold a total of around 1 billion euros annually, and had a combined market share of over 90 per cent. The collusion was quite formally coordinated. According to the Commission's investigation, between 1996 and 1999 the four brewers held numerous unofficial meetings, during which they coordinated prices and price increases of beer. Such activity was successfully hidden from the authorities; however, when the Commission uncovered a cartel in the Belgian beer market one of the players in that case – InBev – provided evidence in order to reduce its fine. This is a tactic – the so-called leniency policy – that the Commission uses with great effect as it essentially faces the cartel members with a Prisoners' Dilemma. After the tip-off from InBev, the Commission raided (conducted a 'surprise inspection' of) brewers in France, Luxembourg, Italy and the Netherlands.

The raids involved collecting handwritten notes taken at unofficial meetings and proof of the dates and places when these meetings, called 'agenda meetings', 'Catherijne meetings' or 'sliding scale meetings', had taken place. The attendees at these meetings coordinated prices and price hikes at bars and stores. The Commission also found evidence that board members, managing directors and national sales managers actually participated in these meetings. Moreover, evidence was gathered that showed that the companies were well aware that what they were doing was illegal. Indeed, they employed cloak-and-dagger techniques to avoid detection (code names, abbreviations and holding meetings in various hotels and restaurants). One wonders whether they brought their own beer to avoid the high prices!

In the words of then-Competition Commissioner Neelie Kroes (the commissioner who oversaw an historic expansion in the effectiveness of the EU's competition policy in the 2000s): 'It is unacceptable that the major beer suppliers colluded to hike up prices and carve up the market between themselves.' The companies were fined a total of about 270 million euros. InBev escaped without a fine.

Perfect collusion

The *COMP* curve in Figure 11.1 assumes that firms do not collude. Both before and after the integration, we assumed that firms engaged in 'normal' competition in the sense that each firm decided on how much to sell, taking as given other firms' sales. In other words, each firm decided its output without coordination among firms.

This assumption of 'normal' competition is quite reasonable for many industries, but it is not the most profitable behaviour for firms. If firms were allowed to collude, they could raise profits by reducing the amount they sell and raising prices. We consider some real-world examples in the policy section below (Section 11.2), but interested readers may wish to go to ec.europa.eu/comm/competition/cartels/cases/cases.cfm for details on the latest cases in which the European Commission has caught firms colluding.

There are many, many forms of collusion in the world. The first form we consider is the simplest to study. Instead of assuming no collusion on output, we consider the extreme opposite of perfect collusion on output.

If all firms could perfectly coordinate their sales, i.e. if they could act as if they were a single firm, they would limit total sales to the monopoly level. This would allow them to charge the monopoly price and to earn the greatest possible profit from the market. After all, the monopoly price–sales combination is – by definition – the combination that extracts the greatest profit from the market. In the diagram, this is shown by the mark-up, μ^m, which corresponds to one firm ($n = 1$). The resulting price is the monopoly price, shown as P^m.

The hard part of collusion is finding a way to divide up the monopoly level of sales among the colluding firms. The problem is that, because the price is so much higher than marginal cost, each firm would like to sell a little more than its share. To keep things simple, we assume that the firms manage the collusion by allocating an equal share to all firms. This type of behaviour can be illustrated in the *BE–COMP* diagram with the 'perfect collusion' line shown in Figure 11.2. This line extends horizontally since it assumes that the mark-up always equals the monopoly mark-up, μ^m, regardless of the number of firms.

Figure 11.2 Perfect collusion

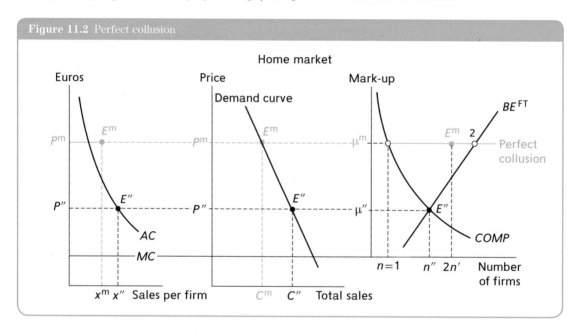

If all firms did charge the monopoly mark-up, then the maximum number of firms that could break even is shown by point '2'. This would involve new entry – an outcome that we rarely observed after liberalization. Another possibility is that all $2n''$ firms would stay in business, without any new firms entering; this is shown as point A'. Note that, at this point, all firms are making pure profits owing to the collusion (since E^m is above the AC curve in the left-hand panel and it is above the BE^{FT} curve in the right-hand panel).

This collusion is good for firms' profits, but it is bad for society as a whole. Comparing the perfect collusion outcome to the long-run outcome without collusion (equilibrium, E'), we see that the price is higher, and consumption and production are lower. Moreover, since firms are smaller (since overall production is lower with collusion, the output of each firm must be smaller), average costs are higher, so the industry is less efficient.

Partial collusion

Perfect collusion is difficult to maintain since the gains from 'cheating' on other colluders are quite high. To reduce the incentive to cheat, the actual degree of collusion may be milder than perfect collusion. This sort of partial collusion restricts sales of all firms but not all the way back to the monopoly level, so the mark-up is lower than the monopoly mark-up but higher than the *COMP* mark-up. With the mark-up lower, it is easier to sustain the collusion since the benefits from cheating are not quite as large.

But how much lower would the mark-up be under partial collusion? As it turns out, an understanding of advanced economics is needed to formalize this notion of 'partial collusion', so we do not address it here explicitly (see Mas-Colell et al., 1995, for an advanced treatment). Fortunately, the basic idea can be easily depicted in Figure 11.3.

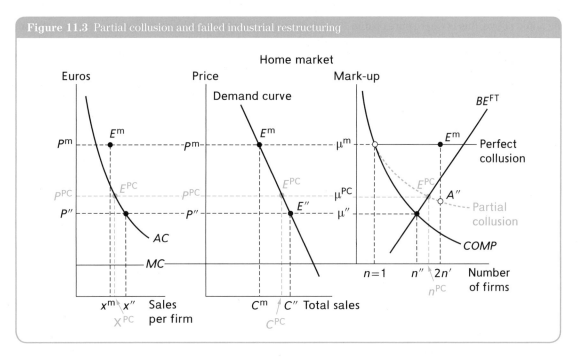

Figure 11.3 Partial collusion and failed industrial restructuring

The curve labelled 'partial collusion' shows a level of collusion where the mark-up is somewhere between the monopoly mark-up and the no-collusion mark-up shown by the *COMP* curve. We do not specify exactly where it lies between the two as it does not change the qualitative analysis. All we need to assume is that the partial collusion curve lies between the *COMP* curve and the perfect collusion curve as shown in the diagram.

If the $2n'$ firms all engaged in this partial collusion, then the mark-up would be shown by point A''. This mark-up is higher than the long-run equilibrium mark-up without collusion (μ''), so we see that this partial collusion offsets, to some extent, the increase in competition induced by integration. (Recall from Chapter 6 that the size of the mark-up is an indicator of the degree of competition.)

Note, however, that although this mark-up is higher than under normal competition, it is not high enough for all the firms to break even. We can see this from the fact that point A'' is below the break-even curve (BE^{FT}). What this means is that, even with partial collusion, some firms will exit the market. In the long run, the number of firms adjusts to restore zero pure profits, and this is where the partial competition curve and the break-even curve intersect, namely, at point E^{PC}.

Point E^{PC} is the long-run equilibrium since with n^{PC} firms the mark-up would be m^{PC} and, with this mark-up, n^{PC} firms would all break even. As before, we can read off all the important aspects from the diagram. The level of consumption in the Home market (which is half of total consumption since Foreign is assumed to be identical) is C^{PC}. Since supply equals demand in equilibrium, we know that C^{PC} is also the total production in each nation. As usual, the equilibrium price also tells us the equilibrium efficiency, i.e. the typical firm's average cost. Using the average cost curve, we also know that the size of the typical firm is x^{PC}.

Now we study the economic implications of such collusion, comparing it to the long-run equilibrium with normal competition, i.e. equilibrium E''. To summarize the price and quantity changes, we note that, compared to the normal competition equilibrium, the partial collusion equilibrium involves firms that are smaller, less efficient and more numerous. The mark-up is higher along with the price, so consumption and total production are lower.

Long-run economic costs of collusion

The first point is that collusion will not in the end raise firms' profits to above-normal levels. Even allowing for the way that partial collusion raises prices above P', the initial number of firms after liberalization, namely, $2n'$, is too high for all of them to break even. Industrial consolidation proceeds as usual, but instead of the zero-profit level being reached when the number of firms has dropped to n'', the process halts at n^{PC}. As noted above, this is where pure profits – which started at zero in the pre-integration long-run equilibrium described in Figure 11.1 – are returned to zero. In other words, the higher prices do not result in higher long-run profits. They merely allow more small, inefficient firms to remain in the market. The welfare cost of the collusion is measured by the four-sided area marked by P^{PC}, P'', E'' and B. This is just the consumer surplus loss, but since there is no change in pure profits (it is zero in the long run with or without collusion), the change in consumer surplus is the full welfare effect.

To summarize, collusion prevents the full benefits of restructuring from occurring. By keeping too many firms in the market, anti-competitive behaviour thwarts part of the industry's adjustment that is the key to the gains from integration.

Having presented a general analysis that suggests why deeper European integration and competition problems tend to go hand in hand, we turn now to considering four types of anticompetitive practices in more detail. We start with cartels.

11.1.2 Anti-competitive behaviour

Firms like to make money. Competition hinders this, so some firms try to limit competition. One age-old way of doing this is to form a cartel with other firms in the industry. For example, one of the best-known cartels, the Organization of the Petroleum Exporting Countries (OPEC), has been controlling the international price of crude oil since the early 1970s.

Horizontal anti-competitive practices: cartels and exclusive territories

The DRAM cartel is a European example (see Box 11.3). As Figure 11.4 shows, the economic effects of cartels are rather straightforward (see Chapter 4 if you need a refresher on this sort of economics). The diagram depicts the impact of the price-raising effects of a cartel.

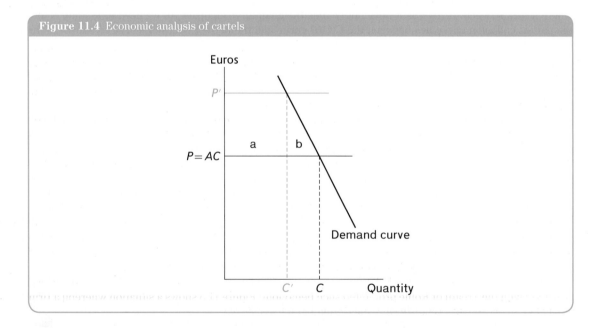

Figure 11.4 Economic analysis of cartels

Box 11.3   The DRAM cartel

Memory chips are a key component in almost every bit of modern electronics – especially Dynamic Random Access Memory, or DRAM. They are used as the main memory for loading, displaying and manipulating applications and data and as such are critical to personal computers, servers and workstations.

The production of DRAMs is extremely capital intensive (the cost of plants runs into the billions), but the marginal cost of each chip is very low. This combination makes collusion especially tempting and the small number of producers globally makes it feasible.

In May 2010, the Commission decided that ten DRAM producers were running a cartel and fined them over 331 million euros. All the convicted companies but one are non-European (Infineon is German), but the case was based on their European sales. The convicted companies were Micron, Samsung, Hynix, Infineon, NEC, Hitachi, Mitsubishi, Toshiba, Elpida and Nanya, but Micron paid no fine as it testified against the others.

The companies ran the cartel between 1998 and 2002 via a network of contacts and the sharing of secret information bilaterally. Specifically, the companies had regular contact whereby they secretly exchanged information on pricing intentions and general pricing strategy. They also swapped commercially sensitive data to identify specific contract customers. In this way, they shared, verified and monitored prices charged to major electronics manufacturers. The companies used the secret information to set their own prices.

Source: This box is based on information from DG Competition's website at http://ec.europa.eu/competition/cartels/cases/cases.html

---

The diagram shows the situation for a particular market, say DRAM, where the price without the cartel would be P. This initial price is shown as being equal to average costs (AC), which indicates zero profits even before the cartel; the analysis follows through even if the initial price were above AC, but this way makes it easier to see the effects. When the cartel raises the price to P' by reducing the volume of sales to C', consumer surplus is reduced by area a + b. The cartel's profit rises by area b. This analysis illustrates the two main problems with cartels: the rip-off effect and the inefficiency effect.

First, the fact that they allow firms to profit at the expense of customers is considered by most people (and by EU law) to be unfair – a rip-off, to put it colloquially. Second, the gain to firms is less than the loss to consumers, so the cartel is inefficient from a purely technical point of view. Specifically, the net economic loss is area b. While few Europeans know or care about the efficiency loss, almost all would believe that the rip-off effect is something their governments should do something about.

Another rather common way of restricting competition is for firms to agree upon so-called exclusive territories. For example, one company would agree to sell only in its local market in exchange for a similar promise by its foreign competitors. One example of this can be found in the market for video games. Nintendo and seven of its official distributors in Europe teamed up in the 1990s to boost profits by dividing up Europe's markets and charging higher prices in those areas where consumers had a higher ability to pay. Under this practice, distributors had to prevent games being shipped from their territory to that of another EU market where prices were higher. Independent customers who allowed such sales among territories were punished by being given smaller shipments next time or cut off altogether. In this way, these companies managed to maintain big price differences for play consoles and games in various EU markets (e.g. Britons enjoyed prices that were 65 per cent cheaper than those faced by the Germans and Dutch). The European Commission fined Nintendo and the seven distributors 168 million euros.

Thinking more broadly, it is clear that such practices offset all the goals of European integration, which is exactly why the Treaty of Rome prohibited such behaviour. Figure 11.5 shows a situation whereby a firm would like to charge different prices in the German and UK markets.

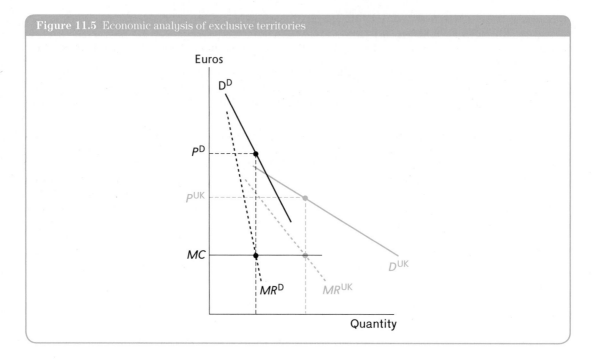

Figure 11.5 Economic analysis of exclusive territories

The diagram shows the two demand curves; the German demand curve D^D is steeper than the British demand curve D^{UK}. The steepness of a demand curve reflects a 'willingness to pay' since it tells us how much consumption of Nintendo products would drop for a given price increase. The German curve is drawn as steeper to reflect the fact that Germans have fewer options when it comes to consumer electronics and games (owing to the smaller number of people who speak German versus English worldwide, and to widespread restrictions on retail outlets in Germany). In economics jargon, German demand is more inelastic, i.e. more unresponsive to price. In this situation, Nintendo would maximize profits by selling the quantities in Germany and Britain that correspond to the intersections of the marginal revenue curves (MR^D and MR^{UK}) and marginal cost curves (MC); see Chapter 6 if this reasoning is unfamiliar. The quantities are not shown explicitly, but the resulting prices are marked as P^D and P^{UK}.

In an integrated market, independent firms, often called 'traders', could arbitrage the price gap by buying Nintendo goods in the UK and shipping them to Germany. Such shipments – which are known as 'parallel trade' – would lower Nintendo's profits and that of its official distributors. To preserve their profits, Nintendo and its distributors attempted, illegally, to prevent such trade.

Bullies in the market: abuse of dominant position

Business leaders and stock markets often evaluate a company's performance based on the growth of its market share, so many firms aim to conquer the market. Firms that are lucky or possess excellent products can succeed in establishing very strong positions in their markets. This is not a problem if the position reflects superior products and/or efficiency – Google's triumph in the market for search engines could be one example. However, once a firm has a dominant position, it may be tempted to use it to extract extra profits from its suppliers or customers, or it may attempt to arrange the market so as to shield itself from future competitors. According to EU law, such practices, known technically as 'abuse of dominant position', are illegal.

The classic example of this is Microsoft. Most computer users are happy that Microsoft has standardized the basics of personal computing around the world – especially those that move between nations or use more than one machine on a regular basis. In other words, computer operating systems are subject to network externalities. That is, computer operating system software becomes more valuable to each user as more people use it.

To understand how and why network externalities work, just think about why the English language has spread so widely and continues to do so; more and more people learn it since so many people speak it. Just as with English, industries characterized by network externalities tend to be marked by a dominant firm, or a handful of firms.

In the case of Microsoft, which has dominated the operating system software market for decades, the question is how it came to dominate applications with products such as Word and Excel. Although it has never been proven in court, many observers believe that the company used frequent updates of its operating system to induce users to drop competing applications (as recently as ten years ago, Microsoft had real competition from rival products such as WordPerfect and Lotus). The details of Windows updates are available to engineers updating Microsoft applications but not to those updating rival applications, so new versions of rival applications often had glitches caused by incompatibilities with the latest version of Windows. Even if a user preferred the other applications, incompatibilities with successive versions of DOS and Windows meant it was easier to switch to Microsoft's applications than it was to deal with the glitches. Moreover, when competing firms came up with innovative programs, Microsoft typically responded with similar programs and gave them away for free. Today, for example, Microsoft charges a high price for Word, where it no longer has any real competitors, but it charges a zero price on software where it has significant rivals, such as media readers and web browsers.

A similar set of issues arose with respect to Google's dominant position in search services. See Box 11.4 for details.

Box 11.4   The Google case

In March 2013, Google was alerted by the Commission that it was under investigation for business practices that potentially violate EU antitrust rules prohibiting the abuse of a dominant position. These included: (1) displaying Google's own specialized web search services more prominently than those of competing companies; (2) using (without consent) other companies' original content; (3) obliging website publishers to obtain most of their online search advertisements from Google; and (4) restricting the transferability of online search advertising campaigns to rival search advertising platforms.

In February 2014, Google was made to change its practice in response to a Commission antitrust investigation. Specifically, Google guaranteed that the services of three rivals would be promoted along with its own specialized search services.

Commission Vice President in charge of competition policy, Joaquín Almunia, said:

> *My mission is to protect competition to the benefit of consumers, not competitors.*
> *I believe that the new proposal obtained from Google after long and difficult talks can*
> *now address the Commission's concerns. Without preventing Google from improving*
> *its own services, it provides users with real choice between competing services*
> *presented in a comparable way; it is then up to them to choose the best alternative.*
> *This way, both Google and its rivals will be able and encouraged to innovate and*
> *improve their offerings. Turning this proposal into a legally binding obligation*
> *for Google would ensure that competitive conditions are both restored quickly and*
> *maintained over the next years.*

The investigation actually began in November 2010 following more than a dozen formal complaints about Google's business practices.

11.1.3 Merger control

In many European industries, the number of firms is falling as they merge or buy each other out. This sort of concentration of market power is a natural outcome of European integration, as Figure 11.1 showed, but it may also produce cartel-like conditions. The basic trade-off can be illustrated with the so-called Williamson diagram in Figure 11.6.

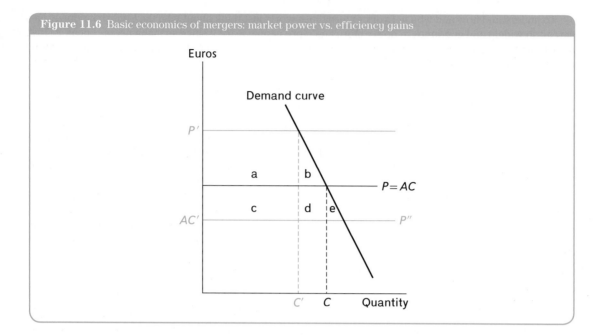

Figure 11.6 Basic economics of mergers: market power vs. efficiency gains

Consider a merger that allows the merged firms to charge a higher price, but which also allows them to lower average cost by eliminating redundant capacities in marketing, accounting, sales representatives, etc. The price rise is shown in the diagram by the increase in price from P to P' (the diagram assumes that the market was in long-run equilibrium at $P = AC$ to start with). The efficiency gain is shown by the drop in average cost from AC to AC'. The gain to the firm's profitability is strongly positive. Before, $P = AC$ meant there were no profits. After, profit is the area a + c. The merger is bad for consumers, since the price hike implies a loss of consumer surplus equal to the area a + b. The overall gain to society, taking profits and consumer surplus together, is the area c − b since area a is merely a transfer from consumers to firms.

There is a point here that is important for understanding the EU's new rules on mergers. Notice that if entry and exit in the industry are unrestricted, and the remaining firms do not collude, then the long-run outcome of this merger will be to drive the price down to the lower average costs, $P'' = AC'$. This is essentially what happens when the equilibrium shifts from E' to E'' in Figure 11.1. In this case, the merger-with-efficiency gain is always positive and equal to area c + d + e since the consumer surplus gain from the lower long-run price, P'', is not offset by any loss of producer surplus; profits were zero to start with ($P' = AC'$) and to end with ($P'' = AC'$). Since entry and exit in most EU industries are fairly unrestricted, there is a presumption that mergers will generally be of the type that boosts efficiency and passes on this efficiency to consumers.

Note that our treatment of competition here is highly simplified. The impact of mergers on pricing and costs can be extremely complicated and highly dependent on the nature of the industry. Examples of such reasoning can be found in the Commission's analysis of actual merger cases on their website: http://ec.europa.eu/competition/mergers/cases/.

11.1.4 State aid

The Figure 11.1 logic linking integration and industrial restructuring presumes that profit-losing firms would eventually leave the industry – that they would be bought out by another firm, merged with other firms or, in rare cases, go bankrupt. All three of these exit strategies may involve important job losses in specific locations, or at the very least an important reorganization that may require workers to change jobs. Since job losses and relocations are painful, governments frequently seek to prevent them. For example, if the firm is government owned, trade unions may force the government to continue to shore up the money-losing enterprise. If it is privately owned, the government may provide subsidies through direct grants or through long-term loans that may not be repaid.

Here, we look at the long-run economics of such subsidies – called 'state aid' in EU jargon – under two distinct scenarios. The first is where all governments provide such support. The second is where only one does.

EU-wide subsidies: thwarting the main source of gains

Start by supposing that both governments provide subsidies that prevent restructuring. To be concrete, we make the additional, more specific assumption that governments make annual payments to all firms exactly equal to their losses. Under this policy, all $2n'$ firms in the Figure 11.1 analysis will stay in business, but, since firms are not making extraordinary profits, no new firms will enter. The economy, in short, remains at point A owing to the anti-restructuring subsidies.

An insightful way to think about this subsidy policy is as a swap in who pays for the inefficiently small firms. Before integration, prices were high, so consumers paid for the inefficiency. After liberalization, competition drives down the price but this comes at the cost of extra pay-outs from the national treasuries, so now the taxpayers bear the burden of the industry's inefficiency. Moreover, since all the firms stay in business, integration is prevented from curing the main problem, i.e. the too-many-too-small firms problem. Firms continue to be inefficient since they continue to operate at too small a scale. As a consequence, the subsidies prevent the overall improvement in industry efficiency that was the source of most of the gains discussed in Chapter 6.

Do nations gain from this liberalize-and-subsidize scheme? As it turns out, both nations do gain overall, even counting the cost of the subsidies. We shall show this with a diagram, but before turning to the detailed reasoning, it is instructive to explain the deep reason for this result. Imperfect competition is inefficient since it leads prices to exceed marginal costs. Recalling from Chapter 4 that the consumer price is a measure of marginal utility, the fact that price exceeds marginal cost implies that the gain to consumers from an extra unit would exceed the resource cost of providing the unit. In short, society tends to gain from an expansion of output when price exceeds marginal cost. Because of this, policies that increase output tend to improve welfare. In the jargon of public economics, the subsidy is a 'second-best' policy since it reduces the negative effects of market-power distortion, even if it does not solve the root of the problem.

Note, however, that this reasoning is very partial. This sort of 'reactive' subsidy turns out to be a very bad idea in the long run. The subsidies are paid to prevent firms from adapting to changed circumstances. While the government may occasionally improve things by preventing change, a culture of reactive interventionism typically results in a stagnant economy. Staying competitive requires industries to change – to adapt to new technologies, to new competitors and to new opportunities. When firms get used to the idea that their governments will keep them in business no matter what, the incentive to innovate and adapt is greatly weakened. Firms with this sort of mindset will soon find themselves far behind the international competition.

Welfare effects of the liberalize-and-subsidize policy

To explain the welfare effects of the liberalize-and-subsidize policy, we refer to Figure 11.7. The policy we consider freezes the economy at point A in the right-hand and middle panels (this point A corresponds exactly to point A in Figure 11.1). We know that the price falls from p' to p^A and consumption rises from C' to C^A. Since the number of firms has not changed but total sales in each market (which must equal total consumption in each market) have increased, we know that the sales of each firm have increased somewhat, from x' to x^A, as shown in the left-hand panel. At this point, firms are losing money, but the government offsets this with a subsidy.

How big will the subsidy be? The easiest way to make this comparison is to adopt a roundabout approach. First, consider the total size of operating profit that the whole Home industry needs to cover all fixed cost before the liberalization. The answer is already in the middle panel. Before the liberalization, the industry broke even by selling a total of C' units at price p'. The operating profit on this was the area A + B in the middle panel of the diagram, i.e. the gap between price and marginal cost times the units sold. After the liberalization, the industry's operating profit is area B + C (the new price–cost gap, $p^A - MC$, times the new sales, C^A). The drop in operating profit is thus area C minus area A. The subsidy we are considering

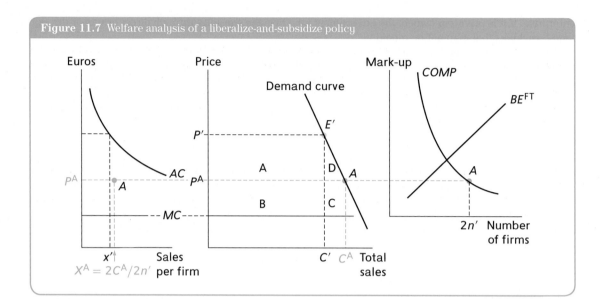

Figure 11.7 Welfare analysis of a liberalize-and-subsidize policy

would have to exactly offset the loss, so the subsidy would equal area A – C. With these facts established, we turn to the welfare calculation.

The consumer part of the welfare calculation is simple. Consumers see a lower price so consumer surplus rises by the area +A + D. To see the overall welfare effect, we subtract the subsidy, which equals A – C. The net welfare effect is A + D – (A – C), which equals D + C. We know this is right since this area is the gap between price and marginal cost summed over all the extra units consumed. Notice that this is the classic gain from partially redressing a market power distortion.

Only some subsidize: unfair competition

The governments of EU Member States differ over how much they can or want to subsidize loss-making firms. Yet, when only some governments subsidize their firms, the outcome of the restructuring may be 'unfair' in the sense that it gets forced upon the firms in nations that do not subsidize, or stop subsidizing before the others. The real problem with this is that it may create the impression that European economic integration gives an unfair advantage to some nations' firms.

To examine this problem more closely while keeping the reasoning as tangible and simple as possible, we continue with the Figure 11.1 example of two nations engaged in an extreme no-trade-to-free-trade integration. The integration moves each identical economy from point E' to point A. At A, all firms in both nations are losing money. Now suppose that restructuring takes, say, five years in the sense that, after that time, the number of firms has adjusted from $2n'$ to n''. In our simple example, there is no way of telling which of the surviving firms will be Home firms and which will be Foreign firms. Symmetry suggests that half the remaining firms would be Foreign, but nothing in the example ensures that this is the case. This is where subsidies can make a big difference.

To be concrete, suppose that prior to the liberalization there were 10 firms in Home and 10 in Foreign, and that after restructuring there will be 12 firms in total. Furthermore, suppose that Home provides a 5-year subsidy to all of its 10 firms, with the size of the subsidy being large enough to offset the liberalization-induced losses. The Foreign government, by contrast, is assumed to pursue a laissez-faire policy, i.e. it allows the market to decide which firms should survive – either because it believes in the market or because it cannot afford the subsidies. In this situation, it is clear that 8 of the 10 Foreign firms will go out of business, while all 10 Home firms will survive. At the end of the 5-year period, the

Home government no longer needs to subsidize its firms since the exit of eight Foreign firms restores the industry to profitability.

From a purely economic perspective, the Foreign nation might have been the winner since having firms in our example brings nothing to national welfare (firms earn zero profit in the best of cases). The Home nation's subsidies were merely a waste of taxpayers' money. Two comments are relevant at this stage. First, this sort of conclusion shows that our simple example is actually too simplistic in many ways. For example, we did not consider the cost of workers having to switch jobs and possibly being unemployed for some time. Second, it shows that economics is only part of the picture.

The politics of state aid disciplines: I'll play only if the rules are fair

From a political perspective, this sort of unfair competition would be intolerable. Indeed, if trade unions and business groups in Foreign anticipated that this would be the outcome, they might very well block the whole integration exercise. To avoid this sort of resistance to liberalization, the EU establishes very strict rules forbidding such unfair competition. In this sense, one of the most important effects of discipline on state aid is the fact that it allows governments to proceed with painful and politically difficult reforms.

11.2 EU competition policy

Having laid out the basic logic of collusion and subsidies, we turn now to considering actual EU policy that constrains such actions by private actors (anti-competitive practices) and governments (subsidies).

EU competition rules are laid out in the Treaty of the Functioning of the European Union and the implementing legislation. The main provisions discipline anti-competitive practices and abusive dominant positions in the market. The Treaty also sets rules on subsidies, or 'state aid' as the Commission calls it. Generally state aids are prohibited unless sanctioned by the Commission.

11.2.1 Institutions: the power of the European Commission

The founders of the EU were fully aware that integrating Europe's markets would result in restructuring and that this would produce incentives for private and public actors to resist consolidation. This is very clear, for example, in the 1956 Spaak Report, which was the economic blueprint for the Treaty of Rome (*Rapport des chefs de délégation aux ministres des affaires étrangères*, Bruxelles, 21 April 1956). Moreover, they feared that the perception that some nations might 'cheat' in an effort to shift the burden of consolidation onto others would, in itself, make deeper European integration politically impossible. To ensure that the prevailing attitude was 'I will reform since the rules are fair' instead of 'I cannot reform since other nations will cheat', the Treaty of Rome prohibited any action that prevents, restricts or distorts competition in the common market.

Importantly, the Treaty puts the supranational Commission in charge of enforcing these strictures. Just as European leaders decided to forgo their control over monetary policy (by making central banks independent) since they knew in advance that short-run politics would lead to bad long-run policy, the Treaty of Rome grants a great deal of power on competition policy directly to the European Commission. The idea was that the politicians in the Council of Ministers might not be able to resist the short-run pressure of special-interest groups opposed to the consolidation that is necessary to obtain the long-run gains from European economic integration. In fact, competition policy is probably the area in which the Commission has the greatest unilateral power.

The Commission has considerable powers to investigate suspected abuses of EU competition law, including the right to force companies to hand over documents. Most famously, the Commission has the right to make on-site inspections without prior warning, which the media often call 'dawn raids'. With a court order, the Commission can even inspect the homes of company personnel.

The Commission has the power to prohibit anti-competitive activities. It does this by issuing injunctions against firms. To back up these demands, the Commission has the right to impose fines on firms found guilty of anti-competitive conduct. The fines vary according to the severity of the anti-competitive practices, with a maximum of 10 per cent of the offending firm's worldwide turnover. When it comes to subsidies, the Commission has the power to force firms to repay subsidies it deems to be illicit.

Unlike most other areas in which it acts, the Commission's decisions are not subject to approval by the Council of Ministers or the European Parliament. The only recourse is through the European Court. This is an area in which Member States truly did pool their sovereignty to ensure a better outcome for all.

11.2.2 EU law on anti-competitive behaviour

EU law on anti-competitive practices was first laid out in the Treaty of Rome and has not been changed substantially (apart from occasional renumbering of the articles, most recently in the Lisbon Treaty). Here, we review the main provisions, but it is important to note that we merely hint at actual policy. EU competition policy has been subject to many decisions of the European Court and one must master the details of these cases in order to fully understand which practices are prohibited and why. Moreover, the Commission publishes its own administrative guidelines so that firms can more easily determine whether a particular agreement they are contemplating will be permitted by the Commission.

Article 101 of the Treaty on the Functioning of the EU, TFEU (as the Treaty of Rome was re-labelled by the Lisbon Treaty) outright forbids practices that prevent, restrict or distort competition, unless the Commission grants an exemption. This article is clearly written and worth reading in its entirety (see Box 11.5).

Box 11.5   Article 101 (Article 81 pre-Lisbon; Article 85 in the original TEC)

1 The following shall be prohibited as incompatible with the common market: all agreements between undertakings, decisions by associations of undertakings and concerted practices which may affect trade between Member States and which have as their object or effect the prevention, restriction or distortion of competition within the common market, and in particular those which:

   (a) directly or indirectly fix purchase or selling prices or any other trading conditions;

   (b) limit or control production, markets, technical development, or investment;

   (c) share markets or sources of supply;

   (d) apply dissimilar conditions to equivalent transactions with other trading parties, thereby placing them at a competitive disadvantage;

   (e) make the conclusion of contracts subject to acceptance by the other parties of supplementary obligations which, by their nature or according to commercial usage, have no connection with the subject of such contracts.

2 Any agreements or decisions prohibited pursuant to this Article shall be automatically void.

3 The provisions of paragraph 1 may, however, be declared inapplicable in the case of:

   ● any agreement or category of agreements between undertakings;

   ● any decision or category of decisions by associations of undertakings;

   ● any concerted practice or category of concerted practices, which contributes to improving the production or distribution of goods or to promoting technical or economic progress, while allowing consumers a fair share of the resulting benefit, and which does not:

   (a) impose on the undertakings concerned restrictions which are not indispensable to the attainment of these objectives;

   (b) afford such undertakings the possibility of eliminating competition in respect of a substantial part of the products in question.

Typically, the restrictions in Article 101 are classified as preventing horizontal or vertical anti-competitive agreements. Horizontal agreements are arrangements, like cartels and exclusive territories, upon competitors selling similar goods. Vertical agreements are arrangements between a firm and its suppliers or distributors (e.g. agreements by retailers to charge not less than a certain price, and tie-in arrangements whereby goods are only supplied if the vendor agrees to purchase other products).

The first part of Article 101 is so categorical that it rules out an enormous range of normal business practices, which can in fact be good for the European economy. The final part therefore allows the Commission to grant exemptions to agreements where the benefits outweigh the anti-competitive effects. The Commission does this for individual agreements notified to the Commission for exemption, but it also has established the policy of 'block exemptions' that grant permission to broad types of agreements. These exist for technology transfer and for R&D agreements. Political pressure has also forced the Commission to grant a block exemption to the anti-competitive practices in the distribution of motor vehicles.

The second major set of policies – restrictions on the abuse of a dominant position – are found in Article 102 of the TFEU (see Box 11.6). A dominant position usually depends upon a firm's market share. Abuse is a general term but it includes refusal to supply, unfair prices and conditions, predatory pricing, loyalty rebates, exclusive dealing requirements and abuse of intellectual property rights.

Box 11.6   Article 102 (formerly Article 82 pre-Lisbon; 86 in original TEC)

Any abuse by one or more undertakings of a dominant position within the common market or in a substantial part of it shall be prohibited as incompatible with the common market insofar as it may affect trade between Member States.

Such abuse may, in particular, consist in:

(a) directly or indirectly imposing unfair purchase or selling prices or other unfair trading conditions;

(b) limiting production, markets or technical development to the prejudice of consumers;

(c) applying dissimilar conditions to equivalent transactions with other trading parties, thereby placing them at a competitive disadvantage;

(d) making the conclusion of contracts subject to acceptance by the other parties of supplementary obligations which, by their nature or according to commercial usage, have no connection with the subject of such contracts.

11.2.3 Control of mergers

The Treaty of Rome did not address the control of mergers. The Commission, however, saw some control of mergers as essential to keeping competition vibrant. The issue was controversial among members. Some doubted that mergers needed controlling and others thought such control should be at the national, not EU, level. Some nations viewed merger policy as an important plank in their industrial policy and not a concern of the Commission provided that state aid and rules on 'abuse of dominant position' were respected. This reluctance shifted during the drive in the 1980s to complete the Single Market and 'European Union Merger Regulation' came into force in 1990 and has been amended occasionally since.

The Merger Regulation does not stand by itself but rather is one pillar in a merger control edifice that also includes guidelines on the assessment of horizontal mergers and on best practice in merger investigations, and reforms within the Commission. The Merger Regulation defines anti-competitive behaviour as: 'A concentration which would significantly impede effective competition, in the common market or in a substantial part of it, in particular by the creation or strengthening of a dominant position, shall be declared incompatible with the common market.' Under the rules, mergers that meet the relevant criteria do not have to be notified to the Commission since they are presumed to be compatible with competition. For details, see Commission (2010).

The current rules also give a prominent role to national competition authorities and courts under the so-called European Competition Network, which facilitates coordination among EU and national competition authorities and courts. Box 11.7 describes the decisions taken by the Commission on two particular mergers.

Box 11.7   Two examples of merger decisions

The European pharmaceutical sector has experienced a wave of consolidation and, as part of this, two mega-mergers were brought to the attention of the European Commission, the Sanofi and Synthélabo link-up and the Pfizer and Pharmacia fusion. The Commission determined that both would lessen competition in certain market segments by limiting the choice of some drugs. The Commission, however, recognized the need for efficiency gains and believed that the mergers could be useful. The outcome was that the Commission allowed the mergers subject to conditions. The firms were required to transfer some of their products to their competitors so as to redress potential anti-competitive effects. For example, Sanofi/Synthélabo sold off certain antibiotics, hypnotics and sedatives.

Another case involved a mainly domestic merger between TotalFina and Elf Aquitaine, which were the main players in the French petroleum sector. The Commission determined that their merger would have allowed them to push up costs for independent petrol station operators (e.g. supermarkets) and the combined company would have operated around 60 per cent of the service stations on French motorways. The combined firms would also have been the leading supplier of liquid petroleum gas. The European Commission believed that this level of market power would be anti-competitive and agreed to the merger only on the condition that TotalFina/Elf sell off a large proportion of these operations to competitors. For example, it sold 70 motorway service stations in France to competitors.

11.2.4 EU policies on state aid

The EU's founders realized that the entire European project would be endangered if EU members felt that other members were taking unfair advantage of the economic integration. To prevent this, the 1957 Treaty of Rome bans state aid that provides firms with an unfair advantage and thus distorts competition. Importantly, the EU founders considered this prohibition to be so important that they actually empowered the supranational European Commission to be in charge of enforcing the prohibition. Indeed, the Commission has the power to force the repayment of illegal state aid, even though the Commission normally has no say over members' individual tax and spending policies.

The Treaty prohibits state aid that distorts competition in the EU, and it defines state aid in very broad terms. It can, for instance, take the form of grants, interest relief, tax relief, state guarantee or holding, or the provision by the state of goods and services on preferential terms. Some state aid, however, is allowed according to the Treaty since subsidies, when used correctly, are an essential instrument in the toolkit of good governance. The permitted exceptions include social policy aid, natural disaster aid and economic development aid to underdeveloped areas. More generally, state aid that is in the general interest of the EU is permitted. For example, the Commission has also adopted a number of bloc-exemption rules that explain which sorts of state aid are indisputable. These include aid to small and medium-sized enterprises, aid for training and aid for employment. More information can be found on the DG Competition website.

Box 11.8   State aid and the global crisis

The global crisis that started in the USA in 2008 spread rapidly to Europe. EU policy makers responded by providing massive state aid to banks to prevent the financial shock from creating a second Great Depression. All these measures had to be approved by the Commission under its state aid policy. In the first 5 years of the crisis, the Commission authorized over 400 state-aid measures to the financial sector. Aid used for recapitalization and asset relief measures amounted to almost 600 billion euros or almost 5 per cent of EU GDP, and aid for guarantees and other forms of liquidity support was almost twice as large. As the crisis has calmed, much of the aid has been repaid.

The Commission duly adopted six 'Communications' providing guidance for Member States regarding what type of aid would be allowed and how it would be monitored. The goal was to allow Member States to underpin financial stability while minimizing distortions of competition between banks and across nations. Financial stability avoids major negative spillovers across EU banking systems and helps banks provide loans to the real economy.

When applying the rules to individual cases, the Commission looks beyond its usual industry-level criteria and takes account of the macroeconomic environment. Key points for the Commission are the long-term viability of the subsidized banks and whether the need for support arose from the crisis or bank-specific risk-taking. This is an ongoing challenge as large parts of the EU financial sector must be restructured.

Source: This box is based mainly on data from http://ec.europa.eu/competition/state_aid/scoreboard/financial_economic_crisis_aid_en.html

A contentious example: airlines in trouble

The Commission is frequently in the headlines regarding its decisions on state aid since these often produce loud protests from firms and/or workers who benefitted from any state aid that the DG Competition judges to be illegal. An excellent example concerns the airline industry – an industry in which there are clearly too many firms in existence and the tendency to subsidize is strong. Many European airlines are the national 'flag carrier' and as such are often considered a symbol of national pride.

Consolidation of the European airline industry has been on the cards for years, but the problem was exacerbated by the terrorist attacks of 11 September 2001. The ensuing reduction in air travel caused great damage to airlines all around the world and led to calls for massive state aid. To prevent these subsidies from being used as an excuse to put off restructuring, the Commission restricted subsidies to cover only the 'exceptional losses' incurred when transatlantic routes were shut down immediately after 11 September. To date, the Commission has managed to resist the desire of several Member State governments to support their national airlines to the same extent that the US government has supported US airlines.

It is easy to see the logic of the Commission's stance. Low-cost airlines, such as Ryanair and easyJet, have done well without subsidies. Moreover, artificial support for inefficient national carriers hinders the expansion of low-cost airlines. As Bannerman (2002) puts it:

No-one will benefit from a return to spiralling subsidies, which damage the industry by encouraging inefficiency. Both consumers and taxpayers would suffer as a result. As for the national carriers, they would probably benefit from some market consolidation, creating fewer, leaner, pan-European airlines – although this process would need monitoring for its competitive effects on key routes. If the airline industry can use the crisis to create more efficient carriers, it will probably be the better for it. But this long-term view cuts little ice with workers who stand to lose their jobs, or with some politicians, for whom a flag carrier is a symbol of national pride. Unfortunately, the benefits of controlling state-aids occur mainly in lower fares and taxes, and are therefore widely diffused among the population. The costs, on the other hand, take the form of job losses, which hurt a small but vocal constituency.

11.3 Summary

Three main points have been made in this chapter:

- One very obvious impact of European integration has been to face individual European firms with a bigger 'home' market. This produces a chain reaction that leads to fewer, bigger, more efficient firms that face more effective competition from each other. The attendant industrial restructuring is frequently politically painful since it often results in layoffs and the closure of inefficient plants. Governments very often attempt to offset this political pain by providing 'state aid' to their national firms. Such state aid can be viewed as unfair and the perception of unfairness threatens to undermine EU members' interest in integration. To avoid these problems, the founders of the EU established rules that prohibited state aid that distorts competition. The Commission is charged with enforcing these rules.

- Private firms may also seek to avoid restructuring by engaging in anti-competitive practices and EU rules prohibit this. Moreover, as integration proceeds and the number of firms falls, the temptation for firms to collude may increase.

- To avoid this, the EU has strict rules on anti-competitive practices. It also screens mergers to ensure that they will enhance efficiency. Again, the Commission is charged with enforcing these rules.

Self-assessment questions

1 Suppose that liberalization occurs as in Figure 11.1 and the result is a pro-competitive effect, but instead of merging or restructuring, all firms are bought by their national governments to allow the firms to continue operating. What will be the impact of this on prices and government revenues? Now that the governments are the owners, will they have an incentive to continue with liberalization? Can you imagine why this might favour firms located in nations with big, rich governments?

2 Look up a recent state aid case on the Commission's website (http://ec.europa.eu/competition/state_aid/register/) and explain the economic and legal reasoning behind the Commission's decision using the diagrams in this chapter.

3 Look up a recent antitrust case (Article 81) on the Commission's website (http://ec.europa.eu/competition/antitrust/cases/index.html) and explain the economic and legal reasoning behind the Commission's decision using the diagrams in this chapter.

4 Using a diagram similar to Figure 11.2, show what the welfare effects would be following a switch from normal competition to perfect collusion. Be sure to address the change in consumer surplus and pure profits.

Further reading: the aficionado's corner

For a very accessible introduction to EU competition policy, see:
Neven, D., P. Seabright and M. Nutall (1996) *Fishing for Minnows*, CEPR, London.

Every interested reader should at least skim through the Commission audiovisual material on Competition Policy (http://ec.europa.eu/competition/consumers/index_en.html). It is well executed and highly accessible.

Useful website

The DG Competition website has several highly accessible accounts of EU competition policy and information on recent cases; see http://ec.europa.eu/dgs/competition/index_en.htm.

References

Bannerman, E. (2002) *The Future of EU Competition Policy*, Centre for European Reform.
Commission (2010) 'EU competition law: rules applicable to merger control, situation as at 1 April 2010', DG Competition, ec.europa.eu/competition/mergers/legislation/legislation.html.
Mas-Colell, A., M. Whinston and J.R. Green (1995) *Microeconomic Theory*, Oxford University Press, New York.

EU trade policy

Chapter Contents

Introduction

The European Union is the world's biggest trader. Counting EU exports both within the EU and to non-EU nations, the Union accounts for approximately a third of world trade – a great deal more than China, Japan and the USA combined. Its dominance of trade in services is even greater. Five of the EU27 members are individually in the top 10 trading nations in the world (Germany, Netherlands, France, Italy and Britain). The EU is also a leader in the world trade system, both as a key player in the World Trade Organization (WTO) and as a massive signer of bilateral trade agreements and extender of unilateral trade concessions to the world's poorest nations.

While the EU has been one of the staunchest supporters of the WTO's trade rules, many observers traditionally viewed EU trade policy – especially that on agricultural goods – as a major roadblock to greater liberalization worldwide. This situation is, however, changing. The EU's reform of its massive Common Agriculture Policy (CAP; see Chapter 9 for details) has greatly reduced the extent to which EU farm policy distorts world markets. For example, as this edition was going to press, the EU was committed to eliminating regular export subsidies for all farm goods by 2017.

This chapter covers EU trade policy by presenting the basic facts on EU trade, describing the EU's institutional arrangements as they concern trade policy, and finally summarizing the EU's policies towards its various trade partners. It is important to note that EU trade policy – like so much about the Union – is mind-numbingly complex. There is a whole army of specialists who do nothing but follow EU trade issues, and most of these have to specialize in one particular area in order to master all the detail. Plainly, then, this chapter cannot come even close to surveying all EU trade policy. Its goal is rather to present the broad outlines and key issues. Readers who are interested in greater detail on a particular trade partner, sector or policy should start with the European Commission's website: http://europa.eu.int/comm/trade/.

12.1 Pattern of trade and tariffs: facts

The EU trades mainly with Europe, as Figure 12.1 shows. The right bar shows the share of EU exports that goes to the EU's various partners. The figures include EU sales to non-EU nations as well as exports from one EU nation to another. This gives perspective on the relative importance of intra-EU trade and external trade. The main points are:

- Two-thirds of EU27 exports are to other EU27 nations. More than 90 per cent of such exports actually occur among the EU15, since the 10 new Member States are fairly small economically (see Chapter 2 for details).

- If we add in other European nations – EFTA (Switzerland, Norway, Iceland and Liechtenstein) and Turkey – the figure rises to three-quarters. In short, three out of four export euros earned by the EU27 are from sales within Europe, broadly defined.

- After Europe, Asia is the EU27's main trading partner, with North America in third place.

- Africa, Latin America and the Middle East are not very important as EU export destinations; their shares are each less than 4 per cent.

The pattern on the import side is very similar (left bar in Figure 12.1). The biggest difference lies with Asia since the EU imports more from Asia than it exports to it. The opposite is true of North America. The EU's trade with the rest of the world is approximately in balance.

It can be useful to take an even closer look by separating out individual nations, as in Table 12.1. Just 10 nations account for about two-thirds of EU27 *external* trade, but the list is slightly different on the import and export sides. The USA is the number one buyer of EU exports by a very large margin, and China is the biggest exporter to the EU. After China and the USA, the next most important market for EU exports is Switzerland, but the Swiss buy only 40 per cent as much as Americans (still, this is a big number given that there are 8 million Swiss and 300 million Americans). Russia, Turkey and Japan round out the top five partners – leaving aside imports from Norway (most oil and gas). This role of the so-called emerging economies in EU trade is quite clear from these numbers. Taking the

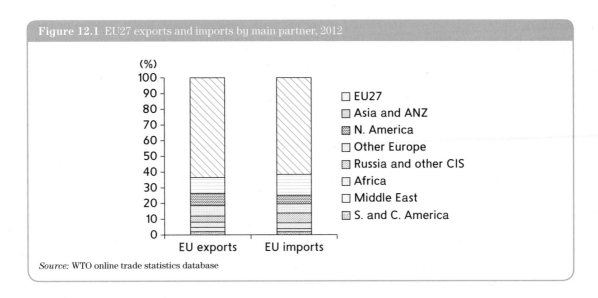

Figure 12.1 EU27 exports and imports by main partner, 2012

- □ EU27
- ▨ Asia and ANZ
- ▨ N. America
- □ Other Europe
- ▨ Russia and other CIS
- □ Africa
- □ Middle East
- ▨ S. and C. America

Source: WTO online trade statistics database

Table 12.1   The EU's top 10 import and export partners, 2010 (€ billions)

Partner	Exports	Share (%)	Partner	Imports	Share (%)
USA	242	18	China	157	10
China	113	8	USA	105	7
Switzerland	105	8	Russia	72	5
Russia	87	6	Switzerland	68	5
Turkey	61	5	Norway	59	4
Japan	44	3	Japan	51	3
Norway	42	3	Turkey	26	2
India	35	3	Korea	26	2
Brazil	31	2	India	22	1
Korea	28	2	Brazil	19	1
UAE	28	2	Libya	16	1
Hong Kong	27	2	Taiwan	16	1

Source: http://epp.eurostat.ec.europa.eu/portal/page/portal/international_trade/introduction

BRICs (Brazil, Russia, India and China) together, they account for 18 per cent of imports and 27 per cent of exports.

12.1.1 Differences among Member States

One of the things that makes EU trade policy a contentious issue is the fact that the various Member States have quite different trade patterns. Some members are landlocked and surrounded by other EU members, while others are geographically and/or culturally close to Africa, North America or Latin America. It is not surprising, therefore, that the importance of various trade partners varies quite a lot across the EU27.

Figure 12.2 illustrates this divergence. The reliance of Member States on imports from the various regions is shown by the 100 per cent bars. The leftmost segment shows the share of imports from non-EU Europe. This ranges from about 5 per cent for Luxembourg to almost 80 per cent for Lithuania. Geography matters a great deal when it comes to trade partners, so it is not surprising that non-EU Europe countries – which include Ukraine and Russia – play a big role in the imports for the central European members such as Poland and the Baltic States. The importance of North America varies almost as much. North America's share in Irish external imports is about 40 per cent, while for the Baltic States it is 10 per cent or less.

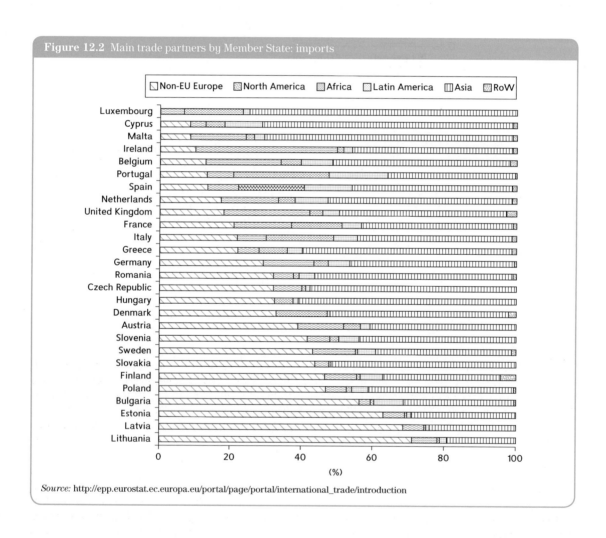

Figure 12.2 Main trade partners by Member State: imports

Source: http://epp.eurostat.ec.europa.eu/portal/page/portal/international_trade/introduction

The figure also shows some fairly natural linkages. The Iberians import a large share of their external trade from Latin America and Africa. Africa's share is also over 15 per cent for Italy and France. Asia's role is more constant, although it tends to be larger for members with easy access to the sea, such as Britain, Denmark and Poland.

12.1.2 Composition of the EU's external trade

What sorts of goods does the EU27 export to and import from the rest of the world? As Figure 12.3 shows, the answer is 'mainly manufactured goods'. The main points from the diagram are:

- Manufactured goods account for almost 90 per cent of EU exports, with about half of all exports being machinery and transport equipment.
- On the import side, about two out of every three euros spent on imports go to buy manufactured goods.
- Being energy poor, the EU27 is a big importer of fuel; about one in every five euros spent on imports goes to pay for fuel.
- Other types of goods play a relatively minor part in the EU's trade.

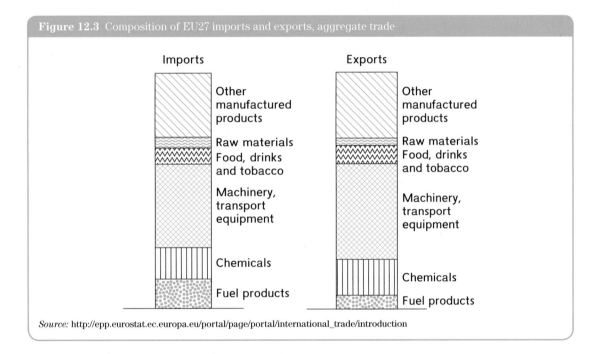

Figure 12.3 Composition of EU27 imports and exports, aggregate trade

Source: http://epp.eurostat.ec.europa.eu/portal/page/portal/international_trade/introduction

About 7 per cent of EU27 exports to the rest of the world consist of food (more precisely, food, drink and tobacco). The EU's imports of such goods account also for 7 per cent of all its imports. As the chapter on the CAP (Chapter 9) showed, Europe's trade in agricultural goods is massively distorted by subsidies to EU farmers, subsidies to EU exports and high barriers against imports. If the CAP were fully liberalized in the direction the Commission is pushing for (see Chapter 9 for details), all trade distortions would be removed and the EU would surely become a net importer of food.

What with whom?

The situation illustrated in Figure 12.3 aggregates all the EU's trade with all partners. This is useful since it gives us an idea of just how dominant manufactured goods are when it comes to EU trade policy. It also provides an important perspective when we turn to EU trade policy, since EU import barriers for manufactured goods are very different from its import barriers on agricultural goods. Moreover, it illustrates quite clearly that agricultural goods play only a minor role in the EU's trade despite the dominance of agriculture in political conflicts both within the EU and with the rest of the world.

The aggregate trade pattern, however, hides a set of facts that are important to understanding the impact of the EU's external trade policy. Simply put, the commodity composition of the EU's *exports* is approximately the same for all of the EU's trade partners, but this is not true for its imports. Figure 12.4 shows the facts.

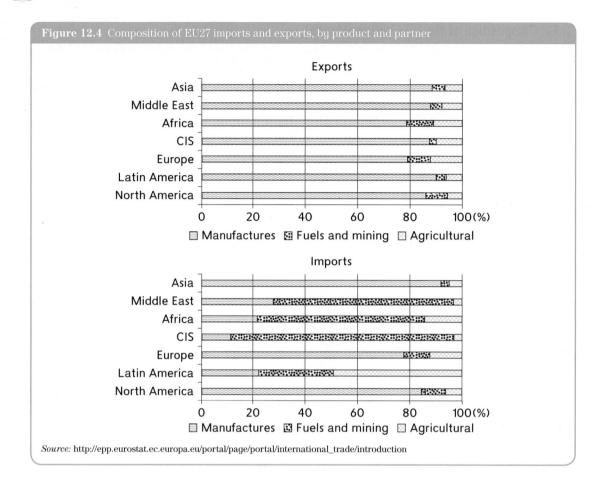

Figure 12.4 Composition of EU27 imports and exports, by product and partner

Source: http://epp.eurostat.ec.europa.eu/portal/page/portal/international_trade/introduction

The diagram gathers EU trade partners into seven groups: Asia, the Middle East, Africa, Commonwealth of Independent States (CIS), Europe, Latin America and North America. The top panel shows the commodity composition of EU exports to these regions, while the bottom panel does the same for EU imports.

- Scanning across the top panel it is easy to see that bars are quite similar. That is, the shares of manufactures in EU exports to all regions are fairly similar, about 80 to 90 per cent.
- The bottom panel, however, shows that the EU's import composition varies a lot by partner. As might be expected, Europe tends to import a lot of primary goods – food and raw materials including fuel – from continents that are relatively abundant in natural resources – Africa, CIS, the Middle East and Latin America. With North America and Asia, the imports consist mostly of manufactures.
- Food is never a dominant import for any of the partners, but it amounts to almost half of the EU's imports from Latin America (and this figure can be much higher for particular nations, especially small, poor nations).

12.1.3 The EU's Common External Tariff (CET)

The EU has been an active participant in the 60-year-long sequence of global tariff-cutting talks known as GATT Rounds or, since 1995, WTO Rounds. As a result, the EU's tariffs are quite low for most goods that were bargained over in these Rounds. Since agricultural tariffs were not included in these Rounds until the end of the twentieth century, EU tariffs on such goods remain much higher.

As the EU defines individual tariff rates for about 10,000 products, we must generalize to get a handle on the numbers. The average CET rate is about 6 per cent, but this hides a wide variation. About a quarter of the rates on all products are set at zero (mostly industrial goods including electronics) and the average for industrial goods is about 4 per cent. The average on agricultural imports is four times this, namely, 16 per cent. The facts for various product categories are shown in Table 12.2.

Table 12.2   EU's Common External Tariff (CET), 2010

	Average (%)	Max (%)	Share of extra-EU imports duty free
Animal products	23	162	10
Dairy products	49	163	0
Fruit, vegetables, plants	11	161	12
Coffee, tea	7	55	78
Cereals and preparations	18	111	2
Oilseeds, fats and oils	6	94	70
Sugars and confectionery	28	118	0
Beverages and tobacco	19	166	15
Cotton	0	0	100
Other agricultural products	5	117	68
Fish and fish products	12	26	5
Minerals and metals	2	12	56
Petroleum	3	5	84
Chemicals	5	13	43
Wood, paper, etc.	1	10	85
Textiles	7	12	2
Clothing	12	12	0
Leather, footwear, etc.	4	17	17
Non-electrical machinery	2	10	53
Electrical machinery	3	14	55
Transport equipment	4	22	17
Other manufactures	3	14	55

Source: WTO online database, 'World Tariff Profiles', www.wto.org

The table's three columns list the average tariff in the relevant product category, the maximum tariff in the category and the share of such imports that come in duty-free. The first column thus gives an idea of the overall protectionist tendency in the category. For example, the average tariff on animal products (meat, etc.) is 23 per cent, which is fairly high, but only half as high as the protection on dairy products (49 per cent).

The maximum tariff in both categories is astronomical – over 160 per cent, as the second column shows. The third column shows the share of the EU's external imports that come in duty-free because of reciprocal or unilateral preference agreements. For example, 10 per cent of EU imports of animal products come in at zero tariffs, but no dairy does. Below we discuss in more detail the various programmes that allow duty-free imports.

Now, looking down the rows we see that imports of primary goods are – with the exception of cotton – taxed at a much higher rate than manufactured goods. The maximum tariffs are also much lower. The share of imports that come in duty-free varies a lot by product. The maximum rates on some manufactured goods are still high, but the average rate on manufactures is always below 5 per cent, except for textiles and clothing where the averages are 7 and 12 per cent, respectively.

12.2 EU institutions for trade policy

Formation of a customs union – which means the elimination of tariffs on intra-EU trade and adoption of a common external tariff – was the EU's first big step towards economic integration. A customs union requires political coordination since trade policy towards third nations is an ever-evolving issue. To facilitate this coordination, the Treaty of Rome granted supranational powers to the EU's institutions as far as external trade policy is concerned – what is known in EU jargon as 'exclusive competence' (see Chapter 3 for details). This delegation of sovereignty has never changed and indeed over the decades the various Treaties have granted the EU more power in the area of trade. The 2009 Lisbon Treaty in particular greatly increased the extent to which EU members have delegated power on trade issues to the EU (see Box 12.1). This section reviews the institutions and practices governing this coordination.

Box 12.1   Lisbon Treaty changes on trade in a nutshell

As far as trade policy goes, the Lisbon Treaty involves three big changes:

1 Big increase in European Parliament power on trade policy. Before Lisbon, the Parliament's power on EU trade policy was minor. Now its power is very nearly equal to that of the Council (i.e. the old Council of Ministers). Specifically:

- All EU trade laws (e.g. imposition of anti-dumping tariffs, granting of trade preferences, etc.) must be adopted by the 'ordinary legislative procedure' (the old codecision procedure). Under this procedure, the Parliament and Council have equal power.

- All trade agreements must now be approved by Parliament, but Parliament does not have the formal right to suggest amendments. However, as the discussion of the EU–Korea free trade agreement showed, Parliament can use its right of refusal to influence the content of agreements.

2 Increased powers for the EU as opposed to EU members.

- Foreign direct investment (FDI) becomes clearly under EU authority, so only the EU can conclude international agreements and adopt laws on FDI.

- The Lisbon Treaty clearly grants power to the EU on issues such as trade in services and commercial aspects of intellectual property, along with trade in cultural, audiovisual, educational and social and health services (in certain sensitive cases, like culture, the EU power is subject to specific voting rules that grant EU members the power of veto).

3 Qualified majority voting for most trade issues.

Qualified majority voting (see Chapter 3 for details) is now the general rule in the Council for actions related to trade policy areas (including the new areas such as investment and services). However, members still retain a veto (i.e. unanimity is required in the Council) in certain cases;

for example, when commitments in trade agreements might undermine the EU's cultural and linguistic diversity, or seriously disturb members' national organization of social, educational or health services. Unanimity is also required if the EU law or trade agreement covers issues that would be subject to unanimity for internal laws (e.g. tax harmonization).

Source: This box draws on European Commission (2011)

12.2.1 EU competences on trade

Trade policy is an EU 'exclusive competence' (see Chapter 3 for details). That is, the EU has the exclusive power to set trade policy with third nations – the so-called Common Commercial Policy. Individual Member States cannot legislate on trade matters or conclude international trade agreements. The logic of a customs union having one trade policy is extremely strong. After all, if each member did bilateral deals on its own, the single market might be undermined by third nations exploiting differences across EU members' external trade policies.

In the twentieth century, the EU's power on trade policy was basically limited to tariffs. This was not an important limitation; back then, tariffs were by far the most important aspect of trade policy. As EU tariffs came down during the course of multilateral trade negotiations, and the nature of international commerce grew more complex, the range of important trade barriers broadened.

As the logic of a unified external trade policy was as strong as ever, this trend created a need to expand the competence of the EU beyond tariffs. This was done in a series of small and practical steps in the Maastricht and Nice Treaties. It took a big step forward with the December 2009 Lisbon Treaty, which extended the Common Commercial Policy to explicitly include trade in services, foreign direct investment and some aspects of intellectual property rights (copyrights, patents, etc.).

Protection and enforcement of intellectual property

A key element in Europe's competitiveness lies in its intellectual property (the general name for things like patents, trademarks, designs, copyrights and geographical indications, like Parma ham or Champagne). To protect these, the EU and its members have signed many agreements establishing international disciplines that protect this intellectual property. These disciplines are meant to deter piracy, counterfeiting and the like.

A key role of EU trade policy is to see that such standards are respected by third countries. The Commission takes the lead here and pursues the objective in the WTO and bilaterally with third nations. Most recently, the EU participated actively in the negotiation of the Anti-Counterfeiting Trade Agreement (ACTA), which was signed in the autumn of 2011.

Investment

In many industries, investment has become an integral part of trade. For example, BMW and Airbus set up production facilities in China as part of their effort to sell goods to Chinese customers. Likewise, the internationalization of supply chains often involves EU companies investing in factories in third nations. Indeed, the EU is the largest generator of foreign direct investment (FDI) in the global economy (FDI is where a company from one nation directly controls an investment in another, say a factory, rather than merely owning some shares in the foreign company).

Such investment is facilitated by clear rules that establish legal rights for investors abroad and for foreign investors in the EU. Establishing, improving and enforcing such rules is the main thrust of EU investment policy. Here, the Commission works with the WTO and third nations in the context of bilateral trade agreements (e.g. the EU–Korea FTA that came into effect in 2011). Currently, the focus is on the negotiation of investment rules in the context of preferential trade agreements that the EU negotiates with third countries. The EU–Korea Free Trade Agreement is the most recent example of an agreement that reflects EU investment policy negotiations.

Prior to the Lisbon Treaty, investment was not part of the EU's responsibility, so Member States signed a large number of bilateral arrangements (called Bilateral Investment Treaties, BITs). It is not yet clear how the EU will deal with this tangle of agreements. For example, Turkey has a BIT with 11 separate EU members. These will presumably be eventually merged into one, but such pre-existing BITs are likely to remain in force for some time.

12.2.2 Allocation of responsibilities

Trade policy in today's globalized world touches on a vast array of issues. Correspondingly, EU trade policy is extremely complex since it has to deal with issues ranging from quotas on men's underwear from China to internet banking to sugar imports. To keep EU policy coherent in the face of this complexity, the Treaties assign to the European Commission the task of negotiating trade matters with third nations on behalf of the Member States (Article 207 of the Treaty on the Functioning of the European Union). In practice, this means that the EU Trade Commissioner (currently Karl de Gucht) is responsible for conducting trade negotiations. These negotiations are conducted in accordance with specific mandates defined by the Council and the Parliament (called 'Directives for Negotiation'). The European Commission also takes the lead in trade policy in the sense that it has the right of initiative on, for example, trade agreements, and it is in charge of enforcement and surveillance of compliance with existing agreements and WTO rules.

The basic frameworks guiding the Commission are jointly decided by the European Parliament and the Council (i.e. what was called the Council of Ministers before the Lisbon Treaty). These decisions are taken on the basis of the 'ordinary legislative procedure' (see Chapter 2), which involves majority voting in the Council and the Parliament. The Council must adopt any agreements negotiated by the Commission after the Parliament has given its consent (i.e. the Parliament can say 'yes' or 'no' but cannot amend the agreements). For agreements that deal with areas under the exclusive competences of the EU, members' national parliaments no longer have to ratify the decision of the Council and Parliament.

The big change in the Lisbon Treaty on trade policy concerns the European Parliament. Specifically, it is now co-legislator with the Council on all basic EU trade legislation, such as anti-dumping tariffs and trade preferences for developing nations. Moreover, the Commission is required to inform the Parliament regularly about ongoing negotiations.

Trade policy and foreign policy

Trade policy has long been one of the EU's most effective foreign policy tools. After Lisbon, the lines between foreign policy and trade policy became even more blurred. The Lisbon Treaty institutes a hierarchy of principles that should be applied to trade policy (as well as other aspects of foreign policy). For example, Article 3 of the Treaty on European Union states:

> *In its relations with the wider world, the Union shall uphold and promote its values and interests and contribute to the protection of its citizens. It shall contribute to peace, security, the sustainable development of the Earth, solidarity and mutual respect among peoples, free and fair trade, eradication of poverty and the protection of human rights, in particular the rights of the child, as well as to the strict observance and development of international law, including respect for the principles of the United Nations Charters.*

It is not yet clear how much practical importance this will have, but it certainly means that the EU's general pro-business view of trade agreements will be tempered with more input from players – such as Members of the European Parliament – who are less concerned with exporting and more concerned with human rights, the environment and so on.

12.2.3 Anti-dumping and anti-subsidy measures

Under WTO rules, tariff liberalization is a one-way street. Once a nation has lowered a tariff in WTO talks (such talks are often called 'Rounds', e.g. the ongoing one is called the Doha Round), it is not allowed to put the tariff back up. This principle of 'binding' tariffs applies to the EU's external tariffs. The principle, however, is subject to some loopholes, the most important of which are anti-dumping and anti-subsidy tariffs.

Dumping is defined as the selling of exports below some normal price. According to WTO rules, a nation, or more broadly speaking, a customs area (i.e. the EU), can impose tariffs on imports if dumping 'causes or threatens material injury to an established industry'. The EU, together with the USA, is one of the world's leading users of such measures, especially in iron and steel, consumer electronics and chemicals.

The European Commission is in charge of investigating dumping complaints. If the Commission finds that: (1) dumping has occurred (this involves intricate and somewhat arbitrary calculations) and (2) material injury to EU producers has happened or might happen, it can impose a provisional duty (that lasts between 6 and 9 months). The Council of Ministers must confirm the Commission's decision before the tariffs become definitive (these stay in place for 5 years). Sometimes the Commission avoids imposing tariffs by negotiating 'price undertakings' with the exporting nation; these are promises by the exporters to charge a high price for their goods in exchange for suspension or termination of the Commission's anti-dumping investigation. In terms of EU welfare, price undertakings are worse than tariffs since the EU collects no tariff revenue. Nevertheless, price undertakings are often more expedient politically since they are a way of 'bribing' the exporting nation into not complaining too loudly about the EU's new protection. (See Chapter 4 for the economic analysis.)

Since dumping duties, like all tariffs, help producers but harm consumers and firms that buy the goods (see Chapter 4), the Commission often faces a tricky balancing act among Member States. Frequently, the EU producers are concentrated in one or a few Member States while there are consumers in every Member State. Typically, the former want the Commission to impose dumping duties while the latter oppose them. For this reason, the Commission implements anti-dumping measures only when it believes that they are in the broader interest of the EU. For historical and institutional reasons, the EU rarely imposes anti-subsidy duties, preferring to deal with such behaviour as 'below normal' pricing.

Many observers believe that both the EU and the USA employ a cynical manipulation of dumping rules – especially the calculation that determines whether imports have been dumped – in order to provide WTO-consistent protection for sectors whose producers are usually powerful politically. The iron and steel industry and the chemical industry are leading examples.

12.3 EU trade policy: broad goals and means

For most of its life, EU external trade policy meant negotiating:

- Reciprocal tariff cuts in FTAs with other Europeans (e.g. the EU–EFTA bilaterals for 1973).
- Reciprocal tariff cuts with non-European rich nations in the GATT/WTO (e.g. the 1967 Kennedy Round or 1994 Uruguay Round).
- Unilateral tariff preferences for developing nations.

This started to change as a result of a 2006 landmark communication from the Commission known as Global Europe. It set out a more global strategy for EU external trade policy as a complement to the renewed 'Lisbon Strategy'. (The Lisbon Strategy was a set of loosely-knit initiatives that EU members were supposed to undertake domestically to improve their growth prospects.) Specifically, Global Europe identified ASEAN, Korea, India and Mercosur as priority partners for new FTAs.

The logic behind these choices is still rock solid. Up until around the end of the twentieth century, about 60 per cent of world growth came from rich-nation markets – the USA, EU, Japan, Canada, etc. That share declined rapidly in the new century even before the global economic crisis. According to IMF forecasts, after recovery from the crisis, China and other developing nations will account for more than three-quarters of global growth.

There was also a shift away from 'shallow' FTAs, i.e. agreements that focused on many tariffs, towards deeper agreements that covered issues such as investment, public procurement, competition, IPR enforcement and regulatory convergence issues (i.e. what would be known as approximation of laws inside the EU). Such matters had to be dealt with in FTAs since the ongoing WTO Round – the Doha Round launched in 2001 – was based on an agenda that included few of these subjects.

Europe 2020 and EU trade policy

In March 2010, the European Commission launched a new ten-year strategy (similar to the Lisbon Strategy) aimed at promoting 'smart, sustainable, inclusive growth' (see http://ec.europa.eu/europe2020/index_en.htm for details). This, of course, included a trade and investment policy component laid out in a 2010 Commission communication titled 'Trade, Growth and World Affairs'. The communication notes that world trade has undergone profound changes, especially with respect to the internationalization of supply chains. For example, two-thirds of EU imports involve intermediate inputs which boost the EU's productive capacity. Keeping ahead of the competition in manufacturing and export services requires EU firms to source parts and services from the most competitive locations.

Owing to these changes, the EU trade policy is to continue the tendency, started by Global Europe, of focusing on deeper integration; cutting tariffs is still important, but the big challenge is more complex. The goal is to tackle market access for services and investment by opening up public procurement, enforcing protection of IPR, removing restrictions on the supply of raw materials and energy, and overcoming regulatory barriers. Readers can follow a public debate on this new strategy on the policy portal www. voxeu.org (just click on the Debate tab and then on 'The Future of EU Trade Policy').

Given this renewed emphasis on 'beyond the borders' barriers to trade – and the continued inability of WTO members to conclude the Doha Round – the EU's emphasis shifts even more towards bilateral FTAs. The Doha Round remains the EU's top trade priority; however, getting more than 150 nations to agree on that complex deal is beyond the EU's power.

12.4 EU trade policy: existing arrangements

The EU's external trade policy is extremely complex. It has or is considering or is negotiating trade agreements with most nations in the world, as Figure 12.5 shows.

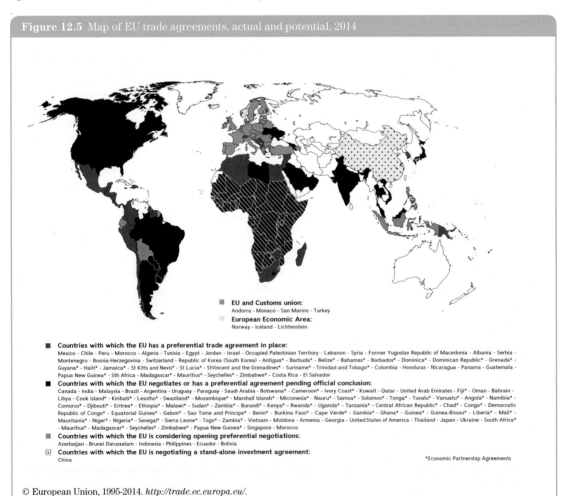

Figure 12.5 Map of EU trade agreements, actual and potential, 2014

■ **EU and Customs union:**
Andorra - Monaco - San Marino - Turkey

European Economic Area:
Norway - Iceland - Lichtenstein

■ **Countries with which the EU has a preferential trade agreement in place:**
Mexico - Chile - Peru - Morocco - Algeria - Tunisia - Egypt - Jordan - Israel - Occupied Palestinian Territory - Lebanon - Syria - Former Yugoslav Republic of Macedonia - Albania - Serbia - Montenegro - Bosnia-Herzegovina - Switzerland - Republic of Korea (South Korea) - Antigua* - Barbuda* - Belize* - Bahamas* - Barbados* - Dominica* - Dominican Republic* - Grenada* - Guyana* - Haiti* - Jamaica* - St Kitts and Nevis* - St Lucia* - StVincent and the Grenadines* - Suriname* - Trinidad and Tobago* - Colombia - Honduras - Nicaragua - Panama - Guatemala - Papua New Guinea* - Sth Africa - Madagascar* - Mauritius* - Seychelles* - Zimbabwe* - Costa Rica - El Salvador

■ **Countries with which the EU negotiates or has a preferential agreement pending official conclusion:**
Canada - India - Malaysia - Brazil - Argentina - Uruguay - Paraguay - Saudi Arabia - Botswana* - Cameroon* - Ivory Coast* - Kuwait - Qatar - United Arab Emirates - Fiji* - Oman - Bahrain - Libya - Cook Island* - Kiribati* - Lesotho* - Swaziland* - Mozambique* - Marshall Islands* - Micronesia* - Nauru* - Samoa* - Solomon* - Tonga* - Tuvalu* - Vanuatu* - Angola* - Namibia* - Comoros* - Djibouti* - Eritrea* - Ethiopia* - Malawi* - Sudan* - Zambia* - Burundi* - Kenya* - Rwanda* - Uganda* - Tanzania* - Central African Republic* - Chad* - Congo* - Democratic Republic of Congo* - Equatorial Guinea* - Gabon* - Sao Tome and Principe* - Benin* - Burkina Faso* - Cape Verde* - Gambia* - Ghana* - Guinea* - Guinea-Bissau* - Liberia* - Mali* - Mauritania* - Niger* - Nigeria* - Senegal* - Sierra Leone* - Togo* - Zambia* - Vietnam - Moldova - Armenia - Georgia - United States of America - Thailand - Japan - Ukraine - South Africa* - Mauritius* - Madagascar* - Seychelles* - Zimbabwe* - Papua New Guinea* - Singapore - Morocco

■ **Countries with which the EU is considering opening preferential negotiations:**
Azerbaijan - Brunei Darussalam - Indonesia - Philippines - Ecuador - Bolivia

▣ **Countries with which the EU is negotiating a stand-alone investment agreement:**
China

*Economic Partnership Agreements

© European Union, 1995-2014. *http://trade.ec.europa.eu/*.

The key agreements underway when this edition went to press are the Trans-Atlantic Trade and Investment Partnership (TTIP), which was analysed in Chapter 5, the EU–Japan trade agreement and the EU's discussions with China on investment protection.

12.5 Summary

This chapter provided a broad introduction to the immensely complex topic of EU trade policy. It started by presenting facts on the EU's trade pattern. The main points were:

- The EU trades mainly with Europe, with itself in particular.
- The EU is primarily an exporter of manufactured goods.
- Most EU imports are manufactured goods, although imports of primary goods are important for Africa, the Middle East and Latin America.

The next topic was EU decision making on trade. In a nutshell, the European Commission is in charge of negotiating the EU's external trade policy, but its efforts are directed by mandates from the Council of Ministers and all deals are subject to Council approval. Before the Lisbon Treaty, the Parliament had a negligible role, but now it is a co-legislator with the Council on issues like anti-dumping duties, and it must give its consent on new trade agreements.

The last section in the chapter addressed the content of the EU's trade policy. The main points were:

- Trade arrangements in Europe can be characterized as hub-and-spoke bilateralism. The hub is formed by two concentric circles (the EU, which has the deepest level of integration, and EFTA, which participates in the Single Market apart from agriculture). These circles form a 'hub' around which a network of bilateral agreements is arranged with almost every nation in Europe (broadly defined) and the Mediterranean. These bilateral deals fall into three groups: the Euro–Med agreements, the Stabilisation and Association Agreements with Western Balkan nations, and the Partnership and Cooperation Agreements with former Soviet republics in the Commonwealth of Independent States.
- The EU has preferential trade agreements with its former colonies – the so-called ACP nations – that are currently asymmetric (the EU charges zero tariffs but the ACP nations do not), but they are aiming at establishing full-blown two-way FTAs in the coming years.
- The EU grants unilateral preferences of various types to almost all developing nations.

Self-assessment questions

1. What is the role of the Member States and the Commission in relation to external trade policy? Be sure to distinguish between trade in goods and more 'modern' trade issues such as trade in services, trade in intellectual property rights and foreign direct investment.
2. What does the EU buy from and sell to the five continents: Europe, Africa, North America, South America and Asia?
3. What is the most protected good in the EU and which is the least protected good?
4. Why did the EU extend unilateral tariff preferences to former French and Belgian colonies, and why did it extend these to former British colonies in the mid-1970s?
5. Explain the term 'hub-and-spoke bilateralism' as applied to the EU's neighbours in Europe and around the Mediterranean.

Further reading: the aficionado's corner

A very lengthy and complete treatment of the EU's trade policy can be downloaded from the WTO's website, www.wto.org (follow links to the Trade Policy Reviews, or use Google with the words EU, Trade Policy Review and WTO). This is an independent review of EU trade policy, which includes detailed presentation of its preferential, multilateral and sector policies. It also provides references to many academic studies on the impact of EU policies.

A very sceptical presentation of EU trade policy that includes explicit economic evaluation is:

Messerlin, P. (2001) *Measuring the Costs of Protection in Europe: European Commercial Policy in the 2000s*, Institute for International Economics, Washington, DC.

For general information on the WTO, see:

Hoekman, B. and M. Kostecki (2001) *The Political Economy of the World Trading System: The WTO and Beyond*, Oxford University Press, Oxford.

Also check out the **WTO**'s website, www.wto.org.

For more on the EU trade policy with poor nations, see:

Hinkle, L. and M. Schiff (2004) 'Economic Partnership Agreements between Sub-Saharan Africa and the EU: a development perspective', *World Economy*, 27(9): 1321–34.

Panagariya, A. (2002) 'EU preferential trade policies and developing countries', *World Economy*, 10(25): 1415–32.

For more on GSP in general, see:

GAO (1994) *Assessment of the Generalized System of Preferences Program*, US General Accounting Office, Washington, DC. Download from www.gao.gov.

Useful websites

The best general site is the European Commission DG-Trade site, http://ec.europa.eu/trade/.

For information on preferential trade agreements worldwide, see www.bilaterals.org.

References

Baldwin, R. (1994) *Towards an Integrated Europe*, CEPR, London.

European Commission (2011) 'What did the Lisbon Treaty change?' Factsheet, 14 June 2011, Brussels. Download from http://trade.ec.europa.eu/doclib/html/147977.htm.

GAO (1994) *Assessment of the Generalized System of Preferences Program*, US General Accounting Office, Washington, DC. Download from www.gao.gov.

Part **IV**

The Macroeconomics of Monetary Integration

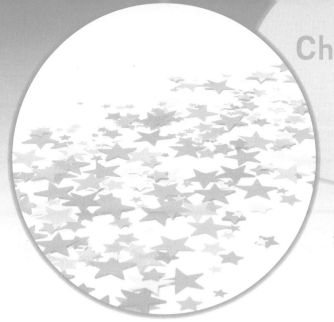

13

*The point is that you can't have it all: A
country must pick two out of three.*

Paul Krugman (1999)

Essential
macroeconomic tools

Chapter Contents

Introduction

This chapter provides the tools required to understand the European monetary integration process. It starts with the textbook case of a closed economy and then introduces the all-important changes resulting from openness to trade and financial flows. It introduces two principles: the interest rate parity condition and purchasing power parity. These principles will serve over and again to help the reader to understand the issues at stake and the policy choices that have shaped the monetary integration process, for better or worse. The required theory is presented as lightly as possible and each step is illustrated by real-life examples.

13.1 The closed economy: a refresher

The macroeconomy is described in the simplest possible way: it consists of a market for goods and services and a financial market. Just one item is traded in each market: *the* good (or service) with a price P and *the* bond with an interest rate i. The goal is to examine how each market functions independently and how both markets interact. We thus study how each market achieves equilibrium on its own – this is called partial equilibrium – and then we ask how both markets simultaneously reach equilibrium – this is called general equilibrium. We start with the case of a closed economy, which does not trade in goods and services with the rest of the world and which is also financially isolated.

13.1.1 Goods markets and the role of fiscal policy

All the country's firms produce a total quantity Y of *the* good. This is the country's gross domestic product (GDP). Demand for this good originates from three categories of customer: households, which consume a quantity C; firms, which invest in a quantity I of the good for production purposes – think of the good being used as machinery; and the government, which purchases a quantity of G for its own needs. Partial equilibrium occurs when demand $C + I + G$ is equal to supply Y:

$$Y = C + I + G$$

Things become interesting when we note two things. First, consumers spend more when they earn more, and they earn more when the firms that employ them produce more. This means that consumption C rises with income Y. Thus, given firms' investment I and public spending G, there is one level of GDP such that consumption C is just right to achieve equilibrium in the goods market. This level is called, unsurprisingly, equilibrium GDP.[1] Second, in order to invest, firms usually borrow on the financial market, at the going interest rate i. When the interest rate rises, the cost of borrowing increases and firms invest less because they borrow less. An interest rate increase will also reduce consumption because some goods – mostly durable goods like cars, home equipment and houses – are often financed, partly at least, through borrowing. The result is that any change in the interest rate will affect demand. This links the two markets.

A simple graphical representation will prove most useful. Start with a level i_1 of the interest rate, which leads firms to invest I_1. Given public spending G, the equilibrium GDP is Y_1. This is shown as point A_1 in Figure 13.1, where GDP is displayed on the horizontal axis and the interest rate on the vertical axis. Now imagine that the interest rate rises to i_2. This discourages investment spending by firms, bringing it down to I_2. Total demand ($C + I + G$) has declined and so does equilibrium GDP, now down to Y_2. The new equilibrium is represented by point A_2. We can repeat this thought experiment over and over again, looking at the whole range of interest rates. Doing so will draw up the curve IS in Figure 13.1. It is represented as a line because its exact shape does not matter for our purposes. The really important point is that it is downward sloping: higher interest rates lead to lower GDP levels, keeping constant consumer preferences – how C varies with Y – and public spending G. The IS curve represents all the possible cases when the goods market is in equilibrium.

Outside IS, the goods market is in disequilibrium. For example, consider point A_3, just above point A_1. Here, the interest rate is i_3 (not shown), higher than i_1. As we move from A_1 to A_3, the interest rate rises and firms spend less on investment, and demand declines. As we move vertically above $A1$, however, we keep output Y_1 unchanged: less demand, same supply – we are thus in a situation where firms do not

---

[1] Formally, equilibrium GDP Y is the solution of equation $Y = C(Y) + I + G$, where $C(Y)$ describes how consumption responds to GDP.

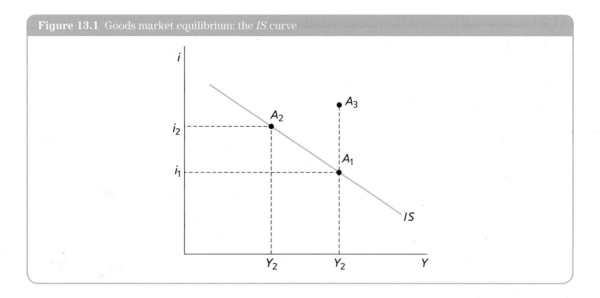

Figure 13.1 Goods market equilibrium: the *IS* curve

sell everything that they produce. Above *IS*, we have a disequilibrium characterized by excess supply or insufficient demand. This situation cannot last very long. If they can't sell, firms will cut production and we will move to the left of *A*3 until we hit the *IS* curve at a lower level of GDP. Similarly, below *IS*, we have a situation of excess demand and firms will respond by increasing production. As a first approximation, we will consider that the economy is always on its *IS* curve.

We can now see how fiscal policy operates. Fiscal policy consists of using the government budget to affect the level of activity. Governments can change their spending, *G*, or they can change how much they collect in tax revenues by varying tax rates (on personal incomes, on corporations, on VAT, etc.). An expansionary policy, for instance, consists of increasing public spending or reducing tax revenues. In the first case, more spending means higher demand *G*, given *C* and *I*. In the latter case, reducing taxes provides higher incomes to consumers or firms, and they will respond by spending more. In both cases, total demand $C + I + G$ rises, for any given interest rate. This means that equilibrium GDP is now larger for any given interest rate. This is represented graphically in Figure 13.2 as a rightward shift of the *IS* schedule to *IS'*.[2] Naturally, a contractionary fiscal policy would do the opposite: move the *IS* schedule to the left.

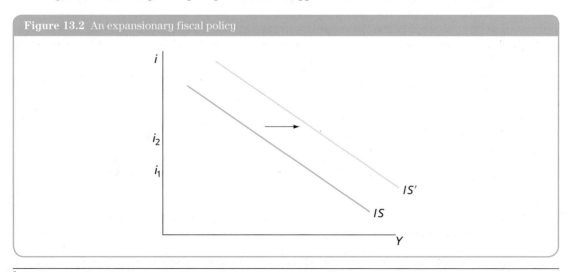

Figure 13.2 An expansionary fiscal policy

---

[2] Later on, we will worry that more public spending or less tax revenues hurt the government budget.

13.1.2 Financial markets and the role of monetary policy

Financial markets involve a vast array of firms and institutions, including banks, investment firms, stock markets, bond markets, etc. Beyond the bewildering details, financial markets perform a relatively straightforward task. They collect savings from households and firms and then lend them to borrowers; again, households and firms as well as public authorities. This activity has a few specific features that matter a lot in terms of understanding European integration:

- *Finance is a risky business.* When financial intermediaries make loans, they take risks. Will they be paid back? No matter how careful they are, they must occasionally bear losses on unpaid debts. When these debts are very large, financial firms may even collapse.

- *Financial intermediaries continuously deal with one another, borrowing and lending.* This is a way of spreading risks or of temporarily parking money that they cannot lend. An implication is that the collapse of one large financial institution can drag down other institutions. A recent example is the collapse of the Lehman Brothers bank in 2008, which led to an immense financial crisis.

- *Risk has a price.* Risky borrowers must offer to pay a higher interest rate to convince reluctant lenders. Conversely, financial intermediaries may be willing to take big risks to collect higher returns while hoping that the risks will not materialize. When they do materialize, crises occur. Financial markets are inherently crisis-prone.

- *Most people keep their savings in financial institutions, usually banks.* They generally ignore how fragile their banks are. When a bank collapses, a large number of innocent depositors stand to lose their savings.

For these reasons, financial institutions are subject to regulations designed to reduce risk-taking, to make them better able to withstand large losses and to protect depositors. Of course, regulations are costly, so financial institutions develop ways of circumventing them. In turn, regulators add new regulations. This leads to an ever more complex process of new regulations and imaginative evasion strategies.

In this chapter, we ignore these aspects. We merely consider the financial market as a whole and imagine that all loans – which we call bonds – are riskless and identical. This means that there is just one interest rate, i, the one that applies to these bonds. It is the interest paid by borrowers and earned by lenders.

As the interest rate rises, lenders are eager to lend more, increasing the supply of loanable funds, while borrowers are deterred by the rising costs and borrow less, as we already saw in the previous section. It stands to reason that there must be an interest rate at which the supply of and the demand for loans are equal. This is the equilibrium interest rate, depicted as i^* in Figure 13.3 – the intersection of the supply of loans, which is upward sloping as explained above, and the demand, which is downward sloping.

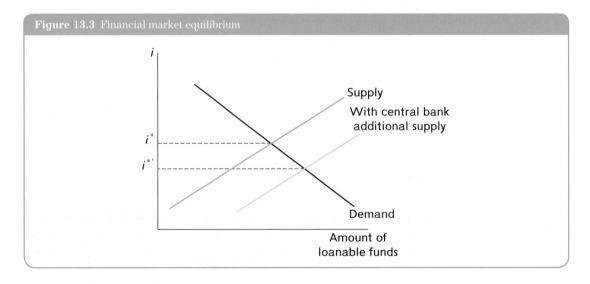

Figure 13.3 Financial market equilibrium

What determines supply of and demand for loanable funds? Wealth is a first important parameter. The richer people are, the more they save, thus increasing supply. Optimism is another determinant. If households and firms are confident that their incomes will rise in the future, they are willing to borrow more, thus increasing demand. Another aspect is the role of governments. They can be large borrowers. When they conduct expansionary fiscal policies, they spend more or tax less and they need to make up the difference by borrowing. This creates a link from the goods market to the financial market.

There is, however, another public institution that matters enormously: the central bank. Its key characteristic is that it can create money at will. When it does, it lends to banks, which increases the amount of loanable funds as banks will seek to immediately relend what they borrowed from the central bank. Central banks can also withdraw money by simply not renewing loans to banks, or even by borrowing. The ability of central banks to create or reabsorb any amount of money means that they can control the interest rate. This is shown in Figure 13.3. An injection of money by the central bank shifts the entire supply curve to the right. This lowers the equilibrium interest rate, which is precisely what an expansionary monetary policy seeks to achieve. More generally, by shifting the overall supply curve, the central bank can achieve whatever interest rate it wishes to see.

The important lesson is that the central bank can decide on the interest rate that it wishes to see, at least in this very simple world in which there is just one interest rate and we do not worry about risk-taking and the threat of financial crises. In other words, once the central bank has an interest rate target, we do not need to worry about what happens to private demand and supply. Obviously, we will need to revisit the question at a later stage. For the time being, in order to understand the implication of the conclusion that has been reached, we need to wonder what the central bank is trying to achieve when it sets the interest rate.

Any central bank has two main objectives: (1) to control inflation, of which more later; and (2) to stabilize the economy, i.e. to avoid large fluctuations in economic activity. The second objective means that monetary policy must be counter-cyclical, meaning that the central bank raises the interest rate when the economy grows too fast and that it lowers the interest rate when the economy is stalling. This can be easily represented graphically, as in Figure 13.4, with an upward-sloping monetary policy schedule, *MP*. It says that, when the level of activity declines, the central bank systematically reduces the interest rate.

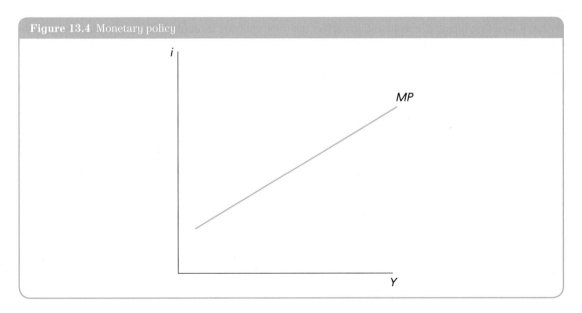

Figure 13.4 Monetary policy

Of course, central banks do not act so mechanically. As we will soon see, they also worry about inflation. Yet this simple description of what central banks do is a realistic place to start. This can be seen in Figure 13.5, which plots the interest rate and GDP for the Eurozone. The *MP* schedule says that they move systematically in the same direction, and this is what has happened since the creation of the euro.

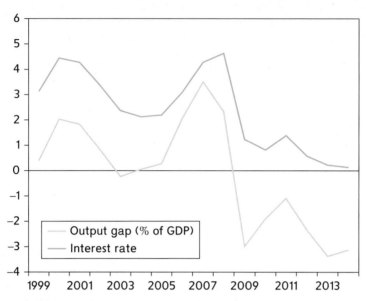

Figure 13.5 The interest rate and output in the Eurozone, 1999–2014

Note: GDP tends to rise continuously following a reasonably stable trend. The figure displays the deviation of actual from trend GDP, which reflects business cycles – precisely what a central bank worries about.

Source: Economic Outlook 95, OECD, May 2014

13.1.3 General equilibrium

We have seen that financial considerations affect the goods market through the impact of the interest rate on firms' decisions about investment spending and consumers' willingness to borrow. We also noticed a link in the opposite direction since government budgets weigh on the demand for loans. This shows that the good and financial markets influence each other. How does the dust settle? Quite simply, when both markets are simultaneously in partial equilibrium. This situation represents the general equilibrium of the economy.

Practically, we simply bring together the two schedules that describe the partial equilibria of the good and financial markets, which is done in Figure 13.6. The intersection point *A* between *IS* and *MP* represents the general equilibrium. This is a very powerful tool, which goes a long way towards understanding business cycles.

The usefulness of this tool can be seen in the case of the 2008 collapse of Lehman Brothers bank in New York. Following this collapse, financial markets panicked, first in the USA and then in the rest of the world. One of the consequences was that households became enormously worried. When people are worried, they save, which means that they cut down on consumption, irrespective of their current incomes. Total spending thus quickly declined, which we represent in Figure 13.6 as a leftward shift of the *IS* curve to *IS′*. The new equilibrium occurs at point *A′*, where GDP has declined and the central bank has reduced the interest rate. This explains the deep recession of 2009, visible in Figure 13.5. Note that, had the central bank not reduced the interest rate, the economy would have moved to point *B*, which corresponds to a deeper recession.

Avoiding a rerun of the Great Depression of the 1930s, following a similar crash on Wall Street, was a paramount objective of the central banks. In fact, they have taken extraordinary actions, including lowering the interest rate over and beyond usual practice. In Figure 13.6, this can be captured as a downward shift of the *MP* curve. For the sake of clarity, this is not shown but you can imagine how the economy moves down along *IS′*, explaining why between 2009 and 2010 the interest rate declines while the level of activity recovers somewhat, as seen in Figure 13.5.

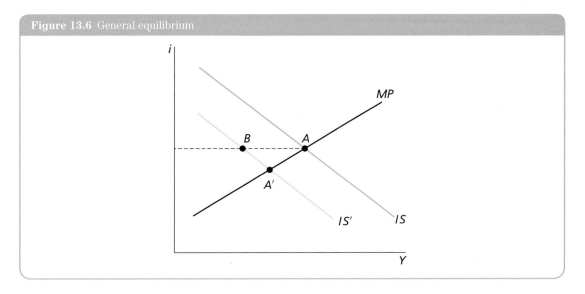

Figure 13.6 General equilibrium

13.2 The open economy

The next step is to take into account that countries are open to exchanges with the rest of the world. Trade in goods and services affect the *IS* curve while capital movements change the nature of financial market equilibrium.

13.2.1 Goods markets

Starting with the simple representation of the goods and services market, we now recognize that *the* good can be exported and imported. Of course, this does not make much sense with just one good, but again the simplification is worth another notch to realism.

The first implication is that we now have foreign customers. Their spending on our production increases demand and this is measured by our exports X. The second implication is that domestic consumers, firms and the government now buy goods from foreign producers. Imports Z therefore represent the share of our spending $C + I + G$ that is spent on domestic production. Domestic demand for the domestically produced good is only $C + I + G - Z$. In the end, total demand addressed to domestic producers is:

$$Y = C + I + G + X - Z$$

The difference $X - Z$ between exports and imports of all goods and services is called the current account.[3] Qualitatively, this does not change the shape of the *IS* curve. An increase in the interest rate still reduces demand for domestic goods as a result of reduced spending on consumption by households and on investment by firms. Since some of this spending is on foreign goods, it will reduce imports so that not all of the impact is borne by domestic producers, but the closed economy result stands and the *IS* curve remains downward sloping as in Figure 13.1.

What matters most is that goods and services markets become interdependent across countries. Changes in foreign spending will affect the demand for Home goods through its exports. A spending boom abroad will translate into more exports, much as a spending boom at home will raise imports and therefore increases demand addressed to foreign producers. A good example of interdependence is the aftermath of the 2008 financial crisis. Financial institutions in the emerging market countries (e.g. the BRICS – Brazil, Russia, India, China and South Africa) were not directly hurt by the crisis because they had not been involved in the risky lending that turned sour in the USA and much of Europe. This led some observers to develop the

---

[3] The trade balance is the difference between exports and imports of goods, excluding services. Although well known, it is not particularly interesting because there is no reason to exclude services like insurance, banking or tourism, which are widely traded internationally.

'decoupling theory' according to which the emerging market countries would not be affected by the crisis that was hurting the developed economies. This view overlooked that part of the spending in the developed countries took the form of imports. A recession in the developed countries had to reduce imports from the rest of the world. Demand from buyers in the developed countries to producers in the rest of the world was bound to decline, and it did – as Figure 13.7 shows. Graphically, their *IS* curves shifted to the left.

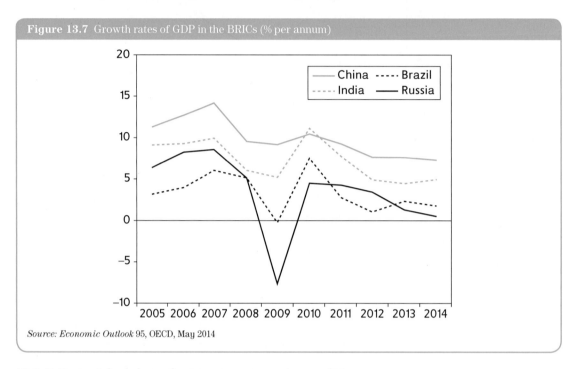

Figure 13.7 Growth rates of GDP in the BRICs (% per annum)

Source: *Economic Outlook* 95, OECD, May 2014

13.2.2 Financial markets: the interest rate parity condition

It is not just goods and services that travel across borders. Financial institutions daily move gigantic sums of money back and forth across countries. They do so routinely as they seek to improve their profits; buying bonds here and borrowing – issuing bonds, for instance – there. These capital flows have a powerful effect on financial market equilibrium around the world.

To see how this works, imagine that you are a trader working for a large bank. You are in charge of a vast amount of money and your job is to achieve the best returns. The world is your playground. As shown in Figure 13.8, you are perfectly informed about all investment opportunities anywhere. Now suppose that the domestic interest rate is low relative to interest rates elsewhere in the world. Shouldn't you invest your money abroad rather than at home? Consider the two options. Investing at home for, say, one year gets you the principal and interest in the domestic currency after the year has elapsed. In order to invest the same amount abroad, you must first buy the foreign currency at the current exchange rate; then, after one year, you receive the principal and higher interest but in foreign currency. To compare this situation with the first option, you will need to convert all that into domestic currency at the then-prevailing exchange rate.

If the exchange rate will not change, maybe because it is fixed, then the interest rates fully capture the difference between the two options and, indeed, you will want to invest abroad. If the foreign currency will appreciate, you will get more domestic currency when you sell the foreign currency in one year's time; by investing abroad you get both a higher interest rate and a capital gain (the additional domestic currency value of your holdings in the foreign currency). Now imagine that the foreign currency depreciates over the year. Then you will get less domestic currency when you convert back at the end of the year, and the loss that you suffer may be even larger than what you gained from the higher interest rate. The conclusion is that you need to compare not just the domestic and foreign interest rates, but also make a bet on the likely evolution of the exchange rate. Box 13.1 provides a formal derivation.

Figure 13.8 A trader ponders his next move

If it is not right there on one of the screens, any information can be obtained on the phone.

© iStock.com/Andrey Popov

Box 13.1   The interest rate parity condition: a formal derivation

A trader wants to invest €1,000 for one year and considers the choice between euros where the interest rate is i, say, 5 per cent, and dollars where the interest rate is i^*, say, 2 per cent. After one year, the euro investment will have become €1,000$(1 + i)$, i.e. €1,050. The investment in dollars requires selling the euros to acquire dollars. The current exchange rate is E_t, defining how many dollars are obtained by selling one euro, for example 1.3. Selling €1,000 gives \$1,000.E_t – \$1300 in our example – which will become \$1,000.$E_t.(1 + i^*)$ in one year's time, \$1,326 when $i^* = 2$ per cent. Then, the exchange rate is expected to be E_{t+1}, so that selling these dollars will yield €1,000.$E_t(1 + i^*)/E_{t+1}$, or €1326/E_{t+1}.

    The interest rate parity condition is achieved when both strategies yield the same revenue:

$$100(1+i) = 100\, E_t\,(1+i^*)\,\frac{1}{E_{t+1}}$$

This will be verified if the expected exchange rate one year ahead is 1.2629. Note that the initial investment, €1,000, appears on both sides of the equation and can therefore be eliminated, which simply means that the interest rate parity condition is independent of the amount involved:

$$(1+i) = (1+i^*)\,\frac{E_t}{E_{t+1}}$$

An approximation yields the condition presented in the text. It involves taking logs on both sides and noting that $ln(1 + i) \approx i$, $ln(1 + i^*) \approx i^*$, and $ln(E_t/E_{t+1}) \approx -(E_{t+1} - E_t)/E_t$:

$$i = i^* - \frac{E_{t+1} - E_t}{E_t}$$

This approximation says that, if the euro interest rate is 5 per cent, the dollar interest rate is 2 per cent; the difference in favour of the euro (3 per cent) must be compensated by an expectation of euro depreciation of (about, because this is an approximation) 3 per cent.

The story becomes even more interesting when you realize that you are not the only trader in the world. Hundreds of colleagues look at the same screens and compare their views about what may happen in the future. If the consensus is that the exchange rate will not change much, they all conclude that investing abroad is the better deal. No one brings money from abroad and all the money available at home leaves the country. Given the huge resources available to international investors, the resulting flowing out of the domestic currency leads to a depreciation of the current exchange rate. In one year's time, the maturing investments in foreign currency will be sold and the proceeds converted into domestic currency. As a result, demand for the domestic currency will swell, so the exchange rate will appreciate. The combination of a weaker exchange rate today and a stronger exchange rate in one year means that the domestic currency is expected to appreciate or, equivalently, that the foreign exchange rate will depreciate. This undermines the attractiveness of investing abroad. In fact, if the expected foreign currency depreciation exactly undermines the higher foreign interest rate, traders become indifferent between the two options. This is when capital flows between the two countries will come to a halt.

International financial markets are in equilibrium when capital flows of this kind are unnecessary because the returns on domestic and foreign assets are equalized, taking into account likely capital gains or losses on currency conversion. This property of international financial markets is called the interest rate parity condition. It can be stated as:

$$\text{Domestic interest rate} = \underbrace{\text{Foreign interest rate} + \text{Expected exchange rate depreciation}}_{\text{Return on foreign assets}}$$

Written this way, it makes it clear that when our exchange rate is expected to depreciate, a higher domestic interest rate is required to prevent massive capital outflows. Conversely, an expected exchange rate appreciation – a negative depreciation – is accompanied by lower interest rates at home than abroad. For example, if the exchange rate is expected to depreciate by 3 per cent and the foreign rate is 2 per cent, the interest rate parity condition requires that the domestic interest rate be 5 per cent.

The smallest deviation from the interest rate parity condition instantly triggers huge capital flows among countries whose financial markets are deeply integrated. These flows promptly affect domestic and foreign interest rates as well as current and expected future exchange rates, and the interest rate parity is instantly re-established. In fact, deviations from the parity condition are fleeting, which is why traders try very hard to spot and act upon them, for they offer profit opportunities to the early birds.

Does the interest rate parity condition actually work? The parity condition cannot be directly observed because we cannot measure the expected exchange rate. Anyway, whose expectation are we talking about? There are thousands of traders, each of whom has her own views. They all play the game of constantly shifting money around. The interest rate parity condition reveals the 'market sentiment', the average of what traders believe will be the exchange rate in the future. In other words, we interpret the interest rate parity condition as revealing the 'market expectation':

$$\text{Expected exchange depreciation} = \text{Domestic interest rate} - \text{Foreign interest rate}$$

This re-interpretation of the interest rate parity condition offers a way of observing indirectly market expectations, under the assumption that the condition is indeed verified. Box 13.2 looks at the indirect evidence and provides a few refinements.

Box 13.2   The interest rate parity condition and risk: lessons from the Greek crisis

Figure 13.9 shows the interest rate on Greek and German public debts. Greece joined the Eurozone in January 2001. Before that, the Greek drachma was a weak currency that was perennially depreciating vis-à-vis the German mark. As the interest rate parity condition predicts, Greek interest rates were above German rates. Once Greece became a Eurozone member, the exchange rate between the drachma and Germany's new currency was fixed. The interest rate parity condition predicts that the interest rates should become equal, which they dutifully did, with the Greek rate gradually converging to the German

Figure 13.9 Government bond interest rates

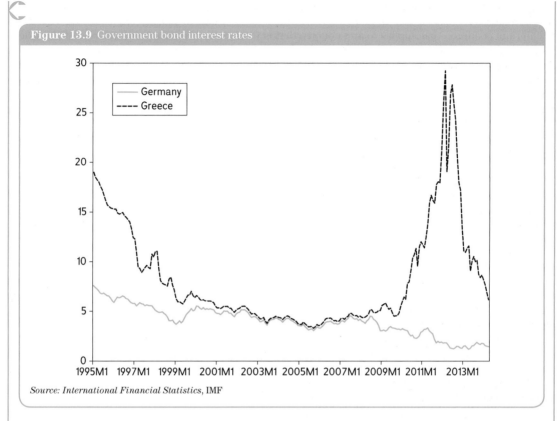

Source: International Financial Statistics, IMF

rate until D-day. This is not the end of the story, though, as Greek rates have again risen. This does not mean that the interest rate parity condition has failed; rather it requires going deeper into the issue.

One interpretation is that the markets expected Greece to leave the Eurozone; this possibility was dubbed 'Grexit'. They expected that the new Greek currency, presumably the old drachma, would soon depreciate vis-à-vis the euro. As interest rate parity would predict, the Greek interest rate rose. Since Summer 2012, however, it has gone down, following the European Central Bank's statement that it would do 'whatever it takes' to keep Greece inside the Eurozone, an important event that is discussed in Chapter 19.

Another interpretation considers the risk factor. As noted above, any loan is risky, and holding bonds or other assets amounts to making a loan to whoever issued these assets because reimbursement is never – or rarely – fully guaranteed. This is why, within a country, rather than just one interest rate, a whole range of rates exists. Top quality borrowers – rated AAA by rating agencies – pay much lower interest rates than risky borrowers. The difference, called the risk premium, is the price of risk, the compensation that not fully trustworthy borrowers must offer to lenders. This can be summarized as follows:

Interest rate of risky asset = Interest rate of safe asset + Risk premium

Moving capital across currencies adds another source of risk: the fact that we do not know what the exchange rate will be when the time comes to transfer back to the original currency. Within a monetary union, there can be no expected change in the exchange rate. Up until the crisis, developed country governments were seen as safe borrowers. In 2005, even though the Greek government was more indebted than the German government, its public debt was rated AA, just a notch below the AAA enjoyed by the German government. The risk premium was very small, hardly visible in Figure 13.9. The crisis changed all that. Already highly indebted governments that went on running large deficits spooked the markets. The Greek debt came to be seen as increasingly risky and, quite naturally, commanded rising risk premia. This in turn fed fears of Grexit, further increasing the risk premium.

Summing up, when capital flows freely in and out of a country, the interest rate parity principle asserts that the domestic interest rate is tied to interest rates abroad and to market expectations. This is an equilibrium condition that applies to any country that is financially integrated with the rest of the world. Indeed, full integration means that there is no point defining financial market equilibrium at the national level, as in the closed country case. This conclusion seriously challenges the view that the central bank can decide the interest rate and that the financial market will find its equilibrium. This is the topic that we now consider.

13.3 The impossible trinity principle

13.3.1 The exchange rate regime

The exchange rate is the price of the domestic currency in terms of the foreign currency. Of course, there are many foreign currencies, and therefore many exchange rates but we keep things simple by imagining just one foreign currency, say the dollar. The euro exchange rate is, for example, 1.3 dollars. This price can change as it freely responds to demand and supply movements on the foreign exchange market, a component of financial markets. Alternatively, the central bank can declare a fixed parity. In that case, the central bank commits to use its reserves of foreign currency to buy or sell any quantity of its currencies to ensure that demand and supply are equal at the chosen parity.

Each country decides which exchange rate regime it wants to adopt. The decision involves many trade-offs and depends on local conditions such as inflation, the development of financial markets or the nature of institutions – especially the central bank. The Annex shows that there are many possibilities. Here, we consider two simple regimes: flexible, when the central bank makes no commitment, and fixed, when the central bank commits to uphold a particular parity relative to the foreign currency. This provides the tool for thinking about the choice of exchange rate regime, of which a monetary union is a special case.

13.3.2 Properties of exchange rate regimes

Figure 13.10 brings together all the previous results. From the closed economy analysis, we represent the goods market equilibrium with the *IS* curve – suitably re-interpreted. We also continue to depict the central bank preferences with the *MP* curve. The horizontal line depicts the interest rate parity (*IRP*) condition as stated above: financial markets are in equilibrium when the domestic interest rate i is equal to the return

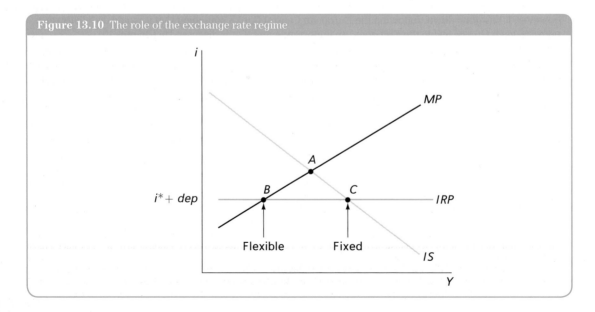

Figure 13.10 The role of the exchange rate regime

from foreign currency bonds expressed in the domestic currency, that is, the foreign interest rate $i*$ plus the expected rate of depreciation (dep) of our currency. For the time being, to keep things simple, we ignore expected depreciation (so we assume $dep = 0$).

General equilibrium requires that both the goods and financial markets be in equilibrium, which means the intersection of *IS* and *IRP*. The central bank chooses the interest rate according to *MP*. As all students of geometry know, however, three lines (or reasonably straight curves) normally intersect pair-wise in three different points. We are therefore stuck with too many possibilities represented by points *A*, *B* and *C*. This is, graphically, the impossible trinity principle, which is stated as follows:

- Only two of the three following features are compatible with each other:
    - Full capital mobility
    - Fixed exchange rates
    - Autonomous monetary policy

Consider first the case of a fixed exchange rate regime. When the goods market is in equilibrium and the central bank acts according to its preferences, we must be at *A*, at the intersection of *IS* and *MP*. As drawn, point *A* lies above the *IRP* line: the domestic interest rate is too high for the international financial markets to be in equilibrium. High returns on domestic currency assets attract capital inflows. Investors buy up the domestic currency, which tends to appreciate. But the central bank must resist the appreciation. To do so, the central bank intervenes on the foreign exchange market: it sells its currency – which it can produce in any amount – and accumulates the foreign currency. This will continue as long as the interest rate remains above the *IRP* line. Given how large the financial markets are, the amounts involved can be enormous and, normally, the central bank will give up before long. Note that if the interest rate is below the *IRP* line, capital flows out and the exchange rate tends to depreciate. The central bank now buys back its own currency, drawing upon its foreign exchange reserves. Evidently, this cannot go on forever because the stock of reserves is bound to be depleted. Either way, monetary policy autonomy is lost and the central bank must admit that it cannot choose the interest rate. The *IRP* line must be respected and the central bank preferences, represented by the *MP* schedule, become irrelevant. The only possible position is point *C*.

Consider now the case when the exchange rate is allowed to float freely. Consider again point *A*. We already know that in this position capital flows in and the exchange rate tends to appreciate, which the central bank no longer opposes. An appreciation means that the foreign currency becomes cheaper, and this applies to imported goods as well. Imports will rise. The opposite occurs abroad as our exports become more expensive because our currency costs more. Exports will decline. Less *X* and more *Z* means a diminishing demand ($C + I + G + X - Z$) for our producers and the *IS* curve shifts to the left. It will continue to do so until it passes through point *B*, where international financial equilibrium is achieved while the central bank is pursuing its chosen policy *MP*. As the economy moves from *A* to *B*, the central bank lowers the interest rate to soften the decline in output. In this case, the central bank can remain on the *MP* schedule and the *IRP* condition is satisfied. It is now the *IS* curve that has to move until it meets the two other schedules. The exchange rate does what it has to do to achieve this outcome.

This analysis explains the impossible trinity principle, which is represented in Figure 13.11 by a triangle. Each angle corresponds to one of the three features listed above and each side represents a feasible combination. The bottom side of the triangle represents the case when the exchange rate floats freely, as just described. The triangle's left side corresponds to the fixed exchange rate case with capital mobility but no monetary policy autonomy. Consider now the right side of the triangle, when capital controls prevent capital mobility – more on controls below. Traders cannot (legally) move their monies freely and the interest parity no longer applies. The *IRP* line does not exist, leaving the central bank free to choose the interest rate that best fits its objectives, irrespective of whether the exchange rate is fixed or not.[4]

---

[4] The reasoning is a little bit trickier than described so far as we assume that expected depreciation is nil ($dep = 0$). Under a fixed exchange rate regime, market expectations that the exchange rate will not change is a sign that the policy is credible, since it means that the financial markets accept the central bank commitment. When the exchange rate floats freely, the markets are likely to expect movements. This means that policy actions are likely to change market expectations, which means that the *IRP* line will shift. We do not pursue this (rather complicated) issue because it does not affect the conclusions reached so far.

The impossible trinity principle is central to the European integration process. It implies that, for a country that maintains full financial integration, the exchange rate policy, i.e. the choice of an exchange rate regime, is simply the same thing as adopting a monetary policy strategy. Fixing the exchange rate means adopting the foreign interest rate; conversely, maintaining the ability to choose the domestic interest rate requires allowing the exchange rate to float freely. Ever since the EU adopted in 1992 the principle of open capital markets as part of the Single Market (see Chapter 1), the choice has been circumscribed to the left or bottom sides of the triangle in Figure 13.11.

One way of escaping the choice between exchange rate stability and monetary policy autonomy is to restrict capital movements. This is one reason why many European countries operated extensive capital controls until the early 1990s when full capital mobility was made compulsory as part of the Single Market. Likewise, many of the new EU members only abandoned capital controls upon accession.

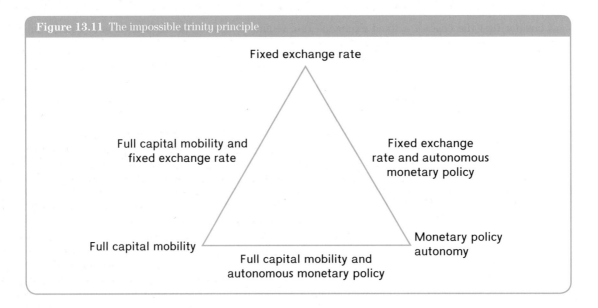

Figure 13.11 The impossible trinity principle

13.3.3 Who does what?

Each side of the impossibility triangle has its real-life supporters. A few examples can illustrate the principle and serve as a warning that there is no universally better exchange rate regime. Governments often want to have all three features at the same time; refusing to choose invariably leads to a crisis.

Full capital mobility and autonomous monetary policy, flexible exchange rate

In this case, monetary policy is effective but the central bank must give up any pretence at steering the exchange rate. The Eurozone as a whole, the USA, Japan, the UK, Switzerland (until 2012) and Sweden, among many others, follow this approach. These countries, which gave up capital controls long ago and are committed to full financial openness, have decided to retain full control of monetary policy.

While retaining monetary autonomy sounds like a good idea, it also has drawbacks. The downside is that the exchange rate can be quite volatile, which affects external competitiveness. For example, the UK has very explicitly decided to retain monetary policy autonomy and negotiated an exemption from the EU obligation to eventually join the monetary union. Switzerland too has long decided that monetary policy autonomy is crucial to its standing as a financial centre with a stable currency. Figure 13.12 describes their experience since 1999, the year when the euro was launched. Until the onset of the financial crisis, both currencies fluctuated vis-à-vis the euro within relatively narrow margins. Once the crisis was under way, the pound promptly depreciated by some 25 per cent. This made imported goods significantly more expensive and redirected spending towards domestic production while boosting exports, which helped cushion the recessionary impact of the financial crisis. At the same time, it raised the price of imports and contributed to a rise in inflation. Exactly the opposite happened in Switzerland, which has long been considered as a safe haven in troubled times. Capital dutifully flew in and the Swiss franc began to appreciate. This worried Swiss exporters because an appreciated currency means that exports become expensive. Ultimately, the staunchly independent Swiss National Bank set a ceiling for its currency in September 2012. *De facto*, the exchange rate is quasi-fixed and autonomy in relation to monetary policy is lost for the time being.

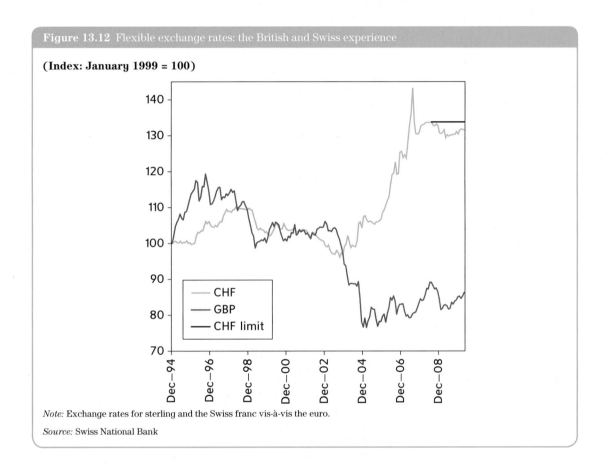

Figure 13.12 Flexible exchange rates: the British and Swiss experience

Note: Exchange rates for sterling and the Swiss franc vis-à-vis the euro.

Source: Swiss National Bank

Full capital mobility and fixed exchange rate

In this case, the central bank must dedicate itself to upholding its commitment to the fixed exchange rate. This was the worldwide regime adopted at the Bretton Woods conference in 1944. When the system collapsed in 1973, many European countries attempted to keep their bilateral exchange rates fixed. This led to the creation of the European Monetary System (explained in full in Chapter 14). A number of European countries now fix their exchange rate to the euro. One of them is Denmark.[5] Figure 13.13 shows that the Danish central bank has essentially adopted all decisions taken by the European Central Bank, except (but only slightly) during the crisis period. The distinction between such a policy and euro

---

[5] In 1992, the Danish people rejected the Maastricht Treaty, against the wishes of the government, because they wanted to keep their currency. Since European treaties are valid only when ratified by all member countries, Denmark was offered an exemption from euro area membership. A second referendum in 1993 was, however, successful. The Danish authorities, who believe that exchange rate stability is crucial, are pegging the kroner to the euro.

> **Figure 13.13** Central bank interest rates: Denmark and the euro area, 1999–2014

(Danish kroner per euro)

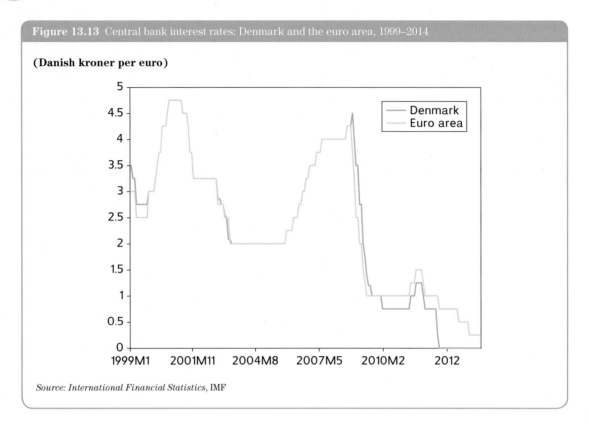

Source: International Financial Statistics, IMF

area membership is tenuous. Euro area member countries have formally given up their autonomy over monetary policy by transferring responsibility for it to the European Central Bank, and Denmark has done the same on an informal basis. Of course, Denmark is not involved in ECB decisions.

Fixed exchange rate and monetary policy autonomy, with capital controls

Capital controls make the interest rate parity principle inoperative. There exist a wide variety of capital controls. Some simply forbid the transfer of funds between a country and the rest of the world, or subject these transfers to limits and sometimes to administration authorization. The result is that traders can no longer take advantage of higher returns abroad or lower borrowing costs. Being restricted, capital flows cannot establish the parity condition. Many developing and some emerging market countries, for instance China, use this type of control. Another form of capital control imposes taxes on international financial transactions. The result is that traders must factor in these taxes when they compare domestic and foreign interest rates. If the tax rate is high enough, it will discourage a significant portion of capital flows. In recent years, Brazil has adopted this mechanism.

Capital controls allow for monetary autonomy but there are costs. To start with, people try to evade the restrictions and the taxes. This means that one has to build an administration to monitor and enforce the controls, and then to punish those who evade them. The more sophisticated the financial sector, the more expensive and eventually self-defeating the enforcement of those capital controls becomes. In addition, while capital flows are occasionally disruptive, they serve a useful purpose. They allow savers to achieve the best returns that the world has on offer, much as they allow borrowers to find the best available loans. Financial autarky prevents these arrangements, which eventually harm investment and economic growth.

The combination of capital controls and fixed exchange rates was widespread under the Bretton Woods system – although some countries such as Germany and Switzerland almost never enforced capital controls. It also characterized Europe's early monetary integration efforts, which led to the European Monetary System. As predicted by the impossible trinity principle, the removal of capital controls made this arrangement non-viable, which eventually led to the adoption of the euro by most EU countries, and to a free floating of the exchange rate in Sweden and the UK.

13.3.4 Can the impossible trinity principle be ignored?

Policy makers naturally do not like the impossible trinity principle because it restricts their room for manoeuvre. It is often tempting to ignore it and keep the exchange rate fixed while using monetary policy actively and freeing capital movements.

What happens when one tries to violate the impossible trinity? The answer is simple: a currency crisis. Sooner or later a speculative attack wipes out the fixed exchange rate arrangement. We will show in Chapter 14 that this is precisely what happened in Europe in 1993. Some more recent and prominent examples include Russia and Southeast Asia in 1997 and, in some way, Argentina in 2001. In all these cases, financial liberalization was undertaken as part of the financial globalization process but the authorities did not want to give up either the fixed exchange rate system or monetary autonomy. Eventually, they had to make this choice but in the midst of traumatic crises.

The impossible trinity principle lies at the heart of the history of European monetary integration. A number of countries consider that a common market for goods and services requires a high degree of exchange rate stability. Until the early 1980s, most countries operated various capital controls so they could have both exchange rate stability and autonomy over monetary policy. With the advent of globalization, these controls were dismantled. The impossible trinity principle sharpened the exchange rate regime choice: either exchange rate flexibility or the loss of monetary autonomy. It took time – and the 1993 crisis – for governments to be willing to face that choice. Losing monetary policy autonomy was the price to pay for exchange rate stability. Once this conclusion was accepted, losing one's own currency looked like a small sacrifice to achieve exchange rate stability. Those countries that favour monetary policy autonomy, in contrast, decided to stay out of the monetary union.

13.4 Monetary neutrality

So far we have ignored prices. A full extension of the previous analysis to also explain price formation is beyond the scope of this book.[6] We take shortcuts by presenting two principles: monetary neutrality and purchasing power. These principles establish a link between money and the price level and between domestic and foreign prices, respectively.

We saw that the central bank decides on the interest rate that it wants to see prevailing. To do so, it makes money more or less abundant. For instance, if it wishes to lower the interest rate, it provides more money to banks, which then lend it on to their customers or invest it in assets at home or abroad. The ability to control the amount of money, on which it has a legal monopoly, grants to the central bank the possibility of enforcing the interest rate of its choice.

This is how things happen in the short run, say, 1-3 years. By lowering the interest rate, the central bank encourages spending, as we saw, which strengthens demand. Beyond that horizon, monetary policy gradually loses its power to influence demand. The reason is that a stronger demand for goods and services tends to lead to higher prices (and wages as firms hire more workers or pay for extra hours). This erodes the purchasing power of money.

Indeed, money is useful because it allows people to buy goods. With a 50 euro note you can buy two restaurant dinners at 25 euros each. If the price of the dinner rises to 30 euros, the same note will only pay for one dinner. its purchasing power has diminished. This is a very general proposition: the purchasing power of money is inversely related to the price level. As the central bank increases the stock of money and raises demand, and then prices rise, the purchasing power of money declines and the policy effect wears off. In the long run, monetary policy is inoperative.

The monetary neutrality principle is stated as follows:

- In the long run, monetary policy loses its effectiveness because the price level increases in the same proportion as the money stock.

---

[6] Standard textbooks provide the extension, the aggregate demand and supply framework.

In the long run, inflation is determined by money growth. For instance, if the central bank increases the money stock by 20 per cent, eventually the price level will rise by 20 per cent and the purchasing power of money will return to its previous position. If you have 60 euros in cash, you can buy two dinners at 30 euros each, exactly as you could afford two dinners at 25 euros each with just a 50-euro note.

Monetary neutrality is very simple and intuitive, but that situation can be deceptive. First, how long does it take to kick in? The answer is that it varies, depending on a host of accompanying circumstances; however, five years is a reasonable rule of thumb. Second, is it that simple and automatic? Well, not quite. It tends to work well, but can be derailed by special circumstances. This is clearly illustrated by the history of the Eurozone in Figure 13.14. Up until the financial crisis that started in 2008, the money stock and the price level moved in an approximately parallel fashion; thus monetary neutrality works. Post-2007, however, it no longer seems to do so. What has happened is that badly hurt banks have curtailed their lending to households and firms, instead building up reserves of money to prepare for a major upheaval. This behaviour has derailed the transmission of monetary policy to the economy as a whole. This is an extraordinary event, however. Once understood, it does not invalidate the general principle.

Figure 13.14 The money stock and the price level in the Eurozone

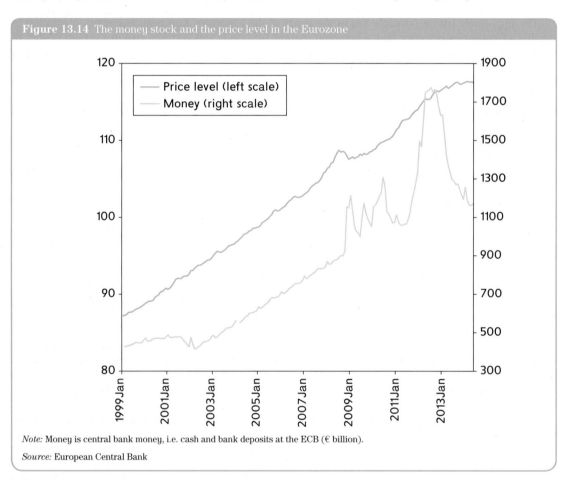

Note: Money is central bank money, i.e. cash and bank deposits at the ECB (€ billion).

Source: European Central Bank

13.5 The real exchange rate and the purchasing power parity principle

13.5.1 The real exchange rate

We already saw that the exchange rate E matters for competitiveness, but we need to be more precise. Obviously, prices must play a role too. We keep assuming that there is a single domestic good, whose price is P. This price is expressed in euros. We need to compare it to the price of the foreign good, P^*, which is expressed in the foreign currency, say, in dollars. We cannot compare them directly because they are in different currencies. To undertake a meaningful comparison, we need to use the exchange rate E to express both goods in the same currency, either euros or dollars. The solution is quite straightforward. Imagine a domestic good whose price is 100 euros:

Price of the European good in euros	P	(e.g. €100)
Exchange rate (dollars per euro)	E	(e.g. 1.3 $/€)
Price of the European good in dollars	EP	(e.g. $130)

Thus we can compare EP with P^*, since both are measured in dollars.

This observation leads to the definition of a new and important variable, the real exchange rate. It is the ratio EP/P^*, also called the relative price of the domestic good in terms of the foreign good. Note that we could instead measure the price of the US basket in euros as P^*/E and compare it to the domestic price in euros as well. When we divide P by P^*/E, we obtain EP/P^* as before. Reassuringly, it does not matter which currency we use. Like price levels, the real exchange rate is an index number, computed to take a simple value (e.g. 1 or 100) in a specified period.

When the real exchange rate increases – we say that it appreciates – it means that domestic goods become more expensive relative to foreign goods: our competitiveness declines. The real exchange rate appreciates when:

- the nominal exchange rate E appreciates;
- domestic prices P rise faster than foreign prices P^*, so that P/P^* increases.

Conversely, a real exchange rate depreciation – a decline in EP/P^* – signals a gain in competitiveness. When we ignored prices, we looked only at the nominal exchange rate E; now we know that this is not enough.

13.5.2 The purchasing power parity principle

The purchasing power parity (PPP) principle asserts that the rate of change of the nominal exchange rate between two countries is equal to the difference between the inflation rates in these two countries, called the inflation differential:

$$\text{Exchange rate appreciation} = \underbrace{\text{Foreign inflation rate} - \text{Domestic inflation rate}}_{\text{Inflation differential}}$$

If inflation at home is lower than abroad, our currency should appreciate. Conversely, a country with higher inflation sees its exchange rate depreciate vis-à-vis the currency of a country with a lower inflation rate.

This principle is known to only hold in the long run – when it holds; the next section gives an important reason why it sometimes fails to hold. An example of PPP is provided in Table 13.1, which compares Italy and Germany over a very long period, from 1960 to 1998, the year before the adoption of the euro by these

Table 13.1   PPP: Italy and Germany, 1960–98

	(%)
Average annual inflation rate in Italy	8.0
Average annual inflation rate in Germany	3.2
Average annual depreciation of the lira	5.3

Source: IMF

two countries. Inflation in Italy had been high, on average 8.0 per cent per year, far exceeding the German average rate of 3.2 per cent. The PPP prediction is that the Italian lira should have depreciated vis-à-vis the German mark by a difference of 4.8 per cent, on average. In fact, the lira depreciated a bit more, at an average rate of 5.3 per cent. This is a good example of how PPP works: it tells us the right story, not always very precisely, but close.

13.5.3 The equilibrium real exchange rate

An important implication of PPP is that the real exchange rate EP/P^* is constant.[7] In the example of Table 13.1, on average over nearly 40 years, the bilateral exchange rate of the Italian lira E declined by 5.3 per cent, P rose by 8 per cent, so the numerator EP increased by 2.7 per cent. During the same period, the denominator P^* rose on average by 3.2 per cent. Thus the bilateral real exchange rate depreciated by 0.5 per cent. This is not exactly zero, but it is small in comparison to the changes in E, P and P^*.

Even that small discrepancy can be explained. Germany is an important economic partner of Italy, but not its only partner. Could it be that the real depreciation of the lira vis-à-vis the mark is offset by a real appreciation vis-à-vis other currencies? In order to look at Italy vis-à-vis the rest of the world, we need to average the nominal exchange rates of the lira and then the euro vis-à-vis all of Italy's partners – or its most important partners – and, accordingly, observe how prices elsewhere change on average. When this is done, we look at what is called the nominal effective exchange rate, E, and at inflation in 'the rest of the world', P^*, which makes it possible to measure the real effective exchange rate, EP/P^*. The left-hand chart of Figure 13.15 shows the evolution of Italy's nominal and real effective exchange rates over a long period. The difference between the nominal and real rates stands out. During the 1970s, the nominal exchange rate depreciated hugely while the real exchange rate moved very little. This confirms that inflation in Italy was much higher than among its partners and that the exchange rate made up the difference. The larger nominal fluctuations affect the real exchange rate in the short run but tend to leave no lasting influence. The real effective exchange rate is certainly not constant year after year, but roughly so over longer periods. The real effective exchange rate was 103.5 in 1970 and 108.0 in 2012 (and 102.4 in 2011). Over 42 years, this is near constancy. This is PPP in the long run.

The long-run stability of the real exchange rate cannot be a fluke and, indeed, there is a good explanation. When its real exchange rate appreciates, a country becomes less competitive. Its current account deteriorates as exports decline – domestic goods are more expensive on foreign markets – and imports rise – foreign goods are cheaper at home. The resulting external deficit – the country buys more abroad than it sells – cannot go on forever because it must be financed by borrowing abroad. Eventually, either the nominal exchange rate must depreciate or prices have to move to re-establish competitiveness. Either way, the real exchange rate must return to its 'normal' level, which is called the equilibrium rate: it is the rate at which trade is balanced. When the real exchange rate is above equilibrium, it is said to be overvalued, and it is undervalued in the opposite case. Over- and under-valuations are instances of misalignment.

This explains why PPP is a long-run concept. External imbalances are possible, indeed they occur all the time, but they must eventually be corrected. It may take a long time for that to happen, as seen in the bottom chart of Figure 13.15.

The PPP principle is simple and intuitive. It is a good point to start thinking about the exchange rate over the long run, but it does not hold very precisely, as we have already noted, nor everywhere and at all times. Not only is it very slow to assert itself but it also suffers from many important exceptions. If it works well among countries at similar stages of development, like the developed countries, it can fail badly in other cases, for well-understood reasons. One key reason, which affects the newer members of the EU, is presented in Section 13.5.4.

13.5.4 The Balassa–Samuelson effect

Italy and Germany compete with each other on broadly similar goods and services, such as cars, insurance and chemicals. These products are very similar, so that competition is primarily a matter of costs, mostly

---

[7] The formal proof of this assertion is as follows. The rate of change (in per cent) of the real exchange rate EP^*/P is $\Delta(EP/P^*)/EP/P^* = \Delta E/E + \Delta P/P - \Delta P^*/P$. It follows that $\Delta(EP/P^*)/EP/P^* = 0$ when $\Delta E/E = \Delta P^*/P^* - \Delta P/P$.

Figure 13.15 Italy, 1970–2012

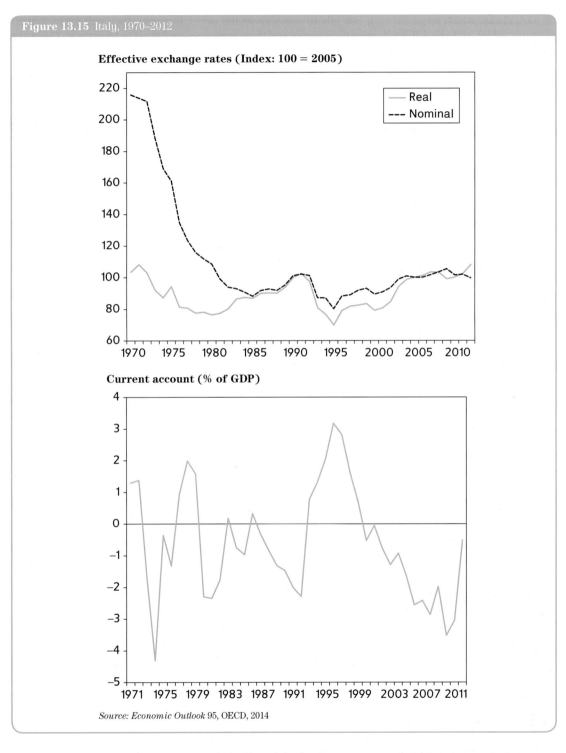

Source: Economic Outlook 95, OECD, 2014

labour costs. India and China also manufacture cars, which they export. Their labour costs are a fraction of those of Italy and Germany, and indeed their cars are considerably cheaper. Yet, Indian and Chinese firms find it hard to enter the European market because these cars are low-tech, which is indeed why they must be very cheap, which requires very low labour costs. Over the years, however, they will upgrade their products, which will allow them to raise their prices and their wages, as explained in Chapter 8. This is the Balassa–Samuelson effect.[8] It can be stated as follows:

- Equilibrium real exchange rates of countries that enjoy lasting fast growth – because they are catching up from a lower level of development – follow an appreciating trend.

Every traveller knows that the cost of living is much lower in poor countries. A low level of development is associated with low physical capital intensity; that is, little and poor quality production equipment. This situation applies to both private and public capital; that is, machinery and production facilities but also public transport systems, telecommunications and administration. In most cases, it is also associated with a relatively limited education level, also called human capital. Development occurs when all that changes. Better-educated workers can utilize more sophisticated equipment to produce higher-quality goods and services, which fetch higher prices. As human, physical, private and public capital grows, the quality and value of products rises, from basic agricultural products to elaborate foodstuffs, for example. In turn, incomes and prices rise. The Balassa–Samuelson effect captures this by-product of the catch-up process, when relatively under-developed countries gradually close the technology gap between themselves and more advanced countries.

This effect implies that the real equilibrium exchange rate EP/P^* of a country that is catching up is steadily increasing as domestic prices P rise relative to foreign prices evaluated in the domestic currency P^*/E, or, equivalently, when domestic prices evaluated in the foreign currency EP rise relative to foreign prices P^*. The real appreciation can take the form of higher inflation at home (P/P^* increases steadily) or a continuous nominal appreciation with possible ups and downs along the way (E is on a rising trend), or any combination of both.

Within the EU, the western countries caught up with the USA during the period 1950–80. Standards of living are no longer very different. Among these countries, we expect PPP to do well. The central and eastern European countries have been transitioning from planned to market economies since the mid-1990s. Starting from a low-income level and poor production capacities, they have been catching up on their western neighbours. As they build up their production potential and adopt the best technologies, they climb up the product quality ladder and produce increasingly more sophisticated products that they can sell at higher prices, which allows their workers to earn higher wages. For instance, in 1997, the average hourly labour cost in Hungary was 10 per cent of that in Germany; by 2012, it had increased to 19 per cent. This process is bound to continue over the coming decades, and Hungary's real exchange rate relative to Germany will keep on appreciating, year in, year out.

Table 13.2 shows how this has played out for the new EU members. For each country, it displays in the first row the inflation differential, the difference between domestic and euro area inflation rates, and

Table 13.2 The Balassa–Samuelson effect: average annual changes (%), 1996–2008

	Bulgaria	Czech Republic	Estonia	Latvia	Lithuania
Inflation differential	29.0	1.6	3.2	3.7	1.4
Nominal appreciation	−19.7	2.6	−0.2	0.0	3.2
Real appreciation	9.3	4.2	3.0	3.7	4.6
	Hungary	Poland	Romania	Slovenia	Slovakia
Inflation differential	6.2	3.3	28.3	3.8	4.1
Nominal appreciation	−2.4	−0.2	−20.6	−2.8	1.5
Real appreciation	3.8	3.1	7.7	1.0	5.6

Source: AMECO, European Commission

---

[8] It is named after Hungarian-born US economist Bela Balassa, who taught at Johns Hopkins University, and Paul Samuelson, Nobel Prize laureate, who taught at MIT; they discovered this effect independently.

nominal exchange rate appreciation vis-à-vis the euro.[9] In all of these countries, inflation has been higher than in the Eurozone. For the real exchange rate to remain constant, they would have had to undergo a nominal depreciation of the same magnitude; in fact, their currencies depreciated by less, even appreciating in the case of the Czech Republic, Lithuania and Slovakia.

13.6 Summary

This chapter has presented two extensions of the traditional closed economy macroeconomic framework: the role of trade and financial openness and the drastic implications of capital mobility. An important aspect of the theoretical framework *IS–MP–IRP* is that it shows the importance of the exchange rate regime, which is what monetary union is all about. The framework creates two essential tools: the interest rate parity condition and the impossible trinity. Two additional tools are developed in this chapter: monetary neutrality and the purchasing power principle.

The interest rate parity condition is a feature of capital mobility and it is met permanently as financial markets constantly reshuffle assets across countries and currencies. International investors are constantly on the watch for the best possible returns. As they shift capital around, they equalize expected returns across countries and currencies. Interest rate parity establishes a tight link between the exchange rate and domestic and foreign interest rates. Relying as it does on market expectations, it recognizes the importance of perceptions, whether or not they are correct, and irrespective of whether these expectations eventually materialize. Welcome to the world of finance!

The impossible trinity principle reveals crucially important implications for monetary and exchange rate policy strategies. It asserts that governments must make coherent choices regarding the exchange rate regime, the use of monetary policy and the capital mobility regime. An important implication is that, when capital is free to move, a central bank cannot control simultaneously the interest and the exchange rates.

The third tool is monetary neutrality. It asserts that, in the long run, inflation is proportional to the rate of growth of money created by the central bank. It will become an important part of the explanation of how a monetary union works.

The final tool, purchasing power parity, is also a long-run property. It establishes a link between domestic inflation and the exchange rate. We have not made use of this principle in the present chapter, but it will play an important role later on.

In practice, genuinely fixed exchange rates and complete free floating are just the two corners of a wide range of intermediate arrangements. These 'soft peg' arrangements either set limits to exchange rate fluctuations – betraying a fear of floating – or seek to introduce some degree of flexibility in fixed rate regimes – revealing a fear of fixing. Attempts to avoid the rigour of fixing and the volatility that comes with floating often amount to violating the impossible trinity principle. In general, the result is a crisis.

Self-assessment questions

1 A currency is called strong when it is usually appreciating. How can a country achieve strong currency status? Which currencies are strong?

2 If the nominal exchange rate appreciates by less than the excess of foreign over domestic inflation, is the real exchange rate appreciating or depreciating?

3 Why are fixed exchange rates believed to impose discipline on monetary policy?

4 Return to Table 13.2 and compute for each country the change in exchange rate we would have observed if PPP were to be satisfied.

---

[9] Following the reasoning in footnote 7, we present $\Delta P/P - \Delta P^*/P^*$ in the first row, $\Delta E/E$ in the second row and the real exchange rate is calculated in the last row as $\Delta(EP/P^*)/(EP/P^*) = \Delta E/E + \Delta P/P - \Delta P^*/P^*$, i.e. the sum of the first two rows.

5 Consider the case where $i > i^* + dep$. Explain the capital flows triggered by this configuration. In which direction are the capital flows likely to push i, i^*, the current exchange rate E, for a given expected future exchange rate?

6 Using the *IS–MP–IRP* framework, examine the effects of an expansionary fiscal policy (e.g. an increase in public spending (G) under a fixed and under a flexible exchange rate regime.

7 Drawing on your results in the previous question, characterize the differences between the fixed and flexible exchange rate regimes: which policies work and which do not?

8 A standard speculation strategy consists of borrowing in the home country, investing abroad and selling the proceeds from the foreign investment to pay back the original loan. Determine when this strategy is profitable. Explain why it helps to re-establish the interest rate parity condition.

9 Link the monetary neutrality and PPP principles to explain how money and the exchange rate are associated in the long run. Then revisit Question 1 above.

10 Does PPP imply that the inflation rate must be the same in every country under fixed exchange rate arrangements?

Essay questions

1 The real, not the nominal, exchange rate is what matters for the real side of the economy. Why don't central banks attempt to control the real rather the nominal exchange rate?

2 It is often believed that a peg encourages residents (households, firms, banks) to borrow in a foreign currency. Then, if the exchange rate is devalued, many residents face the risk of bankruptcy. Explain and comment.

3 The Eurozone crisis has resulted in very different interest rates being applied in different countries, as exemplified by the case in Greece (Figure 13.9). Explain how this has reduced the ECB's ability to conduct monetary policy.

4 Argue why it may be preferable to adopt a fixed exchange rate regime. Now make the argument in defence of a floating exchange rate.

5 In the aftermath of the financial crisis, the exchange rates of Poland, Sweden and the UK have depreciated sharply (by some 20 per cent or more) relative to the euro. These countries are members of the Single Market but not of the monetary union. Discuss the likely effects on these countries and on the Eurozone countries.

Further reading: the aficionado's corner

Purchasing power parity is one of the oldest regularities detected by economists, traced back to the sixteenth century and much studied ever since. A classic review of its various incarnations (absolute PPP, relative PPP) and of the evidence is:

Rogoff, K. (1996) 'The purchasing power parity puzzle', *Journal of Economic Literature*, 34(2): 647–68.

The interest rate parity condition also has a long history. While its logic is strong, 'proving' this condition is much more difficult because it deals with expectations and everyone is entitled to her own views. There is no such thing as the 'expectation of the markets'. A large empirical literature has been and still is grappling with the issue. It has become increasingly technical. A good update is:

Lothian, J.R. and L. Wu (2011) 'Uncovered interest-rate parity over the past two centuries', *Journal of International Money and Finance*, 30(3), 448–73.

The impossible trinity comes under a variety of names such as the unholy trinity, the policy trilemma or the triangle of impossibility. It was made clear by Robert Mundell in his classic development of what has come to be called the Mundell–Fleming model. This link is described in detail in:

Burda, M. and C. Wyplosz (2013) *Macroeconomics: A European Text*, 6th edition, Oxford University Press, Oxford.

A critical view of the impossible trinity asserts that even countries with a flexible exchange rate lose their monetary policy autonomy; see:

Rey, H. (2013) 'Dilemma not trilemma: the global financial cycle and monetary policy independence', VoxEU, 31 August.

The Bank for International Settlements surveys the size and functioning of foreign *exchange* markets every three years. The latest survey is described in:

BIS (2013) *Triennial Survey*, December. Download from www.bis.org.

A description of existing capital controls and an evaluation of their effectiveness can be found in:

Ostry, J.D., A.R. Ghosh, K. Habermeier, L. Laeven, M. Chamon, M. S. Qureshi and A. Kokenyne (2011) 'Managing capital inflows: what tools to use?', IMF Staff Discussion Note, April 5. Download from imf.org /external/ pubs/ft/sdn/2011/sdn1106.pdf.

Useful websites

The IMF presents up-to-date evaluations of exchange rate policies: www.imf.org.

To find out about the exchange rate regime of a particular country, visit the website of its central bank.

Reference

Krugman, P. (1999) 'O Canada', *The Dismal Science*, Slate, http://www.slate.com/articles/business/the_dismal_science/1999/10/o_canada.html.

Annex: Various exchange rate regimes

So far we have mentioned just two exchange rate regimes: fixed and flexible. In practice, exchange rate regimes come in all sorts of shapes and forms. Except when the exchange rate is freely floating, all other regimes require choosing a foreign currency to peg. The main anchors have traditionally been the US dollar and the Deutschmark, now replaced by the euro. This section reviews the various possible arrangements, ranging from full flexibility to full rigidity.

Free floating

The simplest regime is when the monetary authorities decline any responsibility for the exchange rate. The rate is then freely determined by the markets and can fluctuate by any amount at any moment. We have already noted (Section 13.3.3) that most developed countries let their exchange rate float freely because they want to conduct autonomous monetary policies and to put their central bank in charge of inflation.

Managed floating

In small and open economies, the authorities are often concerned that a free float results in excessive exchange rate volatility, a pattern sometimes called 'fear of floating'. At the same time, for reasons that will become clear below, they may not want to commit themselves to a particular exchange rate; this is 'fear of fixing'. What they desire is to intervene on the exchange markets from time to time, as they see fit. They operate a managed float, sometimes called a dirty float, which is a halfway house between a free float and a peg. Central banks buy their own currency when they consider it too weak, and sell it when they see it as too strong, but they refrain from pursuing any particular exchange rate target. They are not making any explicit commitment but they are occasionally present on foreign exchange markets with the aim of smoothing short-term movements. This strategy cannot always be distinguished from a free float. European countries that manage their exchange rates to some degree include the Czech Republic, Hungary, Poland and Romania.

Fixed exchange rates or target zones

In a fixed exchange rate regime, the authorities declare an official parity vis-à-vis another currency, chiefly the US dollar or the euro, sometimes vis-à-vis a basket of several currencies. The arrangement normally specifies margins of fluctuation around the central parity, hence the qualification as a target zone. The wider is the band of fluctuation, the closer is the regime to a free float or a managed float. Practically, the central bank must intervene – and lose policy autonomy – when the exchange rate moves towards the edges of the target zone, but it can also intervene at any time it wishes, even if the exchange rate is well within its band of fluctuation. The main advantage is that the knowledge that the central bank will intervene for sure as the exchange rate moves towards the margins leads traders to become prudent when this is the case, which has a stabilizing effect – unless they believe that the central bank will not be willing to intervene strongly enough, in which case a speculative attack may occur.

It is understood that central parity may be infrequently changed, a procedure called realignment. The realignment option is useful when dealing with serious disturbances. It is also needed when domestic inflation durably exceeds that of the anchor currency, which erodes external competitiveness.[10] The realignment option provides some monetary policy autonomy, mainly the ability for the inflation rate to differ from that in the anchor currency country.

---

[10] If inflation is higher than abroad, P rises faster than P^* and P/P^* increases. When the nominal exchange rate E is fixed, the real exchange rate EP/P^* appreciates. In order to restore competitiveness and lower the real exchange rate, the country must depreciate the nominal rate, i.e. reduce E.

From 1945 to 1973, under the Bretton Woods agreement, fixed and adjustable exchange rates were the rule worldwide. The margins were initially set at ±1 per cent until 1971, and then widened to ±2.25 per cent. This widening reflected a desire to maintain autonomy over monetary policy as capital movements, strictly limited since the end of the Second World War, were gradually liberalized. Fundamentally, it reflected attempts to avoid the implication of the impossible trinity and the Bretton Woods system collapsed in the midst of currency crisis.

Between 1979 and 1993, Europe's Exchange Rate Mechanism (ERM) also operated as a system of fixed and adjustable exchange rates, a situation studied in the next chapter. Here, we merely note that attempts to retain monetary policy autonomy led to a serious crisis in 1993 and to the end of the ERM as originally designed.

Crawling pegs

In a crawling peg regime the authorities declare a central parity and band of fluctuation around it. The characteristic of this regime is that the central parity and the associated maximum and lower levels are allowed to slide regularly: they crawl. The rate of crawl is sometimes preannounced, sometimes not. The difference between a crawling peg and a target zone is not clear cut, since both involve an acceptable range – margins considered narrow enough to qualify as a pegged arrangement are typically less than ±5 per cent around the official parity. Many Latin American countries operated crawling pegs in the 1980s, as did Poland and Russia in the mid-1990s. These arrangements did not last for very long, however, because they really are attempts to escape the logic of the impossible trinity.

Currency boards

Currency boards are a tight version of fixed exchange rate regimes. Under a pegged regime, monetary policy has to be wholly dedicated to the exchange rate target but, as we saw, the possibility to devalue or revalue and the existence of margins of fluctuation introduce some degree of flexibility. Currency boards are designed to remove this flexibility. In order to ensure that monetary policy is entirely dedicated to supporting the declared parity, with no margin of fluctuation, the central bank may only issue domestic money when it acquires foreign exchange reserves. If it spends its foreign exchange reserves, the central bank must retire its own currency from circulation and the money supply shrinks.[11]

Currency boards used to exist in the British Empire, and disappeared with it. They were revived by a number of Caribbean islands as they became independent and by Hong Kong in 1983. They became more widespread in the 1990s when countries with weak political institutions, such as Argentina, Bosnia-Herzegovina and Bulgaria, chose this rigorous arrangement to put an end to monetary indiscipline and its corollary, raging inflation. Freshly independent from the Soviet Union, with no history of central banking, Estonia and Lithuania also adopted a currency board. Argentina's system collapsed in 2002, illustrating the dangers of an inflexible arrangement.

Dollarization/euroization and currency unions

A yet stricter regime is to fix the exchange rate irrevocably, which means adopting a foreign currency, hence the term 'dollarization' (as in Ecuador, El Salvador, Panama and Liberia) or 'euroization' (as in Kosovo and Montenegro). Without a domestic currency, there obviously can be no monetary policy whatsoever. This regime is typically adopted by small countries with very weak political institutions as they simply rely on a foreign central bank to carry out what is de facto their own monetary policy.

A monetary union is very similar since countries that decide to share the same currency give up national monetary policy. The difference between a currency board and a monetary union is that, in the former, monetary policy is carried out by a foreign central bank, which only cares about its own country, while the common central bank of the latter cares about all member countries. In addition to Europe, francophone Africa and some Caribbean islands have formed monetary unions, as described in Box A13.1.

---

[11] The study of the gold standard in Section 14.1.1 provides the logic of this rule.

Box A13.1   Existing monetary unions

In Africa, the CFA zone was created when the former French colonies gained independence in the 1960s.[1] It includes two unions: the West African Economic and Monetary Union (Benin, Burkina Faso, Côte d'Ivoire, Guinea Bissau, Mali, Niger, Senegal, Togo) and the Central African Economic and Monetary Union (Cameroon, Central African Republic, Chad, Democratic Republic of Congo, Equatorial Guinea, Gabon). These countries never created their own currencies (Mali and Equatorial Guinea did, until they joined the CFA zone in 1985). The two monetary unions are formally independent of each other and each has its own central bank, yet both pegged their currency to the French franc at the same rate, and both devalued just once, by 50 per cent in 1994. They have been pegged to the euro since 1999. The arrangement is special, a legacy of colonial times and based on a guarantee by France, but it is a true, modern monetary union. Belgium and Luxembourg formed a monetary union until they joined the euro area.

The East Caribbean Common Market (Antigua and Barbuda, Dominica, Grenada, St Kitts and Nevis, St Lucia, and St Vincent and the Grenadines) forms a monetary union. These are small islands that can hardly be compared to the European monetary union.

Brunei and Singapore also form a currency union.

Other countries have unilaterally adopted a foreign currency and therefore do not actively participate in the running of the central bank. This is the case of Kiribati, Nauru and Tuvalu, which use the Australian dollar; Lesotho, Namibia and Swaziland, which use the South African rand; and the Bahamas, Liberia, the Marshall Islands, Micronesia, Palau and Panama, which have adopted the US dollar. Since 2001, Ecuador and San Salvador have also adopted the US dollar. In Europe, Monaco uses the French franc (now the euro), Liechtenstein the Swiss franc, and San Marino the Italian lira (now the euro). These are not true monetary unions, since the centre country is not committed to taking into account the interests and viewpoints of its 'satellites', and actually never does.

---

[1] The term CFA comes from the old colonial French designation 'Comptoir Français d'Afrique'. The western Africa CFA means *Communauté financière d'Afrique* (Financial Community of Africa), while the central Africa version means *Coopération financière en Afrique centrale* (Financial Cooperation in Central Africa).

It was the 1992 EMS crisis that provided the immediate impetus for monetary unification.

Barry Eichengreen (2002)

Essential facts of monetary integration

Chapter Contents

Introduction

This chapter presents the main steps in the history of monetary integration in Europe. The aim is to reveal the deep logic that has led to the creation of the euro. As we know all too well, the monetary union is far from perfect – more on that in subsequent chapters – and political considerations have been paramount all along, yet there is also an economic logic behind it. Indeed, the concepts developed in the previous chapter provide a powerful interpretation of the main events.

All the countries that completely eschew capital controls are financially integrated already – the interest rate parity condition applies. This is often referred to as financial globalization and it concerns all the developed countries and, increasingly so, the emerging market countries. Monetary integration goes much further as it seeks to achieve a high degree of cooperation in the area of monetary policy. The interest rate parity condition links interest rates in two countries and their bilateral exchange rate. This shows that there is an intimate relationship between monetary policy – setting the interest rate – and exchange rate policy. In fact, one is just the other side of the coin of the other one. Indeed, the impossible trinity principle states that, when capital is freely mobile, a central bank can choose the interest rate, or the exchange rate, but not both at the same time.

This is why monetary integration can be viewed from the perspective of the exchange rate regime. When two countries want to stabilize their bilateral exchange rate, they have to cooperate in the area of monetary policy. The more exchange rate stability they wish to achieve, the tighter must be cooperation. At the end of the spectrum lies a monetary union, where the bilateral exchange rate has disappeared completely or, equivalently, has been set once and for all. In that case, there can be only monetary policy and, therefore, one central bank. A number of European countries have now reached this end of the road. The trip has been eventful and erratic. Part of the reason is that the concepts presented in Chapter 13 were either unknown or ignored. Going back over the events through the prism of current knowledge is not just fascinating; it also reveals the deep logic behind European monetary integration, as well as the reasons why a number of countries have chosen to pursue that process.

The chapter starts far back in the nineteenth century with a brief review of the Gold Standard. Interest in history is justified by the fact that, in many respects, a monetary union works like the Gold Standard. In both cases sovereign countries share the same currency – gold back then, the euro now – and can no longer use the exchange rate to correct imbalances. The correction was achieved automatically through price adjustments, a feature highly relevant to the Eurozone crisis. This is a warning, rather a reminder, that automaticity may be very painful.

The chapter next looks at the inter-war period, that of the Great Depression, currency crises and the dislocation of international trade as the Gold Standard crumbled. Policy mistakes accumulated during these years, providing a large number of important lessons. These lessons, in fact, have played a crucial role in shaping policy makers' thinking, and they still do. For one thing, the Bretton Woods system was shaped to avoid these past mistakes. From a European viewpoint, this system offered exchange rate stability. Its demise left Europe in need of a replacement. The chapter recounts the history of the 'snake' and its much-improved successor, the European Monetary System (EMS).

The EMS worked well as long as capital controls were pervasive. When these controls were removed, as predicted by the impossible trinity principle developed in Chapter 13, the EMS was no longer the solution to the quest for intra-European exchange rate stability. The logical response was a common currency.

We will see that the rise of capital mobility within Europe has forced a choice between monetary policy autonomy and intra-European exchange stability. There is no obviously better alternative; both have advantages and disadvantages, which is the main theme of Chapter 15. With some notable exceptions (Sweden and the UK, so far), some countries still undecided (the Czech Republic, Hungary and Poland) and others not yet ready (Bulgaria, Croatia and Romania), the other countries have opted for exchange rate stability (Denmark is a special case discussed below). Over several decades, this choice, largely driven by past experience, has triggered a series of moves that made the adoption of a common currency a natural step.

14.1 Back to the future: before paper money

Europe's path to complete monetary integration is spectacular but, in many ways, it is just a return to the situation that prevailed before the introduction of paper money. This section reviews the historical record, partly for its own sake, and partly because some important lessons have been learnt and forgotten.

14.1.1 The world as a monetary union

From time immemorial until the end of the nineteenth century, money was metallic (mainly gold and silver) and a bewildering variety of currencies were circulating side by side. Each currency was defined by its content of precious metal and each local lord endeavoured to control the minting of currency in his fiefdom, chiefly because it was a source of revenue, called seigniorage. Exchange rates existed between these coins – recognizable by the face of the lord – but they merely corresponded to the different contents of precious metal in coins. This was the Gold Standard.

In effect, goods were priced in gold (or silver, but we ignore this detail from now on) weight. Buyers and sellers would then exchange various coins whose gold content added up to the price. In practice, gold was *the* currency and monies were merely the materialization of gold. The 'world' was just one monetary union. While there are vast differences between now and then, chiefly the existence of central banks that can create money, the functioning of this monetary union is of more than historical interest.

This system had a very nice property: it automatically restored a country's external balance. This property, which was lost when we adopted paper money, is known as Hume's price–specie mechanism (see Box 14.1 for a note on Hume). The mechanism is well worth a modern visit because it applies to the internal working of a monetary union. It is presented at some length in the Annex. Briefly stated, the mechanism works as follows. A country whose prices are too high is uncompetitive and runs a trade deficit. This means that importers spend more gold money, which is shipped abroad, than importers receive from abroad in payment for their sales. Overall, therefore, the stock of money declines. Long-run monetary neutrality means that eventually prices will decline. The process must go on automatically until competitiveness is restored and the external deficit has been eliminated. The opposite occurs when prices are too low and the current account is in surplus: inflows of gold eventually lead to higher prices and a correction of the surplus. Thus, even though there is no exchange rate, imbalances cannot last forever. They are self-correcting.

Box 14.1 David Hume (1711–76)

Born in 1711 to a well-to-do family in Berwickshire, Scotland, Hume mostly wrote on philosophy, including the *Principles of Morals* (1751), which founded, among other things, the theory of utility. His works were highly influential even though they were denounced at the time as sceptical and atheistic. His economic thinking, mainly contained in *Political Discourses* (1752), had a large impact on Adam Smith and Thomas Malthus.

Source: Library of Congress Prints and Photographs Division

The automatic return to external balance implies that the 'world monetary union' was inherently stable. The underlying reason is the impossible trinity principle. There was no exchange rate as money was everywhere simply gold, so it was a universal fixed exchange rate regime. There were no capital controls; although moving gold across borders was cumbersome and necessarily slow, it was moving. Monetary policy autonomy could not exist, therefore, and it did not since there was no central bank (and no paper money). Beyond what could be extracted from the ground and rivers, the stock of gold money was entirely determined by the balance of payments and interest rates were adjusting according to market demand and supply.

Great, then? Not so fast, please. Note that prices had to do the balancing work. They were going up and down, as did wages. What was bringing prices and wages down were long periods of recession and rising unemployment. Poverty was rampant and was worse during these periods of adjustment. It is easy to admire the automatic world of gold money and to forget the hardship that it imposed. The invention of paper money is a great achievement but, like any invention, it can be misused.

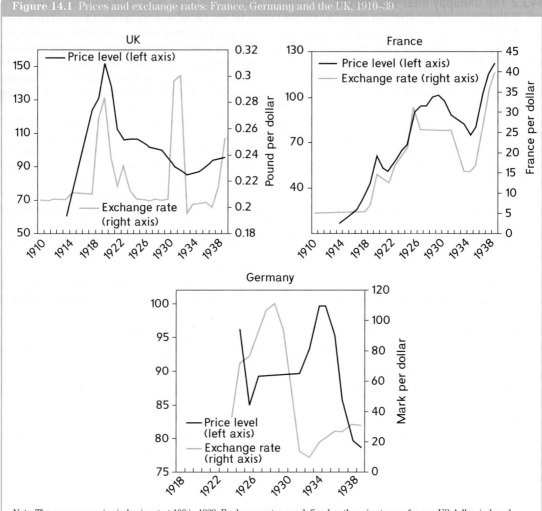

Figure 14.1 Prices and exchange rates: France, Germany and the UK, 1910–39

Note: The consumer price index is set at 100 in 1929. Exchange rates are defined as the price to pay for one US dollar, indexed at 100 in 1929. This means that an increase represents a depreciation, since the dollar becomes more expensive. We choose this presentation because it makes the PPP link between the exchange rate and the price level clearer: a higher price means a depreciation, hence a higher exchange rate as defined here.

Source: Mitchell (1998)

Luxembourg, Italy, the Netherlands, Poland and Switzerland) formed the Gold Bloc, in an attempt to jointly protect their now overvalued currencies. Overvaluation is the channel through which France was finally hit by the Great Depression. Facing speculative attacks, exactly as had the UK ten years earlier, France finally devalued its currency by a whopping 42 per cent.

Germany

In contrast to France and the UK, Germany never considered returning to its pre-war exchange rate. Its domestic public debt was huge, without even taking the massive war reparations imposed in 1919 by the Treaty of Versailles into account. As in France, Germany's post-war inflation was high, but in 1922 it slipped out of control.[3] The result was one of history's most violent hyperinflations. A new Deutschmark – worth

---

[3] This is why pre-hyperinflation prices and exchange rates are not shown in Figure 14.1 – the scale doesn't allow for them!

one million times the old one – was established in 1924 as part of a successful anti-inflation programme. The German economy started to pick up just when it was hit by the Great Depression. Preservation of the restored value of the mark was seen as essential to dispel the ghosts of hyperinflation. Like the franc, the mark became overvalued when more and more countries devalued their own currencies. Germany first suspended its debt and then started to move away from a free trade system. Then capital controls were established. As the depression deepened, the Nazis combined public spending with wage and price increases. This further dented external competitiveness and deepened the trade deficit. The response was to stop the conversion of marks into gold and foreign currencies – an extreme form of capital control – and to impose ever-widening state controls on imports and exports. Germany bypassed completely the foreign exchange market by working out bilateral barter agreements with one country after another.

Lessons

With free capital mobility re-established, once they had restored the Gold Exchange Standard – i.e. when they set a fixed gold value for their paper monies – France and the UK had to forego autonomy over their monetary policies. In the depths of the Great Depression, however, the urge to use monetary policy became too strong. The impossible trinity principle was violated and the result was the end of the fixed exchange rate system. Germany respected the impossible trinity principle, in an extreme way, by severing all market-based relationships with the rest of the world.

Once the Gold Exchange Standard collapsed, exchange rates were left to float, a fairly novel experience. Faced with a deep recession, each country – except Germany – sought to boost its exports by letting its exchange rate depreciate and become undervalued. But one country's undervaluation is another country's overvaluation, hurting foreign exports. The ensuing round of tit-for-tat depreciations, which came to be called beggar-thy-neighbour policies, led nowhere but began to disrupt trade. Protectionist measures soon followed and trade exchanges went into a tailspin, aggravating the depression. The result was political instability, leading to war.

This traumatic period left a deep imprint within Europe, shaping post-war thinking among policy makers who started to realize the complexity of paper money. Among the many lessons learnt, two are relevant for the monetary integration process:

- Floating exchange rates can be manipulated. The resulting misalignments breed trade barriers and eventually undermine prosperity. Most European countries developed a fear of floating, which remains a key concern today.
- The management of exchange rate parities cannot be left to each country's discretion. We need an international order that deals with the fact that one country's depreciation is another country's appreciation. In other words, we need a 'system'.

14.2 Bretton Woods as an antidote to the inter-war debacle

Even before the end of the Second World War, the USA and the UK started to plan the Bretton Woods conference. The aim was to establish an international monetary system based on paper currencies. Gold remained the ultimate source of value, but the dollar became the anchor of the system, and the US government guaranteed its value in terms of gold. All other currencies were defined in terms of the dollar. Exchange rates were 'fixed but adjustable' to avoid both unreasonable adherence to an outdated parity (over- or undervaluation) and an inter-war-type free-for-all. The system was a collective undertaking, with the International Monetary Fund (IMF) both supervising compliance and providing emergency assistance. As supplier of the system's central currency and host of the IMF in Washington, the USA was the ultimate economic and political guarantor of the system. Capital controls were not outlawed and most countries made abundant use of them. This was compatible with the impossible trinity.

The system unravelled when capital controls started to be lifted in the 1960s. The impossible trinity principle required that exchange rates be freed – including the link between the dollar and gold – or that the authorities give up monetary policy autonomy. Most governments – Canada being a rare exception as it chose to let its currency float in violation of the Bretton Woods agreements – refused to make such a choice.

With widespread capital controls in place, most countries actively used monetary policy to prop up growth. The monetary neutrality principle was not yet well established so there was no concern regarding inflation. By the late 1960s, however, inflation started to rise in a number of countries, including the USA. The anchor of the system, the US dollar, gradually became overvalued. The Bretton Woods system came under strain when the USA could no longer guarantee the dollar's gold value because the stock of dollars exceeded the value of its gold reserves. The demise of the system occurred in two steps. First, in 1971, the USA 'suspended' the dollar's convertibility into gold. Then, in 1973, the 'fixed but adjustable' principle was officially abandoned; each country would now be free to choose its exchange rate regime and could retain monetary policy autonomy if it accepted a flexible exchange regime. This effectively ended the Bretton Woods era.

14.3 After Bretton Woods: Europe's snake in the tunnel

In the 1970s, the European countries were focused on developing the Common Market. With fresh memories of the interwar period, they wanted fairly fixed exchange rates and reassurances that competitive devaluations would be held in check. The Bretton Woods system had provided the solution: exchange rates were fixed and the IMF exerted surveillance on all member countries. Once the system fell apart, Europe found itself without a solution. Its early reaction charted the path for the monetary union that was created three decades later.

The first response was the 'European snake', a regional stepped-down version of the Bretton Woods system designed to limit intra-European exchange rate fluctuations by pegging European currencies to the dollar. Under the protection of capital controls, monetary policy was available. Still ignorant of the link between money growth and inflation, many countries used their central banks to expand credit in order to sustain rapid economic growth. The monetary neutrality principle predicts that, with the money stock growing at a sustained rate, inflation should creep up gradually, which is exactly what happened. Germany and Switzerland, which had forfeited capital controls, used monetary policy sparingly and kept inflation in check. Real exchange rates started to move away from their equilibrium levels.[4] PPP implies that this situation cannot last for long. External deficits deepened in those countries experiencing inflation and surpluses emerged in Germany and Switzerland. In the late 1960s, France and the UK, two high-inflation currencies, devalued their currencies. The realization that exchange rates were as adjustable as they were fixed, triggered speculation and more countries devalued. Soon European nominal exchange rates became unhooked, as Figure 14.2 shows. PPP was asserting itself.

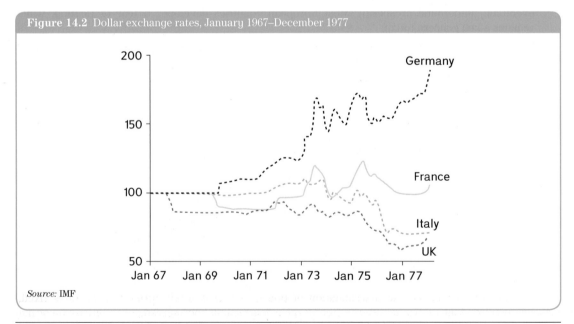

Figure 14.2 Dollar exchange rates, January 1967–December 1977

Source: IMF

---

[4] With fixed nominal exchange rates E, higher increases in the domestic price level led to real appreciation as EP/P^* rose. Low inflation countries, on the other hand, underwent real depreciations as EP/P^* declined.

As explained in Box 14.3 below, the snake was a loose arrangement. It did not deal with the impossible trinity principle: capital controls were often in place but they were not tight and could increasingly be evaded, while there was no restriction on national monetary policies. When inflation rose abruptly in the wake of the first oil shock of 1973–74, the central banks reacted differently. Some (Germany, the Netherlands, Belgium) succeeded at keeping inflation in check, whereas others (e.g. Italy and the UK) did not. Maintaining exchange rate fixity with divergent monetary policies was hopeless and, indeed, several countries had to leave the snake arrangement.

Box 14.3   The snake in the tunnel

In 1971, in a last-ditch effort to save the Bretton Woods system, it was decided to widen the margin of fluctuations vis-à-vis the dollar from ±1 per cent to ±2.25 per cent. Non-dollar currencies, like the mark and the franc, would now fluctuate by as much as 9 per cent vis-à-vis each other, as is shown in the upper part of Figure 14.3. Under the Bretton Woods system, the exchange rates of the franc and the mark were determined in terms of dollars. Consider the case, represented by both points A, where these currencies are at their opposite extremes vis-à-vis the dollar; the mark is 2.25 per cent above the dollar and the franc 2.25 per cent below it. As a result, the mark is 4.5 per cent above the franc. At the opposite extremes (points B), the mark is 4.5 per cent below the franc, with a total amplitude of 9 per cent. A number of European countries (the EC members as well as Denmark, Ireland, Norway, the UK and Sweden) felt that this was too wide a margin and decided to maintain their bilateral rates within a common ±2.25 per cent band of fluctuation. This was called the 'snake in the tunnel' – a colourful representation of their joint movements vis-à-vis the dollar, as shown in the lower part of the figure. Once the Bretton Woods system ended, the tunnel was gone but the EC countries resolved to keep the snake, i.e. to limit the range of variation of their bilateral exchange rates to a maximum of 4.5 per cent. The snake crawled out of the vanishing tunnel and, in doing so, led directly to the EMS.

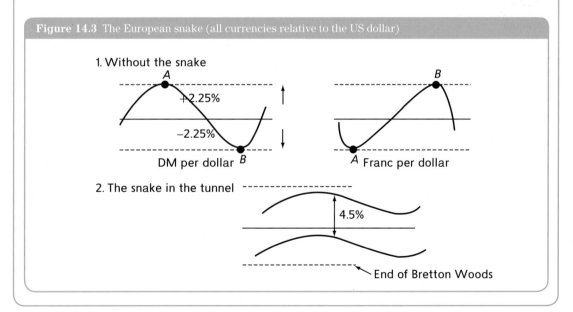

Figure 14.3 The European snake (all currencies relative to the US dollar)

The snake had embodied the determination of policy makers to keep intra-European rates fixed, irrespective of what happened elsewhere in the world. It was meant to be 'an island of stability in an ocean of instability'. It failed because it did not recognize that increasing freedom of capital movements was incompatible with monetary policy autonomy. That lesson was not yet taken on board but another lesson shaped the next step, the creation of the European Monetary System (EMS). It was slowly being recognized that paper money does not need any backing. The Gold Exchange Standard and the Bretton Woods system still retained a link to gold. The snake had given up on gold but replaced it with the dollar. Europe now realized that it did not need the dollar either, much as the dollar was not linked to any superior anchor since 1971. From there on in, the European currencies would be defined vis-à-vis each other.

14.4 The european monetary system

The decision to create the system was taken in 1978 by German Chancellor Helmut Schmidt and French President Valéry Giscard d'Estaing. The heart of the EMS is the Exchange Rate Mechanism (ERM), a system of jointly managed fixed and adjustable exchange rates backed by mutual support. Open to all EU countries, the ERM has seen its membership grow and then decline (see Table 14.1) as countries give up their national currencies for the euro. Several more recent EU member countries have followed this pattern, leaving the mechanism with just one member, Denmark.

Table 14.1 ERM membership

Older EU members	Joined	Left	Recent EU members	Joined	Left
Austria	1995	1999	Bulgaria		
Belgium/Luxembourg	1979	1999	Cyprus	2005	2008
Denmark	1979	Still a member	Czech Rep.		
Finland	1996	1999	Estonia	2004	2011
France	1979	1999	Hungary		
Germany	1979	1999	Latvia	2005	2014
Greece	1998	2001	Lithuania	2004	2015
Ireland	1979	1999	Malta	2005	2008
Italy	1979, 1996	1992, 1999	Poland		
Netherlands	1979	1999	Romania		
Portugal	1992	1999	Slovakia	2005	2009
Spain	1989	1999	Slovenia	2004	2007
Sweden					
UK	1990	1992			

Note: Italy, Portugal and Spain initially operated a wider (±6 per cent) band of fluctuation around the central parity than the normal (±2.25 per cent) band. In 1993, the band was widened to ±15 per cent, but Denmark has retained the narrow (±2.25 per cent) band. All other current members of the ERM operate the wide (±15 per cent) band, except for Latvia (±1 per cent). Luxembourg used the Belgian franc until the euro was created.

Political sensitivities were important in shaping the design of the ERM. Germany would never take the risk of weakening its star currency, the Deutschmark, while France could not be seen to be playing second fiddle to Germany. Additionally, the smaller countries had to be brought along, while the UK was staunchly opposed to any fixed exchange rate regime. The squaring of the circle took the form of an explicitly symmetric arrangement, without any currency at its centre, and it established a subtle distinction between the European Monetary System, of which all European Community countries were de facto members, and the Exchange Rate Mechanism, an optional but operational scheme.

14.4.1 Fixed and adjustable exchange rates

The ERM involves four main elements: a grid of agreed-upon bilateral exchange rates, mutual support, possibility of realignments but subject to unanimity agreement, and the European Currency Unit (ECU).

All ERM currencies were fixed to each other, with a band of fluctuation of ±2.25 per cent around the central parity (Italy was initially allowed a margin of fluctuation of ±6 per cent, in recognition of its higher rate of inflation and internal political difficulties). The resulting bilateral rates formed the grid. The responsibility for maintaining each bilateral exchange rate was explicitly to be shared by both the strong- and the weak-currency countries, thus removing the stigma of one weak and one strong currency. This symmetry ended with the advent of the euro; the common currency has now become the reference for ERM members – the grid has disappeared – and the responsibility to uphold the declared parity belongs to the ERM not the ECB.

Defence of any bilateral parity required central banks to intervene in the foreign exchange markets, buying the weak currency and selling the strong one. Crucially, this commitment was *unlimited*. If the weak-currency central bank had exhausted its reserves, it could borrow those of the strong-currency central bank. Other ERM central banks, even if they were not directly involved, could decide to give a helping hand, by also intervening in the foreign exchange markets.

How long should interventions be pursued? Clearly, if markets remained unimpressed by the artillery lined up against them, there remained the possibility of depreciating the weak currency, appreciating the strong currency, or both. Realignments, as these actions were called, had to be agreed by all ERM members because all parities were defined bilaterally. The consensus rule implied that, in effect, each country gave up exclusive control of its own exchange rate. The history of realignments is shown in Table 14.2.

Table 14.2   ERM realignments

Dates	24.9.79	30.11.79	22.3.81	5.10.81	22.2.82	14.6.82
No. of currencies involved	2	1	1	2	2	4
Dates	21.3.83	18.5.83	22.7.85	7.4.86	4.8.86	12.1.87
No. of currencies involved	7[a]	7[a]	7[a]	5	1	3
Dates	8.1.90	14.9.92	23.11.92	1.2.93	14.5.93	6.3.95
No. of currencies involved	1	3[b]	2	1	2	2

[a] All ERM currencies realigned;
[b] in addition, two currencies (sterling and lira) leave the ERM.

14.4.2 From divergence to convergence and blow-up

Between 1979 and 1987, realignments occurred no fewer than 12 times, once every 8 months on average. Most of them occurred in the midst of serious market turmoil. The reason is that, in violation of the impossible trinity principle, most countries sought to retain monetary policy autonomy. Until the mid-1980s, capital controls were in place in most countries, so policy autonomy was possible. The result was different inflation rates, as indicated in Figure 14.4. As a result, realignments were frequently needed to re-establish competitiveness, an implication of the PPP principle presented in Chapter 13. For this reason, they were

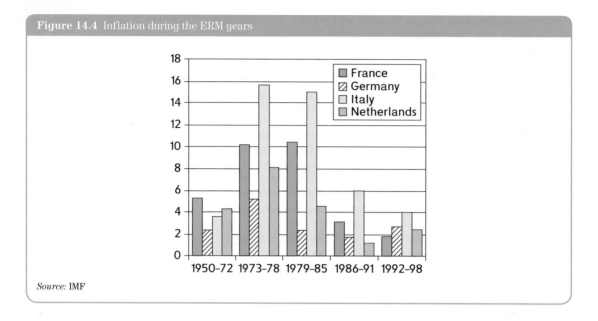

Figure 14.4 Inflation during the ERM years

Source: IMF

easily guessed ahead of time and investors rushed to sell off the currencies up for devaluation, which resulted in speculative crises that often forced the hands of the national authorities.

As capital controls were lifted, realignments became increasingly destabilizing. This pushed high-inflation and depreciation-prone countries to seek to bring down inflation to the lowest rate. The monetary policy of Germany, the perennial low-inflation country, became the ERM standard. The other countries de facto surrendered monetary policy autonomy. The impossible trinity principle was finally accepted.

With all central banks emulating the Bundesbank, inflation rates started to converge. For nearly 6 years, from early 1987 to September 1992, there was no realignment.[5] The link became tighter as capital controls were formally banned as of 1990. The Deutschmark served as anchor, leaving its central bank, the Bundesbank, with full monetary policy autonomy. A system designed to be symmetric, in violation of the impossible trinity principle, had become perfectly asymmetric.

This unplanned evolution had two momentous implications. First, the other countries resented the Bundesbank leadership. The next step in the reasoning was: if we have to give up national monetary policy autonomy, we should share it collectively, not delegate it to one national central bank. Of course, Germany was unwilling to relinquish its lock on ERM monetary policies but, in the end, accepted a political deal in 1991: the monetary union in exchange for its own reunification with the former East Germany. This is when the second event occurred and nearly destroyed the ERM, in 1992–93.

14.4.3 The crisis of 1992–93

The absence of any realignment for about 6 years looked good,[6] but inflation rates never fully converged (see Figure 14.4) because monetary neutrality sets in very slowly. While countries such as Denmark and

---

[5] The 1990 realignment (Table 14.2) was not really a realignment. It was merely a technical adjustment prompted by Italy's decision to switch to the narrow ±2.25 per cent band of fluctuation, a consequence of the 'strong lira' policy. Parity was brought closer (from 6 per cent to 2.25 per cent) to its weak margin.

[6] The Governor of the Banque de France at that time, Jean-Claude Trichet, famously defined his objective as 'competitive disinflation', a reference to the infamous competitive devaluations of the inter-war period.

France indeed moved towards the German inflation rate, others, such as Italy, Portugal and Spain, failed to get close enough because they had started from too far afield. Their real exchange rates kept appreciating, which resulted in a dangerous loss of competitiveness. Any spark could trigger speculative attacks. In short succession, three sparks were ignited.

The first spark came from Germany. Unification represented an inflationary risk. The Bundesbank responded by sharply raising its interest rate. Facing a global economic slowdown, several overconfident European central banks decided not to follow the Bundesbank and to recover some autonomy. The result of this violation of the impossible trinity principle was bound to trigger speculative attacks on the countries that had lost competitiveness.

The second spark came from Denmark. The Maastricht Treaty – the creation of a single currency – had been signed in December 1991 and was to be ratified by each Member State. The first country to initiate the ratification process was Denmark, where law mandates that international treaties be submitted to referenda. For a variety of reasons, some quite obscure,[7] the Danes voted down the Treaty. This created considerable confusion. Box 14.4 provides the details.

The third spark came from France, which also organized a ratification referendum. Negative polls alarmed the exchange markets. Speculative attacks started immediately, initially targeting Italy (the lira was seriously overvalued by then) and the UK, which had finally joined the ERM a year earlier but at an overvalued exchange rate.[8]

In response to the speculative attacks, as mandated by the ERM agreements, the strong-currency central banks initially intervened in support of the embattled Banca d'Italia and Bank of England. By mid-September 1992, the attacks had become so huge that a frightened Bundesbank decided that truly unlimited interventions were not reasonable and stopped its support. Left to themselves, the lira and the pound withdrew from the ERM. The markets concluded that the ERM was considerably more fragile than hitherto admitted. Speculation shifted to the currencies of Ireland, Portugal and Spain. Each of them had to be devalued, twice. Contagion then spread to Belgium, Denmark and France, even though inflation in these countries had converged to below the German level and their currencies were not overvalued.

By the summer of 1993, huge amounts of reserves had been thrown into the battle and, yet, speculation was still going strong. In order to uphold the principle of the ERM, the monetary authorities adopted new ultra-large (±15 per cent) bands of fluctuation.[9] Figure 14.5 shows the ERM history of the French franc/ German mark exchange rate as it moved throughout six realignments within the fluctuation band. The tight ERM was dead.

14.4.4 The EMS re-engineered

The post-crisis ERM agreed upon in 1993 differed little from a floating exchange rate regime. Bilateral parities could move by 30 per cent, a very wide margin. Unsurprisingly, therefore, the (non)system worked well because it left enough room for some degree of monetary policy autonomy. Figure 14.5 shows that the franc/mark fluctuated slightly outside of its earlier narrow ±2.25 per cent range for a few years and then gently converged to its ultimate EMU conversion rate.

One precondition set by the Maastricht Treaty for joining the monetary union is at least 2 years of ERM membership (the other conditions are presented in Chapter 16). This means that the ERM is still in use as a temporary gateway to the Eurozone. Currently, its only member is Denmark, which has a non-official ±1 per cent band. Figure 13.13 shows that it has given up monetary policy autonomy, so the arrangement is stable.

---

[7] The No camp warned that a monetary union would encourage Germans to buy Danish properties along the common border.

[8] The UK had joined the ERM a few months before, soon after John Major replaced Margaret Thatcher as Prime Minister, largely because her opposition to ERM membership appeared anachronistic in the midst of a wave of Euro-optimism.

[9] Germany and the Netherlands independently agreed to keep their bilateral parity within the old ±2.25 per cent margins. Belgium decided on its own to follow the same rule. In effect, these countries had given up monetary policy autonomy.

Figure 14.5 The French franc/German mark exchange rate in the ERM

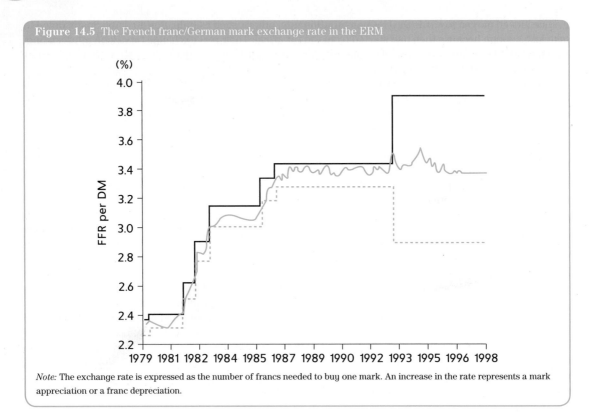

Note: The exchange rate is expressed as the number of francs needed to buy one mark. An increase in the rate represents a mark appreciation or a franc depreciation.

14.4.5 Assessment and lessons

The EMS represents an important step in the European monetary integration process. For the first time, European currencies defined their interrelationship without reference to an external store of value, like gold or the US dollar. It involved deep and comprehensive agreements among sovereign states that remain unmatched elsewhere in the world, with the exception of existing monetary unions. Its unplanned evolution into a de facto Greater Deutschmark Area made the adoption of a common currency a natural next step.

The tools developed in Chapter 13 provide the keys to understanding the ups and downs of the long road to monetary integration. The impossible trinity principle implies that a commitment to exchange rate stability requires the loss of monetary policy autonomy once capital is allowed to float freely. PPP, in turn, explains that lasting inflation differences are unsustainable if the exchange rate is fixed. This too pleads for a close alignment of monetary policies. Once autonomy is given up, the difference between a fixed exchange rate regime and a monetary union is mostly symbolic. Monetary neutrality means that, over the long run, monetary policy autonomy does not matter for economic growth or unemployment; put differently, there are no long-run costs of giving up a currency. However, monetary policy does matter in the short run and the costs can be significant. In the face of serious disturbances, the decision to bypass monetary policy can be painful. The Eurozone crisis has made that fact plain to see (Chapter 19), but it was clear much earlier, at least since the EMS crisis of 1993 as explained above.

Not all European countries have put exchange rate stability at the top of their priorities. The Czech Republic, Poland, Sweden and the UK have chosen monetary policy autonomy and correctly concluded that this precluded fixing the exchange rate or joining the Eurozone. (The UK briefly joined the EMS but withdrew soon thereafter; see above.) Figure 14.6 shows that, following the creation of the euro in 1999, the Czech Republic and Sweden did not make much use of their policy autonomy until 2010, when the Eurozone crisis erupted. The UK, on the other hand, did carry out a different monetary policy.

Figure 14.6 Interest rates

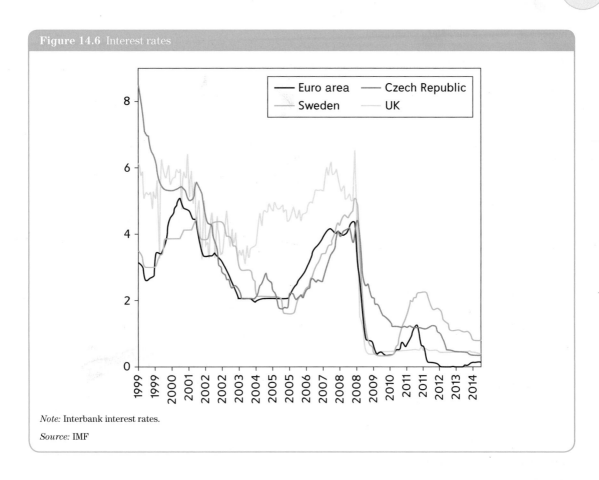

Note: Interbank interest rates.

Source: IMF

14.5 The maastricht treaty

Maastricht – unpronounceable by non-Dutch natives – is a picturesque Dutch town. In December 1991, the 12 heads of state and government of the EU gathered there to sign a treaty that replaced the European Community (EC) with the European Union (EU). The change of name was meant to signal that the Treaty was not just about economics but also included political considerations. Two new pillars – foreign and defence policies, justice and internal security – were added to the first, economic, pillar. Yet, the Maastricht Treaty will remain mostly known for having established the monetary union.

A monetary union was already in the back of the minds of the signatories of the Treaty of Rome in 1957. Chapter 1 describes the first attempt that failed, the Werner Report. The second attempt, the 1989 Delors Report, was successful. The report, commissioned by the European Council, was formally adopted in July 1989. Two intergovernmental conferences followed and their conclusions were presented to the Council meeting held in Maastricht at the end of 1991. Even though the debt crisis that started in 2010 casts a shadow on this achievement – and could lead to the demise of the euro as we know it – the Treaty marks the end of a long road: three decades of attempts to achieve a monetary union, summarized in Table 14.3. Maybe as a bad omen, the Treaty ratification process turned out to be eventful, as recalled in Box 14.4.

The Treaty described in great detail how the system would work, including the statutes of the European Central Bank (ECB). The Treaty specified entry conditions, also described in Chapter 16. These conditions – called the convergence criteria – were established mostly at the request of Germany. Germany, which considered the strong Deutschmark an essential achievement and a key economic success factor, was not willing to swap it for a weaker currency. Against much German public opinion, Chancellor Helmut Kohl was convinced of the paramount importance of European integration and was ready to abandon the mark. In return, he requested

Table 14.3   Steps of monetary integration

Towards Maastricht		Between Maastricht and the single currency		After Maastricht	
1970	Werner Plan	1994	European Monetary Institute (precursor of ECB)	1999	Monetary union starts
1979	European Monetary System starts	1997	Stability and Growth Pact	2001	Greece joins
1989	Delors Committee	1998	Decision on membership	2002	Euro coins and notes introduced
1991	Maastricht Treaty signed	1998	Conversion rates set	2007	Slovenia joins
1993	Maastricht Treaty ratified	1998	Creation of ECB	2008	Cyprus and Malta join
		2014	Banking Union	2009	Slovakia joins
				2011	Estonia joins
				2014	Latvia joins
				2015	Lithuania joins

Box 14.4   The bumpy ratification of the Maastricht Treaty

Any international treaty must be ratified by the signatories. The ratification procedure varies from one country to another: some countries require a referendum, others must obtain parliament's approval, yet others can decide between these two alternatives. The first country to undertake ratification of the Maastricht Treaty was Denmark, and it had to be by referendum. The Danish people chose to reject the Treaty by a small margin. Since European treaties are all-or-nothing, the Treaty looked dead before the other countries even had a chance to consider it. Yet, hoping that a legal solution would be found, it was decided to continue with the ratification process.

France offered to be the second country to consider ratification. In the hope of re-launching the project after the Danish vote, President Mitterrand chose the referendum procedure – he could have followed the more modest parliamentary approval procedure. As the campaign went on, support gradually eroded. When some polls reported a majority against the Treaty, leading to fears of a collapse of the whole project, the exchange markets became jittery and speculation gained momentum. In the event, Italy and the UK were ejected from the ERM and several currencies had to be devalued, some of them many times, as described above. Meanwhile, the French approved the Treaty by a narrow margin.

The Danes were asked to return to the polls, after the Danish government was given the right, included in a special protocol, not to adopt the single currency. This time, the Danes approved the Treaty. Just when the road seemed clear, the German Constitutional Court was asked for an opinion on whether the Treaty was compatible with Germany's constitution. The Court took several months to deliver its opinion, keeping the process hanging. The Court finally decided that the Treaty did not contradict the German Constitution. This allowed Germany to ratify the Treaty in late 1993, the last country to do so.

tough entry conditions.[10] Germany would rather start the monetary union with a small number of like-minded countries than bring on board more countries several of which, in its eyes, had not adopted its culture of price stability. Greece, Italy, Spain and Portugal were not on the list of welcomed members. Neither was France, but Chancellor Kohl decided that politically France could not be kept out. It is striking that these are precisely the countries that ended up being caught in the public debt crisis that started in 2009.

The convergence criteria were designed with this objective in mind. Fulfilment of these criteria was to be evaluated by late 1997, a full year before the euro would replace the national currencies. In the end, partly through window-dressing and creative accounting, all the countries that wanted to adopt the euro qualified, with the exception of Greece, which had to wait for another 2 years.

On 4 January 1999, the exchange rates of 11 countries[11] were 'irrevocably' frozen. The old currencies formally became (odd) fractions of the euro, and the power to conduct monetary policy was transferred from each member country to the European System of Central Banks (ESCB), under the aegis of the European Central Bank (ECB) headquartered in Frankfurt. Ordinary citizens had to wait another 3 years, until January 2002, to see and touch euro banknotes and coins. Since then, 8 more countries (see Table 14.3) have joined the Eurozone, which includes 19 members as of January 2015. Nine European Union members have either decided not to join[12] or do not fulfil the convergence criteria.[13]

14.6 The crisis ⇐

In 2010, a severe crisis initially affected Greece and then moved on to Ireland, Portugal, Spain, Italy and Cyprus. It has profoundly transformed the monetary union, leading to a number of innovations while simultaneously revealing several flaws in the Maastricht Treaty. The first innovation was the creation of a Troika to rescue these countries. Composed of the IMF, the European Commission and the ECB, the Troika set conditions in exchange for large-scale emergency funds. The second innovation was an agreement to reduce the Greek public debt, well into the second year of the crisis. This debt reduction severely hurt Cypriot banks, which found themselves also forced to call in the Troika. In the meantime, pressure on Italy and Spain mounted, but no rescue was needed. This led to the third innovation, a new treaty designed to tighten oversight of national budgets. The ECB then called for a banking union, the fourth innovation. After a long delay, the ECB used its potentially infinite resources to quiet down the panic that had gripped the financial markets. This represents the fifth major innovation and could be the definitive step to grant, temporarily at least, some respite in the face of the raging crisis. Chapter 19 is dedicated to the study of these momentous events.

14.7 Summary

The process of monetary integration that led to the creation of the monetary union has taken decades and was not free of economic crises and political tensions. It is not complete either, as a significant number of countries have not adopted the euro, several of which have no intention of doing so, at least in the near future.

A couple of centuries ago, monetary integration was complete, and not merely in Europe, by default. A monetary union existed as all countries shared the same money – gold. There was no central bank and no monetary policy. The discovery of paper money changed all that. As is often the case with major discoveries, initially paper money was poorly understood. The Gold Exchange Standard experienced a painful dislocation in the inter-war period. The Bretton Woods system, created in 1944, offered what many European countries wanted: a degree of exchange rate stability. There followed various attempts to fix intra-European exchange rates without always paying due respect to the basic principles developed in the previous chapter. The logic of these principles eventually prevailed and led to the adoption of a common currency, with a common central bank, by countries attached to exchange rate stability.

---

[10] Germany also insisted on a strong statute of independence for the European Central Bank. This issue is examined in detail in Chapter 16.

[11] Austria, Belgium, Finland, France, Germany, Ireland, Italy, Luxembourg, the Netherlands, Portugal and Spain.

[12] The Czech Republic, Denmark, Hungary, Poland, Sweden and the UK.

[13] Bulgaria, Croatia and Romania.

The great advantage of the Gold Standard lies in the automatic elimination of imbalances, Hume's price–specie mechanism. Countries with balance of payment surpluses see their money supply increase, which eliminates the surplus first through lower interest rates and capital outflows and then through rising prices that undermine external competitiveness. The same mechanism is at work in the monetary union. But it can be painful, as was the case with gold money and now again in the crisis-hit countries of the Eurozone.

The EMS was adopted in 1979 in an effort to preserve exchange rate stability within Europe following the end of the Bretton Woods system. Initially created to shield Europe from international monetary disturbances, all EU members are members of the EMS. The active part of the system, the ERM, is however optional, in the sense that some countries (Denmark and the UK) have a derogation while the Czech Republic, Hungary, Poland and Sweden have made it clear that they have no interest in joining an arrangement that is now a prerequisite for Eurozone membership.

The initial ERM was based on a grid specifying all bilateral parities and the corresponding margins of fluctuation, normally ±2.25 per cent. ERM members were committed to jointly defending their bilateral parities, if necessary through unlimited interventions and loans. Realignments were possible, but required the consent of all members. This amounted to a tight and elaborate arrangement. Over time, as capital controls were removed, the nature of the ERM changed. At first it was unstable because countries were reluctant to give up on monetary policy autonomy. When they finally bowed to the rigour of the impossible trinity principle, they adopted the Deutschmark as an anchor. Circumstances created a further relapse, which led to the 1992–93 crisis, which effectively brought the arrangement to an end. Two currencies, the Italian lira and the British pound, left the ERM and the others adopted very wide margins of fluctuation, which pretty much made the mechanism irrelevant. By then, the Maastricht Treaty had been adopted, so the ERM had only to nominally survive until the launch of the euro.

The adoption of the common currency led to a new EMS. The euro is now the reference currency and the responsibility to uphold declared parities rests only on individual countries. The ERM is just one of the requirements for joining the Eurozone. As a result, countries join and then leave the ERM as they become candidates for Eurozone membership. Denmark is the only 'permanent' ERM member.

The Maastricht Treaty, signed in 1991 and ratified over the following 2 years, established the monetary union, to start on 1 January 1999. It included entry conditions designed to keep out those countries that were not wed to price stability. In the end, all candidate countries bar one were found to satisfy these conditions. Greece was admitted 2 years later. Cyprus, Estonia, Malta, Latvia, Lithuania, Slovakia and Slovenia have joined subsequently. The euro is now the currency of 19 countries.

Self-assessment questions

1 During the inter-war era, misalignments led to competitive devaluations, which then prompted a tariff war. Explain why.
2 What differences do you see between the Gold Exchange Standard and a monetary union?
3 What is the difference between the EMS and the ERM?
4 How does EMS-2 differ from EMS-1?
5 What are margins of fluctuation? What role do they play?
6 Why was it easy to foresee realignments with the ERM? How could speculators take advantage of that?
7 What do we mean when we say that the EMS-1 had become a 'Deutschmark area'? How did that happen and could it have been foreseen?
8 What did countries gain and lose by transferring from the ERM to monetary union?
9 The non-Eurozone EU member countries currently allow their exchange rates to float (relatively) freely. Denmark is a member of the ERM. Is this in line with the impossible trinity principle?
10 The Danish people have rejected by referendum joining the Eurozone. So Denmark has been a member of the ERM-2 since it was created in 1999, and the krone has almost never moved by more than 1 per cent vis-à-vis the euro. What difference would Eurozone membership make?

Essay questions

1 In retrospect it is claimed that the 1992–93 EMS crisis could have been anticipated. Why/why not? Once the crisis started, could Italy and the UK have stayed in the system, and if so under what conditions?

2 Would the Bretton Woods system have survived had it been constructed more tightly, for example like the ERM?

3 Some suggest a return to the Gold Exchange Standard. Discuss, using the tools developed in Chapter 13.

4 The inter-war decline of Britain is sometimes imputed to the 1924 return to the Gold Standard at the overvalued pre-war parity. Explain how and why lasting overvaluations hurt.

5 Proposals to return the world to the Gold Standard are regularly put forward. Evaluate the pros and cons of this idea.

6 'The creation of the European snake was a sign of US decline in monetary matters.' Comment.

7 Why did the ERM succeed while the snake failed?

8 Britain and Sweden have decided not to adopt the euro. Discuss the economic implications.

9 Some countries are attached to intra-Europe exchange rate stability, others are not. Comment.

10 Imagine a break-up of the euro. What is likely to happen to the exchange rate regimes of the ex-member countries?

Further reading: the aficionado's corner

On the Gold Standard:

Bordo, M. (1999) *The Gold Standard and Related Regimes*, Cambridge University Press, Cambridge. This book offers a comprehensive and modern analysis of the Gold Standard and its relevance to today's discussions.

On early efforts at monetary unification:

Bergman, M., S. Gerlach and L. Jonung (1993) 'The rise and fall of the Scandinavian currency union 1873–1920', *European Economic Review*, 37: 507–17.

Bordo, M. and L. Jonung (2000) *Lessons for EMU from the History of Monetary Unions*, Institute of Economic Affairs, London.

Holtfrerich, C.L. (1993) 'Did monetary unification precede or follow political unification of Germany in the 19th century?', *European Economic Review*, 37: 518–24.

On the evolution of the monetary union in Europe:

Eichengreen, B. (2007) 'Sui Generis Euro'. Download from www.econ.berkeley.edu/~eichengr/sui_generis_EMU.pdf.

Kenen, P.B. (1995) *Economic and Monetary Union in Europe*, Cambridge University Press, Cambridge.

Padoa-Schioppa, T. (2000) *The Road to Monetary Union in Europe: The Emperor, the Kings, and the Genies*, Oxford University Press, Oxford.

On exchange rate regime choices:

Bordo, M. (2003) *Exchange Rate Regime Choice in Historical Perspective*, Working paper no. 03/160, IMF.

Frankel, J. (1999) 'No single currency regime is right for all currencies or at all times', *Essays in International Finance*, International Finance Section, Princeton University.

Two studies show the difference between the officially declared regime and what countries actually do:

Levy-Yeyati, E. and F. Sturzenegger (2005) 'Classifying exchange rate regimes: deeds vs. words', *European Economic Review*, 49(6): 1603–35.

Reinhart, C. and K. Rogoff (2002) 'The modern history of exchange rate arrangements: a reinterpretation', *Quarterly Journal of Economics*, 119(1): 1–48.

A very useful description of the EMS is given in Chapter 1 of:

Kenen, P. (1995) *Economic and Monetary Union in Europe*, Cambridge University Press, New York.

Useful websites

The European Commission publishes annual Convergence Reports that evaluate each country's position relative to the EU: http://ec.europa.eu/economy_finance/publications/european_economy/convergence_reports_en.htm.

The Exchange Rate Mechanism is described on the European Commission's site at http://ec.europa.eu/economy_finance/euro/adoption/erm2/index_en.htm.

References

Eichengreen, B. (2002) *Lessons of the Euro for the Rest of the World*, December. Download from http://repositories.cdlib.org/cgi/viewcontent.cgi?article=1005&context=ies.

Mitchell, B.R. (1998) *International Historical Statistics: Europe 1750–1993*, Macmillan, London.

Annex: Hume's mechanism

Hume's mechanism is based on several results from Chapter 13: the long-run neutrality of money and PPP, and the short-run effect of money on interest rates. The neutrality principle is represented in panel (a) of Figure A14.1 by the upward-sloping schedule, which describes the proportionality between the money stock M and the price level P. In the same panel, we add a horizontal line meant to capture long-run PPP. When all prices are defined in terms of gold, the exchange rate is fixed and simply equal to unity ($E = 1$, as one gram of gold is one gram of gold everywhere!). Imagine that the price of domestic goods P rises while the price P^* of foreign goods remains unchanged. The domestic economy becomes less competitive and must eventually run a current account deficit.[14] The horizontal line corresponds to the price level P at which exports equal imports and the current account is in equilibrium. Above this line, the current account is in deficit, and it is in surplus below the line. Point E represents the external equilibrium where the money stock M is consistent with the price level P.[15]

Where is the gold money stock coming from? Some of it may be dug out from the ground, the rest is imported. Ignoring for the time being financial flows, it is earned through exports and spent on imports. Thus a current account surplus results in an inflow of gold money, the modern-day equivalent of the accumulation of foreign exchange reserves, the counterpart to a balance of payments surplus. Conversely, gold flows out in the presence of a deficit. Now consider point A, where the stock of gold money has been large, resulting in a relatively high price level and, therefore, a current account deficit. The country sends more gold abroad to pay for its imports than it receives for its exports. The stock of gold money declines. This mechanism is represented by the downward-sloping schedule in panel (b) of Figure A14.1. It says that the balance of payments deteriorates as the stock of money increases (because the price level rises, as shown in the top left-hand panel). Point A in both panels describes a situation of external deficit, which corresponds to money stock M'. The deficit means that gold is flowing out and the money stock contracts, which takes us to point A' in both panels. Over time, the price level declines and the deficit is reduced.[16] At A', the deficit is not yet fully eliminated, gold is still flowing out and the money stock keeps contracting, so we continue moving in the same direction. The process will not stop until point E is reached. At point E, the price level is just 'right', the balance of payments is in equilibrium and the money stock is stabilized. Obviously, a surplus such as point B will trigger an inflow of money (specie) and an increase in prices, bringing the economy gradually to point E. This link between money and external balance is Hume's price–specie mechanism.

The mechanism that takes us from a situation of excessively high money and price level (point A) to equilibrium (point E) involves two steps: (1) the link from the balance of payments to the money stock in the right-hand panel, which is instantaneous; and (2) the link from money to the price level in the top left-hand panel, which takes time when prices are sticky. This is a long-run mechanism, as predicted by PPP and monetary neutrality. In the shorter run, most of the action takes place in the financial sector, which has been overlooked so far. To remedy this, we now look at panel (c) in Figure A14.1, which describes the financial market. The downward-sloping schedule describes the fact that an increase in the stock of money results in a lower interest rate. Since the exchange rate is fixed (remember, money is gold, everywhere), the interest rate parity principle presented in Chapter 13 implies that, when the domestic interest rate i is below the rate i^* prevailing abroad, it pays to borrow gold at home where interest is low and ship it abroad for lending at the higher interest rate. The horizontal line represents the interest rate parity condition. Along this line, the domestic interest rate is the same as abroad ($i = i^*$) and the financial account is in equilibrium. Above this line, the financial account is in surplus; below it, it is in deficit. The financial account is balanced

---

[14] It is the trade balance that changes. It is assumed that the other components of the current account remain unaffected.

[15] If we normalize the foreign price index to be $P^* = 1$, with $E = 1$ the real exchange rate is $EP/P^* = P$. Thus the price level P is also the real exchange rate and the horizontal line corresponds to the equilibrium exchange rate.

[16] This is PPP, a long-run proposition. The detailed mechanism involves declining demand because money contracts and interest rates rise. Then, the Phillips curve mechanism predicts declining inflation.

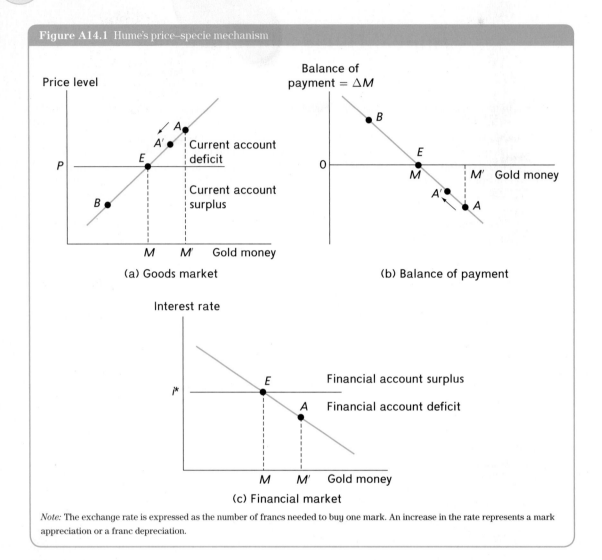

Figure A14.1 Hume's price–specie mechanism

(a) Goods market

(b) Balance of payment

(c) Financial market

Note: The exchange rate is expressed as the number of francs needed to buy one mark. An increase in the rate represents a mark appreciation or a franc depreciation.

when the stock of gold money is M. If the stock of gold exceeds M, the interest rate is lower than i^*, capital flows out, gold is shipped abroad and the money supply contracts back to the equilibrium level M.

Overall, starting at point A in all three panels, where the money stock M' exceeds the long-run equilibrium level M, both components of the balance of payments – the current and the financial accounts – are in deficit. The overall deficit means that gold is flowing out. As the money supply shrinks, over time the price level declines and the interest rate rises. The capital flow route is very fast while the trade route is slower. Panel (b) of Figure A14.1 accounts for both channels. The key result is that they both work towards eliminating the external deficit. Likewise, they would eliminate a surplus if it arose.

*The European countries could agree
on a common piece of paper ... they
could then set up a European monetary
authority or central bank ... This is a
possible solution, perhaps it is even an
ideal solution. But it is politically very
complicated, almost utopian.*

Robert Mundell (1973)

Optimum currency areas

Chapter Contents

Introduction

This chapter presents the optimum currency area theory, a systematic way of trying to decide whether it makes sense for a group of countries to abandon their national currencies. The theory develops a battery of economic and political criteria that recognize that the real economic cost of giving up the exchange rate instrument arises in the presence of asymmetric shocks – shocks that do not affect all currency union member countries. The chapter then examines whether Europe passes these tests. The conclusion is that Europe is not really an optimum currency area, but it does not fail all the tests either. A further consideration is that the adoption of the euro may change the situation. Over time, Europe may eventually satisfy all or most of the criteria.

15.1 The question, the problem and the short answer

It is usually taken for granted that each country has its own currency. After all, like the flag or the national anthem, a currency is a symbol of statehood. National heroes or rulers are proudly displayed on coins and banknotes, much as kings, emperors and feudal lords had their faces stamped on gold and silver coins. And yet, it is worth asking whether it makes good economic sense for each country to have its own currency.

This chapter provides answers to a simple question: If we forget about nations and focus purely on economic relations, how would we redraw the map of the world? To start with, does the world need more than one currency? Could Zimbabwe, Peru and China share the same currency? Probably not. At the other extreme, should each city have its own currency, as was sometimes the case just a few centuries ago? No, of course not. These answers seem obvious, but exactly why? Box 15.1 presents an example that is suggestive of the issues involved.

15.1.1 Why is a large currency area desirable?

Money is one of humanity's great inventions. Economics textbooks tell you that its key feature is to avoid achieving the 'double coincidence of wants', i.e. barter. With money, you can buy what you want without

---

Box 15.1 The case for a Michigan dollar

Michigan is home to Chrysler, Ford and General Motors. For decades, it benefitted enormously from being the motor industry state. It drew workers from around the USA, attracted by secure and well-paid jobs. However, for some time now, the US motor industry has not been doing so well and Michigan has suffered alongside it. As can be seen in Figure 15.1, its annual growth rate has underperformed relative to the USA as a whole. In the wake of the global financial crisis, GDP plunged by more than 8 per cent. Chrysler was sold to Fiat and both GM and the city of Detroit, the state capital, went bankrupt. Factories were closed and tens of thousands of people left, fleeing high unemployment.

Now imagine that the state of Michigan had its own currency. With a battered economy, the Michigan dollar would most likely have depreciated, and significantly so. Cars made in Michigan would have become cheaper to US and foreign customers and, quite possibly, the US motor industry would have been much better able to fend off competition from Japanese, European and Korean manufacturers. But, although its economy differs from that of most other US states, Michigan cannot use the exchange rate to compete. The cost has been huge, earning the state the unfortunate nickname the 'rust belt of the USA'.

Yet, no one in Michigan has seriously proposed a monetary secession. It is not because the Michigan economy is too small to justify a separate currency. Its GDP approximately equals that of Iran, South Africa and Denmark. Somehow, Michigan citizens consider that belonging to the US dollar currency area provides benefits that far outweigh the costs. Or, maybe, no one really asks the question because most assume that one country means one currency.

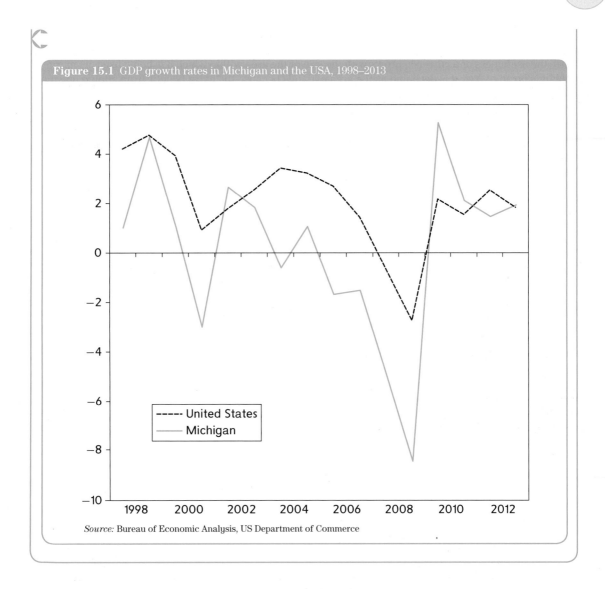

Figure 15.1 GDP growth rates in Michigan and the USA, 1998–2013

Source: Bureau of Economic Analysis, US Department of Commerce

needing to simultaneously sell something else. Money is useful because it both makes commercial and financial transactions much easier than barter and is immediately recognizable. The more people accept a currency, the more useful it is.[1]

In that sense, the world would benefit from having just one currency. There would be no need to exchange money when travelling, exporting or importing. Exchanging currency is not just bothersome – how many unspent foreign coins lie in one of your drawers? – it is also costly. Indeed, if you buy a foreign currency and re-sell it immediately, you are likely to lose 10 per cent or much more. This is how currency dealers and credit card companies get paid for the service that they provide; however, this service would be unnecessary if just one currency existed. In addition, currency transactions are risky as exchange rates fluctuate and seem always to go against you! This is why small currency areas – geographic zones that share the same currency – are clearly not optimal. A currency that is used in a small area is just not very useful.

---

[1] Technically, money is said to generate network externalities. Network externalities are studied in Chapter 18.

The marginal benefit curve in Figure 15.2 symbolically represents this idea. It measures the added advantage of increasing a currency area by one unit, for example one unit of GDP or one more country. Since the usefulness of a currency grows with the size of the area within which it is being used, its marginal benefit is positive. Yet, it is declining as the area expands because the extra benefit from adding one more country to an already large currency area is smaller than when the initial area was small.

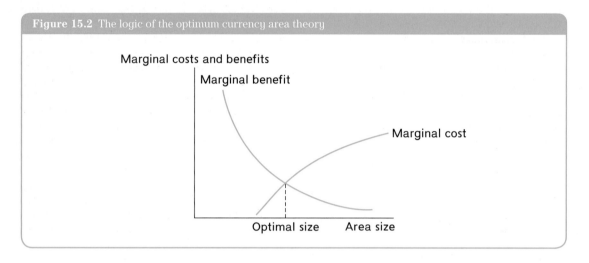

Figure 15.2 The logic of the optimum currency area theory

If the marginal benefit is always positive, is the world the optimal currency area? It would be if there were no costs. What can these costs be? As a currency area grows larger, it becomes more diverse – in standards of living, for instance. If more diversity means more costs when sharing a common currency, the marginal costs are positive and rising with the size of the area. This idea is depicted in Figure 15.2 by the upward-sloping marginal cost schedule. The figure reveals the existence of a trade-off: a large currency area is desirable because it enhances the usefulness of money, but it has drawbacks. The optimal currency area corresponds to the situation whereby the marginal costs and benefits from sharing the same currency balance each other out, as shown in Figure 15.2.[2] The figure is highly symbolic and there should be no pretence that we can actually draw these schedules. Yet, it summarizes what this chapter is about.

15.2 Benefits of a currency area

15.2.1 Transaction costs

With the creation of the euro, Austrian exporters can ship goods to Finland and be paid in their own currency, because that is also the currency of their customers. Before the euro, the exporters and their customers had to negotiate which currency would be used. The exporter much preferred the Austrian schilling, because that is what she uses every day and she would not have to pay a fee to her bank to exchange Finnish markkas for schillings. Of course, the Finnish customer had the exact opposite preference. No matter what, in the end someone would have to bear the transaction costs. This may seem trivial, but it is not. In a famous example, the European Commission looked at what happened when one started with one EU currency – say, 100 worth of it – and exchanged it successively in all the currencies of the EU before returning to the initial currency. The result was that less than 50 of the initial 100 would be left. Of course, no one would ever do that – except maybe teenagers roaming Europe with an InterRail pass – but the point was that transaction costs are not trivial. Unfortunately, we do not have estimates of how big these effects are.

---

[2] We use marginal, and not total, benefits because the highest net benefits (benefits less costs) occur where marginal benefits and costs are equal. Mathematically, net benefits are $NC = B - C$, where B and C represent, respectively, benefits and costs. The maximum value of NC occurs where $dNC = 0$; that is, when $dB = dC$, where d is the differentiation operator so that dB and dC are the marginal benefits and costs, respectively. This assumes that $dB > dC$ below the maximum point.

15.2.2 Price transparency

Another important benefit is that goods prices become directly comparable across countries that are part of a monetary union. Along with reduced transaction costs, this allows for more competition. Stronger competition in turn is expected to benefit consumers and to encourage producers to keep improving their offerings. There is evidence that the adoption of the euro has led small and medium-sized firms to engage in exporting throughout the area. Opening up trade opportunities to the large number of firms that were previously unable to deal with or intimidated by the challenge of exporting can be a very large benefit.

Transparency and competition also affect wage-setting. In most countries, wages are set collectively, either at the national or industry level. It is natural for trade unions to seek wage increases. If the increases are too large, however, firms lose their competitiveness. In effect, workers in different countries compete against each other via exports. When the exchange rate can be changed, either because it is floating or because it is fixed but adjustable, the tendency is to raise wages, and then prices, and then to depreciate the exchange rate to recover competitiveness. This is one source of rampant inflation, but not an efficient one since a depreciation raises the price of imports; along with higher domestic prices, the result is that the purchasing power of wages declines, which calls for another round of wage increases, and so on. Resisting such vicious circles is politically and socially difficult. Closing down the depreciation door makes it clear that any lapse in wage-setting will have to be clawed back through subsequent wage moderation.

Bringing more economic logic to setting wages stands to be another important benefit from being part of a currency area. This requires, however, deep changes in a process that is politically and socially complex. This effect is likely to take a very long time to take hold. The Eurozone crisis is an indication that it requires fairly traumatic conditions to occur, although it is too early to know whether the effects (see Chapter 19) will be lasting.

15.2.3 Uncertainty

Another benefit is the elimination of exchange rate risk. When exports are priced in the currency of the exporter, the importer does not know precisely what the exchange rate will be when the time comes to settle the purchase. If the price is set in the importer's currency, it is the exporter that faces the risk. Alternatively, the party facing the risk may purchase financial insurance (through forward contracts), which adds to the cost of converting currencies. This may deter trade across currency boundaries.

Another area likely to be affected by uncertainty concerns foreign direct investment (FDI), that is, investors acquiring firms, partially or completely. Benefits from FDI include transfers of technology, returns to scale, better production structures and more. Exchange rate fluctuations deter FDI because investors intending to have a presence in foreign countries for the long term may suffer losses as a result.

15.2.4 Trade

With easier and more secure payments and more competition, a common currency encourages more trade. This benefits all citizens in many ways. It provides more choice for customers and more customers for successful producers. More intense competition is bound to cut prices of producers who enjoy some degree of monopoly on their home turf. In a nutshell, a common currency eliminates a number of non-tariff barriers. Part II explains why and how this raises economic welfare.

Figure 15.3 displays the weight of exports in the GDPs of the original 12 members of the Eurozone. These are exports among the countries themselves. Trade has indeed increased, almost as much as following the implementation of the Single Act in 1992. The adoption of the euro may not be the sole factor that has increased trade, but there is other corroborating evidence that it has played a role.

15.2.5 Quality of monetary policy

Joining a monetary union implies a complete loss of national monetary policy autonomy. We will see that this is an important cost. On the other hand, swapping a domestic central bank for a collectively run central bank may bring benefits. This is the case if the domestic central bank lacks a tradition of administering bank policies effectively and if the collective central bank stands to do a better job. Box 15.2 presents the

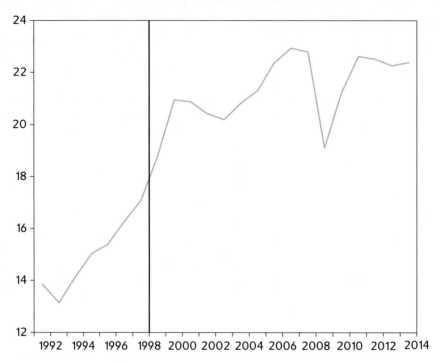

Figure 15.3 Export shares of the original Eurozone countries among themselves (% of GDP)

Source: AMECO, European Commission

Box 15.2   Essentials of central banking principles

The tools presented in Chapter 13 make it easy to understand what central banks try to achieve and how. The impossible trinity principle says that policy autonomy requires a flexible exchange rate regime. The *IS–MP–IRP* framework shows the role of monetary policy in the short run. Monetary neutrality tells us that, in the long run, these short-term effects are eroded by inflation and that, at the end of it all, inflation is directly proportional to the growth rate of the money stock. This is pretty much all that we need to know to understand central banking theory.

Because inflation is eventually driven by money growth, central banks are entrusted with the task of achieving price stability, conventionally defined as an inflation rate of 2 per cent or less – we return to this choice below. This is called inflation targeting. However, we do not live in the long run. In the shorter run, we face business cycles. These are periods of fast growth and low unemployment followed by periods of low, possibly negative, growth and high unemployment. These fluctuations, which last on average between two and five years, are painful as they hurt firms, some of which face bankruptcy, and households, threatened by job losses. Monetary policy can counteract business cycles, at least partly. This is why central bank are also tasked with the responsibility of smoothing cycles, a task captured by the *MP* curve (Section 13.1).

We can now see what central banks do. On a day-to-day basis they change the interest rate in response to economic conditions; they follow the movements of the *IS* schedule along the *MP* curve. To do so, they provide banks with liquidity and banks provide credit to their customers. The money stock is continuously adjusted to enforce the chosen interest rate. But central banks also monitor the evolution of the money stock because they know that its evolution will eventually determine inflation. If the money stock grows too fast, they will raise the interest rate; the *MP* schedule will shift up. This is an important qualification to the framework developed in Chapter 13: the *MP* schedule is not unmovable. For most central banks, inflation is the overriding objective, because it takes time to set in and even longer to combat. When and if money grows at a rate deemed inflationary, central banks move the *MP* schedule up and, conversely, they move it down when they fear disinflation (negative inflation).

The fact that monetary neutrality only occurs in the long run has an important consequence. Central banks must anticipate future inflation because their actions have a much-delayed effect. It may happen that today's conditions call for, say, a lower interest rate as prescribed by the *MP* schedule, but that this requires inflationary money growth.

The interest rate parity condition tells us that the exchange rate will respond to monetary policy. But what if the exchange is fixed? Then the interest rate parity condition implies that the domestic interest rate is just the same as the foreign interest rate – the rate in the country to whose currency we peg – and the central bank's role is just to provide the stock of money that delivers that interest rate. In the long run, PPP says that domestic inflation will be the same as abroad. How does it come about? This is where Hume's mechanism, presented in Chapter 14, comes into play. The central bank will have to increase or reduce the money stock to uphold the declared exchange rate parity, which it will do in response to external surpluses and deficits driven by the under- or overvaluation of the real exchange rate. Thus, a fixed exchange rate regime removes central bank autonomy but the exchange rate peg provides an anchor to long-run inflation.

essentials of central banking theory, which has the following implications under a flexible exchange rate regime:

- The central bank is ultimately solely responsible for inflation. Long-run price stability – however defined (see below) – must be a key objective of monetary policy.

- Monetary policy can be used to smooth cyclical fluctuations. In the shorter run, therefore, the central bank should adjust its interest rate accordingly. This is the justification for the *MP* schedule presented in Chapter 13.

- The short- and long-term objectives can occasionally conflict with each other. The solution is for the central bank to be flexible in the short term and to set the interest rate without undue concern for the evolution of the money stock. In the long term, it must also be determined to keep the money stock growth rate in line with the inflation objective.

- This balancing act between short- and long-run imperatives can often be delicate and even confusing. A first risk is that monetary policy can be misunderstood. Firms and households may then set prices and wages that are incompatible with the objectives of monetary policy. A second risk is that financial markets may destabilize the exchange rate. The response is for the central bank to develop a clear strategy and to be as transparent as possible regarding the implementation of that strategy.

An important additional consideration concerns the relation between central banks and their governments. Money creation is obviously very lucrative as it costs very little to produce money. The resulting seigniorage profits are turned to the government for which it represents a sizeable source of income. Seigniorage is a form of taxation, but a painless one, at least as long as inflation remains low. Many governments can be tempted to raise more income through seigniorage, as a great many historical examples confirm. The result is invariably high, sometimes extremely high, inflation. But since inflation follows money growth with a long lag – at least two years, often much more – the temptation can be irresistible for hard-pressed governments. The best way to resist this temptation is to make the central bank fully independent of its government and to assign monetary policy a clear, unambiguous and legally binding price stability objective.

The upshot is that good monetary policy requires full central bank independence, along with a clear monetary policy strategy and a high degree of transparency.

Central bank independence can be achieved through adequate domestic governance, but laws can always be changed in the face of (actual or perceived) necessity. The adoption of a proper strategy requires adequate human resources and, even if the central bank is independent, old habits die hard. Political pressure and the appointment of malleable officials often prove to be enough to bend the anti-inflation resolve of a central bank. This is especially so if the public is not well informed about the source of inflation, which is often the case in countries that have not experienced price stability long enough to be convinced of the merits of monetary policy discipline.[3]

An important benefit of a monetary union is that a collective central bank is more likely to extract itself from government pressure simply because no government will want to see the common monetary policy used to finance other governments. In addition, central bank independence guaranteed by an international agreement is less likely to be revoked, or simply trampled upon, than in the case of a purely national central bank. In addition, the mission of the common central bank is defined through an explicit agreement, which is likely to be better formulated than often implicit and vague mission statements. This, in turn, favours transparency.

15.2.6 Wrap-up

The benefits from a common currency are very sizeable but diffuse and immeasurable. Some of them, like increased competition, are even politically controversial because they threaten established interest groups, including industries and trade unions. The merits of independent and well-run central banks emerge slowly over time and are often hard to comprehend by the broad public and even governments. Yet, these benefits are very real.

Importantly, the benefits grow with the size of the currency area. This is why the marginal benefits – the additional benefits – are shown as always positive in Figure 15.2, even if their size declines. It is clear as far as trade and competition is concerned: big markets allow for wider choice and larger increasing returns. In that case, the marginal benefits may not even be declining, but we do not know for sure. It also applies for the *quality* of monetary policy since central bank independence and importance grow with its size, although we will see that big currency areas can incur important policy costs. As noted above, the usefulness and convenience of a currency is deeply associated with the number of people who use it. This may seem a mundane point, but it is not. A currency is chiefly an instrument designed to carry out transactions; after all, that is why money was invented in the first place, as explained in Chapter 14. It is very easy to overlook this benefit, and others too.

15.3 Costs of a currency area

Intuitively, it seems obvious that bringing together into a currency area very diverse countries creates difficulties. The intuition is right. Diversity is costly because a common currency requires a single central bank, and a single monetary authority is unable to react to each and every local particularity. The optimum currency area (OCA) aims at identifying these costs more precisely. The basic idea is that diversity translates into asymmetric shocks and that the exchange rate is very useful in dealing with such shocks.

We proceed in three steps:

1 First, we define and examine the effects of asymmetric shocks.

2 Second, we study the problems that arise in the presence of asymmetric shocks in a currency area.

3 Finally, we ask how the effects of asymmetric shocks can be mitigated when national exchange rates are no longer available.

15.3.1 Shocks and the exchange rate

Imagine that the world demand for a country's exports declines because tastes change or because cheaper alternatives are developed elsewhere. This opens up a hole in the balance of trade. To re-establish its external balance, the country needs to make its exports cheaper, which calls for enhanced competitiveness.

---

[3] A quick look at Figure 14.4 readily shows that most European countries have not been particularly good at keeping inflation in check following the abandonment of the fixed exchange rate anchor provided by the Bretton Woods system. The reason is that most central banks were under the direct or indirect control of their governments, which did not resist the temptation of seigniorage.

One solution would be for prices and wages to decline; but what if they do not? In this case, a depreciation will do the trick if the country has its own currency. If, however, the country is part of a wider currency area, there is no alternative to lowering prices. Macroeconomic principles tell us that this requires that the economy slows down, deeply enough for long enough.

In order to examine the situation, we turn to a new tool, closely related to the *IS–MP–IRP* framework of Chapter 13, and developed in some detail in the Annex. World demand for our goods depends on their prices relative to those of competing goods. At the aggregate level, competitiveness is captured by the real exchange rate EP/P^*. The real exchange rate is measured along the vertical axis in Figure 15.4. The aggregate demand (*AD*) curve is downward sloping because a real exchange rate appreciation represents a loss of competitiveness, which weakens demand for domestic goods as exports decline and imports rise. Think of a leftward shift in the *IS* curve.

The aggregate supply (*AS*) curve is very different: it asks 'What will incentivize producers to provide more of the good?' Clearly, they will do so if it brings about more profit. In a nutshell, this requires that they earn more and therefore that the price level increases. Since they often import primary commodities or parts, they need for *P* to increase over and above the price of foreign goods P^*/E. In brief, a real exchange rate EP/P^* appreciation elicits more output. Conversely, a real depreciation will lead to less production. This is the *AS* curve.

A last point. Under normal circumstances, economies tend to grow year in, year out. The existence of business cycles means that GDP fluctuates around a growing trend. Deviations from this trend are called the output gap (for one example, see Figure 13.5). This is the measure of output that is measured along the horizontal axis in Figure 15.4.

Starting from point *A*, an adverse demand shock is represented by the leftward shift of the *AD* curve, from *AD* to *AD'*. If the nominal exchange rate is allowed to depreciate, or if prices are flexible, the short-run effect will be a shift from point *A* to point *B*: the real exchange rate depreciates from λ to λ'. This is a painful move, of course, but an unavoidable one given the adverse shock.

However, the outcome is even more painful if the exchange rate is fixed and prices are rigid. In that case, the economy moves to point *C*, where the output decline is even deeper. At the unchanged real exchange rate λ, domestic producers continue to supply the output corresponding to point *A*, but point *C* represents the new, lower, demand. The distance *AC* represents unsold goods. Obviously, domestic firms will not accumulate unsold goods forever. Something has to give and production will fall. The recession generates incentives to gradually cut prices, eventually bringing the economy to point *B*. But this is likely to be the outcome of a painful and protracted process, in contrast to a rapid exchange rate depreciation.

The example illustrates why exchange rate fixity, when combined with sticky prices, makes an already bad situation worse. In a monetary union, instead of a simple once-and-for-all change in the nominal exchange rate, a real exchange rate adjustment can only come from changes in prices and wages. If prices and wages are sticky, the adjustment can take time, creating hardship along the way. Box 15.3 tells the story of Germany.

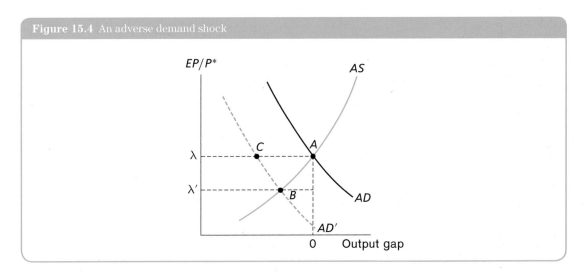

Figure 15.4 An adverse demand shock

Box 15.3 Early pain for Germany

Germany joined the Eurozone in 1999 at an overvalued exchange rate. As in Figure 15.4, the axes in Figure 15.5 represent the real exchange rate and the output gap. PPP predicts that the real exchange rate will have to depreciate. In the absence of its own exchange rate as a member of the monetary union, we expect that this will come about after a prolonged period of poor growth or, equivalently, negative output gaps. For a while, until 2001, Germany benefitted from a worldwide expansion. Once this expansion was over, it went through several years during which GDP remained below trend. This is when *The Economist* famously dubbed Germany 'the sick man of Europe'. The government pushed for a long period of wage moderation, which translated into a low inflation rate, and its real exchange rate depreciated. Germany gradually recovered competitiveness until it was pronounced healthy again in 2007. Like most other countries, following the global financial crisis, Germany underwent a deep recession in 2009 but its hard-won competitiveness bore fruit and allowed a speedy recovery. This recovery, however, generated frustration in other Eurozone countries, which did not recover or did so much more slowly. They stated that they had been unfairly undervalued, to which Germany responded: 'do like we do'. Wage moderation had come to an end by 2013 and Germany is now re-entering the fray, doing as the others do.

Figure 15.5 Germany: the real exchange rate and the output gap, 1999–2014

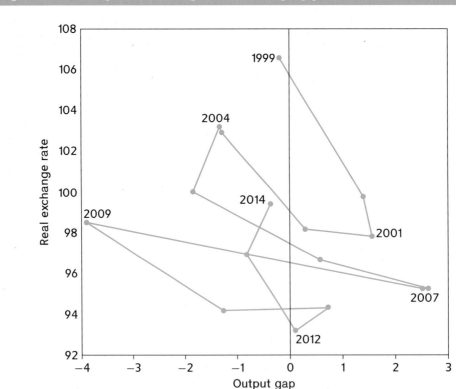

Note: The real exchange rate is the German price level relative to the average price level in the EU15 countries. The index takes the value of 100 in 2005. The output gap, actual less trend GDP, is expressed in percentage of trend GDP.

Source: AMECO, European Commission

15.3.2 Asymmetric shocks

So far we have thought of one country taken in isolation to set the stage. Diversity means that different countries face different shocks. The simplest case is a currency area with two member countries. We call these countries A and B and examine what difference sharing or not sharing the same currency makes. Note carefully that country A has two (nominal and real) exchange rates: one vis-à-vis country B and one vis-à-vis the rest of the world. The same applies to country B, of course.

If countries A and B are hit by the same adverse shock, we know from the previous section that both have to undergo a real depreciation vis-à-vis the rest of the world. If they are similar enough, to a first approximation, there is no need for their bilateral (nominal and real) exchange rate to change. They are in the same boat facing the same headwinds. This reasoning shows that the loss of the exchange rate within a currency union is of no consequence as long as all member countries face the same shocks. In that case, the union simply adjusts its common exchange rate vis-à-vis the rest of the world and its member countries are as well off as if they had each independently changed their own exchange rate.

The situation is very different in the presence of an asymmetric shock. Assume, for instance, that country A is hit by an adverse shock, but not country B. What happens then? The situation is examined in Figure 15.6. The vertical axis measures each country's real exchange rate vis-à-vis the rest of the world: EP_A/P^* and EP_B/P^*, where P_A and P_B are the price indices in country A and country B, respectively, P^* is the price level in the rest of the world and E is the common currency's exchange rate, initially equal to E_0. Points A in both panels represent the initially nicely balanced situation, both countries having a zero output gap. Defining the price indexes such that $P_A = P_B$, the real exchange rates are the same in both countries: $\lambda_0 = E_0 P_A/P^* = E_0 P_B/P^*$. (Prices are assumed to be sticky – otherwise, the exchange rate regime does not matter, as we already noted above.)

The adverse shock that affects country A alone is represented in the left-hand chart by a downward shift of the demand schedule from AD to AD'. If country A is not part of a monetary union and can change its own nominal exchange rate, its best course of action is to let it depreciate to E_1 such that the real exchange rate depreciates to $\lambda_1 = E_1 P_A/P^*$, as represented by the new equilibrium at point B. Country B has no reason to change its nominal and real exchange rates, which remain at E_0 and λ_0, respectively.

Things are very different when countries A and B belong to a monetary union. They cannot have different nominal exchange rates. The now-common central bank must make a choice on their behalf. If it cares only about country A, it depreciates the common exchange rate to E_1. With sticky prices, both countries must share the same real exchange rate λ_1. Figure 15.6 shows that this is not good for country B, which now faces a situation of potentially inflationary excess demand (represented by the distance $B'B''$).

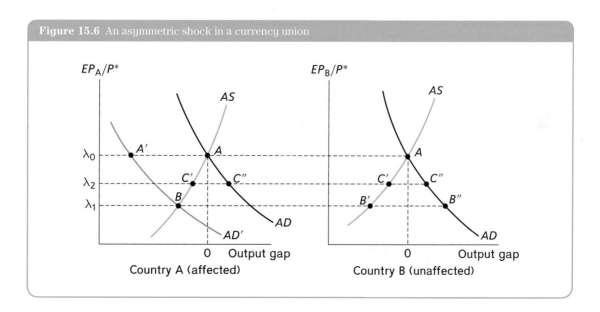

Figure 15.6 An asymmetric shock in a currency union

If the central bank instead favours country B, it will keep the common exchange rate unchanged. Both countries retain the initial real exchange rate λ_0, and stay at the initial point A. This suits country B well, as it does not face any disturbance, but it means excess supply for country A (represented by the distance $A'A$). Clearly, in the presence of an asymmetric shock, what suits one country hurts the other.

If the union's common external exchange rate floats freely, it will depreciate because of the adverse shock in one part of the area, but not all the way to E_1. It will decline to an intermediate level such as E_2, which corresponds to a real exchange rate $\lambda_2 = E_2 P_A/P^* = E_2 P_B/P^*$.[4] The outcome is a combination of excess supply in country A and excess demand in country B (both represented by $C'C''$). Both countries are in disequilibrium. The new exchange rate level is 'correct' on average, but it is too strong for country A, which is in recession, and too weak for country B, which is overheating.

That there is no good outcome is the fundamental and unavoidable cost of forming a monetary union. The logic is very intuitive. With sticky prices, the nominal exchange rate is the only way of adjusting a country's competitiveness to changing conditions. If an asymmetric shock occurs, the common exchange rate cannot insulate all countries that belong to a monetary union.

Disequilibria cannot last forever. Over time, prices are flexible and will do what they are expected to do. Consider the latest case, when the common exchange rate vis-à-vis the rest of the world is E_2. It has no reason to change further since it has already done its job of taking into account the average situation in the union. Country A cannot sell all of its production, so its price level will eventually decline until the real exchange rate depreciates to λ_1 and country A will reach its equilibrium at point B. This will require a recession – remember, country A's goods are in excess supply – and unemployment will rise, putting downward pressure on prices. The price of country A's goods will decline until it reaches level P_A' such that $\lambda_1 = E_1 P_A'/P^*$. Country B is in the opposite situation: facing buoyant demand, the price of its goods will rise to P_B' such that its real exchange rate appreciates back to its equilibrium level, which is the original level $\lambda_0 = E_2 P_B'/P^*$. Recession and disinflation in country A, boom and inflation in country B: these are the costs of operating a monetary union when an asymmetric shock occurs.

15.3.3 Symmetric shocks with asymmetric effects

The analysis has focused on asymmetric shocks, but it applies also to the case of symmetric shocks that produce asymmetric effects. There are many reasons why countries do not react in exactly the same way to the same shock: different socio-economic structures, including labour market regulations and traditions, the relative importance of industrial sectors, the role of the financial and banking sectors, the country's external indebtedness, the ability to strike agreements between firms, trade unions and the government, and so on. A good example is the case of a sudden increase in the price of oil and gas. This shock hurts oil- and gas-importing countries but benefits – or, at least, hurts less – oil- or gas-producing countries, such as the Netherlands, Norway and the UK. It is one reason why the two latter countries have not joined the European monetary union.

Another asymmetry concerns the way in which monetary policy operates. When a common central bank reacts to a symmetric shock, it is not a foregone conclusion that the effect of its action will be the same throughout the currency union. Differences in the structure of banking and financial markets or in the size of firms – and their ability to borrow – may result in asymmetric effects. Chapter 18 examines this issue.

The bottom line is that symmetric shocks can have asymmetric effects. Then the analysis carried out in the previous section fully applies. The situation is similar to the one described in Figure 15.6.

15.3.4 Policy preferences

Countries may disagree on how to deal with each and every possible shock. In practice, there rarely exists a 'best way' to deal with a shock. For example, should we be more concerned about inflation or unemployment? Should we favour the exporters – who wish to have weak exchange rates to buttress competitiveness – or the consumers – who wish to have strong exchange rates to raise their purchasing power? These are trade-offs, which generate the confrontation of opposing interests and are dealt with through the respective

---

[4] Where E_2 exactly lies depends on a host of factors, such as the relative size of the two countries and how sensitive is their trade to changes in the real exchange rate.

influence of political parties, trade unions and lobbies. There is no reason for the resulting decision to be the same across different countries because national preferences are not necessarily homogeneous.

The result is that, traditionally, some countries demonstrate less tolerance towards inflation, budget deficits or unemployment than do others. In Germany, for instance, where the hyperinflation of the 1920s is still painfully remembered, price stability is widely seen as a top policy priority. In contrast, high unemployment and social unrest in France in the 1930s have left a lingering distaste for recessions, with relatively little concern for inflation.

This means that shocks, even if symmetric, may elicit different policy responses. When monetary policy is no longer carried out at the national level, the common central bank will be asked to act differently and its managers, drawn from different countries, may find it difficult to agree. It also means that the other macroeconomic instrument, fiscal policy, may be used in different directions. These issues, long latent, have surfaced in the euro area during the financial crisis, as explained in Chapter 19.

15.4 The optimum currency area criteria

The optimum currency area (OCA) theory brings together the benefits (Section 15.2) and the costs (Section 15.3) to derive practical criteria that can help us answer the question asked at the outset: Which countries should share the same currency? In a way, OCA is a misnomer, for two reasons. First, because the theory does not really deal with optimality (what is best?) as it simply balances costs and benefits. Second, the theory does not even provide yes or no answers to the central question asked above. Rather, it derives criteria that make a common currency acceptable, not optimal; and the criteria are never black or white, they are more or less fulfilled. Box 15.4 provides an example of the OCA criteria at work.

There are three classic economic criteria and an additional three that are political.[5] The first criterion asks what characteristics make it easier to deal with asymmetric shocks within a currency area. The next two economic criteria take a different approach: they aim to identify which economic areas are less likely to be hit by asymmetric shocks or to face shocks moderate enough to be of limited concern. The last three criteria deal with political aspects; they ask whether different countries are likely to help each other when

---

Box 15.4   Should Sweden adopt the euro?

Sweden has carefully debated whether to adopt the euro. The debate ended in 2003 with a referendum that rejected membership. As recalled by Jonung and Vlachos (2007):

> *A Government Commission Report . . . set the stage for the ensuing discussions. . . . The economic analysis of the report was based on the traditional theory of optimum currency areas (OCAs) listing the expected benefits and costs of Swedish membership of the euro area. The main benefits were identified as the efficiency gains from a common currency, in other words the reduction in costs concerning international transactions and the elimination of uncertainty concerning fluctuating exchange rates within the monetary union, which would generate more foreign trade and more competition. The loss of monetary policy autonomy was deemed to be the main cost of full EMU membership. . . . The surrendering of monetary policy autonomy was believed to be associated with high costs for Sweden in the event of asymmetric shocks to the domestic economy. Thus, a Swedish currency with a floating exchange rate was viewed as an insurance device. . . . In its conclusions, the Commission recommended Swedish membership in the long run, but proposed that Sweden should not enter . . . in the short run.*

---

[5] The three 'political' criteria are not part of classic OCA theory. They were introduced in earlier editions of this textbook. The crisis offers a powerful demonstration of their relevance. There is also a tendency toward the proliferation of criteria. In particular, policies are added to the list while the criteria should only reflect existing structural conditions. Policies can – and should – always be adapted.

faced with asymmetric shocks. This section lists and explains the logic of the OCA criteria; Section 15.5 will examine whether they are satisfied in Europe.

15.4.1 Labour mobility (Mundell)

The first criterion was proposed by Robert Mundell (Box 15.5) when he first formulated the notion of an OCA. The idea is that the cost of sharing the same currency would be eliminated if the factors of production, capital and labour, were fully mobile across borders. Since it is conventionally assumed that capital is mobile, the real hurdle comes from the lack of labour mobility.

Mundell criterion

Optimum currency areas are those within which people move easily.

The reasoning behind this statement is illustrated in Figure 15.7, which is based on Figure 15.6. Remember that the adversely affected country A undergoes unemployment while non-affected country B faces inflationary pressure. Both problems could be solved by a shift of the production factors

---

Box 15.5   Founders of the optimum currency area theory

Robert A. Mundell, a Canadian-born economist at Columbia University, won the Nobel Prize in part for having created the OCA theory, in part for having started the field of open economy macroeconomics. The *IS–MP–IRP* framework is often referred to as the Mundell–Fleming model. (J. Marcus Fleming was an economist working at the IMF; he independently developed the same theory.) He now advocates a single worldwide currency.

Ronald McKinnon, (left) from Stanford University, has made major contributions to the international monetary literature. He is known for his critical appraisal of the European monetary union.

Peter Kenen, (right) from Princeton University, was a leading contributor to our understanding of the international monetary system and a keen observer of European monetary integration.

Source: Stanford University

© Office of Communications, Princeton University

(labour and capital), which are idle in country A, to country B, where they are in short supply. This reallocation is shown as a shift of both countries' supply schedules to AS', leftward for country A, rightward for country B. This reallocation changes trend – or potential – GDPs so that the output gap is zero at both equilibrium points C. What is remarkable is that there is no need for prices and wages to change in either country. Once the factors of production have moved, the currency area's nominal exchange rate E_2 delivers the real exchange rate λ_2 that is best for each country.

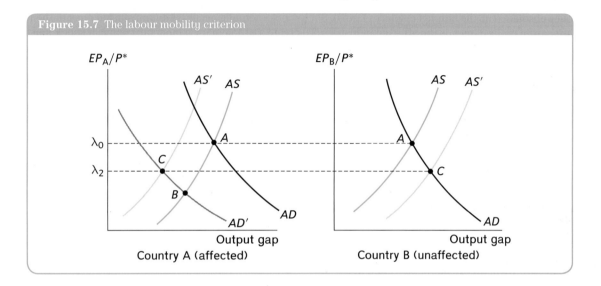

Figure 15.7 The labour mobility criterion

The Mundell criterion makes good sense: why should unemployment rise in some part of a currency area while, in other parts, firms cannot produce enough to satisfy demand? Let people and their equipment simply move!

Criticism

Yet, as always, things are less simple than they look. A few words of caution are warranted. We need to think a bit harder about what shifting production factors really means. First, it is no wonder that actual currency areas generally coincide with nation-states. Common culture and language, right and ease of resettling, schooling systems, retirement systems, etc. make labour mobility easier within a country than across borders. A national currency is not just a symbol of statehood, it is usually justified by labour mobility, which is precisely what the Mundell criterion asserts. Across borders, not only do cultural and linguistic differences restrain migration, but also institutional barriers further discourage labour mobility, as explained in Chapter 8. A response is to change legislation to make cross-border labour mobility easier and thus enlarge the size of optimum currency areas. Indeed, this is part of Europe's quest for closer integration.

Second, the goods produced in country A may differ from those produced in country B. It may take quite some time to retrain workers from country A to produce the goods of country B, if at all possible. If the shocks are temporary, it may not be worth the trouble of moving, retraining, etc. Labour mobility is not a panacea, just a factor that mitigates the costs of an asymmetric shock in a currency union.

Finally, labour needs equipment to be productive. What if all equipment is already in use in country B? The usual answer is that capital is mobile, but this view needs to be qualified. Financial capital can move freely and quickly, unless impeded by exchange controls. Installed physical capital (means of production such as plant and equipment) is not very mobile. Machinery can be transported but it takes time to build plants. Closing plants in country A can be done quickly – although social–political resistance may create stumbling blocks – but creating new production facilities in country B may take months, if not years. Even if labour were highly mobile, which it is not, shifting the supply curves as described in Figure 15.7 may take many years. By then, the asymmetric shock may well have evaporated or even reversed.

15.4.2 Production diversification (Kenen)

Asymmetric shocks are the problem within a currency area, but how frequent are they, really? If substantial asymmetric shocks happen only rarely, the costs are episodic while the benefits accrue every day. The Kenen criterion takes a first look at this question by asking what the most likely sources of substantial and long-lasting shocks are. Most of the shocks likely to be permanent are associated with shifts in spending patterns, which may be a consequence of changing tastes (e.g. German beer consumers find it more fashionable to drink French wine) or of new technology that brings about new products and makes older ones obsolete (e.g. the internet displaces faxes). Such shocks actually occur continuously, but most of them are hardly noticed outside the affected industries. To create a problem for a monetary union, a shock must be large and asymmetric.

The countries most likely to be affected by severe shocks are those that specialize in the production of a narrow range of goods. For example, many of the African countries that are part of the CFA franc zone primarily export a single agricultural product such as coffee or cacao. A decline in the demand for coffee – which may occur because new producers emerge elsewhere in the world – is an asymmetric shock because it affects some countries in the CFA franc zone and not others. Conversely, a country that produces a wide range of products will be little affected by shocks that concern any particular good because that good weighs relatively little in total production.

This explains the second criterion for an optimum currency area, initially stated by Kenen (Box 15.5): in order to reduce the likelihood of asymmetric shocks, currency area member countries ought to be well diversified and to produce similar goods. In that case, good-specific shocks are likely to be either symmetric or of little aggregate consequence, thus lessening the need for frequent exchange rate adjustments.

Kenen criterion

Countries whose production and exports are widely diversified and of similar production structure form an optimum currency area.

Criticism

This is a very broad statement. How much diversification is enough? When are the production structures sufficiently similar? As discussed in Box 15.1, Michigan is probably more different from Texas than Belgium and the Netherlands. The criterion provides a good sense of what is at stake, but it does not allow anyone to draw a clear delineation. One can argue that Greece, with its focus on tourism and agribusiness, is not well-adapted to sharing a currency with industrial Germany, but is that enough to draw a conclusion? Controversies abound.

15.4.3 Openness (McKinnon)

The next relevant question is whether the exchange rate is at all helpful in the presence of an asymmetric shock. If not, little is lost by giving it up. In the analysis so far, the distinction between 'domestic' and 'foreign' goods refers to where the goods are produced and priced. However, many standard goods, such as paper sheets or electric bulbs, although produced in different countries, are virtually identical. In that case, trade competition will ensure that their prices are the same everywhere, or nearly so, and therefore largely independent of the exchange rate. In addition, modern trade takes the form of value chains whereby finished products incorporate many parts produced literally all over the world. It becomes increasingly difficult to talk about national goods.

Consider the example of electric bulbs produced in Sweden and think of the German market. Competition forces the competing producers to set the same price in euros, say €2.5. Pricing to market, as this is called, means that if the krona's exchange rate vis-à-vis the euro changes, Swedish bulbs will still sell for €2.5 in Germany. If the krona depreciates from 9 to 9.5, the Swedish manufacturer will see its selling price rise from SKR 22.5 to SKR 23.75. If the krona appreciates from 9 to 8.5, the Swedish manufacturer will have to absorb the difference as the selling price declines from SKR 22.5 to SKR 21.25. Presumably, the same applies to German goods exported to Sweden. Losing the exchange rate, therefore, is of little consequence and the two countries can form a currency area without suffering much hardship in the presence of asymmetric shocks.

McKinnon criterion

Countries that are very open to trade and trade heavily with each other form an optimum currency area. The criterion can be made more precise, as follows. When two countries A and B do not share the same currency, they each have their own exchange rate vis-à-vis the rest of the world, E_A and E_B. If they are very open and trade intensively with each other, the distinction between domestic and foreign goods loses much of its significance, as competition will equalize the prices of most goods when expressed in the same currency. For example, if the price of country A's domestic goods in domestic currency is P_A, expressed in the rest of the world's currency it is $E_A P_A$, and similarly country B's price is $E_B P_B$. Competition ensures that $E_A P_A = E_B P_B$. Any change in one country's nominal exchange rate, say, E_A, must be immediately compensated by a change in local currency prices P_A such that the world price level $E_A P_A$ remains unchanged. In effect, P_A and P_B are no longer sticky. In that case, the real exchange rates of both countries vis-à-vis the rest of the world are also equal: $E_A/P_A/P^* = E_B P_B/P^*$. When prices are flexible, creating a currency union by giving up the exchange rate entails no serious loss of policy independence.

Criticism

Again, the criterion can be deceptively simple. The exchange rate does not affect competitiveness in the sense that competition forces prices to be the same. Still, the fact that the domestic price of exports (like bulbs) changes with the exchange rate may still have an impact on competitiveness, but in a different way, through profits. When the exchange rate depreciates, for instance, higher domestic-currency export prices (from SKR 22.5 to SKR 23.75 in the previous example) translate into higher profits for exporters. This may induce firms to shift their activities towards exports. Conversely, an appreciation eats into the profit margin of exporters. In that sense, exchange rate changes do affect the economy.

There is an answer to this objection. If more and more goods have little national specificity as value chains spread, a depreciation may raise profits because of higher domestic-currency prices but it also means that imported components could become more expensive because their prices are set internationally. Some gain here, some loss there; once again, we find that exchange rate changes have little or no effect.

This counter-argument is puzzling. If value chains become the dominant form of production worldwide, the McKinnon criterion implies that the whole world is an optimum currency area. The counter-counter-argument is that in most countries about half of total production concerns non-traded goods: goods that are produced and consumed locally. Examples include medical or car mechanic services, house building, public administration, and much more.

15.4.4 Fiscal transfers[6]

An important aspect of the analysis in Section 15.3 is that country B suffers – some inflationary pressure – from the adverse shock that hits country A if they share the same currency. It is therefore in the interest of country B to help alleviate the impact of the shock. One possibility is for country B to compensate country A financially. Such a transfer mitigates both the recession in country A, which receives the transfer, and the boom in country B, which pays out the transfer. This allows time for the shock to disappear if it is temporary, or to work its effects through prices if it is longer lasting. If shocks occur randomly, the country that pays out a transfer today will be tomorrow's beneficiary. In effect, such transfers work like a common insurance against bad shocks.

Transfer criterion

Countries that agree to compensate each other for adverse shocks form an optimum currency area. Transfer schemes of this kind exist across regions in every country. Sometimes they are explicit; most often they are implicit. For example, if a particular region suffers an asymmetric shock, then, as income declines, so do tax payments, while welfare support – chiefly unemployment benefits – rises. This is how the region receives transfers from the rest of the country. These transfers are often implicit, part-and-parcel of the redistributive mechanism at work in the country. Some federal countries, such as Germany and Switzerland, additionally operate explicit transfer systems.

---

[6] This criterion was also developed initially by Peter Kenen.

Criticism

The debt crisis has brought forward the issue of transfers. They are properly seen as a form of insurance against asymmetric shocks. Insurance works if, indeed, shocks are random. If it is always the same countries that suffer from adverse shocks, the other countries might see it as a costly undertaking. Why could that be the case? Because any insurance involves a moral hazard: the possibility of courting adverse shocks to elicit transfer payments. A car driver may be more reckless if he knows that his insurance will pay for all the accidents that he provokes than if he were not insured. This is why car insurance involves deductibles – you pay for some part of the costs – and experience-rated – you pay a higher premium if you are often involved in accidents. Applied to a currency union, countries may take fewer precautions to avoid frequent shocks if they expect transfers. For instance, they may remain too specialized, or too dependent on imports, or they may nurture rigid labour markets that make adjustments long and painful. We will see the importance of this criticism in Chapter 19.

15.4.5 Homogeneous preferences

Political conditions matter even for symmetric shocks. Section 15.3.2 shows that symmetric shocks do not pose any problem as long as each country reacts in the same way to the shock. But Section 15.3.4 explains how symmetric shocks can have polarizing effects akin to asymmetric shocks when currency area member countries do not share the same preferences regarding policy responses. Under such circumstances, whatever the central bank chooses to do will be controversial and will leave some, possibly all, countries

Box 15.6 Germany and Italy: a difficult relationship

The OCA theory starts and ends with the idea that, once a country joins a monetary union, external competitiveness must be maintained the hard way – keeping costs and prices low – rather than through recurrent devaluations. Figure 15.8 makes it clear that Germany worked hard on that (see Box 15.3) while Italy, well, let its competitiveness slip away. Unsurprisingly, Germany's current account accrued a strong surplus while Italy's experienced increasing deficits. Italians called upon the ECB to adopt a policy stance that would prevent the euro from being overvalued. German public opinion did not conceal its annoyance with Italy, insisting that a strong euro is what the monetary union is all about.

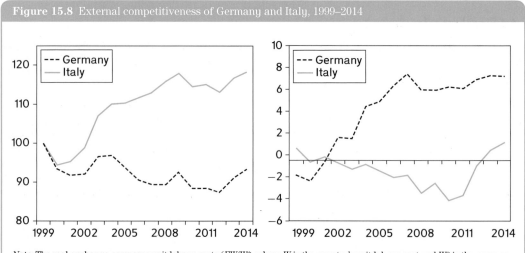

Figure 15.8 External competitiveness of Germany and Italy, 1999–2014

Note: The real exchange compares unit labour costs (*EW/W**, where *W* is the country's unit labour cost and *W** is the average of unit labour costs in 35 industrial countries).

Source: AMECO, European Commission

unhappy. At best, there will be resentment; at worst, the currency union may not survive. Box 15.6 provides a classic example of this kind of tension.

Homogeneity of preferences criterion

Currency union member countries must reach consensus on the best way to deal with shocks.

Criticism

Once again, this is a very broad statement that cannot lead to a precise assessment. Within each country, political parties usually disagree on policies and the official view changes when power changes hand. The criterion must refer to shared values that are not the same from one country to another, which is even harder to pinpoint.

In addition, views and values may change over time. Deep economic crises leave an imprint that can last a very long time. In that sense, lessons can be drawn about which policies work and which do not. Furthermore, it is not just history that matters but also political and social institutions. For example, we have seen that the degree of price and wage flexibility matters a great deal in the presence of shocks, and that identical shocks may have widely different effects. Wage flexibility, in particular, depends on bargaining structures.

15.4.6 Solidarity vs. nationalism

The final criterion goes deeper into political considerations. Since none of the previous criteria is likely to be fully satisfied, no currency area is ever optimum. This is even true for individual countries, which unknowingly operate as currency areas. One consequence is that shocks generate political disagreements regarding the proper response. Such disagreements are a familiar feature in any country. They may be more delicate if asymmetric shocks generate disagreements across regions. In individual countries, the eventual resolution of such debates is usually accepted as the price to pay for living together – the natural consequence of statehood. The outcome is ultimately seen as acceptable because citizens of the same country readily accept some degree of solidarity with one another.

When separate countries contemplate the formation of a currency area, they need to realize that there will be times when disagreements will occur and that these disagreements may follow national lines, especially if the shocks are asymmetric or produce asymmetric effects. For such disagreements to be tolerated, the people who form the currency union must accept that they will be living together and extend their sense of solidarity to the whole union. In short, they must have a shared sense of common destiny that outweighs the nationalist tendencies that would otherwise call for intransigent reactions.

Solidarity criterion

When the common monetary policy gives rise to conflicts of national interest, the countries that form a currency area need to accept the costs in the name of a common destiny.

Criticism

In a way, this is obvious. A currency union is not a free ride and costs are bound to arise now and then, when asymmetric shocks occur. One reason to accept these occasional costs is that, over time, they are more than compensated for by the benefits; this is the essence of OCA theory. Another reason is that solidarity makes some sacrifices acceptable for the better common good. When the benefits are too diffuse to be fully felt, solidarity becomes essential. This supports the view that a monetary union can only come about after a political union. A political union, it is asserted, creates the necessary sense of solidarity. However, a deeper question is whether this sense of solidarity can only be the outcome of a political union. The next section presents an alternative view.

15.5 Endogenous criteria?

The six criteria presented above refer to country characteristics, but these characteristics may change over time. A puzzling question is whether they can change because of membership of a currency area. Put differently, can an area that is not an optimum currency area become one as a consequence of being one? This possibility is called the endogeneity of the OCA criteria.

As we examine each criterion, this is a very logical possibility. The fact that some criteria are not well satisfied implies that asymmetric shocks will be painful. The pain itself may change countries and people.

The six criteria

The following sections describe the possible effects of an asymmetric shock when the six criteria are not fully satisfied.

Labour mobility

The Mundell criterion emphasizes labour mobility. When country A has a high level of unemployment and country B faces labour shortages, the incentive for citizens to move becomes more urgent. A shock may therefore encourage labour mobility in situations where exchange rate adjustments made it previously unnecessary.

Diversification

A high degree of specialization implies that some countries will be especially hard hit when they are affected by specific shocks. As a consequence, many firms will disappear. The displaced managers and employees will undoubtedly seek other ways of gaining a living. They will form new firms in new lines of business, which will reduce the extent of specialization.

Openness

This criterion really refers to the impact of exchange rate changes on economic activity. As noted above, the evolution of trade toward value chains is gradually making this criterion less relevant. This is not endogeneity because the changes occur not as a response to the presence of a monetary union, but to technological changes.

Homogeneous preferences

Experimentation is a great way of learning. As countries deal with similar difficulties, they can learn from each other. For that to happen they must be aware of what others do and they have to be convinced that successful foreign experiments can be applied at home. This process is very much alive in federations where states, provinces, Länder or cantons, whatever they are called, indeed continuously learn from each other. Within a currency area, transparency is a benefit because it enhances competition. It also makes comparisons easier and more convincing. This is particularly the case with a symmetric shock that produces asymmetric effects. Why is it happening? Which country deals better with the shock? What should we change to deal with a shock better in future? In this spirit, shocks reveal underlying weaknesses and they may trigger Darwinian responses.

Transfers

In existing federations, transfers between the centre (the federal government) and the sub-central level(s) are commonplace, as mentioned above. They are intimately related to the structure of taxation, since sub-central authorities may have limited tax or tax collection authority. They also correspond to the co-insurance motive mentioned earlier. This second motivation is directly linked to the risk of asymmetric shocks. Insurance may merely be convenient but in most countries it is justified by either of two issues. The first is solidarity, which is related to the common destiny criterion; the second is common interest: when one country suffers an asymmetric shock and sees its GDP decline, imports from other countries are reduced and thus the shock spreads. Reducing this effect is therefore in every country's interest. Inasmuch as a common currency leads to tighter economic integration, co-insurance is likely to become more appealing. This source of endogeneity is magnified if one country's crisis could be contagious, as happened in the Eurozone after 2010.

Common destiny

The question here is whether living with the same currency increases the sense of common destiny among sovereign countries. The answer can only be speculative because historically the adoption of a common currency has followed the creation of a common state. There seem to be two opposing forces at work. The first is that, indeed, people who share the same currency feel closer to each other, if only because their countries become more economically and financially integrated. The second is that this greater interdependence is seen as a threat because one country's troubles can be costly to the others. In that case, a common currency undermines the sense of common destiny. Much is likely to depend on political considerations.

15.6 Is Europe an optimum currency area?

In principle, the OCA theory should tell us whether it did make sense to establish a monetary union in Europe. As already noted, the answer is most unlikely to be black and white. The benefits are hard to quantify, as are the six OCA criteria, which may be only partly fulfilled. This section distils that rich and unending debate. Box 15.7 reports on the conclusions reached in May 2003 by the British Chancellor of the Exchequer on the basis of five tests inspired by the OCA theory.

Box 15.7   Why Britain is not yet ready for the euro (in 2003)

When he was appointed Chancellor of the Exchequer in 1997, Gordon Brown awarded himself the right to veto the highly political decision of British Eurozone membership. He announced that he would reach a verdict on the basis of five economic tests:

1 *Convergence.* Are business cycles and economic structures compatible so that we and others could live comfortably with euro interest rates on a permanent basis?
2 *Flexibility.* If problems emerge, is there sufficient flexibility to deal with them?
3 *Investment.* Would joining the EMU create better conditions for firms making long-term decisions to invest in the UK?
4 *Financial services.* What impact would entry into the EMU have on the competitive position of the UK's financial services industry, particularly the City's wholesale markets?
5 *Growth, stability and employment.* In summary, will joining the EMU promote higher growth, stability and a lasting increase in jobs?

In May 2003, the Chancellor released his first assessment. He found that the convergence and flexibility tests were not met, that the investment and financial services tests were met, and the fifth test would be met when the first two were met. From this, he concluded that the UK was not yet ready, adding: 'We will report on progress in the Budget next year. We can then consider the extent of progress and determine whether on the basis of it we make a further Treasury assessment of the five tests which – if positive next year – would allow us at that time to put the issue before the British people in a referendum.'[1] There has been no further assessment of this sort.

   Two characteristics of this procedure are striking. First, the heavy and explicit use of OCA economic principles. Test 1 deals with the presence of asymmetric shocks, test 2 with the ability to cope with asymmetric shocks, with heavy emphasis on labour markets, while test 3 looks at capital mobility. Test 5 summarizes the OCA approach. Test 4 is specific to the UK's specialization in financial services. Second, the tests are specified in an obviously intended vague way, leaving the Chancellor free to implicitly weigh the political aspects of the undertaking.

[1] The various documents are available on www.hm-treasury.gov.uk/. They include a large number of specially commissioned studies that are well worth reading.

15.6.1 Labour mobility

There are always people who move, but do they move enough and as the Mundell criterion wants them to, in response to asymmetric shocks? Do they promptly take advantage of any difference in earnings, and move to where they can earn more? Is moving better than being unemployed? There are many impediments to migration.

Migrants have to consider many economic issues, such as:

- the cost of moving, possibly including the selling and buying of dwellings;
- the prospect of becoming unemployed, both in the country of origin and in the country of immigration;
- career opportunities, which means not only current but also future earnings;
- family career prospects, including the spouse and children and sometimes even more distant relatives;
- social benefits, including unemployment, health and retirement;
- taxation of earnings from both labour and savings.

Labour mobility is also subject to non-economic incentives, such as:

- cultural differences (language, religion, traditions, possibly racism and xenophobia) in the country considered for immigration;
- family and friendship links that can be weakened;
- commitment to one's country of origin (nationalism).

For these reasons, labour mobility can only be limited. A natural approach is to compare Europe with existing, well-functioning currency areas, such as the USA. Figure 15.9 shows that mobility across countries is considerably lower in Europe than in the USA. This is not really surprising; moving across countries entails many of the difficulties listed above. What is more telling is to observe that mobility within countries remains much smaller in Europe.

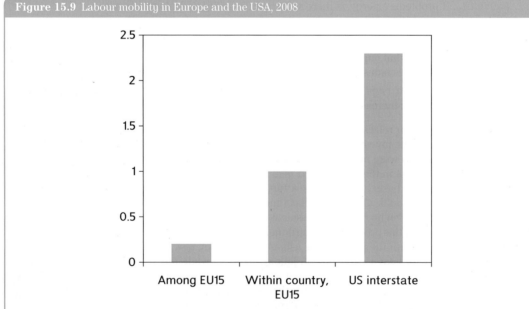

Figure 15.9 Labour mobility in Europe and the USA, 2008

Note: Mobility is measured as the proportion of the population that has moved from another country in Europe, from another state in the USA. The EU15 refers to the 15 members of the Eurozone in 2008.

Source: European Commission, *Geographic Mobility in the European Union*, Directorate for Employment, Social Affairs and Equal Opportunities, April 2008

Why do Europeans move so little? Across countries, there are many reasons, some obvious such as language and tradition, others less well appreciated, such as health insurance, retirement pension systems or the fact that housing tends to be more expensive and the housing market less fluid in Europe than in the USA. But within countries? Cultural issues and welfare protection – which alleviates the pain of unemployment – seem to matter.

Box 15.8   The effects of asymmetric shocks in Europe and the USA

How does Europe's low labour mobility affect the response to an asymmetric shock? A study by Fatás (2000) compares Europe and the USA. Fatás looks at 51 regions in the USA (the 50 states and the District of Columbia) and at 54 regions in Europe (a decomposition of 14 countries, all EU countries with the exception of Luxembourg). He asks what happens when an adverse asymmetric shock occurs, i.e. when it affects just one region. Figure 15.10 shows the result. The figure depicts the joint behaviour of total

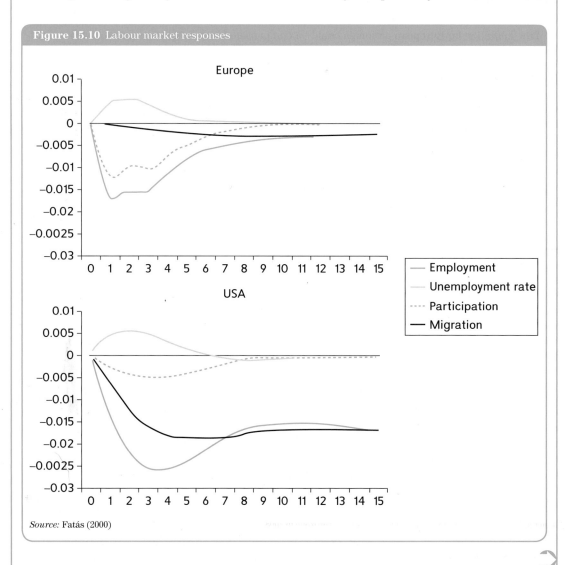

Figure 15.10 Labour market responses

Source: Fatás (2000)

employment, unemployment and the participation rate in each region (all compared with the overall situation in the USA and Europe, respectively).[1] Obviously, employment declines and, for the same shock size, the effect is quantitatively similar in Europe and the USA. The difference lies elsewhere. In the USA, most of the drop in employment is met by regional emigration; people move to more fortunate parts of the country. In Europe, instead, most of the drop in employment is met by a fall in the participation rate; people withdraw from the labour force and stay at home. Interestingly, in the long run, in the USA those who leave do not return, and in Europe those who stop working remain inactive.

This study corroborates a key element of OCA theory: labour mobility crucially affects the response to asymmetric shocks. The twist is that, with low European labour mobility, following an adverse shock, people become unemployed and many others simply give up the hope of working.

[1] Box 8.1 defines employment, unemployment and participation rates.

Low migration by European nationals could be compensated by immigration from outside the EU.[7] If immigrant workers were to move to where job offers exceed supply, some of the costs of a monetary union would be reduced. Even viewed this way, immigration – a big political issue in Europe – is relatively limited in Europe, as shown in Chapter 8.

In summary, Europe is far from fulfilling the labour mobility criterion. An important implication is that asymmetric shocks, when they occur, are likely to be met by unemployment in countries facing a loss of competitiveness. Box 15.8 reports that, indeed, when asymmetric shocks occur, migration plays a smaller role in Europe than in the USA, with the unfortunate result that employment takes most of the burden.

15.6.2 Diversification and trade dissimilarity

The Kenen criterion rests on the idea that asymmetric shocks are less likely among countries that share similar production patterns and whose trade is diversified. Figure 15.11 presents an index of dissimilarity within European trade. The index looks at how each country's trade structure differs from the situation in Germany (old members) or the Eurozone (new members). The index is based on the decomposition of trade into three classes of goods: agriculture, minerals and manufacturing.

Dissimilarity is highest for Latvia and Denmark, two countries that have not joined the Eurozone, but it is also low for non-member countries such as the Czech Republic, the UK and Hungary. Of interest is the case of the Netherlands, a natural gas exporter that sets it apart and yet it is an enthusiastic member of the Eurozone. The Dutch authorities must believe that the costs are outweighed by the benefits since their economy is deeply integrated with the European economy and they wish to be deeply involved in European integration.

15.6.3 Openness

Openness, which may reduce the usefulness of an independent exchange rate, is usually defined as the share of economic activity devoted to international trade. The ratio of exports to GDP measures the proportion of domestic production that is exported. The ratio of imports to GDP measures the proportion of domestic spending that falls on imports. The openness index presented in Figure 15.12 sums up both (and can go beyond 100 per cent). Most European countries are very open, the more so the smaller they are, which explains why the smaller countries have traditionally been the most enthusiastic supporters of the monetary union. This applies to both old and new EU member countries.

As far as the McKinnon criterion is concerned, most EU economies qualify for joining a monetary union. They are very open and well-integrated within Europe.

[7] See Chapter 8 for an analysis of immigration.

Figure 15.11 Trade dissimilarity index

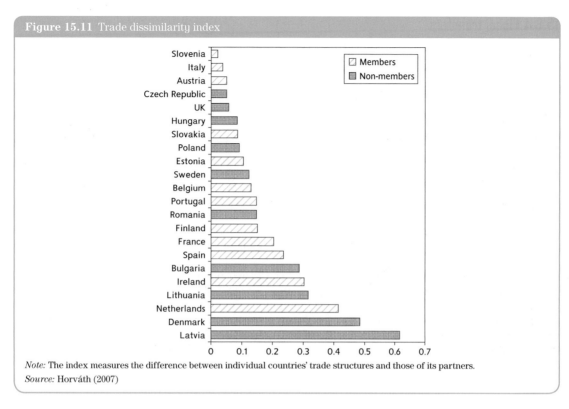

Note: The index measures the difference between individual countries' trade structures and those of its partners.
Source: Horváth (2007)

Figure 15.12 Openness to trade, 2011

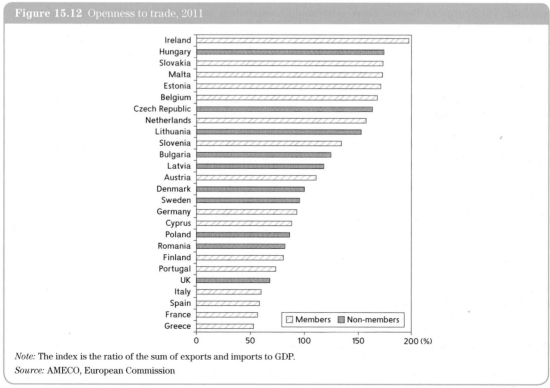

Note: The index is the ratio of the sum of exports and imports to GDP.
Source: AMECO, European Commission

15.6.4 Fiscal transfers

Up until the debt crisis, there was no cyclical transfer system in the EU. The EU budget is small, slightly above 1 per cent of GDP, and almost entirely spent on three items: the Commission's operating expenses, the Common Agricultural Policy and the Structural Funds which support the poorer regions irrespective of whether they are hit by shocks. The crisis has led to the creation of the European Financial Stability Facility (EFSF), transformed into the European Stability Mechanism (ESM), as explained in Chapter 19. Initially designed specifically to deal with public debt crises, the EMS can also be used for bank recapitalization. It may evolve over time to deal with a wider set of disturbances. On this criterion, Europe is definitely not an optimum monetary union, although a first small step has been taken.

15.6.5 Homogeneous preferences

Do all countries share similar views about the use of monetary policy? On the basis of past inflation rates, this does not seem to be the case. Low-inflation Germany and formerly high-inflation Italy or Greece have very little in common. Similarly, looking at public debt (Chapter 18), a gulf separates European countries' approaches to fiscal policy. So, is the verdict negative? It may be too early to tell but the crisis shows that these concerns are real.

Why has the quality of macroeconomic policies been so diverse in Europe? Is it in the genes? Medical research has not yet revealed any clues! But economic research has a lot to say about the incentives facing policy makers. Broadly defined, political institutions shape their reactions to various events, and policy-making institutions differ from one country to another. This includes the respective roles of the executive and the parliament, the number of political parties and trade unions, the role of ideology and much more.

The solution has been to accompany integration steps with the setting up of common institutions. In fact, one reason why the inflation-prone countries have been eager to join the monetary union is that it provides for a degree of monetary policy discipline that has been elusive in the past. As far as the single currency is concerned, Chapter 17 shows that a key preoccupation has been to guarantee macroeconomic stability. The European Central Bank is strongly independent and constitutionally committed to price stability. National deficits are bound by an excessive deficit procedure. Still, although all countries are increasingly operating under common institutions, they do not fully share the same views on each and every issue that arises.

The result is occasional friction among governments and a sense of estrangement expressed in public opinion, which was particularly visible when the Constitution was rejected in the spring of 2005. More seriously, these divergences have been on public display during the debt crisis. As recounted in Chapter 19, they explain the inadequacy of policy responses.

We can conclude that there remains some heterogeneity among national preferences. This criterion is only partly fulfilled.

15.6.6 Solidarity vs. nationalism

How deeply do European citizens feel a sense of solidarity? Put differently, to what extent are they willing to give up elements of national sovereignty in the pursuit of common interest? There is no simple, uncontroversial way to measure the willingness of European citizens. An indication is given in Figure 15.13, however, based on the results of an opinion poll conducted in 2006 that asked respondents whether they felt European.[8] On average, 16 per cent said they 'often' felt that way; 43 per cent said 'never'; and 38 per cent said 'sometimes'. The figure shows the 'often' answer for each country. Clearly, European citizenship is not a widely-felt sentiment. On the other hand, less than half of Europeans never feel European, although this is the case for two-thirds of British citizens! Clearly, the glass is half full or half empty!

The European debt crisis offers a real-life test of this question. As Chapter 19 explains, the initial reaction to the Greek debt crisis was to extend collective support, very explicitly in the name of solidarity. As the crisis deepened, however, nationalistic sentiments started to be expressed. According to Reuters,

---

[8] This is the most recent poll conducted on on this issue. Tellingly perhaps, the question has not been asked since.

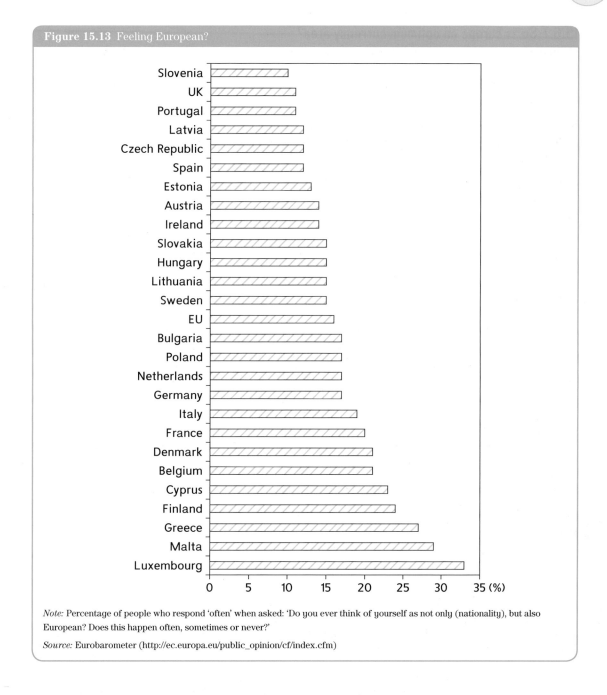

Figure 15.13 Feeling European?

Note: Percentage of people who respond 'often' when asked: 'Do you ever think of yourself as not only (nationality), but also European? Does this happen often, sometimes or never?'

Source: Eurobarometer (http://ec.europa.eu/public_opinion/cf/index.cfm)

the German newspaper *Bild* 'lambasted Greece as a nation of lazy cheats who should be "thrown out of the euro on their ear"'. To which slur some Greek deputies responded: 'By their statements, German politicians and German financial institutions play a leading role in a wretched game of profiteering at the expense of the Greek people.'[9]

All in all, Europe is not scoring very highly on this criterion; neither, however, is it failing badly.

---

[9] http://www.reuters.com/article/2010/02/18/greece-germany-idUSLDE61H1IZ20100218.

15.6.7 So, is Europe an optimum currency area?

In the end, most European countries do well on openness and diversification, two of the three classic economic OCA criteria, and fail on the third, labour mobility. Europe also fails on fiscal transfers, with an unclear verdict on the remaining two political criteria. Table 15.1 summarizes this appraisal. The mixed performance that it reveals can be interpreted in two ways.

Table 15.1   OCA scorecard

Criterion	Satisfied?
Labour mobility	No
Trade openness	Yes
Product diversification	Yes
Fiscal transfers	No
Homogeneity of preferences	Partly
Commonality of destiny	?

First, the table explains why the single currency project has been and remains controversial. Neither the supporters nor the opponents have been able to produce an overwhelming case. That was only to be expected, however. A monetary union entails costs and benefits, neither of which can be measured nor even compared. The OCA criteria themselves are not black or white, entirely satisfied or entirely violated. Ultimately, the economic case is undecided, and the decision to create the monetary union must rest on political considerations.

Second, the partial fulfilment of the OCA criteria implies that, given that the decision to go ahead has been taken, costs will be involved. The OCA theory identifies these costs and suggests two main conclusions: the costs will mainly arise in the labour markets and fiscal transfers will have to be rethought. It is often argued that the Eurozone crisis is a proof that Europe is not an optimum currency area. That, we knew. The crisis simply reminds us that asymmetric shocks do happen and that they can be painful. This is the fate of every large monetary union, as Box 15.1 reminds us.

15.7 Is Europe becoming an optimum currency area?

The endogeneity hypothesis presented in Section 15.5 is puzzling. More than 15 years after the creation of the euro, are there any signs of endogeneity? Much has changed regarding the political criteria, as explained in Chapter 19. Here, we take a brief look at the three economic criteria.

15.7.1 Effects on trade

Many European policy makers strongly believe that stable exchange rates promote trade integration. Indeed, as explained in Chapter 14, this conviction coupled with the impossible trinity principle has driven the process of monetary integration. As time passes, we can start evaluating the impact of the single currency on intra-Eurozone trade.

When the monetary project was initially mooted, this issue was intensely debated. Policy-makers were understandably keen to believe that intra-Eurozone trade would quickly deepen, and they may well have oversold the case. A body of economic research, reviewed in Box 15.9, backed this view.

15.7.2 Effects on specialization

More trade integration within the Eurozone may have a disquieting effect, however. If trade leads to more specialization as each country or region focuses on its comparative advantage, then the Kenen

---

Box 15.9   The Rose and border effects

Andrew Rose, from the University of California at Berkeley, initially found that trade within a pair of countries that belong to a currency area is three times larger than trade within otherwise similar countries (2000). Another approach has been to look at trade in border areas. Engel and Rogers (1996) focused on the border between the USA and Canada. They observed that the prices of the same goods in different cities become increasingly different the further apart are the cities. Their calculations imply that just crossing the border has the same effect as travelling 3000 km within the same country. Further work has shown that, among the various reasons why borders matter, the fact that currencies differ plays a powerful role.

These effects are huge, so huge that they are unbelievable. A large literature has explored the robustness of these results. Reviewing the Rose effect, Baldwin et al. (2008) conclude that, so far, the euro has probably increased trade by some 5 per cent. This is much smaller than initially found, yet it remains a significant effect and the process is likely not to be complete. The same study also attributes to the common currency an increase in cross-border investments and mergers and acquisitions. This means that firms increasingly operate by assembling parts manufactured in different countries.

---

diversification criterion may become less fulfilled as time goes by. If, instead, trade integration takes the form of intra-industry trade, then diversification will increase. This would occur if exports and imports include increasingly similar goods. In that case, every country produces the whole range of goods, simply with different brands, offering customers more choice. The jury is still out, but the evidence accumulated so far seems to support the view that diversification increases with trade integration. In that case, the Eurozone is becoming more of an OCA.

15.7.3 Effects on labour markets

European labour mobility is low and few expect it to increase dramatically in the near future. An alternative to mobility is flexibility, and the argument runs as follows. European labour markets are noticeably less flexible than their US counterparts. For example, in the USA firms are quite free to fire workers when economic conditions worsen, whereas in Europe firing is costly because it entails severance pay and adherence to numerous regulations. In addition, US unemployed workers receive less generous welfare support, which encourages them to find and accept another job as soon as possible, sometimes elsewhere in the country, possibly less well paid and in a different activity. Can the loss of the exchange rate encourage reforms in this area?

One possibility is that the single currency increases the costs involved in the 'European way' and reduces opposition to measures that aim at making labour markets more flexible. When each country had its own currency, workers advocated using monetary policy and the exchange rate to boost the economy. This is now impossible, at least at the national level, and to date there are no pan-European trade unions. In addition, the increasing transparency in goods prices should benefit countries where labour markets are more flexible. Thus, it is believed, economic competition will indirectly lead to competition among individual countries' welfare programmes, which will shift the trade-off between economic performance and labour protection. The opposite, a hardening of labour market rigidities, is possible too. This possibility is based on an increasing emphasis on 'Social Europe'. Advocates of a high degree of labour protection understand well the risk of competition among welfare programmes and have successfully called for the adoption of Union-wide minimum standards.

There is no clear evidence yet of where things are going. The European crisis may act as a trigger. Under heavy pressure, the Greek and Irish governments have pushed forward wage cuts in the public sector. If this is confirmed, it would be an illustration of how OCA principles operate. Non-fulfilment of a criterion makes the common currency difficult and costly, possibly leading to a crisis situation. The crisis in turn breaks down barriers to reform. Of course, an alternative scenario is that it is the common currency that breaks down. At the time of writing, both outcomes are plausible.

15.7.4 Fiscal transfers

Much the same applies to fiscal transfers. In a previous edition of this book we wrote: 'There is at present no political support for established extensive and automatic intra-European transfers, but proposals regularly surface. … It is reasonably certain that, in the not-too-distant future, Europe will have adopted some form of transfer scheme.' Some schemes are currently being hotly debated. They are examined in Chapter 19.

15.7.5 Beyond the OCA criteria: politics

We have reached two important conclusions. First, Europe is not exactly an optimum currency area; it does well on some but not all of the criteria. Second, it is not merely labour mobility that is insufficient; more generally, the labour markets display significant rigidity, especially in the large countries. In these countries, the monetary union may worsen an already painful situation of high unemployment.

It is natural therefore to ask why the European heads of state and government who gathered in Maastricht in 1991 still decided to take the risk and set up a monetary union. The answer is: politics.[10] Interestingly enough, Harvard economist Martin Feldstein, a sharp critic of the single currency, sees it as a source of conflict:

> *Political leaders in Europe seem to be prepared to ignore these adverse consequences because they see EMU as a way of furthering the political agenda of a federalist European political union. … The adverse economic effects of EMU and the broader political disagreements will nevertheless induce some countries to ask whether they have made a mistake in joining. Although a sovereign country could in principle withdraw from the EMU, the potential trade sanctions and other pressures on such a country are likely to make membership in EMU irreversible unless there is widespread economic dislocation in Europe or, more generally, a collapse of peaceful coexistence within Europe.*

> Feldstein, 1997, p. 41

In Feldstein's view, the euro is not only unjustified on economic grounds (it is not an OCA) but its survival will require a major step towards a federal Europe, including common defence and foreign policies as well as a generalized harmonization of taxation and labour market regulations. In every member country of the Union, a large number of people share this view and are adamant in their desire to preserve the nation-state.

Indeed, political considerations have been paramount in launching the euro. It is fair to say that the political leaders who agreed on the monetary union did not consider the OCA theory at all (see Box 15.10). They were largely focusing on the symbolic nature of the undertaking. Precisely because money and statehood are intertwined, their intention was to move one step further in the direction of an 'ever-closer union'.

Box 15.10 The return of the OCA theory

The negotiators who prepared the Maastricht Treaty did not pay attention to the OCA theory. They were first and foremost heeding the impossible trinity principle, focusing on the need to preserve exchange rate stability in the wake of full capital movement liberalization. They were also concerned that the new currency be as strong as the Deutschmark, hence the tough entry conditions detailed in Chapter 16. Overall they believed that, if the countries allowed into the monetary union had sufficiently converged, and if the new central bank was well protected from political interference, then the undertaking would work.

---

[10] For a detailed discussion, see the exchange between Feldstein and Wyplosz in the *Journal of Economic Perspectives*, 11(4): 3–42, 1997.

Price convergence:

Cavallo, A., B. Neiman and R. Rigobon (2013) 'The euro and price convergence: you wanted it … you got it!', Vox EU, http://www.voxeu.org/article/euro-and-price-convergence.

The Hume mechanism at work:

Auer, R. (2013) 'Rapid current-account rebalancing in the southern Eurozone', Vox EU, http://www.voxeu.org/article/rapid-current-account-rebalancing-southern-eurozone.

References

Baldwin, R., V. DiNino, L. Fontagné, R. De Santis and D. Taglioni (2008) *Study on the Impact of the Euro on Trade and Foreign Direct Investment*, European Economy – Economic Papers 321, European Commission.

Engel, C. and J. Rogers (1996) 'How wide is the border?', *American Economic Review*, 86 (December): 1112–25.

Fatás, A. (2000) 'Intranational migration: business cycles and growth', in E. van Wincoop and G. Hess (eds) *Intranational Macroeconomics*, Cambridge University Press, Cambridge.

Feldstein, M. (1997) 'The political economy of the European Economic and Monetary Union: political sources of an economic liability', *Journal of Economic Perspectives*, 11(4): 23–42.

Horváth, R. (2007) 'Ready for euro? Evidence on EU new member states', *Applied Economics Letters*, 14(14): 1083–36.

Jonung, L. and **J. Vlachos** (2007) *The Euro – What's in it for me? An Economic Analysis of the Swedish Euro Referendum of 2003*, European Economy – Economic Papers 296, Directorate General Economic and Monetary Affairs, European Commission.

Mundell, R. (1973) 'A plan for a European currency', in H. Johnson and A. Swoboda (eds) *The Economics of Common Currencies*, George Allen & Unwin, London.

Rose, A. (2000) 'One money, one market: the effects of common currencies on trade', *Economic Policy*, 30: 7–46.

Annex: Aggregate demand and aggregate supply

This annex presents an extended explanation of why the *AD* curve is downward sloping and the *AS* curve is upward sloping.

A15.1 Aggregate demand

Aggregate demand is directly related to the *IS–MP–IRP* framework developed in Chapter 13. Looking at Figure A15.1, we ask what happens when the real exchange rate EP/P^* appreciates, which reduces demand for our good. As we do so, we assume that it is P that rises, not P^* that declines because we take the rest of the world 'as given'. As for the nominal exchange rate E, it is either left to float, and its evolution is part of the analysis, or fixed. Starting from point A in the left-hand chart of Figure 15.6, the *IS* schedule shifts to the left, to the *IS'* position. What happens next depends on the exchange rate regime.

When the exchange rate is fixed, the *MP* schedule is irrelevant because the central bank has lost its autonomy. The economy moves to point B: as expected, the loss of competitiveness leads to a fall in demand. The effect is shown in the right-hand chart: a real appreciation takes the economy from point A to point B. The *AD* schedule is indeed downward sloping.

When the exchange rate is flexible, the *IS* schedule moves passively to meet the intersection of the *MP* and *IRP* schedules. However, the central bank is now autonomous. As explained in Box 15.2, central banks are committed to price stability. As the price level P has increased, the central bank will typically want to counteract this change. To do so, it will raise its interest rate over and above what is warranted by the activity level. This is captured by an upward shift of the *MP* schedule, to *MP'* in the left-hand chart of Figure 15.6. The economy moves to point B. (To keep the chart clean, we assume that *MP'* goes through point B, but that does not have to be the case; anyhow, it will intersect the *IRP* line to the left of point A, which is what matters.) Note that the *IS* curve will meet the two other schedules at point B by moving left, as the monetary policy tightening triggers capital inflows, which lead to a nominal exchange rate appreciation, further raising the real exchange rate. Transposing this result to the right-hand chart delivers the downward-sloping schedule *AD*.

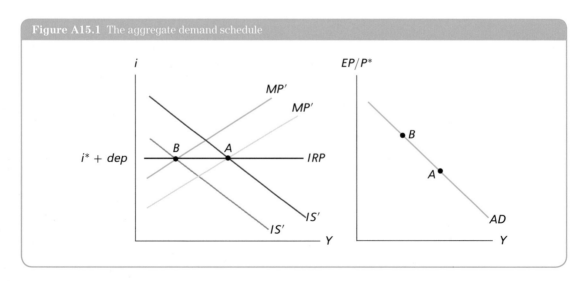

Figure A15.1 The aggregate demand schedule

A15.2 Aggregate supply

We have looked so far at what customers – domestic and foreign households, firms and governments – intend to buy. This is why we refer to the above curve as representing aggregate demand. But how do we know that the producers are ready to supply this exact quantity of goods? Each firm has equipment and a workforce in place. It is set up to produce the corresponding quantity of goods. But if demand is weak, it will obviously produce less, keeping workers idle or working shorter hours and possibly even firing some of them. If demand is strong, it can increase output by hiring more workers or asking for extra hours. In responding to demand, firms look at their profitability: when is it worth changing the level of activity?

A key profitability criterion is the price at which it sells goods. If the price rises, it is worthwhile facing the added costs and producing more. When the price declines, the firm needs to make savings, which means producing less with fewer workers. This is why the aggregate supply (AS) schedule, which represents all the production of all the domestic firms, is shown as upward sloping in Figure A15.2.

A little detail is important: in Figure A15.2, the vertical axis displays the real exchange rate EP/P^*, not just the domestic price level P. The reason is that the production of most goods (and services) involves the use of imported goods, such as parts, energy based on imported oil or gas, possibly licences, etc. For domestic producers, these are costs, measured in domestic currency as P^*/E. If they rise, and EP/P^* declines, profitability declines and firms will reduce the supply. Once again, the relevant measure of external competitiveness is EP/P^*, the ratio of the domestic price level P to the foreign price level P^*/E, both expressed in the domestic currency.

A15.3 General equilibrium with the real exchange rate

We are now equipped with an analysis of aggregate demand AD, derived from the results from Section 15.3, and with the aggregate supply schedule AS. General equilibrium occurs when demand and supply are equal, given equilibrium conditions in the goods market (IS) and in the financial markets (IRP). This is shown in Figure A15.2 as the intersection of AD and AS.

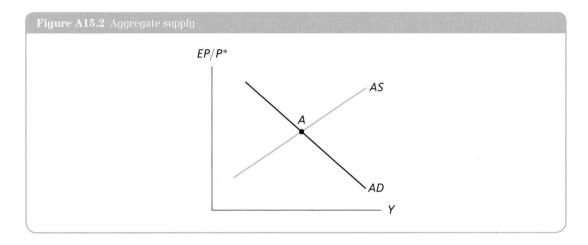

Figure A15.2 Aggregate supply

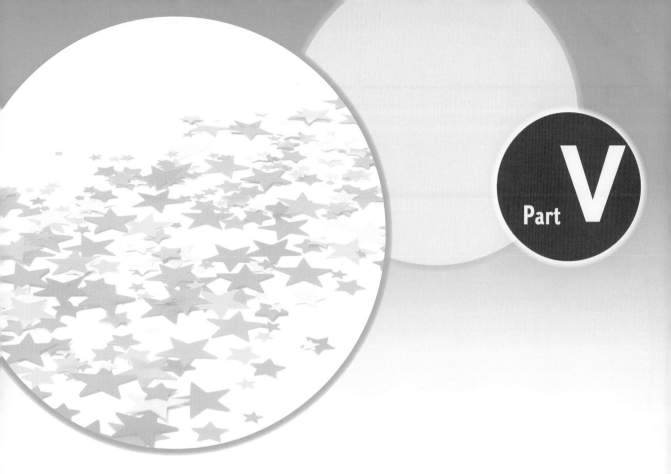

Part V

EU Monetary and Fiscal Policies

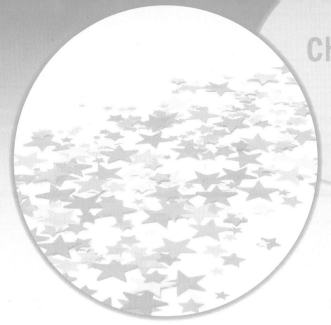

Chapter

16

A normal central bank is a monopolist. Today's Eurosystem is, instead, an archipelago of monopolists.

Tommaso Padoa-Schioppa (Former Executive Board member of the ECB)

The European monetary union

Chapter Contents

Introduction

How the European monetary union functions was established by the Maastricht Treaty. Chapter 14 has explained the genesis of this treaty and its key features. Since the adoption of the euro, a number of difficulties have arisen, which should not come as a surprise. Forming a monetary union among highly developed countries is a first and it is also a complex undertaking. It would have been truly extraordinary to have got it 100 per cent correct right from scratch! Over time, the monetary union is being adapted to deal with problems as they arise and one presumes that this process will go on for decades to come. This chapter presents the current situation.

Section 16.1 lays out the principles that drove the architecture of the Eurozone, emphasizing the priority given to price stability and the need for central bank independence. Accordingly, admission to the Eurozone was based on five convergence criteria; they are presented and interpreted in Section 16.2. The original central banking structure involves a common central bank, the ECB, and the national central banks. Together they make up the Eurosystem, which is described in Section 16.3. Their governance is presented in Section 16.4, while Section 16.5 explains how independence is guaranteed and how democratic accountability operates. The next section explains how the Eurosystem operates and its choice of monetary policy instruments. The last section reviews the experience during the quiet pre-crisis years.

16.1 Principles

The vision of the monetary union reflects its birth as the outcome of a deal between Germany, which agreed to abandon its strong currency, and the other countries, which wished to move away from the Deutschmark-dominated and unstable EMS while keeping exchange rates stable. Highly concerned that the new currency would not be as strong as the mark, Germany requested guarantees. This led to a set of principles.

16.1.1 Price stability

The Maastricht Treaty specifies that the main task of the Eurosystem is to deliver price stability:

> *The primary objective of the ESCB shall be to maintain price stability. Without prejudice to that objective, it shall support the general economic policies in the Union in order to contribute to the achievement of the latter's objectives.*
>
> Article 282-2, Treaty on the Functioning of the European Union

The Treaty does not give an exact definition of price stability. The Eurosystem[1] has chosen to interpret it as follows: 'Price stability is defined as a year-on-year increase in the Harmonized Index of Consumer Prices (HICP)[2] for the Eurozone of close to but below 2 per cent. Price stability is to be maintained over the medium term.' Many central banks typically announce an admissible range for inflation; the Eurosystem's target is not set in this way but it is commonly understood that the implicit objective is to keep inflation between 1.5 and 2 per cent. The meaning of 'the medium term' is also imprecise; but it is understood to refer to a 2–3 year horizon.

The logic behind the price stability objective is the monetary neutrality principle (Chapter 13): in the long run, monetary policy only impacts inflation. Because inflation is ultimately determined by monetary policy, it is the duty of the Eurosystem to achieve price stability. In the shorter run, monetary policy affects other economic variables, chiefly the economic growth rate and unemployment. Thus, while the Treaty considers price stability a 'primary objective', it stipulates that 'without prejudice to that objective', the Eurosystem may pursue 'secondary objectives'.

---

[1] The Eurosystem is defined below. In brief, it is the central bank.

[2] The Harmonized Index of Consumer Prices is an area-wide consumer price index. The same method is also used to compute national HICPs.

These secondary objectives are described above in Delphic terms. The 'general economic policies in the Union' refer to Article 3, which lists many objectives, including 'the sustainable development of Europe based on balanced economic growth and price stability', and more. This leaves the Eurosystem with quite some leeway to decide its strategy. The hierarchy between price stability and other objectives has become standard among many central banks, with some exceptions, including the USA, which puts employment and price stability on the same level.

16.1.2 Central bank independence

In order to fulfil its main task of delivering price stability, a central bank must be free to operate without outside interference. While, in principle, everyone approves of price stability, some important actors occasionally have second thoughts. In particular, financially stressed governments may come to see the printing press as the least-bad option. Likewise exporting firms, whose competitiveness depends on the exchange rate, frequently ask their central banks to relax monetary policy,[3] and they are supported by trade unions, which are concerned with employment. Debtors like inflation for it erases the value of their (non-indexed) liabilities. Financial institutions often make larger profits when liquidity is plentiful. In any democracy, these are formidable coalitions. Experience with high inflation has shown that these effects are temporary – another manifestation of long-term monetary neutrality – while inflation is in fact painful, unfair to the poor and its elimination requires long periods of slow growth and high unemployment. This is why the modern trend of focusing monetary policy on price stability also argues in favour of central bank independence from all segments of society and, in particular, from the political powers.

16.1.3 Fiscal discipline

Even with a strong guarantee of central bank independence, governments may create – intentionally or not – conditions such that monetary policy can be undermined. History shows how to do it. When a government runs budget deficits, it borrows from the financial markets. If the deficits are large enough for long enough, the markets may refuse to offer more loans. This immediately creates a financial crisis. The government can no longer operate, the exchange rate is likely to plummet and the banking system – a big lender to governments – is under threat.

The pressure is now on the central bank: either it creates money to finance the deficit or the country experiences an acute crisis. Citizens flee the domestic currency, which creates an unmanageable situation for the commercial banks. A central bank may turn a blind eye and let the fire consume the economy. Most likely, it caves in and prints money. The result is invariably 'inflation in the long run', but in a panic situation the long run comes about extremely swiftly, a matter of weeks rather than months. This is why there can be no central bank independence without fiscal discipline.

In a monetary union this threat is compounded by the fact that the incentives to follow fiscal indiscipline are even stronger than in a purely national setting. Running budget deficits is politically expedient. Spend now, tax later, after the elections, is already a powerful incentive. In a monetary union the incentive becomes: spend now, then get the collective central bank to pay for it. This is why the Maastricht Treaty includes a fiscal discipline clause. The resulting Stability and Growth Pact is the object of the next chapter.

16.2 The five entry conditions

As noted in the previous chapter, the OCA principles were not much appreciated by the authors of the Maastricht Treaty. Admission to the Eurozone was not based on the OCA criteria, but rather on a very different principle: the coronation theory. According to this view, countries should only join the Eurozone once they have demonstrated that they can live according to the guiding principles set in the Treaty. This has led to the adoption of five entry conditions.

---

[3] The *IS–MP–IRP* framework of Chapter 13 explains why. Under a flexible exchange rate regime, a monetary relaxation is captured by a downward shift of the *MP* curve, which leads to an exchange rate depreciation.

16.2.1 Inflation

The first criterion deals directly with inflation. To be eligible for membership of the monetary union, a country's inflation rate should not exceed the average of the three lowest inflation rates achieved by the EU Member States by more than 1.5 percentage points. Figure 16.1 shows how the 'Club Med' countries of southern Europe managed to bring their inflation rates to below the acceptable limit by 1998. Greece (not shown) failed on that criterion.

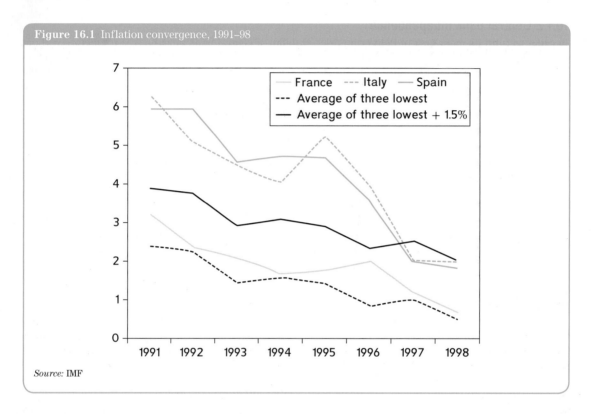

Figure 16.1 Inflation convergence, 1991–98

Source: IMF

16.2.2 Long-term nominal interest rate

An inflation-prone country could possibly squeeze prices temporarily, on the last year before admission – for example, by freezing administered prices (electricity, transport) – only to relax the effort afterwards. In order to weed out potential cheaters, a second criterion requires that the long-term interest rate should not exceed by more than two percentage points the average rates observed in the three lowest-inflation-rate countries. The reasoning is shrewd. Long-term interest rates mostly reflect markets' assessment of long-term inflation for reasons explained in Box 16.1. Achieving a low long-term interest rate therefore requires convincing naturally sceptical financial markets that inflation will remain low 'for ever'.

Box 16.1 The Fisher principle

The Fisher principle is usually stated as follows: nominal interest rate = real interest rate + expected inflation. Since the real interest rate is reasonably constant and set worldwide, the main driving force determining the long-term interest rate is the expected long-term inflation rate.

This principle can be seen as an implication of some of the tools developed in Chapter 13. The interest rate parity condition links the interest rate to expected exchange rate depreciation:

$$i = i* + \text{expected exchange rate depreciation}$$

Domestic   Foreign

interest rate   interest rate

Purchasing power parity links the exchange rate to domestic and foreign prices. If the real exchange rate $EP/P*$ is constant, we have seen that:

$$\text{Exchange rate depreciation} = \pi - \pi*$$

Domestic   Foreign

inflation rate inflation rate

This implies that the expected rate of depreciation is equal to the difference between expected domestic inflation and expected foreign inflation.

Combining these two conditions, we find:

$$i = i* + \text{expected } \pi - \text{expected p*}$$

This relationship says that the nominal interest rate is driven by expected domestic inflation π and by the foreign real interest rate, i.e. the nominal interest rate $i*$ less expected foreign inflation.

16.2.3 ERM membership

The same concern about a superficial conversion to price stability lies behind the third criterion. Here, the idea is that a country must have demonstrated its ability to keep its exchange rate tied to the currencies of its future monetary union partners. The requirement is that every country must have taken part in the ERM for at least two years without having to devalue its currency.[4]

16.2.4 Budget deficit

The three previous criteria aim at demonstrating a country's acceptance of, and ability to achieve, permanently low inflation, but it makes sense to also eradicate the incentives to tolerate high inflation. Mindful of the potentially deleterious effects of fiscal indiscipline on monetary policy (Section 16.1.3), the fourth convergence criterion sets a limit on acceptable budget deficits. But what limit?

Here again, German influence prevailed. Germany had long operated a 'golden rule', which specifies that budget deficits are only acceptable if they correspond to public investment spending (on roads, telecommunications and other infrastructure). The idea is that public investment is a source of growth, which eventually generates the resources needed to pay for the initial borrowing. The German 'golden rule' considers that public investment typically amounts to some 3 per cent of GDP. Hence the condition that budget deficits should not exceed 3 per cent of GDP.[5]

16.2.5 Public debt

Much as inflation can be lowered temporarily, deficits can be made to look good in any given year (for example, by shifting some public spending to next year and some of last year's tax revenues to this year).

---

[4] The Exchange Rate Mechanism is presented in detail in Chapter 14.

[5] This entry condition is formally distinct from the same limit prescribed by the Stability and Growth Pact, which is studied in Chapter 17. There is a logical link between the two limits, though: having joined the monetary union, a country is not allowed to let its budget deficit rise again.

Thus it was decided that a more permanent feature of fiscal discipline ought to be added. The fifth and last criterion mandates a maximum level for the public debt. Here again, the question was: which ceiling?

Unimaginatively, perhaps, the ceiling was set at 60 per cent of GDP because it was the average debt level when the Maastricht Treaty was being negotiated in 1991. An additional reason was that the 60 per cent debt limit can be seen as compatible with a deficit debt ceiling of 3 per cent, as explained in Box 16.2.

Box 16.2   The arithmetic of deficits and debts

Debts grow out of deficits, but how does the debt/GDP ratio relate to the deficit/GDP ratio? A little arithmetic helps. If total nominal debt at the end of year t is B_t, its increase during the year is $B_t - B_{t-1}$, and this is equal to the annual deficit D_t:

$$B_t - B_{t-1} = D_t \qquad (1)$$

The two fiscal convergence criteria refer not to the debt and deficit levels, but to their ratios to nominal GDP Y, denoted as b_t and d_t, respectively. Divide the previous accounting equality by the current year GDP to get:

$$\frac{B_t - B_{t-1}}{Y_t} = \frac{D_t}{Y_t} \text{ or } b_t - \frac{B_{t-1}}{Y_t} = d_t \qquad (2)$$

Then note that

$$\frac{B_{t-1}}{Y_t} = \frac{B_{t-1}}{Y_{t-1}} \frac{Y_{t-1}}{Y_t} = \frac{b_{t-1}}{1+g_t}$$

where

$$g_t = \frac{Y_t - Y_{t-1}}{Y_{t-1}} = \frac{Y_t}{Y_{t-1}} - 1$$

is the growth rate of GDP in year t. We can rewrite the debt growth eqn (2) as:

$$b_t - b_{t-1} = (1 + g_t)d_t - g_t b_t \qquad (3)$$

If the debt-to-GDP ratio b is to remain constant, we need to have $b_t = b_{t-1}$, which from eqn (3) implies:

$$d_t = \frac{g_t}{1+g_t} b_t \qquad (4)$$

The fiscal convergence criteria set $d_t = 3$ per cent and $b_t = 60$ per cent. If nominal GDP grows by 5 per cent, eqn (4) is approximately satisfied. The implicit assumption is therefore that real GDP annual growth is about 3 per cent and inflation is 2 per cent, hence a nominal GDP growth rate of 5 per cent.

If the debt level is constant, the debt/GDP ratio declines as the result of GDP growth, the more so the faster nominal GDP grows. This means that some debt increase, and therefore some deficit, is compatible with a constant debt/GDP ratio, and the tolerable deficit is larger the faster nominal GDP grows.

However, according to what constitutes the definition of average, some countries had debts in excess of 60 per cent of GDP, and some much larger. In particular, Belgium's public debt then stood at some 120 per cent of GDP. Yet, by 1991, Belgium had overhauled its public finances and was adamant that it was now committed to adhering to strict budgetary discipline. Even so, it would take a long time to bring its debt to below 60 per cent.[6] As a founding member of the Common Market in 1957, an enthusiastic European country and a long-time advocate of monetary union, Belgium argued that it could not be left out because of past sins now firmly repudiated. At its request, the criterion was couched in prudent terms, requiring that the debt-to-GDP ratio be either less than 60 per cent or 'moving in that direction'.

For the countries then members of the EU, Figure 16.2 shows the deficits and debts in 1998, the last year before the launch of the monetary union, which is when it was decided whether the entry criteria were being fulfilled. The shaded rectangle shows where countries have strictly fulfilled the two budget criteria. All countries managed to bring their deficits below the 3 per cent threshold, sometimes thanks to accounting trickery.[7] Only a few, however, could report debts below 60 per cent of GDP. In the end, all were saved by the 'Belgian clause'.

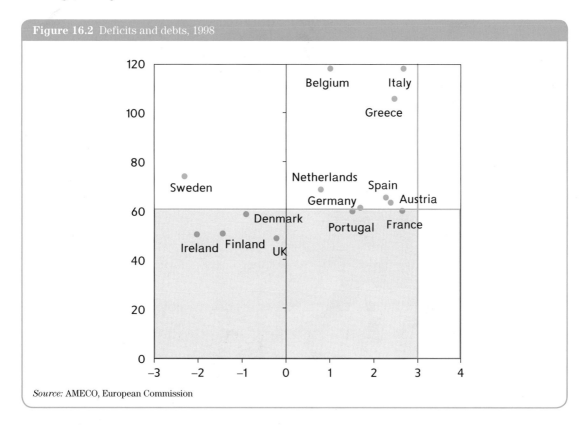

Figure 16.2 Deficits and debts, 1998

Source: AMECO, European Commission

16.2.6 Two-speed Europe

An important aspect of the Maastricht Treaty is that it introduced, for the first time, the idea that a major integration could leave some countries out. The Treaty specifies that all EU member countries are expected to join as soon as practicable. Denmark and the UK were given an exemption. By 2014, 19 of the 27 EU member countries had adopted the euro; see Figure 16.3. These countries include the 11 original members, which were joined by Greece in 2001, Slovenia in 2007, Cyprus and Malta in 2008, Slovakia in 2009, Estonia in 2011, Latvia in 2014 and Lithuania in 2015.

This 'two-speed' arrangement is not without problems. The endogeneity of the OCA view (see Chapter 15) means that the Eurozone countries are becoming increasingly cohesive. Although the crisis has led to divisions

---

[6] Indeed, by 2008, before the collapse of Wall Street, the Belgian debt had been reduced to only 82.6 per cent of GDP.

[7] France privatized part of its state-owned telecommunications corporation, which provided the revenues needed to achieve the deficit target. Italy collected at the end of 1998 some taxes that would normally have been due in early 1999. Even the German government considered selling gold to pay back its debt but backed off as the Bundesbank publicly attacked the idea.

among them, the Eurozone member countries have been encouraged to develop their own consultation mechanisms. Eurozone heads of state and government regularly meet when they attend European Council meetings, occasionally overshadowing the full meeting. The ministers of finance of the Eurozone have created the Eurogroup, whose decisions may have an impact on the non-Eurozone member countries.

Figure 16.3 The Eurozone inside the EU

Source: European Central Bank

16.3 The Eurosystem

16.3.1 *N* countries, *N* + 1 central banks

With a single currency there can be only one interest rate,[8] one exchange rate vis-à-vis the rest of the world, and therefore one monetary policy. Normally this implies a single central bank, but this is not quite the way the euro area was set up! Each member still comes equipped with its own central bank, the last remaining vestige of monetary sovereignty. No matter how daring the founding fathers were, they stopped short of merging the national central banks into a single institution, partly in fear of having to dismiss thousands of employees and partly for political expediency.

---

[8] During the crisis, interest rates sharply diverged, however. Still, the Eurosystem sets a single interest rate. This question is taken up in Chapter 19.

The solution was inspired by federal states like Germany and the USA where regional central banks coexist with the federal central bank. But the EU is not a federation, and the word 'federation' is highly politically incorrect in Europe. Inevitably, therefore, the chosen structure is complicated. The newly created European Central Bank (ECB) coexists with the national central banks, one of which did not even exist prior to 1999 since Luxembourg, long part of a monetary union with Belgium, only established its own central bank to conform to the new arrangement.

16.3.2 The system

The European System of Central Banks (ESCB) is composed of the European Central Bank (ECB) and the national central banks (NCBs) of *all* EU Member States (see Figure 16.4). Since not all EU countries have joined the monetary union, a different term, Eurosystem, has been coined to refer to the ECB and the NCBs of Eurozone member countries.[9] The Eurosystem implements the monetary policy of the Eurozone. If needed, it also conducts foreign exchange operations, in agreement with the finance ministers of the member countries. It holds and manages the official foreign exchange reserves of the EMU Member States. It monitors the payment systems and is involved in the prudential supervision of credit institutions and the financial system.

As shown in Figure 16.5, the ECB is run by an executive board of six members, who are individually appointed by the heads of state or governments of the countries that have joined the monetary union, following consultation with the European Parliament. The Eurosystem is run by the Governing Council of the ESCB. It comprises the six members of the Executive Board and the governors of the NCBs of monetary union member countries. The Governing Council is the key authority deciding on monetary policy. Its decisions are, in principle, taken by majority voting, with each member holding one vote, although it seems to operate mostly by consensus. Another body, the General Council, includes the members of the Governing Council and the governors of the NCBs of the countries that have not joined the monetary union. The General Council is in essence fulfilling a liaison role and has no authority.

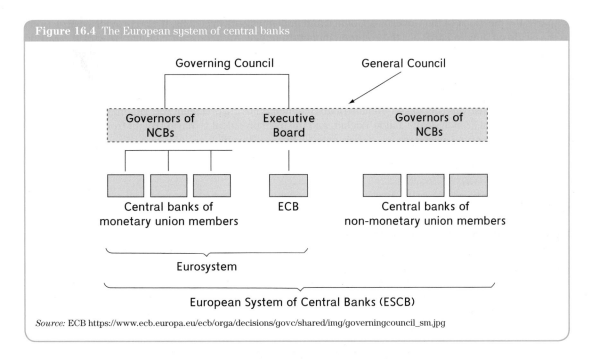

Figure 16.4 The European system of central banks

Source: ECB https://www.ecb.europa.eu/ecb/orga/decisions/govc/shared/img/governingcouncil_sm.jpg

---

[9] For a full and formal description, see the ECB website at http://www.ecb.int/ecb/html/index.en.html.

Figure 16.5 The Governing Council, February 2014

Although the Governing Council takes decisions, the ECB also plays an important role. Its president chairs the meetings of the Governing Council and reports its decisions at press conferences. The ECB prepares the meetings of the Governing Council and implements its decisions. It also provides instructions to the NCBs on how to carry out the common monetary policy. An important characteristic of the ECB is that its Executive Board members are not representing their countries: they are appointed as individuals, even though the large countries (France, Germany, Italy and Spain) all had a national sitting on the first Executive Board appointed. This implicit right of the large countries has been maintained upon successive renewals with one exception so far (in 2012, a Spaniard was replaced by a citizen of Luxembourg). In general, there is also one (out of six!) female Board member. The first president was Dutch, Wim Duisenberg, his successor was French, Jean-Claude Trichet, and the third president is Mario Draghi from Italy. All three have previously served as governors of their own NCBs (see Box 16.3).

Box 16.3   ECB presidents

Wim Duisenberg (1998–2003)
Wim Duisenberg, the first president of the ECB, was born in 1932. He held a PhD in economics, worked at the IMF and was professor of macroeconomics at the University of Amsterdam before entering politics in the Labour Party and serving as Minister of Finance. Later on, he joined De Netherlandsche Bank, and became its governor in 1982. In 1997, he was appointed President of the European Monetary Institute, in charge of preparing the introduction of the single currency.

Jean-Claude Trichet (2003–11)

His successor, Jean-Claude Trichet, was also a central bank governor prior to taking over the ECB. Born in 1942, he studied economics and civil engineering before attending the elite Ecole Nationale d'Administration. He capped a distinguished career in the French Finance Ministry by becoming head of the Treasury and, in 1993, Governor of the Banque de France. While at the Treasury, he designed the 'franc fort' policy of disinflation.

Mario Draghi (2011–19)

The third president is Mario Draghi, who was Governor of the Bank of Italy from 2005 to 2011. He graduated from the University of Rome and received a PhD in economics from the Massachusetts Institute of Technology. His career was mostly in the Italian Treasury, where he rose to be director general, with a stint in the private sector at Goldman Sachs International. He also taught economics at the University of Florence.

© European Central Bank, Frankfurt am Main, Germany

16.3.3 Voting rights in the Eurosystem

The Governing Council has $6 + N$ members, where N is the number of countries that have adopted the euro. This is a large body, whose size increases when new members join the union. Following the entry of Lithuania in January 2015, the Governing Council now has 25 members. In the light of the previous agreement, this increase in size triggered a change in voting procedure. Until the Council reached 25 members, each member had one voting right, irrespective of whether (s)he sat on the Board or represented an NCB, and in the latter case on whether (s)he hailed from a large or small country.

The new system works on a rotation basis. An index is computed for each country, based on its GDP (5/6 of the weight) and the size of its financial sector (remaining 1/6). The resulting ranking classifies all countries into two groups:

- The five largest countries (Germany, France, Italy, Spain and the Netherlands) form the first group, with four voting rights.
- The remaining countries make up the second group, with 11 voting rights.

This means that, at any meeting, one large and four of the other countries do not vote. Their NCB governors may still attend and contribute to the discussion, however. The rotation takes place each month. Figure 16.6 summarizes the situation. More details are available in the *Monthly Bulletin* of the ECB, May 2003.

16.4 The monetary policy strategy

The Eurosystem decides on the interest rate. In the *IS–MP–IRP* framework of Chapter 13, the strategy is captured by the *MP* schedule, which indicates that the central bank leans against the wind, raising the interest rate when the economy booms and lowering it during slowdowns. In Chapter 14, the strategy is complemented by the price stability objective: when inflation rises, the central bank raises the interest rate and the *MP* curve shifts up; when inflation is low, the central bank reduces the interest rate and the *MP* curve shifts down. These are the broad principles, widely shared among central banks. The Eurosystem has developed a detailed strategy to address these principles.

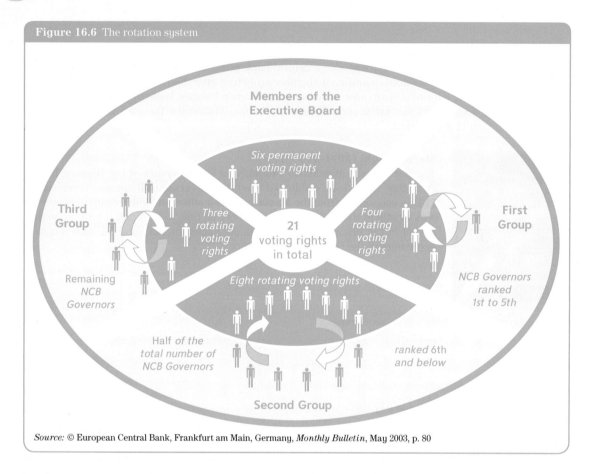

Figure 16.6 The rotation system

Members of the Executive Board

Six permanent voting rights

Third Group

Three rotating voting rights

21 voting rights in total

Four rotating voting rights

First Group

Remaining NCB Governors

Eight rotating voting rights

NCB Governors ranked 1st to 5th

Half of the total number of NCB Governors

ranked 6th and below

Second Group

Source: © European Central Bank, Frankfurt am Main, Germany, *Monthly Bulletin*, May 2003, p. 80

Before examining the strategy, an important issue needs to be addressed. The Eurozone comprises many countries and it would be extraordinary if the economic situation (inflation, growth, unemployment) were the same everywhere, always. Divergences of economic situations are likely, which underlines the importance of the OCA theory developed in Chapter 15. How can the Eurosystem deal with asymmetries, then? The response is clear: the Eurosystem does not look at individual countries but at the Eurozone as a whole. It monitors overall inflation, overall growth, overall employment, etc. and studiously avoids focusing on any one country. In principle, within the Governing Council NCB governors are not supposed to discuss their own countries. This is logical. From a political viewpoint, taking the needs and desires of individual countries into account would be very divisive because opposing views will always exist. Like a good mother, the ECB cannot have a favourite daughter.

Figure 16.7 shows the overall inflation rate within the Eurozone (looking only at the original 12 members) together with the highest and lowest inflation rate recorded each year among the member countries. It provides a vivid graphical example of the great diversity of economic conditions evident from one country to another. With low inflation as its primary objective, obviously the Eurosystem cannot have one policy that fits all.

The strategy relies on three main elements: the definition of price stability, and two 'pillars' used to identify risks to price stability.

The first pillar is what the Eurosystem calls 'economic analysis'. It consists of a broad review of the recent evolution of and likely prospects for economic conditions (including growth, employment, prices, exchange rates and foreign conditions). The second pillar, the 'monetary analysis', studies the evolution of various monetary aggregates (M3, in particular) and of bank credit, which, in the medium to long term, moves in proportion to inflation, in line with the neutrality principle. In the words of the Eurosystem, 'these two perspectives offer complementary analytical frameworks to support the Governing Council's overall

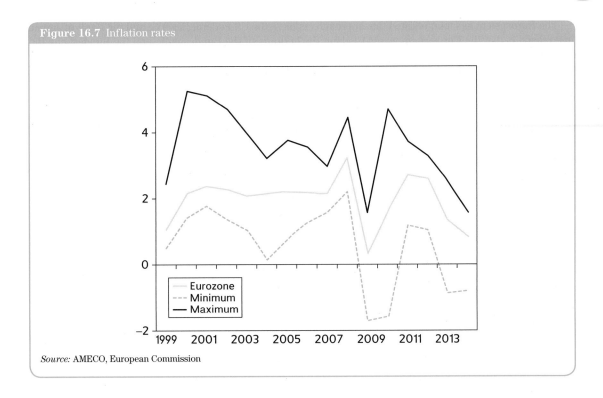

Figure 16.7 Inflation rates

Source: AMECO, European Commission

assessment of risks to price stability. In this respect, the monetary analysis mainly serves as a means of cross-checking, from a medium- to long-term perspective, the short- to medium-term indications coming from economic analysis' (ECB, 2003).

What does this mean in practice? Given that monetary actions affect first growth and employment, with a lag of at least a year, and then inflation, with an additional one or more years, the central bank must anticipate the evolution of the situation over at least a 3-year period. Importantly, it must act now on the basis of forecasts, not on the basis of the current situation because it is too late for that. Given that inflation is its primary long-run target, the Eurosystem must take into consideration expected future inflation. Given that its secondary target, roughly growth and employment, is impacted after one year or so, the Eurosystem must also foresee 'economic conditions' over that intermediate horizon. Of course, the associated forecasts must be consistent with each other over time, hence the need for 'cross-checking'.

At the policy meeting, the Chief Economist – one of the six Board members – presents to the Governing Council a broad analysis of the situation, including forecasts of inflation and growth. Monetary conditions – the association between money growth and inflation – are then used to qualify the forecasts and allow the Council to form a view of where inflation is heading. Then the real debate starts: What should happen to the interest rate? Should it be raised because inflation is perceived as excessive? How much weight should be attached to other considerations, such as growth and employment, or the exchange rate and stock markets? The strategy guides the answers. Importantly, the Eurosystem does not take any responsibility for the exchange rate, which is freely floating.

Is the Eurosystem's strategy special? Over the past decade, many central banks have explicitly adopted the inflation-targeting strategy, which links interest rate decisions to growth in the short run and inflation over the longer run (this is the *MP* schedule that shifts in response to expected inflation). In Europe, this is the case of most non-monetary union member central banks (including those of the Czech Republic, Hungary, Norway, Poland, Sweden and the UK). Inflation targeting comprises announcing an inflation target, publishing an inflation forecast for the relevant policy horizon (usually 2-3 years ahead) and adjusting the interest rate according to the difference between the forecast and the target. For example, if the inflation forecast exceeds the target, the presumption is that monetary policy is tightened, i.e. that the interest rate is raised.

The Eurosystem has long resisted this approach, as have the US Federal Reserve and the Bank of Japan. One reason is that the Eurosystem wants to claim the heritage of the Bundesbank, and the Bundesbank did not target inflation; it targeted money growth, which explains the second pillar. The justification for monetary targeting is that money growth eventually determines inflation. The shortcoming is that, in the shorter run, it also affects growth and employment. The two-pillar strategy is an attempt to deal with these two considerations. What the Eurosystem seems to reject is giving the impression that it acts mechanically and puts the secondary objective on the same footing as the primary objective (as does the *MP* schedule). In practice, the Eurosystem's strategy resembles inflation targeting: there is an implicit target (the 2 per cent definition of price stability) and its inflation forecast is published twice a year. Box 16.4 examines this issue in more detail.

Box 16.4 How different is the ECB?

Inflation-targeting central banks set the short-term interest rate with one eye on inflation forecasts and the other on the expected activity level, measured as the output gap; that is, the deviation of actual GDP from its 'normal' level. This approach – the 'shifting-*MP* curve' – is formalized as the Taylor rule.[1] This rule simply posits that the central bank chooses the actual interest rate as a function of (1) the deviation of inflation from its (implicit or explicit) target; and (2) the output gap, which is the difference between actual and potential GDP, measured as a percentage of potential GDP.

Formally, this is written as:

$$i_t = a(\pi_t - \pi^*) + b(y_t - y_t^*)$$

where i_t is the interest rate at time t, π_t is the inflation rate, π^* is the inflation target, y_t is GDP and y_t^* is potential GDP.[2] The parameters a and b are weights that reflect the relative importance attached by the central bank to its two objectives (b is the slope of the *MP* curve and a tells us how much it shifts in response to inflation).

Figure 16.8 looks at the Eurosystem (and its predecessor, the Bundesbank), the Swedish Riksbank and the Bank of England. For each central bank, it displays two short-term interest rates: the actual rate and the rate that would have been chosen if the central banks had followed the same Taylor rule.[3] We see that central bank behaviour has increasingly conformed to the Taylor rule. This also applies to the Bundesbank until 1999; despite its tough rhetoric, it was an early practitioner of the Taylor rule.

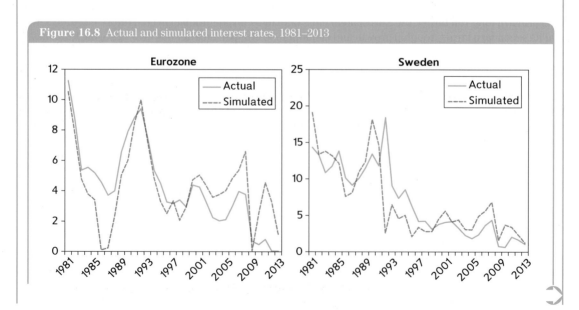

Figure 16.8 Actual and simulated interest rates, 1981–2013

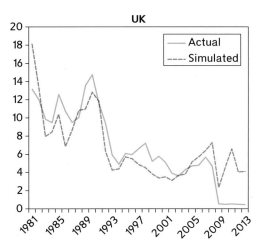

Sources: IMF and *Economic Outlook*, OECD

We also see that the Eurosystem followed suit and that its actions do not differ from those of explicit inflation-targeters, such as the Riksbank or the Bank of England. Following the global crisis, however, central banks have all behaved somewhat differently, as explained in Chapter 19.

[1] This formalization was first proposed by John Taylor, a Stanford University economist who has served as Under Secretary of the Treasury.

[2] A more precise description involves the forecasts, not the current values, of inflation and the output gap. This detail is ignored here.

[3] The weights are $a = 1.5$ on inflation and $b = 0.5$ on the output gap. In the simulation that follows, we use actual inflation and output gaps. We also 'smooth' the simulated interest rate, as central banks seem to do, by computing it as a weighted average of the previous year's interest rate and the interest rate predicted by the Taylor rule, putting equal weights on each.

16.5 Independence and accountability

16.5.1 Independence

The importance of central bank independence is stressed in Section 16.1.2. The Eurosystem is characterized by a high degree of independence. This is achieved through a number of characteristics specifically crafted to that effect.

Institutional arrangements

The Treaty explicitly states that the ECB and all NCBs are strictly protected from political influence. Before joining the Eurozone, each country must adapt the statutes of its NCB to match a number of common legal requirements to that effect. In particular, the EU Treaty explicitly rules out any interference by national or European authorities:

> *When exercising the powers and carrying out the tasks and duties conferred upon them by this Treaty and the Statute of the ESCB, neither the ECB, nor a national central bank, nor any member of their decision-making bodies shall seek or take instructions from Community institutions or bodies, from any government of a Member State or from any other body. The Community institutions and bodies and the governments of the Member States undertake to respect this principle and not to seek to influence the members of the decision-making bodies of the ECB or of the national central banks in the performance of their tasks.*

Article 130, Treaty on the Functioning of the European Union

Status of Eurosystem officials

The personal independence of Executive Board members is guaranteed. They are appointed for a long period (8 years) and cannot be reappointed, which reduces the opportunity to pressurize them while in office. Similar conditions apply to the NCB governors, although they differ slightly from one country to another, but their mandates must be for a minimum of 5 years. No central bank official can be removed from office unless he or she becomes incapacitated or is found guilty of serious misconduct; the Court of Justice of the European Communities is competent to settle disputes.

Policy objectives and instruments

The Treaty sets the objectives in terms vague enough to allow the Eurosystem to decide on what it wants to achieve, as explained in Section 16.4, but price stability is paramount and the rest is 'without prejudice to price stability'. As long as it can relate its actions to the objective of price stability, the Eurosystem cannot be challenged. Indeed, since its inception, the Eurosystem takes great care to systematically relate every decision that it takes to price stability. Even so, some of its critics have mounted a legal challenge to its actions during the Eurozone crisis; see Box 16.5.

The Treaty further leaves the Eurosystem completely free to decide which instruments it uses, and how. Other central banks sometimes have instrument independence only. This is the case of the Bank of England, which is instructed to pursue an inflation target set by the Chancellor of the Exchequer.

Financial independence

The ECB is financially independent. As a legal personality, it has its own budget, independent from that of the EU. Its accounts are not audited by the European Court of Auditors, which monitors the European Commission, but by independent external auditors.

Box 16.5 A challenge from the German Constitutional Court

The main risk to central bank independence is that it could be coerced by government into money creation, a threat to price stability (see Box 15.2). During the Eurozone crisis, like many other central banks, the Eurosystem has taken bold new steps. In particular, it has created previously unheard of quantities of money and even committed to supporting the market value of public debts of those countries offered combined IMF and European support.[1] A number of German legal scholars have taken the view that these actions bring the Eurosystem far too close to governments and thus threaten price stability. They have asked the German Constitutional Court to decide whether these actions violate the German constitution (the so-called primary law). The Eurosystem is strictly prohibited from financing governments but it is explicitly allowed to buy public debts on the so-called secondary market.[2]

After more than one year of deliberation, the Court issued an ambiguous decision in February 2014: 'Subject to the interpretation by the Court of Justice of the European Union, the Federal Constitutional Court considers the . . . decision incompatible with primary law. . . . Another assessment could, however, be warranted if the . . . decision could be interpreted in conformity with primary law.'[3]

One legal issue to address is that the ECB is an international organization not subject to German law. This is why the petitioners asked the Court its opinion regarding German law, which also prohibits financing of the government. This is also why its decision explicitly recognizes that the Court of Justice of the European Union must first settle the matter. However, the German Court puts the European Court on notice that it disagrees with the actions of the ECB. Should the European Court issue a ruling that does not address the concerns of the German Court, the latter could still decide that the German constitution is being violated. For the German government, such a decision would be binding. It could create a major crisis.

[1] The programme in question, Open Market Transactions, is described in Chapter 19.

[2] When a government issues fresh debt, that debt is up for sale; this is the primary market. Afterwards, the bonds are regularly traded in the secondary market.

[3] https://www.bundesverfassungsgericht.de/pressemitteilungen/bvg14-009en.html.

16.5.2 Accountability

Monetary policy affects citizens of the monetary union in a number of ways. The interest rate directly impacts on the cost of borrowing and on the returns from saving; the exchange rate, which is affected by the interest rate (see Chapter 13), directly impacts on the competitiveness of firms and on the purchasing power of citizens. In effect, by granting independence to their central bank, the citizens delegate a very important task to a group of individuals who are appointed, not elected, and who cannot be removed unless they commit grave illegal acts. In a democratic society, delegation to unelected officials must be counterbalanced by democratic accountability.

Democratic accountability is typically exercised in two ways: reporting and transparency. Formally, the Eurosystem operates under the control of the European Parliament. Its statutes require that an annual report be sent to the Parliament, as well as to the Council and the Commission. This report is debated by the Parliament. In addition, the Parliament may request that the President of the ECB and the other members of the Executive Board testify to the Parliament's Economic and Monetary Affairs Committee.[10] In practice, the President appears before the committee every quarter and the members of the Executive Board also do so quite often. In addition, the President of the EU Council and a member of the European Commission may participate in the meetings of the Governing Council but without voting rights.

At the end of the day, the question is whether the Eurosystem, and the ECB in particular, is subject to effective control by elected officials. Beyond the formal requirements, so far at least, the European Parliament has never really challenged the ECB. The quarterly testimonies of the ECB President in front of the relevant European Parliament committee, aptly called 'Monetary Dialogue', are almost never even vaguely controversial and, when they are, the MPs soon publicly disagree among themselves. Divide and conquer.

16.5.3 Transparency

Transparency contributes powerfully to accountability (see Box 16.6). By revealing the contents of its deliberations, a central bank conveys to the public (the media, the financial markets and independent observers) the rationale behind and difficulties faced by its decisions. Currently, the Eurosystem does not provide detailed reports of the meetings of its Governing Council. Instead, the President of the ECB holds a press conference immediately after the policy-setting meeting to present its decisions in highly standardized terms. Table 16.1 shows how major central banks reveal the work of their decision-making committee meetings. Several of them publish the committee meeting's minutes within a month, but since they can be heavily edited, minutes are not necessarily very informative. Very few (the US Federal Reserve and the Bank of Japan) publish extensive records of the discussion, but with very long delays, which makes the publication irrelevant except for historical purposes. Many central banks report on individual votes, which is a clear way of indicating how certain policy-makers feel about their collective decisions. The Eurosystem is almost alone in doing none of that. It considers that revealing individual votes could be interpreted in a nationalistic manner that does not, in fact, correspond to the thinking of members of the Governing Council who are duty bound to look only at the Eurozone as a whole.

[10] The European Parliament may not order NCB governors to testify because NCBs are not European institutions.

Table 16.1   Provision of information on monetary policy meetings

	Public debt	ESCB	Bank of Japan	Bank of England	Bank of Canada	Swedish Riksbank
Interest-rate decision immediately announced	Yes (after 1994)	Yes	Yes	Yes	Yes	Yes
Supporting statement providing some rationale for change	Yes	Yes	Yes	Sometimes	Yes	Yes
Release of minutes	5–8 weeks[a]	No	1 month	13 days	n.a.	2–4 weeks
Official minutes provide full details of:	Yes	No	Yes	Yes	n.a.	No
Internal debate	Yes	No	No	Yes	No	No
Individuals' views						
Verbatim records of MP meetings are kept	No	Yes	No	No	No	Yes
Verbatim records released to the public after:	5 years	n.a.	10 years	n.a.	n.a.	n.a.

[a] The minutes are released after the following FOMC meeting.

Source: Blinder et al. (2001)

At the time of writing, however, the Eurosystem has signalled its intention to publish 'accounts' of the deliberations of the Governing Council as of 2015.

16.6 Instruments

In order to meet its objectives, any central bank must use some instrument to affect aggregate demand. They universally seek to influence the cost of credit. Like most other central banks, the Eurosystem uses the short-term interest rate. The reason is that central banks have a monopoly on the supply of cash. Very short-term assets – 24 hours or less – are very close to cash, so central banks can control very short-term rates with a high degree of precision. Changes in the short-term interest rate have a knock-on effect on longer-term interest rates (and thus on the cost of credit), on asset prices (and thus on capital costs of firms) and on the exchange rate (and thus on foreign demand for domestic goods and services). These effects, however, are not very precise as they depend on market expectations of future inflation and future policy actions. Expectations are beyond the direct control of the central bank but being clear about longer-run aims and intentions is part of the art of central banking.

The Eurosystem focuses on the overnight rate EONIA (European Over Night Index Average), a weighted average of overnight lending transactions in the Eurozone's interbank market. Control over EONIA is achieved in two ways:

1 The Eurosystem creates a ceiling and a floor for EONIA by maintaining open lending and deposit facilities at pre-announced interest rates. The marginal lending facility means that banks can always borrow directly from the ECB (more precisely, from the NCBs) at the corresponding rate; they would never pay more on the overnight market, so the marginal lending rate is in effect a ceiling. Similarly, since banks can always deposit cash at the ECB's deposit rate, they would never agree to

Box 16.6   Independence and transparency

In principle, the more independent is a central bank, the more accountable it should be, and transparency is one key element of accountability. Since there is mounting evidence that inflation tends to be lower where central banks are more independent, a good central bank should be very independent and very transparent. Using legislation and other information, a number of studies provide quantitative estimates of central bank independence and transparency. The numbers are inevitably arbitrary but nevertheless plausible. An example is presented in Figure 16.9, which looks at 29 countries around the world. It suggests that the ECB is indeed very independent but only ranks seventeenth as far as transparency is concerned. Note that there is no apparent link between independence and transparency.

Figure 16.9 Independence and transparency indices, 2008

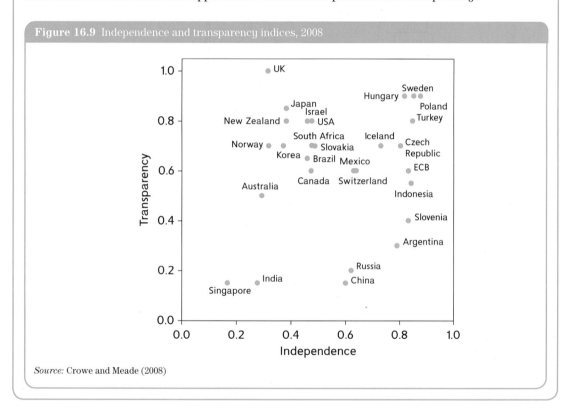

Source: Crowe and Meade (2008)

lend at a lower rate, and this rate is the floor. Figure 16.10 shows that, indeed, EONIA moves within the corridor thus established.[11]

2 The Eurosystem conducts, usually weekly, auctions at a rate that it chooses. These auctions, called main refinancing operations, are the means by which the ECB provides liquidity to the banking system and the chosen interest rate serves as a precise guide for EONIA.

How does liquidity flow from the Eurosystem to all corners of the Eurozone banking system? As noted above, the Eurosystem organizes auctions on a regular basis. Each NCB collects bids from its commercial banks and passes the information to the ECB. The ECB then decides which proportion of bids will be accepted and instructs the NCBs accordingly. The commercial banks can then disseminate the liquidity on

---

[11] Note that from 2009 onward, EONIA was kept close to the floor. This was intended; see Chapter 19.

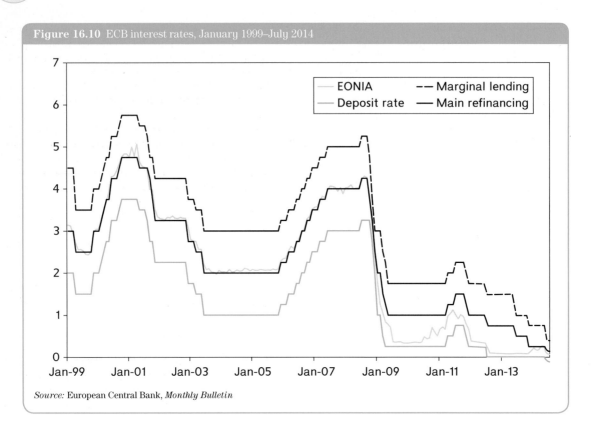

Figure 16.10 ECB interest rates, January 1999–July 2014

Source: European Central Bank, *Monthly Bulletin*

the interbank market. It does not matter where the initial injection is made: since there is a single interest rate throughout the Eurozone, the area-wide interbank market ensures that money is available where needed.

16.7 The first years, until the Great Crisis

This section looks at how the Eurozone has operated since its creation. Because the crisis has been so unusual, we defer its study until Chapter 19. Here we just look at the 'normal' pre-crisis years.

16.7.1 Inflation

When the euro was launched in January 1999, inflation was very low, partly because all member countries had been working hard at meeting the Maastricht convergence criteria presented in Section 16.2. Soon thereafter, oil prices rose threefold in 2000. An oil shock means both more inflation and less growth, a classic dilemma that all central banks fear. Simultaneously, stock markets worldwide fell, marking the end of a long-lasting financial bubble fed by unrealistic expectations of what the information technology revolution could deliver. Within months, the US economy went into recession, and Europe's economy slowed down. Then, the terrorist attacks of 11 September 2001 shook the world economy. There followed a mellow period – dubbed the Great Moderation – until oil prices again rose to record levels. The Great Global Recession, which started in the USA in mid-2007, culminated with the Wall Street meltdown of September 2008. The Eurozone sovereign debt crisis came about in late 2009.

As indicated, price stability is the Eurosystem's primary objective and the Eurosystem has demonstrated that it interprets this objective as a rate close to but below 2 per cent. Figure 16.11 shows that, until the crisis, the inflation rate has almost always been above the 2 per cent ceiling. Yet, it would be wrong to conclude that the Eurosystem has failed to deliver price stability. Until late 2007, the inflation rate remained close enough to 2 per cent for comfort. An interesting observation is that professional forecasters have systematically anticipated that inflation would remain close to but very slightly above 2 per cent, even though they could see that it was not the case. It is also important to note that no member country – including Germany – has enjoyed such a long period of such low inflation since the Second World War. It is surprising, therefore, that in nearly every country a large number of people are convinced of the opposite, namely, that the adoption of the euro has resulted in inflation. This phenomenon is discussed in Box 16.7. On the other hand, the euro area is not unique in having experienced low inflation.

Figure 16.11 Inflation in the Eurozone (%), 1999Q1–2014Q2

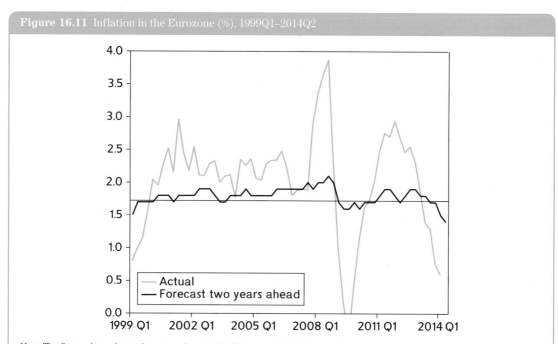

Note: The figure shows for each quarter the actual inflation rate (over the previous four quarters) and forecast inflation over a two-year horizon, computed by the ECB as the average of forecasts produced by professional forecasters.

Sources: IMF and *Survey of Professional Forecasters*, ECB

Box 16.7   For the public, inflation is up

When euro coins and banknotes were introduced in early 2002, a number of retailers rounded up prices. This created a perceived jump in the price level. The jump has been confirmed by HICP measures but its amount – about 0.5 per cent – is trivially small in comparison with public perception. Figure 16.12 shows actual inflation as measured by the HICP and an estimate of perceived inflation by citizens. Not only is the gap large in the months following the introduction of euro notes and coins, but it has not disappeared. Public opinion polls keep revealing that Eurozone citizens believe that the euro has been a major source of high and enduring inflation. In fact, many people believe that the official measure of inflation is deeply flawed since it is much lower than what 'they see'.

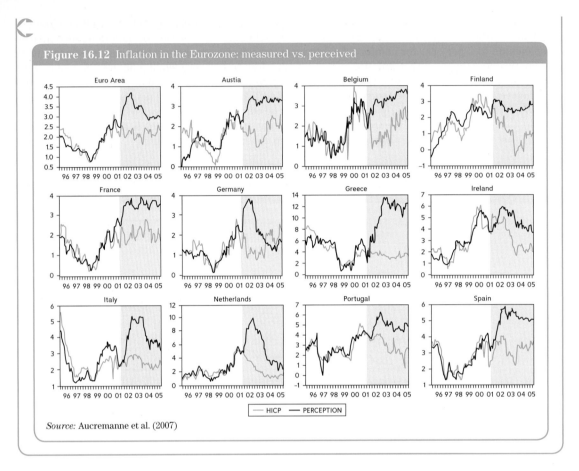

Figure 16.12 Inflation in the Eurozone: measured vs. perceived

Source: Aucremanne et al. (2007)

Many studies have been conducted to ascertain that the official index is not flawed and to try to explain why perceptions can systematically differ from 'facts'. One explanation is that rounding up has mostly affected cheap goods (an increase in €0.50 for a cup of coffee that costs €1.50 is indeed a 33 per cent increase) that people purchase frequently, which keeps reminding them of the jump. Another explanation is that people still evaluate prices by computing their value in the old currency (liras, francs, pesetas, etc.). Not only is it a long time since that currency was used, but people also appear to make rounding-up errors. In truth there is still no satisfactory explanation of the phenomenon.

16.7.2 Growth

Until the crisis growth was generally slow in the Eurozone; of course, the situation was disastrous afterwards. This has prompted criticism of the Eurosystem, including by some member governments. The criticism may be unfair for the pre-crisis years. To start with, the neutrality principle says that monetary policy cannot have long-lasting effects on economic growth. Then, while growth has been slow on average, this has not been the case in every Eurozone country. Some countries have even grown very fast, as Figure 16.13 shows, although many of these countries were those worst hit by the crisis after 2008. Critics also blame the Eurosystem for 'excessive growth' that ended badly. The growth rate of the overall Eurozone is low because some of the largest members – chiefly Germany and Italy, with France only slighter better – have managed a disappointing performance. The Eurosystem has argued that this performance is not the result of an over-restrictive stance on monetary policy. It has a point.

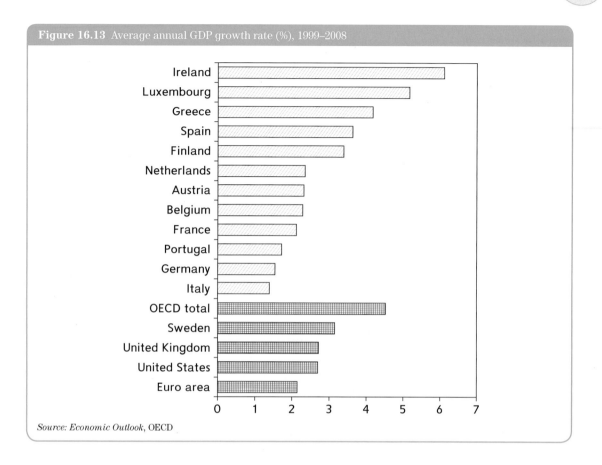

Figure 16.13 Average annual GDP growth rate (%), 1999–2008

Source: *Economic Outlook*, OECD

16.7.3 The exchange rate

The Eurosystem has faced another vexing issue. Just when the euro was launched in early 1999, the dollar started to rise vis-à-vis all major currencies, including the euro and, to a lesser extent, the pound sterling. Given that the US dollar has long been the world's standard, this situation was generally interpreted as meaning that the new currency was weak. This created the impression that the Eurosystem was unable to deliver the strong currency that had been predicated upon its price-stability commitment, following the PPP logic presented in Chapter 13. Then, from late 2002 onwards, the value of the dollar started to fall. Instead of praising the Eurosystem for having finally delivered a strong currency, critics then complained that the euro was overvalued and hurting European exporters. Yet, as Figure 16.14 shows, the movements of the dollar/euro exchange rate have not been particularly out of step with the past, at least until 2007.

From the start, the Eurosystem clearly announced that it would take no responsibility for the exchange rate. Its view is that the euro is a freely floating currency. Since capital movements are completely free, this position accords well with the impossible trinity principle. The discussion of exchange rate regimes in Chapter 13 suggests that very large and relatively closed economies, like the Eurozone, have little interest in stabilizing their exchange rates. This choice may occasionally suggest unpleasant implications, however, and critics have seized on these adverse effects to blame the Eurosystem. It is also true that the exchange rate between the euro and the dollar is as much driven by US as by European events. In that sense, it is not the euro that is too strong but the dollar that is too weak, or the other way round. Undoubtedly, this debate will go on for many years to come.

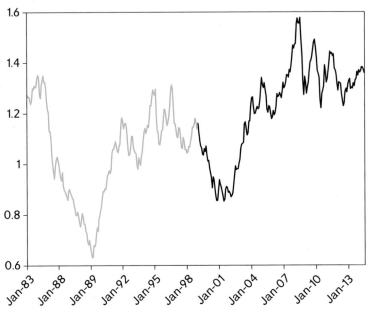

Figure 16.14 The dollar/euro exchange rate, January 1983–June 2014

Note: Before 1999, there was no euro. The 'synthetic euro' used here is the value of the ECU, a basket of EU currencies. An increase of the index indicates a euro appreciation.

Source: European Central Bank

16.7.4 One money, one policy

Lasting differences in inflation

How about the much-feared asymmetric shocks emphasized by the optimum currency area (OCA) theory? The Eurozone crisis is an example of an enormous asymmetric choice, which renders discussions of the pre-2009 situation mundane. Yet, in many respects, the crisis itself is partly the consequence of asymmetric changes that were relatively small but persistent enough to create tensions within the monetary area.

Figure 16.7 documents fairly sizeable differences in inflation. The Eurosystem was then eager to point out that inflation rates differ no more among the Eurozone member countries than across broad regions in the USA. The problem is that US regions alternate in their respective positions while, in the Eurozone, the same countries have persistently exhibited lower or higher inflation rates. A country that faces continuously higher inflation than others is bound to face a loss in competitiveness as its real exchange rate appreciates.[12] If this process persists, the country would then have to undergo several years of lower inflation to restore competitiveness. This is an implication of the self-equilibriating Hume mechanism presented in Chapter 14. Figure 16.15 shows that large inflation differentials have occurred. Inflation has been lower than average in Germany, Finland and France, and higher than average in Ireland, Spain, Portugal, the Netherlands and Italy. Not surprisingly, the four countries with the highest inflation rates are those that eventually faced the debt crisis first.

What are the reasons for such a divergence? The potential explanations are:

- *The Balassa–Samuelson effect.* This effect, presented in Chapter 13, predicts that the real exchange rates of catching-up countries appreciate. Within a currency area, real appreciation can only be

---

[12] Higher domestic inflation means that P/P^* increases. With the nominal exchange rate E permanently fixed, the real exchange rate EP/P^* appreciates.

Figure 16.15 Change in price levels relative to the Eurozone, 1999–2008

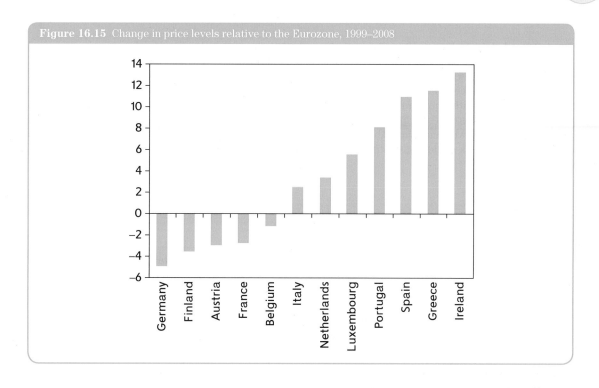

achieved through higher than average inflation.[13] This higher inflation rate does not imply a loss of competitiveness; quite the contrary. It is actually a consequence of rising productivity. This effect could be part of the explanation for the cases of Ireland, Spain and Portugal.

- *Wrong initial conversion rates.* Each currency was converted into euros at the ERM parity that prevailed in 1998, but there was no certainty that these conversion rates were fully adequate. For instance, it is now generally accepted that Germany's conversion rate was overvalued; this may explain why, from 1999 to 2008, its consumer price index declined by 4.5 per cent relative to the Eurozone's HICP. Similarly, Greece may have used an undervalued rate for the conversion of drachmas into euros.

- *Autonomous wage and price pressure.* Wage increases in excess of labour productivity gains eat into competitiveness. This basic truth may be lost when factors other than economics drive wage negotiations. For example, minimum wages can be raised to reduce inequality; civil servants – who do not face any foreign competition directly – may be well-organized in terms of extracting wage increases; administered prices – electricity, transport – may be pushed up to avoid losses in state-owned companies. Such price increases next filter down to all wages and prices because they raise production costs and the general price level. These factors seem to have played a role in Greece, Italy, the Netherlands, Spain and Portugal.

- *Policy mistakes.* Through excessively expansionary fiscal policies or public sector price and wage increases, mentioned above, governments may, temporarily at least, contribute to inflationary pressure. Once prices are up, it is difficult to bring them down.

- *Asymmetric shocks.* This is the scenario that lies at the centre of the OCA theory. Oil shocks have not affected all Eurozone member countries to the same extent. Many other factors may have played a role, even though none has been identified so far.

---

[13] A Eurozone country's real exchange rate vis-à-vis the zone is EP/P^*. With a common currency the nominal exchange rate is $E = 1$, so the real exchange rate is P/P^*. A real appreciation requires that the domestic price level P increases faster than the foreign price level P^*.

Diverging current accounts

The left-hand chart in Figure 16.16 shows that, until 2008, the external accounts of some countries had been increasingly unbalanced. While Germany's surplus kept widening, the deficits of Greece, Italy and Spain continuously deepened, reaching huge sizes in Spain and especially Greece. The same can be said of Ireland, as shown in the right-hand chart, which also indicates that initial disequilibria remained unchanged in the Netherlands, with a continuing surplus, and Portugal, with a continuing deficit. The chart also shows that the Finish surplus was slowly closing. Taken together, Figures 16.14 and 16.15 indicate that the Hume mechanism was not working. Quite the contrary, inflation was lower in surplus countries and higher in deficit countries. This could not continue forever, and it did not, but it took a major crisis to induce a correction.

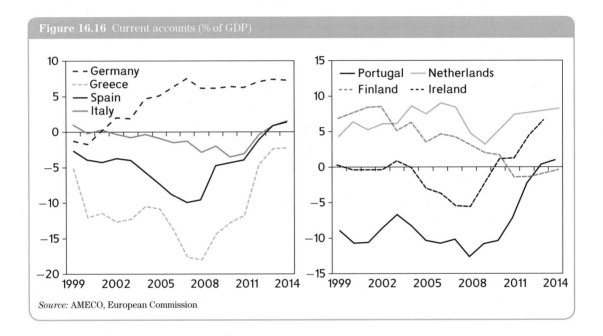

Figure 16.16 Current accounts (% of GDP)

Source: AMECO, European Commission

What could have been done?

As indicated earlier, the Eurosystem has wisely decided not to tweak its policy to meet the particular needs of individual countries. This means that it cannot deal with asymmetric conditions. It is precisely the reason why the OCA principle sees asymmetries as the central risk in a currency area. The implication is that the treatment of these growing divergences could not be undertaken by the central bank.

Normally, in a currency area, countries that undergo higher inflation and see their real exchange rate appreciate face declining exports and rising imports. This is indeed what happened, as shown above. This should reduce demand for domestic goods and lead to a decline in activity and rising unemployment. As predicted by the Hume mechanism, this should exert downward pressure on wages and prices until inflation is lower and the correction takes place. Why was this process stunted? There is no single answer.

In some high deficit/high inflation countries – Greece, Ireland, Spain – demand did not decrease because domestic spending remained strong, for reasons developed in Chapter 19. Here, fiscal policy could have been used to cool down the economy. In others – Italy, Portugal – demand did decline but wages and prices did not respond. This suggests that the markets, especially the labour market, were malfunctioning; governments would have been well advised to introduce adequate reforms. In various countries, the governments benefitted from a windfall effect but they handled it poorly; Box 16.8 describes this effect in the case of Italy.

Box 16.8   Italy's windfall gain from Eurozone membership

Italy joined the Eurozone with a very large public debt (see Figure 16.2). At the time when the Maastricht Treaty was agreed upon, its government was spending some 12 per cent of GDP on debt service, about one-quarter of its total expenditures. Debt service is approximately equal to the product of the interest rate and the debt value (iB, where i is the interest rate and B the debt). This means that part of the debt burden was associated with a high interest rate. Figure 16.17 shows how the Italian interest rate steadily declined in the years following the Maastricht agreement. The decline is explained by the disinflation process, as Italy strived to meet the convergence criteria. It is also explained by the credibility associated with Eurozone membership and its price-stability-oriented central bank. The remarkable feature of this evolution is the parallel decline in debt service, which has declined to about 40 per cent of what it used to be. Most of this huge windfall gain, worth 7.5 per cent of GDP, has been used by the Italian authorities to increase spending in many areas, not to reduce the debt.

Figure 16.17 The interest rate and net debt service as a percentage of GDP in Italy, 1992–2011

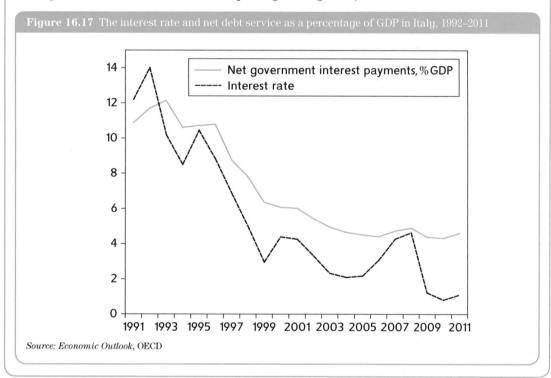

Source: Economic Outlook, OECD

16.8   Summary

The monetary union is an elaborate construction carefully mapped out in the Maastricht Treaty. The Treaty was signed in 1991 and the single currency started to operate, as planned, in 1999, even though the new currency was not issued until 2002. This long process was part of a careful approach that recognized the unique nature of the undertaking.

    The main objective assigned to the Eurosystem is price stability; in practice, the Eurosystem aims at an inflation rate close to but below 2 per cent. The secondary objective, growth and employment, is to be pursued only if price stability is not in jeopardy. In order to meet these objectives, the Eurosystem has been granted considerable independence. Independence, in turn, calls for democratic accountability and a high degree of transparency.

Central bank independence can be threatened by fiscal policy indiscipline. The Treaty explicitly recognizes this requirement. It is the objective of the Stability and Growth Pact.

The OCA theory has a lot to say about the creation of the Eurozone and its membership. The Maastricht Treaty, however, studiously ignored these principles. Instead, it envisioned a gradual convergence process based on the adoption of 'a culture of price stability' and of the discipline that goes with it. In practice, this involves a number of provisions:

- Monetary union membership is not automatic. Admission is assessed on the basis of five convergence criteria: low inflation, low long-term interest rates, ERM membership, low budget deficits and a declining public debt.
- While all EU members are expected to join the currency area, two countries (Denmark and the UK) were given opt-out clauses.
- Eurozone members must continuously display fiscal discipline as required by the Stability and Growth Pact.
- The common central bank is to be completely independent.

This was the first time that the possibility of a 'two-speed Europe' was accepted.

A monetary union implies that monetary policy is delegated to a single authority. Yet the EU is not a federal system, so it was decided to maintain the national central banks. The resulting Eurosystem formally brings together the newly created ECB and the national central banks of all Eurozone countries. Decisions are taken by the Governing Council, chaired by the President of the ECB, which includes the ECB's Executive Committee and the governors of the central banks of the Eurozone countries. The Governing Council is very large, and is getting larger as new members join the Eurozone. It has been agreed to eventually cap its size to 25 through a rotation procedure that takes into account country size. Rotation starts in 2015 following the accession of Lithuania.

The Eurosystem has also adopted the common practice of steering the short-term interest rate of the euro through three channels: the marginal refinancing facility sets a ceiling, the deposit facility sets a floor, and the interest rate is kept close to the middle of that range through regular auctions that establish the main refinancing rate.

Logic has it that the short-term interest rate affects the economy through a number of channels that operate via credit availability and the money supply, the long-term real interest rate, asset prices and the exchange rate. Thus, the effect of monetary policy on the economy, and on inflation in particular, is indirect and the Eurosystem must factor in these various effects, all of which take time to produce results.

This requires a strategy. The Eurosystem's approach is to rely on two pillars: economic analysis (the medium-term impact of current conditions on inflation) and monetary analysis (the longer-term impact of monetary aggregates on inflation). In addition, the strategy recognizes that in a monetary union there can only be one monetary policy. This is why the Eurosystem explicitly cares only about the whole Eurozone, not about individual member countries. In addition, it takes no responsibility for the exchange rate that is freely floating.

The Eurosystem enjoys considerable constitutional independence, both in defining its objectives and in deciding how to conduct monetary policy. It is not allowed to take instructions from any other authority, be it European or national. This independence is a condition for guaranteeing price stability, but it raises an important issue: in a democracy, every authority has to be accountable to its citizens for its actions. The solution adopted by the Maastricht Treaty is to make the Eurosystem formally accountable to the European Parliament. Accountability takes the form of an annual report and the Parliament's Committee on Economic and Monetary Affairs receiving regular hearings from the ECB president and members of the Executive Board.

Between 1999 and 2007, until the advent of the global financial crisis, economic conditions in the Eurozone apparently worked smoothly. But there were disquieting signals. Having converged as a requirement of admission, a number of countries started to diverge. Lasting differences in inflation affected competitiveness. Growth was brisk in some countries, sluggish in others. External accounts became unbalanced. The shortcoming predicted by the OCA theory duly appeared and remained largely ignored.

Self-assessment questions

1. What shape is the *MP* schedule and how does it shift if the central bank cares only about price stability and ignores growth? Answer the same question for a central bank that cares only about growth and disregards price stability.
2. Consider a bank that cares only about price stability. Use the *IS–ML–IRP* framework under a flexible exchange rate regime to see what happens when inflation is rising.
3. A Eurozone member has a fixed exchange rate. Use the *IS–ML–IRP* framework to see what happens when:
   – demand for domestic goods declines;
   – interest rates abroad rise;
   – the government carries out an expansionary fiscal policy.
4. Why are central banks ultimately responsible for inflation? How can they achieve this objective?
5. Why do central banks have to anticipate future economic developments?
6. What are the five convergence criteria and what is the logic behind each of them?
7. Why can inflation rates differ across the EMU member countries? What are the consequences?
8. What is the difference between Denmark and Sweden regarding monetary union membership? Which one, if any, is likely to adopt the euro first?
9. What happens to a country's interest rate when it joins the Eurozone?
10. Why can't the Eurosystem take responsibility for national inflation rates?
11. What is the rationale of the Taylor rule?
12. Is the lack of real convergence a serious danger?

Essay questions

1. Devise the entry conditions using OCA principles.
2. The Eurosystem asserts in its deliberations that it never pays attention to local (i.e. national) economic conditions. The reason is that there is a single monetary policy and that 'one size fits all'. Discuss this approach and imagine alternative approaches.
3. The Maastricht Treaty describes in minute detail the creation of the Eurozone but is silent on a possible break-up. Imagine that a country is suffering from a severe loss of competitiveness. Could it leave? How? What could the other countries do to try to keep it in?
4. Why are transparency and accountability so important for the Eurosystem? What kind of difficulties can you envision if the system is perceived as not sufficiently accountable? Not sufficiently transparent?
5. The convergence criteria concern nominal conditions (inflation, deficits and debts) but not real conditions (GDP per capita, growth). This was understandable for the original founders but should the same criteria still apply?
6. 'The crisis that started in 2007 has shown that central banks cannot just focus on price stability. Financial stability is as important.' Comment.
7. A perception exists that the ECB is too far away from people's concerns. Comment.

Further reading: the aficionado's corner

The first decade of the euro as reviewed by the ECB:

European Central Bank, www.ecb.int/pub/pdf/other/10thanniversaryoftheecbmb200806en.pdf?a2a06e7f1ee81c0d422 49ee63d0ce0e8.

And by independent observers:

Aghion, P., A. Ahearne, M. Belka, J. Pisani-Ferry, J. von Hagen and L. Heikesten (2008) *Coming of Age, Report on the Eurozone*, BRUEGEL, Brussels. Download from www.bruegel.org.

Fatás, A., H. Flam, S. Holden, T. Japelli, I. Mihov, M. Pagano and C. Wyplosz (2009) *EMU at Ten: Should Denmark, Sweden and the UK Join?*, Stockholm: SNS-Centre for Business and Policy Studies. Download from www.sns.se.

Mongelli, F.P. and C. Wyplosz (2009) 'The euro at ten: unfulfilled threats and unexpected challenges', in B. Mackowiak, F.P. Mongelli, G. Noblet and F. Smets (eds), *The Euro at Ten – Lessons and Challenges*, European Central Bank, Frankfurt am Main.

Wyplosz, C. (2010) 'Ten years of EMU: successes and puzzles', in J.F. Jimeno (ed.), *Spain and the Euro: The First Ten Years*, Banco de España, Madrid.

For presentations of the Eurosystem, see:

European Central Bank (2011) *The Monetary Policy of the ECB*.

European Commission, http://ec.europa.eu/economy_finance/euro/index_en.htm.

Padoa-Schioppa, T. (former member of the Executive Board of the ECB) An Institutional Glossary of the Eurosystem. Download from www.ecb.int/press/key/date/2000/html/sp000308_1.en.html.

On Taylor rules, see:

The Economist (2005) 'Monetary policy in the Eurozone has been looser than critics think', 14 July. Download from http://www.economist.com/node/4174785.

Useful websites

The ECB website: www.ecb.int.

The Treaty of Maastricht: http://europa.eu/eu-law/decision-making/treaties/pdf/consolidated_versions_of_the_treaty_on_european_union_2012/consolidated_versions_of_the_treaty_on_european_union_2012_en.pdf.

The President of the ECB reports every quarter to the Committee of Economic and Monetary Affairs of the European Parliament. The transcripts of the meetings, politely called 'Monetary Dialogue', as well as background reports can be found at: http://www.europarl.europa.eu/activities/committees/editoDisplay.do?language=EN&id=3&body=ECON.

A website dedicated to EONIA and interest rates in the Eurozone: http://www.euribor-rates.eu/.

References

Aucremanne, L., M. Collin and T. Stragier (2007) *Assessing the Gap between Observed and Perceived Inflation in the Eurozone: Is the Credibility of the HICP at Stake?* Working Paper No. 112 , National Bank of Belgium.

Blinder, A., C. Goodhart, P. Hildebrand, D. Lipton and C. Wyplosz (2001) 'How do central banks talk?', *Geneva Reports on the World Economy* 3, Centre for Economic Policy Research, London.

Burda, M. and C. Wyplosz (2012) *Macroeconomics*, 6th edition, Oxford University Press, Oxford.

Crowe, C. and E. Meade (2008) 'Central bank independence and transparency: evolution and effectiveness', *European Journal of Political Economy*, 24(4): 763–77.

ECB (2003) 'The ECB's monetary policy strategy', Press release, 8 May. Download from www.ecb.int.

I know very well that the Stability Pact is stupid, like all decisions which are rigid.

Romano Prodi (EU Commission President), Le Monde, 17 October 2002

Over the last months, Europe has gone through a serious financial crisis. Although economic recovery in Europe is now on track, risks remain and we must continue our determined action. We adopted today a comprehensive package of measures which should allow us to turn the corner of the financial crisis and continue our path towards sustainable growth.

Conclusions of European Council, 24–25 March 2011

Fiscal policy and the Stability Pact

Chapter Contents

Introduction

With the loss of monetary policy as a macroeconomic stabilization instrument, fiscal policy may assume greater importance in a monetary union. However, national fiscal policies affect other countries in a number of different ways. Do these spillover effects also call for sharing the fiscal policy instrument? This chapter first reviews how fiscal policy operates across national boundaries and presents the principles that can help to decide whether some limits on national decisions are in order. This lays the ground for an understanding of the Stability and Growth Pact. The chapter next examines the Pact's impact on policy choices and the controversies that have arisen as its shortcomings become more evident. It concludes with a description of a new pact, the Euro Plus Pact.

17.1 Fiscal policy in the monetary union

17.1.1 An ever more important instrument?

When joining a monetary union a country gives up one of its two macroeconomic instruments – monetary policy – but retains full control of the other – fiscal policy. Without national monetary policy, fiscal policy is the only instrument remaining with which to deal with asymmetric shocks when they arise. From this perspective, fiscal policy becomes more important for smoothing national output and employment fluctuations and, through the impact of prices, inflation too. As seen in Chapter 13, in a rigidly fixed exchange rate regime like the monetary union, the *MP* schedule is irrelevant given the loss of monetary autonomy, but the *IS* schedule can be shifted with fiscal policy.

Unfortunately, fiscal policy is unlikely to be a good substitute for monetary policy. It is a very different instrument, more difficult to activate and less reliable than monetary policy. Importantly, it can be misused, and is often misused when governments ignore the need to eventually balance their budgets.

Indeed, changes in public spending and/or taxes impact on the budget balance, which immediately raises the question of the financing of public debt. Consider, for instance, a cut in income taxes designed to increase private spending. A tax cut creates a budget deficit. The government will have to borrow and thus increase the public debt, but how will this new debt be reimbursed? If, as is plausible, taxes are eventually raised, the policy action is properly seen as the combination of a tax reduction today and a tax increase later. This is an action unlikely to boost private consumption once taxpayers realize that the benefit today will be offset by an equivalent cost in the future.[1]

In comparison with monetary policy, fiscal policy faces a major additional drawback: it is very slow to implement. A central bank can decide to change the interest rate whenever it deems it necessary, and can do so in a matter of seconds. Not so for fiscal policy. Establishing the budget is a long and complicated process. The government must first agree on the budget, with lots of heavy-handed negotiations among ministers. The budget must then be approved by the parliament, a time-consuming and highly political process. Then spending decisions must be enacted through the bureaucracy, and taxes can be changed only gradually as they are never retroactive. For example, income taxes can only affect future incomes, implying long delays, even though, once implemented, fiscal policy actions tend to have a more rapid effect on the economy (6 to 12 months) than does monetary policy (12 to 24 months). Ultimately, fiscal policy is like a tanker; it changes course very slowly. The delay may even be such that, when fiscal policy finally affects the economy, the problem that it was meant to solve has disappeared.

In much the same way as unrestrained monetary policy eventually delivers inflation, undisciplined fiscal policy results in high public indebtedness. The crisis has shown that allowing debts to grow can destabilize a country and that the phenomenon may be contagious within the Eurozone. The inflation bias, the tendency to use monetary policy unwisely, has been reduced by making central banks independent from governments that tend to favour short-term gains (revenue from inflation) at the expense of long-term pain (getting rid of inflation once it has been unleashed). The same political instincts are the source of a deficit bias, which is examined in Section 17.2.4. The deficit bias remains a feature of several Eurozone countries, which calls for remedial action. This is the raison d'être of the Stability and Growth Pact, presented in Section 17.4.

---

[1] The extreme case whereby consumers save all of the tax reduction to pay for future tax increases is called Ricardian equivalence. It is explained, and its empirical validity assessed, in, for example, Burda and Wyplosz (2012).

17.1.2 Borrowing instead of transfers

Another way of looking at fiscal policy is that the government borrows and pays back on behalf of its citizens. During a slowdown, the government opens up a budget deficit that is financed through public borrowing. In an upswing, the government runs a budget surplus in order to pay back its debt. A government that borrows to reduce taxes now and raises taxes later to pay back its debt is, in effect, lending to its citizens now and making them pay back later. Individual citizens and firms could, in principle, do it on their own, borrowing in bad years and paying back in good years. This would have the same stabilizing effect as fiscal policy. Is fiscal policy a futile exercise or, worse, a bad political trick? Not quite.

To start with, in the previous example the government simply acts as a bank vis-à-vis its citizens. The reason why it may make sense is that, when the economy slows down, lending becomes generally riskier and banks become very cautious. Many citizens and firms cannot borrow in bad times, or can only borrow at high cost. Indeed, their banks consider workers who lose their jobs as a bad risk, and the same applies regarding firms that face sagging profits or even losses. When governments are considered a good risk, they can borrow at all times at reasonably low cost. This is why counter-cyclical fiscal policies can be effective.

An additional reason is related to one of the optimum currency area criteria examined in Chapter 15, the desirability of substantial inter-country transfers. In that dimension, Europe was found to do very poorly. Using fiscal policy can alleviate this problem. When a country faces an adverse asymmetric shock, its government can borrow from countries that are not affected by the shock. This is the equivalent of a transfer: instead of receiving a loan or a grant[2] from other Eurozone governments or from 'Brussels', the adversely affected country's government borrows. In this way, fiscal policy makes up for the absence of 'federal' transfers in a monetary union.

17.1.3 Automatic stabilizers and discretionary policy actions

Automatic stabilizers

Fiscal policy has one important advantage, though: it tends to be spontaneously counter-cyclical. When the economy slows down, individual incomes are disappointingly low, corporate profits decline and spending is rather weak. This all means that tax collection declines: revenues from income taxes, profit taxes, VAT, etc. are less than they would be in normal conditions. At the same time, spending on unemployment benefits and on other subsidies rises. All in all, the budget worsens and fiscal policy is automatically expansionary. These various effects are called the automatic stabilizers of fiscal policy.

Table 17.1 shows how much the budget balance deteriorates when the economy slows down. Roughly, on average, a 1 per cent decline in growth leads to a deterioration of the budget balance of about 0.5 per cent of GDP. There are some differences from one country to another that reflect the structure of taxation and welfare payments.[3] This, in turn, represents an automatic fiscal expansion.

Table 17.1   Sensitivity of government budget balances to a 1 per cent decline in economic growth

Country	%	Country	%	Country	%	Country	%
Germany	0.5	Austria	−0.5	Greece	−0.6	Portugal	−0.4
France	−0.5	Belgium	−0.5	Ireland	−0.4	Spain	−0.5
Italy	−0.4	Denmark	−0.7	Netherlands	−0.6	Sweden	−0.5
UK	−0.6	Finland	−0.5				

Source: Economic Outlook, OECD, 1997

---

[2] A grant is not to be reimbursed, but a collective system of grants implies that any country is supposed to be alternately giving and receiving, the total hopefully averaging zero over the long run. This is no different from long-term borrowing – receiving now, paying back later.

[3] For example, the more progressive are income taxes, the more tax collection declines during a slowdown, hence the greater the stabilization effect. Similarly, the automatic stabilizers are stronger, the larger are the unemployment benefits.

Discretionary fiscal policy

The automatic stabilizers just happen. Discretionary fiscal policy, on the contrary, requires explicit decisions to change taxes or spending. As noted above, such decisions are slow to be made and implemented. This is why, in some countries, the budget law sets aside some funds – called rainy day funds – that can be quickly mobilized by the government if discretionary action is needed. Even then, the amounts are small and their use is often politically controversial.

An implication of the existence of automatic stabilizers is that the budget figures do not reveal what the government is doing with its fiscal policy. The budget can change for two reasons. It can improve, for example, because the government is cutting spending or raising taxes – this is called discretionary policy – or because the economy is booming – the automatic stabilizers. In order to disentangle these two factors, it is convenient to look at the cyclically-adjusted budget. This procedure is based on the output gap concept. A negative gap, for instance, indicates that the economy is underperforming – that it operates below its potential. The cyclically-adjusted budget balance is an estimate of what the balance would be in a given year if the output gap were zero. When output is below potential, i.e. when the output gap is negative, the actual budget balance is lower than the cyclically-adjusted budget balance and, conversely, when the output gap is positive. The difference between the evolution of the actual and cyclically-adjusted budget balances is the footprint of the automatic stabilizers.

The cyclically-adjusted budget balance is a reliable gauge of the stance of fiscal policy since it separates discretionary government actions from the cyclical effects of the automatic stabilizers. An improvement indicates that the government tightens fiscal policy whereas an expansionary fiscal policy worsens the cyclically-adjusted budget balance. If the government never changed its fiscal policy, the cyclically-adjusted budget balance would remain constant, at least to a first approximation.[4] Box 17.1 illustrates this point in the case of the Netherlands. These two issues – the role of the automatic stabilizers and the distinction between the actual and cyclically-adjusted budgets – play a crucial role in what follows.

Box 17.1 The automatic stabilizers at work in the Netherlands

Figure 17.1 displays the output gap along with the actual and cyclically-adjusted budget balance of the Netherlands. We can see that the actual balance generally moves in tandem with the output gap, an indication that the automatic stabilizers are at work. Note also the steady improvement in the budget that occurred during the convergence years 1995–99. This occurred partly as a result of government efforts to meet the Maastricht entry conditions, as shown by the reduction of the cyclically-adjusted deficit, and partly because a rising output gap made it easier to meet those conditions. It is also interesting to observe that the sharp deterioration in the budget over 2001–05 – which caused the Netherlands to violate the Stability and Growth Pact – is the consequence of a serious slowdown, and occurred in spite of visible government efforts to avoid this outcome. The financial crisis that began in 2007 then caused the Dutch economy to contract sharply. Both actual and cyclically-adjusted balances in parallel developed large deficits, an indication that little discrete action occurred. The government then moved sharply to close the cyclically-adjusted balance, which had contributed to a dramatic fall in output. With the economy in a deep recession, the actual budget modestly improved.

Note that the cyclically-adjusted budget, which is a measure of discretionary actions, also tends to move in the same direction as the output gap. In good years, when the output gap rises, the government conducts restrictive fiscal policies, while its policy is expansionary when the output gap declines. Put differently, fiscal policy tends to be used in a counter-cyclical way, which dampens the business cycle. Looking carefully at the figure reveals numerous exceptions, however.

---

[4] Why to a first approximation? Because, as the economy grows, more people climb the income ladder and face higher tax rates. Also, the structure of the economy changes, possibly changing the way taxes are collected.

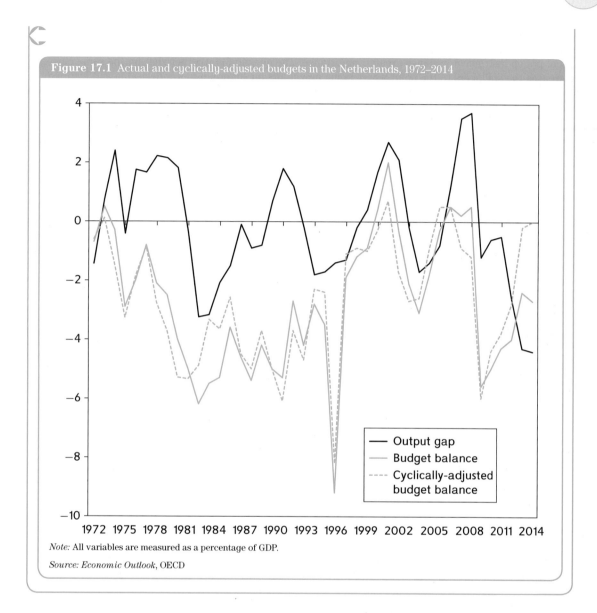

Figure 17.1 Actual and cyclically-adjusted budgets in the Netherlands, 1972–2014

Note: All variables are measured as a percentage of GDP.

Source: Economic Outlook, OECD

17.2 Fiscal policy externalities

17.2.1 Spillovers: a case for policy coordination

So far, the discussion has concerned individual countries. But fiscal policy actions by one country may spill over to other countries through a variety of channels, such as income and spending, inflation, borrowing costs and financial distress. Such spillovers, called externalities, mean that one country's fiscal policy actions can help or hurt other countries. Countries subject to each other's spillovers stand to benefit from coordinating their fiscal policies. In principle, all concerned countries could agree on each other's fiscal policy to achieve a situation that benefits them all. This is what policy coordination is all about.

While, formally, fiscal policy remains a national prerogative, it is natural to ask whether the deepening economic integration among Eurozone countries calls for some degree of coordination. On the one hand, the setting up of a monetary union strengthens the case for fiscal policy coordination as it promotes deeper ties. On the other hand, fiscal policy coordination requires binding agreements defining who does what and when. Such detailed arrangements would limit each country's sovereignty, precisely at a time when the fiscal policy instrument assumes greater importance. The question is whether sharing the same currency increases the spillovers to the point where some new limits on sovereignty are desirable and justified. To answer this highly controversial question, we review the channels through which spillovers occur and examine what difference the Eurozone makes.

17.2.2 Cyclical income spillovers

Business cycles are transmitted through exports and imports. When Germany enters an expansion phase, for instance, it imports more from its partner countries. For these partner countries, the German expansion means more exports and more incomes. This is how the expansion tends to be transmitted across borders. Figure 17.2 displays output gaps for a number of countries. The countries in the left-hand chart are all Eurozone members and have been EU members since the Treaty of Rome; their business cycles are highly synchronized, and were so long before the adoption of the euro. Those exhibited in the right-hand chart are more recent partners and two of them have not adopted the euro. Their cycles are much less synchronized. Quite obviously, the spillover is stronger the more the countries trade with each other, and sharing the same currency enhances income spillovers. This observation is a reminder of the endogenous OCA hypothesis presented in Chapter 15. A high degree of synchronization means fewer asymmetric shocks.

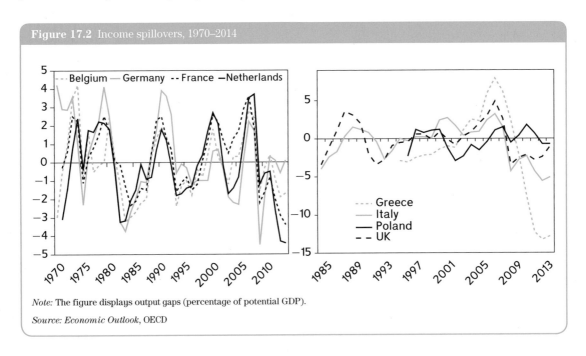

Figure 17.2 Income spillovers, 1970–2014

Note: The figure displays output gaps (percentage of potential GDP).

Source: Economic Outlook, OECD

What does this mean for fiscal policy? Consider, first, the case when two monetary union member countries undergo synchronized cycles, for example both suffer a recession. Each government will want to adopt an expansionary fiscal policy, but to what extent? If each government ignores the action of the other, their combined actions may be too strong; if, instead, each government relies on the other to do most of the work, too little might be done to pull each economy out of recession. Consider next the case when the cycles are asynchronized. An expansionary fiscal policy in the country undergoing a slowdown stands to boost spending in the already booming country. Conversely, a contractionary fiscal policy move in the booming country stands to deepen the recession in the other country.

What all these examples have in common is that there is ample room for mutually beneficial cooperation. This conclusion is a particular case of the general result of Section 17.2.1.

17.2.3 Borrowing cost spillovers

A fiscal expansion increases public borrowing or reduces public saving. As the government is usually the country's biggest borrower, large budget deficits may push interest rates up. Once they share the same currency, Eurozone member countries share the same interest rate. One country's deficits, especially if the country is large and its deficits sizeable, may impose higher interest rates throughout the Eurozone.[5] As high interest rates deter investment, they negatively affect long-term growth. This is another spillover channel.

As stated, the argument is weak, however. Since Europe is fully integrated in the world's financial markets, any one country's borrowing is unlikely to make much of an impression on world and European interest rates. On the other hand, heavy borrowing may elicit capital inflows. This could result in an appreciation of the euro, which would hurt the area's competitiveness and cut into growth. Borrowing costs thus represent another channel for spillovers.

17.2.4 Excessive deficits and the no-bailout clause

Even before the crisis, it was clear that debt sustainability could not be taken for granted in Europe. As Figure 17.3 shows, overall public indebtedness (as a percentage of GDP) in the Eurozone had more than doubled between 1977 and 1996, just before the check on admission criteria.[6] In the distant past, public debt

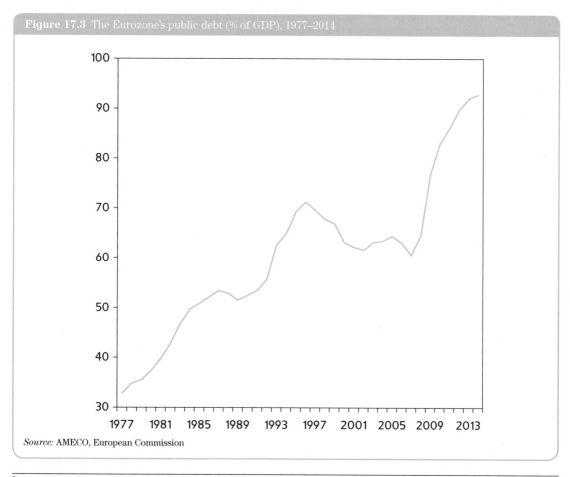

Figure 17.3 The Eurozone's public debt (% of GDP), 1977–2014

Source: AMECO, European Commission

---

[5] According to Jürgen Stark, a high-level German official who was influential in designing the Stability and Growth Pact: 'The state's absorption of resources which would otherwise have found their way into private investments results in higher long-term interest rates' (2001, p. 79).

[6] This is the debt for the whole zone. The situation differs from country to country.

had occasionally risen but only in difficult situations, mostly during wars. The post-war build-up of debt, partly related to the oil shocks of the 1970s and 1980s, illustrates what is sometimes called the 'deficit bias'. This bias reflects a disquieting tendency for governments to run budget deficits for no other reason than political expediency. Does it call for a specific collective measure?

In principle, it is in each country's interest to resist the deficit bias and there is no need for collective measures, unless spillovers can be identified. The founding fathers of the euro identified four spillovers. The first concerns the tendency of financially hard-pressed governments to call upon the central bank to finance their deficits. Debt monetization, as this is called, is the traditional route to inflation. Central bank independence from government is the proper response and, as noted in Chapter 16, the Eurosystem indeed enjoys very strong independence.

Second, heavy public borrowing by one country is a sign of fiscal indiscipline that could trouble the international financial markets. If markets believe that one country's public debt is unsustainable, they could view the whole Eurozone with suspicion. The result would be sizeable capital outflows and euro weakness. This is precisely what happened in 2010–11 within the Eurozone.

There is a third potential spillover. A government that accumulates a debt that it can no longer service must eventually default. Experience of public debt defaults shows that the immediate reaction is a massive capital outflow, a collapse of the exchange rate and stock markets, and a prolonged crisis complete with a deep recession and skyrocketing unemployment. Being part of a monetary union changes things radically. It is now the common exchange rate that is the object of the market reaction. The spillover can further extend to stock markets throughout the whole monetary union.

A further fear is that the mere threat of one member country's default would so concern all other member governments that they would feel obliged to bail out the nearly bankrupt government. This last risk has been clearly identified in the Maastricht Treaty, which included a 'no-bailout' clause. Article 125 of the European Treaty forbids all public institutions, including governments, to provide direct support to a Eurozone government. Article 123 does the same regarding the ECB. Yet it always was an open question whether, in the midst of an emergency, some arrangement could still be found to bail out a near-bankrupt government. For example, the ECB could be 'informally' pressed to relax its monetary policy to make general credit more abundant at a lower cost, which would result in inflation. More generally, it was feared that a sovereign default would badly affect the Eurozone and undermine its credibility. We will see in Chapter 19 that the no-bailout clause was ignored in May 2010.

17.2.5 The deficit bias and collective discipline

Why do many governments seem to have a deficit bias, and why does this bias seem to differ from country to country, as can be seen in Table 17.2? Deficits allow governments to deliver goods and services today, including jobs to civil servants and transfers to the needy, without facing the costs, passing the burden of debt service

Table 17.2   Public debt within Europe (% of GDP), 2014

Austria 80.3	Belgium 101.7	Bulgaria 23.1	Croatia 69.0	Cyprus 122.2	Czech Rep. 44.4
Denmark 43.5	Estonia 9.8	Finland 59.9	France 95.6	Germany 76.0	Greece 177.2
Hungary 80.3	Ireland 121.0	Italy 135.2	Latvia 39.5	Lithuania 41.8	Luxembourg 23.4
Malta 72.5	Netherlands 73.8	Poland 49.2	Portugal 126.7	Romania 39.9	Slovakia 56.3
Slovenia 80.4	Spain 100.2	Sweden 41.6	United Kingdom 91.8	EU 89.5	Eurozone 96.0

Source: AMECO, European Commission

to future governments or even to future generations. It is tempting to do so, especially when elections are near, but adequate democratic accountability should prevent governments from indulging in doing so. Even though future generations are not here to weigh in, the current generation may reasonably expect to be called upon to service the debt, and anyway most people care about the next generation. A debt build-up often reflects a failure of democratic control over governments. Why has this been happening in Europe's democracies?

Public spending is an important source of income for all sorts of citizens, organizations and firms. Taxpayers, current or future, must pay for it. Those who receive money from the government hope that they will not pay the corresponding taxes, or at least not fully. It is in the interest of every recipient of public spending to ask for more. In fact, they often form well-organized and influential interest groups. Democratically elected governments are naturally inclined to please the interest groups without raising taxes. This is what lies behind the widespread bias towards deficits. The importance of the bias depends on the electoral process. For instance, parliamentary regimes that involve large coalitions seem to be doing less well at keeping deficits in check.

Changing the democratic regime (the form of democracy, how elections are organized, etc.) could help, but it is a rather intractable endeavour. This is why some governments find it appealing to seek external restraint and to invoke 'Brussels' as a scapegoat that can be blamed when resisting interest groups and political friends. Collective discipline, even if not necessarily justified by spillovers, can be used as a substitute for adequate domestic institutions.

17.3 Principles

The existence of spillovers is one argument for sharing policy responsibilities among independent countries but powerful counter-arguments exist. The broader question is, at which level of government – regional, national, supranational – should policies be conducted? The theory of fiscal federalism deals with this question. The principle of subsidiarity is another way of approaching the issue. Both approaches are presented in detail in Chapter 3; they are briefly recalled in this section with a particular emphasis on fiscal policy.

17.3.1 Fiscal federalism

The theory of fiscal federalism asks how, in one country, fiscal responsibilities should be assigned between the various levels (national, regional, municipal) of government. It can be transposed to Europe's case, even though Europe is not a federation, by asking which tasks should remain in national – possibly regional in federal states – hands and which should be a shared responsibility, i.e. delegated to Brussels. There are two good reasons to transfer responsibility to Brussels and two good reasons to keep it at the national level. An additional concern is the quality of government at the national and supranational levels.

Two arguments for sharing responsibilities: externalities and increasing returns to scale

As noted before, spillovers lead to inefficient outcomes when each country is free to act as it wishes. Sometimes too much action is taken, sometimes not enough. In addition some policies are more efficient when carried out on a large scale. Increasing returns to scale can be found in the use of money,[7] in the design of commercial law or in defence (army, weapons development and production), among others.

One solution is coordination, which preserves sovereignty but calls for repeated and often-piecemeal negotiations, with no guarantee of success. Another solution is to give up sovereignty, partly or completely, and delegate a task to a supranational institution. In Europe, some important tasks have already been delegated to the European Commission under the name of shared competences (the internal market and trade negotiations) and to the Eurosystem (monetary policy).

Two arguments for retaining sovereignty: heterogeneity of preferences and information asymmetries

Consider the example of common law concerning family life (marriage and divorce, raising children, dealing with ageing parents, etc.). Practices and traditions differ across countries, sometimes to a considerable

---

[7] Chapter 15 explains why this is a key benefit resulting from forming a currency area.

extent. In this domain, preferences are heterogeneous and a supranational arrangement is bound to create much dissatisfaction.

Now consider decisions regarding roads: where to build them, how large to make them, where to set up traffic lights, etc. These require a thorough understanding of how people move, or wish to move, in a specific geographic area. It is a case of information asymmetry: the information is more readily available at the local level than at a more global level.

Heterogeneity of preferences and information asymmetries imply that, in these matters, it would be inefficient to share competence at a supranational level. Much of the criticism levelled at 'Brussels' concerns cases where either heterogeneity or information asymmetries are important: deciding on the appropriate size of cheese or the way to brew beer is best left to national governments, even to local authorities, no matter how important are the externalities (public health is the mantra used by the Commission to expand its power in food-related matters) or even the existence of important increasing returns to scale.

The quality of government

An implicit assumption so far is that governments always act in the best interest of their citizens. While this may generally be the case, there are numerous instances when governments either pursue their own agenda or are captured by interest groups. In addition, like any institution, governments often wish to extend their domain, possibly in order to increase their own power or because they genuinely believe that they do a better job than lower-level jurisdictions. One can question whether there is such a thing as 'the best interest of citizens': some citizens favour some actions which others dislike. Governments exist in part to deal with such conflict and do so under democratic control, but elections cannot sanction every one of the millions of decisions that favour well-connected interests. In spite of all the good things that can be said about democracy, it is not a perfect system.

What to conclude?

Good reasons exist for both centralizing and decentralizing particular tasks. The theory of fiscal federalism does not provide a general answer; rather, it argues in favour of a case-by-case approach and suggests that, often, we face trade-offs with no compelling answer. To make things even murkier, the observation that governments are not perfect, merely human, means that we need always to keep in mind that a good solution may transpire to be bad if the government is misbehaving. In particular, the quality of both government and democratic control ought to be brought into the picture. The practical question here is whether Brussels performs better than the national governments.

17.3.2 The principle of subsidiarity

It should be clear by now that the four arguments for and against centralization at the EU level are unlikely to lead to clear-cut conclusions, and the warning about the quality of government further complicates the issue. Weighing the various arguments and trading off the pros and cons is often mission impossible, hence another question arises: where should the burden of proof lie? The EU has taken the view that the burden of proof lies with those who argue in favour of sharing sovereign tasks. This is the principle of subsidiarity (presented in Chapter 3) and it is enshrined in the European Treaty:

> *In areas which do not fall within its exclusive competence, the Community shall take action, in accordance with the principle of subsidiarity, only if and insofar as the objectives of the proposed action cannot be sufficiently achieved by the Member States and can therefore, by reason of the scale or effects of the proposed action, be better achieved by the Community.*

(Article 5)

In other words: unless there is a strong case of increasing returns to scale or of externality, the presumption is that decisions remain at the national level.

17.3.3 Implications for fiscal policy

A key distinction: microeconomic vs. macroeconomic aspects of fiscal policy

It is helpful to separate two aspects of fiscal policy. The first aspect is structural, that is, mainly microeconomic. It concerns the size of the budget, what public money is spent on and how taxes are raised, i.e. who pays what. It also concerns income redistribution and the need to reduce inequalities or to provide incentives to particular individuals or groups. The second aspect is macroeconomic. This is the income stabilization role of fiscal policy, the idea that it can be used as a counter-cyclical instrument.

Here, we focus on the macroeconomic stabilization component of fiscal policy, ignoring the structural aspects, which clearly are a matter for national politics, with very limited macroeconomic impact. To simplify, we look at the budget balance and ignore the size and structure of the budget and the resulting evolution of the public debt. We apply the principles of fiscal federalism to ask whether there is a case for limiting the free exercise of sovereignty on national budget balances and debts.

The case for collective restraint

Section 17.2 identifies a number of spillovers: income flows, borrowing costs and the risk of difficulties in financing runaway deficits, possibly leading to debt default. Some of these spillovers can have serious effects across the Eurozone, as the crisis has shown. In addition, some countries have not established political institutions that are conducive to fiscal discipline so it may be in their own best interest to use Brussels as an external agent of restraint. On the other hand, it is difficult to detect any scale economy in these matters.

These externalities call for some limits on national fiscal policies, and such limits can take various forms, ranging from coordination and peer pressure to mandatory limits on deficits and debts.

The case against collective restraint

Working in the opposite direction are important heterogeneities and information asymmetries. Macroeconomic heterogeneity occurs in the presence of asymmetric shocks. A common fiscal policy, on top of a common monetary policy, would leave each country with no counter-cyclical macroeconomic tool. Heterogeneity can also be the consequence of differences of opinion regarding the effectiveness of the instrument. Some countries (e.g. France and Italy) have long been active users of fiscal policy whereas others (e.g. Germany) have a tradition of scepticism towards Keynesian policies. Finally, national political processes are another source of heterogeneity. In some countries, the government has quite some leeway to adapt the budget to changing economic conditions, whereas in others the process is cumbersome and politically contentious.

Information asymmetries chiefly concern the perception of the political implications of fiscal policies. Each government faces elections, and economic issues often weigh heavily in shaping voter preferences. Whether and how to use fiscal policy at a particular juncture is part of a complex political game, which makes national politics highly idiosyncratic. While politicians clearly understand each other's electoral plight, they have a hard time absorbing the many fine details of foreign national politics.

Finally, a number of countries have built institutions that effectively contain the deficit bias. Table 17.2 shows that this is the case in the Nordic countries as well as in some central and eastern European countries. These arrangements include national budget rules, oversight committees (wise-persons) or limits to parliamentary initiatives that tend to raise spending or cut taxes. If it is possible to achieve fiscal discipline locally, then the subsidiarity principle indicates that this is where measures have to be taken in the first place.

Overall

It is far from clear that the macroeconomic component of fiscal policy should be subject to common limits. Quite clearly, a single common fiscal policy is ruled out, but what about some degree of cooperation? The debate is ongoing and is unlikely to be settled in the near future. The subsidiarity principle implies that, as long as the case is not strong, fiscal policy should remain fully a national prerogative. On the other hand, the spillovers that could result from *excessive* deficits are important; this is the logical basis for the Stability and Growth Pact.

17.3.4 What does it all mean for fiscal policy in the Eurozone?

In true federal states, there is a powerful federal government and sub-federal governments are usually restrained in their ability to run deficits and hence to use fiscal policy as a macroeconomic instrument. In the Eurozone, in contrast, the Commission budget is far too small (1 per cent of GDP) to play any macroeconomic role. This is why a number of proposals aim at establishing an 'economic government for Europe', including a European Finance Minister. The idea is that decentralized fiscal policies would be subject to overall coherence objectives. There is a strong logic to it, but how does it deal with sovereignty in fiscal matters?

Applying the principles of fiscal federalism to the Eurozone leaves us with few uncontroversial conclusions. There always were valid reasons for imposing fiscal discipline, and the debt crisis has made it clear that it is a survival condition for the euro. The case for policy coordination is also convincing but there are equally valid arguments in the opposite direction. All in all, the case for further transfer of sovereignty is weak.

Start with fiscal discipline. Since one country's lack of fiscal discipline may create havoc throughout the Eurozone, as has happened, a natural reaction is to limit the sovereignty of member countries, at least during periods of instability. At the same time, parliamentary control over budgetary matters is a very fundamental principle of democracies ('no taxation without representation'). Challenging this principle can be justified only if there is no other way of imposing fiscal discipline through member countries. But, as noted above and further explained in Box 17.2, a number of countries have alleviated their own deficit biases by reforming their budgetary processes. This indicates that national solutions can deliver fiscal discipline.

Box 17.2   The deficit bias and the common pool effect

The deficit bias is a frequently observed feature of otherwise well-functioning democracies. Is there a systematic reason for this tendency? The common pool effect provides a convincing interpretation. Its name refers to a medieval practice: villages often included a field – the commons – where peasants could freely bring their cows and sheep to pasture. Each peasant had an incentive to bring as many animals as possible since grass was free. The (possibly inaccurate) result was that the commons could not feed all the animals that were grazing. Collectively, the peasants should have agreed to limit the number of animals that anyone could bring, but individually each peasant wanted the others to take the first step. Herds were decimated and the peasants starved.

Much the same applies to taxation: let the others pay more! It also applies to government spending: I want more public spending that is a benefit to me, so cut spending elsewhere if need be. In a democracy, voters require governments to do things for them and to pay for them with taxes paid by others. They often organize themselves in powerful pressure groups that lobby the government. In that way, many specific expenditures become political sacred cows. Since tax increases are politically unsavoury, budget deficits emerge as a natural outcome.

Once the source of the problem is identified, a solution can be envisioned. The common pool effect suggests that the budget process must be straightened out. Some countries legally limit the size of deficits; others require the government to decide on the deficit first, and only then to decide on spending and taxes; and yet others request a high degree of transparency, which undermines the influence of lobbies.

Table 17.3 documents the track record among a number of developed countries. For each country, it provides two pieces of evidence: in the first row, the proportion of years when the budget was in

Table 17.3   Deficit years during 1960–2014 in the OECD area (%)

	Australia	Austria	Belgium	Canada	Germany
% Last surplus	81 2008	83 1974	96 2006	74 2007	77 2012
	Denmark	Spain	Finland	France	UK
% Last surplus	51 2008	79 2007	25 2008	91 1974	85 2001
	Greece	Ireland	Italy	Japan	Netherlands
% Last surplus	81 1972	81 2007	100	70 1992	89 2008
	Norway	New Zealand	Portugal	Sweden	USA
% Last surplus	4 2014	48 2008	100	42 2008	92 2000

Sources: Economic Outlook, OECD and Eichengreen and Wyplosz (1993) for older data

deficit over more than half a century and, in the second row, which year the budget was last in surplus, if that occurred after 1960. The deficit bias is widely confirmed as most countries have experienced deficits for at least four years out of five. The exceptions are Norway (which benefits from huge oil and gas income), Denmark, Finland, New Zealand and Sweden, countries that display a high degree of both transparency and collective responsibility. It is also interesting to note that some countries have recently adopted some of the anti-bias solutions mentioned above; while their track record is poor, it is improving, as indicated by recent surpluses.

There is no doubt that policy coordination is desirable, but it is also very difficult to implement. Ideally, all governments would discuss their macroeconomic needs and the Eurosystem would indicate its contribution to overall inflation and output stabilization. The governments would then agree on what each one would do, both to deal with domestic conditions and to achieve the collective best. This is a tall order. First, because assessing each country's needs and identifying the collective best is largely beyond current knowledge. Second, because in each country the politics of fiscal policy are often conflictual. Often the outcome of the budgetary process is unpredictable until the parliament has finished voting. Finally, governments are likely to be highly reluctant to relinquish such an important political tool.

A step was taken in 2011 with the adoption of a 'European semester'. The arrangement is described below. One objective is to synchronize budgetary planning in the EU, opening the door to cooperation. Another objective is to move ahead of national budgetary processes in the hope of framing them in accordance with the obligations of the Stability and Growth Pact. The European semester triggers discussions among governments and in the European Parliament and leads to jointly agreed recommendations by the Council.[8] Time will tell whether the European semester succeeds in injecting some degree of coordination effective enough to take into account the spillovers described in Section 17.2. Since this new coordination mechanism

---

[8] 'The Council' here refers to the Ministers for Economic and Financial Affairs and is called ECOFIN. For Eurozone decisions, ECOFIN includes only Ministers from member countries, casually referred to as the Eurogroup. The Eurogroup usually meets on the day before ECOFIN meetings.

Box 17.3   Fiscal policy coordination in the Eurozone

Following the crisis of 2010 and subsequent years, recovery was anaemic in 2014. A large number of countries, not merely the crisis countries, have again been asked to cut their budget deficits. This means a restrictive fiscal policy that stunts recovery. Policy coordination would deal with this situation by encouraging deficit reduction where needed while promoting a stronger recovery through spillovers from expansionary fiscal policies where the situation allows. In this exercise, the focus is on large countries that have a stronger income spillover effect on the Eurozone. Germany is in this situation, but the German authorities are still concerned that their budgetary situation is still fragile and worry about a return of inflation if growth is too rapid.

Without coordination, therefore, Germany will not adopt an expansionary fiscal policy and other countries will limit efforts at deficit reduction. The European semester is designed to promote coordination. At the conclusion of the 2014 exercise, the July European Council stated that '[it] is of the opinion that public finances in Germany remain sound overall as the medium-term objective is forecast to continue to be maintained and the debt rule respected'. In other words, there is no suggestion that Germany should change its fiscal policy stance. Earlier, when it concluded its annual review of German policies, the IMF considered that 'policies should focus on increasing growth in Germany while at the same time supporting the recovery in the euro area'.[1] This is more in line with coordination.

[1] The European council statement is available at: http://register.consilium.europa.eu/pdf/en/14/st10/st10783.en14.pdf. The IMF statement can be found at http://www.imf.org/external/np/ms/2014/051914.htm.

---

does not limit national sovereignty in any way, it is hard to imagine that much will be gained. Box 17.3 provides an example of the difficulties.

Ultimately, the debate has been ongoing for a decade and is unlikely to disappear for some time yet.[9] It pits those who attach much importance to spillovers and think that macroeconomic coordination is both promising and relatively easy to implement against those who see it as a collusion of self-interested governments.

17.4 The stability and growth pact

17.4.1 From convergence to the quest for a permanent regime

As explained in Chapter 16, admission to the monetary union requires a budget deficit of less than 3 per cent of GDP and a public debt of less than 60 per cent of GDP, or declining towards this benchmark. But what about afterwards, once in the monetary union? Could countries achieve the two fiscal criteria, join the monetary union and then freely relapse into unbridled indiscipline? Doing so would be against the spirit of convergence. The founding fathers of the Maastricht Treaty were keenly aware of this risk and, indeed, Article 126 unambiguously states that 'Member States shall avoid excessive government deficits' and then goes on to outline an 'excessive deficit procedure'. The Treaty left the practical details of the procedure to be settled later – and this is the task fulfilled by the Stability and Growth Pact (SGP) and its excessive deficit procedure (EDP).[10]

---

[9] Some references are provided in the further reading section at the end of this chapter.

[10] The initiative was taken by Germany in 1995 and the Pact adopted in June 1997 by the European Council. Informed by its own inter-war history, Germany was always concerned that fiscal indiscipline could lead to inflation. This is why it insisted on a clear and automatic procedure. It wanted to make full use of the provisions of the Maastricht Treaty, which allowed for fines in the case of excessive deficits. The other countries were less enthusiastic but Germany was holding the key to the Eurozone. France, in particular, was unhappy with the German proposal. It obtained the symbolic addition of the word 'growth' to what Germany had initially called the Stability Pact.

Adopted in 1997, the EDP was meant to be strictly enforced. However, because fiscal policy remains a national competence, the final say was given to the Council of Finance Ministers of the Eurozone, the Eurogroup. Acting on proposals from the Commission, which assumed the responsibility of being the Pact's 'tough cop', the Eurogroup has been loath to make decisions that would strongly antagonize its members, especially the finance ministers from the large countries. In November 2003, France and Germany were about to be sanctioned. Under pressure from the French and German finance ministers, the Eurogroup recanted and placed the SGP 'in abeyance'. This incident is recounted in Box 17.5. This episode confirmed the view that the SGP was not well designed. Recognizing that it was too rigid to be enforceable, governments and the Commission prepared a reformulation of the Pact. The new version was adopted in June 2005.

Then came the great financial crisis. Obviously, this was not the time to insist on a strict application of the SGP and nearly all countries were technically in excessive debt. The Commission issued a European Economic Recovery Programme, which implicitly accepted that it would take time to respect the SGP. At the same time, the Commission proposed to strengthen and expand the SGP, acknowledging that it had not delivered its promises even before the crisis.

This has led to yet another re-engineering of the SGP. Two new agreements, the so-called Six Pack–Two Pack, and one new Treaty, the Treaty on Stability, Coordination and Governance (TSCG, also called the Fiscal Compact) have added complexity and technicality to an already intricate arrangement.

17.4.2 The stability and growth pact

The SGP consists of five elements:

1 A definition of what constitutes an 'excessive deficit'.

2 A preventive arm, designed to encourage governments to avoid excessive deficits.

3 A corrective arm, which prescribes how governments should react to a breach of the deficit limit.

4 Procedures designed to embed each country's budget process within a European framework that is meant to be over-riding.

5 Sanctions.

The SGP applies to all EU member countries but only the Eurozone countries are subject to the corrective arm.

Excessive deficits and debts

The Stability and Growth Pact considers that deficits are excessive when they are above 3 per cent of GDP. The public debt is excessive when it exceeds 60 per cent of GDP. These are the two convergence criteria described in Chapter 16, which also explains the logical connection between these values (Box 16.2).

The weakness of the deficit threshold is the existence of automatic stabilizers (see Section 17.1.3). When an adverse asymmetric shock occurs, the limit can be breached. At the same time, an adverse shock is just when a fiscal policy expansion is desirable. This is why the SGP also takes into account the structural budget balance, defined as the cyclically adjusted balance net of exceptional spending or revenues. The SGP requires that the structural budget always be in balance or surplus, with a deficit not in excess of 0.5 per cent of GDP.

The preventive arm

As explained in Section 17.2.4, many governments exhibit a deficit bias because of domestic pressure and political expediency. The SGP can exert counter-pressure in the form of peer pressure, called mutual surveillance. The preventive arm is designed to submit finance ministers to a collective discussion of one another's fiscal policy in the hope that doing so will help with budgetary discipline. This preventive arm is meant to circumvent using the politically sensitive corrective arm.

In 2013 a new version of the SGP was enacted; now each country defines its Medium Term Objective (MTO), the budget balance that it commits to achieving within a 3-year period. It must be compatible with 'minimum benchmarks' estimated by the European Commission. The benchmarks recognize the starting point for every country (budget balance, debt, growth). They are updated every 3 years.

Table 17.4   Minimum benchmarks and forecasts of structural budget balances (% of GDP)

	2012 Benchmarks	2014 Forecasts of 2013	2015 Forecasts of 2014
Belgium	−1.5	−2.3	−2.5
Germany	−1.5	0.3	0.0
Estonia	−1.8	0.2	−0.7
Ireland	−0.9	−4.8	−4.2
Greece	−1.8	2.0	−0.4
Spain	−1.4	−5.5	−3.4
France	−1.5	−2.3	−2.0
Italy	−1.5	−0.7	−0.7
Cyprus	−1.7	−5.1	−4.3
Latvia	−1.8	−1.5	−1.9
Lithuania	−1.8	−2.8	−1.3
Luxembourg	−1.6	0.3	−1.3
Malta	−1.8	−3.7	−2.9
Netherlands	−1.4	−2.3	−0.8
Austria	−1.8	−1.7	−1.1
Portugal	−1.8	−2.0	NA
Slovenia	−1.7	−3.3	−2.4
Slovakia	−1.9	−2.4	−1.8
Finland	−0.7	−0.5	−0.3

Sources: Columns 1 and 2: European Commission, Public Finances in EMU, 2013. Column 3: AMECO, European Commission

Table 17.4 presents the first benchmarks established in late 2012, and therefore for the 2015 horizon, along with the Commission's forecasts produced in 2013 for 2014 (forecasts for 2015 were not available then) and those of 2014 for 2015.

The 2011 reform of the SGP also introduced the European semester. This semester begins in January with the publication of the SGP's forecasts for the years to come, which is a way of harmonizing expectations and limiting unduly optimistic national forecasts that lead to unrealistic budget previsions. Then, in early spring, each EU government submits its Stability and Convergence Programme. Along with other policy objectives, the programme includes 'medium-term budgetary strategies', essentially a statement of intentions covering the next 3 years. The crucial issue at this stage is how each government intends to achieve its MTOs year by year. The Commission assesses these programmes and determines whether they are realistic and compatible with the MTOs. If they are not, the government is asked to adjust its intentions in good time before the next annual budget is submitted to parliament. The adopted budget is then evaluated by the Commission, which then forwards its views to the Council. The Council then examines each country's budget and makes public recommendations in early July, which concludes the exercise. The Council's recommendations are meant to shape the next steps, when budgetary proceedings revert back to the national level.

What happens if a country adopts a budget that is not in conformity with the requirements put forward by the Council? This triggers a procedure summarized in Figure 17.4: warnings and recommendations follow in quick succession. The ultimate sanction is a fine of 0.2 per cent of the country's GDP, which takes the form of an interest-bearing deposit; these resources are frozen until the procedure is lifted. Importantly, the decision is adopted by the Council, following a recommendation by the Commission, through a procedure called reversed qualified majority voting (RQMV). This means that the Commission's proposal is adopted unless a majority of votes, weighted by country size, decides against it.[11] The intention is to make Commission proposals more likely to be adopted.[12] The preventive arm applies to all EU countries but fines can only be imposed on Eurozone member countries. In effect, the SGP is binding only on these latter countries.

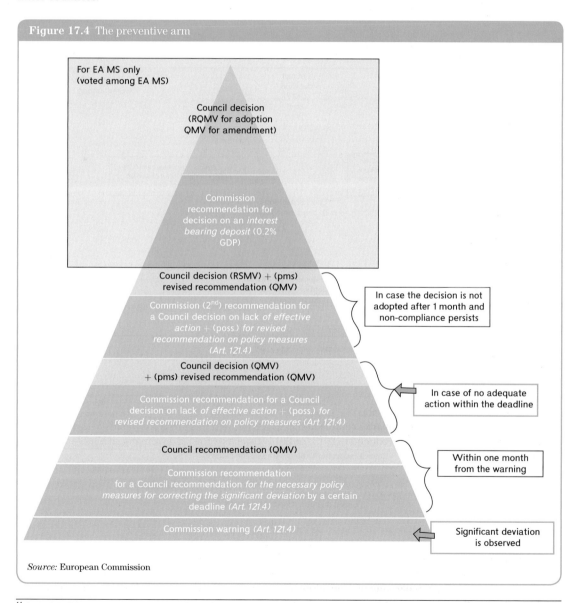

Figure 17.4 The preventive arm

Source: European Commission

---

[11] A qualified majority requires at least two-thirds of the votes cast.

[12] This is a direct response to the 2003 decision not to sanction France and Germany. The two largest countries mustered enough votes to fail to approve the Commission's proposal.

The corrective arm

When a country does not meet the requirements of the SGP – the 3 per cent deficit and 60 per cent debt limits – it is declared in excessive deficit by the Council. The decision is made through qualified majority voting (QMV) upon a recommendation from the Commission. Given that most Eurozone countries have debts vastly in excess of 60 per cent, the EDP only applies if a country above the threshold has not reduced its debt by at least 0.5 per cent of GDP on average over the previous 3 years.

The Council applies gradually increasing peer pressure, described in Figure 17.5. In brief, the Council adopts recommendations that are increasingly detailed and urgent when the recommended course of action is not followed. After several failures to comply, a sanction procedure is triggered. Following a next-to-final

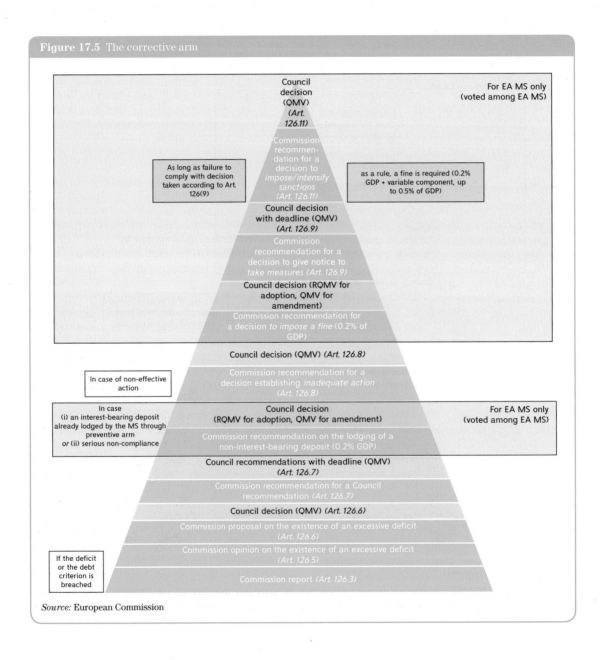

Figure 17.5 The corrective arm

Source: European Commission

warning adopted by RQMV, the Council imposes a sanction by QVM. The sanction is a deposit worth 0.2 per cent of the delinquent country's GDP. Further non-compliance may result in additional fines up to a maximum of 0.5 per cent of GDP.

Appraisal

Several aspects of the EDP are noteworthy. First, formally, it does not remove fiscal policy sovereignty. Governments are in full control; they only agree to bear the consequences of their actions. The procedure involves recommendations, not orders by the Council. At the end of the day, governments and their parliaments decide fiscal policy, and policy-makers care about voters not about 'Europe'. Sanctions are intended to weigh in. It remains the case that both recommendations and sanctions may result in hardening public opinion against 'Europe'.

Second, the intent is clearly pre-emptive. The preventive arm is designed to avoid reaching the stage of corrective action and even then a lengthy procedure is involved between the time a deficit is deemed excessive and when a fine is imposed. Finally, all decisions are in the hands of the Council, a highly political body that can exploit many of the 'ifs' included in the SGP.

As already indicated, the EDP applies to all EU countries but fines can only be imposed on Eurozone member countries. By mid-2014, 17 EU countries were declared to be in excessive deficit (the exceptions were Bulgaria, Germany, Estonia, Italy, Hungary, Latvia, Lithuania, Luxembourg, Romania, Finland and Sweden). At the depth of the crisis, in the spring of 2011, 24 of the 28 EU Member States were declared to be in excessive deficit. No sanction has ever been imposed.

17.4.3 The Treaty on Stability, Coordination and Growth

Most of the elements of the Treaty on Stability, Coordination and Growth (TSCG), adopted in 2012, are included in the SGP. There is one novel element that is of a different nature, however. It requires that every country adopt a budget rule enshrined in high-level legislation. It also mandates the setting up of a watchdog council composed of independent experts. The intent is to further strengthen the SGP by making fiscal discipline a national obligation, not just a requirement set and implemented at the European level.

Inadvertently, perhaps, this treaty could change the situation. The heavy machinery of the SGP (European semester, Commission surveillance and Council decisions) is designed to affect national debates about fiscal policy. Yet national debates are national, filled with unavoidable domestic considerations often far removed from taking into account the importance of fiscal discipline. The Commission easily emerges as the villain that encroaches on an area of national sovereignty. The Commission's response, that it merely implements agreements voluntarily adopted by member countries, often elicits hostility to these agreements, if not toward European integration. The TSCG shifts the debate: it is national laws that must be respected.

The TSCG actually specifies what type of rule is required. Its prescription is the 'debt brake' arrangement inscribed in the German constitution in 2009. This arrangement, inspired by the Swiss debt brake of 2001, is described in Box 17.4. It is based on a simple rule: the cyclically-adjusted budget must never exceed 0.35 per cent of GDP. As explained in the box, the rule is flexible in the short run and strict in the long run. Fiscal policy can be used counter-cyclically when needed but fiscal discipline is non-negotiable and enforceable.

Unfortunately, the TSCG is not very precise. It recommends 'in principle' the German rule and asks that it be written 'in principle' into each country's constitution, which would provide a strong guarantee of enforceability. Early indications are that implementation of the treaty is very much à la carte, with many countries adopting complex rules not written into the constitution (perhaps because they are too complex). Complexity and lower-level law make it possible to ignore the rule.

Another prescription of the TSCG is that each country subjects its budget laws to the scrutiny of a committee of independent experts before adoption. A growing number of countries have established such fiscal councils worldwide. They can play an important role. They usually are tasked to examine how the budget is constructed and to spot unreasonable assumptions and calculations. They can also bless

Box 17.4   The German debt brake

The German debt brake rule requires that the budgets of the federation and of the Länder be in balance. This requirement is deemed satisfied if the federal structurally-adjusted deficit does not exceed 0.35 per cent of GDP. The Länder have no such derogation. If, for unforeseeable reasons, the deficit exceeds the threshold, the corresponding excess is noted down as a debit in a control account. Better outcomes are credited positively into the control account. If the account debit exceeds 1.5 per cent, the federal government must empty the account 'in a manner appropriate to the cyclical situation'.

The arrangement has many advantages over the EDP. First, it is simple and therefore not subject to interpretation. Second, being defined in cyclically-adjusted terms, it allows the automatic stabilizers to fully operate. Third, even better, deviations are allowed, which leaves room for some discretion; later, however, these deviations must be corrected. Fourth, again in contrast to the SGP, the correction does not have to be executed immediately, only 'in a manner appropriate to the cyclical situation', which leaves space in which to wait for better times. Importantly, the obligation to correct accumulated lapses implies that bygones are not bygones; the government knows ex-ante that it will have to compensate any slippage through subsequent surpluses. Finally, the rule is a constitutional requirement. The all-powerful Constitutional Court of Karlsruhe will see to it that the rule is respected.

The debt brake is being progressively applied, so it is too early to observe its full effect. The Swiss debt brake, which served as a model for Germany, has been in place since 2002. Figure 17.6 presents the evolution of the Swiss federal government debt. Obviously, fiscal discipline did not exist in Switzerland before the adoption of the debt brake. However, the impact of a simple and clever rule has led to a clear break from the past.

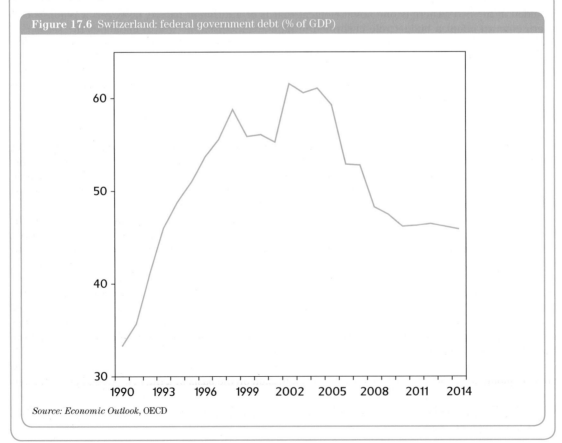

Figure 17.6 Switzerland: federal government debt (% of GDP)

Source: Economic Outlook, OECD

temporary flexibility in bad years – deviations from the rule, when it exists – while insisting on rigorous discipline in good years.[13] Here again, while some countries have established high quality fiscal councils, others have made sure that the government will not be subject to strong criticism.

17.4.4 Why the pact is controversial

Counter-cyclical fiscal policies: how much room to manoeuvre?

The automatic response of budget balances to cyclical fluctuations, recalled in Section 17.1.3, is a source of difficulty for the EDP because much of its machinery, including the sanction mechanism, focuses on the 3 per cent deficit and the 60 per cent debt limits. The logic is that, in normal years, budgets should be balanced or in surplus to leave enough room for the automatic stabilizers to come into play in bad years without breaching the 3 per cent limit.

Mindful of this problem, the reforms of the SGP have put increasing weight on the structural budget. As it conducts surveillance, the Commission interprets the budgetary situation by recognizing that a budget balance can deteriorate automatically when the economic situation worsens. Indeed, the corrective arm urges governments to aim at surpluses during good years (with a formal definition of what a good year actually is). Still, when a country is declared in excessive deficit, it is not allowed to let the automatic stabilizers play their shock-absorbing role. The same applies to countries with debts in excess of 60 per cent of GDP, which are required to cut indebtedness by 0.5 per cent per year, a requirement that applies to 13 out of 18 Eurozone member countries (as of mid-2014).

The upshot is that many member countries are forced to conduct pro-cyclical fiscal policies in bad times, with a contractionary effect. The result is shown in Figure 17.7, which plots changes in the output gap between 2008 (before the Eurozone crisis) and 2014 on the horizontal axis, and of the cyclically-adjusted budget balance (net of debt service) on the vertical axis. If fiscal policies are counter-cyclical, a decline in the output gap should be associated with a worsened structural balance as fiscal policy becomes expansionary. Figure 17.7 shows that output gaps have worsened everywhere in the Eurozone and that the structural balances have increased everywhere except Finland and Germany. In fact, the worse has been the decline in output gap, the more the structural budget has improved. Put differently, the countries that adopted the more contractionary fiscal policies are those where the recession has been deeper. This suggests a two-way causality: the recession has subjected all countries to the excessive deficit procedure and the SGP has promoted contractionary fiscal policies. These policies, in turn, have led to deeper falls in output gap.

Controversies

The Stability and Growth Pact is the arrangement adopted to establish much needed fiscal discipline in the EU in general, and especially in the Eurozone. Its logic is to provide a strong incentive for each government to bring its budget into balance, or even surplus in good years, so that fiscal policy can be used as a counter-cyclical instrument in bad years. This is a good principle, for all countries anywhere in the world. Yet, the SGP has become intensely controversial, and not simply because of the crisis.

A first hurdle is the starting position. Had all countries achieved budget surpluses before adopting the euro, it would have been much easier to operate the SGP as intended. The convergence criteria, however, only required a deficit of less than 3 per cent and, as Figure 16.2 shows, many did marginally better. The early years of the euro were mostly good years, sometimes even very good years, but 'Maastricht fatigue' – efforts to meet the criteria – set in and few countries took advantage of the economic situation to carry out the required clean-up. This eventually led to the adoption of the preventive arm, but the crisis occurred before the budgets had been suitably improved. The impact of the SGP during the crisis, following a serious tightening of the rules in 2011–12, led to the adoption of pro-cyclical policies at the worst possible time (Figure 17.6). This is the 'bad luck' interpretation of the SGP. It implies that the efforts of the crisis years represent a good start and have to be sustained until surpluses are achieved.

When the SGP was under discussion, one view was that it should be entirely automatic, with each step, including sanctions, to be decided by the Commission on the basis of a transparent and unambiguous

---

[13] During the crisis, the Swedish committee asked for a more expansionary fiscal policy than planned by the government. The government dutifully obliged.

Figure 17.7 Pro-cyclical fiscal policies during the crisis, 2008–14

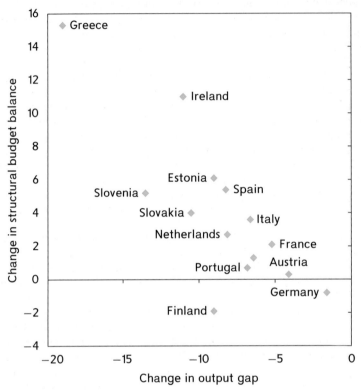

Note: Vertical axis: change in the ratio of output gap to GDP (%); horizontal axis: change in the ratio of cyclically-adjusted balance to GDP (%).

Source: Economic Outlook, OECD

roadmap. On the other hand, in every democracy, deciding who will pay taxes and how much, and how public money is to be spent, is in the hands of elected officials. An automatic application of the SGP, including detailed mandatory recommendations, would clearly violate this basic principle of democracy. This is why, in the end, enforcement of the SGP was entrusted to the Council of Economic and Finance Ministers. But finance ministers are, by definition, politicians. As such, they make elaborate calculations involving tactical considerations. Another view is that governments will never want to humiliate each other, as in 2004, as recalled in Box 17.5. A related view is that it is wrong to rely on external pressure in a process that remains in the domain of domestic sovereignty.

Box 17.5   The Commission vs. the Council

The Stability Programme presented by Germany at the end of 2000 anticipated a deficit of 1.5 per cent of GDP for 2001; the final figure was 2.7 per cent. Following pledges from the German government, the Council decided not to follow the Commission's recommendation of an early warning. But then, contrary to the government's previous promises, the 2002 budget deficit stood at 3.8 per cent of GDP. The German government argued that this was the result of floods in eastern Germany, an unforeseeable exceptional event. This explanation did not cut much ice with the Commission and the Council, and Germany, the promoter of the SGP, became the second country to be declared in excessive deficit, two years after Ireland.

For 2001, France had announced a deficit of 1.4 per cent of GDP, but the outcome was 2.7 per cent. In 2002, the deficit reached 3.2 per cent of GDP. By June 2003, a further deterioration was visible, partly because President Chirac reduced income taxes in both years following an election campaign promise. The Council accepted the Commission recommendation to trigger the excessive deficit procedure.

By November 2003, it had become clear that France and Germany were not heeding the recommendations. Their 2003 deficits, not yet known, both transpired to be 3.7 per cent of GDP, and forecasts for 2004 and 2005 did not envision a return to below 3 per cent. This led the Commission to issue mandatory recommendations, the last step before sanctions. After intense lobbying by France and Germany, the Council decided by qualified majority to 'hold the excessive deficit procedure for France and Germany in abeyance for the time being'. An outraged Commission took the Council to the Court of Justice of the European Communities. The Court subsequently annulled this decision, mostly on legal technical grounds. It considered that the wording of the Council decision was not laid out in conformity with the treaty. The Council promptly confirmed the substance of its decision with adequate wording. The Commission claimed victory. By then, however, deficits had declined and the issue was moot.

An amusing episode followed. In 2003, the Dutch deficit stood at 3.2 per cent, the result of a long slowdown. As it was expected to fall below 3 per cent in 2004 and afterwards, no action should have been taken. But the Dutch government, which had led the resistance against the French and German whitewash in November 2003, was keen to restore credibility to the EDP. It asked to be declared in excessive deficit and its request was granted.

The abeyance episode was a lesson well learned. It led to the first major revision of the SGP, in 2005. The lesson drawn then was that the SGP was too strict, leaving the Commission with no choice but to recommend the EDP for France and Germany. Flexibility was achieved by introducing the cyclically-adjusted balance as an additional criterion in 2005. Indeed, as Figure 17.8 shows, neither country breached the 3 per cent limit under this criterion in 2003–04. Afterwards, however, while Germany endeavoured to achieve fiscal discipline, France did not. By the time of the next revision, in 2011, it was concluded that the SGP had been too flexible.

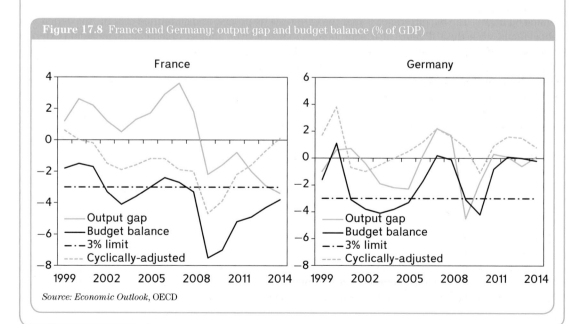

Figure 17.8 France and Germany: output gap and budget balance (% of GDP)

Source: Economic Outlook, OECD

Implicit liabilities

Another difficult issue is related to the phenomenon of an ageing population. It is currently expected that the share of people aged 65 years and above will rise to 30 per cent of total population in the Eurozone by 2060, up from 17.2 per cent in 2009. This development will have profound budgetary implications. Spending on health and retirement is expected to increase very significantly. At the same time, the burden of caring for more elderly people will fall on a smaller proportion of the population. The old-age dependency ratio (the number of those aged 65 and over divided by those of working age (15 to 64 years)) will increase from 25.6 per cent in 2009 to 53.5 per cent in 2060.

These expenditures represent entitlements, sometimes called implicit liabilities. They are true liabilities of the governments because they are enshrined in existing welfare programmes. They are implicit because they appear nowhere in existing accounts. They are a source of concern for fiscal discipline because they will eventually increase public expenditures while the corresponding revenues are not provided for. The eventual solution will have to combine a delaying of the age at which people retire, a reduction of pension payments and possibly of health provision, and higher taxes and contributions to the welfare system. Needless to say, each solution is controversial. Some countries have already taken important steps in that direction; others prefer to ignore the issue.

The SGP requires that member governments start planning for the ageing phenomenon. But there is no hard data, merely forecasts focused on decades into the future. As a result, enforcement is impossible and, indeed, the Commission only uses this consideration to colour its diagnosis. Yet, the amounts involved are potentially huge, possibly even dwarfing current debt levels.[14] Why focus the whole pact on existing deficits and debts, then? The answer – because they are measurable – is not particularly convincing.

17.5 The macroeconomic imbalance procedure

Figure 16.16 shows that the external balances of Eurozone countries have increasingly diverged since they adopted the euro. In theory, such imbalances should be self-correcting but the Hume mechanism has not worked well. Institutional arrangements and politics have stood in the way of wage and price adjustments made necessary by the absence of national exchange rates. Something must be done about it. The response is the macroeconomic imbalance procedure (MIP) introduced in 2012 alongside the reform of the excessive deficit procedure.

The formal apparatus of the MIP parallels that of the EDP. It has both preventive and corrective arms and can lead to sanctions after graduated admonitions proposed by the Commission and adopted by the Council by RQMV. The big difference is that the EDP rests on precise and quantified criteria, the deficit and debt ceilings, while the MIP relies on a 'scoreboard', that is, a large number of indicators, including external balances, the evolution of labour costs, unemployment, financial conditions and more. All EU countries are subject to the MIP but only Eurozone countries can be fined.

The heart of the MIP is the Alert Mechanism Report, which is published once a year. It identifies countries that the Commission considers to be in potential difficulty. This triggers an in-depth review, which can lead to recommendations and, ultimately, to possible sanctions of up to 1 per cent of GDP. In 2014, the Commission identified 16 EU countries that required an in-depth review.

17.6 Summary

The loss of national monetary policy leaves fiscal policy as the only macroeconomic instrument for each Eurozone member country. Its importance is reinforced by the absence of intra-Eurozone transfers, one of the OCA criteria not satisfied in Europe.

Fiscal policy operates in two ways:

- The automatic stabilizers come into play without any policy action because deficits increase when the economy slows down, and decline or turn into surpluses when growth is rapid.
- Discretionary policy results from explicit actions taken by the government.

---

[14] Some estimates put the implicit liabilities at 100–300 per cent of GDP.

However, undisciplined fiscal policy results in high public indebtedness. Indeed, there is a well-documented budget deficit bias as governments are eager to please voters with generous spending not financed by commensurate tax revenues.

Within a monetary union, fiscal indiscipline in one country affects other countries through a number of spillover channels:

- Income flows via exports and imports.
- The cost of borrowing, as there is a single interest rate.
- The fear that a default by a government on its public debt would hurt the union's credibility.

The presence of spillovers argues in favour of coordination of fiscal policies within a monetary union. In practice, however, fiscal policy coordination is difficult. Member States have retained full sovereignty in budgetary matters and budgets are both highly political and a key element of democratic oversight by national parliaments.

The theory of fiscal federalism provides arguments for and against the sharing of policy instruments. On the one hand, the presence of spillovers and of increasing returns to scale argues for policy sharing. On the other hand, the principle of subsidiarity suggests exercising caution in the centralization elements of fiscal policy. The existence of national differences in economic conditions and preferences, and of asymmetries of information, argues against policy sharing. The quality of government also matters.

The Stability and Growth Pact (SGP), an application of the excessive deficit procedure (EDP) envisioned in the Maastricht Treaty, is based on five organizing principles:

- A definition of what constitutes an 'excessive deficit'.
- A preventive arm, designed to encourage governments to avoid excessive deficits.
- A corrective arm, which prescribes how governments should react to a breach of the deficit limit.
- Procedures designed to embed each country's budget process within a European framework, the European Semester, which is meant to constrain national parliaments.
- Sanctions.

The difficulties encountered in the implementation of the SGP can be traced to both economic and political considerations:

- From an economic viewpoint, targeting the annual budget deficit can lead to pro-cyclical policies, i.e. policies that reinforce either a slowdown or a boom. Revisions of the SGP have moved the focus somewhat to cyclically-adjusted budgets and the debt level.
- From a political viewpoint, the SGP faces a formidable contradiction. Fiscal policy is a matter of national sovereignty, in the hands of democratically elected governments and parliaments. At the same time, fiscal policy is recognized as a matter of common concern.

The EDP has been complemented with a Macroeconomic Imbalance Procedure (MIP) that runs in parallel to it. It rests on a scoreboard of indicators designed to identify early on unsustainable external deficits, excessive labour costs and prices that cannot be corrected though exchange rate depreciation and a host of other potential threats to macroeconomic stability.

Self-assessment questions

1 What is the difference between actual and cyclically-adjusted budgets? Why are discretionary actions visible only in changes of the cyclically-adjusted budget balance?
2 In Figure 17.1, identify years when fiscal policy is pro-cyclical, and years when it is counter-cyclical.
3 What are externalities and spillovers? How do they operate in the case of fiscal policy?

4 Explain the no-bailout clause.

5 What is the intended purpose of the Stability and Growth Pact?

6 In Table 17.4 identify countries that have performed better than their medium-term targets and countries that have performed less well.

7 Compare the Stability and Growth Pact and the German debt brake.

8 Explain why fiscal policy would be strictly confined to the automatic stabilizers if the SGP required that the cyclically-adjusted budget be balanced every year. What difference would it make if the cyclically-adjusted budget had to be balanced on average over business cycles?

9 Why are fines under the Stability and Growth Pact sometimes described as pro-cyclical fiscal policy?

10 Why is there a contradiction between the Stability and Growth Pact and sovereignty in budgetary matters?

Essay questions

1 Compare majority voting, qualified majority voting and reverse qualified majority voting.

2 Does a debt default by a member country make it impossible for this country to remain in the Eurozone?

3 Some countries argue that the monetary union needs a common fiscal policy to match the common monetary policy. Evaluate this view.

4 In making its decision on whether to join the Eurozone, the UK Treasury studied the Stability and Growth Pact and stated:

> *Where debt is low and there is a high degree of long-term fiscal sustainability, the case for adopting a tighter fiscal stance to allow room for governments to use fiscal policy more actively is not convincing. Provided that arrangements are put in place to ensure that discretionary policy is conducted symmetrically, then long-term sustainability would not in any way be put at risk.*

Fiscal Stabilization and Eurozone, HM Treasury, May 2003

Interpret and comment.

Further reading: the aficionado's corner

The European Commission's website provides a detailed presentation of the SGP and the MIP. See, for instance:
http://ec.europa.eu/economy_finance/economic_governance/sgp/index_en.htm
http://ec.europa.eu/economy_finance/economic_governance/macroeconomic_imbalance_procedure/index_en.htm.

On the tendency of governments to not always serve their citizens' interests and what it means for the EU, see:

Persson, T. and G. Tabellini (2000) *Political Economics*, MIT Press, Cambridge, MA.

Vaubel, R. (1997) 'The constitutional reform of the European Union', *European Economic Review*, 41(3–5): 443–50.

On the role of the SGP during the crisis:

M. Larch, P. van den Noord and L. Jonung (2010) *The Stability and Growth Pact: Lessons from the Great Recession*, European Economy – Economic Papers 429, European Commission.

On ways to reform the SGP:

Wyplosz, C. (2011) 'Fiscal discipline: rules rather than institutions', *National Institute Economic Review* 217, August.

A defence of the SGP, by one of its creators (J. Stark):

Schuknecht, L., P. Moutot, P. Rother and J. Stark (2011) *The Stability and Growth Pact: Crisis and Reform*, Occasional Paper No. 129, European Central Bank.

The **VoxEU** website contains a wealth of relevant analyses, among them:

On austerity policies:

http://www.voxeu.org/debates/has-austerity-gone-too-far.

On the difficulty faced by fiscal policies because of poor information and what it means for the SGP:

http://www.voxeu.org/article/do-fiscal-policymakers-know-what-they-are-doing.

The Commission's view in June 2014:

http://www.voxeu.org/article/delivering-eurozone-consistent-trinity.

On the benefits of policy coordination:

http://www.voxeu.org/article/spillovers-why-macro-fiscal-policy-should-be-coordinated-economic-unions.

On the role of independent fiscal agencies:

http://www.voxeu.org/article/fiscal-forecasts-governments-vs-independent-agencies.

On the cyclical behaviour of fiscal policy, see:

European Commission (2001) 'Fiscal policy and cyclical stabilization in the Eurozone', *European Economy*, 3: 57–80.
Hallerberg, M. and R. Strauch (2002) 'On the cyclicality of public finances in Europe', *Empirica*, 29: 183–207.
Melitz, J. (2000) 'Some cross-country evidence about fiscal policy behaviour and consequences for the Eurozone', *European Economy*, 2: 3–21.

For analyses on the politico-economic aspects of fiscal policy, see:

Alesina, A. and R. Perotti (1995) 'The political economy of budget deficits', *IMF Staff Papers*, 42(1): 1–37.
Hagen, J. von and I.J. Harden (1994) 'National budget processes and fiscal performance', *European Economy Reports and Studies*, 3: 311–408.
Persson, T., G. Roland and G. Tabellini (2000) 'Comparative politics and public finance', *Journal of Political Economy*, 108(6): 1121–61.

For an introduction to the theory of fiscal federalism, see:

Oates, W. (1999) 'An essay in fiscal federalism', *Journal of Economic Literature*, 37(3): 1120–49.

On fiscal rules:

Bordo, M., L. Jonung and A. Marliewicz (2011) 'A fiscal union for the Euro: some lessons from history', VoxEU, http://www.voxeu.org/index.php?q=node/7007.
IMF (2009) 'Fiscal rules – anchoring expectations for sustainable public finances', http://www.imf.org/external/np/pp/eng/2009/121609.pdf.
Wyplosz, C. (2011) 'Fiscal discipline: rules rather than institutions', *National Institute Economic Review*, 217: R19–R30.

On independent fiscal policy watchdog committees:

OECD (2013) *Principles for Independent Fiscal Institutions*,
http://www.pbo-dpb.gc.ca/files/files/Revised%20IFI%20Principles_EN%20-%2013-Feb-13.pdf.

References

Burda, M. and C. Wyplosz (2012) *Macroeconomics: A European Test*, 6th edition, Oxford University Press, Oxford.
Eichengreen, B. and C. Wyplosz (1993) 'Unstable EMS', *Brookings Papers on Economic Activity*, 1: 51–144.
OECD (1997) *Economic Outlook*, OECD, Paris.
Stark, J. (2001) 'Genesis of a pact', in A. Brunila, M. Buti and D. Franco (eds) *The Stability and Growth Pact*, Palgrave, Basingstoke.

The big payoff on the Euro is, of course, in the capital markets. . . . It will move from the dull bank-based financing structure to big-time debt markets and markets for corporate equities that offer transparency for the mismanaged or sleepy European companies. Capital markets are good at kicking butt.

Rudi Dornbusch (2000), p. 242

The crisis has highlighted a fundamental inconsistency between the single monetary policy of the euro area and the responsibility of national authorities for financial policies. The single currency needs a single financial system that is not fragmented along national lines.

Mario Draghi (2012), Frankfurt European Banking Congress

The financial markets and the euro

Chapter Contents

Introduction

This chapter looks at the integration of European financial markets. Adoption of the euro was expected to encourage further integration of Europe's capital markets, providing savers and borrowers alike with more and better opportunities. This, in turn, was expected to improve the overall productivity of the European economy. More generally, businesses and tourists would save the substantial costs involved in changing currencies as they trade, travel and park their savings in another Eurozone country. This was then, before the sovereign crisis. Some of these hopes have evaporated but the single currency is now reshaping the financial sector.

This chapter starts with an overview of the role and characteristics of financial markets. Section 18.2 then examines how far the existence of the euro has integrated the national financial markets. As this process was under way, the global financial and Eurozone's sovereign debt crises fragmented the financial markets. Section 18.3 looks at the evidence and pinpoints the difficulties that these events have created for the single monetary policy.

Section 18.4 focuses on one part of the financial markets – banking. It also presents the newly adopted Banking Union, designed to remedy the many shortcomings of the original blueprint of monetary union. Finally, Section 18.5 looks at the issue of the supremacy of the US dollar as the world's international currency and the possibility of the euro issuing a challenge to this supremacy.

18.1 Essentials of financial markets

18.1.1 What are financial institutions and markets?

The financial markets are central to long-term growth, as explained in Chapter 7. Their task is to make savers and borrowers meet to achieve the best possible mutual deals. This task is in the hands of a variety of financial intermediaries. Banks borrow from some customers and lend to others. Bond markets arrange for borrowers to issue debt instruments – bonds – that savers acquire. Stock markets perform a similar function but the borrowers are private corporations that raise money by offering ownership – shares or stocks.

Borrowers and lenders have very different needs, and those needs can change over time. The challenge for the financial markets is to cater to every single need in the most efficient and cheapest way. To do so, they perform three main functions:

1 *Intermediation.* Savers and borrowers do not meet face to face. Savers deposit their funds in financial institutions, which re-lend them to borrowers. The trip may be long, going through many financial institutions that borrow from and lend to each other, often even across many national borders.

2 *Maturity transformation.* Savers typically do not like to part with their money. They want assets with short maturities. Borrowers, on the other hand, typically prefer to obtain stable resources. They look for liabilities with long maturities. Financial intermediaries stand in-between: they issue short maturity instruments (bank deposits, bonds) for savers and accept long maturity instruments (bank loans, bonds) from borrowers.

3 *Risk taking and diversification.* A loan implies providing money on the promise of future repayment. In the meantime, the borrower may face difficulties that make repayment partly or totally impossible, and some borrowers may simply be dishonest. Every single financial transaction is therefore risky. The financial markets deal with risks in many ways, including offering baskets of instruments that are collectively less risky than their individual components; this is called risk diversification.

18.1.2 Types of financial institutions and markets

Banks, funds, insurance companies

The best-known financial institutions are banks: they receive deposits, in effect borrowing from their customers; they offer loans; and they often provide assistance with managing portfolios. In contrast to these universal banks, investment banks specialize in managing portfolios; they do not accept deposits and sometimes cater only to wealthy customers. Fund management firms do not even deal with individuals; they offer 'wholesale' services to banks and insurance companies. Insurance companies are also considered to be financial institutions. Part of their activity is to provide insurance, which, strictly speaking, is not a financial service. Yet, in order to deal with potentially high payments, they accumulate large reserves, which they want to manage in order to obtain returns that are as high as possible. In effect, they take 'deposits' – the insurance premia paid by their customers – that they use to 'make loans' as they invest in financial assets. In addition, many insurance companies provide pension schemes and life insurance, which can be seen as deposits with very long maturities. In fact, some financial conglomerates combine classic universal banking, investment banking and insurance.

Markets

The bond and stock markets represent the other component of the financial system. Like banks, they are designed to collect savings and lend them back to borrowers, with the crucial difference that the users – lenders and borrowers – 'meet' each other on the markets. Bonds are debts issued by firms and governments for a set maturity at an explicit interest rate. Stocks (also called shares) are ownership titles to firms: they have no maturity since they last as long as the firm itself; borrowers receive dividends, which fluctuate depending on firms' performance.

When bonds and shares are created, they are initially sold on the primary market. Thereafter, they can endlessly change hands on the secondary market. The possibility of disposing of their assets is a great convenience to lenders because they can retrieve their money when they need it. The ability to promptly buy and sell bonds or shares results from the depth of the market: it relies on the continuing presence of a very large number of investors, from individuals to banks, funds and insurance companies. Market depth differs from market breadth, which describes the variety of instruments and issuers available to investors. Depth and breadth are the essential qualities of a financial market; these desirable attributes grow with market size, which explains why Wall Street and the City of London are so powerful.

Lenders (also called investors) usually operate through intermediaries – brokers, banks, investment banks – whom they instruct to buy or sell assets on the markets on their behalf. Most small investors, and many large ones too in fact, purchase funds, which are ready-made baskets of shares and/or bonds managed by financial intermediaries. Each fund has particular characteristics: the relative importance of bonds and stocks, the industry or country where they invest, the degree of risk and associated guarantees, and more.

Financial institutions come in all shapes and sizes. A few huge international banks coexist with small, strictly local ones. Some financial markets attract lenders and borrowers from all over the world (New York's Wall Street and the City of London are the two largest), whereas others deal in a very narrow range of local assets.

18.1.3 What do financial markets do?

Matching lending and borrowing needs: maturity

Imagine an individual who wants to put aside a given amount. She can always deposit this amount with her bank and withdraw whatever she wants whenever she wants, but the interest rate offered is quite low. She can do better by choosing term deposits; in that case she will have to pay a penalty if she needs to withdraw before maturity is reached. On the other hand, term deposits offer more attractive interest, which grows with maturity. The bank thus encourages its customers to choose longer-term deposits. Why? Because the bank will re-lend the deposit to another customer who will be ready to pay a higher interest rate for loans of longer maturity. Time has a value, and the market sets its price.

Bank deposits are not the only way to save. The saver could buy bonds, with various maturities, or stocks, which are of unlimited duration. In that case, she would lend directly – albeit via her broker and the market – to the borrowers who issue bonds and stocks. The returns will be higher than bank deposits of the same maturity because these bonds and stocks are typically riskier than bank deposits.

Matching lending and borrowing needs: risk

Governments, banks and firms issue bonds as a counterpart to borrowing. Their maturities range from the very short term – 24 hours or less – to the very long term – 10–20 years or more. Firms issue stocks; the holder owns a share of the firm and is entitled to the corresponding portion of profits. Bonds and shares are risky: if the issuer goes bankrupt, at best they are worth a fraction of their face value and at worst nothing.[1] How do financial markets deal with risk?

Consider the return from investing in a particular project, say, a new factory. When the investment is made, there is usually no way of knowing for certain whether the project will yield profits. Even if the venture proves profitable, the future profit level is uncertain. Customer tastes, exchange rates, prices and the level of competition can change unexpectedly, thereby altering profits. Of course, one can make a reasonable guess as to what the profit will be, on average, but a guess is just that and the investor is inevitably concerned with the risk taken. Two projects may have the same expected return, but the profit flow may be more variable (i.e. riskier) for one than for the other. Investors typically prefer the less risky project. 'A bird in the hand is worth two in the bush' is the colloquial way of expressing the common-sense principle that people tend to value less risky projects more. Markets put a value on risk.

Firms that plan new investments raise money by issuing bonds and/or shares. Bondholders and shareholders bear the investment risk. For them to be willing to buy a risky asset, there must be a reward. This is why the rate of return incorporates a risk premium. For each asset, the law of demand and supply will determine a risk premium such that borrowers can convince savers to bear the risk. Savers obviously prefer no or little risk, but they may be attracted by a higher return. The interest offered on each asset typically rises with the risk of the asset, as shown in Figure 18.1. The curve describes the trade-off faced by investors between the return and the safety of an asset. Depending on her appetite for risk and return, the saver will choose where on the curve she would like to be.

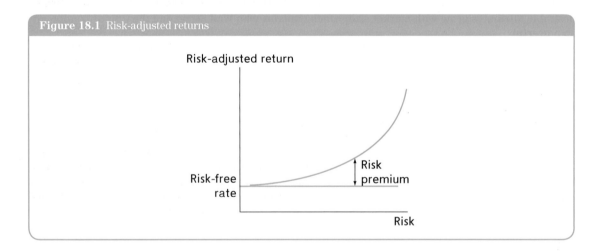

Figure 18.1 Risk-adjusted returns

Different savers will pick different points on the risk–return trade-off schedule because they have different degrees of aversion to risk. Financial markets allow every saver to find an asset that meets her preference and every borrower to find the resources that he needs.[2] Markets thus put a price tag on risk and all assets fit nicely on the risk–return schedule shown in Figure 18.1. The schedule reflects the collective preferences of investors and borrowers. This is how markets price risk.

---

[1] Bonds issued by trustworthy governments are considered riskless.

[2] Well, not every borrower. Very risky borrowers are usually unable to raise funds. Graphically, in Figure 18.1 the curve eventually becomes vertical.

Diversification

Not only do markets price risk, they also allow for risk diversification. The basic issue can be illustrated with an example. Ask yourself, 'How risky is betting on red at the roulette table?' You might answer that you can win almost half the time because all numbers on a roulette wheel, except for 0 and 00, are either red or black. This is the correct answer if you consider the bet-on-red 'project' in isolation. But suppose that you add a bet-on-black 'project' to your 'portfolio'. In addition to betting on red with each roll of the ball, you also bet on black with each roll. Now the effective risk of this betting venture is much reduced. You almost always win, except for when the ball lands on 0 or 00, in which case you lose both bets to the house. Two 50 per cent chance bets become a 100 per cent bet. This is a particular example as most bets do not simply add up, but it highlights the power of diversification.[3]

The lesson to be learned from this example is that the risk of a particular project must not be evaluated in isolation. It must be looked upon in conjunction with the investor's total portfolio of projects. If some projects will do well when others do badly, the average return to the portfolio is less risky than the individual projects.

Financial markets can offer almost unbounded possibilities for diversification, the more so the bigger they are. By increasing the variety of projects, i.e. assets, large financial markets allow savers to hold relatively riskless portfolios composed of very risky assets. Both savers and borrowers stand to benefit from the situation. Because well-diversified portfolios bear little risk, the risk premium is reduced and this reduction is shared between savers, who receive higher returns, and borrowers, who face lower borrowing costs.

18.1.4 Characteristics of financial markets

Scale economies

Matching the needs of borrowers and lenders and risk diversification are both easier when there are a large number of borrowers and lenders. The finance industry is subject to massive scale economies, which affect banks and financial markets. Where small banks and markets survive, it is not difficult to find some barriers to competition. The existence of different currencies is one such barrier. Indeed, before the advent of the euro, an Irish saver who purchased Portuguese assets faced currency risk in addition to the normal lending risk, and this made Irish assets more attractive to her. The creation of a single currency removes this particular barrier to competition.

Networks

Financial institutions and markets can be seen as a network of borrowers and lenders. This is another reason why financial markets tend to become ever larger. When a financial firm receives funds from a saver, it needs to re-lend these funds as soon as possible because 'time is money'. With some luck, it will find among its customers a borrower with matching needs and preferences, but more often not. The solution is to re-lend the saver's money to another financial firm that may have spotted a borrower or identified another financial firm that may have spotted a borrower, etc. This is why financial markets may be described as networks. Indeed, money passes quickly from financial firm to financial firm until it finds a home – a suitable borrower – somewhere in the network, quite possibly in a very different corner of the world.

Asymmetric information

A fundamental characteristic of financial activities is that the borrower always knows more about his own riskiness than the lender. This information asymmetry carries profound implications. Borrowers may intentionally attempt to conceal some damning information for the sake of obtaining a badly needed loan. As a consequence, lenders are very careful, not to say suspicious. They may simply refuse to lend rather than take unknown risks. Alternatively, they may set the price of risk very high, i.e. they ask for very

---

[3] In finance jargon, the red and black 'projects' are perfectly negatively correlated (their correlation coefficient is –1), which means that one pays off when the other pays nothing. More generally, risk diversification is higher the more negatively correlated are the assets that make up a portfolio.

large risk premia. This, in turn, may discourage low-risk borrowers who cannot convincingly signal their true riskiness. If this process goes unchecked, only bad risks are present in the market and, knowing that, lenders withdraw.[4] At best, the price of risk is excessive, at worst the financial market dries up. Box 18.1 illustrates this phenomenon.

Box 18.1   Asymmetric information at its worst: the global financial crisis

House prices started to fall in the USA in late 2006. Why should that destroy, a year or two later, some well-established banks in New York, London and Frankfurt? Because a bank that lent money to a homeowner in Nebraska had resold this loan to a bank in, say, New York, which then resold it to another bank in, say, Frankfurt, which could have resold it to a bank in New York. In the end, many banks were indirectly lending a little bit to the Nebraskan homeowner. This is risk-diversification at its best: if the homeowner defaults on his loan, every bank will suffer a minute loss. This is also information asymmetry at its worst: what does a big international bank in Paris know about the small Nebraskan borrower? Worse, these loans were not just cut into small pieces; the small pieces were repackaged together. So a bank in Brussels could hold a package of portions of loans to tens of thousands of totally unknown American homeowners. It would not really know, or even care to know, who the borrowers were. In fact, it could not investigate the long chain of slicing and repackaging that had produced the assets that it had bought. When the housing market experienced a downturn and tens of thousands of homeowners stopped paying for houses that were worth less than the loans they owed, banks around the world abruptly discovered that these packages had become toxic. Too late.

A new information asymmetry then hit the markets. Bank A knew that it had a pack of toxic assets. It suspected that Bank B was in the same, possibly even worse, situation. Not knowing for sure, and already worried about its own situation, Bank A stopped doing business with Bank B, which would not lend anything to Bank A or any other bank anyway. The interbank markets, where banks lend to each other, seized up (see Section 18.3.1). The interbank markets are often referred to as the mother of all financial markets, since this is where liquidity is redistributed. With liquidity all but frozen, the crisis was on its way.

Asymmetric information is a fact of life, unavoidable and widespread. It tends to undermine the development of financial institutions and markets. This phenomenon explains many features of the financial services industry presented below. One general response is regulation, i.e. legislative measures that aim at reducing the overall riskiness of financial markets and institutions.

18.2 Effects of a monetary union

18.2.1 EU policy on capital market integration

Until the 1986 Single European Act and a 1988 directive that ruled out any remaining restriction on capital movements among EU residents, EU capital markets were not integrated. Although the Treaty of Rome explicitly provides for the free movement of capital, several loopholes allowed EU member countries to impede capital mobility. One reason was that they wanted to protect their financial institutions from foreign competition. Another reason is that many EU nations just did not believe that unrestricted capital mobility was a good idea. They saw capital flows as responsible for repeated balance-of-payment and banking crises.

In the early 1960s, the European Commission promoted a partial liberalization but included numerous opt-out and safeguard clauses, which were in fact extensively used by EU members. The emphasis was on facilitating cross-border business activity, for example international transfers of capital or the repatriation of profits or wage earnings. The Single European Act 1986 went further: it established the principle that all

---

[4] This phenomenon is called adverse selection. Borrowing in a desperate situation is sometimes called 'gambling for resurrection'.

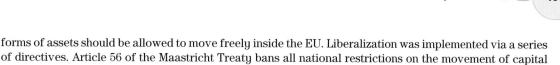

forms of assets should be allowed to move freely inside the EU. Liberalization was implemented via a series of directives. Article 56 of the Maastricht Treaty bans all national restrictions on the movement of capital except those required for law enforcement and reasons of national security.

Finally, the adoption of the euro eliminates the currency risk within the Eurozone. In principle, therefore, savers do not have to worry about where the asset is issued as long as it is denominated in euros, and borrowers can tap the whole area by taking on euro-denominated debt. There is no longer any reason for financial markets to be Finnish, Greek or German. We now look at the evidence.

18.2.2 Effects of the single currency on banks

Banks compete to attract deposits and to make loans. The market for bank services is segmented along national lines for several reasons. First, before the adoption of the common currency, different currencies tended to make national markets fundamentally distinct. The adoption of the euro has eliminated this source of fragmentation. Second, customers do not change banks easily. Like changing address, moving to a new bank complicates things as one must warn countless debitors (bills that you pay automatically) and creditors (e.g. employers). Third, banks often develop personal relationships with their customers to better know their needs and means (and reduce the information asymmetry) and to develop loyalty. Fourth, proximity is important, although less so with the spread of internet banking and of automatic teller machines. Still, a bank that wants to develop its activity in a new country must invest heavily to set up a network of branches. Finally, regulations have long implied that using the services of a foreign bank may result in lower legal protection. The various reforms of recent years have sought to establish a level playing field; see Box 18.2.

Box 18.2 Harmonization of banking regulation in Europe

Efforts at building a unified banking market in Europe go far back in history. The main steps are as follows:

- In 1973, a directive on the abolition of restrictions on freedom of establishment and freedom to provide services for self-employed activities of banks and other financial institutions established the principle of national treatment. All banks operating in one country are subject to the same non-discriminatory regulations and supervision as local banks. Yet, widespread capital controls limited competition and, in the absence of any coordination of banking supervision, banks were deterred from operating in different countries.

- In 1977, the First Banking Directive on the Coordination of Laws, Regulations and Administrative Provisions Relating to the Taking Up and Pursuit of Credit Institutions established a gradual phasing in of the principle of home country control. Under this principle, it is the home country of the parent bank that is responsible for supervising the bank's activities in other EU countries. The directive left open a number of loopholes, including the need to obtain authorization from the local supervision authorities to establish subsidiaries and continuing restrictions on capital movements.

- In 1989, the Second Banking Directive was designed to apply to the banking industry the provisions of the Single European Act 1986, which mandated the elimination of capital controls. The directive stipulates that any bank licensed in a EU country can establish branches or supply cross-border financial services in the other countries of the EU without further authorization. It can also open a subsidiary on the same conditions as nationals of the host state. The parent bank must now consolidate all its accounts for supervision by its own authority. Yet, the host country can impose specific regulations if they are deemed to be 'in the public interest'.

- Facing a lack of progress, a Financial Services Action Plan (FSAP) was adopted in 1999. This plan called for the harmonization of prudential rules, the establishment of a single market in wholesale financial services and efforts to unify the retail market.

- Limited results led to the adoption in 2001 of the Lamfalussy process.[1] This process involves four steps: (1) the adoption of common core legal values; (2) the adoption of detailed proposals at the national level; (3) the consolidation of these measures at the European level, including the creation of a Committee of European Securities Regulators (CESR), which brings together a newly created regulator, the European Securities Committee (ESC), and the national regulators; and (4) enforcement of the agreements by the European Commission.

- The financial crisis has accelerated the process. New institutions have been created; see Section 18.4.

[1] Named after Alexander Lamfalussy, former Chairman of the European Monetary Institute (the predecessor of the ECB), in his capacity as Chairman of a Committee of Wise Men.

Bank deposits by Eurozone non-banks (households and corporations) in foreign Eurozone banks have nearly doubled, as can be seen in the left-hand chart of Figure 18.2. The figure shows that this evolution has been driven by bank loans to non-residents elsewhere in the Eurozone: as people took out loans from new banks, they were encouraged to move their business, at least part of it, to these banks. Most of the increase happened between 2005 and 2008, the years of the Great Moderation and associated optimism. A key part has been loans by German banks to Spanish borrowers and, mostly perhaps, to German residents buying properties in Spain as the housing market was booming (and the sea was blue). The figure shows that this all came to a halt in the autumn of 2008 when the financial crisis erupted. Since then, there has been a reversal, but a relatively muted one.

The right-hand chart displays deposits by and loans to other banks in other Eurozone countries. After the adoption of the euro, both cross-border deposits and loans among banks have grown rapidly, quadrupling as far as deposits are concerned. The crisis has provoked a sharp reversal but current levels are still much higher than in 1999.

What has not happened, or only to a surprisingly small extent, are cross-border mergers of banks within the Eurozone. According to the ECB, the number of banks – more precisely, credit institutions – has declined from 8320 on the eve of the creation of the euro to 5708 in June 2008. This may be an effect of heightened competition, but the numbers of banks have declined pretty much everywhere in the developed countries.

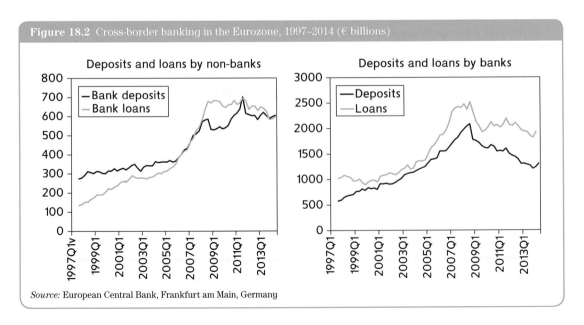

Figure 18.2 Cross-border banking in the Eurozone, 1997–2014 (€ billions)

Source: European Central Bank, Frankfurt am Main, Germany

Banks have typically merged with one another to become larger and thereby gain increasing returns to scale, but very few of these mergers have combined banks from different countries within the Eurozone.

18.2.3 Effects of the single currency on bond markets

We first look at the market for public bonds, issued by governments, where the evolution is well documented and spectacular. Remember from Chapter 13 that the interest parity principle asserts that, when markets are well integrated, interest rates between two assets issued in different currencies differ by: (1) the expected change in the exchange rate, and (2) a premium reflecting different risks. Up until the crisis, rightly or wrongly, EU governments were believed to be highly trustworthy, financially at least. As a result, there was no significant risk premium and the only difference should have been expected exchange rate changes. With the adoption of the common currency, the currency risk was eliminated and financial integration should have resulted in identical rates across the Eurozone.

This conjecture was fully verified, until the Eurozone crisis. Figure 18.3 displays the evolution of interest rates on long-term government bonds. For decades, interest rates had been lowest on German bonds because of the strong currency status of the Deutschmark. As the date of the launch of the single currency drew nearer and more certain, the currency risk declined and gradually became irrelevant. The figure shows an impressive convergence of Italian rates towards the German level by January 1999. Exactly the same happened to all other counties, including for instance Greece, which joined the Eurozone in January 2001, and Slovenia, which adopted the euro in January 2007. It is also interesting to observe that the UK rate did not quite converge because the UK decided not to adopt the euro, but the difference was small, as markets believed that the exchange rate between the euro and the pound would be mostly stable. All of that came to an end when the sovereign debt crisis hit the Eurozone, as further explained in Chapter 19.

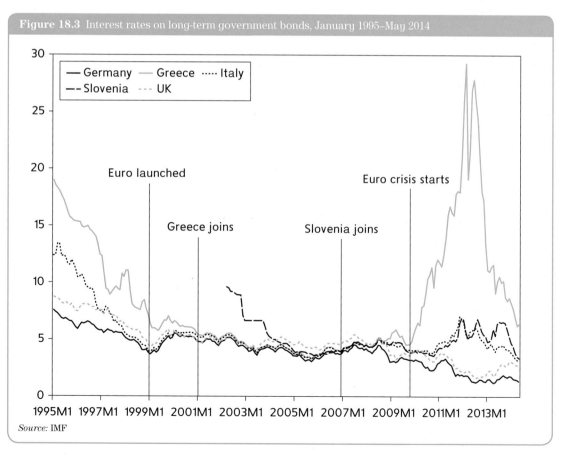

Figure 18.3 Interest rates on long-term government bonds, January 1995–May 2014

Source: IMF

18.2.4 Effects of the single currency on stock markets

The stock market is where large – and some medium-sized – firms raise the financial resources they need to develop their activities. They issue shares, many of which are held by individuals or by large institutional investors, such as pension funds and insurance companies. Increasingly, individuals buy shares from collective funds designed to offer good risk–return trade-offs through extensive diversification, as explained in Section 18.1.3. Yet, for all the hype about globalization, it is striking that stock markets are characterized by a strong 'home bias': borrowers and savers alike tend to deal mostly on domestic markets and to hold domestic assets.

One reason for the home bias is information asymmetry: investors (believe that they) know more about domestic firms. This is changing because individual investors increasingly rely on financial intermediaries to manage their wealth and financial intermediaries are becoming increasingly global. The other reason for the home bias is currency risk. This obstacle to capital mobility has been eliminated within the Eurozone, so we would expect less of a home bias.

Is it happening? Apparently, yes, as seen in Figure 18.4. The figure displays how Eurozone investment funds invest. The proportion of home shares is declining, while the proportion of shares issued in other Eurozone countries has risen, as did the proportion issued elsewhere in the world. Here, again, the onset of the Eurozone crisis has changed previous trends, with an acceleration of investments in shares issued in the rest of the world. Until then, though, the fastest growing segment was investment in shares issued in other Eurozone countries.

Another piece of evidence is provided by the evolution of stock exchanges, the marketplaces where shares are traded. Most European countries have one stock exchange each, or more. This was natural when

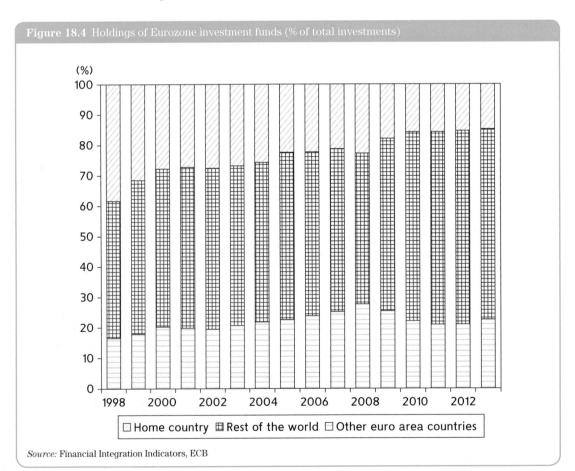

Figure 18.4 Holdings of Eurozone investment funds (% of total investments)

Source: Financial Integration Indicators, ECB

currency risk was segmenting the various national markets. Are things changing with the advent of the euro? Table 18.1 displays the sizes of stock markets in the Eurozone and in a few large financial centres. Size is measured by market capitalization, i.e. the total valuation of all the firms listed on the exchange. In comparison to the USA, Eurozone exchanges remain small, and therefore likely to suffer from limited scale economies. Even London, which hosts the largest European stock market, pales in comparison with the USA.

Table 18.1   Size of stock markets (total capitalization), 2010

	$ bn	% GDP		$ bn	% GDP		$ bn	% GDP
France	967	38	Ireland	60	29	United States	30,455	209
Germany	686	21	Portugal	43	19	Japan	2,126	39
Italy	477	23	Austria	32	8	UK	1,864	83
Spain	462	33	Slovenia	5	10	Switzerland	554	106
Netherlands	402	51	Estonia	2	13	Hong Kong	463	206
Finland	139	58	Slovakia	2	2			
Belgium	128	27	Cyprus	2	6			
Greece	69	23	Malta	1	13			

Source: US Census Bureau

The USA, which is similar to the Eurozone in economic and geographic size, has 15 stock exchanges; only 2 or 3 are significant, however, and the New York Stock Exchange (NYSE) is by far the largest. In the Eurozone, each country insists on having its own exchange. Because stock markets display strong scale economies, the Eurozone should be evolving towards one major centre and a handful of secondary exchanges. The question is where will they be located? Each country seems keen to retain its own stock exchange, for reasons of prestige and because it may be a major economic activity.

For a while, it was thought that the Frankfurt stock exchange would benefit from the location of the ECB, but this has not happened. In fact, the London and Frankfurt stock exchanges tried to merge in 1998, but this attempt failed for reasons explained in Box 18.3. In order to challenge both London and Frankfurt, a number of exchanges have merged. Euronext was created in 2000 by the exchanges of Amsterdam, Brussels and Paris, maintaining physical operations in each city. Then, in 2007, Euronext merged with the New York Stock Exchange but activities remained on both sides of the Atlantic. The two separated again in 2014 after the NYSE merged with Intercontinental Exchange (ICE), a US electronic trading platform.

In 2003, Stockholm and Helsinki merged into OMX, which has since linked up with Copenhagen and the Baltic States (Riga, Tallinn and Vilnius), also maintaining physical operations in each of these cities. Clearly, the currency issue is not driving market consolidation.

Box 18.3   Consolidation of stock markets

Some consolidation is taking place among traditional stock markets. The most noticeable example was the creation of Euronext in September 2000, the result of a merger of the Amsterdam, Brussels and Paris stock exchanges. Euronext is subject to Dutch legislation and has a subsidiary in each of the participating countries. Each subsidiary holds a local stock market licence that gives access to

trading in all the participating countries. Euronext has integrated many market functions, but the local markets are not legally merged, which implies, for example, that the regulatory body in each of the participating countries retains its prerogatives. From the beginning, Euronext was not intended to be a closed structure and was eager to finalize agreements with other stock exchanges. In 2001, this resulted in the acquisition of Liffe, the London derivatives trading platform, and the agreement to also integrate the Portuguese exchanges of Lisbon and Porto.

Before Euronext, another, even larger, merger between stock exchanges was attempted. In 1998, the Deutsche Börse (DB) and the London Stock Exchange (LSE) were planning to merge in an attempt to gain a leadership position in Europe. While the negotiations between the two stock exchanges were still in process, the OM Gruppen, owner of the Stockholm stock exchange, tried to take over the LSE. This event critically affected the projected merger between DB and LSE, which was subsequently rejected by the LSE board. Now and then, rumours of negotiations between the LSE and DB resurface.

Source: Adapted from Hartmann et al. (2003)

18.2.5 Overall effects of the single currency

There are clear signs that the creation of the euro was accompanied by further integration of all financial market components until 2008. However, these were also the years of globalization when financial markets and investors took an increasingly worldly view of finance. They were eager to reap the benefits of globalization: returns to scale and diversification. In most cases, faster integration has been the tendency within the Eurozone. The global financial crisis has put a (temporary?) stop to financial globalization, reminding us that usually benefits come with costs. The Eurozone sovereign debt crisis has had a particularly strong adverse effect on financial integration within the Eurozone, the topic of the next section.

This section has examined a number of indicators of financial integration, but what is the complete picture? One answer comes from an indicator produced by the ECB that brings together two types of integration measure: quantitative measures, as shown in Figures 18.2 and 18.4, and price measures (inspired by the interest parity condition) shown in Figure 18.3. This synthetic indicator is displayed in

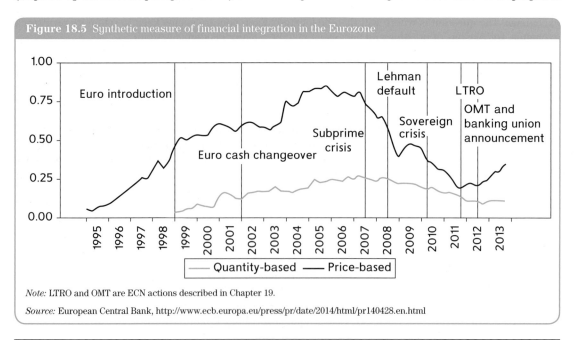

Figure 18.5 Synthetic measure of financial integration in the Eurozone

Note: LTRO and OMT are ECN actions described in Chapter 19.

Source: European Central Bank, http://www.ecb.europa.eu/press/pr/date/2014/html/pr140428.en.html

---

[5] SYNFIT (Synthetic Financial Integration) relies on a large number of measures.

Figure 18.5.[5] The picture is quite clear. Financial integration rose between 1999 (even before, as markets anticipated the creation of the euro) and 2008 and then declined. Still, the Eurozone is now significantly more integrated financially than before the advent of the euro.

One possible negative aspect of the euro, however, is that the potential for diversification shrinks. Before the advent of the euro, a Belgian saver could diversify her portfolio by acquiring German, Italian and other European assets. Now these assets are less diverse because they all share the same currency and as cyclical conditions become more homogeneous. To achieve a high degree of diversification, investors may have to look further, toward less well-known parts of the world.[6] All in all, however, the positive effects of scale economies in a wider unified market are likely to outweigh the negative effects of reduced diversification.

18.3 Fragmentation during the crisis

The Eurozone has faced two crises in short succession: the global financial crisis that started in 2007 in the USA and its own, home-made sovereign debt crisis. The evidence presented in Section 18.2 shows that these crises have led to a significant reduction in financial integration. The result is a step backward and a serious challenge to one of the key benefits expected from the monetary union. Anticipating a complete analysis of the crisis in Chapter 19, this section explains how financial markets have become fragmented during the crisis. One solution has been the creation of the Banking Union, which is presented in Section 18.4.

18.3.1 Banks and the interbank market

At any moment in time, commercial banks grant loans and witness customers making deposits or withdrawing money from their accounts. Cash comes in and cash goes out; banks are alternatively flush with and short of cash. The imbalances can last a few hours or a few days, rarely more. For large banks, the amounts can be huge and earning interest on excess reserves, as these imbalances are called, even overnight, can net substantial income at the end of the day.[7] Naturally, commercial banks find it mutually beneficial to exchange these imbalances among themselves. They do it on a network called the interbank market. The interbank market is the heart of the banking system. In normal time, it works smoothly, setting an interest rate that is the basis for all other interest rates. The interbank market interest rate is the one that the central bank focuses on, and the interbank market is where the central bank intervenes on a routine basis.

In the summer of 2007, interbank markets froze in many developed countries, including the USA, Britain and, of course, the Eurozone (see Box 18.1 for details). Banks stopped lending to each other. Whatever activity took place on the interbank market was driven by ECB interventions, which declined as an increasing number of banks were not able to operate on the market. More ominously, these banks were increasingly from the crisis-hit countries. Figure 18.6 shows how the fragmentation of the Eurozone banking system has worsened and had not recovered several years later.

Banks have become increasingly unable to fulfil a key task: lending to firms and households. Large firms have been less affected, if only because they can borrow internationally, but households and smaller firms are still dealing with a credit crunch. Even though the ECB has provided them with huge amounts of cash, the banks have faced very different situations and this fragmentation has hit the more fragile borrowers. This is illustrated in Figure 18.7. Banks usually charge a higher interest rate on smaller loans, largely because the information asymmetry is more important for loans to small borrowers. Normally, the difference, called spread, is around 1 per cent (or 100 basis points). It has grown in the wake of the global financial crisis, following a period of decline during the benign Great Moderation years. The left-hand chart shows that the spreads returned to normal in the non-distressed countries but have remained very large in the distressed countries. A small or medium-sized enterprise (SME) in Portugal faces higher borrowing costs than in Germany. That is, if it can borrow. The right-hand chart shows that loan applications have

---

[6] This is not a serious concern. As globalization develops, so do the possibilities for diversification. Over the past few years, Chinese and Indian assets have joined Brazilian and Korean assets in well-diversified portfolios.

[7] In many countries, banks are required to hold a minimum of cash to meet unexpected needs. Elsewhere, banks do it anyway. These minima are called reserves.

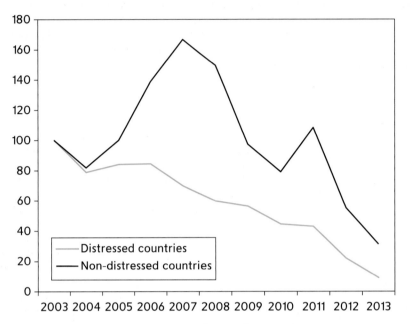

Figure 18.6 Bank borrowing on the interbank market (Index: 100 = 2003)

Note: The distressed countries are: Cyprus, Greece, Ireland, Italy, Portugal, Slovenia and Spain.

Source: Financial integration indicators, ECB, May 2014

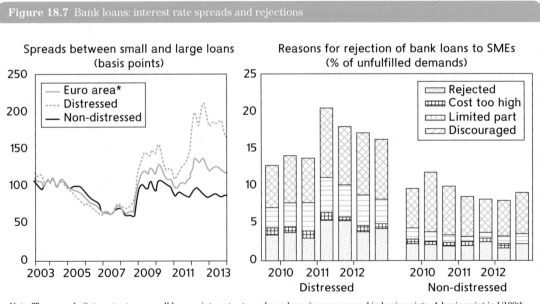

Figure 18.7 Bank loans: interest rate spreads and rejections

Note: The spreads (interest rate on small loans – interest rate on large loans) are measured in basis points. A basis point is 1/100th of a per cent. Loans for less than €1 million are classified as small.

Source: © European Central Bank, Frankfurt am Main, *Financial integration in Europe*, April 2014, Charts 53a and 55

been rejected at a much higher rate in the distressed countries. This situation directly challenges the notion that there exists a single market in Europe: how can firms compete if they face such different conditions?

In addition, money held in banks stopped being common. Indeed, depositors are protected by a state guarantee, but some governments were in dire financial straits, so the guarantee did not have the same value. One euro held in a bank in Finland, say, was not the same as one euro held in an Irish bank. As a result, there were some transfers away from banks in distressed countries. In fact, Cyprus was forced to establish limits on cash withdrawals and imposed capital controls.

18.3.2 Bond markets

It is a fact that, in any country, private issuers of bonds have to offer an interest rate that is higher than the rate applied to government bonds. Public debt is considered the safest debt in any country, often perfectly safe. Indeed, hard-pressed governments can raise money by increasing taxes or cutting expenditures, in effect transferring the debt burden on to the private sector.

As Figure 18.3 shows, interest rates on several Eurozone government debts started to diverge when the global financial crisis began and bounced back when the sovereign debt crisis got underway. The creation of the euro unified the government bond markets and the crises fragmented them. The result was a total fragmentation of the markets for private bonds. A further illustration is offered in Figure 18.8, which plots the average interest rate in the countries that form the Eurozone as well as the difference between the highest and lowest interest rates observed each month. It confirms the unification of the markets between 1999 and 2007 and the subsequent fragmentation, which was at times much more profound than before the creation of the single currency.

The divergence between public bond rates reflects two risks. First, the fear that some governments could default, introducing a risk premium; and, second, the fear that some countries could leave the Eurozone and

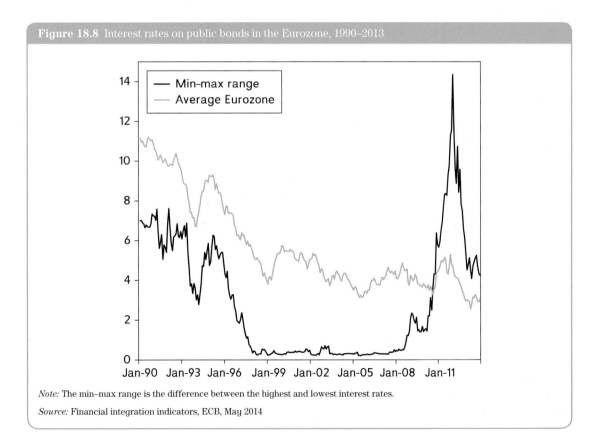

Figure 18.8 Interest rates on public bonds in the Eurozone, 1990–2013

Note: The min–max range is the difference between the highest and lowest interest rates.

Source: Financial integration indicators, ECB, May 2014

restore their own currencies, the redenomination risk. In the latter case, the interest rate parity condition implies that expected depreciation has to be factored in.

18.3.3 Stock markets

How did Eurozone stock markets behave during the crisis? One way to answer this question is to look at the average profitability of shares exchanged in each country and ask how different it has been from the average performance in the whole Eurozone. Figure 18.9 provides the answer, distinguishing between distressed and non-distressed countries. Except for a brief episode in 2008 at the height of the financial crisis, the returns in the non-distressed countries have been more dispersed than in normal years. Among the distressed countries, however, dispersion has hugely and durably increased during the sovereign debt crisis.

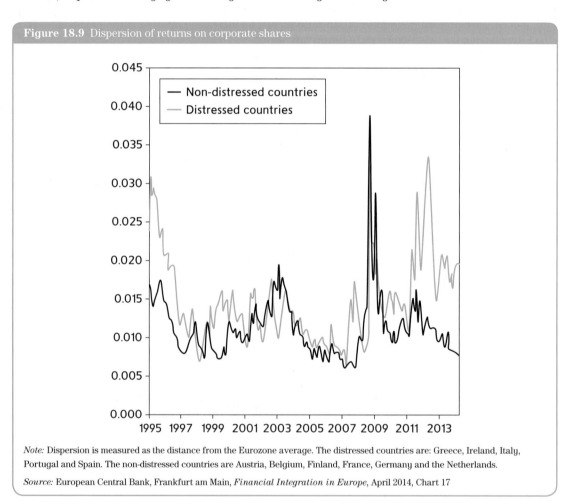

Figure 18.9 Dispersion of returns on corporate shares

Note: Dispersion is measured as the distance from the Eurozone average. The distressed countries are: Greece, Ireland, Italy, Portugal and Spain. The non-distressed countries are Austria, Belgium, Finland, France, Germany and the Netherlands.

Source: European Central Bank, Frankfurt am Main, *Financial Integration in Europe*, April 2014, Chart 17

18.3.4 Monetary conditions in Eurozone countries

Even though each component of the financial markets has become more nationally orientated during the crisis, there is still one central bank caring for a single currency. The damning observation is that monetary policy has stopped being common. As previously explained, monetary policy works through two channels: the cost and availability of credit to households and firms, and the exchange rate. The role of the exchange rate is examined in Chapter 19. Regarding credit conditions, we already know that bank lending has been very different across the Eurozone (Figure 18.6).

It follows that monetary policy dealing with the channels through which credit is provided has been very different across the Eurozone. In the presence of an asymmetric shock, the common monetary policy cannot be adequate for every member country; this is a well-understood implication of a monetary union, the starting point of the OCA theory studied in Chapter 15. The countries not affected by the sovereign debt crisis have been growing quasi-normally while a historically deep recession has afflicted the crisis-hit countries. The common monetary policy was therefore too lax for the first group and far too tight for the second group. The fragmentation has made matters much worse. Countries like Greece, Ireland, Portugal and Spain needed very low interest rates. Figure 18.10 shows that the ECB did cut its interest rate but that it did not have the desired effect. The actions by the ECB succeeded in reducing the interest rate in countries like Germany, where there was no need for such relaxation, while interest rates kept rising in the crisis-hit countries. In effect, monetary policy broke down where it was most needed. In response, the ECB eventually took extraordinary actions, which succeeded in lowering the hugely high interest rates in the crisis-hit countries; see Chapter 19.

Figure 18.10 The ECB policy rate and national interest rates, January 2007–June 2014

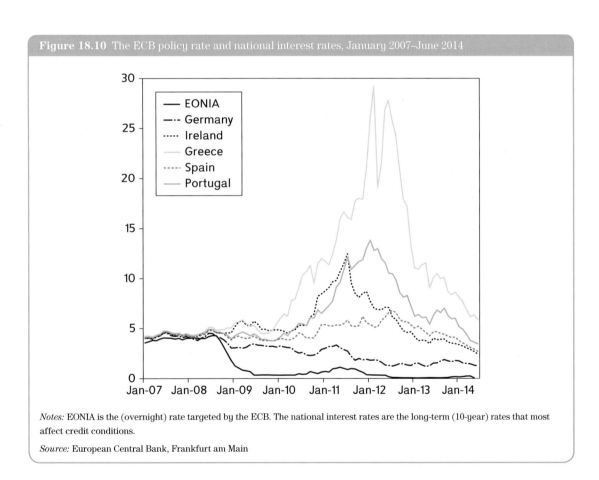

Notes: EONIA is the (overnight) rate targeted by the ECB. The national interest rates are the long-term (10-year) rates that most affect credit conditions.

Source: European Central Bank, Frankfurt am Main

18.4 The Eurozone and its banks

18.4.1 What is special about banking?

Section 18.1 identifies a number of characteristics specific to financial markets that also concern the banking industry: they display important scale economies, they operate as networks and they suffer from information asymmetries.

The presence of scale economies implies that a few large banks eventually dominate the market. The tendency for competition to become monopolistic challenges the perfect competition assumption.[8] It also means that economies are vulnerable to difficulties suffered by one or two of these important players. This vulnerability is sharpened by the two other characteristics. As part of networks, banks are continuously dealing with each other. They routinely borrow and lend huge amounts among each other. If one of them fails, all the others may be pulled down too. Failures tend to be systemic, meaning that one bank's misfortune stands to drag down the entire banking system. Large banks are systemically important. The third characteristic, the presence of information asymmetries, means that all banks routinely take risks. This is why banks are inherently fragile and prone to panics and crises. Another implication is that bank outsiders do not know how healthy each bank is. Outsiders are other banks, many of which have extensive financial relationships with each other. Other important outsiders are banking authorities, whose task is to monitor each bank and, if need be, to require corrective action. In the end, each bank is in the dark about its customers, its partners and the authorities.

At the same time, most people and firms have deposited significant parts of their wealth in banks. Worse, the better-off can use the services of advisers and sophisticated intermediaries, while the less-well-off hold much of their savings in banks and are typically ill-informed about the risks that they take. A bank failure, therefore, can have dramatic implications for the whole country, with disproportional effects on a majority of the population and on many SMEs. For this reason, banks cannot just be allowed to go bankrupt like any other corporation. One way or another, the state must protect people … and their banks. The banks know that, of course, and this encourages them to take even more risks. This is a vicious cycle, wherein protection from risk results in more risk taking, and is a phenomenon called moral hazard.

This brief review of banking theory reveals how special the banking industry is. Indeed, the history of banks is also a history of bank failures that have severe and lasting effects on the overall economy. It is well understood that banking suffers from 'market failures', i.e. deviations from the textbook description of perfect markets. In the presence of failures, markets may malfunction, which justifies interventions by the authorities. Indeed, in every country, banks are tightly regulated and closely supervised. In addition, the authorities systematically intervene when a bank fails.

18.4.2 Regulation, supervision, and resolution

In order to reduce the incidence and consequences of catastrophic events, banks are regulated. Over the years, regulation has changed and become increasingly sophisticated, which unfortunately does not necessarily mean effective. The general thrust is to ensure that financial institutions adopt prudent strategies and, when the need arises, are able to withstand shocks. The collapse in 2008 of Lehman Brothers, one of the most highly reputed banks on Wall Street, reminded us just how fragile banks can be. It also demonstrated that existing regulation was inadequate.

Regulation, in turn, requires supervision. It is not enough to adopt good rules; it is essential to make sure that they are respected. Since financial conditions can quickly deteriorate, supervision must be continuous. Given the complexity of modern finance, and the possibility of hiding emerging problems, supervisors must be as sophisticated as the financiers themselves, and they need to exercise their duties with great diligence and firmness. Over 2007–08, it emerged that supervisors were ill-informed, ill-prepared or technically unable to cope with the crisis. In the same vein, some of the events that led to the sovereign debt crisis – chiefly excessive credit granted by banks in Ireland and Spain – originated in inadequate regulation and poor supervision.

Even with perfect regulation and supervision, there will always be bank failures. As explained before, banks cannot be just left to fold, wiping out the money entrusted to them by their customers. Someone must step in, declare that the bank has failed, provide resources to protect the depositors and organize an orderly liquidation of the failed bank, in effect deciding who will suffer losses and who will be protected, if need be with taxpayers' money. If the amounts are very large, the central bank is the place where they can be found in case of emergency. In order to avoid depositor panic, failing banks are usually dealt with over a weekend, when only ATMs can be emptied.[9] This process is called bank resolution. At stake are huge amounts of money, and therefore huge private interests. Where a failing bank has been active in different countries,

---

[8] As explained in Chapter 6, monopolistic competition describes the situation whereby a small number of large firms dominate the market.

different resolution authorities become involved, each of which is subject to national legislation and likely to face national interest groups. The cases described in Box 18.4 show just how messy the result can become.

Box 18.4 Fortis and Dexia

Fortis Bank was a bank owned by a Belgian and Dutch parent company, with a significant presence in Luxembourg. Like many other European banks, it had accumulated large amounts of assets comprised of subprime loans. In 2007, it acquired part of a major Dutch bank, ABN AMRO, which strained its resources. To make things worse, it had large loans to Lehman Brothers outstanding. By late September 2008, following the demise of Lehman, Fortis required emergency support. The Belgian, Dutch and Luxembourg supervisory authorities could not agree on a unified response and each went its own way. The Dutch authorities nationalized the Dutch part of Fortis and ABN AMRO; the Belgian authorities nationalized the rest, i.e. the non-Dutch part of Fortis, and sold most of it to French bank BNP Paribas. Why was Fortis thus split? According to Claessens et al. (2010), 'Belgian and Dutch authorities have had a long tradition of cooperation, but Fortis was systemically important in both Belgium and the Netherlands. The Belgian authorities wanted to rescue Fortis as a whole, keeping the home base in Brussels while the Dutch authorities wanted to return ABN AMRO, which had just been acquired by Fortis, to Dutch control.'

Dexia is a Belgian bank, the outcome of the merger of a Belgian and a French bank, both specializing in lending to local authorities. Dexia bought a US financial institution that was exposed to both Lehman and the subprime market and faced acute losses in late September 2008. Days after Fortis was in trouble, Dexia also needed rescuing. This time, the Belgian and French authorities cooperated and injected funds to save Dexia and keep it intact.

These two almost simultaneous events showed that there was no Eurozone doctrine on how to deal with failed banks, which makes these traumatic events even more perilous. The different responses are explained by Pisani-Ferry and Sapir (2010) as follows: 'First, Dexia was (and still is) owned by a single holding company headquartered in a single country whereas Fortis was owned by two parent companies located in two separate countries. Second, the shareholders of Dexia were closely connected to governments.' In other words, truly European banks die more easily than national banks, especially if they do not have well-connected friends.

A deep overhaul was in order. Because banking is a global industry, core principles of regulation are agreed within the framework of the Basel Committee of Bank Supervision, which brings together regulators from countries with significant banking systems.[10] It issues recommendations that are meant to be adopted worldwide. A new institution that examines all financial institutions, the Financial Stability Board, was created in 2009. It is also based in Basel. It has issued a number of recommendations, some of which have been taken on board, after some unavoidable adjustments, by countries around the world.

What about Europe and its single market? Heated debates regarding whether regulation, supervision and resolution should be carried out at the EU or national level have always occurred, and still do. These debates concern the following issues:

- *Regulation.* In fact, the regulation debate has been settled, for both banks and other financial institutions: the rules are largely[11] designed at the EU level. This assignment is based on the 'four

---

[9] When many banks fail simultaneously, more time is needed. It is customary then to declare a 'bank holiday'. A famous example is the 1933 bank holiday in the USA that succeeded in stopping a run on banks.

[10] These countries are: Argentina, Australia, Belgium, Brazil, Canada, China, France, Germany, Hong Kong SAR, India, Indonesia, Italy, Japan, Korea, Luxembourg, Mexico, the Netherlands, Russia, Saudi Arabia, Singapore, South Africa, Spain, Sweden, Switzerland, Turkey, the UK and the USA.

[11] More precisely, EU-level regulation sets minimum standards, leaving individual countries free to establish more stringent – but not more lenient – rules. Within this principle, national-level rules are subject to the principle of mutual recognition, i.e. foreign rules are recognized as substitutes for domestic rules.

freedoms': free mobility goods, services, assets and people. For financial services to be freely traded, financial institutions need to be allowed to operate throughout the EU, if they so wish. If national regulations differed too much, financial institutions would have to register in each and every country in which they wished to operate. This would greatly hamper the mobility of financial services. Savers, unsure about the quality of foreign regulations, would prefer to keep their money in domestic institutions.

- *Supervision.* One argument for keeping supervision at the national level is the existence of another kind of information asymmetry, this time between supervisor and supervisee. Obviously each bank knows more about its business, and the risks that it is taking, than its supervisor. Quite likely, most banks wish to hide their difficulties, especially if disclosure would lead to fines or even outright closure of the bank. It is argued that these information asymmetries are lower at the national than at the union level. National supervisors claim that they know their banks well, and that they have developed a relationship over the years that allows for a smooth process. Another argument for decentralized supervision is subsidiarity: unless proven impossible or inefficient, supervision should remain at the national level. Powerful arguments also exist in favour of centralized supervision. First, banks are likely to become multinational; after all, this is what the single market is all about. In that case, they cannot be subject to just one supervisor or to several supervisors that operate differently. Indeed, supervision is a complex and expensive process and supervisors cannot avoid making subjective judgements. Second, closeness between supervisor and supervisee is beneficial in terms of reducing information asymmetries but can lead to capture. Third, a level playing field requires equality of treatment. Finally, and probably the decisive argument, the ECB is bound to be involved when a troubled bank requires quasi-instantaneously large amounts of money. Committing collective resources requires collective oversight, before and after resolution.

- *Resolution.* When a bank fails, a number of decisions must be made. They usually include: the type and amount of bank liabilities that will be protected and who will benefit from such protection; how large losses will be imposed and on whom; and whether management will be discharged and, if so, who will take over. In some case, the bank can even be nationalized. These are very significant political decisions, which involve potentially large resources. In a democracy, only elected officials have a mandate to take such decisions. This calls for delegating bank resolution authority to a national administration that operates under the authority of its government. Three arguments work in the opposite direction. First, banks are powerful and often exercise strong influence on their governments. Taxpayers may not be well protected. Second, many governments like to defend their national champions, a form of protectionism that runs against the spirit of the single market. Finally, as already indicated, the amounts can be such that the ECB may have to provide resources. As noted above, for the ECB to act as lender of last resort, the use of its resources cannot be left in purely national hands. Box 18.5 explains in more detail the role of the central bank in bank resolution.

Box 18.5 Lending in last resort

When a bank runs into trouble, prompt intervention is essential. At this stage, however, information asymmetries usually play a deleterious role. Bank customers fear for their money and proceed to withdraw cash – this situation is called a bank run – which the bank does not have in sufficient quantity as it typically lends most of what it receives. The bank then wants to borrow from other banks, but they too fear for their money and refuse to lend. Within days, sometimes hours, the bank is unable to operate. A rescue is urgently needed.

The government must decide what it will do. Much depends on the source of the trouble. It is customary to distinguish between illiquidity and insolvency. Illiquidity occurs when the bank does not have enough cash at hand to honour its commitments. A bank run, prompted by unjustified rumours, is a good example of illiquidity; there is nothing wrong with the bank but it cannot pay out deposits. Insolvency occurs when a bank has suffered a loss sufficient to exceed its capital, so that it is effectively bankrupt.

In the case of illiquidity, all that the bank needs is cash, and the central bank can provide it immediately. Acting as a lender of last resort, the central bank solves the problem by lending money to the bank against collateral, which means that the bank pledges or sells assets in exchange for cash. In that case, the central bank takes no risk. If the bank is insolvent, cash injections will not suffice. Some emergency money may be needed to protect depositors but the bank needs to be resolved. This is a risky operation and central banks are not supposed to take risks. The responsibility falls entirely on the government, which must commit its own resources, in effect passing the risk on to taxpayers. Inasmuch as emergency lending is needed, the central bank may provide cash but the government typically provides a guarantee to its central bank that it will cover any resulting loss.

This is the theory. In practice, finding out within hours whether or not a bank is insolvent is impossible. Most of the time, the supervisors are unable to make such a judgement. Worse, a bank may experience illiquidity but then find itself insolvent as a result of the crisis for a variety of reasons: it can lose a significant number of customers; some of its lenders can request immediate repayment; its assets can lose value because investors, alarmed about the general situation in the country, sell assets in large amounts; and so on. Because the distinction between illiquidity and insolvency is weak, it is often difficult to follow the rule that central banks only intervene in the case of illiquidity. In many cases, the central bank must first act as a lender of last resort, and then analyse the actual situation.

The monetary union creates a special difficulty for the ECB. If it intervenes as lender of last resort and, as a consequence, suffers losses, who will pay? Normally, it is for the government to provide a guarantee. Within the Eurozone, however, there are many governments, and no one wants to pay for the losses caused by a foreign bank. Yet all governments own the ECB collectively. The logical solution is for the government of the failing bank to provide the guarantee, but how good is the guarantee if the government is already deeply indebted?

When the euro was created, the solution was to establish some common minimum regulation with decentralized supervision and national resolution authorities. The financial crisis that engulfed Europe in 2008 showed that this system was not adequate (Box 18.4). The decision by Ireland to fully guarantee all deposits and other liabilities of its banks forced the government to borrow an amount in excess of 30 per cent of its GDP, because the ECB was not acting as lender of last resort. This led the country directly into a debt crisis.[12] The other countries, which offered limited guarantees, became concerned that their own banks would be at a disadvantage at a crucial moment. One by one, and each in its own way, all countries ended up temporarily offering unlimited guarantees to deposits at their own banks. These events led to a rethink of the initial arrangements and led to profound changes.

The first step was the appointment of a task force. The ensuing de Larosière[13] Report (2009) dutifully noted that national supervisors did not share information with one another, leaving governments in the dark when emergency decisions had to be made. The report also revealed that the ECB, tasked with the function of lender of last resort, was no better informed regarding the true situation of stressed banks. Following the proposals of the de Larosière Report, the European System of Financial Supervision (ESFS) was created, which includes four new institutions:

- The European Banking Authority (EBA), which is charged with collecting detailed information on all EU banks.

- The European Securities and Market Authority (ESMA), which brings together all EU bond and stock market regulators and supervisors.

---

[12] Much the same occurred in Spain.

[13] The task force was chaired by Jacques de Larosière, a former Governor of the Banque de France and also former Managing Director of the International Monetary Fund.

- The European Systemic Risk Board (ESRB), which looks at the overall picture, especially the cross-border links among financial institutions that heretofore were unknown. The ESRB, which is chaired by the president of the ECB, can issue binding recommendations.

- The European Insurance and Occupational Pensions Authority (EIOPA), which is like the ESRB but with a focus on insurance companies and pension funds.

- The Joint Committee of the European Supervisory Authorities (ESA), which brings the national supervisors together with a view to improving transparency.

The second step was the creation of a banking union, to begin operations at the end of 2014. It is presented in the next sub-section.

18.4.3 The Banking Union

It should be clear by now that central banks are unavoidably involved in banking and finance. Because monetary policy operates through the financial markets, a central bank is in daily contact with the banks and other financial institutions under its jurisdiction. It has to know what they are, how they operate and how healthy they are. It has a direct interest in financial stability and, in particular, in a well-functioning banking system. In addition, whether they like it or not, all central banks are *de facto* the lender of last resort to banks that fail. The Maastricht Treaty ignored these considerations, largely because delegating monetary policy to the ECB was perceived as a huge loss of national sovereignty. Going further and giving up bank supervision and resolution was just too much to tolerate. This decision was politically wise but economically unreasonable. A price had to be paid, and it became due during the sovereign debt crisis. The price was so enormous that the debate was reopened. The result is the Banking Union.[14]

With regulation already dealt with at the European level, the Banking Union involves the other two functions, supervision and resolution. Since regulations have also changed significantly, we review the still-evolving situation as of mid-2014.

Regulation

In 2013, the EU adopted its own version of the Basel III measures suggested by the Basel Committee.[15] The key requirements are:

- *Bank capital.* Banks must have an amount of capital equal to 8 per cent of 'risk weighted assets'. Capital is the amount of shares issued by the bank and represents the value of the bank to its owners. The bank itself assesses the quality of its assets and safer assets are weighted at less than 100 per cent of their value to determine the total amount subjected to the capital adequacy ratio. The rationale is as follows. A bank stands to suffer losses if some of its assets lose value. These losses are borne by the bank owners. If the losses exceed the capital, the bank is technically bankrupt. The regulation requires that there be enough capital to serve as a buffer. The measure, therefore, makes banks more resilient in case of heavy losses.

- *Leverage ratio.* A bank often borrows to invest. If the cost of borrowing is lower than the (expected) returns on its investments, the bank makes profits. The more it borrows and invests, the larger are the profits. It is very tempting to climb the leverage mountain, but it is also very dangerous if the returns transpire to be disappointing. The leverage ratio relates borrowing to capital. In order to reduce risk taking, the leverage ratio of each bank will be closely monitored and the authorities can require that it be reduced.[16]

- *Liquidity ratio.* This is the ratio of assets that can be promptly and safely sold to obtain cash as a proportion of payments that a bank expects to make over the next 30 days. This ratio will have to be progressively raised to 100 per cent, starting at 60 per cent in 2015.

Discussions are under way to impose higher capital requirements on the large banks deemed 'too big to fail'.

---

[14] Surprisingly perhaps, the Banking Union is a set of agreements, not a treaty. The European leaders were fearful of the political implication of a full-blown treaty. In mid-2014, a number of German citizens petitioned the German Constitutional Court to decide on whether the Banking Union is unconstitutional.

[15] The UK has adopted additional measures as the City is a major financial centre.

[16] Banks strenuously resist plans to impose a limit on leverage ratios.

Supervision

As of late 2014, supervision for the 134 largest banks of the Eurozone is centralized and under the authority of the ECB. This is the Single Supervision Mechanism (SSM). Non-Eurozone countries may choose to join the SSM. The SSM is managed by a Supervisory Board, which is part of the ECB. The decision represents a sharp but incomplete move to centralization since the smaller banks remain subject to national supervision.

The ECB won this responsibility because it is an independent institution with considerable credibility.[17] The decision was, and remains, highly controversial. Critics worry about the ECB facing a conflict of interest between its monetary policy and bank supervision duties: would it not be tempted to relax monetary policy to help out banks, possibly very large ones, that it knows are in a precarious situation? In addition, supervision is more art than science and any supervisor stands to make a wrong judgement call now and then; will that not affect the credibility, and therefore the independence, of the ECB?[18]

As a pre-condition for assuming this expanded role, the ECB has obtained the right to conduct an in-depth analysis of the state of health of the banks that it will supervise. This analysis includes an Asset Quality Review (AQR), designed to challenge banks on their own evaluation of the risk that they bear. The AQR is followed by stress tests: the situation of each bank is examined in relation to hypothetical financial and economic shocks to determine their resilience. The stress tests are conducted by the EBA (see above) in liaison with the ECB. The results of the AQR and stress tests are to be made public before the end of 2014. The EBA and the SSM will be able to request those banks that fail the tests to take precautionary measures.

Resolution

The bank resolution regime has also been transformed. In parallel with the SSM, a new Supervisory Resolution Mechanism (SRM) has been created. It will come into play at a date not yet decided. This is another partial step toward centralization, although less extensive than the SSM. The SRM will operate under the authority of a Single Resolution Board (SRB) composed of the European Commission, the Council and the national resolution authorities, as well as its own members. The ECB is an observer, not a full member of the SRB.

A few aspects of the new regime are noteworthy:

- Resolution of a bank will be decided by the SRB and carried out by the relevant national resolution authority. Centralization is therefore partial and decision making could be complicated in emergency situations.

- Funding for any cash injection will be provided by a new resolution fund to which banks will contribute starting in 2016 and ending in 2024.

- The ECB has kept its distance from the SRM because it believes that supervision, which it now manages through the SSM, and resolution ought to be firmly separated. This arrangement is to avoid a conflict of interest between these two functions and also because resolution is about the distribution of losses, which is a government responsibility, as noted above.

- The creation of the SRM is complemented by the Bank Resolution and Recovery Directive, which applies to all EU countries. The stated intention of the directive is to minimize costs to taxpayers. To that effect, bank losses will be paid for by the stakeholders in a predetermined order, the so-called 'pecking order': first the shareholders, then owners of junior bonds ranked from more to less liquid. All deposits by households and SMEs will be fully protected up to 100,000 euros.

For the resolution fund, the objective is to collect 55 billion euros. This sum is unrealistically small. The Commission has estimated the cost of supporting banks during the financial crisis at 1600 billion euros. Some of this amount has been injected slowly to restructure failed banks, but some has been needed as a matter of urgency. Together with the weak distinction between illiquidity and insolvency, this means that the resolution fund may lack resources, in which case the ECB will have to be lender of last resort.

---

[17] Its main competitor was the European Commission. The Commission is much less independent from governments.

[18] In some countries, the central bank is the bank supervisor and in others it is not. The poor performance of many supervisors under government authority during the global financial crisis has led several countries to shift bank supervision partly (e.g. in the USA) or fully (e.g. in the UK) to the central bank. The Eurozone is part of that worldwide trend.

18.5 The international role of the euro

The classic attributes of money apply to its international role. Externally, a currency can be a medium of exchange used for international trade, a unit of account used to price other currencies or widely traded commodities, and a store of value used by foreign individuals and authorities. Domestically, these attributes are underpinned by the legal status of money; internationally, they have to be earned.

In the nineteenth century, sterling was the undisputed international currency. It was displaced by the US dollar in the early part of the twentieth century. Clearly, only large economies can expect their currency to achieve an international status, a condition that the Eurozone fulfils. Currently, some 340 million people live within the Eurozone, and new membership could eventually bring this number to 480 million; compare this with the 310 million people living in the USA. The EU's GDP is 75 per cent of that of the USA. Another condition is that the currency must be stable. The Eurosystem's commitment to price stability further suggests that, eventually, the euro can aspire to playing a large international role. Will it, and if so, when? Would it be a good thing? These are the issues that we consider in this final section.

18.5.1 Medium of exchange: trade invoicing

For every export, an agreement must be reached on the currency that will be used to set the price and then carry out payment. Will it be the exporter's, the importer's or a third currency? Each side of the trade would rather use its own currency to avoid exchange costs and uncertainty. In that sense, the Eurozone stands to benefit from a wider acceptance of its currency.

Figure 18.11 presents some evidence that European firms increasingly invoice trade in euros. Yet the bulk of primary commodities (oil, gas, raw materials) are priced in US dollars in specialized markets, and

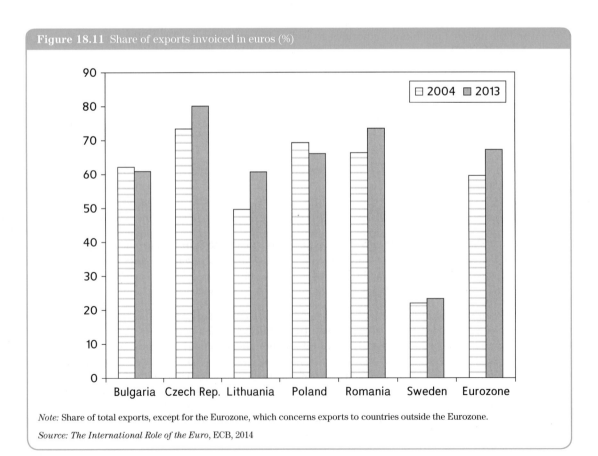

Figure 18.11 Share of exports invoiced in euros (%)

Note: Share of total exports, except for the Eurozone, which concerns exports to countries outside the Eurozone.

Source: The International Role of the Euro, ECB, 2014

this is unlikely to change in the foreseeable future. Even if European firms can now more often avoid exposure to currency risk by using the euro, the dollar is and will remain the currency of choice among countries that are neither the USA nor euro currency areas. The exception is countries in the EU or in the rest of Europe.

18.5.2 Unit of account: vehicle currencies on foreign exchange markets

The foreign exchange market is a network of financial institutions that trade currencies among themselves. This is a huge market in which an average *day* in April 2013 saw currency exchanges worth US$5,300 billion (this amounts to about a quarter of US *annual* GDP). Most of the world currencies are not really traded, as explained in Box 18.6. The bulk of transactions involve a vehicle currency. Table 18.2 reports the percentage of trades that involve, on one side or another, the three main world currencies as well as the pound sterling or the Chinese yuan, an up and coming currency in this league (the sum for all currencies would be 200 per cent since each transaction involves a pair of currencies). The share of the euro in 2013 was much smaller than the sum of the former shares of its constituent currencies. This simply reflects the elimination of exchange rate transactions among the currencies that joined the Eurozone. Overall, the table reveals considerable stability. The pre-eminence of the dollar remains unchallenged.

Table 18.2　Currency composition of exchange trading volume (%)

	US dollar	Euro	Yen	Deutsch-mark	French franc	ECU and other ERM currencies	Pound sterling	Chinese yuan
1992	82.0		23.4	39.6	3.8	11.8	13.6	
1998	87.3		20.2	30.1	5.1	17.3	11.0	0.0
2010	84.9	39.1	19.0				12.9	0.9
2013	87.0	33.4	23.0				11.8	2.2

Note: If all currencies were listed, the sum would be 200 per cent since each exchange involves two currencies.
Source: Triennial Central Bank Surveys, BIS, 2014

Box 18.6　Vehicle currencies

Each transaction must involve two currencies. Since there exist more than 180 currencies in the world, there are about 16,000 bilateral exchange rates.[1] If all these bilateral rates were traded, most of them (think of the exchange rate between the Samoan tala and the Honduran lempira) would involve very few trades, resulting in a host of shallow, hence inefficient and volatile, markets. This is why foreign exchange markets use the property of triangular arbitrage to considerably reduce the number of currency pairs that are traded.

The idea is simple and illustrated in Figure 18.12. Consider two currencies, A and B, and their bilateral exchange rate, e_{AB}. Currency A has an exchange rate vis-à-vis the dollar, $e_{A\$}$, and so does currency B, $e_{B\$}$. Once these two rates are known, the bilateral rate can be identified as $e_{AB} = e_{A\$}/e_{B\$}$. In this example, the dollar is used as a currency vehicle and the implied bilateral rate e_{AB} is called a cross-rate. In practice, cross-rates are rarely traded and very few currencies are used internationally.

[1] With n currencies, there exist $n(n-1)/2$ bilateral exchange rates. Here, $16,110 = (180 \times 179)/2$.

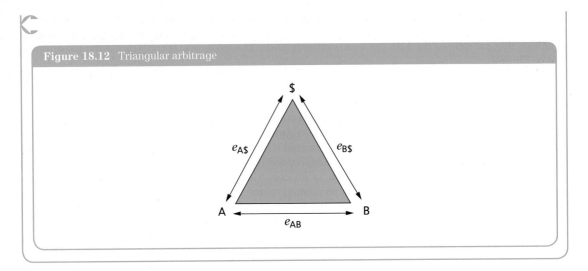

Figure 18.12 Triangular arbitrage

18.5.3 Store of value: bond markets

Large firms and governments borrow on the international markets by issuing long-term debt, i.e. bonds. This is an enormous market. Figure 18.13 shows that, following the launch of the euro, the share of bonds issued in that currency rose. This is not surprising in view of the market integration that has taken place, as explained in Section 18.3.2. Given the recent turmoil, however, it is also not surprising that the share of euro-denominated bonds has now declined. Interestingly, the City of London has become the leading marketplace for this instrument whereas New York seems uninterested.

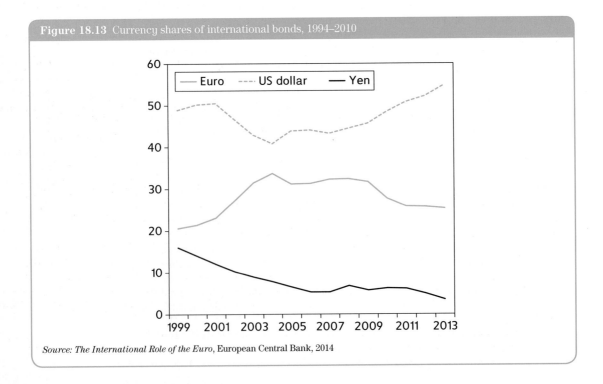

Figure 18.13 Currency shares of international bonds, 1994–2010

Source: The International Role of the Euro, European Central Bank, 2014

18.5.4 Store of value: international reserves

All national central banks hold foreign exchange reserves to underpin trust in their currencies and, if need be, to intervene on foreign exchange markets. Currencies appropriate for this store of value role must be widely traded; they must also be perceived as having long-term stability. Figure 18.14 shows that the euro has made some progress since its creation, but the dollar seems firmly entrenched as the leading currency.

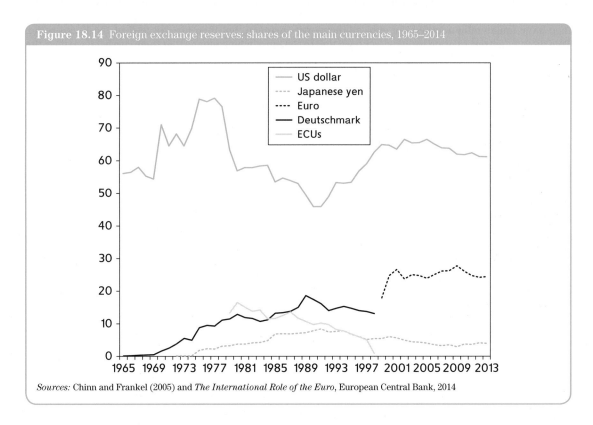

Figure 18.14 Foreign exchange reserves: shares of the main currencies, 1965–2014

Sources: Chinn and Frankel (2005) and *The International Role of the Euro*, European Central Bank, 2014

European countries at the periphery of the Eurozone (including the UK) are gradually replacing dollars with euros. A number of developing countries have also announced their intention to do so, largely for political reasons. Recently, various Asian authorities, including China, who accumulated vast reserves in dollars, have diversified into the euro.

Why should the euro eat into the dollar's market share? Besides politics, central banks are traditionally unwilling to change the currency composition of their reserves. In particular, large-scale sale of dollars could precipitate a depreciation of the US currency, with two adverse effects: the depreciation would alter international competition in trade – favouring the US economy – and it would create losses for dollar-holders, including for the central banks themselves. This is why, even if the euro may be an attractive store of value, a major shift would require a serious deterioration in the dollar's own quality as a store of value. Even though inflation rose in the USA to double-digit levels in the late 1970s, the dollar retained its supremacy. The financial crisis that originated in 2007 in the USA did not challenge the dollar's supremacy in the least. Surprisingly perhaps, given rumours that the Eurozone could break up, the euro has also held its own. Much more would be needed to affect the existing hierarchy.

18.5.5 The euro as an anchor

When a country does not let its exchange rate float freely, it must adopt an anchor; that is, a foreign currency to which its own currency is more or less rigidly tied. The anchor, which works as a unit of account, can be a single currency or a basket of currencies. The link can be deliberately vague – known as a managed float – or quite explicit, ranging from wide crawling bands to the wholesale adoption of a foreign currency (for details, see Chapter 14).

A number of currencies use the euro as an anchor in one way or another, as indicated in Table 18.3. Most of the countries listed in the table are geographically close to the Eurozone (central and eastern Europe, northern Africa) or have historical ties to one of its constituent legacy currencies (e.g. French-speaking Africa). Two former members of the Yugoslav Federation, Kosovo and Montenegro, have 'euroized', i.e. they have unilaterally adopted the euro as their own currency, but they are not part of the Eurosystem. Two more countries operate a currency board tied to the euro, which means that their currency really is the euro but under a different name. A number of countries around the world are pegging their currencies to a basket composed of a few important currencies, of which the euro is quite naturally part.

Table 18.3   Countries using the euro as an anchor (as of May 2014)

ERM 2	Peg to euro	Peg to basket including the euro	Managed floating with euro as reference currency	Euro-based currency boards	Unilateral euroization
Denmark	CFA Franc Zone	Algeria	Croatia	Bulgaria	Kosovo
Lithuania[1]	Cape Verde	Belarus	Czech Rep.	Bosnia-Herzegovina	Montenegro
	Comoros	Botswana	Macedonia		Micro states[2]
	São Tomé and Príncipe	Fiji	Romania		
		Iran	Switzerland		
		Kuwait			
		Libya			
		Morocco			
		Russia			
		Samoa			
		Singapore			
		Syria			
		Tunisia			
		Vanuatu			

Notes: (1) Lithuania adopts the euro in January 2015; (2) The micro states are: Republic of San Marino, Vatican City, Principality of Monaco, Andora.

Source: The International Role of the Euro, European Central Bank, 2014

18.5.6 Parallel currencies

Foreign currencies are also sometimes used alongside the domestic currency, fulfilling all three functions of means of payment, unit of account and store of value. Parallel currencies, as the phenomenon is called, emerge in troubled countries where the value of the domestic currency is eroded by very rapid inflation or political instability. In most cases, the parallel currency circulates in cash form, but a number of countries also allow bank deposits.

The dollar is the universal parallel currency of choice, but the Deutschmark used to circulate widely in central and eastern Europe and in Turkey, as did the French franc in northern Africa and parts of sub-Saharan Africa. The euro has now replaced the Deutschmark and the franc. The problem with the use of parallel currencies is that little is known about this system, if only because it is highly informal and not captured by official statistics. The ECB estimates that some 145 billion euros – 15 per cent of all euro banknotes in circulation – are outside the Eurozone. As a comparison, the Federal Reserve estimates that 500 billion dollars are circulating outside the USA, about half of the total.

Another 'parallel' use of banknotes concerns illegal activities, both within and outside the country. A distinguishing feature of euros is that they exist in very large denominations, which makes it easy to pack vast amounts of money in a small suitcase. Figure 18.15 shows the value of the different banknote denominations in circulation. The banknote of choice in the Eurozone (e.g. in ATMs) is the 50 euro denomination, ahead of the 20 dollar denomination that dominates in the USA. These are the denominations that fill up wallets, purses and cash registers. One suspects that the largest denominations are more often in the hands of people carrying out criminal activities of one variety or another, including corrupt dictators. The popularity of the 500 euro and 100 dollar banknotes is difficult to understand otherwise.

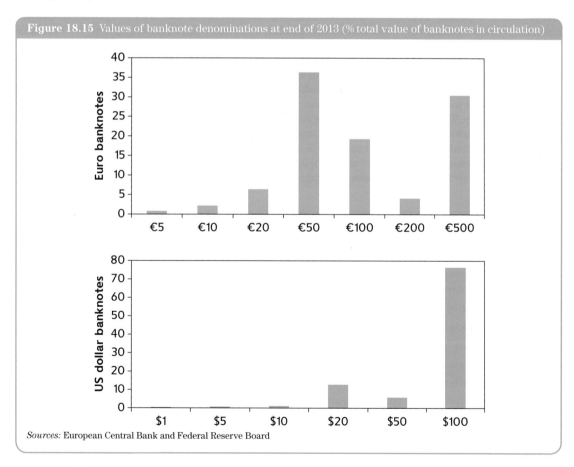

Figure 18.15 Values of banknote denominations at end of 2013 (% total value of banknotes in circulation)

Sources: European Central Bank and Federal Reserve Board

18.5.7 Does it matter?

In the minds of some Europeans, the euro should be challenging the supremacy of the dollar. The wish to displace the dollar is no doubt driven by political sentiment, but what about the economic advantages?

When international trade is invoiced in a foreign currency, importers and exporters face an exchange risk. Many months can elapse between the signing of a commercial contract and the making of a payment. In the intervening period, the exchange rate may change, imposing a risk on traders. They can purchase insurance (in the form of forward exchange contracts), but at a cost. US firms, which mostly carry out international transactions in dollars, thus enjoy some advantage. In addition, 'greenbacks' are conspicuous all over the world. Paper money is virtually costless to produce but, of course, is not freely provided, being exchanged against goods, services or assets. The profit earned by the central bank, known as seigniorage, is a form of tax. When it is levied on residents, it is just one form of domestic taxation, but when levied on foreigners, it represents a real transfer of resources. The value of expatriate dollars is about 3 per cent of US GDP – a nice sum. However, once we realize that it has been accumulated over several decades, it is not really a significant source of revenue.

All in all, the economic benefits resulting from having a world currency are quite modest. This explains why the ECB considers that a possible international role for the euro is something that it should neither encourage nor discourage. Beyond some legitimate pride, it does not really care.

18.6 Summary

The financial markets are special. They are subject to economies of scale, they operate as networks and they face important information asymmetries. One consequence is that they are prone to systemic instability. This instability, as well as other market failures, explains why financial systems are regulated and supervised.

The adoption of a common currency has contributed to the further integration of the various components of the financial market. The crises that started in 2007 have led to a fragmentation of these markets. This fragmentation has also affected banks, which undermines the single monetary policy.

The crises have also made it clear that the Eurozone was inadequately equipped to deal with turmoil in the banking system. This has led to a host of new Eurozone institutions, culminating in the establishment of a Banking Union, which goes some way toward centralizing bank supervision and resolution.

The euro has some potential to challenge the US dollar as an international currency, but old habits die hard and, despite some changes, the dollar's supremacy has not been seriously challenged. Still, at the periphery of the Eurozone, it plays a dominant role as an anchor for local currencies and, possibly, as a parallel currency.

Self-assessment questions

1. What is depth in financial markets? What is breadth? What are network externalities?
2. Describe the phenomenon of information asymmetry. How can it explain why banks refuse credit to some customers? How can it contribute to systemic risk in financial markets?
3. What is maturity transformation? Why is it risky?
4. How do financial markets establish a risk premium for each and every asset that is traded?
5. Diversification: is it always the case that holding more assets reduces risk?
6. What is bank resolution? How is it conducted?
7. What is the difference between bonds and shares?
8. How do we know that bond markets were unified in the Eurozone upon the launch of the euro? Why has this not happened for stock markets?
9. Why can't the ECB conduct a single monetary policy when the financial system is fragmented?
10. What is the SSM? The SRM?
11. What is capital requirement? What is a leverage ratio?
12. Explain how the three functions of money apply at the international level.

13 What is the difference between regulation and supervision?

14 Why is centralization of bank supervision in the Eurozone resisted?

15 What is the difference between a parallel and a vehicle currency? Is the bitcoin a parallel currency?

Essay questions

1 'The real reason why Eurozone countries can't agree on a single supervising agency is that each one wants to protect its own financial institutions.' Evaluate this view.

2 What is the case for centralization of bank supervision in the Eurozone? The case against?

3 The ECB has been given a major role in bank supervision. Is it a good thing?

4 Suppose that you are in charge of resolving a failing bank. How would you go about it?

5 Finance is a major industry in the UK, accounting for some 5 per cent of its GDP. Does this characteristic make membership of the Eurozone more or less appealing?

Further reading: the aficionado's corner

On the evolution of financial markets in the Eurozone:

European Central Bank, *Financial integration in Europe*, an annual publication available on the ECB website.

Lane, P. (2009) 'EMU and financial integration', in B. Mackowiak, F.P. Mongelli, G. Noblet and F. Smets (eds) *The Euro at Ten – Lessons and Challenges*, ECB.

On bank regulation and supervision:

Pomerleano, M. (2010) 'The Basel II concept leads to a false sense of security', VoxEU, http://www.voxeu.org/debates/commentaries/basel-ii-concept-leads-false-sense-security.

On fragmentation during the crisis:

Al-Eyd, A. and S.P. Berkmen (2013) 'Fragmentation and monetary policy in the euro area', Working Paper 13/208, IMF.

Brunnermeier, M., J. De Gregorio, P. Lane, H. Rey and H.S. Shin (2012) 'Banks and cross-border capital flows: policy challenges and regulatory responses', Vox EU, http://www.voxeu.org/article/banks-and-cross-border-capital-flows-policy-challenges-and-regulatory-responses.

Coeuré, B. (2014) 'Completing the single market in capital', ECB, http://www.ecb.europa.eu/press/key/date/2014/html/sp140519_1.en.html.

Merler, S. (2013) 'Home-(sweet home)-bias and other stories – a look into banks' assets with an update on financial fragmentation', BRUEGEL, Brussels.

On the Banking Union:

A set of short contributions is summarized, with a link to the full publication, in:

Beck, T. (2012) 'Banking union for Europe: risks and challenges', Vox EU, http://www.voxeu.org/content/banking-union-europe-risks-and-challenges.

Other studies:

Gros, D. (2013) 'Banking union for Europe: risks and challenges', CEPS, Brussels, http://ceps.eu/system/files/Banking_Union.pdf.

Sapir, A. and G.B. Wolff (2013) 'The neglected side of banking union: reshaping Europe's financial system', BRUEGEL, Brussels.

The Commission's dedicated website:

http://ec.europa.eu/internal_market/finances/banking-union/index_en.htm.

The ECB's dedicated website regularly publishes studies and data: https://www.ecb.europa.eu/ssm/html/index.en.html.

On the international role of the euro and other challengers, see:

Chinn, M. and J. Frankel (2005) *Will the Euro Eventually Surpass the Dollar as Leading International Reserve Currency?*, NBER Working Paper 11510. Download from www.nber.org/papers/w11510.

ECB, *The International Role of the Euro*, an annual publication available on the ECB website.

Eichengreen, B. and M. Kawai (2014) 'Issues for Renminbi internationalization: an overview', Working Paper No. 454, Asian Development Bank.

Useful websites

Websites concerned with regulation and supervision:

Basel Committee on Banking Supervision: www.bis.org/bcbs/aboutbcbs.htm

Basel Financial Stability Board: http://www.financialstabilityboard.org/.

References

Chinn, M. and J. Frankel (2005) *Will the Euro Eventually Surpass the Dollar as Leading International Reserve Currency?*, NBER Working Paper 11510. Download from www.nber.org/papers/w11510.

Claessens, S., R.J. Herring and D. Schoenmaker (2010) *A Safer World Financial System: Improving the Resolution of Systemic Institutions*, Geneva Reports on the World Economy 12, ICMB and CEPR.

Dornbusch, R. (2000) *Keys to Prosperity, Free Markets, Sound Money and a Bit of Luck*, MIT Press, Cambridge, MA.

Hartmann, P., A. Maddaloni and S. Manganelli (2003) 'The Eurozone financial system: structure, integration and policy initiatives', *Oxford Review of Economic Policy*, 19(1): 180–213.

Pisani-Ferry, J. and A. Sapir (2010) 'Banking crisis management in the EU: an early assessment', *Economic Policy*, 62: 341–73.

Chapter 19

We knew that a storm was brewing but, admittedly, we did not know exactly where. Neither did we know what would trigger it, or when it would come.

Jean-Claude Trichet, President of the ECB, Fifth ECB Central Banking Conference, Frankfurt, 13 November 2008

The euro is like a bumblebee. This is a mystery of nature because it shouldn't fly but instead it does. So the euro was a bumblebee that flew very well for several years. Probably there was something in the atmosphere, in the air, that made the bumblebee fly. Now something must have changed in the air, and we know what after the financial crisis. The bumblebee would have to graduate to a real bee.

Mario Draghi, President of the ECB, Global Investment Conference, London, 26 July 2012

The Eurozone in crisis

Chapter Contents

Introduction

The Eurozone was just celebrating its first decade of existence when the global financial crisis that had started in 2007 morphed into a public debt crisis concentrated on the area. The second stage of the great crisis has not merely marred the early achievements of the single currency, it has also revealed deep flaws in the construction of the Eurozone – described in earlier chapters. This concluding chapter looks at the crisis, which is bound to leave a profound imprint on the history of the monetary integration in Europe. Some expect the Eurozone to emerge tighter and stronger while others foresee a break-up, and possibly the end of the euro.

This chapter is being completed in August 2014, at a time when the worst of the crisis appears to be over; that belief may transpire to be wishful thinking, however. After years of controversy, often along national lines, a reasonably shared understanding of what happened is at hand. The chapter presents the results of this analysis, as well as some of the debates, past and present, in Section 19.1 (the global financial crisis) and Section 19.2 (the specific Eurozone crisis). Section 19.3 presents the policy responses, Section 19.4 looks at the special case of banks and Section 19.5 examines the lessons learnt, and not learnt.

19.1 Stage one: the global financial crisis

Between 2001, the year of the high-tech crisis, and 2007, the year of the financial crisis, the USA and much of the rest of the world enjoyed an unprecedented period of prosperity, the combination of sustained growth and declining inflation. The Great Moderation lasted longer and was more widespread than any previous cyclical upswing. Policy makers were quick to claim responsibility for this achievement, ignoring the silent build-up of tensions that have led to the worst economic crisis since the Great Depression. Knowledge of what had caused the Great Depression helped to contain the crisis that originated in the USA and promptly spread to Europe, but it led to rapid increases in public debt. This, in turn, set the stage for the second phase of the crisis, which has been concentrated in the Eurozone.

19.1.1 Financial deregulation

Following the Great Depression, for which US financial markets were blamed, strict regulation was designed to limit risk-taking by banks and financial institutions. The deregulation phase started in the 1980s and culminated in 1999 with the repeal of the Glass–Steagall Act of 1933. There followed a rapid expansion of the financial sector in the USA, and Europe soon followed with its own deregulation process associated with the Single European Act adopted in 1986 (although deregulation in Europe never went as far as in the USA).

A first result of deregulation was that banks developed activities not directly related to their traditional role of collecting deposits and making loans. Increasingly, banks became active investors themselves. In order to expand this lucrative activity, they borrowed globally and short term to invest globally in long-term financial instruments.[1] Doing so created two mismatches:

- The *maturity mismatch* between their short-term borrowings and long-term investments. As a result, they had to continuously renew their borrowings; they became vitally dependent on their ability to do so.
- The *currency mismatch*, between borrowing and lending in different currencies, meant that they could run into difficulty should exchange rate movements reduce the value of their lending relative to the value of their borrowing.

The result was to increase the fragility of banks. The good years of the Great Moderation hid the build-up of risk, as did Basel II regulations that allowed banks to determine themselves the degree of riskiness of their assets. As explained in Chapter 18, because ordinary customer deposits are crucial to everyday economic life, banks cannot simply go bankrupt; if they fail, they must be bailed out. Thus, the major risks taken by banks were implicitly borne by their governments (and taxpayers), which naturally encouraged banks to take even more risks (this situation is called moral hazard). Avoiding the potential socialization of losses had been a key motivation of the Glass–Steagall Act, including restricting the banks to the dull – and not very

---

[1] In the terminology of Chapter 18, banks became highly leveraged.

profitable – business of deposit taking. Deregulation made banks more profitable, as long as the economic conditions were benign. Finance became ever more sophisticated, so much so that top bank managers lost track of what their rocket scientists[2] were cooking; they did not mind as long as profits were fat. Much as the roaring twenties preceded the 1929 Wall Street crash, golden boys (and girls) were running the quick money show until it collapsed.

19.1.2 The roots of the financial crisis

Part of this inventiveness was directed at US mortgages. Keen to encourage individual homeownership – the famed American dream – the US authorities adopted measures that made it possible and lucrative to lend to people long considered a bad risk. As the Great Moderation was taking hold, and with it the perception that growth was sure to persist forever, bankers became less sensitive to risk. They approached people who until then could never hope to borrow[3] and offered them the now-infamous subprime loans. These very special loans are explained in Box 19.1.

Box 19.1   The subprime mortgage loans

Low (or no) income households cannot borrow because regulation and banking practice establish a minimum ratio between debt service and income. Subprimes circumvented that restriction by offering loans with an initially low interest rate – and, therefore, low debt service – that would be significantly increased after two or three years. When the interest rate was stepped up, a new, similar, loan would be granted to enable the debtor to pay back the previous loan. If the price of the house had increased, the borrower could borrow even more, again at the initially low rate, and thus keep some cash after repaying the previous loan. Everyone loved this system, especially the US consumers who used houses like ATMs.[1]

As house prices kept rising, refinancing before step-up was easy. However, if prices were ever to fall, the amount that could be borrowed before step-up would be lowered because the guarantee – the house itself – would be worth less money. For a long while, prices did keep increasing as abundant mortgage loans – both subprimes and others – fed strong purchases. The increase was spectacular – Figure 19.1 shows that house prices doubled between early 2000 and early 2006 – drawing ever more borrowers. A (very small) number of experts started to talk about a housing bubble, but nobody wanted to listen.[2] Prices paused in 2006. Doubt set in and lending slowed down markedly, which pushed house prices down. Borrowers could not avoid the step-up and many stopped servicing their debts. House prices started to decline precipitously, bankrupting borrowers and lenders alike. It took four years for prices to find a floor. By then, the world was in crisis.

Were the lenders crazy? This is where things become complicated but interesting. Specialized mortgage companies sprang up during the years of the Great Moderation. They borrowed money, granted loans and promptly sold the loans to banks. In this way, they were passing the risk of non-repayment to the banks while being able to lend again and again. Were the banks that purchased the loans crazy? Things now become even more complicated but also even more interesting. Banks that accumulated the loans, in turn sold them to other banks, which sold them to yet other banks with a twist, called securitization.

The securitization process consists of lumping together a large number of individual mortgage loans into one big bundle, which is less risky than any of its constituent loans taken separately; doing so is called diversification (see Chapter 18). Next, the bank divides the bundle into formally independent

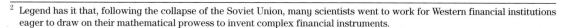

[2] Legend has it that, following the collapse of the Soviet Union, many scientists went to work for Western financial institutions eager to draw on their mathematical prowess to invent complex financial instruments.

[3] These people have been mischievously characterized as NINJAs (No Income, No Job or Address).

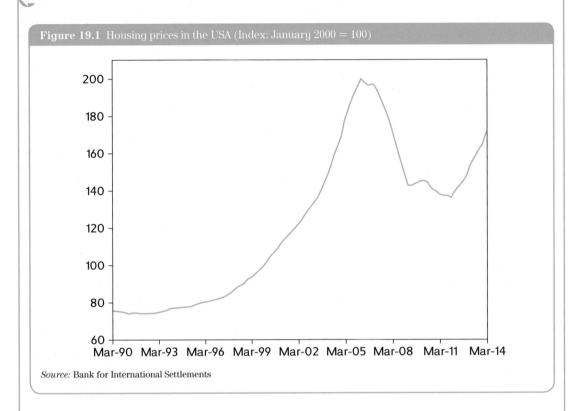

Figure 19.1 Housing prices in the USA (Index: January 2000 = 100)

Source: Bank for International Settlements

'tranches', which it then ranks. Thus if some mortgage loans were to be defaulted upon, the loss would go to the lowest tranche. If the losses exceeded the value of the lowest tranche, they would go to the next lowest one, and so on. The top tranches were accordingly considered perfectly safe; a great many loans would have to sour for these tranches to be affected, and that was considered impossible. The top tranches received an AAA ranking and sold at a high price. The lowest tranches sold for much less, but still at a nice price given the unbounded optimism of the Great Moderation years. The ultimate buyers were often the world's largest and most prestigious banks.

These banks bought into the diversification argument: the individual loans were very different because they were granted to different people whose abilities to pay back were unrelated. This meant that the likelihood that many loans would sour together was negligible, even though the likelihood that any one of them would not be repaid was quite high. The problem was that the subprime loans transpired to be very similar – they all relied on continuously rising house prices. When prices started to fall, the supposedly unlikely event of all loans going bad at the same time proved to be reality. This meant that the AAA tranches were junk, as the ultimate holders then discovered.

---

[1] A number of mortgage companies have since been prosecuted for deceptive selling practices. Some of them actually remunerated people who were bringing new clients to them, irrespective of their borrowing ability.

[2] Yale economist and co-author of *Irrational Exuberance*, Robert Shiller famously earned the nickname Mr Bubble in 2005 when he stated: 'It's worthwhile to reflect that although home prices have gone up a lot in the recent years, they are just the same houses, right? There's no change in the services they provide. It's just the value we put on them. And so a house's value can just evaporate overnight, too. If people suddenly get very wary of investing in houses because they don't think the prices are going to go up or if they think they're going to fall, then that will cause home prices to fall' (http://www.npr.org/templates/story/story.php?storyId=4679264).

Subprime mortgages only existed in the USA, largely because consumer protection legislation in Europe and elsewhere would not allow people to engage in the highly dangerous step-up mechanism. But why did the collapse of housing prices in the USA result in a global financial crisis? After all, the subprime mortgage market was small relative to the US financial system. This reasoning proved to be wrong because it ignored the linkages between financial institutions.

Many of the world's largest banks had eagerly played the subprime game; now they faced heavy losses and looked alarmingly fragile. These banks were mainly from the USA, the UK, France, the Netherlands, Belgium and Germany, because banks in other countries (Spain and Italy, for instance, as well as in Asia and Latin America) were instructed by their supervisors not to wade into such unknown business. Hoping to weather the shock, they tried hard to conceal their situation from each other, and from their supervisors. They could do so because many of their now-toxic assets were owned by subsidiaries – the so-called shadow banking system – that were not banks and therefore not subject to tight supervision and regulation. As each bank was using the same trick to claim good health, each suspected all others of doing the same. This asymmetric information game led to widespread suspicion among banks, and halted their mutual borrowing and lending, as explained in Chapter 18.

19.1.3 Banks: meltdown and rescues

In April 2007, one of the largest US mortgage lenders, New Century Financial Corporation, declared bankruptcy. In July, one of the jewels of Wall Street, Bear Stearns, announced that it would stop honouring the commitments of one of its funds. When BNP Paribas did the same in August 2007, the US interbank markets froze, as did those in other major financial centres around the world in which large banks were active. Many banks could not find the cash that they needed for routine daily operations. Central banks scrambled to provide liquidity directly to these banks in the hope of maintaining normal banking operations.

For a while, things seemed to quieten down, but just below the surface trouble was really brewing. As house prices quickly fell, loan delinquency rose and banks faced growing losses. These losses were moderate but banks were increasingly unable to operate. Global banks are tightly linked by a myriad of mutual loans so that the chain is as strong as its weakest link. Between September 2007 and the spring of 2008, several major banks failed, including Britain's Northern Rock and Wall Street's Bears Stearns, which was taken over by JPMorgan Chase with the help of the US Treasury.

The failure of Lehman Brothers on 15 September 2008 triggered the worst financial crisis since 1929. This time, the US authorities refused to intervene. They considered that Lehman had taken huge but highly profitable risks, and they did not want taxpayers to pay for the consequences. It took only a few hours to realize that Lehman owed considerable sums to nearly every financial institution that mattered, both in the USA and Europe.

Actively cooperating, central banks around the world scrambled to support their banks. They offered cash, they bought tons of toxic securities derived from mortgage loans, and they experimented with various innovative rescue measures. Within a few months, the US Federal Reserve Bank more than doubled the size of its balance sheet, while the ECB's own balance sheet increased by more than 50 per cent (see Figure 19.11 below), something never achieved before.

The contagion from the obscure subprime market, largely in the hands of hardly known, local mortgage-lending companies, to the largest financial establishments in both the USA and Europe is striking. Banks found themselves unable to honour their maturing borrowings. They were forced to sell some of their assets, quickly and at whatever price they could fetch. Fire sales, as this panic strategy is called, meant that a wide range of fine assets lost value, which triggered losses several times bigger than those directly linked to the subprime-backed securities. Interestingly, Asian and Latin American banks, badly burnt in previous financial crises, had stayed out of the subprime business. This allowed them to ride out the crisis relatively unscathed. This was a stunning change in fortune.[4]

---

[4] Most of the financial crises of the 1980s and 1990s occurred in Latin America and East Asia, as they deregulated their markets to join the global system. These countries, from the top leader to the woman in the street, deeply resented the conditions attached to IMF rescue programmes as well as being lectured to by US and European policy makers. By 2008, these countries could hardly conceal their glee.

As in the USA, house price bubbles also occurred in Europe, including in Ireland, Spain and the UK. House prices stabilized and then started to decline at about the same time as in the USA. Although subprime-like mortgages are unlawful in Europe, many banks or mortgage lenders found themselves overextended and faced mounting losses. Lenders like Northern Rock in the UK, Allied Irish Bank in Ireland and numerous Spanish *cajas* (regional saving and loan banks) in Spain had to be rescued.

19.1.4 Avoiding a new Great Depression

When house prices peaked in the USA and it emerged that the subprime edifice would crumble, the authorities – governments and central banks – were more exasperated than concerned. They resented what they saw as reckless risk taking. They particularly disliked investors stating that the crisis would only worsen until troubled banks were bailed out. They initially wanted to resist what they saw as a form of blackmail.[5] However, they soon remembered the lessons learned from the Great Depression:

- Large financial institutions – called systemic, because their failures can drag the whole financial system and the economy into a tailspin – must be rescued
- Deep distress in the financial system is soon followed by a profound and long-lasting recession
- Central banks must provide liquidity to the financial system and adopt sharply expansionary policies
- Governments must use fiscal policy to prevent a vicious cycle of recession and large budget deficits.

The authorities did all of that. Central banks provided massive amounts of liquidity, interest rates were slashed to the zero lower bound and banks were kept afloat. Everywhere, the recession that followed the financial crisis sharply reduced tax revenues. The London G20 Summit in 2009 called upon all governments to urgently adopt expansionary policies: 'We are undertaking an unprecedented and concerted fiscal expansion, which will save or create millions of jobs which would otherwise have been destroyed, and that will, by the end of next year, amount to $5 trillion, raise output by 4 per cent, and accelerate the transition to a green economy. We are committed to deliver the scale of sustained fiscal effort necessary to restore growth.'[6]

© European Union, 2014

The impact on budget deficits was dramatic; see Figure 19.2. Among the few countries that had paid great attention to fiscal discipline before the crisis, Ireland (not shown) and Spain apparently lost control of their budgets because they had to rescue their banks; in 2010, the Irish government spent more than 30 per cent of its GDP on bank bailouts. The build-up of public debt is the immediate cause of the next crisis, the Eurozone debt crisis, to which we now turn. However, it must be pointed out that the UK and the USA let their budgets deteriorate to the same extent as the Eurozone countries in the left-hand chart, which experienced a crisis.

19.2 Stage two: the public debt crisis in the Eurozone

19.2.1 The legacy of the financial crisis: the Great Paradox

If the goal was to return quickly to positive growth, by early 2010 things looked good, as Figure 19.3 shows. The recession had been deep but relatively short-lived by previous standards. However, while the USA went on growing, the Eurozone underwent a 'double dip'. At the time of writing, the Eurozone is expected to renew positive growth but current forecasts anticipate a fairly anaemic recovery.

---

[5] Initially, Mervyn King, the Governor of the Bank of England, famously refused to bail out Northern Rock: 'The provision of such liquidity support undermines the efficient pricing of risk. . . . That encourages excessive risk-taking and sows the seeds of a future financial crisis' (Letter to the Treasury Select Committee, 12 September 2007).

[6] G20 Leaders Statement (https://www.g20.org/sites/default/files/g20_resources/library/London_Declaration.pdf).

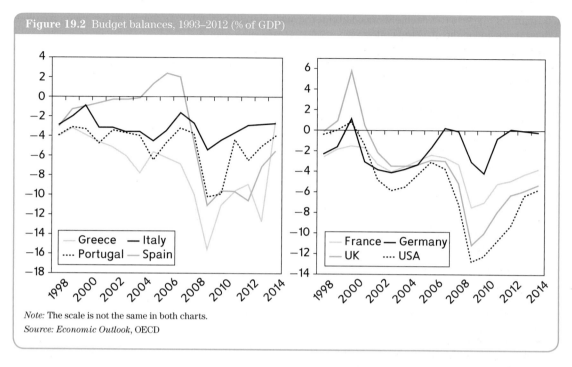

Figure 19.2 Budget balances, 1993–2012 (% of GDP)

Note: The scale is not the same in both charts.
Source: Economic Outlook, OECD

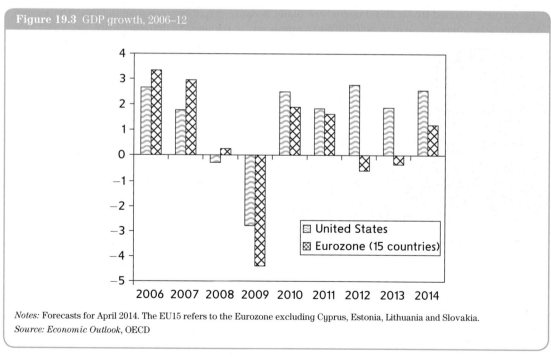

Figure 19.3 GDP growth, 2006–12

Notes: Forecasts for April 2014. The EU15 refers to the Eurozone excluding Cyprus, Estonia, Lithuania and Slovakia.
Source: Economic Outlook, OECD

Negative growth and large budget deficits resulted in fast increases in public debts when measured as a ratio to GDP. (This is the right measure, because debts must be paid for by taxes, and taxes are essentially levied on the incomes that make up GDP.) The result is an amazing paradox: the financial crisis led governments to run considerable budget deficits to contain the recession, which worked, but the deficits

led financial markets to become worried about the sustainability of public finances, which then provoked a deep recession in the affected countries.

In fact, governments and banks are tied strongly together. Banks hold bonds issued by their governments because, traditionally, these bonds are considered safe. They are used on the interbank market and in exchanges with the central bank because they are 'good assets'. An implication is that banks will suffer large losses if a government defaults on its debt obligations. At the same time, governments must rescue banks in difficulty. The debts of the banks then become debts of the government. If the government itself is in a fragile position, the situation becomes pretty desperate. To make things worse, in a recession governments become more indebted and bank profits decline. Bigger budget deficits and deeper bank losses create a vicious cycle, as explained in Box 19.2.

Box 19.2   The phenomenon of multiple equilibria

Why did markets start to worry about Greek debt? One interpretation is that the rapid deterioration of public finances, after decades of neglect, convinced the markets that Greece could not honour its public debt. In addition, the 'discovery' by the new government of debts hidden by its predecessor contributed to market alarm.

An alternative interpretation is that market participants started to worry about what might happen if other market participants were worried. They realized that the Greek government might have to pay a higher interest rate to keep borrowing and the cost of servicing the debt could rise quickly, adding to the deficit. This would trigger further interest rate increases, larger deficits, and so on.

The subtle, but crucial, difference between the two interpretations is that the first considers that a debt default had become unavoidable, while the second implies that the crisis occurred because the markets worried that it could occur, not really because it had become unavoidable. The second interpretation thus involves a self-fulfilling prophecy. It recognizes that there are (at least) two possibilities:

- Markets worry and the crisis occurs.
- Markets remain sedate and the debt level is not considered as lethal.

This scenario is referred to as a case of multiple equilibria: a crisis may or may not occur, depending on what markets worry about.

Multiple equilibria cannot be proven or disproven because they happen only when there is a reason for markets to worry. There is always a cause, but the cause may not be serious enough to make the crisis unavoidable. Multiple equilibria reflect the fact that the financial markets are driven by expectations of the future. This is yet another aspect of financial fragility.

Multiple equilibria are suspected in numerous crises, including the collapse of Lehman Brothers which triggered the global financial crisis. One view is that the bank had suffered losses beyond reparation; it was effectively bankrupt. The alternative view is that Lehman's failed because other banks refused to lend it cash because they feared it might fail. Ex post, Lehman was surely bankrupt, but beforehand?

19.2.2 Greece: crisis and bailout

By late 2007, Greek public debt stood at 105 per cent of GDP, more or less the same as in 2000. It was a large amount, but for a long period markets did not express particular concern about it, at least according to the data in Figure 13.8. By late 2009, the debt had jumped to 127 per cent of GDP. This is when the view of financial market participants shifted. Figure 13.8 shows that this is when the interest rate faced by the Greek government, long quasi-identical to the German bond rate, started to rise. While one may quibble about whether the Greek government could honour its debt at the pre-crisis interest rate, there is little doubt that borrowing at a rate of 10 per cent, then 15 and 20 per cent, imposes an unbearable debt burden. By early 2010, the Greek government was facing a desperate situation.

When a government finds itself unable to borrow, or only at punitive rates (see Figure 18.3), the normal solution is to apply to the International Monetary Fund (IMF) for emergency assistance. The IMF provides conditional loans; it requires the government to take remedial action. Promptly reducing a budget deficit under IMF monitoring is painful, but the alternative, to completely close the deficit for lack of any financing, is even more painful. A particularity of IMF lending is that it is arranged through the central bank, following a letter of agreement signed by the finance minister. Greece's central bank is part of the Eurosystem. The ECB publicly voiced opposition to an IMF intervention in Eurozone affairs. In line with Eurozone governments, the ECB promoted a purely European solution. After several announcements of increasingly larger financial packages failed to sway the markets, in May 2010 the European Council decided a joint IMF–EU–ECB (called the Troika) rescue operation. It also created a new institution, the European Financial Stability Facility (EFSF), designed to deal with other similar cases should they arise.

Greece was offered a 110 billion euro loan under conditions set and monitored by the Troika. The conditions emphasized public spending cuts and enhanced tax revenues, as well as a bevy of structural reforms aimed at boosting competitiveness. But a fiscal contraction acts fast while structural reforms take years to produce effects. Unsurprisingly, one year later the Greek economy was gripped in a severe recession, its tax revenues were falling, the deficit situation was not seriously improved and Greece needed a fresh financial injection. The Troika declared itself disappointed and requested stronger measures in exchange for a new 100 billion euro loan.

19.2.3 Contagion inside the Eurozone

The bailout of Greece in May 2010 was a turning point. The official reason for a decision that may be incompatible with the Treaty (see Box 19.3) was that it would avoid highly dangerous, contagious effects. This goal proved elusive, as Figure 19.4 shows. In total five countries had to be bailed out, one way or another.

Figure 19.4 Time line of financial assistance

Greece €110 bn.	Ireland €85 bn.	Portugal €78 bn.	Greece €130 bn. PSI: €106 bn.	Spain €100 bn.	Cyprus €10bn.
May 2010	Nov. 2010	May 2011	March 2012	July 2012	Apr. 2013

Box 19.3   Do the country bailouts violate the Treaty?

Two articles of the European Treaty were interpreted as making it impossible for the ECB and governments ever to lend directly to Eurozone governments. The idea was to buttress fiscal discipline and warn governments that they would have to fend for themselves (e.g. by applying to the IMF for emergency assistance) if they found themselves unable to borrow from financial markets, banks and individuals. The first article concerns the ECB:

> *Article 123(1): Overdraft facilities or any other type of credit facility with the European Central Bank or with the central banks of the Member States (hereinafter referred to as 'national central banks') in favour of Union institutions, bodies, offices or agencies, central governments, regional, local or other public authorities, other bodies governed by public law, or public undertakings of Member States shall be prohibited, as shall the purchase directly from them by the European Central Bank or national central banks of debt instruments.*

The second article concerns governments and the Commission:

> *Article 125(1): The Union shall not be liable for or assume the commitments of central governments, regional, local or other public authorities, other bodies governed by public law, or public undertakings of any Member State, without prejudice to mutual financial guarantees for the joint execution of a specific project. A Member State shall not be liable for or assume the commitments of central governments, regional, local or other public authorities, other bodies governed by public law, or public undertakings of another Member State, without prejudice to mutual financial guarantees for the joint execution of a specific project.*

This prescription was widely called the no-bailout clause. The official answer was to invoke the solidarity principle from yet another article:

> *Article 122:*
> *1. Without prejudice to any other procedures provided for in the Treaties, the Council, on a proposal from the Commission, may decide, in a spirit of solidarity between Member States, upon the measures appropriate to the economic situation, in particular if severe difficulties arise in the supply of certain products, notably in the area of energy.*
> *2. Where a Member State is in difficulties or is seriously threatened with severe difficulties caused by natural disasters or exceptional occurrences beyond its control, the Council, on a proposal from the Commission, may grant, under certain conditions, Union financial assistance to the Member State concerned. The President of the Council shall inform the European Parliament of the decision taken."*

The other official argument is that the ECB has not lent directly to governments but only bought existing debt on financial markets, as authorized by Article 123. Neither have governments become 'liable for or assume[d] commitments' of other governments as forbidden by Article 125; they have only offered loans. However, large ECB bond purchases are not in the spirit of the no-bailout clause and, by lending to governments that may default, the lenders have made some commitments.

The German Constitutional Court has been asked to rule on the decision. In September 2011, the court formally stated that the bailouts were not violating the German constitution but did request more parliamentary control. It did not specifically address the case of the European Treaty. French ministers have offered their own evaluation. Europe Minister Pierre Lellouche stated, 'It is expressly forbidden in the treaties by the famous no-bailout clause. De facto, we have changed the treaty';[1] Finance Minister Christine Lagarde (a professional lawyer) said, 'We violated all the rules because we wanted to close ranks and really rescue the euro zone. . . . The Treaty of Lisbon was very straightforward. No bailout.'[2]

[1] *Financial Times*, 27 May 2010.
[2] Reuters, http://www.reuters.com/article/2010/12/18/us-france-lagarde-idUSTRE6BH0V020101218.

19.2.4 Why contagion within the Eurozone?

Contagion within the Eurozone is highly troubling, as is the fact that no other developed country elsewhere faced a debt crisis over that period. There must be something special about the monetary union. It may be a fundamental implication of any currency area, or a flaw in the design of the Eurozone, or policy mistakes, or all of these factors. The explanation matters a great deal because it clearly has policy implications. Unsurprisingly, controversies abound. The main interpretations are presented here.

Indebtedness

Figure 19.5 indicates that public indebtedness in 2009, on the eve of the Eurozone crisis, alone cannot explain why these countries, and not others, have faced the wrath of the financial markets. Ireland, for instance, has been one of the most fiscally disciplined countries in the EU. As explained above, its public finances deteriorated suddenly when a massive banking crisis was met with a government rescue. Portugal, on the other hand, had a poor record of fiscal discipline and low growth prospects, suggesting that it would be difficult to reduce its public indebtedness within a short time period. Greece, Ireland and Portugal were not in an obviously worse situation than many other developed countries. The key is the existence of multiple equilibria: it just so happened that markets focused their attention on these three countries; given their weaknesses, they were unable to turn the tide. Still, why only Eurozone countries? The indebtedness interpretation follows.

No lender of last resort

Countries with their own currencies have a national central bank that may help their governments. For instance, the US Federal Reserve and the Bank of England, two central banks in countries with a higher level of public debt than Ireland (Figure 19.5), have acquired vast amounts of government debt. Financial

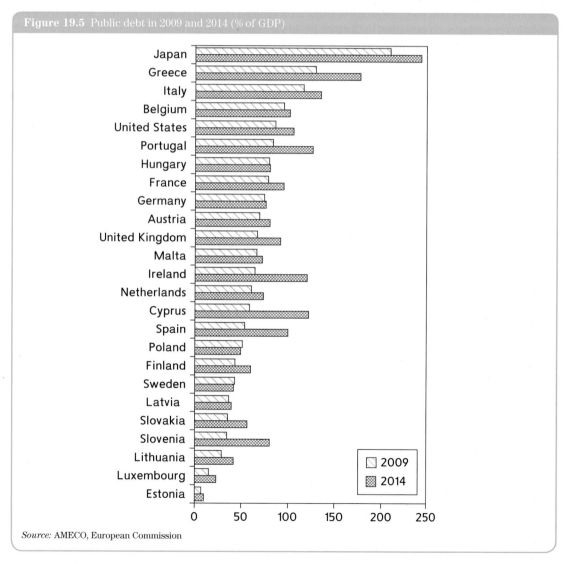

Figure 19.5 Public debt in 2009 and 2014 (% of GDP)

Source: AMECO, European Commission

markets may have been reassured that these central banks would not stand idle in the face of a debt crisis. Indeed, most central banks are understood to be ready to act as lender of last resort for their governments. In a world of multiple equilibria, such beliefs make the difference between crisis and no crisis. In the Eurozone, instead, the ECB is admittedly more distant from member countries. In that respect, the euro is a foreign currency for its member governments.[7] In fact, several Eurozone governments, from countries not in crisis, have strenuously opposed large-scale purchases of public bonds by the Eurosystem. They also rejected the issuance of Eurobonds, national public debts jointly guaranteed by all Eurozone members. In both cases, they fear both moral hazard – an encouragement to continue with budget deficits – and the possible sharing of losses if a government were to default. Such opposition has led the ECB to repeatedly state that it has no inclination to help out stressed governments. As we will see, the ECB has abandoned this view, with spectacular results.

Not only the role of the central bank as lender of last resort to governments has been at stake. Three of the five countries listed in Figure 19.5 – Cyprus, Ireland and Spain – have faced urgent and huge increases in their public debts as a result of bailing out some banks. Had the ECB acted as lender of last resort to banks, it could have provided some of the needed funds. Here again, considerations of moral hazard and of potential losses prevented the ECB from taking on this role. Moral hazard, the fact that banks take more risk when they know that they are protected, can be contained through proper regulation, supervision and resolution procedures, as explained in Chapter 18. As for losses, they can be limited, possibly even avoided, at resolution time. Box 19.4 relates how the Swiss government and central bank actually made a profit when they teamed up to save UBS bank.

Box 19.4 The bailout of UBS

UBS was Switzerland's (and the world's) largest bank, with global operations and assets worth close to four times the country's GDP. UBS had acquired vast amounts of assets based on US mortgages, including the infamous subprimes. Following the collapse of Lehman Brothers, UBS appeared to be in serious difficulty. Since it was too big to fail, the Swiss authorities promptly decided to bail it out. However, they did not want to offer a gift to UBS. Quite the contrary, they imagined a clever arrangement that would both protect taxpayers and potentially be profitable. The November 2008 bailout of UBS included two steps.

First, the Swiss federal government recapitalized UBS. This took the form of a loan that could be transformed into shares at the discretion of the government. Thus, either UBS would reimburse the government, including interest on the loan, or the government would become a shareholder – and then sell its shares to make a profit – whichever was better for taxpayers. In fact, the government sold its loan to UBS to private investors in August 2009 and made a 20 per cent profit from the transaction.

Second, the central bank, the Swiss National Bank (SNB), created a subsidiary called the Stabfund. Its construction is rather complicated but essentially it is designed to both limit potential losses to the SNB and provide the possibility of making a profit. It works as follows. The fund bought much of UBS's toxic assets at market price, at a time when the market was depressed. The Stabfund received 90 per cent of its resources from a loan issued by the SNB, the remaining 10 per cent being provided by UBS. The Stabfund, under direct SNB control, was then asked to sell its portfolio of assets – acquired at a low price – at its discretion over a period of several years, with the objective of protecting the SNB. If the Stabfund suffers losses, the first 10 per cent is to be borne by UBS. If losses exceed 10 per cent, the SNB will not be fully reimbursed. If the sales transpire to be profitable, the SNB will receive the full amount of the loan, including interest, plus 50 per cent of the profits. Recent valuation indicates that the SNB is making a profit, but a few years need to pass before the conclusion to the story is known.

---

[7] According to de Grauwe (2011), '[m]embers of a monetary union issue debt in a currency over which they have no control'.

Competitiveness

A different explanation emphasizes competitiveness. With exchange rates irremediably fixed, a Eurozone country that has let its competitiveness deteriorate must regain it the hard way, through wage and price moderation. This situation is precisely what the OCA theory, presented in Chapter 15, identifies as the main cost of a monetary union.

Figure 19.6 shows the results for two indicators of competitiveness during 1999–2009, the first decade of the euro: unit labour costs and the consumer price index. Unit labour costs measure how much, on average, firms must spend on labour – wages and associated taxes – to produce one unit of GDP. Firms tend to pass higher labour costs onto their prices in order to maintain their profitability. The figure reveals that, with the notable exception of Luxembourg – a very special case – the crisis countries are those where inflation has been higher. These countries have undergone a real exchange rate appreciation relative to other Eurozone countries, which results in a loss of competitiveness. Note that the differences, accumulated over a decade, are very large: labour costs in Ireland, Spain and Greece increased by 30 percentage points faster than in Germany.

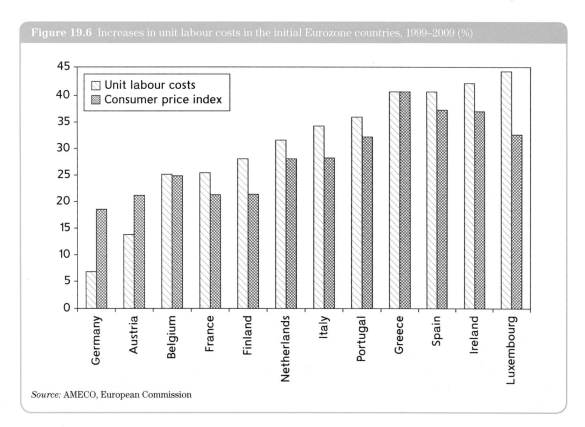

Figure 19.6 Increases in unit labour costs in the initial Eurozone countries, 1999–2009 (%)

Source: AMECO, European Commission

We would expect that the higher inflation countries would see their current accounts (exports less imports, both broadly defined) deteriorate and the opposite effect in the lower inflation countries. This is exactly what happened, as confirmed by Figure 19.7.[8] Note that the counterpart of the external deficits were capital inflows, which added to inflation pressure. Investors and banks were willing to temporarily shield these countries from their growing loss of competitiveness.

According to this view, a number of Eurozone countries had lost competitiveness during the first decade of the monetary union. Without an exchange rate of their own, recovering competitiveness

---

[8] Other Eurozone countries (not shown) also saw their current accounts steadily improve (Austria) or remain strongly positive (Finland, the Netherlands). Chapter 16 also covers this issue.

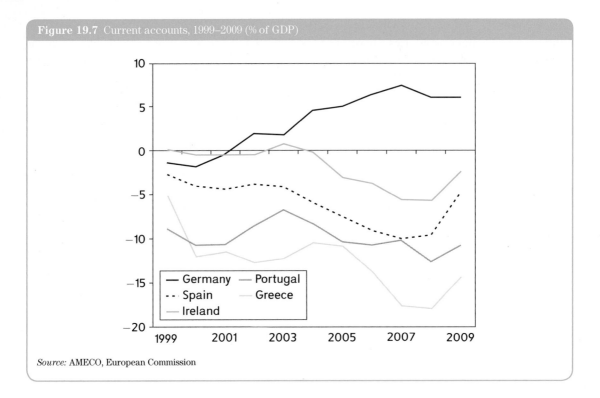

Figure 19.7 Current accounts, 1999–2009 (% of GDP)

Source: AMECO, European Commission

would be a painful process. This vulnerability so worried the markets that they stopped lending to these countries. The problem with this view is that the external deficits had turned around before the crisis, as did labour costs.

Policy mistakes

The dithering responses to the Greek crisis (Section 19.2.2) had alarmed the markets. Governments believed that the conditional bailout would allay these fears. In fact, the opposite happened. Figure 19.8 displays the differences between public bond interest rates (ten year bonds) of the stressed countries relative to the German bond interest rate. We already saw that these differences – called spreads – are a measure of market perceptions regarding the risk of default and/or exit from the Eurozone (Figure 18.3). Figure 19.8 shows that the spreads continued to rise, sometimes even accelerated, after the decision to bail out Greece. One interpretation of this situation is that the authorities may have inadvertently encouraged the markets to focus attention on the Eurozone. Other mistaken policy choices, discussed in Section 19.3, may have further worsened a bad situation.

Appraisal

No agreement has been reached regarding which of these explanations identifies why the debt crisis occurred in the Eurozone, and there only. It is tempting to answer that each explanation holds an element of truth. It takes a multiplicity of several adverse developments to produce such a disastrous outcome. It is worth noting, however, that the indebtedness interpretation indicates that a number of governments did not fully understood the need to abide by strict fiscal discipline, while the competitiveness view suggests that wage-setters (employers, employees, the government as an employer and tax-setter) did not recognize the constraints imposed by monetary union membership. If these are the reasons for the Eurozone crisis, chances are that the message has now been heard. Whether the right conclusions have been drawn is another issue; Chapter 17 describes changes in the excessive deficit procedure intended to strengthen fiscal discipline. It also discusses the new macroeconomic imbalance procedure designed to prevent large

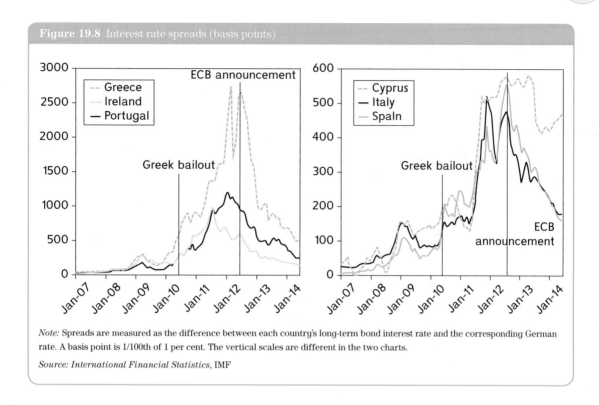

Figure 19.8 Interest rate spreads (basis points)

Note: Spreads are measured as the difference between each country's long-term bond interest rate and the corresponding German rate. A basis point is 1/100th of 1 per cent. The vertical scales are different in the two charts.

Source: International Financial Statistics, IMF

wage differentials. Chapter 18 describes the creation of a single supervisor (for large banks) and a Single Resolution Mechanism as a step in the right direction. The ECB, however, is still not recognized as a lender of last resort to both banks and governments. We return to this issue in Section 19.5.

19.2.5 Not all crisis countries are alike

We have examined several interpretations that can potentially explain all the cases at hand. Yet, each country has its own characteristics. An alternative approach is to explain each crisis country individually. This has been the view taken by many policy makers. Indeed, a constant feature of the crisis is that it was a long time coming and governments remained in denial until they finally caved in. 'We are not Latin Americans,' said the Greeks; 'we are not Greek,' said the Irish, and so on. In a way, they were right. Explanations for why the crisis occurred vary from one country to another. However, it is very difficult to argue that these were separate events that simply occurred at about the same time in the same currency area. Yet, for the sake of completeness, this section examines some interesting national specificities.

Some countries have a poor history of fiscal discipline, as shown in Table 17.3. Markets doubted that Greece and Portugal could continue adding more debt to an already high mountain without eventually defaulting. Greece came first, probably because a newly elected government revealed that the accounts of its predecessor were untruthful. Ireland and Spain, on the other hand, had displayed an impressive degree of fiscal discipline. For them, the problem resulted from the banking system and the necessity of providing bank bailouts. Markets may have trusted the Irish government to roll back this sudden debt increase, but they were worried that this would not be the end of the story. Indeed, in a now-classic erroneous move, the Irish government did not merely guarantee all bank deposits, it also guaranteed all bank liabilities in 2008.[9] The potential cost of this guarantee was unknown, and in fact was immeasurable. The resulting uncertainty triggered the crisis. The same applies to Spain.

---

[9] Who did it? Irish commentators maintain that the government was ordered to do it by the ECB. The ECB says it was the European Commission. The Commission claims that it was not involved.

For a decade, Italy had managed to stabilize its public debt at about 110 per cent of GDP. It did not let it grow a great deal during the crisis; in fact, it relied on expansionary fiscal policies elsewhere to contain the recession. Was this a sign of fiscal discipline? Not quite, because the debt remained very large and had not been reduced in better years. Italian banks had not accumulated subprime-based assets – they were not allowed to by the central bank – nor had Italy experienced a house price bubble. But Italy is not growing, which is a source of fragility for banks and makes debt reduction difficult. This is why Italy has been in the danger zone all along.

France, too, has a poor record of fiscal discipline (Table 17.3) but its debt is comparatively moderate. It has experienced a house price bubble, which has not (yet?) burst. French banks had accumulated toxic assets and whether the clean-up is complete will not be known until the Asset Quality Review is completed at the end of 2014. Germany shares with France the problem of banks badly hit by the US subprime crisis and maybe not thoroughly cleaned up. Its reputation as a fiscally disciplined country may not be fully justified in the light of the history of the past two decades, but it is buttressed by the adoption in 2009 of a constitutional zero-budget rule (see Chapter 17). Belgium also has a problem with its banks and, like Italy, has a lingering huge public debt. France and Italy, and even Belgium and Germany, can be seen as in-between countries, which could be pushed into the danger zone if their circumstances deteriorate.

19.3 Policy responses

The financial markets continuously warned policy makers that determined action was needed to stop the debt crisis. Much like the situation before the eventual collapse of Lehman Brothers, they asked for a comprehensive solution. Policy responses were partial and half-hearted, and a growing rift was evident within the Eurozone. Markets had long questioned the strategy of imposing fiscal restraints in the midst of a severe recession. They were also concerned about the limited resources and tools put in place, the situation of European banks and the role of the ECB. Things changed radically in July 2012 when the ECB took resolute action. The national governments, however, had yet to rise to the challenge.

19.3.1 Why did financial markets fret?

From the start, the financial markets worried that some governments might partly repudiate their public debts, thus imposing large losses on investors. They also worried about the wider repercussions, including bank failures and a possible break-up of the Eurozone. More than anything, however, markets hate uncertainty. In that respect, half-hearted policy responses have had a deleterious effect on financial markets, which in return have increased the pressure on governments. Many of the steep increases in interest spreads (Figure 19.8) can be traced back to policy decisions that markets perceived as 'too little, too late'. A good example is the creation of the European Financial Stability Facility (EFSF) in May 2010, at the time of the Greek bailout. The idea was to build a war chest big enough to 'shock and awe' the financial markets. The national governments announced that they had put together a package worth 750 billion euros. In addition to the 440 billion euros provided by the EFSF, the package also included 60 billion euros from the European Commission and 250 billion euros from the IMF. It quickly transpired that the 440 billion euros really meant 250 billion euros, that the Commission could not really provide 60 billion euros (about half of its annual budget) and that the IMF had made no ex ante commitment. The markets interpreted this situation as an indication that governments were either not aware of the risks ahead or were unwilling to recognize them. They concluded that the crisis would be left to fester.

19.3.2 Fiscal policy strategy

The response to the Greek crisis became a template for the other Eurozone countries. In cooperation with the IMF – which so far has never co-organized emergency lending – the EU provided Greece with a loan to cover approximately one year's budgetary needs. As with all IMF loans, stiff conditions were attached. They called for public expenditure cuts and tax increases, and established a host of structural requirements designed to improve the performance of the economy: a reduction of the size of the civil service along with wage reductions, the privatization of state-owned companies, improvement of tax collection, elimination of closed-shop professions, pension reform and much more.

The wisdom of requiring fiscal austerity when the economy was in recession, however, was met with considerable doubt. Would not fiscal austerity prevent a return to positive growth? If the recession were to continue and possibly deepen, tax revenues would decline and the deficits would not be reduced. The debt would just keep growing, defeating the very purpose of the policy.

Figure 19.9 presents the standard multi-year real GDP forecasts for Greece and Ireland produced by the IMF at the time of a programme agreement, together with subsequent annual updates. The two Greek programmes were considered the least successful while the Irish programme was arguably the most successful. In the case of Greece, successive forecast revisions have led to large downward adjustments, each time further worrying the financial markets. The 2013 target for the Greek debt to GDP ratio was set in 2010 at 149 per cent; even after a debt cancellation worth 27 per cent of GDP, the outcome was 176 per cent. Ireland, on the other hand, slightly bettered the target.

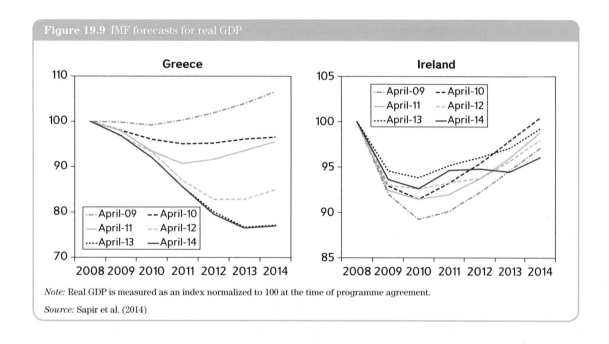

Figure 19.9 IMF forecasts for real GDP

Note: Real GDP is measured as an index normalized to 100 at the time of programme agreement.

Source: Sapir et al. (2014)

Why did the IMF (and the Commission, working together) get it so systematically wrong? The technical aspects of the answer are presented in Box 19.5. Here, we quote from a report commissioned by the European Parliament:

> All four countries have by and large adopted the fiscal consolidation measures prescribed by the Troika. However, debt-to-GDP levels increased more than originally foreseen. This was mostly due to the larger-than-expected fall in economic output. A combination of factors is responsible for this substantial error in judgement: (a) the larger-than-expected fiscal multipliers, (b) the unexpected deterioration in the external environment, including an open discussion about euro area break-up undermining investor confidence, (c) an over-optimistic assessment of the initial conditions, (d) an underestimation of the weakness of some administrative systems and a lack of political ownership.

Sapir et al. (2014)

Box 19.5   The battle of the multipliers

The Troika requested exacting fiscal policy contractions. The logic was as follows. Countries that asked for support did so because they had lost market access, meaning that their governments could no longer borrow from banks or the bond markets. Without official help, therefore, strictly speaking they were unable to run budget deficits because they could not borrow to plug the hole. The aim of the programmes was to restore market access as soon as was practicable. This was interpreted as a requirement to close the deficits as soon as was practicable.

The debate starts with the word 'practicable'. The Troika wanted that to be within three years. With some countries starting with very large deficits (Figure 19.2), the objective implied a massive fiscal policy contraction (in terms of Chapter 13, a large leftward shift of the *IS* curve). The debate quickly focused on the size of the fiscal multiplier. The fiscal multiplier is a number that answers the following question: if a government cuts its deficit by 1 per cent of GDP, by how much will GDP growth be reduced? The exact value of the number depends on circumstances and the details of the policy action, but a rule of thumb is that the multiplier is between 1 and 1.5. When the IMF and the Commission required that the deficits be cut by several percentage points, they did not forecast severe contractions. They suggested that the multiplier was very small. This assertion led to optimistic forecasts of GDP growth and deficit outcomes.

In 2012, the IMF acknowledged the problem quite openly in its flagship publication:

> *The main finding, based on data for 28 economies, is that the multipliers used in generating growth forecasts have been systematically too low since the start of the Great Recession. . . . Informal evidence suggests that the multipliers implicitly used to generate these forecasts are about 0.5. Actual multipliers may be higher, in the range of 0.9 to 1.7.*
>
> *World Economic Outlook*, October 2012, p. 41

The European Commission was far less forthright in recognizing this 'error', which arguably caused huge pain in the affected countries. The Commissioner in charge of the Troika programmes is reported to have argued that the multipliers were zero. In 2012, he sought to blame monetary policy:

> *It is correct that fiscal consolidation can have a dampening effect on growth in the short term. Attempts to quantify this effect through the so-called 'fiscal multiplier' have been much in the news in recent days. This issue merits analysis. But we should be cautious about drawing conclusions too quickly. Fiscal multipliers may indeed be larger on average in this crisis than in normal times. . . . That is not to say they are larger in every case. And we should ask whether worse-than-expected recessions in certain countries can be attributed only, or even mainly, to the effects of fiscal consolidation. Other factors have played a role in each slowdown. . . . The countries whose growth was revised most sharply down at a time when they were tightening fiscal policy were also those experiencing large rises in spreads and suffering the effects of the breakdown in monetary policy transmission in the euro area – a problem the European Central Bank has recognized.*
>
> Olli Rehn, 'Foundations for growth', European Commission, 2012

The debate affected not merely the crisis countries under Troika programmes but the whole Eurozone. The European Commission emphasized the urgent need to reduce deficits throughout the Eurozone, thus implementing the Stability and Growth Pact. As indicated in Chapter 17, most Eurozone countries were placed under the EDP procedure. Figure 19.10 shows the average cyclically-adjusted budget balances[10] of the Eurozone as a whole alongside those of the USA and the UK over the crisis period. The comparison reveals that fiscal policy was much less expansionary in the Eurozone.

---

[10] Section 17.1.3 explains that the cyclically-adjusted budget balance is the correct way of interpreting government action.

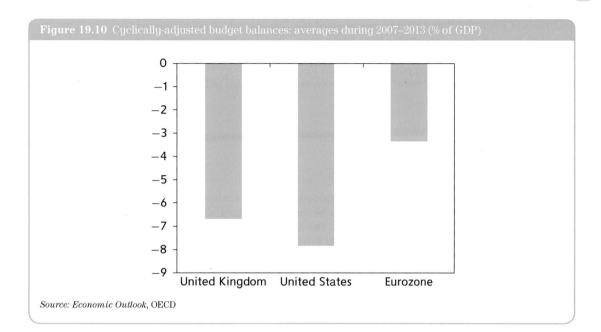

Figure 19.10 Cyclically-adjusted budget balances: averages during 2007–2013 (% of GDP)

Source: Economic Outlook, OECD

19.3.3 The bailout institutions

The creation of the EFSF (see Section 19.3.2) was meant to provide policy makers with readily available resources in case of contagion. The fund was considered a temporary arrangement for dealing with emergency bailouts. Its lending capacity was limited to 250 billion euros and the EFSF was only allowed to lend directly to countries, excluding the purchase of existing debts. As the crisis spread, it was decided to replace the EFSF with a bigger, permanent and more versatile fund, the European Stability Mechanism (ESM).

The ESM replaced the EFSF in 2012. Based in Luxembourg, the ESM has a lending capacity of 500 billion euros. It belongs to the Eurozone countries, which contribute to its capital. Starting capital is 80 billion euros, but it can be increased to 700 billion euros if the need arises. It borrows the amounts that it lends; since it can only lend less than its capital, it is considered very safe.

The EFSF contributed to the bailouts of the 'first wave': Greece, Ireland and Portugal. The ESM lent to Spain and Cyprus (Figure 19.4). Spain has been an interesting case. By mid-2011, the markets were worrying that many Spanish banks were in need of a rescue, especially the regional banks called *cajas*. As pressure grew (see Figure 19.9), it seemed that Spain would be the next country to be bailed out. Fearful of the conditions imposed previously, the Spanish government vehemently refused to apply for a Troika programme. Yet, it needed money to rescue some banks and did not want to borrow on the markets, fearful of the Irish precedent. After long negotiations, in order to avoid another shock it was agreed to allow the ESM to lend money for bank rescues under a lighter programme called Precautionary Financial Assistance.

19.3.4 Monetary policy

Chapter 18 covers a number of monetary policy issues, including the problems created by the fragmentation of the financial markets. This section focuses on the macroeconomic aspects of monetary policy.

Like the Federal Reserve and the Bank of England, the Eurosystem has reduced its interest rate to zero, just more slowly, as the left-hand chart of Figure 19.11 indicates. This action has been controversial because recovery has been stronger in the USA and the UK than in the Eurozone, which is still facing (in mid-2014) an inflation rate of 0.5 per cent, significantly below its 'close to but below 2 per cent' definition of price stability. Critics have accused the Eurosystem of being 'behind the curve', reacting slowly to the turn of events rather than being proactive. The Eurosystem has reminded such critics that its mandate requires that it take no risk in terms of price stability, that the sovereign debt crisis is due to misguided government policies and that deep asymmetries (the conjuncture, financial market fragmentations) have undermined the effectiveness of monetary policy. Box 19.6 describes one such controversy.

Box 19.6   The ECB in July 2008

By August 2007, the Federal Reserve understood that the situation was precarious. The Bank of England initially refused to help out banks, because it felt they should face the consequences of their risky bets, but gave in in January 2008. The ECB did not move. In July 2008, when the Federal Reserve and Bank of England were quickly bringing their interest rates down to zero, the ECB even raised its interest rate (Figure 19.11). When Lehman Brothers collapsed in September 2008, however, the ECB changed its mind. It then followed the actions of the two other central banks, although not going all the way down to zero until June 2014, even though the Eurozone entered a deep recession in 2009 and the sovereign debt crisis, which started in early 2010, provoked a second recession a year later.

The Chairman of the ECB, Jean-Claude Trichet, thus explained the July 2008 decision:

> On the basis of our regular economic and monetary analyses, we decided at today's meeting to increase the key ECB interest rates by 25 basis points. . . . Inflation rates have continued to rise significantly since the autumn of last year. They are expected to remain well above the level consistent with price stability for a more protracted period than previously thought. . . . Against this background and in full accordance with our mandate, we emphasise that maintaining price stability in the medium term is our primary objective and that it is our strong determination to keep medium and long-term inflation expectations firmly anchored in line with price stability. This will preserve purchasing power in the medium term and continue to support sustainable growth and employment in the euro area.
>
> Press conference, 3 July 2008

Commodity prices, including oil, had been rising for months, which was filtering down to higher inflation. The ECB chose to fight inflation at a time when the world was descending into the worst financial crisis in several generations. Of course, awareness of the gravity of the forthcoming situation was still limited, but the two other central banks were obviously more worried than the ECB. And they turned out to be right.

In order to deal with the freezing of the interbank market in the wake of the collapse of Lehman Brothers, the ECB undertook to lend directly to banks, face to face rather than through the market. Panicked banks wanted to amass vast amounts of liquidity to avoid the fate of Lehman Brothers, which fell because it could not borrow the money necessary to deal with rising withdrawals. The ECB responded. Within a few weeks, the size of its balance sheet – which measures the total amount of its loans – increased by an unprecedented 40 per cent. The right-hand chart in Figure 19.11 shows that, during the same period, the Federal Reserve and the Bank of England allowed their balance sheets to more than double and triple, respectively. In 2011, when the recovery proved weak (and the Eurozone was entering a recession) and banks were still so fragile that they could not lend to their customers, all three central banks further doubled the size of their balance sheets, but the action of the ECB was again more muted.

Figure 19.11 Monetary policies: a comparison

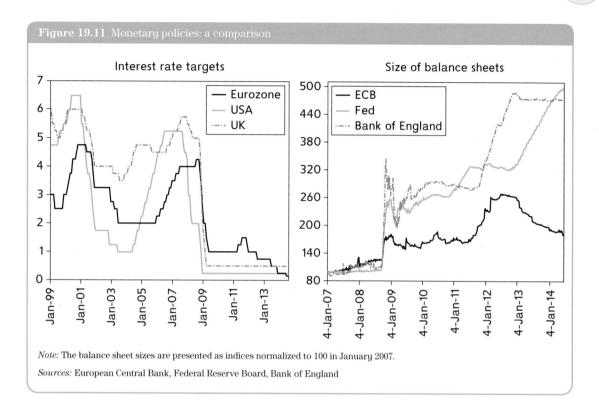

Note: The balance sheet sizes are presented as indices normalized to 100 in January 2007.

Sources: European Central Bank, Federal Reserve Board, Bank of England

As it lent to banks, the ECB took compensating steps – called sterilization – to prevent its balance sheet from increasing. Over time, its actions took many forms and it became increasingly resolute. All along, however, the ECB was careful to recall that price stability was its main priority and that it was not acting as lender of last resort to governments and banks. Its prudence reflected deep disagreement among member countries. Somewhat schematically, one can say that the northern countries, not under market pressure, were opposed to many of the central bank innovations. They worried that the risk inherent in these actions could create losses at the ECB. Since all Eurozone countries share ECB benefits and losses, they feared that they would have to pay for the mistakes of others. Most of the southern countries were mired in the crisis and did not understand that the ECB was being careful. This divergence of opinions, which reflected the asymmetry of the economic situation, considerably constrained the Eurosystem. At stake was the notion of policy dominance, which is presented in Box 19.7.

Box 19.7   Monetary or fiscal dominance?

As explained in Chapter 16, high inflation invariably occurs when the central bank is forced to finance large budget deficits. This observation is the reason why central bank independence is essential. But what does 'forced' really mean? The issue is quite subtle.

Imagine an independent central bank deeply committed to price stability. Now imagine that its government is fiscally undisciplined and accumulates a large public debt as it runs large budget deficits. Sooner or later, the government will lose market access. Plagued by growing risk premia, domestic interest rates will rise. This will bring about a recession and quite possibly destabilize the banking system.

Financial markets will crumble too and the exchange rate will begin to depreciate. The independent central bank will flatly refuse to print money for the government. As the situation deteriorates and banks begin to fail, the government will point its finger at the uncooperative central bank.

At that stage, the question is who will blink first. If it is the government, which then cuts its deficit, this is a case of monetary policy dominance. The central bank will have won the battle of will and inflation will be contained, quite likely at the cost of a deep recession. If the central bank blinks first and provides cash to the strapped government, fiscal dominance leads to runaway inflation.

No matter how independent is the central bank, it must be accountable to elected politicians. It can resist pressure, but its ability to do so will eventually depend on which side public opinion supports. The best protection against fiscal dominance is fiscal discipline. This is why efficient institutions of the kind presented in Chapter 17 are so important. Some observers consider that the bailout of Greece, partly financed by the ECB, is an instance of fiscal dominance.

When the sovereign debt crisis deepened, the Eurosystem undertook to buy bonds issued by the crisis governments. This undertaking caused much consternation in the northern countries. Doing so half-heartedly, however, did not stop the crisis, causing much consternation in the southern countries. Thus, one criterion of an optimum currency area, homogeneity of preferences, was found to be missing entirely, with crippling consequences (see Chapter 15).

Ultimately, the ECB ended the crisis, its acute phase at least. In July 2012, its president announced that 'the ECB is ready to do whatever it takes to preserve the euro'. This announcement was understood as a promise to buy as many crisis countries' public bonds as necessary to bring down the interest rates shown in Figure 19.8. In September 2012, this announcement was formalized as the Open Market Transactions (OMT) programme. This was a drastic step because it came close to financing deficits and because the purchases were not to be sterilized. Sensing opposition, the ECB imposed a condition on those countries from which it would buy bonds; they had to be in a Troika programme.[11]

As Figure 19.8 shows, the effect was both immediate and long-lasting. Even though the ECB did not actually make any purchases under the OMT programme, the spreads still declined quite dramatically. Its mere announcement that it was accepting its role as lender of last resort to national governments moved the Eurozone from a bad to a better equilibrium. This is how financial markets work.

Since then, an emboldened ECB has set up other programmes designed to reduce financial fragmentation. Yet, as the right-hand chart in Figure 19.11 shows, unlike other central banks, the ECB has refrained from providing injections of money – so-called quantitative easing. At the time of writing, such a step is being openly contemplated – officially, to bring inflation to its desired level 'within the mandate' of the Eurosystem; in practice, to try to revive the Eurozone economy.

19.3.5 Outcome

The combination of austerity-oriented fiscal policies and a monetary policy long 'behind the curve' of financial market panic means that the Eurozone differs from comparable countries. Figure 19.12 compares the evolution of the GDPs of the Eurozone, the UK and the USA since 1999. In each case, the evolution is shown alongside the corresponding long-run trend. Both GDPs and trends are indexed to take the same value in 2007, the year before the first crisis. In all three countries, the 2009 recession unhinged GDP from it secular trend. The striking observation is that, in the Eurozone and the UK, the gap kept growing while growth almost resumed its secular path in the USA. While the UK achieved a modest recovery, GDP remained flat in the Eurozone.

Both monetary and fiscal policy orientation in the Eurozone can be related to the primacy of the price stability objective. This is quite directly so for monetary policy. For fiscal policy, the link is the fear of fiscal

---

[11] Opposition came in the form of a complaint lodged with the German Constitutional Court; see Box 16.5.

dominance. Has the price stability performance been better in the Eurozone, then? Figure 19.13 shows that this is not the case relative to the USA. Inflation rates have been nearly identical throughout the crisis but, at the time of writing, there is mounting concern that inflation is too low in the Eurozone and is heading toward negative territory.

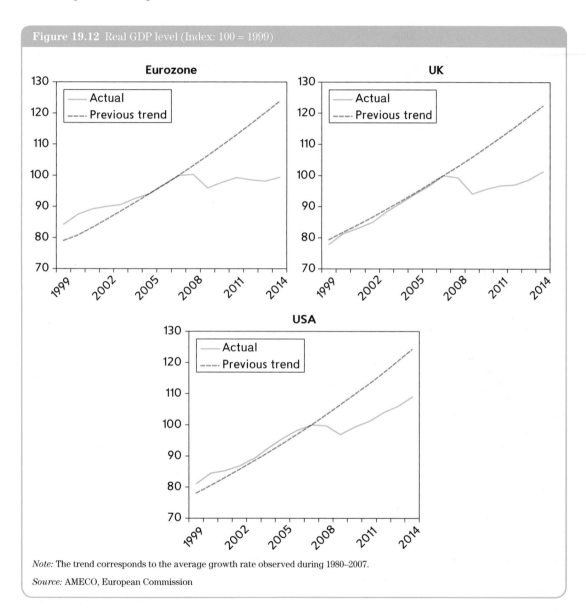

Figure 19.12 Real GDP level (Index: 100 = 1999)

Note: The trend corresponds to the average growth rate observed during 1980–2007.

Source: AMECO, European Commission

19.4 Banks and public debt

19.4.1 The diabolic loop

Many European banks suffered heavy blows during the global financial crisis. Some had bought into the US mortgage market, as explained in Chapter 18. In other countries, chiefly Ireland and Spain, the cause was home grown. Excessive bank lending led to local overheating of the housing market; when the bubble burst and house prices promptly fell, many borrowers could not, or would not, service loans whose values

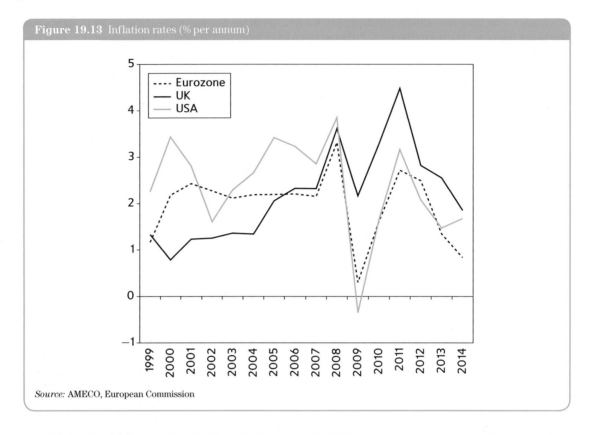

Figure 19.13 Inflation rates (% per annum)

Source: AMECO, European Commission

were higher than the houses they had bought. As a result, in 2008 many governments injected resources into their banks. Everywhere, taxpayers asked why their governments could find money for banks and not for schools, hospitals, and so on.

Next, the 2009 recession made it harder still for borrowers, who now found themselves in a precarious economic condition, to service their debts. The last straw was the sovereign debt crisis. Many banks were holding government bonds, whose prices were falling sharply. In parallel, governments had already seen their debts rise during the 2009 recession and were also facing a delicate financial situation. The last thing they wanted was to face another bank crisis, which would force them to pour more money into banks thus further angering taxpayers.

The outcome was the 'diabolic loop'. Governments saw to it that supervisors viewed the situation of stricken banks with sympathy. In return, banks were 'encouraged' to buy public bonds as a means of upholding their value. As a result, Greek banks normally held large amounts of Greek government debt, German banks held German public debt, and so on. As the crisis deepened, so the concentration of national debt in the portfolios of banks continuously increased, another symptom of the fragmentation of the Eurozone banking system already described in Chapter 18.

The diabolic loop thus locked governments and their banks in a dangerous embrace. Banks depended on light government supervision but also on their countries' public debt reputation. Governments needed banks to support their bonds and were highly motivated to help banks minimize their risks. As long as the good equilibrium prevailed, calm would be maintained. Unfortunately, a bad equilibrium loomed. At any moment, the financial markets could stop financing a government and the attendant fall in bond prices would trigger a bank crisis. Alternatively, the markets could consider a bank doomed. The bank would quickly need public support, which would create a fiscal crisis. This is what happened in some countries, but very rare were the other countries that could not fall in the bad equilibrium. Even if the good equilibrium were to prevail, the precedent of the Japanese crisis of the early 1990s, briefly described in Box 19.8, meant that the situation was precarious indeed.

Box 19.8   Japan's lost decade(s) and zombie banks

Much like China today, Japan achieved impressively high growth rates in the 1950s and 1960s, as a poor and war-torn country became a rich economic powerhouse that established brand names like Toyota, Sony and Matsushita. Much like China in the future, growth remained high but slowed down in the 1970s and 1980s as Japan was catching up with the most advanced countries in terms of technology and productive equipment. This is the normal growth catch-up process. What the Japanese called the lost decade of the 1990s has now become more than two decades of near-zero growth over the 1990s and 2000s, as Table 19.1 shows.

Table 19.1   GDP growth and inflation rates in Japan (average % per annum)

	Growth	Inflation
1960–69	10.1	5.4
1970–79	5.2	9.0
1980–89	4.4	2.6
1990–99	1.5	1.2
2000–09	0.7	−0.3

Source: Economic Outlook, OECD

This did not have to happen. Following the bursting of a house price bubble fed by reckless mortgage lending, the Japanese authorities reacted by bringing the interest rate to zero and adopting strongly expansionary fiscal policies. It did not work because a string of weak governments did not force near-bankrupt banks to restructure. 'Zombie banks', as they were called, were unable and unwilling to lend. As a result, monetary policy was unable to restart the economy, since it mostly operates through bank credit. With a negative inflation rate, even a zero interest rate is not expansionary, however. More surprising is the ineffectiveness of fiscal policy; maybe it was not expansionary enough to counteract the paucity of bank credit. The result is that Japanese public debt, at about 240 per cent of GDP in 2014, is the world's highest.

19.4.2 Stress tests I

The situation in the USA was little better than that in the Eurozone. However, fairly early on, the government decided to bite the bullet to avoid what had happened in Japan. It organized a series of stress tests. These tests, already mentioned in Chapter 18, examined what happens to a bank in response to adverse outside events. The tests were strict and those banks found to be fragile were ordered to take remedial action, mostly to increase their capital to the consternation of their shareholders. Many of the largest US banks or subsidiaries of European banks were found unfit and complied immediately. The US authorities now conduct stress tests annually. The result is that US banks are now considered reasonably safe.

In the Eurozone, after much delay, the newly created European Banking Authority (EBA) was also tasked with carrying out stress tests.[12] A first wave was carried out in 2010. The results identified six banks as failing the test and therefore in need of recapitalization. Importantly, the stress tests did not include any risk of sovereign default. If anything, these tests raised the level of market anxiety because they were seen as proof that governments, which specified that the 'outside events' be simulated, were first and foremost interested in 'proving' that their banks are healthy. A second wave was carried out a year later and the results released in July 2011, just when the public debt crisis was worsening. This time, the risk of a sovereign default was included in the simulations, but the size of the default (15 per cent) was seen as much too small at a time when Greek debt was selling at half its value. Again, most banks were deemed in good health, including Dexia, which had to be rescued for the second time two months later.

---

[12] The EBA is covered in Chapter 18.

19.4.3 Stress tests II

As part of the creation of the Single Supervision Mechanism (SSM) which is under its authority, the ECB requested that demanding stress tests be conducted jointly with the EBA in 2014. Chapter 18 presents some details of the new exercise underway at the time of writing. The ECB has announced that new tests will be strict enough to re-establish the credibility of the Eurozone banking system and, hopefully, bring its fragmentation to an end.

19.5 What have we learned from the crisis?

It would have been an extraordinary piece of luck if the Maastricht Treaty had produced a perfect blueprint for the monetary union. The creation of the euro was complex and had no real precedent to rely upon. In addition, political considerations, heterogeneous preferences and unavoidable technical mistakes were sure to interfere. The creation of the euro is a historical undertaking that will need continuous improvement as its flaws are slowly revealed and understood. It is perhaps sad that crises are needed to stimulate improvement, particularly as most flaws had already been identified ahead of time. It is even sadder that some improvements are still not complete or correct, but at least much has changed as the result of the crisis. These changes are described in previous chapters. This section appraises only the most important.

19.5.1 Fiscal discipline and public debt

The need for fiscal discipline was recognized early on, leading directly to the creation of the Stability and Growth Pact. Chapter 17 explains that the pact suffers from a fundamental contradiction: it seeks to impose discipline on national governments but member countries maintain sovereignty in this matter. Over the years, the pact has been 'strengthened', which has involved encroachments on national budgetary sovereignty. Europe, however, is not a federation and there is thus no central government. Except where sovereignty has been transferred to the Commission, it cannot bypass national governments.

A clean solution would be to create a fiscal union, which would necessitate a central authority with its own resources and some power over national governments. This is a tried and tested solution and has been suggested many times. It may happen – eventually. Unsurprisingly, the notion of a fiscal union is opposed, often obliquely, by governments (and parliaments) loath to give up, or simply share, power. The crisis has given both 'Europe' and 'Brussels' a bad name. Even if people do not quite grasp the details of the crisis, it is plain for all to see that its management has been awkward, as recounted throughout this chapter. It is no surprise, therefore, that trust in the European Union has declined over the last 10 years, as shown in Figure 19.14. Even though the EU remains slightly more trusted than national governments and parliaments, a fiscal union is very unlikely to emerge in the foreseeable future.

The implication is that the Eurozone will have to remain 'messy' – neither a federation nor fully sovereign states. This situation directly affects fiscal discipline. Chapter 17 explains the current working of the strengthened Stability and Growth Pact, which seeks to increase the power of the Commission through reverse qualified majority voting (RQMV). It also notes the as yet unexploited promises of the Treaty on Stability, Coordination and Growth (TSCG), which opens the door to the possibility of better fiscal institutions. Fiscal discipline remains a work in progress.

A most disquieting legacy of the crisis is the level of public debt. Public debt has increased in every Eurozone country since 2009 (Figure 19.5), when they were already high enough to create a crisis of their own accord. In some cases (Cyprus, Greece, Ireland, Portugal, Slovenia and Spain), increases in public debt have been very large indeed. Very high public debt creates serious difficulties:

- Servicing it requires high tax revenues.
- It limits the potential of counter-cyclical fiscal policy.
- It represents a potential challenge to central bank independence.
- It is a source of asymmetry.
- It creates vulnerability in the presence of multiple equilibria.
- It acts as a brake on growth (although this view is controversial).

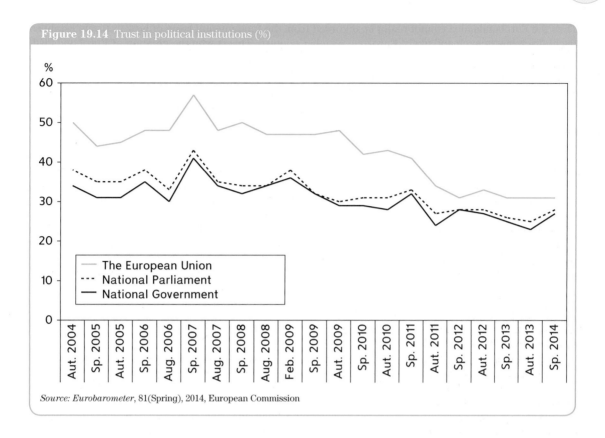

Figure 19.14 Trust in political institutions (%)

Source: *Eurobarometer*, 81(Spring), 2014, European Commission

Whether the debt legacy is bearable is an open question, which has triggered heated debate. Numerous controversial solutions have been put forward – two of which are reviewed below.

Eurobonds

One idea is the creation of Eurobonds, collectively issued and guaranteed by Eurozone governments. They could replace some current national bonds or could be used to finance future deficits.[13] Eurobonds have several appealing features:

- They would cement solidarity.
- A single market for Eurobonds would develop, allowing Eurobonds to compete effectively with US Treasury bonds as the instrument of choice for other countries wanting to accumulate foreign exchange reserves.
- Being guaranteed by all Member States, Eurobonds would probably be considered very safe, in contrast to bonds of high-debt countries.
- They would end the fragmentation of Eurozone financial markets.

Opposition to Eurobonds, however, appears overwhelming. No government would underwrite the debt of another government without an unbreakable guarantee that fiscal profligacy will not occur elsewhere.

---

[13] One creative proposal is that countries be allowed to issue Eurobonds – called 'blue bonds' – to a value of up to 60 per cent of their GDP. The rest, 'red bonds', would remain purely national, be inferior to 'blue bonds' and offer no collective protection. Thus the collective signature would only guarantee the first tranche, which is reasonably safe. This proposal, made by Jakob von Weizsäcker and Jacques Delpla, is available at: http://www.bruegel.org/publications/publication-detail/publication/509-eurobonds-the-blue-bond-concept-and-its-implications/.

Thus the Eurobonds idea cannot really be divorced from the fundamental issue of how to firmly establish fiscal discipline in each and every Eurozone member country. This is why the creation of Eurobonds will have to wait until the fiscal discipline problem is solved once and for all.

Public debt restructuring

The seemingly easiest way to deal with large debts is to cancel them, at least partly. Debt restructuring, as this is called, has been used frequently over many decades. It raises a host of serious issues. It imposes a cost on bondholders. Beyond the legality and fairness of the process, it could trigger a new crisis. As noted above, national bonds have now been concentrated in national banks. A fundamental restructuring could destroy some banks and require national governments to once more borrow, this time to finance the rescues, which would defeat the purpose of the exercise. In addition, governments that default find it difficult to borrow in future. Finally, it is sometimes felt that a default would break the Eurozone.

   Opposition to debt restructuring is very strong. When the debt crisis began, restructuring was proposed and immediately rejected by many governments and by the ECB. Yet, 2 years later, a significant portion of the Greek debt was 'voluntarily' cancelled by banks in a process called Private Sector Involvement (PSI); see Box 19.9.

   The high level of debt in several countries demonstrates that the crisis cannot yet be declared over. These debts will have to be reduced. The official plan A is fiscal discipline. Plan A necessitates large budget surpluses over a period of many years, decades in fact. Many believe that such a situation is

---

Box 19.9   Restructuring Greek debt

'In regard to your question on so-called rescheduling, "haircuts" and so forth . . . we are very clear we don't trust that, provided the two first conditions [implementation of Troika conditions and strict Troika surveillance] I have mentioned are there, there is a need for restructuring or for haircuts. And we would say it is not appropriate,' said Jean-Claude Trichet, then President of the ECB (interview with the Canadian Broadcasting Corporation, 6 June 2011).

   Trichet made this observation following the 'Deauville statement': in October 2010, recognizing that things were not going well in Greece, Angela Merkel and Nicolas Sarkozy came back from a long walk along the sea and opined that some debt restructuring was unavoidable. This statement took everybody by surprise and sent a huge shock through the financial markets. Right from the start, the markets had thought that, though painful for investors, such a step was inevitable – hence the risk premia seen in Figure 19.8 – but the ECB and national governments had been strongly opposed to it. Now, all of a sudden, debt restructuring seemed possible. But a restructuring needs to be carefully prepared, and secretly so as to avoid market panic. Obviously, the statement was merely an idea; there had been no preparation. Telling investors that they will lose money is a sure way to create a panic.

   The Deauville statement met a great deal of resistance, and not just from the ECB. Meanwhile Greece entered a deeper and deeper recession, other countries were hit by contagion and the Greek debt kept mounting, including as a result of the bailout, which was not a present but a loan, hence a new debt. In the end, after long negotiations with banks and groups of investors, the restructuring, called Private Sector Involvement, was agreed at the end of 2011. Almost all of the debt owed to private creditors, about half of the total, was reduced by some 75 per cent. Investors were willing to accept the certainty of a large immediate loss rather than the uncertainty of a future, possibly even larger, loss.

   Among the losers were two large Cypriot banks, which had accumulated a vast amount of Greek bonds. A year later, these banks collapsed and Cyprus became the next country under a Troika programme.

not achievable and fear that a further crisis will be needed to force the hand of national governments (and the ECB). Officially, no plan B exists. A number of proposals have been mooted but officials deem them unrealistic. The likely outcome is simply muddling through. Small, insufficient, debt cancellations could be accepted, leading to painful negotiations between the defaulting government and investors, with considerable interference by other governments keen to protect their own banks. It will then take some time to realize that the size of the default was insufficient, triggering yet another default, and then another.

19.5.2 Bank fragility

The other lesson to be learnt is how fragile banks are. This has been a well-known fact for years; the crisis merely confirmed it. At the global level, new regulations have been put forward by the Basel Committees and are gradually being enacted in national laws. Supervision has been strengthened too, often by delegating it to central banks. Chapter 18 provides the details.

Chapter 18 also explains why Eurozone banks are in a particularly delicate situation. The crisis has led to a surprising degree of fragmentation of the banking system. The policy response, the Banking Union, is a major step forward, yet an incomplete one. Only the large banks are part of the Single Supervision Mechanism (SSM). As for the Single Resolution Mechanism (SRM), it is more a getting together of national regulators than a single mechanism with a single authority. The resolution fund is to be built over a long period of time and its eventual size is unimpressive. Furthermore, the ECB is not yet quite prepared to act resolutely as lender of last resort. Time will tell whether another crisis is needed to complete these steps.

19.5.3 Governance

A spectacular feature of the crisis has been its de facto management by the Eurozone's two largest countries, France and Germany, and then only when they could agree. The Commission has been largely passive. Tension has always existed between the community principle and intergovernmentalism; see Chapter 2. In principle, the Commission assumes the executive role and Member States jointly hold the ultimate authority since the Council acts as the legislative branch of European government. The community principle is that the Commission takes initiatives and member governments approve or disapprove. Intergovernmentalism instead relies on governments to take and negotiate initiatives. The crisis has witnessed a shift to intergovernmentalism, often reduced to a dominating role by the two largest countries.

The obvious reason for this shift is that a crisis requires prompt decision making and the 19 Eurozone countries cannot collectively deliberate effectively. In addition, the Commission's mandate is not limited to the Eurozone, so it has no particular authority in terms of Eurozone affairs. In order to improve effectiveness, the Lisbon Treaty created the post of President of the Council, but his or her brief also extends to the whole EU.

The crisis has thus made it clear that the Eurozone needs its own system of governance. For a while, this role was assumed by the Eurogroup, which brings together the Finance Ministers of the Eurozone. However, given the importance of the issues needing to be addressed during the crisis, it has now been decided that the heads of state and government of countries within the Eurozone will meet twice a year. This structure is obviously unable to handle emergencies, because of its size and frequency of meeting; however, it does represent a symbolic step given reluctance to formalize a 'two-speed Europe'.

A number of other propositions have been advanced and the debate is sure to continue. For instance, the former ECB President, Jean-Claude Trichet, has suggested that a new position be created: the Economic and Finance Minister of Europe. This person would have some, as yet undefined, authority to enforce fiscal discipline in Member States, which may require a new Treaty.

19.5.4 Survival of the euro

Having observed the weaknesses inherent in the euro architecture, a number of people have concluded that the Eurozone is doomed. Several arguments have been presented to back up this claim:

- The failure to establish fiscal discipline throughout the monetary union – both the ineffectiveness of the Stability and Growth Pact and the loss of the no-bailout clause – means that countries in a strong

position have good reason to leave in order to avoid having to pay for those that have let their debts grow to the point where they can no longer honour them.

- Countries with high debts need to grow fast to generate tax revenues. In general, defaulting countries undergo a sharp exchange rate depreciation, which provides the demand boost that they need to recover and grow. There is no room for depreciation in a monetary union.

- The crisis has exposed a gap between a well-functioning North and a badly-wounded South. Solidarity between these groups has been strained.

- Many international investors do not believe that the euro can survive. Whether they are right or not, this belief can become a self-fulfilling process, as explained in Box 19.2.

- Finally, Europe is not an optimum currency area (see Chapter 15). Right from the start it was an experiment doomed to fail.

Powerful arguments are also presented from the opposite perspective, however:

- A break-up of the Eurozone would have catastrophic implications. Some countries would face a deep depreciation, which would make it difficult or even impossible to honour public and private debts contracted in euros. The precedent of Argentina (see Box 19.10) illustrates how disturbing the situation can become. The other countries would face a strong appreciation, which would severely hurt their international competitiveness.

- A new currency would have to be printed and reintroduced. It took three years to introduce the euro and it is likely that reintroducing national currencies would also take a long time. How would transactions be carried out in the meantime?

- It may well be that some countries will have to default, but that does not require an exit from the Eurozone. As a part of the Eurozone, a country is protected from a simultaneous currency crisis involving serious risks for its banking system.

- There is no legal procedure enabling a country to leave – or to be expelled from – the Eurozone; adopting the euro was meant to be a one-way street.

- The crisis has made it clear that the euro architecture needs to be improved, and solutions do exist.

- The Eurozone may not be an optimum currency area, but neither is it hugely ill-suited to operating a common currency. Arguably, the bigger problem has been the political mishandling of the crisis.

Box 19.10   Giving up a currency: Argentina in 2001

In 1991 Argentina declared that the peso would be worth US$1 and that this parity would never be changed. The convertibility law, as the arrangement was called, was solid because it required that the central bank hold as many dollars as it had issued pesos. Full coverage of domestic currency is meant to make the arrangement unassailable, in theory at least. Over the next few years, inflation – Argentina's scourge for decades – disappeared and the economy grew quite fast. People came to see the peso and the dollar as equivalent currencies. However, because inflation did not quite decline to the US rate, Argentine goods became gradually too expensive and the economy started to suffer, as Figure 19.15 shows. Without the ability to depreciate and restore competitiveness, the situation became increasingly desperate. A political crisis set in and, in the midst of intense social turmoil, Argentina abandoned the convertibility law in late 2001.

The peso instantly lost half of its value. Millions of contracts set in dollars, from loans to rents and sales, were in total disarray. If they remained in dollars, borrowers, people with house rentals and large industrial producers would become bankrupt. If they were switched into pesos, the losses to lenders, house owners and sellers would be immense. It took months, and a devastating banking crisis, to sort the situation out. GDP contracted by more than 10 per cent in 2002, after having declined

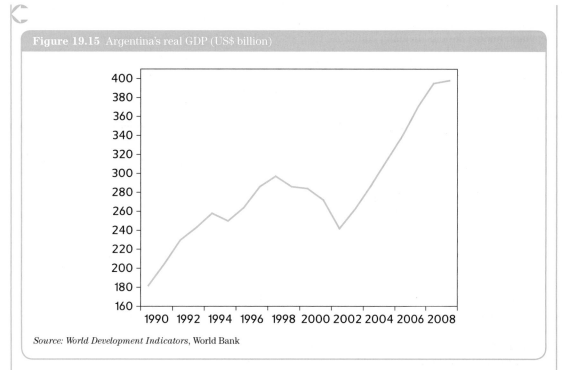

Figure 19.15 Argentina's real GDP (US$ billion)

Source: World Development Indicators, World Bank

by nearly 20 per cent over the previous 5 years. Yet, the depreciation of the peso boosted Argentina's competitiveness and the economy turned around in 2003. From there on, it grew very fast.

In many respects, the Argentine case is similar to an exit from a monetary union. It shows how difficult it is to abandon a currency but also how helpful a depreciation can be. One difference with a monetary union is that, during the currency board years, the peso continued to circulate alongside the dollar: not all contracts were in dollars, vending machines accepted mostly pesos, and the peso did not have to be reintroduced from scratch.

Ultimately, the creation of the euro was partly justified by economic reasons and partly promoted for political reasons (see Chapter 15). Leaving the Eurozone would not represent a clear-cut economic gain and would have serious drawbacks in the short run, which is why no government is likely to do so for economic reasons. The crisis has shown the strength of the political determination to defend the euro. Many believed that Greece would exit – and coined the expression Grexit – but it did not. Despite the enormous hardship that they suffered, most Greeks still want to stay in, and have shown it through successive voting rounds. Likewise, a number of Germans have called for Grexit, but an overwhelming majority of voters supported the mainstream parties during the 2014 elections to the European Parliament. Still, opponents of the EU and the euro, in all countries, have won a significant number of seats. They appear to be on the ascendency.

19.6 Summary

Europe has experienced two successive crises: the global financial crisis that began in the USA, and the Eurozone sovereign debt crisis.

Bank deregulation in the 1980s and 1990s changed the US financial industry. In particular, it made it possible for banks to take more risk to achieve better profits. While banks were becoming more sophisticated, a segment of the market developed risky mortgage loans. Repackaged, these loans ended up in the hands of the world's largest and most highly reputed banks. When house prices turned down, this construction unravelled.

Central banks took vigorous measures to provide banks with liquidity and to cut interest rates. Governments too intervened quite forcefully. They used fiscal policy to avoid a protracted recession, deepening budget deficits. In many countries, they also bailed out banks, sometimes at great cost.

The result was a rapid increase in public debt, which led directly to the second leg of the crisis. Strikingly, this crisis has only affected countries within the Eurozone. Several reasons have been advanced to explain why. They either point to policies incompatible with Eurozone membership or to flaws in its architecture.

With financial markets in panic, the authorities vacillated for too long. National governments aimed at austerity policies that led to a double-dip recession without succeeding in stemming debt increases. The Eurosystem remained 'behind curve' for an extended period, more concerned about inflation than about the quickly deepening recession.

The ECB recovered the initiative by declaring its intention to buy, if needed, an indefinite amount of distressed public bonds. This declaration brought the acute phase of the sovereign debt crisis to its end.

All in all, the Eurozone's economic performance has been poor and inflation has declined significantly below the ECB's own definition of price stability.

The Eurozone banks and governments have been locked in a diabolic loop. Banks bought large amounts of domestic public debt in return for lenient supervision. Governments faced the risk of yet another bank crisis, but the high debt levels reduced their ability to bail out banks in case of need.

As the ECB has taken over the supervision function – for large banks only – it has requested that banks undergo challenging stress tests. If the ECB delivers, the banking system will recover its credibility. This should lead to a progressive end of its fragmentation.

The crisis has shown that the Eurozone construction suffered from important weaknesses. These weaknesses include the lack of fiscal discipline in some member countries, the absence of Eurozone-wide banking regulation, supervision and resolution, the ECB's difficult position as lender of last resort, and poor economic governance. Some progress has been achieved on all these fronts.

The legacy of very large public debts in a number of countries remains.

Self-assessment questions

1 Why did bank deregulation create the conditions for a financial crisis?
2 Why were subprime mortgage loans so dangerous?
3 Explain why the phenomenon of multiple equilibria may lead to self-fulfilling crises.
4 List the possible reasons why the sovereign debt crisis has been limited to the Eurozone.
5 Explain why banks and governments have been caught in a situation whereby they can weaken each other.
6 What are the possible reasons behind the outcomes shown in Figures 19.13 and 19.14?
7 What are stress tests? How are they related to trust in the banking system?
8 Explain the debate surrounding the fiscal multipliers.
9 What is the problem with large public debts?
10 What is the OMT programme? Why has it been so successful?

Essay questions

1 Why has the sovereign debt crisis spread only within the Eurozone?
2 Should subprime lending have been subject to rigorous consumer protection and, if so, what would you propose?
3 Imagine a break-up of the Eurozone. What might be the consequences?
4 Austerity has been a very controversial approach. What else could have been done?
5 Develop the case for (or against) a fiscal union.

Further reading: the aficionado's corner

On financial crises in general:

Reinhart, C. and K. Rogoff (2009) *This Time is Different*, Princeton University Press, Princeton, NJ.

A Nobel Prize winner arguing that this has not been a crisis of macroeconomics as a body of knowledge:

Akerlof, G. (2013) 'The cat in the tree and further observations: Rethinking macroeconomic policy', Vox EU, http://www.voxeu.org/article/cat-tree-and-further-observations-rethinking-macroeconomic-policy.

On the crisis in the Eurozone:

Eichengreen, B. (2009) 'Ireland's rescue package: disaster for Ireland, bad omen for the Eurozone', VoxEU, http://www.voxeu.org/article/ireland-s-rescue-package-disaster-ireland-bad-omen-eurozone.

Grauwe, P. de (2011) 'The governance of a fragile Eurozone', *Australian Economic Review*, 45(3): 255–68.

Lane, P. (2012) 'The European sovereign debt crisis', *Journal of Economic Perspectives*, 26(3): 49–68.

Wyplosz, C. (2011) 'A failsafe way to end the Eurozone crisis', VoxEU, http://www.voxeu.org/article/failsafe-way-end-eurozone-crisis.

On the ECB policies:

Grauwe, P. de (2011) 'The European central bank as a lender of last resort', VoxEU, http://www.voxeu.org/index.php?q=node/6884.

On austerity policies:

Blanchard, O. and D. Leigh (2013) 'Fiscal consolidation: at what speed?', Vox EU, http://www.voxeu.org/article/fiscal-consolidation-what-speed.

On fiscal discipline in the Eurozone:

Bordo, M., L. Jonung and A. Marliewicz (2011) 'A fiscal union for the Euro: some lessons from history', VoxEU, http://www.voxeu.org/index.php?q=node/7007.

IMF (2009) 'Fiscal rules – anchoring expectations for sustainable public finances', http://www.imf.org/external/np/pp/eng/2009/121609.pdf.

Wyplosz, C. (2013) 'Europe's quest for fiscal discipline', *European Economy Economic Papers*, 498, European Commission.

On the Greek PSI:

Xafa, M. (2013) 'Life after debt, the Greek PSI and its aftermath', *World Economics*, 14(1): 81–102.

Zettelmeyer, J., C. Trebesch and M. Gulati (2013) 'The Greek debt restructuring: an autopsy', Working Paper 13-8, Peterson Institute for International Economics, Washington, DC.

On the diabolic loop:

Beck, T., D. Gros and D. Schoenmaker (2012) 'Banking union instead of Eurobonds – disentangling sovereign and banking crises', Vox EU, http://www.voxeu.org/article/banking-union-instead-eurobonds-disentangling-sovereign-and-banking-crises.

Brunnermeier, M., L. Garicano, P. Lane, M. Pagano, R. Reis, T. Santos, S. Van Nieuwerburgh and D. Vayanos *(2011)* 'ESBies: a realistic reform of Europe's financial architecture', Vox EU, http://www.voxeu.org/article/esbies-realistic-reform-europes-financial-architecture.

On governance of the Eurozone:

Grauwe, P. de (2011) 'The governance of a fragile Eurozone', unpublished paper, University of Leuven, http://www.econ.kuleuven.be/ew/academic/intecon/Degrauwe/PDG-papers/Discussion_papers/Governance-fragile-eurozone_s.pdf.

On governance, a bold plan for redesigning the Eurosystem:

Burda, M. (2013) 'Redesigning the ECB with regional rather than national central banks', Vox EU, http://www.voxeu.org/article/redesigning-ecb.

Gros, D. (2014) 'A fiscal shock absorber for the Eurozone? Lessons from the economics of insurance', Vox EU, http://www.voxeu.org/article/ez-fiscal-shock-absorber-lessons-insurance-economics.

On a breakup of the Eurozone:

Eichengreen, B. (2010) 'The Euro: love it or leave it?', VoxEU, http://www.voxeu.org/index.php?q=node/729.

Levy Yeyati, E. (2011) 'How Argentina left its Eurozone', VoxEU, http://www.voxeu.org/index.php?q=node/7055.

On stress tests:

House of Commons (2009) 'US bank stress tests', www.parliament.uk/Templates/BriefingPapers/Pages/BPPdfDownload.aspx?bp-id=SN05066.

On the public debt legacy and plans to organize debt restructuring in the Eurozone:

Crafts, N. (2013) 'The Eurozone: if only it were the 1930s', VoxEU, http://www.voxeu.org/article/eurozone-if-only-it-were-1930s.

Bofinger, P., L. Feld, W. Franz, C. Schmidt and B. Weder di Mauro (2011) 'A European redemption pact', VoxEU, http://www.voxeu.org/article/european-redemption-pact.

Eichengreen, B. and U. Panizza (2014) 'Can large primary surpluses solve Europe's debt problem?', VoxEU, http://www.voxeu.org/article/can-large-primary-surpluses-solve-europe-s-debt-problem.

Mody, A. (2014) 'The ghost of Deauville', Vox EU, http://www.voxeu.org/article/ghost-deauville.

Pâris, P. and C. Wyplosz (2014) 'The PADRE plan: Politically Acceptable Debt Restructuring in the Eurozone', Vox EU, http://www.voxeu.org/article/padre-plan-politically-acceptable-debt-restructuring-eurozone.

Vihriälä, V. and B. Weder di Mauro (2014) 'Orderly debt reduction rather than permanent mutualisation is the way to go', Vox EU, http://www.voxeu.org/article/orderly-debt-reduction-rather-permanent-mutualisation-way-go.

On whether the euro makes any sense at all:

The 'yes' answer:

Wyplosz, C. (1997) 'EMU: why and how it might happen', *Journal of Economic Perspectives*, 11(4): 3–21.

The 'no' answer:

Feldstein, M. (1997) 'The political economy of the European Economic and Monetary Union: political sources of an economic liability', *Journal of Economic Perspectives*, 11(4): 23–42.

References

Mackowiak, B., F.P. Mongelli, G. Noblet and F. Smets (eds) (2009) *The Euro at Ten – Lessons and Challenges*, ECB.

Sapir, A., G.B. Wolff, C. de Sousa and A. Terzi (2014) 'The Troika and financial assistance in the euro area: successes and failures', Economic and Monetary Affairs Committee, European Parliament.

INDEX